LINGUISTICS IN SCHOOL PROGRAMS

Officers of the Society
1969-70
(Term of office expires March 1 of the year indicated.)

ii

LINGUISTICS IN SCHOOL PROGRAMS

The Sixty-ninth Yearbook of the
National Society for the Study of Education

PART II

By
THE YEARBOOK COMMITTEE
and
ASSOCIATED CONTRIBUTORS

Edited by

ALBERT H. MARCKWARDT

Editor for the Society

HERMAN G. RICHEY

 *1 9* NSSE *7 0*

Distributed by THE UNIVERSITY OF CHICAGO PRESS • CHICAGO, ILLINOIS

The responsibilities of the Board of Directors of the National Society for the Study of Education in the case of yearbooks prepared by the Society's committees are (1) to select the subjects to be investigated, (2) to appoint committees calculated in their personnel to insure consideration of all significant points of view, (3) to provide appropriate subsidies for necessary expenses, (4) to publish and distribute the committees' reports, and (5) to arrange for their discussion at the annual meeting.

The responsibility of the Society's editor is to prepare the submitted manuscripts for publication in accordance with the principles and regulations approved by the Board of Directors.

Neither the Board of Directors, nor the Society's editor, nor the Society is responsible for the conclusions reached or the opinions expressed by the Society's yearbook committees.

Published 1970 by

THE NATIONAL SOCIETY FOR THE STUDY OF EDUCATION

5835 Kimbark Avenue, Chicago, Illinois 60637

Copyright, 1969, by HERMAN G. RICHEY, Secretary

The National Society for the Study of Education

First Printing, 10,000 Copies

Printed in the United States of America

The Society's Committee on Linguistics in School Programs

SUMNER IVES
Professor of English
New York University
New York, New York

STANLEY B. KEGLER
Assistant Vice President
Professor of English Education
University of Minnesota
Minneapolis, Minnesota

ALBERT H. MARCKWARDT
(Chairman)
Professor of English and Linguistics
Princeton University
Princeton, New Jersey

HAROLD G. SHANE
University Professor of Education
Indiana University
Bloomington, Indiana

JAMES R. SQUIRE
(Chairman)
National Council of Teachers of English
Urbana, Illinois

Associated Contributors

NATHAN S. BLOUNT
Associate Professor in English
and in Curriculum and Instruction
University of Wisconsin
Madison, Wisconsin

v

J. DONALD BOWEN
Professor of English
University of California
Los Angeles, California

RICHARD W. DETTERING
Professor of English and Education
San Francisco State College
San Francisco, California

WALLACE W. DOUGLAS
Professor of English and Education
Northwestern University
Evanston, Illinois

RICHARD E. HODGES
Associate Professor of Education
University of Chicago
Chicago, Illinois

JOSEPHINE P. IVES
Professor of Educational Psychology
New York University
New York, New York

VERA P. JOHN
Associate Professor of Psychology and Education
Yeshiva University
New York, New York

SAMUEL R. LEVIN
Professor of English
Hunter College; The City University of New York
New York, New York

RAVEN I. MCDAVID, JR.
Professor of English and Linguistics
University of Chicago
Chicago, Illinois

SARAH MOSKOVITZ
Instructor
University of California
Los Angeles, California

WILLIAM G. MOULTON
Professor of Linguistics
Princeton University
Princeton, New Jersey

GENE L. PICHÉ
Associate Professor, Department of Speech, Communication and Theatre
Department of Secondary Education
University of Minnesota
Minneapolis, Minnesota

RICHARD L. VENEZKY
Associate Professor, English and Computer Sciences
University of Wisconsin
Madison, Wisconsin

KENNETH G. WILSON
Professor of English
and Dean, College of Liberal Arts and Sciences
University of Connecticut
Storrs, Connecticut

H. REX WILSON
Associate Professor of English
University of Western Ontario
London, Canada

Preface

In 1965, the Board of Directors, after reviewing the sixty-five-year publication record of the National Society, noted that, except for a considerable number of excellent chapters by Hosic, Charters, and others in various yearbooks and for seven volumes on reading, the language arts were represented only by *On the Teaching of English in Elementary and High Schools* (1906), *English Composition: Its Aims, Methods, and Measurements* (1923), and *Teaching Language in the Elementary School* (1944). It had become apparent that research in old, new, and related areas, as well as an increasing awareness of changing social forces, had been shaping for many years new emphases and, to some extent, a new curriculum for language instruction.

In February, 1966 the Board decided to explore further the need for a yearbook on language in the classroom, a volume which would take into account the new developments in the field including those in the rapidly growing discipline of linguistics.

Harold G. Shane, a member of the Board, was asked to examine further the several problems and issues discussed by the Board, to consult with knowledgeable persons in the field, and to prepare a report to be discussed at the following meeting. He consulted with James R. Squire, then of the National Council of Teachers of English, and met informally with several groups of interested persons. After hearing Mr. Shane's report, the Board voted to bring out a yearbook on "linguistics and mother-tongue instruction"; appointed Albert H. Marckwardt chairman of the yearbook committee; confirmed Mr. Marckwardt's nominations of Mr. Shane, Mr. Squire, Stanley B. Kegler, and Sumner Ives to membership on the committee; and authorized a meeting of the committee and representatives of the Board to complete the plans for the yearbook, to be published in 1970.

This excellent committee under the dynamic leadership of Mr. Marckwardt has produced, with the assistance of a number of other outstanding scholars, a yearbook that will be read eagerly by teachers of English at all levels and influence the thinking and behavior of all teachers. It will enlighten the lay public with respect to what the schools are doing and should try to do. It will be used extensively in teacher-education programs and will leave its mark on the textbooks of the future.

In all, *Linguistics in School Programs* will have a major impact upon the nature and methods of language instruction in American schools.

HERMAN G. RICHEY
Editor for the Society

Table of Contents

SECTION I

The Dimensions of Language

Introduction

ALBERT H. MARCKWARDT

Of the various disciplines commanding public attention over the past thirty years which may be considered to have relevance for school programs, linguistics is clearly among those in the forefront. On the surface it is reasonable to suppose that a systematic knowledge of the structure and history of the English language on the part of the teacher is a prerequisite to developing in his students a competence in its use. Parallels can be found in any number of fields. In actual practice, however, it has turned out that what one decade regarded as a basic knowledge of the discipline comes to be considered quaintly outmoded or somewhat irrelevant in the next. Like many disciplines, linguistics has been and still is in something of a state of ferment.

Yet, ferment is a sign of life. And it is because of the quality of development and growth in the science of language that it seems important at this time to present an account of the present state of the discipline and to point out its many implications for what goes on in the classrooms of the nation's schools. Such is the purpose of this collection of essays by well-known scholars in the field and by schoolmen who have been alert to recent developments and their potential applications.

The book opens with a prologue broadly concerned with the entire field of human communication and the place of linguistics in that field. The first of the volume's two sections, "The Dimensions of Language," deals with linguistics in its current state, organized topically in terms of the principal branches of the discipline. As with every discipline which is alive, there are obviously some ends that remain loose, some issues which are still unresolved. These are dealt with frankly and fairly. The authors of the individual chapters have attempted, as well, to distinguish clearly between (*a*) the tools and special knowledge which the linguist employs in the practice of his discipline and (*b*) the concepts and conclusions which may usefully be passed on to teachers. Unfortunately these have often been confused in the past.

Section II, "Learning and Language," consists of a series of chapters dealing specifically with linguistics in the school context, in terms both of its content and its implications for teaching strategies. It is our hope that the authors have succeeded in setting forth the major implications of linguistic scholarship for school instruction and in narrowing the gap between research in a live and exciting field and its potential contribution to what takes place in the classrooms of the nation.

THE DIMENSIONS OF LANGUAGE

The Study of Language and Human Communication

WILLIAM G. MOULTON

Language and Human Communication

COMMUNICATION AND HUMAN BEINGS

Human beings communicate constantly and in a vast variety of ways. It is next to impossible for two or more human beings to be together without communicating in one way or another—most obviously through language, but just as often in other, less obvious ways. Even when we are alone, we continue to make use of communication: perhaps we read a book or a newspaper (communication!), or listen to the radio or watch television (still more communication!), or even in rare moments engage in that silent self-communication that we call "thinking." A significant proportion of our population is professionally engaged in the various communication industries: radio, television, theater, moving pictures, publishing, and advertising, as well as that greatest "communication industry" of them all—our educational institutions.

Much of this communication is voluntary and purposeful. The teacher in front of the classroom purposely uses both audio aids (mostly language) and visual aids (perhaps only the humble blackboard) to communicate the lesson of the day. And the pupil who comes to school tries to communicate with other pupils through his or her manner of dress, his haircut, her hairdo, and numerous sorts of social behavior. Much of this communication is also involuntary and inadvertent. The job applicant who uses unaccepted forms of language in either grammar or pronunciation may inadvertently disqualify himself for the job that he is seeking; and the dinner guest who eats with his knife or wipes his mouth on his sleeve may inadvertently mark himself as one to whom no future invitations will be extended.

Let us define human communication as the transmission of information from one person to another. Such a definition immediately gives the three elements which must be present: first, there must be a *sender;* second, there must be a *receiver;* and third, there must be some sort of *medium of transmission.* As their medium of transmission, human beings have available to them the familiar five senses—those of taste, smell, touch, sight, and hearing—either singly or in various combinations. Though all of these senses are used in one way or another for purposes of communication, human beings in the course of their evolution have developed one particular type of communication to such a high degree that it far surpasses all others in its flexibility, expressiveness, creativity, efficiency, and sheer elegance. This type, of course, is human language, which uses sound as its medium of transmission. Its use by human beings is so all-pervasive, and the role that it plays in human society is so essential, that it justifies us in distinguishing man from all other living beings by describing him as the "talking animal."

It is interesting to speculate about why human beings should have developed as their primary means of communication a system that uses sound as its medium of transmission rather than one of the other four senses. Why, for example, did they not use the sense of touch? Or, since it is especially acute in human beings, the sense of sight? The choice of sound is all the more remarkable because of the rather surprising source from which it is universally produced in human languages, namely, the respiratory tract—that area of the human body that extends from the diaphragm and the lungs out through the larynx, the pharynx, the mouth, and the nose. This area contains the so-called "organs of speech." Yet their use in producing the sounds of speech is surely a secondary development in terms of human evolution; they function primarily as the organs of breathing and, in part, of eating.

Though we can only speculate, it seems likely that sound produced by the respiratory tract came universally to be used as the medium for communication via language because it possesses a double versatility. First, the use of sound does not require the receiver of our message to be right next to us (as is the case with touch) or in our direct line of vision (as is the case with sight); he can just as well be beside us, behind us, or some distance away; and we can communicate with him in any of these positions even in the dark. Second, the use of the respiratory tract to produce sound does not require us to use our hands to communicate messages (as would most likely be the case if we used touch or sight); and this means that we can transmit messages via sound at the same time that we are doing just about anything else. The only drawback is that, as we transmit messages via sound, we must occasionally pause for breath; and some human beings seem almost able to overcome even this limitation.

NONVERBAL COMMUNICATION

This book is concerned primarily with the use of language as a means of transmitting information, that is to say, with what we customarily call "verbal communication." In order to put this topic in proper perspective, however, it is helpful to consider at least briefly some of the ways we transmit information *without* using language—to discuss various types of "nonverbal communication." This is all the more important because we are often unaware of some of these many other kinds of communication.

Do we ever use the sense of taste to transmit information? We surely do—though only to a very limited extent. The host who serves a well-chosen wine, and the hostess who serves a well-cooked meal, are surely communicating to their dinner guests. To prove the point, we need only consider what the reaction of the guests will be (what the "information" communicated to the guests will be) if the wine is cheap and tasteless and the meal is hastily and carelessly prepared.

Do we ever use the sense of smell to communicate information? Again, we surely do, though it is difficult to discuss the matter because our society places a strong taboo on most discussions of smells. Body smells, in particular, are negatively valued in our society; and the intensity of their negative "communication" can be judged by the fact that it supports a considerable part of the cosmetics industry. Curiously, a well-cooked head of cabbage may possess considerable positive "taste" value; but its "smell" value is highly negative—and again has led to a flourishing industry devoted to its suppression. Perfumes and flower smells, on the other hand, are positively valued; they also have produced flourishing industries.

Though we unquestionably use the senses of taste and smell in order to communicate (though not always intentionally), we do so only to a very limited degree. Far more extensive is the use that we make of the sense of touch. Parents fondle children (and psychologists tell us that this subtle communication is highly important in rearing children); lovers hold hands; campaigning politicians kiss babies; strangers, upon being introduced, shake hands; the more extrovert among us slap old friends on the back; and when we try to comfort someone in grief or pain, we stroke his hand or smooth his brow. In these and many other cases we use the sense of touch as an effective medium for communication, though in no case is its use developed to the point where we can say that it truly constitutes a "system" of communication.

Still more extensive is our use of sight as a medium for communication. Here, however, we must be careful to distinguish clearly between visual symbols which signal meaning directly, and those which signal it only indirectly, through the intermediary of language. We can illustrate these two very different types of visual symbols by considering two common sorts of road signs:

Though the meanings of both signs are ultimately the same, they signal this same meaning in quite different ways. Sign (1) does so directly, without the intermediary of language; hence it can be read equally well by speakers of all languages. Sign (2), on the other hand, signals its meaning only indirectly: the four letters of *LEFT* stand for the sounds of the spoken English word *left*; and it is only this spoken word which stands for the meaning of the sign. Signs of this type can of course be read only by people who happen to know English, and know how to read it.

"Indirect" visual symbols, which go from sight to meaning only through the intermediary of language, will be considered elsewhere in this book. We wish to consider here only those visual symbols that go directly from sight to meaning. There are many examples:

traffic lights, railroad signals, barber poles, smoke signals, and the like. In a few cases the use of visual symbols is perhaps elaborate enough to warrant our calling it a genuine "system." Examples are: Indian sign languages, the system of gestures used in some societies (though hardly in our own), the pennants used by yachtsmen, and European road signs. Note that all of these systems are quite independent of spoken language. They must again be carefully distinguished from such language-dependent systems as the hand-signals of the deaf, the semaphore signals used by Boy Scouts, and the blinking-light signals used for communication from ship to ship at sea. These latter types of signals symbolize letters of the alphabet; combinations of letters, in turn, symbolize the spoken words of language; and it is only these latter that contain the intended "meanings" of messages communicated in this way.

As a final type of visual signal, we need to consider briefly the communicative value of body movements—the study of which has recently come to be called *kinesics*. Some of these movements accompany language, and though they are not a part of language, we use them constantly and to a surprising extent. In order to appreciate the great role that they play as an accompaniment to language, it is helpful and amusing to try the following experiment: turn off the sound track on a television set and watch the constant body movements of the speakers as they talk. They scowl, smile, roll their eyes, shift their weight, gesture with their hands, tilt their heads— and almost *never* stand stock still. Or, as another experiment, watch a couple at a nearby table in a restaurant. The communicative effect of their body movements is so strong that we can often see quite clearly whether they are happy, sad, in love, having a fight, or perhaps concocting some dire plot.

Body movements can be equally communicative even when they do not accompany language. A job applicant waiting for his interview may look around the room, scratch the back of his head, adjust his necktie (for the hundredth time), flick a bit of lint off his jacket, rub his hands together, and the like. And when his turn finally comes, the body movements of his interviewer may communicate very powerfully how well things are—or are not—going. At first the interviewer's body movements will probably be conscious and intentional: he may smile and motion the applicant to a chair.

But soon unconscious body movements begin to convey their power-ful messages—and woe to the applicant who cannot read them prop-erly. If, after some minutes, the interviewer begins to cross and recross his legs, shift his weight in his chair, "fiddle" with his pencil, move a paper clip on his desk, or repeatedly rub his hand across his mouth, a wise applicant will know that his time is up and that he must leave.

THE UNIQUENESS OF LANGUAGE

In the preceding discussion we pointed out that human beings have developed one type of communication which far surpasses all others, namely, language. Yet we also noted that human beings com-municate—often very effectively and subtly—in many other ways. We now need to ask: What justifies us in saying that language "far surpasses" all other types of communication? What, in short, is unique about language?

The answer is easily given: Language permits us, quite literally, to transmit an infinite number of messages. In order to appreciate this unique quality of language, we need only compare it with some of the other communicative devices we use. A barber pole transmits only one message, something like: "This is a place where a man can get a shave and a haircut." A traffic light transmits only three mes-sages: green for "go," amber for "caution," red for "stop." European road signs transmit a score or two of messages dealing with the control of traffic, but they cannot be used for discussing politics. Indian sign language can be used for discussing politics, but not for explaining how an internal combustion engine works. And so on. Only language can be used for all the kinds of messages human beings have occasion to communicate: telling someone where he can get his hair cut, discussing politics, explaining the workings of an internal combustion engine, describing the structure of the atom, and so on and on, quite literally without end.

Some notion of the extraordinary creativity and productivity of language can be given by the following simple yet somehow sur-prising observation: most of the sentences that (via language) we say and hear are sentences that we have never said or heard before. There are exceptions, of course—sentences like *What time is it?*, *I love you*, and *Please pass the butter*. Yet these are truly exceptions. Most of the sentences that we hear in daily conversation, or that occur in this book, are quite literally sentences that we have never heard or said (or seen or written) before—and probably never will again.

Many of the uses that we make of language strike us as valuable and important—for example: a classroom discussion of the Constitution of the United States, a trial in court, a plea for assistance. Others strike us as unimportant, even trivial—for example, the babbling of a group of teen-agers in a drugstore. The really classic example of trivial use of language comes not from teen-agers, however, but from adults: it is the American cocktail party. The ideal, perhaps, is to produce messages that are interesting and witty; but the most important thing is just to *use* language—to keep talking, with little regard to the content of the messages communicated. The guest who remains silent is regarded as "queer"; and the guest who really tries to communicate a serious message is considered a "bore."

In all of these uses of language—from the sublime to the ridiculous—there is one common denominator. The essential function of language is that of taking an idea (whether profound or trivial) that exists inside the head of the speaker, shaping it so that it can be transmitted as a message, then actually transmitting the message— and hoping that approximately the same idea will somehow miraculously reappear inside the head of the listener. The wonder of it all is not that the system does not work perfectly, but that it works as well as it does.

How are human beings able to use language in this remarkable way? One answer—and, in a very real sense, it is the only honest answer—is to say: As speakers of a language, we all carry around inside our heads a knowledge of this language; and it is this knowledge that enables us to accomplish this remarkable feat. Ideally, we should now try to get inside our heads and examine this knowledge of language directly. But of course we cannot do this. The best we can do is to try to guess from the outside what seems to be going on inside our heads.

We often think of language as consisting essentially of two ingredients: *sound* on the one hand, and *meaning* on the other. Yet sound and meaning are really not language itself, but only its two external manifestations. Suppose, for example, that we are watching two people speak a language we do not know. We can hear all of the sound, and in lucky cases we can even make shrewd guesses as to the meaning. Yet knowing that a given babble of sound will signal a given meaning is not what we would call "knowing" a bit of that language. We must know not only *that* sound signals meaning, but more particularly *how* it signals meaning; that is to say, we must understand the *correlation* between sound and meaning. This correlation between sound and meaning is the essence of language; and since it takes place inside our heads, none of it is directly observable. Nevertheless, by examining the external aspects of this correlation in any given language, we can deduce many details of its internal workings. It is to this topic that we shall now turn.

Language as Structure

THE TWO EXTERNAL ENDS OF LANGUAGE

We can best think of language as an abstract structure that is connected with concrete reality at two external ends. At one end it is connected with sound—all the noises the speakers of a language make when they talk. At the other end it is connected with human experience—all the things the speakers of a language talk about when they use language. And language itself, as we have just said, is the *correlation* between these two external ends.

The truly remarkable fact about language is, now, the following: *Outside* of language, in the areas of sound and experience, there is no clear structure. We cannot say that the sound of a spoken sentence consists, in any objective sense, of a certain number of pieces in a certain arrangement; and we cannot say that human experience consists, in any objective sense, of a certain number of pieces in a certain arrangement. (It is true that scientists have been able to analyze tangible matter into a certain number of "pieces" in certain "arrangements." But they keep discovering new pieces and arrangements; and, in any case, tangible matter is only a very small part of human experience.) *Inside* of language, on the other hand (insofar as we understand the "inside of language"), everything is neatly structured and consists of units of specific sorts in arrangements of specific sorts. Let us consider how this system seems to work. We shall begin with the end of language where it is connected with sound, since this is the end that we understand the best.

LANGUAGE AND SOUND

The sound that reaches our ears when someone speaks to us does not have any clear and consistent structure. Instead of consisting of a specific number of "pieces" of sound in a specific order, as we normally think of it, it is a continuum—an uninterrupted stream of sound. This is precisely the impression we get when we listen to a language we do not know, and acoustic phoneticians have expensive instruments which demonstrate that this impression is entirely correct. Viewed objectively, spoken language is a continuum of sound. As we *understand* spoken language, however, it *does* consist of a specific number of "pieces" in a specific order. Our spoken English word *at* consists of two such pieces, *cat* consists of three, *flat* of four, *blast* of five, and so on. As these examples show, our whole writing system—with all its imperfections and inconsistencies—is based precisely on this principle: we understand spoken language as consisting of "sounds" strung along in a row.

Since these "sounds" do not exist as such in the external, physically observable world, the only place they can exist is inside our heads, as part of our knowledge of our language. It might therefore be useful to call them "internal sounds"; instead of this, the linguist uses the technical term *phonemes*. The essential point to understand about phonemes is this: every bit of spoken language we hear must be interpreted as consisting of a sequence of phonemes, in a particular order. If we cannot make this conversion of a stream of (external) sound into a sequence of (internal) phonemes, then we cannot understand what has been said to us. Suppose, for example, that a friend introduces someone to us by saying: "This is Mr. Gri--on," pronouncing in the middle of the name a consonant sound that we do not hear properly. What can the name be? English offers us precisely twenty-one possibilities, since it has precisely twenty-one consonant phonemes that can occur in this position: *Grippon, Gribbon, Griffon, Grivon, Grimmon,* etc., through all twenty-one possible choices.

We can think of a language as a device which, at the end where it is connected with audible sound, consists of a sieve with a specific number of holes in it, representing the number of phonemes inside the language. In order to enter language and be "understood," the stream of speech outside of language must be filtered through this sieve. Outside of language, speech consists of a stream of sound; inside of language, it consists of a precise sequence of phonemes. We may therefore say that, in this sense, language gives "structure" to sound—a structure that it does not possess in any objectively observable way. And the same stream of sound may be structured differently by different languages.

Language also "structures" sound in another way. We can illustrate this by listing the twenty-four consonant phonemes that occur in all standard varieties of English:

p	t	č	k	*p*ail	*t*ail	*ch*ain	cane
b	d	ǰ	g	*b*ail	*d*ale	*j*ail	*g*ale
f	θ	s	š	*f*ail	*th*in	sail	*sh*ale
v	ð	z	ž	*v*eil	*then*	*z*eal	a*z*ure
m		n	ŋ	*m*ail		*n*ail	ri*ng*
	l	r			*l*ane	*r*ain	
w		h	y	*w*ail		*h*ail	*Y*ale

The letters to the left represent phonemic symbols; the choice of such symbols is unimportant, though we try to keep as close as possible to the regular letters of the alphabet. The examples to the right are given in regular spelling; italicized letters illustrate typical spellings of the phonemes in question.

These twenty-four consonant phonemes of English do not represent a random selection from among all the various types of consonant sounds that the vocal organs are capable of producing. Instead, they represent an economical system composed of a small number of distinctive phonetic features. Though we cannot go into all details here, we can at least mention the following. The set /p t č k f θ s š/ have the feature *voiceless* (pronounced without simultaneous vibration of the vocal cords); this distinguishes them from the set /b d ǰ g v ð z ž/, which are *voiced* (pronounced with simultaneous vibration of the vocal cords). Further, the set /p t č k b d ǰ g/ are *stops* (pronounced by stopping the breath stream momentarily at some point in the mouth); this distinguishes them from the set /f θ s š v ð z ž/, which are *fricatives* (pronounced by forcing the breath stream through a narrow opening so as to produce friction). All sixteen of these consonants are also *oral* (pronounced without a flow of air through the nose); this distinguishes them from the set /m n ŋ/, which are *nasal* (pronounced with a flow of air through the nose).

All languages also "structure" sound in still another way: in the sequences of phonemes that are permitted in the language. For example, the first twenty-one English consonants can occur after short stressed /i/ and before an unstressed vowel, as in the name *Gri--on;* but the last three consonants (/w, h, y/) cannot occur in this position. Of the twenty-four consonants, twenty-two may occur at the beginning of a word before a vowel; but two of them (/ž/ and /ŋ/) may not. As many as three consonants may occur at the beginning of a word. If so, the first must be /s/; the second must be one of the set /p t k/ (cf. *spring, stroll, scream*); and the third must be one of the set /r l y w/ (cf. *strip, split, skew, squeeze*). These are very strict rules, they cannot be violated and still produce genuine English.

LANGUAGE AND EXPERIENCE

We have just seen how, at one end of language, the infinite number of sounds that the vocal organs can produce are structured, within language, into a small set of abstract phonological units called phonemes. When we now turn to the other end of language, where it is connected with human experience, we find that the infinite number of things human beings talk about are again structured, within language, into a set of abstract units—semantic units, this time. There are, however, two great differences. First, the number of semantic units at this end of language is far, far greater than the number of phonemes. Second, this end of language is much less well understood.

Perhaps the easiest way of understanding how language gives structure to experience is to consider how the same general area of experience can be structured in different languages. There is an area of experience which we in English symbolize by means of the single word *know*; we use it both for persons ("I *know* him") and for facts ("I *know* where he lives"). French, on the other hand, treats these uses as distinctly different "meanings" and has two quite different words for them: *connaître* for persons ("Je le *connais*") but *savoir* for facts ("Je *sais* où il habite"). Here two words in another language correspond to one word in English. An example of the opposite sort is provided by the Russian word *ruká,* which refers to that part of the human body which extends from the shoulder through the fingertips. In English we structure this into two "meanings" through our words *arm* and *hand*. There is no single word for *ruká* in English any more than there is a single word for *know* in French.

Because we are so used to the way in which our own language structures experience, we are often inclined to think of this as the only "natural" way of handling things. Yet a little thought will reveal innumerable examples within our own language to show that its handling of meaning is not "natural" at all, but highly arbitrary— even whimsical. One example is provided by the words *watch* and *clock*. It would seem "natural" to have a single word to refer to all devices that tell us what time it is; yet we in English insist on dividing such objects into two semantic classes, depending on whether or not they are customarily portable. If such a device *is* customarily portable, it is a *watch;* if it is *not* customarily portable, it is a *clock*. Or consider the words *bush* and *shrub*. These are clearly two different semantic units in English; yet if someone pointed to two objects in our garden and asked us to tell him which was a *bush* and which was a *shrub*, most of us would be unable to do so.

In showing how languages give structure to sound, we assume that it is possible to devise a universal phonetic grid on which all the speech sounds of all languages can be more or less accurately plotted. We can then determine which areas of this grid are used to reflect, in audible sound, the various phonemes of a particular language; and this, in turn, allows us to describe the phonetic structure of the system of phonemes in the language, in terms of distinctive phonetic features. In showing how languages give structure to experience, we would like to use a similar method. We would like to devise a universal semantic grid on which all the meanings of all languages could be more or less accurately plotted; and we would then like to determine which areas of this grid are used to reflect, in meaning, the various semantic units of a particular language. If we could do this, we could then describe the semantic structure of the system of semantic units in the language, in terms of distinctive semantic features.

Though this might be an ideal way of handling meaning, it is far beyond our capabilities at present—and probably will always remain so. Constructing a "universal semantic grid" would be a task of staggering complexity, and we have no hope of ever being able to accomplish it. The best we can do is to try to describe tiny areas of this total theoretical grid. One such area which has been investigated in many languages is that represented by kinship terms. Interestingly enough, it serves as a classic example of the very different ways in which languages handle one and the same area of experience. In English we find it "natural" that we have a term *brother* to denote a male child of the same parents as ourselves; yet many languages have no word for this, but only for *older brother* or *younger brother*. We also find it "natural" that kinship terms should reflect the difference between male and female: *brother* vs. *sister, father* vs. *mother, uncle* vs. *aunt*, etc.; yet we in English fail to make this distinction in the case of "child of sibling of our parent" and have only the single word *cousin*. Dutch makes this sex distinction in its words *neef* "male cousin" and *nicht* "female cousin"; but it fails to make the generational distinction that we find so "natural," since *neef* also means "nephew" and *nicht* also means "niece."

Semantics—the study of the way in which each language structures the world of human experience—is an enormously complicated field, about which we know far too little. The one point that we wish to make clear here is: the world of human experience has no clear structure as such; but it receives structure as it is filtered through into language, and each language gives it its own peculiar structure.

LANGUAGE AND SYNTAX

The essence of language, we have suggested, is the correlation between sound on the one hand and meaning (or experience) on the other. We have now seen how sound filters through into language so as to give a set of meaningless abstract units (phonemes), and how experience filters through into language so as to give a set of meaningful abstract units (semantic units). The correlation between these two types of units takes place in that part of language called *syntax;* and the units within this part of language are customarily called *morphemes* (from Greek *morphḗ* "form").

The relation between morphemes and phonemes is relatively clear: by and large, a given morpheme is converted into a sequence of phonemes. Thus the English morpheme *if* is converted into two phonemes: /if/; *push* is converted into three phonemes: /puš/; *chest* into four phonemes: /čest/; *thrift* into five: /θrift/; *splint* into six: /splint/; and so on. Sometimes there are complications. The English morpheme "Past Tense" is converted sometimes into /-t/, as in *kept;* sometimes into /-d/, as in *played;* sometimes into /-ed/, as in *waited;* and sometimes it is fused with the verb stem, as in *took* (past tense of *take*), *wound* (past tense of *wind*), etc. Nevertheless, the principle is clear: morphemes are converted into "strings" of phonemes (one phoneme, or sequences of more than one phoneme).

The relation between morphemes and semantic units is less clear, because our understanding of semantics is so rudimentary. By and large, one morpheme corresponds to one semantic unit: cf. *faith, faith-ful, un-faith-ful, un-faith-ful-ness.* Sometimes, however, a single morpheme seems to correspond to more than one semantic unit. This is presumably the case with such morphemes as *eleven* and *twelve,* which seem to be made up of the semantic units "10 + 1," "10 + 2." (But a one-to-one correspondence between semantic units and morphemes presumably exists in *thir-teen, four-teen,* etc.) Sometimes, on the other hand, more than one morpheme seems to correspond to a single semantic unit. This is presumably the case with *get up,* which clearly consists of two morphemes but seems to be only a single semantic unit; and also with *receive,* which consists morphemically of the prefix *re-* plus the stem *-ceive,* though presumably it is again only a single semantic unit.

The function of syntax is that of arranging morphemes in such a way as to produce meaningful sentences. Because of its central position within language, we assume that syntax shows two different types of structure, corresponding to the structure that language gives to sound on the one hand, and to the structure that it gives to meaning on the other. Because sound is *linear* (through the dimension of time), we assume that the *surface structure* of syntax is also linear: it must consist of strings of morphemes, just as phonology consists of strings of phonemes. We can illustrate this with the sentence *The man wound up the clock:*

Surface Structure:	*the man wind Past up the clock*
Phonemic Structure:	/ðə mæn waund ʌp ðə klak/
Sound Structure:	[a continuous stream of sound]

Meaning, on the other hand, does *not* seem to be linear in structure. We do not understand the sentence *The man wound up the
clock* as consisting simply of the meaning of *the*, plus the meaning
of *man*, plus the meaning of *wind*, plus the meaning of *Past Tense*,
etc. Instead, we understand meanings to be arranged in a *hierarchical*
structure that we can diagram for this sentence (omitting *Past Tense*
for simplicity) as follows:

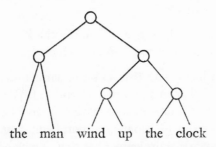

the   man   wind   up   the   clock

That is to say, we understand *the* and *man* as belonging meaningfully
together in the construction *the man; wind* and *up* as belonging
meaningfully together in the construction *wind up;* and *the* and
clock as belonging meaningfully together in the construction *the
clock*. Furthermore, we understand the construction *the man* as the
"subject" of this sentence, and the construction *wind up the clock*
as the "predicate" of this sentence. And we understand the subject
the man as being in construction with the predicate *wind up the
clock* so as to form (with the addition of *Past Tense*) the sentence
The man wound up the clock.

This hierarchical arrangement of morphemes is the part of syntax
called *deep structure*. Whereas surface structure represents the way
we *say* a sentence, deep structure represents the way we *understand*
it. In between the deep structure and the surface structure we can
assume a set of syntactic *transformations* which map the one type
of structure into the other.

The assumption that syntax consists of deep structure and surface
structure, connected by transformations, allows us to account for a
great many facts of language that would otherwise be puzzling. Consider the following pair of sentences:

(1) The man wound up the clock.
(2) The man wound the clock up.

We would like to be able to say that in one sense these two sentences are "the same," but that in another sense they are "different." We can now do so by saying that they have the same deep structure (representing the single way we understand them); that they have different surface structures (representing the two different ways we say them); and that different transformations from deep structure to surface structure account for these differences. Consider now the following two sentences:

(3) Did the man wind up the clock?
(4) Did the man wind the clock up?

We would again like to say that, in some sense, these two sentences are at least very similar to sentences (1) and (2). We can now do so by assuming that all four sentences have the same basic deep structure, but that (1) and (2) contain a morpheme *Statement* whereas (3) and (4) contain a morpheme *Question*. Transformations delete these two morphemes in going from deep structure to surface structure, but their effect is still present in the very different word order of the surface structures. Consider finally the following two sentences:

(5) The clock was wound up by the man.
(6) Was the clock wound up by the man?

Again we would like to say that in some sense these two sentences are "the same" as all the others. We can do so by assuming that the first four sentences contain, in their deep structures, the morpheme *Active*, whereas these last two contain the morpheme *Passive*. Transformations again delete these morphemes as such in going from deep structure to surface structure, but their effect is still present in the very different word order of the surface structures (as well as in the presence of the word *was*, in the fact that *wound* is now past participle rather than past tense, and in the presence of the word *by*).

THE INFINITE PRODUCTIVITY OF LANGUAGE

In discussing the uniqueness of language, as opposed to other forms of human communication, we noted that language is infinitely productive: that it permits us, quite literally, to transmit an infinite number of messages. In concluding this section, "Language as Structure," we must mention briefly the two design features that make this infinite productivity possible. Both features are disarmingly simple: they involve what is known in mathematics as *recursion*. First, two or more sentences may simply be joined together in the deep structure; this is syntactic *coordination*. Second, one sentence may be embedded inside another sentence in the deep structure; this is syntactic *subordination*.

Coordination can be illustrated by the following sentences:

    (1) John told Bill, and Bill told Jim, and Jim told Joe, . . .
    (2) Henry bought a hat, a tie, some handkerchiefs, . . .

In (1), the sentence structures *John told Bill, Bill told Jim, Jim told Joe* have been conjoined by means of the word *and* so as to give a single sentence; such conjoining can obviously go on indefinitely. In (2), the sentence structures *Henry bought a hat, Henry bought a tie, Henry bought some handkerchiefs* have been conjoined by means of the word *and*, first giving *Henry bought a hat and Henry bought a tie and Henry bought*; transformations now delete all but the first occurrence of *Henry bought* and (normally) all but the last occurrence of *and*. As written above, we have omitted this last *and* to indicate that here also conjoining can go on indefinitely.

Subordination can be illustrated with the following famous example:

This is the cat	(1) This is the cat.
that killed the rat	(2) The cat killed the rat.
that ate the malt	(3) The rat ate the malt.
that lay in the house	(4) The malt lay in the house.
that Jack built.	(5) Jack built the house.

Here sentence (5) has been embedded within sentence (4); the resulting sentence has been embedded within sentence (3); the resulting sentence has been embedded within sentence (2); and the resulting sentence has been embedded within sentence (1). A whole cycle of transformations has thus produced the single sentence to the left. Recursion of this sort can of course also go on indefinitely.

Another, more intricate example of embedding is illustrated by the following sentence:

The man was troubled by	(1) Something troubled the man + Passive.
his son's	(2) The man had a son.
being accused of	(3) Someone accused the son of something + Passive
stealing.	(4) The son stole something.

A whole cycle of transformations has again converted the sentence structures labeled (1), (2), (3), (4) into the single sentence to the left.

Coordination and subordination are very powerful devices for combining two or more sentence structures into a single sentence. They have a triple effect: (a) there is in any language an infinite number of sentences; (b) there is no such thing in any language as a "longest sentence"; and (c) it is now easy to understand how it is possible that most of the sentences we say and hear are sentences we have never said or heard before.

Language, Society, and the Individual

LANGUAGE AND SOCIETY

Language is a social institution. More than any other social institution, it serves often (though by no means always) to bind its speakers together into a cohesive group with common ideals and aspirations, and with a common way of looking at the world about them. The child first learns his native language in the microsociety of the family, but he soon expands this learning into ever widening circles: first to his playmates; then to his neighborhood, school, or village; and beyond this to even larger groups. Theoretically, at least, the linguistic society to which an individual belongs is limited only by the number of other persons who also speak his "language" (a slippery term; see below). In our modern world some of these "linguistic societies" are enormous in size. The forty-two largest (including all those with ten million speakers or more) are listed in Table I. In one respect these figures are very misleading: two people who are said to speak "the same language" may not actually be able to talk to each other at all, since many languages include varieties that are not mutually intelligible. This is especially true of what is labeled here as "Chinese." (It might perhaps better be divided into

TABLE 1

THE FORTY-TWO LARGEST LINGUISTIC SOCIETIES
BY NUMBER OF SPEAKERS

Language	Millions of Speakers	Language	Millions of Speakers	Language	Millions of Speakers
Chinese......	619	Ukrainian....	35	Oriya.........	15
English.......	250	Korean.......	33	Persian........	14
Hindi-Urdu...	154	Polish........	33	Rajasthani....	14
Spanish......	140	Tamil........	32	Pashto........	13
Russian......	130	Marathi......	31	Serbo-Croatian.	13
German......	100	Bihari........	30	Sundanese.....	13
Japanese.....	95	Turkish......	25	Swahili........	13
Arabic........	80	Vietnamese...	24	Hungarian.....	12
Bengali.......	75	Gujarati......	19	Czech.........	10
Portuguese....	75	Rumanian....	18	Greek.........	10
French.......	65	Thai.........	18	Malay........	10
Italian.......	55	Dutch-Flemish	17	Visayan.......	10
Javanese.....	45	Burmese.....	16		
Telugu.......	37	Kanarese.....	16		
Punjabi......	36	Malayalam...	15		

Source: Data from *Anthropological Linguistics*, Vol. 3, No. 8, 1961. Number of speakers estimated as of the beginning of 1961.

Mandarin with 460 million speakers, Wu with 50 million, Cantonese and Min each with 46 million, and Hakka with 17 million—though even within these groupings there are many mutually unintelligible varieties.) Even within English there are of course mutually unintelligible varieties. An Arkansas farmer and a Yorkshire farmer would probably not be able to understand each other at all if each spoke his local variety of English; and a New Yorker and a London Cockney would not fare much better.

The development of such large "linguistic societies" is something very new in the history of the human race. A few thousand years ago, before the rise of cities and states, there were surely already a great many different languages in the world, but each of them probably had (from our modern point of view) only a tiny number of speakers—from a few hundred to a few thousand. For us as speakers of English (with some 250 million fellow-speakers), it is hard to imagine such a situation: hundreds, even thousands of languages, each with only a few hundred or a few thousand speakers. Yet the truth of the matter is that this is still the typical linguistic situation today. No one knows how many languages are now spoken in the world (in part because it is so difficult to say just what a "language" is), but the usual estimates place this number at between three and six thousand. The source cited above lists only 128 languages with a million or more speakers each. This means that each of the remaining 96-98 percent of all languages is spoken by *fewer* than a million speakers; and this, in turn, means that the "average" or "typical" language is still spoken by only very small numbers of people. Because such "tiny" languages are spoken largely by primitive tribes in such places as the jungles of the Amazon or the island of New Guinea, we are inclinded to scoff at them as unworthy of serious consideration. Yet for an understanding of human language as a means of communication, they are every bit as valuable as such "huge" languages as Chinese and English. Though there are indeed such things as "primitive societies," there are no such things as "primitive languages." The languages of the most primitive societies and of the most advanced civilizations are all, each in its own way, equally intricate and complex.

All languages exist in more than one variety. The one universal source of variety is *style*. Even the sole surviving speaker of an American Indian language, for example, will use one style when he is asked to show how his tribe used to carry on everyday conversation, another style when he is asked to tell the tales that his tribesmen used to tell, and perhaps still another style when he is asked to describe religious rituals. A second source of variety, which is universal just as long as there are still two surviving speakers of a language, is *skill*. Some speakers are able to use a language more skillfully than others, and this is universally recognized both in primitive societies and in our own complex society. Much of the teaching of English in our schools is aimed at developing skill in the use of language.

As the geographical area in which a language is spoken becomes larger, and as the social structure of its speakers becomes more complex, two further sources of variety emerge. Because every language is constantly changing, a given language will normally develop differently in different geographical areas and in different social strata, giving rise to the varieties customarily called *dialects:* geographical dialects and social dialects. In the course of time these varieties may become so different that speakers can no longer understand each other (assuming that they speak only their local or social dialects) even though they live only a few score miles apart, or even though they live in the same large urban center.

As long as no great need is felt for communication among speakers of these many different varieties, this situation can continue indefinitely. But if a need for communication *is* felt, the speakers of the language are faced with a difficult problem: they must somehow devise some sort of superdialect (technically called a *standard language*) that can be used for communication among all speakers, regardless of their native local and social dialects. Sometimes this comes about without conscious effort on the part of the speakers. Thus, the local dialects of London and Paris came gradually to be used as Standard English and Standard French, respectively, because each of these cities was a great political, economic, and cultural center. In other cases, a group of speakers may struggle for many decades trying to agree on a common standard language. This has been the case with the Norwegians (some four million speakers): they formerly used Danish as their standard language; national independence led them to seek a standard of their own, but they still have not reached full agreement as to just what this Standard Norwegian should be. In still other cases, a standard language is somewhat arbitrarily fashioned out of one or more local varieties and then simply proclaimed as "the standard." This is the case with Bahasa Indonesia, intended to become the standard language of Indonesia. The whole notion of a "standard language" is unfamiliar to Americans because, in effect, we have never lacked one. Though many of our early English settlers must have been dialect speakers, the one variety common to all of them was the Standard London English of the time. This was then the only variety that survived, though it has since—like any language— developed differently in different geographical areas and social strata.

An interesting example of the relationship between standard language and local dialect is provided by Dutch-Flemish and German. From the point of view of local dialects, the entire area from northern Italy (so-called Southern Tyrol), Austria, much of Switzerland, part of France (Alsace and some of Lorraine) on up to the Baltic and North Sea coasts of Germany, Holland, Belgium, and a bit of adjacent France is a single *dialect area*. Though local dialects vary everywhere from village to village, transitions from one village to the next are always gradual, and nowhere is there a sharp linguistic border—unless one crosses into the French-speaking parts of Switzerland, France, and Belgium, or into the Frisian-speaking part of Holland. Within this large area, two standard languages have developed: Standard Dutch-Flemish (now officially called "Netherlandic") in Holland and northern Belgium, and Standard German in the rest of the area. This now leads to the following curious situation. Let us suppose that we visit (as the writer of these lines once did) two villages about two miles apart, one in Holland and one in Germany. The dialects of these two villages are to all intents and purposes identical—except that on the Dutch side prices are given in guilders and cents, whereas on the German side they are given in marks and pfennigs. Should we now say that one and the same variety of language is in one village a dialect of Dutch, in the other village a dialect of German? This is of course absurd, yet it is what we customarily do. We give this example only to show the arbitrariness of saying that there are one hundred million speakers of "German" and seventeen million speakers of "Dutch-Flemish"—and similarly with just about every other "language."

The development of a standard language means that at least some speakers (always including those holding positions of prestige in the society) can speak a variety of the language that has a more or less uniform pronunciation, grammar, and vocabulary; and in modern times it also means that they write the language in a more or less uniform spelling. It does *not* mean, however, that such persons must necessarily give up their local dialects. The German-speaking Swiss, for example, use Standard German for writing and for certain "public" uses of speech: radio and television broadcasts, church sermons, public lectures, and conversations with German speakers from other countries. In daily talk with other Swiss, however, they always use local dialects, and they would find it inconceivable to use Standard German on such occasions. At universities, a professor lectures in Standard German; but if a student comes up to the professor after the lecture to ask a question, both of them always speak local dialect with one another. Further, all pupils are taught Standard German in school, and Standard German is the language of instruction after the first year or two. But outside of the classroom, children talk local dialect not only with each other but also with the teacher. As a result, all Swiss Germans are at least bilingual: they speak both local dialect and (with varying degrees of skill) Standard German; many are, in fact, multilingual since they speak more than one local dialect.

LANGUAGE AND THE CHILD

All normal human beings possess a truly extraordinary ability to learn language during their childhood years. We do not *teach* a language to small children; they learn it by themselves—and we could not keep them from doing so even if we tried, short of locking them up in a room where they would never hear any language whatever. They do not even *learn* a language in the usual sense of the word, as they later learn reading, writing, and arithmetic— through conscious effort and application; they just pick it up, most of the time without even realizing that they are doing so. They seem to possess an inborn faculty for language which, like a film, merely needs to be exposed to language in order to become imprinted. Furthermore, this is a faculty for language generally, not for any one particular language. The language that a child learns has nothing whatever to do with genetic inheritance but depends entirely on the language—or languages—to which he is exposed during childhood. In the normal case, perhaps, he learns only one language; but this is merely because he is *exposed* to only one language. In many parts of the world, children typically grow up speaking two or more languages; and probably all of us know American families who lived abroad for some time and whose children picked up not only the English of their parents but also the Japanese, French, Arabic, or whatnot of their playmates or nurse. All of this has little or nothing to do with what we normally call "intelligence." Language is learned in this way by bright children, by stupid children, by morons—by all but out-and-out imbeciles.

For the adult who tries to learn a new language, there are two aspects of this childhood ability to pick up language that are frustrating and exasperating. First, the child seems to learn his one or more languages effortlessly. He does not struggle with verb endings and noun genders; though he always makes mistakes with such things at first, given sufficient exposure he masters them all to perfection. He acquires what is called a "native speaker's knowledge" of these things—the kind of knowledge that no adult learner can ever hope to match. Second, he learns all these things not only without apparent effort, but also far better than the struggling adult. This is most obvious in the case of pronunciation. The child who has had as little as half a year of genuine exposure to, for example, French, will pronounce it just like his French playmates—down to the minutest details. On the other hand, many of us know foreigners who came to the United States as young adults, who have since lived here for twenty, thirty, or forty years, but who still speak English with a thick foreign accent—the accent of the language that they learned in childhood. To their dying days they will never learn English as well as a child can. This again has nothing whatever to do with what we usually call "intelligence."

How long do children retain this extraordinary ability to pick up a language—effortlessly and perfectly? Though individuals of course vary, the average child retains this ability until about the age of puberty and then quickly loses it. Where the typical child of ten can still "pick up" a language without apparent effort, the typical child of fourteen must already "learn" it—consciously and with effort, and he will almost never acquire a true native speaker's knowledge of it.

Two reservations must be made concerning these observations on a young child's ability to pick up any language. First, he will do so only under what might perhaps be called "natural" learning conditions, as when he speaks the language constantly with one or both parents, with a nurse, or with playmates. This is vastly different from exposing a child to twenty minutes a day of, let us say, Spanish, in third, fourth, and fifth grades. Under these latter conditions, some children come close to attaining native facility in pronunciation, and they gain an easy familiarity with the language so that it need never again be truly "foreign" (all of which makes this type of instruction highly valuable); but they do not acquire genuine native ability in the overall use of the language. Second, the mere fact that a child achieves native control over a language does not mean that he will forever after *retain* this control; he will not, unless he continues to use the language in one way or another.

Language-learning in young children is a matter of "easy come,
easy go." The child of eight who learned such perfect Tagalog
during the four years his family spent in Manila will very soon
forget nearly every word of it unless he is somehow able to continue
using it.

Though the typical child loses his inborn language learning
faculty at around the age of puberty, there is one other ability
which many people retain on up to college age and often beyond:
the ability to learn a new *variety* of a language, especially its pronunciation. Many American families have experienced this when
with teen-age children they have moved, let us say, from Boston to
Atlanta (or vice versa): the children very soon come home from
school with new words and new pronunciations—often to the dismay of the parents. After a year or so of residence in the new
locality, the children's language will be almost indistinguishable
from that of their schoolmates, though usually a few earlier features
still survive. Similarly, many a young American goes to college in
a different section of the country from that in which he was brought
up, and he quickly adapts his language to some new variety that
he finds there.

LANGUAGE AND THE SCHOOLS

The teaching of English in our schools presents us with a curious
paradox. We have just seen that small children possess an extraordinary innate faculty to learn language, any language. By the time he
is five or six years old, the child already has a marvelous control over
his native language—*as he has learned it from his family and playmates*, though not necessarily as we might wish he had learned it.
Within this variety of his native language, he has an almost perfect
control over pronunciation—far better than the typical adult can
ever achieve. He has an excellent, though not yet perfect, control
over syntax. He has learned many thousands of words (estimates of
the active and passive vocabulary of six-year-old children run as
high as 24,000 words). He can speak this variety of his native
language with dazzling—sometimes annoying—fluency. And he
is able to say and understand, with complete ease, an infinite number
of sentences that he has never said or heard before. In short, he al-

ready possesses a "native speaker's knowledge" of his language, in the variety that he has learned.

These remarks may seem exaggerated. They are not. If you have doubts about their correctness, there is an easy remedy: Try out your French on a five-year-old French child.

But now comes the paradox. Precisely when the child is five or six years old, we send him to school; and for the next twelve years the one compulsory type of instruction he will receive year in and year out is instruction in his native language—whether we call this instruction "English," "language arts," or whatnot. Since the child already has such a marvelous ability to speak English (assuming that this is his native language), why do we do this? What do we think we are teaching him?

A number of things that we teach him go *beyond* language, in the strict sense of the term. First, we teach him to read and write—and children do *not* possess an innate faculty to learn these skills effortlessly but must work hard at them. Second, we teach him how to handle the special styles of written English, which are by no means simply the styles of spoken English put down on paper. Third, we teach him such practical uses of written English as how to open and close letters, how to write and answer invitations, and the like. Finally, we teach him how to read and understand some of the great things that have been written in the English language.

We also teach the child many things that *are* directly part of language—for example, the two sources of variety that are present in all languages: style and skill. Because his experience with language has been so brief, he still has much to learn in these two areas, and we try to guide him. In addition, we teach him things that have to do with the two sources of variety that are present in all but the very "tiny" languages: local dialects and social dialects. If we are not satisfied with the variety of English that he has learned so fluently (and we seldom are satisfied), we say to him in effect: "I know that you handle English with native fluency. But your variety of English is not widely accepted. If you want to get ahead in the world—if you want to fulfill the democratic ideal of developing your abilities to the fullest possible extent—you must learn another variety of English." That is to say, he must learn "Standard English"

—the kind of English that will permit him to hold a job at any level in any part of the country.

We have now broached the topic of what is and what is not "correct" English. Since most Americans—especially educated Americans—find it difficult to discuss this topic objectively, let us pretend that we are observing a similar situation in some other language. We visit the mythical land of Transylvania. We observe that its inhabitants speak a number of different varieties of Transylvanian—different local and social dialects. For reasons not clear to us as outsiders, one of these varieties is accepted as standard for the country as a whole. This is the variety that is used in writing, that is spoken in parliament and taught in the schools, and that is regularly used by the better-educated and more influential members of the community (though many of them also use other varieties on certain occasions, as when they are talking with family and friends). To distinguish this variety from all others, let us call it Standard Transylvanian.

We now notice a curious fact. Transylvanians in general have a very peculiar way of talking about the difference between Standard Transylvanian and the various nonstandard varieties. They say: only Standard Transylvanian is "correct" and "really has a grammar." Nonstandard varieties are "incorrect," have no real "grammar," and exist only because the speakers of these nonstandard varieties are lazy and sloppy and—of course—uneducated.

As outsiders, we are not fooled. It is perfectly clear to us that each nonstandard variety has a fully developed grammar, pronunciation, and vocabulary of its own. Each has its own structure, and each can be used to say and understand an infinite number of sentences. What more can one ask of a language? There are some respects in which Standard Transylvanian seems to be more effective: it is somehow better adapted to the style of public speaking (though this is probably because it is the only variety ever *used* for public speaking). But there are other respects in which the nonstandard varieties are more effective: they have a "homier" feeling about them, they give their speakers a precious sense of belonging together, and they are far better suited to many ordinary uses of language such as telling jokes, passing the time of day, gossiping, playing, making love, talking to children, and the like. As a final observation, we note that for us, as foreigners, all of these varieties —standard and nonstandard—are equally hard to learn.

As *language*, then, all varieties of Transylvanian are equally effective and useful, each in its own sphere. They differ not in their value as language, but in the attitudes which the Transylvanians hold toward them. The Transylvanians attach prestige *only* to Standard Transylvanian, and insist that this particular variety is the one that really ought to be used by all speakers at all times— though they belie this by their actual behavior. This seems to be an important fact about the Transylvanian language as a whole; but it is of course a sociological fact, not a linguistic fact.

If we were teachers of Transylvanian in Transylvanian schools, how would we handle this problem? Two things, at least, seem clear. First, we would try to teach all our pupils to speak (and write) Standard Transylvanian. Only in this way could we equip them to play their full role in the adult society that they were soon to enter. Second, we would not perpetuate the obviously nonsensical myth that only Standard Transylvanian is "correct" and "really has a grammar." For one thing, this myth is simply not true; every dialect *does* have a grammar, and standard forms used in dialect are just as "incorrect" as are dialect forms used in the standard language. For another, telling children that the variety of language they learned before coming to school is "incorrect," and that it is the result of inherent laziness and sloppiness, is hardly likely to win us their cooperation. More probably, this attitude will make the pupils afraid to talk at all—since the only way they can talk is the way we call incorrect, ignorant, and sloppy.

If we agree that all pupils must be taught Standard Transylvanian, a further problem arises. Should we teach them to speak Standard Transylvanian *instead of* their nonstandard variety; or should we teach them to speak it *in addition to* their nonstandard variety? In our eagerness to prepare them for successful adult life, it may at first seem preferable to have them get rid of their nonstandard variety altogether and to speak *only* Standard Transylvanian. Some of us might indeed adopt this solution; but many of the rest of us would feel unable to do so—not for reasons of linguistics or pedagogy, but as a matter of conscience and morality. To teach everyone to speak in just one way would be, for many of us, as objectionable as teaching everyone to dress in just one way, to behave in just one way, and to think in just one way. Furthermore, to deprive a child of his native variety of language would make him a stranger in his own home. His own circle of family and friends might then stand in awe of him, or they might make fun of him; in either case he would have lost his most precious means of communication with them. For these reasons, then, many of us would surely prefer to teach our pupils Standard Transylvanian *in addition to* their nonstandard variety. There is no reason to believe that this would make our teaching problem any more difficult (it might well make it easier), and it would not run counter to strong feelings of conscience and morality.

Let us now leave Transylvania and return to the United States. Though the language situation we have been describing is in many respects similar to that in this country, it is by no means identical with it. In some ways we are just as rigid as the Transylvanians, particularly in our attitudes toward what is and what is not "standard" grammar. We are quite unyielding in our condemnation of such forms as *them things* and *he done it*, even though they are widely used—perhaps by a majority of the population. We even plague ourselves with "superstandard" problems such as the distinction between *I will* and *I shall*, or the admissability of *It is me* vs. *It is I*. In another way, however, we are far less rigid than the Transylvanians, namely in matters of pronunciation: we do not insist on a single standard pronunciation that must prevail throughout the entire land. Instead, we permit great variety. We even elect to the highest office in the land persons whose pronunciations are strikingly different, as witness three successive presidents during the 1950's and 1960's: Dwight D. Eisenhower (with a midwestern variety of pronunciation), John F. Kennedy (with a Boston variety of pronunciation), and Lyndon B. Johnson (with a Texas variety of pronunciation). We may have had our personal likes and dislikes regarding these three very different pronunciations, but no one of them was in any sense "nonstandard." There are of course limits to our tolerance. We are not too much concerned (though we may have strong personal preferences) whether a speaker uses the same vowel or different vowels in *Mary, merry, marry,* or in *cot* and *caught,* or in *pin* and *pen;* and we will even let him use the same *s,* or a different *s*, in *easy* and *greasy*. But let him once use the same initial consonants in *den* and *then*, or in *tank* and *thank*, and he has stepped across the thin, fine line between standard and nonstandard.

In another respect we are neither less rigid nor more rigid than the Transylvanians, but simply different. In order to make the point more realistic, however, let us compare ourselves not with the mythical Transylvanians but with the real and very live Swiss. We mentioned above that every German-speaking Swiss, practically without exception, can speak two varieties of his language: Standard German, like that spoken to the north in Germany and to the east in Austria; and also local dialect, which is a strictly Swiss phenomenon. Depending on the situation, he can switch back and forth from the one variety to the other—a practice often called "code-switching." In the United States, again practically without exception, code-switching is neither approved nor disapproved; it is simply unknown. In actual fact there are probably a good many people who *do* engage in code-switching; but somehow we are unaware of it— it is just never talked about. We simply take it for granted that, though a person of course speaks in several different *styles* of English, he speaks only one *variety* of English.

Perhaps the greatest problem today concerning the teaching of language in our schools is the language of the so-called disadvantaged in our urban schools. Aside from those whose native language is not English, these children come to school completely fluent (like all human beings of their age) in the variety of English that they have learned from their family and their playmates. As soon as school starts, however, they are immediately faced with the local variety of Standard American English; the result is confusion and dismay on both sides. Sensing that something is somehow wrong with their variety of English, the children speak as little as possible. As a result, the teacher gains the impression that these children are "disadvantaged" not only socially and economically, but even linguistically. He reports that they can hardly express themselves, that they have a vocabulary of barely a hundred words, and the like. If these observations were correct, they would be anthropologically sensational: nowhere in the world—whether in the most advanced civilizations or in the most primitive tribes— has anyone ever found a human society where five- and six-year-old children were unable to speak their native language (in the native variety) fluently. These disadvantaged children are surely no exception. Their problem is not that they cannot speak *the language*, but that they cannot speak *the standard language*.

In German-speaking Switzerland, and in many other parts of Europe and the rest of the world, this situation is not a cause for confusion and dismay; it is simply one of the recognized facts of everyday life. Realizing this, the teacher knows how to cope with it. He uses his twelve years of school to teach his pupils the standard language not *instead of* their native dialect, but *in addition to* their native dialect. That is to say, he teaches them how to become successful code-switchers.

This system works well. Can we adopt it in our own country? Perhaps we can—though there is one great difficulty. In Switzerland (and many similar areas of the world), the teacher can not only speak the standard variety of the language; he can also speak much the same nonstandard variety of the language as his pupils, and he does so in all normal daily uses of language outside of school. More important, the pupils know this; and they know that their nonstandard variety of the language is entirely appropriate for ordinary, everyday use. Their nonstandard dialect is nothing to be ashamed of. The situation in our own country is very different from this. In most cases the teacher is totally ignorant of the nonstandard variety of English spoken by so many of his pupils. Hence he cannot speak it; and he probably would not want to speak it in front of the children even if he could. Hence, from the point of view of the pupils, their nonstandard dialect *is* something to be ashamed of.

Can we change this situation? Can we make it clear that a nonstandard variety of English is *not* something to be ashamed of, and —at the same time—that Standard English *is* something worth learning? And can we then train our pupils to become successful code-switchers? The writer of these lines can present these matters only from the one-sided viewpoint of a linguist. He cannot pretend to give the answers. But he would be derelict in his duty if he did not at least ask the questions.

CHAPTER I

The Structure of Language

J. DONALD BOWEN

Introduction

Language is without question the most universal of human characteristics. It has occurred in a wonderful variety of forms wherever man has lived in the world, regardless of the level of sophistication shown by any other human activities or developments. Nor can any correlation be found in terms of relative complexity between language and other aspects of human culture. It is certainly not true that so-called primitive peoples have "primitive" or underdeveloped languages. On the contrary, the languages of many aboriginal peoples seem, from the point of view of the speaker of an Indo-European language, to be enormously complicated systems. About the only generalization we can safely make about language and culture is that they are mutually self-sufficient. The language expresses the needs of the culture and the culture develops the language it requires. If a culture changes, the language will have the resources to change with it. In fact the creative capacity of language to adjust to the expressive needs of its speakers is one of the distinguishing marks of human communication.

Man has probably been interested in language for as long as language has existed. As far as we know, language has always been a means of social control, and it continues to be such up to the present time. Leaders wield their influence through speech and are judged by how well they do so. Speech and magic have always been closely associated—a secret word could work miracles. The great door of the mountain affords admission only to the person who knows the magic words "Open sesame."

The Judeo-Christian tradition attests the power of speech. The Gospel of St. John records a most direct association between speech and power, opening with the statement: "In the beginning was the Word, and the Word was with God, and the Word was God." The creative power of words is shown in Genesis, when God says "Let there be light: and there was light." The entire world was created by the mere expression of divine will.

Human interest in understanding language is recorded as early as the fourth century B.C. (or earlier—some scholars say 600 B.C.) in the writings of one of the most remarkable grammarians of all time, Panini, whose description of Sanskrit holds the admiration of linguists to this day. Panini is thought to have been the best of a flourishing school of language students, not a lone scholar whose work just happened to survive.

The Greeks were very much interested in language, primarily their own language, and it is to the Greek philosophers that we owe many of the concepts still used in describing languages. The Romans followed the Greeks, absorbing their interests, but adding little by way of new ideas. The early established Greco-Latin tradition of language analysis was a strong one and had enormous influence on subsequent grammarians and linguists.

The traditional interest was in the "classical" languages; other languages were thought to be of no importance—an attitude that has its counterpart in our own times as many aboriginal languages die out unstudied and unmourned. (Compare the classical attitude with the attitude toward using American Indian languages in our schools today—even in schools that serve Indian students.) It was not until late in the fifteenth century that a grammar of a modern language was written, the Spanish grammar of Nebrija. He anticipated the modern English grammarians by well over two hundred years; but Spanish, English, and all other European grammarians, when they wrote, followed the tradition of medieval scholarship and conceived of their tasks in terms of the patterns and structures of Latin.

Review of Existing Grammars

EARLY GRAMMARS

The first grammars of English were written for a very specific purpose. Scholars looked enviously at the stability of Latin and observed that it had a "grammar"—a formulated body of descriptive information that could be appealed to for answers to questions of usage, a set of rules that any writer could follow to produce acceptable and correct sentences. The scholars also observed that English was by comparison little short of chaotic—there was no agreement on spellings, style, or usage. English had no "grammar," no authority one could appeal to in order to resolve questions of correctness. Latin had a grammar and stability; English lacked both. The solution seemed to lie in the provision of a grammar for English, and the scholars set out to write one.

The justification for our early grammars was a desire to fix, standardize, prevent change—to provide canons against which writing could be compared and judged. This was considered necessary to prevent the unrestrained and capricious deterioration of the language at the hands of inadequately schooled writers. The provision of a grammar would permit all writers to observe the standards of good writing.

Another difference between Latin and English seems not to have been noticed—that Latin was a dead language and English was very much alive. It was easier to lay Latin on a marble slab and dissect it. Not only did English have a rich variety of dialects, but also these were changing as all live languages do. The model for the new English grammar was, of course, classical Latin, and if English did not fit the Latin mold it was forced a bit. This introduction of a Latin model into English grammar has had a continuing influence. It was not entirely inappropriate, since Latin is a language related to English (though not its ancestor language, as many once assumed). But still there are differences. It makes no real sense to talk about vocative forms in English, for example, since they are always the same as the nominative (cf. the English grammatical term "nominative of address"). In Latin, vocative and nominative forms could be different, and it was necessary to recognize the difference.

English was not alone in developing a Latinate grammar tradition. The same concepts of conservatism and respect for classical languages were evident in other European countries. One frequent result was the establishment of official academies to compile dictionaries and grammars and to watch over standards of usage. The three best known were the Italian Accademia della Crusca founded in

1546, the French Académie française in 1635, and the Spanish Real Academia Española in 1714. An academy for England was discussed but never did develop beyond the idea stage, perhaps because the appearance of Johnson's dictionary in 1755 and Lowth's grammar in 1762 seemed to meet some of the needs an academy could satisfy. Johnson's dictionary, although not the first, was surely the most influential early English dictionary, and Lowth's grammar set a pattern of authoritarianism, subordinating usage to logic or "universal grammar."

There were a number of English grammars written in the second half of the eighteenth century. These were synthesized in the grammar of Lindley Murray, which appeared in 1795. With this very popular book the Latinate grammar tradition was firmly established, and it changed very little during the next century.

The school grammar tradition, inspired in its initiation by a desire to control the use of the language (to eliminate or at least minimize change), found a ready acceptance in the developing society. The new middle class, recruited from among those whose language stigmatized them, were anxious to "improve" their use of the language as a sign of their new social status. They were a ready audience, well disposed to accept the prescriptions of the authorities, to endeavor to conform to standards they felt were authentic. The teachers wanted to prescribe, the students wanted their prescriptions, and a series of texts and grammars appeared to cater to the need.

SCHOLARLY GRAMMARS

Scholarly language study became more scientific in the second half of the nineteenth century with the work of the neogrammarians, whose interest was in comparative studies of languages and in tracing genetic relationships back through time. The sound correspondences described by the neogrammarians as phonetic laws are now the basis of historical linguistics, and their laws, somewhat modified and refined, enable us to posit relationships between languages, to define among others the family of Indo-European languages. The neogrammarians helped establish a tradition of close and careful observation in their reconstructions of earlier forms.

Their method and the insights they provided did much to establish linguistics as a science among the humanities.

About the middle of the nineteenth century a scholarly project of monumental proportions was undertaken, the *Oxford English Dictionary on Historical Principles*, or as it is more frequently called, the *Oxford English Dictionary*, or the *OED* (32). This is an impressive work, compiling the labors of many scholars over a period of seventy-five years. It was published in twelve volumes spread over forty-four years, from 1884 to 1928. It remains a monument to lexicography for its completeness and accuracy.

The scope and quality of the *Oxford English Dictionary* seem to have had an influence on contemporary grammarians. Like the big dictionary, the scholarly grammars of the early twentieth century are notable for their size, detail, and comprehensive coverage of usage in English. They are multivolume works, often containing thousands of pages. Three of the best of these, though published in English, were written by speakers of other European languages. Two were written by Dutch scholars, Poutsma, *A Grammar of Late Modern English* (5 vols.) (34) and Kruisinga, *A Handbook of Present-Day English* (4 vols.) (25). The third, *A Modern English Grammar on Historical Principles* (7 vols.) (24) was written by Jespersen, a Dane, but was published in Germany. Two other very influential English grammars were written in German, those of Krüger and Wendt, and additional studies in the same tradition continue to appear, such as those of Curme (9, 10), Zandvoort (50), and others.

The descriptive, historical, analytical work done in the first years of the present century was derived in large part from written sources—from published writings—representing mainly the usage of written English. This orientation influenced and reflected the concepts of second-language study of the time, which was devoted to a study of reading and writing.

STRUCTURAL GRAMMARS

In 1921 an important book by Sapir was published, titled *Language: An Introduction to the Study of Speech* (42). This was a valuable and learned work, still important and readable. Twelve years later another significant book appeared—*Language* by Bloomfield—which has been called the bible of American structural linguistics (6). By the time of the publication of Sapir's work, as the title indicates, the orientation was toward speech rather than writing, with particular attention to language as systematic human behavior, studied on levels of increasing complexity from sounds to forms to words and sentences to meaning. Writing was seen as a secondary system of representation, imperfect and incomplete and therefore inadequate as a systematic representation of speech.

With the concept of the phoneme (a distinctive unit of sound) as a working tool, a fairly complete description of the phonology or sound system of a language was possible. The same techniques which worked quite well in phonology (the identification of distinctive units by contrast, formal similarity, and complementary distribution) were applied to grammar, but the greater complexity of the data made analysis more difficult and less successful. Certain patterns in inflectional morphology were describable in distributional terms (e.g., the noun plural affix, the verb past tense affix, etc.), but sentence patterns could not easily be analyzed.

1. *Immediate-constituent analysis.*—The structuralists, as members of the new school came to be called, were represented by such scholars as Bloch (4, 5), Trager (5, 49), Hockett (18), and Hill (17). They felt that they must rely only on the data they were using, that neither the speaker's feel for the language nor the referential meaning of forms should be utilized (it would be unscientific, subjective, mentalistic). The prime analytic tool for grammar descriptions was a procedure called immediate-constituent analysis. An assumption was made that not all morphemes or meaning-bearing units in a sentence are related to each other in the same way. In "The boy came home" the word *the* is more closely related to *boy* than to *came* or *home*. Likewise *home* is more closely related to *came* than to *boy* or *the*. The first cut in dividing this sentence would be between *boy* and *came*, giving as immediate constituents *the boy* and *came home*. Succeeding cuts would produce the constituents of each half of the sentences until one finally arrives at the ultimate constituents, the smallest meaning-bearing units. Note the analysis of the following sentence by successive binary cuts:

The girls were playing in the yard.

Any further division moves the analysis from grammar to phonology.

The analysts needed a procedure, a set of steps by which they could move from primary data—samples of utterances from the language—to the constituent parts which make up the message. A description of the language consists of all the parts, with statements that reveal how the parts are put together to make sentences that communicate. Meaning *per se* was assumed, as it had to be, but very little was done to study how meaning was signalled or carried. Some analysts felt that meaning or semantics might eventually be described but would have to be postponed until the necessary preliminary work in grammar could be refined. Others felt that meaning was a "humanistic" concern and should not even be included in the science of linguistics.

2. *Tagmemic analysis.*—Immediate-constituent analysis usually presumes binary cuts, but this is not a necessary condition. Another group of structuralists formed among a group of linguists sponsored by a missionary organization known as the Summer Institute of Linguistics. This group, led by Pike, working from field analysis conditions, developed a system and procedure which they called tagmemics (33). This is essentially a slot-and-substitution grammar. A language can be said to be adequately described when all of the possible sentence patterns have been listed and the lexical items which can appear in each slot have been identified.

The limitations of these grammars are obvious. They utilize native-speaker intuition while trying not to refer to meaning, claiming reliance only on distributional characteristics. A sentence like "He rolled up the rug" can only be analyzed adequately if we know whether the more important cut is before or after *up*, and morpheme distribution does not tell us this. In this case a complete notation would include information about phrasing, and this information would enable us to make a correct interpretation, but some ambiguities, such as "Shooting stars can be exciting," cannot be resolved by the physical data they contain; the analyst must know if the speaker plans just to watch a heavenly display or to locate his position by means of a sextant. There are other serious limitations, the chief of which are (*a*) the lack of explicitness, (*b*) an enormous descriptive inefficiency, and (c) the lack of procedures to evaluate claims made in terms of actual accomplishment.

3. *Signals analysis.*—The analyst notes that some words in a stream of conversation have a more or less direct reference to items in the surrounding environment, the content words. We have no trouble pointing to an example of a *tree*, a *stone*, or a *house*, or illustrating the actions *run, sit, eat*; but it is much more difficult to describe or define words like *some, the, by, could*, etc., the function words. The conclusion is that the content words carry a lexical meaning, but that the sentence also contains signals that enable the hearer to interpret what he hears—to relate the lexical meanings of content words in ways that reveal the semantic intentions of the speaker.

These signals include the affixes used with different classes of content words, the use of function words (which have only "grammatical" meaning), intonation patterns, and word order. The signals tell little or nothing about how the sentence is formed; they contain or imply bits of information which facilitate the hearer's task of interpretation, because they effectively increase the amount of redundancy in an utterance and thereby reduce the potential for ambiguity. This is basically the rationale of signals grammar, worked out by Fries (12,13). It is interesting and relevant to note that Fries used the spoken language as the corpus from which he described his grammar—fifty hours of recorded telephone conversations. It is appropriately a grammar for a hearer.

One distinction can be noted between immediate-constituent analysis and tagmemic and (more especially) signals analysis largely as a consequence of the preference of the former for binary cuts in analyzing a sentence. By ordering the sequence of the cuts, a clustering of words and morphemes is produced, revealing the degrees of closeness between the various adjacent elements. If all cuts are made at once (or are made at word or phrase boundaries in linear order) this feature is much less obvious. The signals-oriented grammarian thus looks at word order in a somewhat different way—as an independent signal to interpret meaning. He looks at two sentences like "We suggest the following analysis" and "We suggest following the analysis" and is likely to see merely a different relative order of *following* and *the*, noting that it is associated with a

difference in meaning. The structuralist who is oriented to immediate-constituent analysis knows by the order of cuts that *following* clusters with *analysis* in the first sentence, with *the analysis* in
the second:

We suggest	the following analysis.
We suggest	following the analysis.

This is not the most revealing explanation but improves on a more
vague concept of word order as a matter of relative sequence. Immediate-constituent analysis shows cluster patterns; signals analysis
shows only order patterns.

4. *Stratificational analysis.*—One relatively recent theory of
grammar is called stratificational grammar, associated with the name
of Lamb (30). As publicly described, it is highly tentative and very
complex, treating the levels and relations that mediate between
semiology and phonology. Sounds and meanings are recognized
as patterning in different ways, since sounds must be produced in
a linear order, but thought patterns are multidimensional. The
theory seeks economy of description by providing for maximum
generalization of descriptive statements and for a separate system
of syntax for as many as six structural layers, or strata. The lowest
stratum has about fifteen elements; the highest has thousands. Very
little work has been done with stratification analysis, perhaps because it is so new, and no applications to grammar teaching have
been suggested.

GENERATIVE-TRANSFORMATIONAL GRAMMAR

By far the most promising grammar theory to appear in the
last decade or so is one that has been called transformational or
generative-transformational, originally formulated by Chomsky
(7, 8). It is a theoretical model or description, not of a corpus from
a language, but of the human capacity for meaningful communication through language, i.e., of certain abilities that can be assumed
to underlie the production and recognition of sentences. It is the
responsibility of an adequate grammar, then, to describe explicitly
what the speaker of a language does.

Language is defined as an abstract self-contained system of rules,
some optional and others obligatory, which generate sentences that

permit communication between persons who have a mastery over the same set of rules. The system of rules has three subsystems, described as follows:

1. The core subsystem of rules, the abstract medium: syntax
2. The expressive subsystem of rules, the physical medium: phonology
3. The interpretative subsystem of rules, the cultural medium: semantics

Thus the syntactic rules are central to speech. They find expression through phonological productions and are interpreted through relationships to patterns in the culture.

Transformational analysis is concerned with several areas of theory that have been neglected by other grammatical analyses: (a) the innate human capacity for language mastery at an appropriate age, with or without any specific instruction; (b) the ability of a speaker to produce an infinite number of sentences he has not heard before; (c) a concern for and an attempt to define linguistic universals; and (d) a definition of the difference between competence and performance, explained as the difference between an idealized system and the limitations in evidence when speakers actually use the system.

Transformational analysis has had frequent recourse to logic, philosophy, and traditional scholarly grammar—all, sources that were shunned by the structuralists. No attempt is made to restrict conclusions to inferences drawn solely from the data. The intuition of the analyst is used at every point, and indeed a solution that is not in accord with intuition is suspect. The insights provided in the scholarly grammars with their detailed and extensive treatments are accepted and made explicit.

Transformational analysis can best be illustrated by an example. The two English sentences "Mary is anxious to paint" and "Mary is difficult to paint" look very much alike on the surface: a proper noun plus is plus an adjective plus an infinitive. But every native speaker knows that these sentences have interpretations that are different in structure, not just in dictionary meaning. In one case Mary does the painting, and in the other case she is the model and someone else does the painting. To account for the difference, transformational grammar assumes two levels of structure: one on the surface which can be directly observed (heard or seen), and an abstract level beneath the surface. Meaning comes from this deep structure level, and this postulation helps account for ambiguities that cannot otherwise be reasonably explained.

The role of transformations is to mediate between deep and surface structures, or between meaning and pronunciation. The transformations take the string or strings of elements in the deep structure and apply procedures which delete, add, rearrange, or combine elements to produce a surface string that preserves and transmits the meanings originally assigned. On the surface, pronunciation (or writing) rules are applied, and the string becomes a pronounced (or written) sentence.

The characteristic which no other grammar has attempted to provide is: Given a properly correct set of instructions, all the grammatical sentences of the language and only these sentences can be derived. The claim of "all" and "only" is a strong one—a claim never attempted by any other grammar. In the present state of development, transformational grammar cannot fulfill this claim; if, as the transformationalists claim, it will at some future time even approximate its promise, it will be a very powerful tool indeed.

Language Teaching in Recent Times

TRADITIONAL LANGUAGE CLASSES

A number of reasons have been cited as to why we include the study of language or grammar in our schools, some perhaps more valid and more logical than others. One reason is to help students prevent errors and, thus, to reduce the rate of deterioration (i.e., read "change") in the language itself. This reason may still motivate some teachers of English, but a permissive attitude is more prevalent than was formerly the case. Many fewer teachers conceive of their jobs as guardians of purity of expression; rather a wide range of dialect difference is recognized as acceptable English.

There are, however, some dialects that are considered non-standard, especially among Negroes who are striving for the full exercise of their civil rights. Language usage, rightly or wrongly, marks these students, and many educators are occupied in activities that are essentially remedial—to help teach Standard English as a second dialect. A similar situation exists among our linguistic minorities, such as the Spanish-American and American Indian students. These, however, are second-language situations, and we recognize the source of the undesirable distortions from interference patterns between their native languages and English.

The most commonly cited and probably the most valid reason for teaching English grammar in our schools is the aim of increasing the students' versatility as users of the language. They need to learn to control the formal registers, to increase their sensitivity to style levels, and in general to improve their oral and written expression in a wide variety of situations.

Other reasons for studying grammar have been advanced at various times. One traditional justification is that it teaches a student to think logically—provides exercise for mental discipline. More recently it has been suggested that the study of language, especially one's own language, is an indispensable part of a general education. One cannot understand the world unless he understands man, and one cannot understand man without knowing something about the way he communicates. Grammar is the formalized study of the science of communication.

What one studies in a language class is necessarily related to the kind of grammar assumed by the course. There have always been adapters, authors willing to interpret the work of the scholars into activities for the schools. The early motives of standardization spawned a tradition of prescriptivism that has lasted to our day, passing on to modern English speakers a set of rules more appropriate to Latin than to English.

It has frequently been suggested to American students that the study of a foreign language, and especially of Latin, is an excellent way to learn about English. This would be true in any case, because seeing another language in operation gives a student a vantage point from which to observe his own—the points of contrast come forcefully to one's attention. It is also true that traditional English grammar, shaped as it was by Latin, became more understandable when one could observe Latin. Still it does seem logical to study English, not Latin, to learn more about English.

Traditional grammars served the needs of students through

many years. They were similar but not identical, each author seeking to make his approach more relevant and more attractive. One example is what is called "functional" grammar, an approach in which the teacher (or the text author) looks at the work done by the students to discover just which details and patterns are most in need of remedy. Then the course is planned to emphasize these needs and correct the deficiencies. The logic is appealing: specify that part of the grammar which is not under full control and work on it—a procedure that should be efficient and effective. In practice, it turns out to be a piecemeal approach, a little here and a little there, with no opportunity to integrate the bits of information into a unified whole. No comprehensive understanding was likely following this method, but none was considered necessary.

Over the years, and especially as the voices of criticism grew, new ideas were applied to teaching English, and more particularly to foreign-language teaching. Grammar was alternately emphasized, neglected, ignored, etc., to fit a particular teaching philosophy. Mackey lists (and briefly describes) some twenty types of methods that have been espoused in recent times: direct, natural, psychological, phonetic, reading, grammar, translation, grammar-translation, eclectic, language control, mimicry-memorization, practice-theory, cognate, dual-language, situation, simplification, conversation, film, laboratory, and unit (31:151-53). He then points out that the lists could be considerably expanded by listing the methods that carry persons' names.

1. The "Army" method.—The applications of structural linguistics to language teaching were first felt in the fields of teaching foreign languages and teaching English as a second language.

During World War II the United States Army was faced with the need for training men to speak languages in a hurry, not only the commonly studied languages of Western Europe, but also languages never before offered in the schools and colleges of the United States. Relying for advice on the enthusiastic new school of structural linguistics, the army established special training courses in what was called the Army Specialized Training Program, where languages were taught intensively to military personnel. Special characteristics of the training included: native-speaking teachers (albeit often unsympathetic to the new methods, poorly trained, and inadequately supervised), extensive contact (several hours daily), small classes (about twelve students), and high student motivation (failing out meant a quick trip to the war zone). Grammar patterns were to be internalized from repetitions of model sentences, developed inductively, though in practice linguistically oriented descriptions were given where a linguist was on the scene, and traditional explanations were given where traditional teachers had inadequate guidance and supervision. The results were excellent and overpublicized, leading a lot of people to think that the army had found the answers to efficient language training. Applying the same conditions to general school education was, of course, something different, but a lot of interest was stimulated in better methods of language teaching, and a considerable amount of new-style text materials were produced.

2. *The reverse-English series.*—Shortly after World War II, the American Council of Learned Societies sponsored the production of a series of textbooks to teach English to students of certain language backgrounds—a series which came to be known as the reverse-English series (1, 2). These texts were to bring to the language classroom the insights and descriptions of recent linguistic research, with explanatory material presented in the language of the students. The texts especially emphasized pronunciation, with extensive minimal-pair drills and a very complex modified phonemic transcription of English as an aid to listening. The students were to be given authentic and realistic samples of English to memorize, from which it was assumed a working understanding of the grammar would be developed inductively.

The sequence of patterns presented in the reverse-English texts was mainly determined by a prototype text called the "General Form," written to serve as a model for the overall project. Adaptations were made in each text, however, on the basis of contrastive analyses between English and the particular language involved. The setting was in terms of a foreign student attending an American university, with situations and dialogues typical of this context. The learning problems of each background-language group were identified, and the course treated these in the priority of their importance. The method of presentation in the classroom was guided imitation, with a native-speaking model (or the best substitute available) as a teacher or tutor. Grammatical information was kept to a minimum —only that necessary to follow the course.

These courses were ponderous. The book was big, heavy, and lengthy, and in great part the activities recommended consisted of extensive repetition practice. Sequencing was always based on linguistic considerations; pedagogical requirements were secondary. These sets of materials were never conspicuously successful. They were often dull and boring; students could not be stimulated to give their best efforts. One commercial school in Miami which had enthusiastically adopted these materials for teaching English to what should have been hordes of eager Cubans found that students could not be induced to stay for a series of three free come-on lessons, let alone continue and pay for a longer series. The linguists turned out to be mediocre pedagogues.

3. *The English Language Institute course.*—About the same time some interesting work was being done by a group at the University of Michigan working with Fries and Lado. They published from 1943 to 1958 a series, "An Intensive Course in English for Latin Americans," with parallel series of lessons in pronunciation, structure, and vocabulary (26, 27, 28, 29). The course using extensive repetition and minimal-pair contrast drills was based strictly on the spoken language, with considerable time and attention devoted to pronunciation. Mastering the sound system was given first priority, with a limited vocabulary introduced in the early stages. New sentences and patterns were developed first orally, with reading postponed for later consideration. In the grammar, special attention was given to the signals which the hearer utilizes to interpret the relationships among content words and ultimately the meanings of sentences. Fries felt that "A person has 'learned' a foreign language when he has thus first, *within a limited vocabulary* mastered the sound system . . . and has, second, made the structural devices . . . matters of automatic habit." (14:3).

The Michigan materials are said to be scientifically selected and arranged for students whose first language is Spanish; but the rationale was never made explicit, no separate contrastive analysis was published, and the same materials were used for students of any foreign language background. Specific patterns and vocabulary items were marked for productive or receptive mastery, in order not to overburden memory during the period when automatic habits were being developed.

4. *Contributions of tagmemics.*—The tagmemicists devoted most of their time to language analysis, with only a limited effort given to language teaching. Working among peoples whose language had never been studied, they often had the problem of learning a language themselves. They did this largely by the immersion method, learning as they elicited and collected data. When they did write textbooks for the languages they studied, these usually resembled the courses of other structuralists—heavy on dialogues and pattern practice.

The missionary linguists who have made up a majority of the tagmemicists have been involved in two special kinds of language teaching of considerable interest. After studying and describing a heretofore unwritten language, they devise a writing system that reflects the phonological and grammatical systems of the language and promptly begin to develop literacy materials. The native speakers, those who can be interested in doing so, are helped and encouraged to learn to read and write their language, in the hope that eventually they will be able to read the translations of the Bible that are prepared for them. The second teaching activity is an outgrowth of the first: bilingual education for the school-age children. The Summer Institute of Linguistics programs in Peru and Ecuador have been especially helpful to local governments, bringing many new students into the schools where they are taught first in their own language and soon after are introduced to Spanish as a second language so that they can more easily be integrated into the national life. Linguistics and dedicated linguists have made an enormous contribution to language teaching in parts of the world very remote from us.

5. *Applications of structural analysis.*—Structural linguistics has had an influence in recent years on the kind of grammar taught to first-language speakers of English. One of the best known grammars was by a very skilled popularizer, Paul Roberts, whose books *Patterns of English* in 1956, *Understanding English* in 1958, and *English Sentences* in 1962, managed to blend many of the ideas of structural linguistics, particularly Fries syntax and Trager-Smith phonology,

for the instruction of high school and college students (38, 40, 36). But this new way of looking at grammar was not easily accepted in the schools (the publishers claim they gave away more of Roberts' 1956 book than they sold). Structural grammar made inroads but is now rapidly coming to be replaced by the more sophisticated and currently popular generative-transformational grammar.

6. *Transformational presentations.*—The influence of transformational analysis on the schools has been considerable and has taken place in an amazingly short period of time. In one decade after the appearance of Chomsky's *Syntactic Structures* in 1957, there have been numerous texts that have attempted to incorporate his insights and some genuinely new approaches. The new grammar has been brought to the elementary schools by *The Roberts English Series, A Linguistic Program*, which appeared in 1966 (39). The series presently consists of seven volumes and is designed for Grade III through Grade IX. The concepts of sentence generation, the derivation of complex sentences from simpler ones, the nature of syntactic relations are presented (complete with formulas and technical terminology) to elementary school students. Grammar is conceived and taught as a mechanism for generating sentences which a student can understand and refine in order to improve his skill for expressing himself in his own language.

On the upper-secondary and college level, Roberts contributed another book, *English Syntax* published in 1964 (37). This is a programed introduction to transformational grammar, which attempts to present grammar as a theory of the nature, use, and acquisition of language. Another interesting introductory presentation appeared in 1967 in two small but well-prepared texts, *Grammar 1* and *Grammar 2*, by Jacobs and Rosenbaum (22, 23). A text of special interest for its pedagogical orientation appeared in 1965 (*Transformational Grammar and the Teacher of English*, by Thomas) which was written, the author stated, with the "hope that teachers will learn something valuable about the nature of English from this text and that this knowledge will improve their teaching and help their students" (48:vii). Thomas addresses schools of education, departments of English, and practicing teachers and presents a clear exposition of the new grammar with suggestions about how it can be put to use.

Another recent book attempts to interpret linguistics to the English teacher—to illustrate how it is related to literature, to composition, and to grammar, and to show how new information and insights can be put to use. This is *Linguistics and English Grammar* by Gleason published in 1965. It contains excellent sections on historical background and on applications to the practical problems of the language classroom (15).

Transformational grammar has also found its way into second-language textbooks. It has become fashionable to use transformational terminology and to include drills which change sentence patterns and combine two simple sentences into a single complex sentence. One recent book, *Modern English: A Text for Foreign Students* by Rutherford, stands out as an illustration of how the relationships between sentences can be used to present the rule system of English to speakers of other languages in a way that will encourage the development of insights into English structure (41). It will undoubtedly serve as a model for more texts to come.

What is most significant about all of this activity is that it has taken place entirely in a little over a decade. Transformational analysis has fired the enthusiasms of scholars, pedagogues, and teachers, and the prospects are that we have seen only the beginning of relevant research. All of the books discussed above will probably have to be updated or supplanted in the years ahead; many problems of analysis remain unsolved or are only partially or tentatively explained, but the theoretical tools to undertake the job appear to be available.

Recent Pedagogical Research and Experimentation

THE NEED FOR BETTER LANGUAGE TEACHING

Teachers are people with immediate problems, however, and they neither can nor want to wait for solutions. One of the problems that cries out most loudly for improvement is the teaching of English to American students. That past efforts have been less than successful is not denied anywhere but is most conspicuous in the class which is treated as a stepchild in most colleges and universities: "Subject A," the remedial, noncredit English course demanded of entering freshman who do not pass the English section of the matriculation examination. Teaching a section of "Subject A" is considered a grave misfortune by most college instructors and is usually pushed off on the newest and youngest members of the English department. There is no pleasure in working with students who were not able to do satisfactory work in their high school English classes and need remedial work in college.

Nobody questions the importance of being able to write clearly and effectively. This is a skill that is certainly necessary to the university student, who must write reports, papers, and examinations. The question is how to teach somebody else to write, and everybody who has tried has fallen short. "Subject A" has a record of built-in failure; little wonder no one enjoys teaching it. The aim is the same today as it was in 1898 as reported in a University of California report: "to secure to the student the ability to use his mother tongue correctly, clearly, and pertinently on all the lines upon which his thought is exercised," which has been interpreted as a requirement that undergraduates demonstrate a "minimum level of proficiency" in composition, "the ability to write English without gross errors in spelling, grammar, diction, and punctuation." (11:20). According to Freeman, "The result of this approach all too often is what I like to call SAP—Standard Academic Prose, lifeless, bloodless, voiceless—but correct—which can be transshipped, nine-tenths fine from Subject A to bland undergraduate term papers, to the flaccid patois of organizational life in the PTA and the corporation." (11:20). Yet "Subject A" has failed to reach even this modest goal.

Why has the teaching of English been so spotty? In part it may be due to the separation of the trivium of language, literature, and composition in the English curriculum. This disjunction has been true at all levels, but is the hallmark of university English departments, which like to presume that certainly composition and probably language should be mastered in the lower grades—that English study on the level of higher education should really be limited to literature and literary criticism.

There is an obvious relationship between language (or grammar) and composition; a knowledge of grammar should provide an understanding of language as a system, and composition is an opportunity to apply that knowledge. It is obvious, then, that if grammar is to sustain composition, a grammar must be provided that will be capable of the task. Grammar should provide a complete, explicit, and consistent description of the English language—one capable of explaining the processes by which language is produced—in short, a theory of language. Transformational analysis looks promising, but many English teachers are understandably reluctant to accept uncritically this latest announced panacea for their ills. They have been told before that linguistic research holds the key to the answers to their problems, only to be disappointed in the classroom.

The present situation differs from the past in at least one significant respect. There is now more than ever before a readiness to seek new answers—to try new solutions. Experimental programs have been commonplace in teaching foreign languages and in teaching English as a second language, but the traditional English curriculum has been little affected. One difference today is the current research interest and the availability of funds to support new investigations and to try out new ideas and programs. Much of the impetus comes from the U.S. Office of Education, through its administration of the National Defense Education Act and the Elementary and Secondary Education Act.

1. *Project English.*—In 1961, with support from the Cooperative Research Branch of the U.S. Office of Education, a multiprogram effort to provide a better quality of education in the field of English was launched under the title "Project English" (44, 43, 46, 19). Significantly, this project was launched and developed with professional initiative, with support from English teachers at all educational levels from elementary to graduate schools. Research answers were to be sought to some of the many questions teachers had been asking for many years, often with little hope of ever finding answers. An administrator was selected from the ranks of the profession to oversee what was to grow into a major program.

Early activities included the establishment of six curriculum centers and four demonstration centers to try out and test materials developed at the curriculum centers. This number ultimately grew to fifteen curriculum centers and seven demonstration centers located at some of the nation's strongest schools. There have been curriculum centers at Carnegie Institute of Technology, Hunter

College, University of Minnesota, University of Nebraska, Northwestern University, University of Oregon, Florida State University, University of Georgia, Teachers College (Columbia University), University of Wisconsin, Indiana University, University of Illinois, Gallaudet College, Purdue University, and others. Each of these centers was given approximately a quarter of a million dollars from federal funds, with unspecified but considerable local support funds in addition.

Of the first thirty research projects approved, ten were in composition, six in reading, five in linguistics, and nine in other (or in combined) areas. This distribution probably represents quite fairly the general concerns of the profession about which areas were in most immediate need of improvement. As time has passed, more projects and other areas have been funded, until the amount of activity and the results have become truly astonishing—unthinkable only a decade earlier.

In 1964 the National Defense Education Act was extended and amended to include, among other areas, reading and English. In the following three years, the number of institutes and teachers trained in summer institutes were as follows:

1965	105 institutes	4800 teachers
1966	192 institutes	5300 teachers
1967	152 institutes	3400 teachers

In all, about 10 percent of the country's English teachers have been given this type of training.

During the summers of 1965 and 1966, an English Institute Materials Center was housed in the Modern Language Association headquarters in New York. Its function was to help distribute the materials produced at the curriculum centers as a way of disseminating new ideas, stimulating new thinking at the NDEA Institutes. But not only is there a demand for materials; studies and research reports are also sought after by large numbers of scholars, program administrators, and teachers (not only in English, but also in allied fields). The job of dissemination has assumed major proportions, and it is now anticipated that an Educational Research Information Center (ERIC) in English will be established to facilitate the exchange of reports and bibliographies of the mounting number of research and curriculum projects.

There is other encouraging evidence of a new attitude and new activity in research and the development of improved curriculum methods and materials. In September of 1965, legislation was passed establishing the National Foundation on the Arts and Humanities, with a ten-million-dollar endowment and an annual operating budget of five million dollars.

2. *Regional educational laboratories.*—In the same year the Elementary and Secondary Education Act of 1965 was passed providing for the establishment of twenty regional educational laboratories, in an effort to close the gap between research and the adoption of new techniques and materials; their aim: research, innovation, dissemination. These laboratories are independently organized, with boards of directors representing local universities, industry, community, and so on. They have considerable latitude of action and can define and work on problems that are most pressing and most important in the area served.

Many of the current projects carried out in the educational centers and research laboratories are designed for the production of curriculum materials, almost always in series form, and usually in a sequence for an entire school level. Almost always these materials are fieldtested (usually on a vast scale), evaluated for effectiveness, and then revised as indicated by weaknesses revealed in the tryouts. Error analyses of student work built on many thousands of students' papers, have been conducted on a comprehensive scale. Information and data are piling up at an unprecedented rate, and we now know more about the schools and their conduct than we are ready to assimilate and apply.

It is interesting and instructive to take a brief look at the research being done at some of the centers (35). There is emphasis on the nature of language and a concern for the role linguistics and linguistic research are to play in the language curriculum at all levels—especially with respect to composition, reading, and oral language activities. Also there is an interest in the interrelationships of language skills. Does achievement in one skill enhance achievement in another? Does an improvement in oral expression, for example, generate an increase in reading comprehension? Does the same innate aptitude govern all language skills? Does a knowledge of the structure or grammar of a language improve students' composition skills?

58   THE STRUCTURE OF LANGUAGE

What effect does the "quality" of contacts, especially of adult contacts, have on the linguistic development of young children? These are not new questions; they have been asked many times in the past, but with support, interest, and the new results of continuing research, the chances of finding reliable answers are very enhanced. A small sample of some of the interesting research in progress is reported in the paragraphs that follow.

RESEARCH AND DEVELOPMENT PROJECTS

1. *Measuring syntactic maturity.*—Kellogg W. Hunt has asked some interesting questions about the quantitative measures of syntactic development of school children in the hope of encouraging change and hastening growth (20, 21). He has offered new suggestions on measures of syntactic maturity—refinements on the older measures of sentence length, clause length, proportion of dependent to main clauses, and relative frequency of different dependent clause types. His contribution is a new syntactic unit which he calls a T-unit, a kind of minimal independent sentence structure. The mean length of T-units turns out to be the most reliable index of syntactic maturity, followed by mean length of clauses, followed by the subordination ratio—all better than the mean length of sentences.

He further points out that growth in the area of clause length comes early and therefore needs relatively little attention in composition classes. But growth in the number of clauses per T-unit comes later and is a more legitimate area of concern for the composition teacher.

Hunt's work has been criticized because he fails to distinguish between grammatically well-formed and malformed sentences and because he does not consider the specific linguistic structures in the sentences he analyzes. But if these are crucial, they can easily be introduced in further analyses. The value of Hunt's work is that it allows the teacher to focus his efforts on the specific areas where growth is normal and can be hastened by concentration and effort.

2. *The interrelationship of language skills.*—Bateman and Zidonis at Ohio State University have attempted to answer questions of the interrelationship of language skills and knowledge (3). Does grammar enhance the ability to write: select and express ideas and details, state these clearly and effectively? Does it improve the

ability to read: recognize and recall meanings, make inferences? Does it improve ability to think: recognize assumptions, make deductions, determine accurate interpretations, evaluate arguments? If the answer to any of these questions is affimative, the teaching of grammar will be justified.

In one of the most interesting of their studies, Bateman and Zidonis have concentrated on the effects that high school students' study of transformational grammar has had on composition. Their results show higher but not significantly higher scores in structural complexity, reduction in number of errors, and variety of structures for those exposed to the new grammar. More important is a significant increase (unambiguously attributable to the study of grammar) in the proportion of well-formed sentences. It is interesting that they report no correlation of gain and IQ, and that by their rigid standards almost half of the sentences written by beginning ninth-graders were malformed.

3. *Comprehensive curriculum development.*—The products of the curriculum centers have been extensive and in many cases impressive. Proposed curriculums are comprehensive and original. Excellent results have come from the centers at the universities of Minnesota, Nebraska, and Oregon, and at Florida State. Others concentrate on specific problems at a given level in the school system. An example of a comprehensive effort is provided by the Wisconsin English-Language-Arts Curriculum Project, directed by Robert C. Pooley. Three detailed guides, *Teaching Literature in Wisconsin, Teaching Speaking and Writing in Wisconsin,* and *Teaching the English Language in Wisconsin* have been produced by invited committees of twenty or so members (47). They are highly integrated volumes in a closely planned sequence from kindergarten through Grade XII. It is not practical to try to describe these volumes in detail, but they contain an abundance and variety of ideas, information, bibliography, and advice that cannot help but inspire and support any serious teacher.

4. *Independent research.*—Sponsored projects are helpful, but they should not replace independent research or make new studies become the province of organizations. Individual efforts should be continued and encouraged. An example of a recent study was cited earlier (11). Freeman, in discussing the problems of teaching "Sub-

ject A," one of our most conspicuous failures in the past and an area that needs the most serious consideration we are capable of, suggests that we widen our area of investigation in looking for solutions. He particularly points to British linguistic studies for ideas and insights that have been lightly treated or overlooked in the United States— particularly an awareness and systematic description of registers (16). He feels that much student writing exhibits an insufficiently discriminating sense of appropriateness and consistency, that field, role, mode, and style should be properly expressive of subject matter, task, medium, and audience.

This is the slightest sample of research recently completed and in progress. There is much going on, and we can look forward to changes that will make the curriculum at every level unfamiliar to one who has been away from the schools for a few years. The day of rapid obsolescence will then be the problem for educators that it has been for engineers, and education will indeed become a continuing, lifelong process.

Conclusion

It is good that we are looking in many directions for solutions to our educational problems, because we face a crisis: There is too much knowledge for one person to learn, and the amount is growing at a staggering rate. This is not a new problem. We have faced it in the past with two solutions: specialization and a longer period of formal education. Neither of these solutions will work in the future. We are specialized to a point where we have become compartmentalized; we produce *trained* but not *educated* men and women. And certainly we cannot further lengthen the number of years a student spends in school. Already this preparation represents too long a period of dependency before a graduate becomes productive.

The best hope for a solution seems to lie in increasing the efficiency of the schools—especially in getting a better return on our investment in early education. Many observers agree that time can be more efficiently spent in public school education, and it is inevitable that we move much of the information we teach to lower levels in the school schedule. If we are to accomplish this, language skills become more important than ever, for not only do we have more to communicate, but also there are more people in the range of communication. Much greater efficiency is needed in the use of our language in all of its skills—expressive and receptive. Students especially need to be more effective in writing and in oral expression. But reading and listening comprehension are hardly less important.

We also need to be concerned about learning languages other than our own, for we cannot avoid the need to communicate with other peoples. Many speakers of other languages will be interested in learning English, and we must be prepared to help them, for the incentives are great. English contains a rich literature of experience and information which will continue to attract students from all over the world. We should be prepared to meet them halfway, teaching them English and learning their languages.

Our chances for survival as rational human beings will be closely related to the improvement of our efficiency in the communications skills. Indeed, our survival as physical creatures may depend on it.

BIBLIOGRAPHY

1. AGARD, E. B., y ayudantes. *El inglés hablado, para los que hablan español*. New York: Henry Holt & Co., 1953.
2. American Council of Learned Societies. *Spoken English Textbooks*. Edited by Martin Joos. 10 vols. 1954–55. (English for Burmans, Greeks, Indonesians, Iranians, Koreans, Speakers of Mandarin Chinese, Speakers of Vietnamese, Speakers of Thai, Turks, Yugoslavs.)
3. BATEMAN, DONALD R., and ZIDONIS, FRANK J. "The Effect of a Study of Transformational Grammar on the Writing of Ninth and Tenth Graders," NCTE *Research Report No. 6*. Champaign, Ill.: NCTE, 1966.
4. BLOCH, BERNARD. "A Set of Postulates for Phonemic Analysis," *Language*, XXIV (January-March, 1948), 3-46.
5. BLOCH, BERNARD, and TRAGER, GEORGE L. *Outline of Linguistic Analysis*. Baltimore: Linguistic Society of America, 1942.
6. BLOOMFIELD, LEONARD. *Language*. New York: Henry Holt & Co., 1933.
7. CHOMSKY, NOAM. *Aspects of the Theory of Syntax*. Cambridge, Mass.: M.I.T. Press, 1965.
8. ———. *Syntactic Structures*. The Hague: Mouton & Co., 1957.
9. CURME, GEORGE O. *Parts of Speech and Accidence*. Boston: D. C. Heath & Co., 1935.

62 THE STRUCTURE OF LANGUAGE

10. ———. *Syntax*. Boston: D. C. Heath & Co., 1931.
11. Freeman, Donald C. "Subject A: Subject A," *Experiment and Innovation*, 1 (January, 1968), 19-31.
12. Fries, Charles C. *American English Grammar. The Grammatical Structure of Present-Day American English with Especial Reference to Social Differences or Class Dialects*. New York: D. Appleton-Century Co., 1940.
13. ———. *The Structure of English: An Introduction to the Construction of English Sentences*. New York: Harcourt, Brace & Co., 1952.
14. ———. *Teaching and Learning English as a Foreign Language*. Ann Arbor; University of Michigan Press, 1945.
15. Gleason, H. A., Jr. *Linguistics and English Grammar*. New York: Holt, Rinehart & Winston, 1965.
16. Halliday, M. A. K.; McIntosh, Angus; and Strevens, Peter. *The Linguistic Sciences and Language Teaching*. London: Longmans, 1964.
17. Hill, Archibald A. *Introduction to Linguistic Structures, From Sound to Sentence in English*. New York: Harcourt, Brace & World, 1958.
18. Hockett, Charles F. *A Course in Modern Linguistics*. New York: Macmillan Co., 1958.
19. Hook, J. N. "Project English: The First Year," *PMLA*, LXXVIII (September, 1963), 33-36.
20. Hunt, Kellogg W. *Sentence Structures Used by Superior Students in Grades Four and Twelve, and by Superior Adults*, Cooperative Research Project No. 5-0313.
21. ———. "A Sequence of Clause-to-Sentence Length Factors," *English Journal*, LIV (April, 1965), 300-9.
22. Jacobs, Roderick A., and Rosenbaum, Peter S. *Grammar 1*. Boston: Ginn & Co., 1967.
23. ———. *Grammar 2*. Boston: Ginn & Co., 1967.
24. Jespersen, Otto. *A Modern English Grammar on Historical Principles*. 7 vols. Heidelberg: Carl Winters, 1922-42.
25. Kruisinga, Etsko. *A Handbook of Present-Day English*. 4 vols. Gronigen: Noordhoff, 1911.
26. Lado, Robert, and Fries, Charles C. *English Pattern Practices, Establishing the Patterns as Habits*. Ann Arbor: University of Michigan Press, 1943. (Contains charts)
27. ———. *English Pronunciation, Exercises in Sound Segments, Intonation, and Rhythm*. Ann Arbor: Michigan University Press, 1958.
28. ———. *English Sentence Patterns, Understanding and Producing English Grammatical Structures, An Oral Approach*. Ann Arbor: University of Michigan Press, 1957.
29. ———. *Lessons in Vocabulary*. Ann Arbor: University of Michigan Press, 1956.

30. LAMB, SYDNEY M. *Outline of Stratificational Grammar.* Washington: Georgetown University Press, 1966.

31. MACKEY, WILLIAM FRANCIS. *Language Teaching Analysis.* London: Longmans, 1965.

32. *Oxford English Dictionary on Historical Principles.* Edited by J. A. H. Murray *et al.* 12 vols. London: Oxford University Press, 1884-1928.

33. PIKE, KENNETH L. *Language in Relation to a Unified Theory of the Structure of Human Behavior.* 3 vols. Glendale, Calif.: Summer Institute of Linguistics, 1954-1960.

34. POUTSMA, HENDRIK. *A Grammar of Late Modern English.* 5 vols. Gronigen: Noordhoff, 1904-1926.

35. *Research in Oral Language.* Edited by Walter T. Petty. National Committee on Research in English, 1967.

36. ROBERTS, PAUL. *English Sentences.* New York: Harcourt, Brace & World, 1962.

37. ———. *English Syntax.* New York: Harcourt, Brace & World, 1964.

38. ———. *Patterns of English.* New York: Harcourt, Brace & World, 1956.

39. ———. *The Roberts English Series, A Linguistics Program,* Books 3-9. New York: Harcourt, Brace & World, 1966.

40. ———. *Understanding English.* New York: Harper & Row, 1958.

41. RUTHERFORD, WILLIAM E. *Modern English: A Text for Foreign Students.* New York: Harcourt, Brace & World, 1968.

42. SAPIR, EDWARD. *Language: An Introduction to the Study of Speech.* New York: Harcourt, Brace & World, 1921.

43. SHUGRUE, MICHAEL F. "New Materials for the Teaching of English: The English Program of the USOE," *PMLA* LXXXI (September, 1966), 1-36.

44. SHUGRUE, MICHAEL F., and CRAWLEY, THOMAS F. "The Conclusion of the Indian Phase: The English Program of the USOE," *PMLA,* LXXXII (November, 1967), 15-32.

45. SMITH, HENRY LEE, JR. *Linguistic Science and the Teaching of English.* Cambridge: Harvard University Press, 1956.

46. STEINBERG, IRWIN R. "Research on the Teaching of English Under Project English," *PMLA,* LXXXIX (September, 1964), 50-76.

47. *Teaching Literature in Wisconsin, Teaching Speaking and Writing in Wisconsin, Teaching the English Language in Wisconsin.* The Wisconsin English-Language-Arts Curriculum Project, 1965-67.

48. THOMAS, OWEN. *Transformational Grammar and the Teacher of English.* New York: Holt, Rinehart & Winston, 1965.

49. TRAGER, GEORGE L., and SMITH, HENRY LEE. *An Outline of English Structure.* Norman, Okla.: Battenburg, 1951.

50. ZANDVOORT, R. W. *A Handbook of English Grammar.* London: Longmans, 1957.

CHAPTER II

The Geography of Language

H. REX WILSON

Introduction

THE REALITY OF DIALECT

A recent addition to American folklore tells of a Texan who welcomed the presidency of Lyndon Johnson with the comment, "At last we have a President who doesn't talk with an accent." As English speakers move about and talk to other English speakers in our mobile society, they discover that the English-speaking world is full of people who "talk with an accent." The less sophisticated are apt to deplore the fact that so many speak English so badly as compared to themselves and the people with whom they were brought up.

The more inquisitive may wonder why this should be—that everywhere you go, people speak differently. There are many reasons why people who can understand each other more or less well speak their language differently. There are such factors as education, social group, and age, but one of the most striking ones is difference of location. This does not mean that climate, soil types, or differences in mineral deposits in the geological substrata—or even the stars—dictate the way in which we speak. Separation of two groups which once spoke alike can guarantee that in time they will develop different ways of speaking their language. These ways of talking may be further differentiated by association with other groups of speakers of the same or another language, but separation alone is enough.

THE PHYSICAL PRODUCTION OF SPEECH

Drift in muscular effort.—Language is a marvelous but very human activity. *Why* we talk, *when* we as animals started to talk, and *how* we formulate what we say, present us with difficult problems, but the means we use to project our utterances upon the unoffending air is not at all mysterious. Speech sounds are the product of human muscles. Athletes know that they cannot always produce the same result with apparently the same effort and concentration. True, there is the equipment and the conditions of the field, but even a highly skilled pitcher cannot put the ball twice in succession through quite the same frame, and on the driving range, once hooks and slices have been corrected, the same make of ball will not go the same distance each time. And even in typing we do not always hit the key we intended to strike, as any reader of the first draft of this chapter could confirm.

Self-correction.—In the activities just suggested we are correcting ourselves more or less consciously all the time, but in speech we cannot operate freely and effectively if we are indulging in conscious self-criticism and correction. Of course, we do correct ourselves, and the necessity of being understood keeps our variations in pronunciation within surprisingly narrow bounds. But little by little and generation by generation the way we say things will shift—just as a nasty tendency to slice may gradually distort a player's golf game unless he pays strict attention to the problem. In this way a whole set of English long vowels drifted away from their earlier pronunciation. If they had not, we would be pronouncing the word "boat" with a vowel rather like that of "father," "meat" something like "mate," "time" something like "team"; and we should not have a clear distinction between "mouse" and "moose."

People who talk together a lot will tend to talk in more or less the same way. The speech community provides automatic and largely unconscious correcting factors. But people do not continue talking as a group in the same way generation by generation. They simply drift along together. If they separate, the separated groups will develop different drifts in their pronunciation and lay the foundations of different dialects.

Dialect into language.—As far back as we can trace language, this process has been going on. The ancestors of the speakers of most of the European languages and a number of those of Asia apparently once all spoke the same language, but they moved apart physically, and gradually each group of them changed so much that they could not understand most of the others. The result was what we call today the Indo-European family of languages, a group of dialects so different from one another that the speakers of one cannot understand the speakers of another. This ultimate dialect relationship has been recognized by at least one French scholar who called a book on this group of languages, *The Indo-European Dialects* (22).

Types of dialect differences.—Different drifts in pronunciation are often the first dialect differences recognized because they cut right across the stream of speech, but often the most striking differences may be in the names that we use for things. Different cultural histories result in different vocabularies. A thoughtful young lady from the Chicago area was visiting a home in New England. Her offer to help get supper ready was accepted by her hostess, who said, "Reach up in that cupboard there. . ." This the young lady did. ". . . and you'll find a spider." The hand came back suddenly— empty. But all the hostess wanted was a perfectly ordinary frying pan.

Or perhaps we may use a different sort of sentence to say the same thing. In parts of the American Midwest the question, "Is that all the further you can throw a baseball?" is readily accepted as a query about the extent of one's ability. But this appeared in a textbook used in New England as a sentence to be corrected— which of course resulted in its being added as a temporary novelty to the speech of a whole class of junior high schoolers.

THE DIALECTS OF ENGLISH

Importation of English dialects into Britain.—That we should have dialects is not surprising in view of human physical tendencies and varying cultural histories; that there should be English dialects was assured from the moment of the importation of our ancestral language into Britain. In a sense there were dialects of English before there was an English language, for England was settled from the European continent by speakers of Indo-European languages belonging to a branch called the "Germanic." But they did not all speak one dialect. Traditionally they are known by such names as Angles, Saxons, Jutes, and Frisians, and they seem to have settled in various places and with varying relationships with one another.

Before too long, Scandinavians, whose language was more or less intelligible to the earlier settlers, intruded. All these ingredients, in the absence of easy transportation and mass communications to smooth the mixture, guaranteed the marvelous patchwork of local dialects in the Britain of today. The early settlement of English-speaking North America was roughly parallel to that of England in the fifth and subsequent centuries.

Literary recognition of dialect.—Throughout England, for centuries not only did people speak the dialect of their region, but also records were kept and literature was written in the English of the region where it originated. (Manuscripts copied in a region other than that of their origin were at least partially changed into the second dialect, providing a host of interesting puzzles for scholars of our day.) As London rose steadily to dominate the commercial and administrative life of England, its speech, or at least forms of speech not too confusing to residents of the metropolis, came to dominate literature. The idiom of people outside the London region was known from visitors which the center attracted and was used by Chaucer for artistic effect in "The Reeve's Tale" (38: 688; note line 1, 4022) where Northern speech forms are used to add point to the story in an episode in the feud between the Reeve and the Miller.

When Shakespeare went up to London from Warwickshire as a young man, he must have made an adjustment to the predominant speech of his new surroundings. He was certainly very much aware of "provincial" speech which, in a very generalized way, he used for comic effect to enhance his characterization of bumpkins. Similarly, the more obvious tags of Cockney speech showed up in Mrs. Quickly and her gossips. A tighter artistic use of regional dialect is the conversation of the Irish, Scottish, and Welsh captains in *Henry V*, Act III, scene 2 where amusement at their outlandish speech is subordinated to the symbolism of the unity of England, Scotland, Ireland, and Wales. (9:35-46)

In more recent times, of course, the use of dialect by numerous writers (including Dickens, Tennyson, Lowell, and Twain) comes readily to mind. And, of course, there is the rendition of whole stories in dialect, as most endearingly represented by Joel Chandler Harris.

Professional and social recognition.—That Shakespeare could find dialect differences within the capital to use in his Cockney portrayals—a situation still capable of exploitation four hundred years later in George Bernard Shaw's *Pygmalion*—showed that the dialect of the capital was far from homogeneous. The differences exploited by Shakespeare and Shaw were largely differences of social class; but within one class—the commercial community which gathered in London toward the end of the century before Shakespeare's—there was considerable mixture of which Caxton, the father of English printing, complained in his preface to his edition of *Eneydos.*

As the power and importance of the metropolis grew, more and more provincials were drawn there by the necessities of trade or the attractions of professional careers, and with the industrial revolution a new moneyed class emerged which was led by its womenfolk to London for the winter "Season"—and to other fashionable spots, such as Bath. Either the established members of the class of fashion and affairs of that time were less tolerant of provincial speech than their ancestors had been in Queen Elizabeth's time, or the majority of newcomers lacked the confidence of Sir Walter Raleigh, who is said to have persisted in his own Devon speech even at court (9:8). At any rate, the newscomers to the fashionable world expressed again the puzzlement of Caxton, not only as to what words they should use, but also as to how they should pronounce them.

This pressure, added to unrelated developments in human inquiry, led to the rapid proliferation of works designed to set the unsure upon the path to socially acceptable English. Thomas Sheridan, father of the playwright, combined an acting career with a serious—indeed humorless—study of elocution, a field in which he became a highly successful teacher not only of the socially ambitious but also of the sons of the aristocracy. His teaching and studies eventually led to a very popular pronouncing dictionary (34) which was followed by a rival work by Walker (36), who differed with Sheridan on some points of theory. Under the conditions of publication prevailing at the time, they both became strong influences on the work of Noah Webster and so made their influence felt throughout the whole English-speaking world (33) and contributed a major factor to the widely held notion that accept-able speakers of English "speak without a dialect."[1]

"Standard" dialects.—In fact, what we have glimpsed in the development of London English and the standards imposed upon it by eighteenth-century writers is simply the development of an-other dialect, differing from the others of the English-speaking world only in the reverence with which it is regarded.

In one way or another, by the nineteenth century such standard dialects were to be found in all the major languages of Europe. Yet, very obviously, such preferred ways of using the language were not the only ones prevailing. Romanticism both in England and on the continent turned the attention of poets toward humble and rustic life, and "a selection of language really used by men," to use Wordsworth's terms. There was a great upsurge of interest in folklore, and ultimately a curiosity developed about the finer details of nonstandard language.

Dialectology

ORIGINS

Early studies.—Whatever good use literary men may have made of dialect material, their purpose was artistic and not scientific. Not even the careful markings of the vowels in Tennyson's "The North-ern Farmer" can tell us all we would like to know. The description of dialect requires a far more searching examination and controlled method of reporting than any poet can be expected to use. This method, now called *dialectology*, traces its beginnings to Germany in the first quarter of the nineteenth century.

In its first stage, dialectology was confined to individual dialect studies, starting with Johann Andreas Schmeller's grammar of Bavarian in 1821. This type of study is still an honored tradition, as represented by Orton's *The Phonology of a South Durham Dialect* (1933), but it was only a step in the direction of the type of survey which sets out to provide information about language on a number of dimensions, especially the geographical.

The geographical dimension.—The immediate ancestor of mod-

1. Sheldon (33) provides an excellent discussion of the influence of the work of Sheridan and Walker.

ern linguistic geography is a German scholar who, in 1876, began a survey of the local dialects of Germany with a survey of the area around Düsseldorf (3, 16).[2] Georg Wenker later extended his survey to include more than forty thousand localities in Germany. By modern standards Wenker's method was primitive. He wrote to the schoolmasters in each of the localities asking them to translate forty sample sentences into the local dialect. The result was a network of comparable material whose closeness has never been surpassed. The actual records are often rather gross, since the agents were untrained in linguistic matters, but they are the responses of educated people on the spot and they are more or less standardized.[3] The German spelling conventions of the time were sufficiently exact to give a reasonable approximation of pronunciation (25)—something which is almost hopeless in mailed questionnaires concerning English.

The next great survey was one conducted for French by Jules Gilliéron, who devised a questionnaire of two thousand items and sent out a trained phonetician to record the answers in more than six hundred localities. Publication was completed in 1908. Because the records are the work of one highly trained man, Edmond Edmont, they are especially valuable on the level of pronunciation. In this and other ways, this survey is almost the converse of Wenker's: where his was very approximate in the matter of pronunciation, the French survey was precise and consistent; where Wenker's sample was short, Gilliéron's was long; where Wenker's network was fine, Gilliéron's was coarse; where Wenker's results give ample grammatical material, Gilliéron's yields very little.

Both these early surveys established principles on which modern studies are based.

Geographical Studies of English

RESEARCH DESIGN AND METHODOLOGY

When the *Linguistic Atlas of the United States and Canada* was planned in the late 1920's, two Europeans working in the tradition

2. Bloomfield (3: chap. xix) and Lehmann (16: chap. viii) present comprehensive historical summaries of linguistic geography.

3. An interesting reassessment of Wenker's results is to be found in Moulton (25).

of Gilliéron were brought in to serve as consultants and trainers of field workers for the *Linguistic Atlas of New England* (13: xii). The aim on this continent has been to combine the maximum of information with the closest possible sampling by trained field workers actually interviewing the informants.

The mail questionnaire has not been forgotten and serves as a valuable preliminary sampling for more detailed surveys. Because this type of survey must deal with untrained observers often reporting on their own speech (which most of us listen to least), it is of necessity confined almost entirely to matters of vocabulary, usage, and grammar. It is almost impossible to convey precise notions of pronunciation in this way.

The more recent surveys of local speech have not only been designed to provide information on vocabulary (lexical items), pronunciation (phonological items), and grammar, but they have also recognized that geography is not the only dimension affecting speech difference. Age and social factors are taken into account as well (13: 39 ff).

In reporting the responses of the individuals interviewed (informants), the interviewers (field workers) note carefully not only what is said but also the circumstances. If the pronunciation is overly careful, whether it is corrected, whether it arose spontaneously (conversationally) rather than as the result of questioning, or whether it could only be had as the result of suggestion—all must be noted for future evaluation, along with evaluative or explanatory comments by the informant. Most prized of all, of course, are the purely conversational remarks which supply answers to the questionnaire. The aim of the field worker is to make the interview as conversational as possible, leading the informant into a general area of conversation with as little direct questioning as possible. Direct questions are, of course, frequently necessary; but these are never *direct* in the sense that they ask for a yes-or-no answer, and they must under no circumstances mention the term sought. This is, of course, fraught with uncertainty. The writer once thought he had a simple way of eliciting local terms for *frying pan* by simply asking: "What do you fry your eggs in?" Of course in time he got the reply, "Butter," and revised his method.

The importance of conversational items and the near impossibility of garnering all the unguarded conversational gems in writing have made the tape recorder a blessing—but not an unmixed one. Experience has proved that "as an aid to an inexperienced field worker who makes his preliminary transcription as he goes along, the tape recorder can be extremely useful" (18: 493–94) but as the sole device for field recording, it is a doubtful resource (37).

SURVEYS AND PUBLICATION

Field recording whether manual or electrical (or ideally a combination of both) is not, of course, the end. Editing and interpretation are required to produce such studies and atlases as have been published. Field work for the *Linguistic Atlas of New England* was completed in 1933 and the *Atlas* and *Handbook* appeared in 1939 (13: 14). Although field work continued in the area covered by the thirteen original colonies and over much of the rest of the United States, this is the only atlas to be published to date. The materials for the Middle and South Atlantic states are now being edited under the direction of Raven I. McDavid, Jr. at the University of Chicago, and those for the Upper Midwest are being brought out at the University of Minnesota under the direction of Harold B. Allen. A beginning for Canada is being undertaken by Murray Wanamaker (of the University of Winnipeg) and the writer, who are editing materials for Southwest Nova Scotia which were gathered in 1939-40 by Henry Alexander (then of Queen's University) and which are being augmented by their own field work carried out from 1950 to 1963. Beyond the historically important coastal states, controlled investigation of some sort has touched almost every major region of the United States. In Canada, field work has been done in the Atlantic provinces, in Ontario, and in parts of British Columbia. Although only one regional atlas has yet appeared, materials from other regions have been published in special studies. Three works covering the Eastern Seaboard have appeared (11, 1, 12) treating the vocabulary, verb forms, and pronunciation of this area.

DIALECT REGIONS OF THE UNITED STATES

Revision of old assumptions.—The analyses of the material collected in the field that have resulted in these studies show a need for

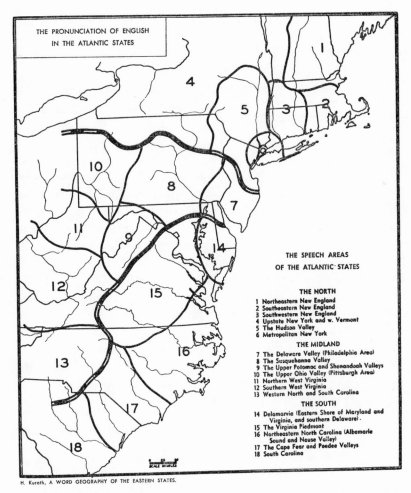

THE PRONUNCIATION OF ENGLISH
IN THE ATLANTIC STATES

THE SPEECH AREAS
OF THE ATLANTIC· STATES

THE NORTH
1 Northeastern New England
2 Southeastern New England
3 Southwestern New England
4 Upstate New York and w. Vermont
5 The Hudson Valley
6 Metropolitan New York

THE MIDLAND
7 The Delaware Valley (Philadelphia Area)
8 The Susquehanna Valley
9 The Upper Potomac and Shenandoah Valleys
10 The Upper Ohio Valley (Pittsburgh Area)
11 Northern West Virginia
12 Southern West Virginia
13 Western North and South Carolina

THE SOUTH
14 Delamarvia (Eastern Shore of Maryland and
   Virginia, and southern Delaware)·
15 The Virginia Piedmont
16 Northeastern North Carolina (Albemarle
   Sound and Neuse Valley)
17 The Cape Fear and Peedee Valleys
18 South Carolina

SCALE IN MILES

H. Kurath, A WORD GEOGRAPHY OF THE EASTERN STATES.

a revision of some common assumptions about American English.
By drawing lines called *isoglosses* around features of vocabulary
and pronunciation, the dialectologists have found that they cluster
together to give the eastern United States three major speech areas—
Northern, Midland, and Southern—terms which might seem to
parallel the often-heard groupings of "New England," "Southern,"
and "General American" (2:446–47). (See map.) However, Northern does not equal New England, since it includes all of New York
State and parts of Pennsylvania and New Jersey, areas popularly
thought of as General American. And furthermore, more than half

of Vermont is grouped with upstate New York in the subtler sub-divisions of this major area. Another avoidance of political bound-aries is seen in the boundary of the Southern area which shuns Mason and Dixon's famous line by starting in the southern part of Delaware, moving westward across Maryland and then bending largely southward, cutting off the western part of Virginia. "The South" of popular linguistic folklore, in fact, is confined chiefly to the region between the Blue Ridge and the coast.

Subareas.—As has been implied, the three main dialect regions of the eastern states by no means account for the remarkable diver-sity of speech to be found in the region. Eighteen subareas can be detected. The North has six, and although New England has the largest single subarea (consisting of all of Maine and New Hamp-shire and parts of Vermont and Massachusetts), it is not as dialectally homogeneous as outsiders often think but contributes to four of the remaining five subareas of the North. The Midland not only has seven subareas, but there is a strong boundary cutting these into two groups, North Midland and South Midland. The South has five subareas.

Chief features of the major regions.—The boundaries for each of the major areas and for the subareas have been set up after the study of the geographical extent of hundreds of items. Only a few can be given here as representative (18:513ff.)

North—A distinction in pronunciation between such items as *hoarse: horse, mourning: morning,* in contrast to a failure to distinguish these in the adjacent North Midland area, a feature which in-vades the North in New York City and the Hudson Valley.

The New York City area shares with Eastern New England a tendency to lose/r/ except before vowels.

In Eastern New England there is also a tendency to insert /r/ before vowels (Cuber is . . .). But *not* just haphazardly (. . . on the island of Cuba).

The border between the North and Midland is especially well marked by the isogloss separating those who pronounce *greasy* with /-s-/ (North) and those who pronounce it with a /-z-/ (Midland and South).

The vocabulary of the North is marked by a preference for the term *pail* where the Midland and South have *bucket.* In the North *bucket* is found consistently only on the coast north of Boston. And of course there is the *spider* for *frying pan* referred to above. This is gradually going out of use inland.

The past tense of *dive* is *dove* (rarely *dived*) in this area. In the Midland and South this is either consistently *dived* (or *dived* and *dove* compete).

Northerners who overindulge are consistently sick *to* their stomachs, whereas in the other areas *at* is more common with *in* or *on* competing. The *at* type of expression is spreading into the New York City area and southern New England.

Midland—The more obvious pronunciation features of the Midland region are implied in the borders described for the North. It is, strikingly, an area where /r/ is not lost in contrast with Eastern New England and the South. Occasionally an unexpected /r/ may be found in *wash* and *Washington*.

The vocabulary of the Midland is marked by the term *skillet* for *frying pan* which, unlike *spider* in the North, is spreading rather than receding.

The term *snake feeder* for *dragon fly* is distinctive for the North Midland, but comes into competition with one of the southern terms, *snake doctor*, in the South Midland, and contrasts with the northern *(devil's) darning needle*.

Poke is used from western Pennsylvania and southward in competition with *sack*. *Sack* alternates with *toot*, borrowed from Pennsylvania German in the southeast corner of Pennsylvania and northern Maryland.

All the further for *as far as* is a marked feature of Midland speech which has spread westward to the Midwest. *I want off* (*in*, *out*, etc.) is a frequent rival for the standard construction with *to get*.

South—As we have noted, the South (like Eastern New England) is a prominent area of *r*-loss. However, the insertion of /r/ before vowels is rare.

The name *Mary* and words like *dairy* have the vowel of *May* rather than that of *merry*, as in Midland speech.

The honorific *Mrs.* in this area is shortened to /miz/ to the confusion of outsiders who have to learn that the /-z/ sets this off from *Miss* which has /-s/.

A particularly desirable type of pitchy kindling is known by the descriptive term *lightwood* with the unexpected pronunciation *lighted*. *String beans* are known as *snap beans*.

The best known of the South's regional expressions is the familiar *y'all*, but this is shared with the South Midland and can be found throughout most of West Virginia and down the rest of the Mountain areas.

Verbal expressions such as *it wan't me* (also typical of the North) and *he belongs to do it* (ought) set this area off from both Midland areas.

Sources of American dialects.—Just as the dialects of England existed from the time of settlement, so those of North America date back also to the earlier settlers. As early as the latter part of the seventeenth century, English visitors to the colonies were commenting on the barbarous corruption by the colonists of the proper language of Englishmen (24:chap. i). Most of these colonists' "bad habits," however, went back to dialects of Old England other than that of the critic. The points at issue were usually items of vocabulary, for Englishmen visiting this country were struck by the lack of distinctly local pronunciation (sometimes referred to as "dialect"). Relative to England, of course, there was a good deal of truth in this observation, but as we shall see, some peculiarities of North American pronunciation find their way back to the old country.

Words which Englishmen tended to find offensive were new additions from languages with which the Americans had come into contact in their new conditions of life, such as *woodchuck* (of Indian derivation) or *portage* (from the French), or were survivals of words which had become unfamiliar in England (30).[4] For instance, the word *creek* for a stream, while less frequent in British usage where it more generally means an inlet of some other body of water, especially the sea, is cited by the *Oxford English Dictionary* as in use in 1555. *Upland* for land other than marshes and valleys is listed by the *OED* as "now arch." but was in British usage as late as 1857. *Spur* as a term describing hills and mountains was in good use in British English as early as 1652.

Naturally, as years have gone by, the North American dialects have diverged in their development from that of their cousin dia-

4. Cited in Mencken (23).

lects in England, and we must not expect to find "pure Elizabethan English" (or, more confused, "pure Anglo-Saxon") (23:459) in even the most conservative, remote speech area of this continent. Comparison of modern North American dialects with those of England is hampered by the fact that, however slow its progress, dialectology on this continent has always been at a more advanced stage than the work in Great Britain. Thus, of the three major works based on the field work in the eastern United States, only one, *The Pronunciation of English in the Atlantic States*, makes use of English materials.

In 1937-38, Guy S. Lowman, who had done much of the field work for the eastern states, did a wide-meshed survey of the southern and South Midland counties of England, using the same techniques as he had in the eastern states. Thus, for a limited area of England, we have a good basis for comparison. Since the publication of *The Pronunciation of English in the Atlantic States* in 1961, the results of a survey of the six northern counties of England have been appearing in tabular form, edited by Orton and Halliday (29), and in map form, edited by Kolb (10), so that gradually fuller comparison with the dialects of England is becoming possible. The less well-advanced work in Scotland and Northern Ireland will be particularly helpful in interpreting the speech of the American Midland.

Such comparison as has been possible has shown a number of interesting parallels with the speech of southern England. New England is especially rich in links—and puzzles. Many features show clear connections with rather specific areas of England, as in the pronunciation of *aunt* with the /a/ of *father* and not the /æ/ of *man*, which points clearly (with other evidence) to Middlesex-Essex. But whether this particular vowel is the result of initial settlement or later cultural and commercial contact is not clear (12:135-36). This same problem exists for coastal Virginia.

In many words where there is a good deal of variation in pronunciation to be found alongside the assumed standard types, the competing forms seem to have come right from the old country. *Rather* with the widespread pronunciation using the vowel of *hat* is linked with the southwestern counties. "Ruther" (to rhyme with *brother*), a common folk pronunciation of the South and South Midland, is linked with East Anglia. "Rether" (to rhyme with

heather)—of scattered occurrence, though somewhat more prominent in New England, upstate New York, parts of the North Midland and Lower South—is linked with the central counties of the
English Midland. Finally, the pronunciation rhyming with *father* in
cultivated use in New England, Metropolitan New York, and parts
of Pennsylvania seems to be the result of contact with the prevailing
British English after the period of settlement (12:138).

The pronunciation of *stamp* as "stomp" (to rhyme with *romp*)
is an inheritance from the Middlesex-Essex region, but it has given
way among educated speakers to the pronunciation which rhymes
with *camp* which Standard British English derived from the southwestern counties of Somerset, Dorset and Devon (12:138). A similar
fate befell *catch*, rhyming with *ketch*, which was respectable in
England until late in the 18th century (12:140).

The English of this continent has clearly gone its own way, nor
all the piety nor all the wit of British critics could do a thing about
it. Yet there is little reason to fear that, like the descendants of Proto-
Indo-European, these will become two different languages.

Tennyson's "Northern Farmer" and Hardy's Wessex country-
folk may have problems understanding one another and the New
York cabdriver would be baffled by both of them; but on the level
of practical affairs, educated people of many professions are drawing together in their language, following up the now legendary exchange in World War II in which the British dropped *lorry* and
adopted *truck* in return for the Americans' use of *petrol* in place of
gasoline. The term "Middle Atlantic English" is hardly adequate
to describe this phenomenon, since at the educated level the language of all English-speaking areas is following the same trend (17).

Dialectology in Education

IN THE CLASSROOM

A foundation study.—Interesting as some of the findings of dialectology may be, their place in any general scheme of education
would seem at first glance to be marginal. Perhaps some of these
quaint anomalies belong in an enriched program for students who
are strong enough to resist being influenced by them. Against this
first impression, the idea that dialectology should be applied to the

very foundations of English studies will sound misguided if not heretical. But this idea is, in fact, held by responsible scholars, who have long been in contact with the teaching profession as advisers, course-designers, and teachers of teachers.

The function of dialectology in education is not merely to provide the student with objectively derived "don'ts." This matter could be taken care of by means of a list. A knowledge of the principles and main findings of English dialectology, and, if possible, some experience in dialect research belong in the education of every teacher who expects to teach English at any level. For dialectology, far from being merely the recording of the quaint sayings of funny little old people in out-of-the-way places, is potentially a great teaching museum of our language. Through its exhibits, earlier stages of the language are revealed. When these are properly evaluated, they bring to the teacher a clearer perspective of the origin of nonstandard features which he may encounter in the work of his students. Similarly, regionally restricted features may be pointed out.

In the teacher's classroom.—Direct teaching application of these and other resources may be devised, but the fundamental value of a teacher's knowledge of dialectology is the resulting reorientation toward our language and to its tremendous regional and social variety. The result should be a therapeutic one—replacing the traditional, somewhat priggish attitude toward "correct" English and "debased" variants with a clearer view of the true nature of the variants and the arbitrary and accidental nature of some of our most cherished rules. (Admittedly the older attitude is no longer popular, but it tends to be deeply rooted despite lip service to a more "liberal" attitude.)

An understanding of the realities and interrelations of dialect will remove a number of perplexities from the minds of teachers and improve their ability to use good materials effectively and guard against the hazards of imperfect ones. (That is, regionalisms like "all the further" will not be untaught where they do not exist, and their occurrence in misguided texts will be passed over, or explained upon request.) Complementary awareness of the social dimension of dialect coupled with a sound historical perspective of the language will supply a firm base from which to deal with students' individual problems. (See chapters iii and iv.)

In the student's classroom.—The introduction of elementary study of dialectology in the classroom might seem like a "frill," but it is as valuable to the average student as it is to the teacher, although most students will not put it to direct vocational application. It is difficult to see how a dialectally informed approach to the teaching of English can be instituted without some teaching of dialectology. The initial insights into the nature of dialect diversity usually awaken in the teacher an urge to share, and this spontaneous charity should be allowed full rein, unchecked by any feeling that it is an intrusion at the expense of the "real" curriculum. Indeed, unless an adequate place is provided for it so that the subject can be dealt with clearly and methodically—ideally as a continuing thread throughout the curriculum for a number of years after its introduction—there is a danger that dialect study will never be more than an Old Curiosity Shop or Believe-It-or-Not Museum of language, providing at best no educational profit and perpetuating at worst a false view of the relationship of "dialects" to "correct" English.

A READING COURSE IN DIALECTOLOGY

The ideal of training in dialectology, including not only a full historical survey and a study of the methodology of dialect field work and editing but also training in phonetic notation and the gathering and processing of data, is not possible for most teachers, especially those already embarked upon their profession. There are, however, a number of books or parts of books which can put the principles and main findings in the field within the reach of the non-specialist.

A useful start would be an introductory book in linguistics, such as Hall's popular introduction *Linguistics and Your Language* (8), to help the reader become at home with the attitudes and principles of the modern linguist. Perhaps the most readable scholarly introduction is Gleason's *Introduction to Descriptive Linguistics* (7), and in brief compass, Francis P. Dinneen describes the scope and nature of linguistics clearly in his *Introduction to General Linguistics* (4), chapter i, "Linguistics as a Scientific Study of Language." Most introductory books in linguistics touch on dialectology but, for clarity and historical completeness up to the time of its publication, Bloomfield's chapter xix in *Language* (3) has not been surpassed. (This has also been republished in *Language History* (15), edited by Hoijer.) A book which demonstrates the interrelations of dialectology and another fascinating field of language study, comparative linguistics, is Lehmann's *Historical Linguistics* (16). (See especially chapter viii). *The Handbook of the Linguistic Atlas of New England* (13) by Kurath and others describes the adaptation of classical dialectology to the American scene, and McIntosh demonstrates a later adaptation in his *An Introduction to a Survey of Scottish Dialects* (21), and Orton shows us another in the "Introduction" to his *Survey of English Dialects* (28).

The chief findings in the field in the Eastern United States are displayed in Kurath's *A Word Geography of the Eastern United States* (11), Atwood's *Verb Forms of the Eastern United States* (1), and Kurath and McDavid's *The Pronunciation of English in the Atlantic States* (12). (The chief features of the dialect regions are summarized by McDavid in chapter ix of Francis' *The Structure of American English* (18).) Orton and Halliday's *Survey of English Dialects: Six Northern Counties and the Isle of Man* performs something of the same function for northern England (29), but it is in simple list form and requires a fairly advanced grasp of phonetics, as does Kolb's *Phonological Atlas of the Northern Region* (10) which supplies maps for many features included in the survey.

Undoubtedly the most genial overview of the English language in the United States is Mencken's *The American Language* (23). In the form as abridged and edited by McDavid, this work (24) is not only more convenient than the original but also more up to date. Reed's *Dialects of American English* (31) is a recently published brief but useful summary.

Much of the material just referred to could be used profitably by mature students, but in recent years materials designed specifically for classroom use have been produced. These are listed in *Resources for the Teaching of English* (32), issued by the National Council of Teachers of English, and cover both the regional and social dimensions of dialect. The chief works in dialectology are Shuy's *Discovering American Dialects* (35) and a pamphlet and record prepared by Muri and McDavid under the title *Americans*

Speaking (20). "The Geography of Language" is one of the topics covered by a set of filmstrips and records entitled *Linguistic Backgrounds of English,* which also concerns itself with such matters as names and language history.

Of interest chiefly to teachers is *On the Dialects of Children* (edited by Davis) (26), a symposium dealing with the linguistic backgrounds of school children in relation to their school experience.

BIBLIOGRAPHY

1. ATWOOD, E. BAGBY. *A Survey of Verb Forms in the Eastern United States.* Ann Arbor: University of Michigan Press, 1953.
2. BAUGH, ALBERT C. A *History of the English Language.* New York: D. Appleton-Century Co., 1935.
3. BLOOMFIELD, LEONARD. *Language.* New York: Henry Holt & Co., 1933.
4. DINNEEN, FRANCIS P. *An Introduction to General Linguistics.* New York: Holt, Rinehart & Winston, 1967.
5. FRANCIS, W. NELSON. *The Structure of American English.* New York: Ronald Press Co., 1958.
6. "The Geography of Language," *Linguistic Backgrounds of English.* (Filmstrips and records). Chicago: Society for Visual Education.
7. GLEASON, H.A. *Introduction to Descriptive Linguistics.* New York: Holt, Rinehart & Winston, 1961.
8. HALL, ROBERT A., JR. *Linguistics and Your Language.* New York: Doubleday & Co., 1960.
9. KÖKERITZ, HELGE. *Shakespeare's Pronunciation.* New Haven: Yale University Press, 1953.
10. KOLB, EDUARD. *Phonological Atlas of the Northern Region.* Bern: Francke Verlag, 1966.
11. KURATH, HANS. *A Word Geography of the Eastern United States.* Ann Arbor: University of Michigan Press, 1949.
12. KURATH, HANS, and McDAVID, RAVEN I., JR. *The Pronunciation of English in the Atlantic States.* Ann Arbor: University of Michigan Press, 1961.
13. KURATH, HANS and OTHERS. *Handbook of the Linguistic Atlas of New England.* Providence, R.I.: American Council of Learned Societies, 1939.
14. ———. *Linguistic Atlas of New England.* (Three Volumes and a Handbook. [See preceding footnote.] Providence, R.I.: American Council of Learned Societies, 1939.)
15. *Language History.* (A reprint of chaps. 17–27 of Bloomfield's *Lan-*

guage). Edited by Harry Hoijer. New York: Holt, Rinehart & Winston, 1965.

16. LEHMANN, WINFRED P. *Historical Linguistics*. New York: Holt, Rinehart & Winston, 1962.

17. MARCKWARDT, ALBERT H., and QUIRCK, RANDOLPH. *A Common Language*. London: British Broadcasting Corporation, 1966.

18. McDAVID, RAVEN I., JR. in W. NELSON FRANCIS. *The Structure of American English*. New York: Ronald Press Co., 1958.

19. McDAVID, RAVEN I., JR. "Tape Recording in Dialect Geography: A Cautionary Note," *Journal of the Canadian Linguistic Association*, III (March, 1957), 3–8.

20. McDAVID, RAVEN I., JR., and MURI, JOHN T. *Americans Speaking* (Pamphlet and recording). Champaign, Ill.: National Council of Teachers of English, 1967.

21. McINTOSH, ANGUS. *An Introduction to a Survey of Scottish Dialects*. Edinburgh: Thomas Nelson & Sons, 1952.

22. MEILLET, A. *Les dialectes indo-européens*. Paris: Société de linguistique de Paris, 1908.

23. MENCKEN, H. L. *The American Language*. New York: Alfred A. Knopf, 1936. Supplement I, 1945, and Supplement II, 1948.

24. ———. *The American Language* (Abridged with annotations and new material by Raven I. McDavid, Jr., with the assistance of David W. Maurer). New York: Alfred A. Knopf, 1963.

25. MOULTON, WILLIAM G. "Structural Dialectology," *Language*, XLIV (September, 1968), 451–66.

26. *On the Dialects of Children*. Edited by A. L. Davis. Champaign, Ill.: National Council of Teachers of English, 1968.

27. ORTON, HAROLD. *The Phonology of a South Durham Dialect*. London: Kegan Paul, Trench, Trubner & Co., 1933.

28. ———. *Survey of English Dialects: Introduction*. Leeds: University of Leeds, 1962.

29. ORTON, HAROLD, and HALLIDAY, WILFRID J. *A Survey of English Dialects: The Six Northern Counties and the Isle of Man*. Vol. 1 in 3 parts. Leeds: University of Leeds, 1962–63.

30. READ, ALLEN WALKER. "British Recognition of American Speech in the Eighteenth Century," *Dialect Notes*. VI, Pt. VI, 1933.

31. REED, CARROLL E. *Dialects of American English*. Cleveland: World Publishing Co., 1967.

32. *Resources for the Teaching of English, 1968–1969*. Champaign, Ill.: National Council of Teachers of English, 1968.

33. SHELDON, ESTHER K. "Walker's Influence on the Pronunciation of English," *Publications of the Modern Language Association*, LXII (March, 1947), 130–46.

34. SHERIDAN, THOMAS. *A Complete Dictionary of the English Language*. London: Charles Dilly, 1789.

35. SHUY, ROGER W. *Discovering American Dialects*. Champaign, Ill.: National Council of Teachers of English, 1967.
36. WALKER, JOHN. *A Critical Pronouncing Dictionary and Expositor of the English Language* (London, 1791).
37. WILSON, REX. "The Implications of Tape Recording in the Field of Dialect Geography," *Journal of the Canadian Linguistic Association*, II (March, 1956), 17–21.
38. *The Works of Geoffrey Chaucer*. Edited by F. N. Robinson. Boston: Houghton Mifflin Co., 1957.

CHAPTER III

The Sociology of Language

RAVEN I. MCDAVID, JR.

Introduction

THE CONCEPT OF A LINGUISTIC STANDARD

Much of the problem of developing a language program for the schools grows out of a widespread acceptance of the assumption that there is a standard variety of the language which for various reasons has become a model of usage. Unfortunately, however, this assumption is not always based on an examination of the facts of usage; indeed, many of those who discuss the need for a standard do not understand the rationale from which standard languages have developed, consciously and otherwise.

In a tribal society, without literacy and the need to preserve permanent religious or commercial or literary records, there is little overt reason for a generally recognized standard. Its need is fulfilled, if at all, in two ways: first, by the attempt to preserve intact, in oral tradition, texts of cultural importance, even though over a period of time there arises considerable divergence between the language of the texts and that of everyday use; second, by the recognition by the tribe, in a situation of linguistic free trade, that certain of its members—usually those vested with roles of some traditional importance—are better models of usage than their fellow tribesmen. Neither of these situations need happen; in some speech communities, various bands or tribal groupings may dispute vociferously about which variety of their language is correct. Those who have worked with the Ojibwa-Ottawa of the Great Lakes, or with the various peoples of Malaita in the Solomons, report all kinds of dialectal prejudices arising from the relative power of groups whose language is mutually intelligible or out of the history of blood feuds and civil wars. Still, within a particular tribe, one of these two developments will probably occur.

The situations described above continued with the development of writing and of more highly structured political units. Writing was at first the possession of a tiny minority (even today, less than half the population of India is literate); it was devised for what the culture considered practical ends—maintenance of commercial records and preservation of sacred texts. It would naturally be established on the basis of the most prestigious form of the language, and its use for religious texts would make this form even more prestigious. (We will leave to other contributors the problem of a writing system's becoming outdated in terms of the current state of the language). As states became wealthier, there was increasing need for a standard language by which the more important business of the community could be transacted. Increasing literacy tended to increase the demand for a standard; the development of printing— and of other media for providing identical copies of a text in large numbers at low cost—made it more useful to have a linguistic frame of reference generally recognized as standard; the rise of technology made uniformity of vocabulary and syntax more desirable to prevent misunderstanding.

The prestige of literary models, too, has strengthened the appeal of a standard language, though not in all respects. For, as anyone knows, many of the most prestigious works, in whatever language, do not reflect current usage. The Homeric poems were recited in Periclean Athens in an archaic variety of Greek; the idiom of Chaucer or of Shakespeare is not that of twentieth-century America; and many of our contemporaries feel that the only legitimate text of the Bible is the King James Version completed in 1611, archaic even then in grammatical practice, and in some details (such as the use of the second-person pronouns) more archaic than the fourteenth-century language of Chaucer. As Charles C. Fries (2) was wont to say, while it is true that such writers as Chaucer and Shakespeare helped to give cultural prestige to London English, it is also true that they wrote in London English because it was already the most prestigious variety of the language. In general, then, a variety of the language becomes the standard because it is used by the people who make the important decisions for the speech com-

munity, and over the years it will change not only with the ineluct-
able passage of time but also with changes in the membership of the
group of decision-makers.

There is, of course, no reason why the standard language must
be an everyday spoken language of the territory in which it is used.
There are numerous examples of contrary situations in the past. In
Asia Minor, *circa* 1000 B.C., Akkadian—the language of Assyria—
was widely used in countries where other languages were spoken.
The conquests of Alexander the Great spread Greek as an administrative language into Egypt and as far east as India; it retained this
status in much of this area until the Islamic conquests, while Latin—
once a local Italic dialect—was established in the western half of
the Roman Empire. Similary, with the Islamic conquests, the classical Arabic of the Koran became the standard for the Caliphate and
its successor states. And even today, despite the liquidation of colonial empires, English and French are languages of higher education
and of much intercommunication in parts of Asia and Africa where
local languages are numerous and of minimun mutual intelligibility.

Nor does the standard language have to be a contemporaneous
spoken tongue; it may represent the usage of a bygone era. Hiero-
glyphic Egyptian, used as late as the period of Greek domination,
was an archaic variety, considerably removed from the popular
Demotic. Among practicing Moslems, there is a widespread feeling
that the only standard for the language is the seventh-century
variety in which the Koran is written; all twentieth-century varieties
of Arabic, no matter how widely spread, are adjudged as no language at all (4). And in present-day Greece, there is a powerful
movement to value usage good to the extent that it rejects contemporary practice and "purifies" itself according to ancient models.

Sometimes what has become the standard language (even though
not consciously archaic) is sharply different from the everyday
language of affairs. The literary Latin we study in schools today
was probably pronounced much the same way as the everyday
Latin of Caesar's time, and it seems to have had the same system of
inflections of noun and verb and other parts of speech; but because
it was consciously shaped by rhetoricians according to the models of
Greek excellence, its syntax was not that of everyday use, and its
vocabulary was strikingly different. For instance, the everyday

word for "horse" was *caballus,* from which descended all the present-day Romance designations for the animal; but in literary Latin it was *equus.*

As we have suggested before, most of the standard languages of today have arisen by the process of trial and error—by the establishment of the prestigious speech of one community or area that had, itself, already established commercial or political leadership over other communities in which varieties of the language were spoken. Latin followed the march of the Roman legions—first throughout Italy and then over Western Europe—and later the paths of the Christian missionaries. The standard varieties of Italian, French, Spanish, Russian, and British English reflect the cultural and economic preeminence—of various kinds—won by Rome and Florence, Paris, Toledo, Moscow, and London. And though the German-speaking community had been atomized politically for more than six centuries before the founding of the Second Reich in 1870, the prestige of the imperial court was such that the variety of German used in its chancellery gradually became accepted as a standard in northern Germany and in southern Germany as well.

In recent years, however, there has been some conscious thought as to the shape a national tongue might take. In Norway, after the personal union under the Swedish crown was substituted in 1814 for the Danish sovereignty that had endured since the fourteenth century, champions of cultural autonomy—and later of independence—felt that the national tongue should bear a closer relationship to the speech of the people than did the slightly modified Danish, or Dano-Norwegian, that had served so long as a standard. Led by a group of folklorists, a movement arose to establish a *Landsmål,* based on the folk dialects; a countermovement naturally developed toward keeping the older standard or *Riksmål,* though modifying it somewhat in the direction of everyday speech. The debate continued until, in effect, the two varieties of Norwegian—now known as *Nynorsk* and *Bokmål* respectively—were both recognized as standard, though each has since been modified in the direction of the other, and the industrialization and urbanization of Norway has given *Bokmål* a heavy preponderance of present-day speakers. In Prague, after the liberation of Czechoslovakia in World War I, Czech linguists took an active part in determining the directions the standard language—the first standard variety of modern Czech—would take. More spectacular have been some of the instances of deliberate language engineering after World War II, in the new nations of Africa and Asia. Practical decisions have often been made in terms of establishing a standard tongue that would be intelligible to the greatest number of speakers of the various dialects. And at least one decision, in Indonesia, was based on political considerations: It was desirable to have, as a national language, a variety of Malay that was equally intelligible to speakers of Javanese and Sumatran dialects; it was also desirable—in view of the long rivalry between the two major islands—to base the new standard on a dialect that was neither Javanese nor Sumatran. The result was the selection of a dialect spoken by relatively few people, a dialect without political connotations, and therefore generally accepted throughout the republic. Now, thanks to a centrally directed educational system, it is well on its way to general use, and native speakers of the new standard are appearing, since it is encouraged in the homes of the educated.

As standard varieties of language have become established, a demand has arisen for some sort of arbiter which should strive to keep the standard pure and free from the contaminations of unbridled change. Usually the demand has been for an academy of the élite, the authority of whose judgment might be thought to outweigh the taste of the uneducated masses. The first of the important academies was the Accademia della Crusca, of Florence; more famous, probably, has been l'Académie française, established by Cardinal Richelieu. Its forty "Immortals," meeting once a week, work through a small segment of the alphabet at each session, and a word they do not recognize is supposedly consigned to linguistic limbo until its turn comes up again, some thirty or forty years later. Other countries, such as Spain and the Soviet Union, have their academies, too; all are charged with the awful responsibility of resisting the deleterious effects of uncontrolled linguistic change. In practice, of course, their influence has been far less than their creators expected; words come and go, and meanings change, regardless of official decisions. And in fact the academies themselves may take a liberal (or at least a realistic) attitude toward the problems of linguistic change.

The English-speaking peoples, so far, have never established such

an academy. During the Restoration period (1660-1685), there was
a strong feeling that an English academy might be desirable; but even
among those who wished for it, there was so strong a rivalry as to
who would be the presiding officer that it was impossible to agree
on the articles of incorporation. Later, it was felt that Dr. Johnson,
through his *Dictionary*, had fulfilled the aims of an academy. But
even the authority of this work waned with the passing of time,
and the English settled down to adjudging the acceptability of language on an unspoken consensus of the educated and well-bred.

The American search for a standard was almost schizoid in its
beginnings. On the one hand, with the national feelings of a newly
independent country, there was a desire to establish an American
standard, independent of British models; on the other, the awareness
of national immaturity encouraged an almost slavish deference to
British opinion. There were several movements toward an academy,
all unsuccessful. Noah Webster, the prototype of American free
enterprise, sought to set himself up as linguistic arbiter. As many
observers have noted, he rejected British authority, not because he
rejected the notion of authority but because he wished to establish
his own. Yet, he did succeed in convincing Americans that models
of good usage must be sought among themselves and not in Britain.
With national maturity, it became evident (*a*) that American standard English must be based on American practice, (*b*) that there was
a healthy variety on the standard level, since each region was bound
to select its model from those whom it considered the most prestigious speakers and writers, and (*c*) that linguistic changes—both
obsolescence and innovation—were not only inevitable but also
healthy, responding to the inexorable passage of time. Still, there
was always a minority who sought to arrest the inevitable, such as
the editorial writer for the late *Saturday Evening Post* who in 1946
called for an authoritarian lexicographer who would purge the
language of the superfluous words created by frontier wits and
saloon columnists. And the ordeal of the Merriam *Webster's Third
New International Dictionary*, following its publication in 1961,
suggests that American authoritarianism is more vigorous than many
of us would like to think.

Yet academies, in the long run, have relatively little influence on
the course of a language. French purists may deplore the corruption

of their language by the inundation of Americanisms; but if an American term is useful in the everyday business of Parisians, they are not going to wait until its next alphabetical turn before the Immortals of the Académie, nor are scientists and technicians likely to be constrained in their invention of new terms, A language, after all, must respond to the needs of the people who use it. If the lack of a guiding authority is likely to encourage an uncontrolled efflorescence of vocabulary and syntactic structures, each innovation still has to prove itself in the marketplace; the test of its fitness is the practical one of whether or not people are willing to use it.

In fact, one should worry less about inadequate control than about too much. We have a striking example of the latter in the fate of Latin as a language of international communication. During the Middle Ages it had proved vigorous and adaptable, capable of taking in new words to deal with new concepts—however inelegant it might have been by Ciceronian standards. Then, in the Renaissance, more elegant models of Latinity were provided, and an author's Latin—regardless of his message—came to be deplored if it failed to measure up to classical excellence. Latin was no longer a working language, adaptable to any number of practical situations; it was a social ornament, with a standard of excellence that could be achieved only by a tiny minority. And despairing of achieving a satisfactory standard of Latinity, scholars and scientists gradually turned to the vernaculars, where there was no Cicero against whom the style, if not the content, of their message would be measured. Of course, other forces—the growing wealth of the middle classes, the extension of education, and the Protestant movement to make the Scriptures available in the vernacular—had already ended, to some extent, the traditional domination of Latin; but the ossification of Latin style did nothing to delay the disuse of the language.

THE STANDARD AND ACTUAL USAGE

It should go without saying that—except for highly codified situations, such as communications between aircraft and ground installations—there is considerable variety in the way a standard language is used by its speakers; and the larger the speech community, the greater the amount of variety possible. In some instances striking differences in pronunciation, in vocabulary, and even in grammar—especially in the spoken variety of the language—may be permissible as the subject of discourse becomes more homely and intimate. But in all standard languages there will be variety, and there will be change with the passing of time. To take British Standard English as an example, since the eighteenth century there have been important changes in the pronunciation system (notably the loss of post-vocalic /-r/ in *barn, beard, board,* and the like); in the incidence of particular sounds, such as the "broad a" /a/; and in the development of new syntactic structures, such as the progressive passive *a new house is being built on our street*—to say nothing of changes in the vocabulary and in the meanings of words.

Attitudes toward usage vary widely in a speech community. In the more traditional societies with rather clearly defined classes, the aristocratic tradition prevails that a person has the right, even the obligation, to shift according to his social situation; a person will be suspect if he is too conspicuously "correct" in situations demanding informal usage. But where there is social mobility, it is the wont of the newly risen to become very rigid in their attitudes, especially toward the informal usage of the group from which they have risen. In communities settled heavily by immigrants with a foreign-language background, the English is likely to be more formal and bookish than where there is a native English colloquial tradition.

Public-school teachers are likely to be more rigid in their attitudes than graduate professors, and newspaper columnists are likely to be even more rigid; the editors of women's magazines are most rigid of all. In all these instances, there is likely to be a limited training in the actual structure and history of the language, a reliance on such older artifacts as the "Blue Back Speller" and on such newer ones as lists of common grammatical errors and words most commonly mispronounced. Moreover, there is a tradition in America that the English teacher has an obligation to impose a rigid standard on his students, so that the revelation of one's professional identity in a social situation is likely to curdle the conversation with such remarks—not always in jest—that the others had better watch their grammar. This tendency, to be sure, is also reinforced by the fact that most English teachers—indeed, most teachers—are drawn from the newly risen lower-middle class, the group most unsure of their own status and therefore most concerned with imposing a rigid standard. But many of the laymen—chiefly, also, of lower-middle-class origins despite their current prosperity—are even more restrictive in their attitudes; they feel that all those who have to do with the language professionally have not only the right but also the duty to impose rigid standards on everyone else. It is amusing that in the controversy over the "lowered standards" of the Merriam *Third* (1961-64), editorial writers, newspaper columnists, and casual critics-at-large were the most violent in their condemnation; litterateurs and teachers in the schools were often perturbed, but the professional students of the language generally accepted the principles upon which the new dictionary had been constructed, even though they were not always happy about the way these principles had been put into practice.

It is not surprising that most people are not fully aware of their own usage. It is a commonplace for a field investigator to have an informant deny that a given word is used in the community—only to hear it five minutes later, or to have an informant sternly condemn a grammatical construction he habitually uses in his own unguarded conversation. In the controversy over the Merriam *Third*, *The New York Times* editorially condemned President Kennedy for using the verb *finalize*, which the *Third* had recognized as standard, only to have it revealed that some of the citations upon which the acceptance of the word had been based were found in the columns of the *Times*. And in casual reading, early in 1969, I encountered in the *Times*—zealously guarded by Theodore Bernstein, one of the most scrupulous of word-watchers—a half-dozen examples of the confusion of *who* and *whom*, nonstandard agreement of subject and verb, and other deviations from the purist's canon of good usage.

Social Dialect and Social Class

DIALECT AND CLASS MEMBERSHIP

As we have pointed out, the prestigious social dialect originates in the upper-class usage of a culturally important part of the speech community. In various ways, differing from one speech community to another, a number of the features of this standard language will spread from its original focus to the upper classes in satellite communities. Then, as new groups rise in the social scale, they will assimilate these models of good usage. But even members of lower-class groups may assimilate the prestigious variety of the language, at least for situations in which they come in contact with the public. It is notorious in England that butlers and club stewards are among the most meticulous speakers of British Received Pronunciation. And in the older South, no one could speak the standard variety of English more elegantly than Negro house servants ministering at a formal dinner.

What seems to be the case is that a person's habitual social contacts will provide him an opportunity to develop a range of linguistic behavior. The wider the range of contacts, the greater the social assurance, the sharper the intelligence and powers of observation of a speaker, the greater the likelihood of his being able to switch not only from one degree of formality to another, but from standard to nonstandard language as well.

And, of course, if individuals rise from one social class to another, they will take with them some of their language practices, even while they are assimilating the practices of their new environment. In this way, upper-class usage escapes petrification and continues to express the range of experience of those who make the important decisions in the speech community.

SOCIAL AND REGIONAL DIFFERENCES, AND OTHER MODES OF VARIATION

In many language communities, where a more or less rigid standard is established (or at least assumed), the word *dialect* is pejorative, describing a form of the language that an educated person would never condescend to use. In others, it is applied to the speech of quaint old people in out-of-the-way places. In still others, it describes the funny way everybody talks but me and those I grew up with. Scientifically, a dialect is simply a habitual variety of a language—regional or social or both—set off from other such habitual varieties by a complex of features of grammar and pronunciation and vocabulary. But despite the attempts of linguists to provide adequate definitions and descriptions, the term *dialect* is still too often used pejoratively, and some of the best-known materials devised for coping with striking social differences in language still set up an opposition between standard language and "local dialect."

For this reason, as Haugen has suggested, it is probably best to drop the term *dialect* altogether and confine oneself to a discussion of regional and social variations in language (3).

Regional varieties, however exotic from one's personal point of view, are not corruptions of primordial excellence. Rather, each regional and local variety, on whatever level, has its own history, and is the result of a complex of forces such as (*a*) settlement history, (*b*) routes of migration and communication, (*c*) prestige or isolation of the community, and (*d*) its social structure and educational system. In the United States, every local variety of English—to say nothing of the more important regional ones—has developed from a mixture of various British dialects, plus foreign-language settlements, plus varying degrees of contact with the Standard English of the British Isles and with other varieties of American English. In each area, thanks to the tradition of cultural and political autonomy of the various colonies and states, a prestige group developed. And one might say that in each community the standard variety of speech is basically a modification of the basic local type of speech by the tradition of Standard English. This influence of Standard English, as has already been pointed out, is such that the vocabulary of the most formal varieties of discourse, oral and written (especially the vocabularies of science and technology), is fairly uniform throughout the English of the Western Hemisphere, indeed throughout the English-speaking world. And grammar is pretty much the same among educated speakers, especially in formal writing. There are very few tags—one of them being *woken* as a participle, where Americans would use *woke* or *waked*—that tell us a book is by a Briton and not a North American. In educated informal usage there are a few more touchstones—Britons will say *have you any?* whereas Americans will say *do you have any?*—but even these are not numerous. Nor do we find many grammatical differences, on the standard level, among the various regional types of American English. In pronunciation, however, and in the more familiar parts of the vocabulary, these differences are much more numerous.

Social differences, on the other hand, are rather striking so far as the extent of the vocabulary is concerned, simply because the less educated have a narrower cultural experience. These differences are not likely to be reflected per se in the humble part of the vo-cabulary; a Southerner of whatever degree of education is likely to know a dragon fly as a *snake doctor* or *mosquito hawk*, if he comes from an environment where the insect is seen in everyday life. As far as pronunciation is concerned, all classes of speakers in a given community—with few exceptions—are likely to have the same system of vowels and vowels of the same phonetic quality, but there may be social differences in the way these vowels occur in different words. Thus, in eastern Massachusetts or in the Pitts-burgh area, such pairs of words as *cot* and *caught*, *collar* and *caller*, are homonyms on all levels of usage, and in most of the upland South all speakers dipthongize the /æ/ of *can't*—when they do not replace it with /e/ so that it rhymes with *paint*. But in New York City the homonymy of *coil* and *curl* is a feature of old-fashioned speech, and in such words as *bad* and *dog* a lower variety of the vowel is felt to be more elegant than a higher. Everywhere the substitution of the /ai/ diphthong for /ɔi/, as in *boil, joint* and *join*, is felt to be a bit quaint, despite the fact that it is hallowed by the rhymes of Alexander Pope.

Differences in the consonants have been studied less intensively than those in the vowels, but it is possible that some of these differ-ences may be of greater social significance. Certainly, the lack of /θ ð/ as distinct from /t d, f v, s z/ is a clear social marker, and the omission of intervocalic /-r-/ in such words as *barrel* and *tomorrow* is likely to be, as is the use of a bilabial variety of /f v/ instead of the usual labiodental kind. (This last feature, like the equally stig-matizing dentalization of /t d n s z r l/, is usually associated with the imperfectly acculturated speaker from a home in which a foreign language is spoken.) Yet the homonymy of *Hugh* and *you*, or of *whales* and *wails*, is a matter of indifference.

But differences in grammar are the clearest indices of social dif-ference. Various lists have been provided (one of the most useful is that published by the Southeastern Educational Laboratory, of Atlanta). It is sufficient to indicate a few of the types of grammati-cal differences:

1. Absence of inflectional endings for noun plurals, noun genitives, third-singular present indicative, past tense, present participle, past participle

2. Analogical forms such as *hisself, theirselves* and the absolute genitives *ourn, yourn, hisn, hern* and *theirn*
3. Double comparatives and superlatives, such as *more prettier, most lovingest*
4. Omission of the copula *be* with predicate nouns, predicate adjectives, present and past participles
5. *Be* as a finite verb
6. Differences in the principal parts of verbs, such as *growed, drawed, taken* as a past tense, *rid* as the past participle of *ride, clum* or *clim* as the past tense or past participle of *climb*

The ways in which social varieties of a language differ are essentially the same as those which distinguish regional varieties. The difference is that in one instance certain linguistic forms are shared by an entire area or region, regardless of class, and in the other, forms are shared by the users of the standard language, regardless of region. For standard usage is much more uniform than nonstandard.

Since we are all more or less ethnocentric, and since the pronunciation of such a community as Charleston, South Carolina, may seem as strange as the idiom of Hell's Kitchen, we can be pardoned our occasional assumption that Charlestonians do not speak good English. To one who knows the self-assuredness of the proper Charlestonian, however, such an assumption is ludicrous on the face of it. It is necessary to be sure of the class of the speaker, in relation to the traditions of his community, before judging his language.

Clearly, social varieties of a language, like regional ones, are not deviations from a uniform and pristine standard. Each has its own history. Cockney, a nonstandard variety of London English, has a long history, developing parallel with standard London speech, occasionally giving words and usages, occasionally taking them. The same is true of the rural uneducated speech of the Southern Appalachians, alongside Southern upland standard, or of any local nonstandard variety of the language alongside its standard counterpart. Neither is a corruption or derivative of the other; though they have undoubtedly influenced each other, each is a legitimate variety of the language in its own right.

It is also important to distinguish social varieties of language, in their habitual sense, from other kinds of language variation. Formal language is not necessarily better than informal; in fact, as J. S.

Kenyon and others have pointed out, there is a formal substandard, marked by the use of such hyperforms as *I have went* instead of the more informal *I done gone*. Slang is a matter of vogue, not of social class. And though the pungent argot of lower-class teen-age gangs is sometimes described as a class idiom, it is the same kind of phenomenon one finds in any closely knit group with a common set of interests, whether safe-crackers, model-railroad fans, or Anglo-Catholic clergy. And the most important features that set off nonstandard usage from standard are often very old in the language, though (like the features of standard usage) they often appear in new combinations.

Methods of Investigation

One should expect the techniques of investigating social varieties of language to have grown from those developed for investigating regional varieties. In fact, one is justified in saying that some serious work with regional varieties of language is necessary if one is to interpret social varieties intelligently. The first linguistic atlases—those of Germany and France (and those modeled on them)—were really studies of regional differences in substandard usage, with the standard language everywhere taken as a given norm: only the "characteristic local dialect" was sought by these projects. Not until the *Atlas* of Italy and Southern Switzerland was there any attempt to assay social differences, and then only for the larger communities.

In the United States, the first two systematic studies of social differences in usage were *American English Grammar*, by Fries (2), and the *Linguistic Atlas of New England*, by Kurath and his associates (5). Fries's study involved the analysis of a large body of correspondence directed to a government bureau during World War I. Since the letters dealt with personal or family hardships, one could assume that each writer was on good linguistic behavior, attempting to achieve his notions of proper style. Furthermore, since the dossiers provided a great deal of biographical information about each writer, it was possible to classify them on extralinguistic evidence as written by users of Standard, Common or Vulgar English (or as unclassifiable). Those that were classifiable were then examined for their grammatical practices, so that it was possible to state objectively what were the actual differences between standard and vulgar usage. Though some of the details of the study may be out of date (after all, the body of users of Standard American English is quite different from what it was fifty years ago), it remains a model. Furthermore, its statement of the obligations of the schools in the matter of teaching standard usage is still one of the clearest, most precise, and most emphatic.

The *Linguistic Atlas of New England* was the first study of its kind to investigate systematically the social variations in a speech community (the other regional atlases, still unpublished but in various stages of completion, have been modeled on the New England study). Instead of seeking speakers of "the local dialect," Kurath sought three local cultural types who were alike only in naturalness of utterance and in identification with their community for at least two generations and for as many more as possible:

1. In every community, an attempt was made to interview a representative of the oldest living native generation with a minimum of formal education, travel, and other outside interference.

2. In every community, likewise, an attempt was made to interview a middle-aged speaker with about a high school education, and somewhat greater reading, travel, and general sophistication.

3. Finally, in about one community of every five, the field workers interviewed a cultivated speaker, who was usually a college graduate and a member of one of the oldest families—presumably a representative of the best local cultural traditions.

Although any student of social structure would concede that every community probably has more than three social classes, this selection of informants does provide an opportunity to examine the differences between cultivated speech and the extreme uneducated types, and (by including the intermediate group) to suggest the probable direction of change. Traditionally, the sharpest break in such democratic communities as the small towns of the Middle West has been found between the first and second groups; in such communities as those in the Old South, where the existence of an élite has been taken for granted, the break occurs between the middle group and the cultivated. However, changes in the economic and social structure of a community may produce changes in values: With the spread of higher education and industrialization in the South, the new decision-makers are increasingly drawn from outside the traditional élite, and new models of language prestige are arising alongside the old. Conversely, in northern cities, massive immigration of lower-class speakers from outside the region—whether from foreign countries or from other regions of the United States—may have created sharper social distinctions in language. Nevertheless, the framework provided by studies on the *Atlas* model makes it possible to interpret recent changes in the social status of language varieties, however the structure of the community may have changed.

Outside of drawing conclusions from the existing body of *Atlas* data, as in McDavid (9,10), there have been various modifications of method; Pederson's study of pronunciation in Chicago (12) involved a closer network of informants, with attention to descendants of the ethnic minorities that have settled in the metropolitan area. Some younger informants—high school students—were interviewed with an abbreviated questionnaire to permit a more accurate judgment on the possibility of increasing linguistic cleavage between Negroes and whites, but, like the primary informants, all these were natives of the metropolitan area. Pederson also introduced a more complicated socioeconomic classification of informants, by which one can determine more easily where or whether linguistic fault-lines are developing in a speech community. The follow-up study (11) sought to polarize the distinctions between standard and nonstandard speech in the Chicago area by concentrating on the two extremes and eliminating the middle group. Since the problems of the schools had been aggravated by recent immigration from other sections, the design of this project included recent arrivals as well as natives. It was noted in both of these surveys that there were no appreciable differences between middle-class Negroes and middle-class whites; furthermore, the oldest generation of Chicago-born Negroes, of whatever class, differed more among themselves than they did from their white contemporaries. However, with the patterns of residential segregation and decreasing economic opportunity (through the phasing-out of the unskilled jobs on which earlier immigrants had always counted for getting a leg up), the speech of the younger generation of Chicago-born Negroes often differed very sharply from the Middle Western speech norms of younger Chicago-born whites, (a) in the tendency to lose postvocalic /–r/, (b) in such structural contrasts as that between such pairs as *morning* and *mourning,* (c) in phonemic incidence, as /–z–/ in *greasy* rather than the characteristic Chicago /–s–/, and (d) in the use of a number of nonstandard verb forms that are practically unknown in the Middle West. Furthermore, by an accompanying instrument designed to evaluate the status of pronunciations, it was revealed that, in Chicago, Southern varieties of pronunciation—regardless of the race or education of the speaker—were usually characterized as rural, uneducated, and Negro.

The studies of William Labov, of Columbia University, have concentrated on a smaller number of linguistic features but have used a relatively large number of informants, a variety of styles, and judgments about the social status of the speakers (6). A pilot study of the dipthongs /ai au/, as in *ride* and *cloud,* on Martha's Vineyard disclosed a tendency for the centering beginning of the diphthongs (which has been recorded in the New England *Atlas*), to be lost to the degree that a speaker was oriented away from the island; that is, it was likely to be lost among those of the younger generation who had most of their contacts with off-island people and who intended to make their careers on the mainland. Conversely, it was retained among those who had identified themselves with the island and intended to remain.

In his study of the Lower East Side of New York (7), Labov concentrated on five linguistic variables: postvocalic /-r/, the initial consonants /θ ð/ of *think* and *then,* the vowels /æ ɔ/ of *bad* and *dog.* A range of formality was sought, from the reading of potentially homonymous pairs of words to accounts of children's games or of an incident in which the narrator thought he might be killed. Since the informants were selected more or less at random, in the follow-up of a previous sociological analysis of the neighborhood, Labov was able to include such ethnic groups as Negroes, Italians, and Jews, whose families had arrived too recently to be considered for the *Atlas* investigations of New York (conversely, by *Atlas* standards he included no cultivated speakers, and the older white Protestant stock of New York was not represented). His conclusions were: (a) that postvocalic /–r/ was being reestablished in New York, (b) that the substitution of affricates or stops for the spirants /θ ð/ was particularly characteristic of lower-class speech, and (c) that in *bad* and *dog*, lower vowels had more prestige than higher ones. These conclusions were reached both on the basis of the characteristic utterances of each social class and on the basis of formality, it being assumed that the more careful the style of utterance, the greater the likelihood that the reader would approach the real or fancied linguistic norm of the community. Furthermore, New York respondents tended to value styles of speech in terms of this scale, and to attribute to their own speech a higher ranking on this scale than it actually had. Whether or not speakers in other communities are so much aware of a scale of values as New Yorkers seem to be, let alone of the same scale, Labov has clearly introduced an interesting new dimension into the evaluation of social differences in language.

The study of Detroit by Shuy and his associates (13) combines the techniques of the *Linguistic Atlas* and those of Labov with a careful demographic investigation beforehand and a sophisticated computer program afterward. Employing a selection of elementary schools, public and parochial (by census tracts, with special care that no major ethnic group was slighted), his team of investigators completed more than 700 hour-and-a-half interviews in one summer, including a generous sample of free conversation and responses to a selection of the most significant items from the questionnaire for the *Linguistic Atlas of the North-Central States*. For each household selected, there were interviews with an upper-grade student and a parent; and, whenever the situation permitted, there were interviews with an older sibling, a grandparent, or both. Although the processing of the data had not been completed at the time this book went to press, preliminary examination suggests that social differences are more a matter of incidence than of fundamental typology; that is, social groups differ in the frequency with which they use certain linguistic forms rather than in the structure of their varieties of language. For instance, though the less educated Negroes—thanks to historical forces—seem to show the sharpest divergence from the local standard, there seem to be no forms used exclusively by Negroes or whites. Again, there were attempts to elicit evaluations of the race and social class of selected speakers; Detroiters seem to judge race correctly some 80 percent of the time (there were, however, no specimens of Southern poor-white speech on the tapes

used for this purpose, though the group is an important numerical
fraction in metropolitan Detroit), with the greatest number of in-
accuracies in the evaluations of the educated Negroes. Social class
was judged less accurately; there was some tendency to downgrade
the class of Negroes and upgrade that of whites. Modifications of
Shuy's approach have been introduced in other projects, notably by
Pederson and his students in metropolitan Atlanta and in other
Georgia communities.

Since *Linguistic Atlas* techniques have concentrated on short-
answer questions, they provide a less satisfactory body of evidence for syntax, stress, intonation, and paralanguage than they do
for vocabulary, vowels and consonants, and inflections. Even the
modifications by Labov are not completely satisfactory in these
respects; Shuy's are somewhat better. Since syntactic differences
create some of the most painful classroom difficulties for Negroes,
there have been several recent investigations designed to provide
extensive corpora of connected discourse which could be analyzed.
Perhaps the most important of these in print is *Conversations in a
Negro American Dialect* (8), a by-product of the Urban Language
Study of the District of Columbia. The study reveals—as does
almost every study of a similar population—striking differences between the syntax of lower-class urban Negro adolescents and that
of middle-class Midwestern white adults.

What is yet unanswered, however, is the question as to whether
these differences are really typological or—as Shuy suggested in
Detroit—merely statistical; informal observation of the unguarded
speech of Southern whites (even highly educated ones) suggests
that at least some of these differences may be due to a greater difference in the South, among all social groups, between formal and
informal speech than one finds elsewhere. The current study of
adolescent white speech in Cullman County, Alabama—an area
almost without Negroes—may provide some of the clues; yet there
is a possibility that the rural life-style may not be as conducive to
the kind of highly verbal juvenile gang-life that one encounters in
cities. Perhaps what is necessary is the simultaneous study, with
identical techniques, of Negro and Southern white groups under
similar conditions of translation to a northern industrial environment, such as one might find in Akron or Detroit or Cincinnati.

Perhaps some of the answers will be suggested in Dunlap's study (1) of the syntax of a hundred fifth-grade students in Atlanta. In any event, the studies recently made and those in progress show the need for dropping rigid dogmas about language standards and for examining the speech of many communities and social groups on their own merits.

Two other kinds of studies might be mentioned—the British investigations by David Abercrombie of Edinburgh and by Basil Bernstein of London. As we have observed, in addition to being a superb descriptive and instrumental phonetician, Abercrombie has made a number of shrewd observations on the relative status of various British "accents," or patterns of pronunciation. Upper-class London pronunciation, or RP, is accepted everywhere, though in Edinburgh or Dublin it may have no edge on cultivated Scots or Anglo-Irish. What constitutes this upper-class standard, however, is as subject to change as any other standard; with the rise of the welfare state and the current prestige of such public figures as Harold Wilson, Twiggy, and the Rolling Stones, it is difficult to imagine that the older speech values of country estates and gentleman's club will survive intact, and with the expansion of higher education and economic opportunities, there may be changes analogous to those that have taken place in the prestigious speech of New York City or the American South.

Bernstein has shown less interest in the taxonomy of linguistic forms than in cognitive styles. In a series of articles he has pointed out that the differences in such styles reflect the essential differences in world outlook between the middle classes and the working classes, the former being more verbal and more inclined to reason, the latter being more inclined to simple answers or physical responses. The cognitive styles of the two groups he labels respectively as an *elaborated code* and a *simple code* with the former susceptible to more variations in style and more amenable to abstract thinking. This division is a plausible one; to some extent it replicates the conclusions of Fries in his *American English Grammar* (2) that the essential difference between Standard English and vulgar English is less in the details of usage than in the greater richness of the former—in vocabulary, in sentence patterns, and in the variety of conjunctions and prepositions. But there are exceptions: we can all recall the prosperous citizen—and literature is full of such characters as Fielding's Squire Western—who despite all kinds of outward advantages seems able to discourse on only a limited range of topics, such as farming, hunting, or finance. And as every college teacher knows, the ability to use abstractions glibly is not necessarily accompanied by any depth of understanding.

Not all aspects of social differences in communication have been adequately studied; there is nothing sensible we can say about stress, intonation, and paralanguage until the long-overdue regional comparisons have been made. But in the generation since Fries's pioneering study we have accumulated a generous amount of data and an understanding of the psychological and sociological correlates. And —unlike such findings in the past—a great deal of this information is already beginning to appear in materials for the schools.

Implications for the Schools

THE NATURE OF LANGUAGE DIFFERENCES

What we have found out about language differences, regional and social, should keep us from repeating some of the old clichés about the degeneration of language in the mouths of the people. If the speaker of nonstandard varieties of the language generally has a smaller vocabulary than his more highly educated neighbor, he has far more than the five hundred words that were once alleged to be the limits of peasant speech. What is more important is the realization that all habitual varieties of language are learned in the same way—through contacts with other speakers. The differences between standard and nonstandard varieties can be explained, not in terms of intellectual or moral differences, but simply in terms of differences in social and cultural experience. An awareness of this fact should be the foundation of any program in the language arts. Furthermore, since any educational program is subject to external pressures, it is the responsibility of the teacher of the language, especially the university scholar, to communicate the nature of language differences to parent-teacher associations, school administrations, citizens' boards, newspapers, and the other instrumentalities by which public opinion is formed on educational issues.

The same message might well be used in the classroom, so that dialect differences, whether regional or social, become a source of enrichment of the curriculum. After all, a person's language is one of his most intimate possessions, something that he associates with his family and friends and neighborhood. As such, it is to be respected by all who encounter it—especially in those situations in which a student may be called on to supplement his native variety of the language with another form of discourse for public occasions. So long as the situation is handled with respect for every person's speechways, there is no reason why one should not use the varieties of grammar, pronunciation, and vocabulary found in the classroom population to show that language, the most characteristic feature of human behavior, can come in a wide range of patterns. For by the time any child enters the first grade, he has already achieved his most important feat of learning; though he is not yet in control of all the details, he has a tolerable mastery of a variety of his native language—nearly all of the pronunciation features, most of the inflectional patterns (such as they are), and a large number of syntactic structures. What happens thenceforth depends on the opportunities he is given. And whatever the variety of the language, as a simple instrument of intercommunication it is as good as any other variety, and—in the hands of a literary artist—it is capable of expressing all the knowledge and emotions, all the inmost experience of humanity.

FROM NONSTANDARD TO STANDARD

But if this is true, why should children be expected to master the standard language, whatever it is? Again, the fact is that some varieties of the language are "more equal" than others. Most of the exchange of public information on which the functioning of our society depends—including almost all of what is found in print—is through the standard language. The extension of one's education, the functioning on the job, the handling of one's affairs with the ever expanding governmental bureaucracy, the coping with leases and installment contracts—all these activities demand an ability to understand the formal variety of the standard language, especially in writing. If one's job involves writing, a productive command of it is necessary as well. And if one's job involves meeting all kinds of citizens, this command must extend to the spoken mode. It is all very well to argue that a minority group—any minority group—has the right to its own form of speech; but the argument is hollow if restriction to a single given form of speech shuts this minority off from the economic and educational opportunities they seek. Here the minority group as a whole is often wiser than its self-appointed spokesmen; parents in such groups are the most insistent that the schools teach their children the kinds of language behavior that will better enable them to cope with the demands of society.

But what is important is that the schools get rid of the notion that a home dialect—regional or social—is something loathsome, from which the children must be purged, so that a new kind of speech (and writing) may be imposed upon them. Not merely the poor (of whatever race), but all those who differ linguistically from the model the teachers have set up as a rigid standard of perfection, have suffered in the past from this attitude. Many Americans, of excellent family and superior educational background, have been ridiculed and patronized by those who would provide them with an allegedly better kind of English—so that the English teacher becomes not merely a busybody but also a sadist. Psychologists as well as linguists have taught us better; we no more have to destroy the home idiom to teach the standard one (itself with many varieties) than we have to forbid playing football to those who are trying to learn tennis. The end, in the long run, is greater fluency, facility, and versatility; our world is not homogeneous, and no student should be expected to use a single kind of discourse in coping with all kinds of problems. In this sense, language education is the work of a lifetime; we should at least hope that those who direct the language programs in the schools should not inhibit students from exploiting the resources of the language.

BIBLIOGRAPHY

1. DUNLAP, HOWARD G. "The Syntax of Fifth-Grade Schoolchildren in Atlanta." Unpublished Ph.D. dissertation, Emory University, 1969.
2. FRIES, CHARLES C. *American English Grammar*. New York: Appleton-Century-Crofts, 1940.
3. HAUGEN, EINAR. "Dialect, Language, Nation," *American Anthropologist*, LXVIII (1966), 922-35.
4. JOOS, MARTIN. "Homeostasis in English Usage," *College Composition and Communication*, XIII (October, 1962), 18-22.

5. KURATH, HANS, *et al. Linguistic Atlas of New England.* 3 vols. (6 parts) and *Handbook.* Providence, R.I.: American Council of Learned Societies, 1939-43.

6. LABOV, WILLIAM. "The Social Motivation of a Sound Change," *Word,* XIX (1963), 273-309.

7. ———. *The Social Stratification of English in New York City.* Washington: Center for Applied Linguistics, 1966.

8. LOMAN, BENGT A. (ed.) *Conversations in a Negro American Dialect.* Washington: Center for Applied Linguistics, 1967.

9. McDAVID, RAVEN I., JR. "Dialect Geography and Social Science Problems," *Social Forces,* XXV (1946), 168-72.

10. ———. "Postvocalic /r/ in South Carolina: A Social Analysis," *American Speech,* XXIII (1948), 194-203.

11. McDAVID, RAVEN I., JR., and AUSTIN, WILLIAM M. *Communication Barriers to the Culturally Deprived.* Final Report, Cooperative Research Project 2107, U.S. Office of Education, 1966.

12. PEDERSON, LEE A. *The Pronunciation of English in Chicago: Consonants and Vowels.* Publication of the American Dialect Society, No. 44, 1964.

13. SHUY, ROGER W.: WOLFRAM, WALTER A.: and RILEY, WILLIAM K. *Linguistic Correlates of Special Stratification in Detroit Speech.* Final Report, Cooperative Research Project 6-1347, U.S. Office of Education, 1966.

CHAPTER IV

The History of Language

KENNETH G. WILSON

The History of the English Language

INTRODUCTION

The English language is usually said to have begun in the sixth and seventh centuries, when the Germanic Angles, Saxons, and Jutes invaded and settled the Celtic island of Britain.[1] With the techniques of historical linguistics and philology, in spite of the lack of written records, we have been able to reconstruct the older forms, sounds, and vocabularies of the invaders' language in remarkable detail, working mainly from later written sources and from our knowledge of linguistic change. The Celtic language, together with most of the Roman linguistic remains, disappeared from England, except for a few place names. The history of English had begun.

THE ANCESTRAL HISTORY

The shift into a new territory of a large number of speakers of a language, isolated from the homeland and in contact with a new language and culture, sets in motion its own rates and kinds of change, so that although the home language may continue strong and pursue its own life, the two strains—here two strains of a West Germanic language—will develop independently and will eventually become different enough from each other as to be no longer mutually intelligible. As a result there will be two separate languages.

The continental origins are important: there the Germanic languages were already fully formed; they belonged to a family of languages, Indo-European, which was already important in the history of the world, both in influence and in numbers of speakers.

Although we have never heard or seen it, scholars have managed

---

1. The first section of this chapter relies heavily on three good histories of English: Baugh (2); Robertson and Cassidy (19); and Pyles (18).

to reconstruct much of Indo-European; from the study of many related languages they have been able to recreate the sounds, the grammar, and the vocabulary of this ur-language from which so many of the modern western and some of the eastern languages have come. The reconstruction itself is a fascinating story, but here we can say only that somewhere in the period 3500 to 2000 B. C., there was a people living probably in northeastern Europe who spoke a language we now call Indo-European. Centuries of migrations, conquests, divisions, and expansions splintered this language (which had itself probably splintered off from another, earlier language) into new languages, some of which in turn spawned still more languages, not regularly or predictably in time, but gradually or spasmodically, as the vagaries of human society drove the people apart. Today we find descendants of the Indo-European language family stretched over almost the entire globe, and we recognize the ancient history of the family in its name. Indo-European languages are native to a wide swath from northern Europe across the eastern Mediterranean into India, and more recently they have been planted in North America, Africa, and Australia.

Through historical linguistic techniques, English can be traced to its origins. It belongs to the Germanic subdivision of a major subgroup of Indo-European. Sound shifts—systematic evolutions in what happened to certain sounds of the Germanic languages only—plus certain grammatical characteristics, such as the loss of nearly all inflectional signs of tense and aspect except the distinction between the present and the preterit, distinguish the Germanic languages. And similar differences distinguish the West Germanic languages from those of the East and North. Thus English traces its history from the West Germanic group to an Anglo-Frisian group and finally to English itself.

THE HISTORY OF THE SPEAKERS OF ENGLISH

In the eighth and ninth centuries we begin to find texts in English written by Englishmen; it is then that we begin the documented history of the language. We have some convenient names: Old English or Anglo-Saxon is the language of the early Middle Ages, roughly from the beginnings to 1000 or 1100. Middle English is the language from 1100 or so to the Renaissance, to about 1500 or 1550. Early Modern English is Renaissance English, lasting perhaps until 1700, and Modern English is the language from the beginning of the eighteenth century until today. These "periods" are arbitrary; more often they measure the social history of its speakers rather than characteristic differences in the language itself, although the differences are there: the English of Alfred, of Chaucer, and of Shakespeare differed markedly, just as our own differs from Shakespeare's. Conventional histories of English examine and try to account for the gross differences in the language at each of these periods.

But the history of *what* is the history of English? Certainly the history of its vocabulary, of its words and their meanings, would be a major consideration. But there are other important aspects too.

In some ways, the history of the speakers themselves is the most important part of the history of a language. Who were the people, how did they live, what did they speak about, whom did they meet, and what happened to them? Social history will be reflected above all in the vocabulary, since a people will invent and adapt words and their meanings to fit its daily requirements; as these change, so will the vocabulary change.

To the student of language history, however, there are other kinds of historical study which are equally important: the history of the sounds of the language, and the development of its grammar —the forms of the words, their inflections and the grammatical meanings they contain, and the constantly evolving rules of the syntax—these too can be historically traced. In this brief account we can only offer reminders of the social history and of the military, economic, political, and religious activities of the English people which affected the history of their language.

We must study the effects of the Scandinavian invasions, wherein a similar Germanic people came into close (and eventually submerged) relationship with the English. The Norman invasion and the several centuries of Norman and French domination of government and upper-class life left their marks, as did the migrations of people from the Low Countries into London in the later Middle Ages. The Renaissance, that time of expansion and invention, inquiry and experiment—political, geographical, social, military, scientific, and religious—affected the quality of English life and left its marks on the language. The development of the Empire in the eighteenth and nineteenth centuries is important: Englishmen began to know the whole world, and the scientific and commercial prowess of the industrial revolution made England the great mercantile and naval power we now think of as Victorian. And then came the great wars of the modern era, with the tremendous social, economic, and political upheaval they left in their wake: all these forces and events have left their marks on the English language.

THE AMERICAN SPEAKERS OF ENGLISH

We need more than a simple footnote, too, to pick up the American version of this social history, which from the seventeenth century on began to run a separate course.[2] Important are the very facts of the arrival of the English on this continent. For example, both the New England and Virginia settlements spoke dialects from the English Home Counties—from the area around London—but different social class dialects; hence the language in these two locations, though essentially Elizabethan at the outset, differed markedly.

And the English encountered other Europeans when they came: in the Great Lakes and Mississippi areas they found the French had been there first, naming the places and animals and tribes, and pronouncing the Indian words in a French that the English could only anglicize. In lower New York, the Dutch had left their mark on the social and topographical order, and in Florida and the Southwest, the Spanish had long since named the geographical parts. And everywhere there were the Indians, not many people in all but speaking many dialects and languages. All these facts of social and political history have left their signs on the American varieties of English, just as they have left them on American life itself.

Later history is important too. A nation of immigrants, we owe something to the kinds of people who settled the various sections of the country: to the Germans in Pennsylvania and the lower Ohio Valley, to the Scotch in the lower Midwest and the uplands of the Border States, to the Scandinavians in the upper Midwest, and to the Irish in Boston and the Italians in New York, just to name a few. As the country assumed the role of inspiration to the down-

2. The best account is by Marckwardt (14).

trodden, thousands of the economically and politically "out" came from the countries of central and southern Europe. And the Negro deserves our attention: he made little mark on the language at first, so low was his social status; but in recent years his words, his dialects, and his special meanings have made a solid impact—on the life of Americans and the American version of English.

All these contacts had their effects—some major, some trivial. But there is much more. We began by being a rural country, with a frontier which stayed open until the First World War. But now we are a great industrial power, an urban society, and these changes have changed the language too.

Hence one vital part of the history of the language is the history of its speakers—who they were, whom they met, how they lived, and what they did and thought and strove for; these things shape speakers' words and the way they say them and even the way they string them together.

THE HISTORY OF THE ENGLISH VOCABULARY

When we study the history of the vocabulary, we can see the importance of social history; vocabulary changes most quickly of all the aspects of language. English in the seventh century displays a predominantly Germanic vocabulary. There are a few Roman words dating from continental encounters with the Romans, and there are a few others picked up from the Roman remains the English found in Britain. But the words are mostly Germanic.

Since the English drove out the British Celts, the latter added almost no Celtic words to the language—a few place names and little more. Missionary culture from Britain's conversion to Christianity added Latin names for religious things. But when the Vikings came and settled down, the two Germanic strains borrowed freely from each other. Actually, many of their words were similar, and sometimes the two similar words were both kept, a shift being made in the meaning of one or the other: *shirt* and *skirt* were originally the same Germanic word; both versions were kept, with different meanings (2: 113). Occasionally, the Scandinavian word displaced the English one: *egg* replaced the English *ey*, first in the Northern dialect and then in all English.

With Norman and later massive French influences in the Middle

Ages, the English vocabulary changed markedly. It borrowed wholesale from French. With Christianity it had accepted Latin words; now it often borrowed the same words again, this time in their French forms and with their French meanings. It borrowed the names of all sorts of French ideas: words for government, law, dress, food, manners, and the like. Chaucer's fourteenth-century vocabulary looks very different from King Alfred's ninth-century one, mainly because so many of Chaucer's words were borrowed from French.

The renaissance brought a different sort of change:[3] scholars and writers deliberately added words or made them up from Latin and Greek, and travelers brought back Italian names for exotic things (2: 113). As English explorers, businessmen, and soldiers went farther and farther afield, even some eastern Mediterranean and New World words began to appear in the language.

In this country, immigration had an effect on the vocabulary, though not in proportion to the numbers of immigrants. The Germans were the most numerous of the non-English-speaking immigrants, yet they have left us only many words for food and drink, a few words for educational matters, and surprisingly little else. The Italians illustrate the whole pattern nicely. When in the seventeenth and eighteenth centuries, the English milords began to take the grand tour, Italian words for music and painting and other aspects of art and cultivation were added to English; we cannot discuss music and painting without using borrowed Italian terms. But when the poor Italians came to New York in the early twentieth century, they had little interest for us except as laborers. We did not ape their language except in jest; they hurried instead to learn ours. As a result, American English added the names of a few Italian dishes to its vocabulary from this contact, and little more.

The point is important: when two cultures come into contact, everything seems to depend upon who is master, or at least upon who feels inferior. Hence English borrowed massively from French during the Middle Ages, when French power and culture seemed demonstrably superior. But in the past two centuries, English has borrowed from French only the terms for hairstyles and women's dress and the like, while terms of technology and the names of soft drinks the French have borrowed from us.

3. The best account is by Baugh (2:240-305).

THE HISTORY OF THE SOUNDS OF ENGLISH: PHONOLOGY

We can also study the history of the *sounds* of English. Using written records from the Middle Ages and the early Renaissance, we can tell from the unfixed spelling a good deal about how the words were pronounced. The histories of English sounds have been elaborately worked out, and the changes are regular, according to generalizable patterns. It is possible to reconstruct these changes, so that we can make reasonable guesses at what Shakespeare's language (or Chaucer's or Alfred's) actually sounded like.

Once the spelling became fixed, we lost a good bit of the information previously provided when each man spelled the way he spoke, but in literature—Hardy's Wessex novels, for example—we find evidence in the author's attempt to suggest or imitate the sounds of the spoken language by unconventional spelling. Mark Twain did this sort of thing well in *Huckleberry Finn*.

With nineteenth- and twentieth-century skills in phonetic notation, and most recently with the development of the phonograph and wire and tape recorders, scholars have learned to record permanently the sound of the language. The history of English sounds before modern times was often a matter of scholarly deduction; henceforth it will be able to rely on accurate recordings.

THE HISTORY OF ENGLISH WORD-FORMS: MORPHOLOGY

We are on even more elaborately detailed ground when we turn to the history of English forms and inflections. Old English was a highly inflected language, as were its Germanic progenitors. It still carried distinctive endings (*a*) for four forms of the verb, (*b*) for number in several parts of speech, (*c*) for case in nouns and adjectives (including both weak and strong declensions in adjectives), and (*d*) for person, number, and case in pronouns. It inflected its demonstratives.

There are useful generalizations we can make about the history of English morphology: we can say first of all that the general trend has been for inflections to disappear and be "replaced" by other means of giving the needed grammatical information. Nouns illustrate the pattern: Alfred's nouns had four cases—nominative, genitive, dative, and accusative. But the case distinctions began to drop off, perhaps partly because the heavy forward stress characteristic of Old English (words tended to be stressed on the first or root syllable) began to make it hard to distinguish among unstressed endings like *–an, –en, –em, –am,* and the like, and partly because other devices began to serve the same purpose. Word order was becoming fixed, so that one looked for nominative case nouns towards the beginning of sentences, and therefore soon one did not require the reassurance of a case ending to know one had a subject before a verb. By Chaucer's time, of case in nouns, only an all-purpose nominative form, a genitive form, and a few relic dative-accusatives were left. Today, although we still have both the "nominative" all-purpose form and the genitive, the datives and accusatives are gone; there are now only two cases in nouns, and for the genitive there is an alternative: a periphrastic construction with *of* which permits us to say *the road's surface* without the genitive inflection, as *the surface of the road.*

Pronouns also show the disappearance of some case inflections since Old English. Middle English still distinguished some of the datives and accusatives: *hine* was accusative, *him,* dative. Now we have coalesced these two into *him,* a form we might logically call a dual-purpose objective case form.

The pattern of deteriorating inflections is felt everywhere: case has disappeared from adjectives, and even some of the signs of tense in verbs are coalescing. Only the third person singular still maintains a distinctive inflection in the present tense: *he swims,* but *I, you, we, you,* and *they* merely *swim.*

Old English had two very different schemes for signalling the past tense and the past participle. The strong verb system had eight distinctive classes of vowel change to signal tense; we see one class pattern reflected in the forms of the Modern English verb *drink, drank, drunk,* (OE *drincan, dronc, druncon, druncen*). The strong verb system was very large in Old English; but the weak system, which ended both preterit and past participle with a dental suffix, also included large numbers of verbs, and in the end it has come to dominate. Hundreds of our formerly strong verbs have taken on the weak pattern: *grip, gripped, gripped; gleam, gleamed, gleamed,* and so on. The increasing dominance of the weak pattern is clear in the child's language: he usually says *swimmed* at first, until he learns the older strong form which we now retain as a kind of exception

to the trend. And when we make new verbs—*televise*, for example
—we make them on the weak system model; the preterit is *televised*,
with the dental suffix.

Changes of this sort, reflecting the general replacement of much
of the inflectional system by other grammatical devices, might lead
us to attempt too hasty a generalization. It is true that inflections
have been disappearing, and that distinctive forms like those of the
subjunctive have been diminishing in use. But there is another
tendency to be considered too: the smaller the number of inflections
left, and the higher the frequency of their occurrence in our speech
and writing, the more likely we are to retain them. Hence the
pronouns retain more of case than do the nouns, and most of those
that remain seem fairly strongly entrenched. And while much of
the subjunctive is weakening (one seldom hears "If he arrive early"
any more), other parts of it seem as strong as ever ("If I were you"
and "I asked that he come tomorrow" seem firmly entrenched).

Hence we can see that the history of English morphology does
permit generalizations; but it is also clear that students of the language need to realize the importance of looking at individual words
and individual grammatical devices in great detail if they would
have an accurate appreciation of this aspect of linguistic history.

THE HISTORY OF ENGLISH WORD ORDER: SYNTAX

An oversimplified statement of a thousand years of syntactic
change might go something like this: Word order and function
words (prepositions and conjunctions and the like) were already
grammatical devices in Old English, but fewer in number and apparently simpler and less forceful in operation than they are today;
by the Middle English period, these devices were beginning to be
more powerful and more numerous, and the closer we get to the
Modern English period, the more these devices take on the force
of overriding signals of grammatical meaning, capable in many instances of canceling out the significance of the inflections that remain.

Case is no longer so important as is the *word order* component
of syntax: "Him hit John" is not really ambiguous today; we ignore the small boy's error of case, and we know unquestionably
who hit whom. But in Old English, had *John* carried a nominative

inflection, the roles of striker and struck would clearly have been reversed.

English syntax has, then, an increasingly complex history; nor are we always entirely sure of the degree of complexity or the true force of word order and function words in Old English. There are many open questions here. But we do know that the subject-verb-object and subject-verb-complement patterns have become very powerful. Positions for modifiers too have developed distinctive patterns, since we must rely on position to tell us which adjective goes with which noun, now that inflections are no longer doing the job.

Our question patterns involve either (*a*) reversal of subject and verb, a pattern more common in Early Modern English and before than it is today (*Rides he to the wars?*), or (*b*) the use of auxiliaries in the reversed position with the verb itself tagging along later (*Can I come too? Does he ever ride?*). We also have a list of question-asking function words which fall into normal subject position, often with a reversal of subject and verb, to make questions: *Whom is he calling? Where are you going? What happened?*

Major patterns of syntax then have developed over the past thousand years of English; they are laws which govern the way we string our words together. When case is gone, we pick out the indirect object in one of two syntactic ways: word order (John gave *his brother* the book) or function word (John gave the book *to his brother*) where the prepositional phrase replaces the indirect object construction.

The history of English syntax illustrates the trend toward fixed patterns in English; it also illustrates two important principles for any language study: (*a*) we must always examine particulars and test the accuracy of generalizations; and (*b*) it helps to understand the English of today or any other day if we can see how the pattern under study evolved over the centuries.

The History of English Grammars [4]

INTRODUCTION

Prior to the eighteenth century there were no full-dress attempts to describe the structure of English. Since then, grammarians and

4. In this section, I have relied heavily on Gleason (10: 67-87).

laymen both have struggled with each other in attempting to understand its structure and to "improve" it. Many of the misunderstandings have arisen from the term *grammar* itself: English grammar is first of all the system of patterns and rules which enables us to use the language. Whether we can describe and state these patterns and rules or not, they do exist: even little children and the mentally defective can speak English; they "know" English grammar even if they cannot tell us what it is they know. But *an* English grammar is also any specific attempt to *describe* the structural system of English. And finally, to confuse the situation further, English grammar in the schools and to the layman has also come to refer simply to points of difficulty and variation, to the choices on which we have placed strong values—in short, to usage. Here we shall concern ourselves solely with the second of these uses of the term *grammar*: the history of attempts to describe the structure of English.

UNIVERSAL GRAMMAR

Systematic study of the structure of English had to await both the "coming of age of English," when it had gained respectability, and the eighteenth-century zeal for order, regularity, and the power of generalization. Universal grammar was a logical beginning, based as it was on ideas of the similarities (and the classical authority) of Latin and Greek. If English seemed to lack something to be found in this universal grammar, it must be a flaw, and it must be corrected.

Pioneer grammarians like Robert Lowth and Joseph Priestly leaned heavily on universal grammar: Lowth's extremely influential *A Short Introduction to English Grammar* (1762) reported variations between English and Latin constructions, and cited English authorial practices to illustrate the rules for English structure. Everywhere Lowth (like Dr. Johnson in his *Dictionary*, 1755) assumed that universal grammar should be the guide to English grammarians; he sought usually to bring English into line (10: 68–70).

Modern linguistic scholarship had until a recent reawakening of interest, very largely disproved the old universal grammar. Part of the problem was that of the blind men and the elephant: comparative grammarians had arrived at their conclusions about universal grammar from an examination of many languages—ancient and modern— but as luck would have it, nearly all were Indo-European. Hence, they found so many similarities that principles seemed obvious. But as anthropologists began to describe the languages they encountered in Asia, Africa, and the Pacific, as well as the Indian and Eskimo languages of the Western Hemisphere, almost all the principles of universal grammar turned out to be unsound.

SCHOOL GRAMMARS

Despite the fact that the most influential of the old school grammars was written in England, school grammars are a peculiarly American phenomenon, fostered by the American zeal for popular education. Lindley Murray's *English Grammar Adapted to the Different Classes of Learners* (1795) was the most widely used and widely imitated of the school grammars. An American who moved to Britain after the Revolution, Murray composed a grammar which was oversimple, dogmatic, and logical at the expense of accurate observation. It laid out "the rules" of English grammar, treating syntax, parts of speech, rules for parsing, spelling, and a number of other topics. It was clear, forceful, and incredibly successful. Gleason remarks:

> Murray frankly appeals to expediency in determining his rules. He recognizes that there are only two case forms in the noun, but considers it easier to teach three, since there are three in the pronoun. His grammar deals almost entirely with words—their classification and forms comprising etymology, and their uses constituting syntax. . . . Almost nothing is said about the order of words (10:71-72).

Within the tradition of school grammars, others began to try to show graphically the structure of the English sentence. Alonzo Reed and Brainerd Kellogg perfected a scheme for diagraming which combined the analytical features of parsing with earlier and clumsier attempts at graphic display of sentence structure. It too caught on (10: 73-74).

The chief problems with school grammars were that they oversimplified and that they stressed logic at the expense of accuracy. They were teachable grammars, and in the schools they were—and are—used prescriptively. In the effort to be clear and firm, they often obscured complexities and falsified the facts of English structure in the effort to be orderly and "complete."

TRADITIONAL GRAMMARS

In continental Europe, the nineteenth and early twentieth centuries provided a fine group of scholarly English grammars. Not textbooks, these were fresh, exhaustively detailed examinations of the structure of English. Conservative and careful, the traditional grammarians closely examined the language, especially the written language, classifying meticulously, never glossing over difficulties, always reporting the details that did not seem to fit.

These grammars were traditional in that they were organized around the conventional classifications of parts of speech, elements of the sentence, and types of sentence. Whatever their descriptions lack in power (that is, in strength of generalization) is made up in detail of description. The classics are Poutsma's *A Grammar of Late Modern English*, Kruisinga's *A Handbook of Present-Day English*, and Jespersen's *A Modern English Grammar on Historical Principles*. Jespersen's seven-volume work is both typical and innovative: he was a thoroughly trained historical linguist, and he had the fine ability of the small boy in *The Emperor's Clothes;* he could observe accurately and though he worked within a tradition, he was seldom bound by it (10: 77–78).

The great European reference grammars have flaws. But their quality has never really ceased to be admired, and they have more recently been given new praise by the transformational-generative grammarians, who see in their attention to detail and in their insistence on dealing with total meaning a kindred spirit of investigation into English structure.[5]

STRUCTURAL GRAMMARS

Structural grammars depend on the work of descriptive linguists, particularly in that they work wholly from real samples of English. The key document is Charles Carpenter Fries' *The Structure of English*, which begins by reclassifying the parts of speech into four form-classes and fifteen groups of function words. Fries makes some good distinctions: for example, he finds that auxiliaries clearly are not like traditionally classified verbs because they neither

5. Gleason cites three modern works in this tradition: Zandvoort (26); Jespersen (13); and Curme (7, 6).

display the full formal patterns of verb morphology nor do they distribute themselves as traditional verbs do. He concludes that they are function words.

His attempts at more rigorous adherence to schemes of classification based first on form and then on position or function, rather than on all three intermixed, were a major contribution, since they permitted grammars to deal more powerfully with the details observed.

This reassessment of the parts of speech caused much of the furor which Fries' book stirred up, particularly among teachers, but the main thrust of the book was its attempt to deal with syntax, especially with the patterns of English word order (10: 79–80).

Much pedagogy has been developed from combining Fries' close look at real samples of language and his efforts at generalizations about syntax with the strong emphasis on the spoken language which stems from the linguists, especially from the work of Trager and Smith (20). This combination has led to solid attempts at fairly full structural grammars, such as W. Nelson Francis' *The Structure of American English* (8), the most widely used text for the training of English teachers in grammar during the past decade.

THE CONTRIBUTIONS OF AMERICAN LINGUISTS

Beginning with Leonard Bloomfield, American anthropologically oriented linguists began to apply to the English language the descriptive methods they used in dealing with exotic languages among Pacific islanders, Eskimos, and Indians. What followed was a series of studies, among them the Smith-Trager *An Outline of English Structure* (1951) (20). It was the first full treatment of English sound structure—including stress, pitch, and juncture—together with a brief but perceptive account of morphology; it did not go far into syntax (10: 82–84). The spoken language was the key; hence the linguists of the forties and fifties attacked the traditional grammarians for their reliance upon the written language and for dealing with meaning as a whole.

Intonation patterns were seen as components of grammar, and this led to what some linguists call "phonological syntax," the elaboration of the grammar of the spoken language. Archibald Hill's *Introduction to Linguistic Structures* (1958) developed this line of descriptions further, although, like much structural analysis, it was not always well received (12).

Eugene Nida, *A Synopsis of English Syntax* (16), concentrated exclusively on syntax; the scheme of immediate constituent analysis which he employed has been widely modified and developed. Gleason says:

> Each construction was described as consisting of two parts (very rarely three or more) of specific types and in a definable relation. Long sentences are described in terms of many layers of such simple constructions, one within another (10:85).

In the end we find people like Francis developing fairly comprehensive descriptions, in which the immediate constituent technique is elaborately worked out, and in which four kinds of structure are described: predication, complementation, modification, and coordination (8:291ff). Francis and others have polished these approaches for use in teaching, but they have by no means resolved all the problems of describing English structure, particularly syntax.

TRANSFORMATIONAL-GENERATIVE GRAMMARS

Beginning with assumptions by Noam Chomsky and others, a whole series of new schemes for describing the manufacture of English sentences has begun to appear recently. None has actually presented a full grammar as yet, and all differ in detail, in completeness, and in some of their assumptions, but they also have some assumptions in common:

1. That there are some universal principles describing what it is that people know when they know (i.e., use unconsciously) any natural language.

2. That the structure of the language itself can be stated in a detailed hierarchy of rules for making sentences.

3. That such a set of rules will generate *all* English sentences, not just those already available for analysis, but others yet unspoken and unwritten.

Most of the attempts at writing such generative grammars begin from Noam Chomsky's idea that the structure of a language has three parts: (*a*) a small "kernel" of sentence types, or short distinctive formulas involving subjects, verbs, and complements; (*b*) a large number of rules for transforming these types by substitution, reordering, and combining their parts; and a list of morphophonemic rules which will enable us to turn into actual sentences the "structured strings" of terms which result from the application of transformational rules to one or more of the kernel types(4).

The structures revealed by this kind of grammatical description are exceedingly complex, as are the systems of rules, and thus far no complete grammar has been written, although a number of broadly successful efforts have been made at describing the gross patterns and at working out some of the details of specific parts such as the structures involving English nominals, or those which generate English questions.

CONCLUSION

The history of the attempts to describe English structure has been relatively short but incredibly active in recent years. Since the development of transformational-generative theories, we have seen many revisions, not only of the details but of basic assumptions. Not all grammarians accept the tripartite scheme described above.

Furthermore, the attention given to total meaning by this kind of grammar, in great contrast to the bell-jar atmosphere which structural grammarians try to create in separating grammatical meaning from total meaning, has led to a number of elaborate new schemes of description which are still in the hands of the theorists: *stratificational grammar*, for example, separates "deep structure," or meaning, from "surface structure" or the actual final syntax of the sentence.

What some students of language conclude from this lively recent series of developments is that although we are not yet "home free," we are eventually going to be able to write a full grammar of this language from a transformational-generative point of view. Others disagree, although they admit that in the attempt we will continue to to learn much more about how people "know" languages and what the psycholinguistic facts truly are.

Meantime it is clear that teachers of English must know at least three broad schemes of structural analysis—the scholarly traditional, the structural, and the transformational-generative. All give useful

information about the structure of English, and all offer methodological advice to those whose job it is to teach English.

The History of English Lexicography

THE BEGINNINGS

Lexicography, the art of dictionary-making, has always had a
very practical purpose, right from the very beginning.[6] From the
very first word-books to the wide diversity to be found in the
many kinds of modern dictionaries, all have been made primarily as
practical tools. The dictionary is not a particularly old idea, moreover; and an examination of some of the practical purposes and of
the books that have resulted shows us several threads:

1. Medieval scholars constantly sought to compile treatises
which would incorporate all that was known about everything:
these encyclopedias grew into alphabetical lists of the names of
things, of natural phenomena, and of man's institutions; they often
resembled dictionaries, and their development into the modern encyclopedia has at several points intertwined with that of the dictionary.

2. A more direct ancestor of the dictionary is the word-list,
the gloss of "hard" or foreign words assembled to help the medieval
reader with a difficult text. In Latin manuscripts of important works,
English monks wrote marginal glosses in Latin and English, explaining the meanings of unfamiliar Latin terms. In the fourteenth and
fifteenth centuries, collections of these glosses were separately compiled, to help students read important books, and to help the English scholar discover the proper Latin term for an English idea.
Hence the *glossarium* was a first in the lineage of modern English
dictionaries.

3. During the sixteenth and seventeenth centuries, Englishmen
were traveling, exploring, studying, and doing business all over
Europe, the Near East, and even the New World, and to help them
make their way, experienced people began to put together English–
foreign-language phrase books and dictionaries. Some of the earliest
and best were for English-French, English-Spanish, and English-
Italian.

6. A useful summary is found on pages 4-9 of Guralnik (11).

4. Still another practical book resulted from Renaissance interest in the English vocabulary. Many scholars, irked by the seeming inelegance and imprecision of English, began consciously to manufacture English words on Latin, Greek, Italian, and French models. They borrowed especially from the classical languages: words like *contiguate, splendente, adjuvate,* and *panion* were coined or borrowed in great numbers, and the reader soon needed help. While many of these coinages soon disappeared, others remained in the language, so that today we find it difficult to imagine how strange such words as *relinquish, antique,* and *illustrate* must have looked to sixteenth-century readers. The dictionary of "hard words" was created to help.

5. The wholesale manufacture of new words also contributed to the development of dictionaries indirectly: men of letters were split into two camps during the Renaissance—those who favored and those who hated these coinages. This quarrel over "inkhorn terms" focused attention on the vocabulary and gave impetus to the production of lists and essays from both attackers and defenders. More groundwork was being laid for the production of the modern dictionary.

6. Finally, the rise of the middle class, and later, the industrial revolution produced still other markets for dictionaries—the same practical markets which letter-writers and books of etiquette were serving; somehow they were all to help the new bourgeoisie acquire the gentle patina.

THE FIRST GREAT MODERN DICTIONARIES

We have space here to mention only four of the great dictionaries which first wove together the several threads described above; two were English, two American; all four have shaped the art of lexicography as we know it today.

1. Nathaniel Bailey's *Universal Etymological Dictionary of the English Language* (1721) was the first. It was "the first to pay attention to current usage, the first to feature etymology, the first to syllabify, the first to give illustrative quotations, the first to include illustrations, and the first to indicate pronounciation."[7]

2. Samuel Johnson used Bailey's work and many others when

7. Guralnik (11) as reprinted in *Harbrace Guide to Dictionaries* (25:4).

he wrote his own great *Dictionary* (1755). He began his enormous task in the hope of recording, repairing and fixing once and for all the vocabulary of English. When he had finished, he ruefully concluded that change was inexorable; he came to a view of the lexicographer's task which is still one of the most accurate—and poignant. He tried to fix orthography, and he used English authors of reputation for his illustrative citations. His work is often idiosyncratic and sometimes erratic, especially in the etymologies. But above all, he made a truly comprehensive dictionary, and he wrote good definitions, avoiding circularity and seeking precision and clarity. His book was the first great "authority," and in its many subsequent editions and imitations, both in Britain and the United States, it came to play the very role of arbiter that Johnson had originally intended but had despaired, in the end, of achieving.

3. In 1828, leaning heavily on Johnson and Bailey, Noah Webster published the first of his "big" dictionaries, *An American Dictionary of The English Language*. In his early dictionaries, Webster too had a program: he sought to distinguish American spelling, pronunciation, and meaning from those of British English. Like Johnson, Webster greatly improved the style of definition-writing, seeking succinct, accurate statements and using American illustrations wherever he could. His later editions were more conservative, and he gave up his spelling reforms, but like his famous spelling book, Webster's later dictionaries became household words, particularly after the Merriam family began to publish them. His name, more than any other, is still synonymous with *dictionary*.

4. One of the main reasons American lexicography pushed forward so rapidly in the nineteenth century was the great commercial rivalry which grew between Webster and Joseph Worcester, whose *Comprehensive Pronouncing Dictionary of the English Language* appeared in 1830. It leaned heavily on Webster's 1828 edition, but, as Harold Whitehall points out, it "was characterized by the additions of new words, a more conservative spelling, brief, well-phrased definitions, full indication of pronunciation by means of diacritics, use of stress marks to divide syllables, and lists of synonyms (24:xxxiii)." From the 1840's on, the Webster and Worcester dictionaries, first edited by the famous men themselves and later by their successors in their names, multiplied and grew in fame. In the

end, Webster's successors won out, but not before both dictionaries were placed throughout this westward-marching nation. The frontier brought with it the first popular movements in education, and with the Bible and Webster's "Blue Back Speller" as both the tools and the symbols of this zeal for universal literacy, reliance on "the dictionary" as the arbiter of taste, the judge of meaning, and the authority on spelling and pronunciation was permanently fastened on the American character.

LEXICOGRAPHY TODAY

English today offers its users the most complete and varied array of dictionaries in the world. We can give here only the briefest account of the variety, but what is most significant is the ready availability of continually updated dictionaries of the very highest quality, and at relatively low cost. We lean heavily on our dictionaries, and competition keeps them good.

We have fine *historical dictionaries;* the *Oxford English Dictionary*[8] is the greatest of these. This ten-volume work prints long entries with dated citations in context for every word in the vocabulary. A work of enormous scholarship, its qualities have become the model for all historical considerations of the vocabulary of English. No lexicographer can work without the *Oxford* at his elbow. Its work on pronunciation is British and minimal and its supplement is dated 1933; but for history it is unmatched. Other historical dictionaries use it as a point of departure: for American English differences from British English, we have the four-volume *A Dictionary of American English on Historical Principles* (5), and Mathews' two-volume *Dictionary of Americanisms* (15). Historical dictionaries of Middle English, Early Modern English, and Scottish are all either being published or prepared. For accurate, detailed, complete information about the history of an English word, these are the works to consult.

Our commercial *unabridged dictionaries* are a unique type. The most famous currently is the Merriam-Webster Third Edition of the *New International* (23). At their best, the great commercial unabridged dictionaries offer incredibly complete information about

8. This dictionary (17), sometimes called the *New English Dictionary*, was published in ten volumes between 1884 and 1927; a corrected reissue with a one-volume supplement was published in 1933.

spellings, pronunciations, meanings, usage, synonyms, and brief etymologies. Some are encyclopedic, like the old *Century* (3) of 1889 and 1909; though badly out of date now, the *Century* is remembered as displaying the highest standard for the quality of its definitions. Most of the commercial houses which make unabridged dictionaries maintain files and revise regularly; almost all produce smaller, abridged dictionaries, based on the big book.

Desk and *collegiate* dictionaries are also uniquely American, one-volume books which are the most widely used of all. Their virtues are their currency and their compactness. Competition keeps their editors revising regularly, and they are noted for excellent definitions, up-to-the-minute information on spelling, pronunciation, and usage, and a surprising amount of encyclopedic information. The current best are probably Merriam-Webster's *Seventh New Collegiate* (21), Funk and Wagnalls' *Standard College Dictionary* (9), the *American College Dictionary* (1), and the college editions of *Webster's New World Dictionary of the American Language* (22) and the Random House dictionary (1). Each has its peculiar virtues and defects, but competition keeps each trying to outdo the others. Sold on the strength of the American need for reassurance, they are a remarkable kind of lexicography.

There are also dozens of other kinds of dictionaries, each for a special purpose: graded school dictionaries abound, many of them of good quality; the dictionaries of usage, which (like the old "hard word" books) deal only with problems which they discuss in little illustrated essays, have multiplied; there are special-vocabulary dictionaries, covering the technical vocabulary of special fields; and there are dictionaries of synonyms, to name only a few.

CONCLUSION

Not just the usual problems plague the lexicographer today—the selection of entries, the documentation of his findings, the wording of definitions, and the like; he also faces a very basic decision when he sets out to make a dictionary. On the one hand, modern linguistic science has given him clear evidence that the best dictionary is the one which records the language as it is, warts and all. Where the pattern of usage is unclear or divided, he must let his readers know that this is so. On the other hand, however, the layman insists that there must be right answers to his questions about language, and he expects the dictionary to give him these. The lexicographer expects to *describe* standards; the layman wants him to *set* them, and he uses his dictionary as though it were a law book, not a report of current custom. The quarrel over *Webster III* illustrates this quandary all too clearly: the scholar of language wants full information, wants shade and nuance clearly delineated—not just in meanings, but in every aspect of every entry. He wants as many minority reports as possible. The layman (and many other professional users of language too) insists that the dictionary ought to set a standard to which everyone may adhere.

The lexicographer is not a scientist; he is a writer, an editor, an artist. He must draw conclusions, and even as he tries to distinguish two shades of meaning in a definition, he is creating, not just reporting. Yet he must be careful not to display his personal crotchets about the language he wishes English were, to the detriment of his description of the English we actually have.

To use his dictionaries, therefore, teacher and student alike need full awareness (*a*) of how he works, (*b*) of the information he has to work with, and (*c*) of the problems of choice posed him by limitations of taste, space, and time. Once he has that, any user of dictionaries can use them intelligently, both as a guide to what the world expects of his English, and as a clear picture of how others actually use theirs. Among other things, he will realize that, depending on his purpose, not one, but many dictionaries can help him.

Teaching Language History in the Schools Today

We are having a kind of Renaissance in interest in language history today. As suggested at many points in the discussions above, there are many kinds of history of language and language-related matters, and nearly all can be made interesting to the student.

Two things are happening: first, through the teacher-training programs, summer linguistic institutes, and in-service programs, the English teachers themselves are studying the history of the language, filling themselves with lore. And such study stresses everywhere the need both for information and for generalization; it lays emphasis both on trends and on the importance of specific investigations.

Second, the teachers in turn are changing the curriculum. Materials are being developed, texts being written, and lessons being created to introduce pupils at all levels to the various aspects of the history of their language. The curriculum centers in several states are publishing materials to aid the teacher. School libraries are acquiring the dictionaries and reference works. And teachers themselves have come to see what enormous curiosity nearly everyone, properly stimulated, has.

In its own right, and for the kind of social perceptivity we seek to foster in school children, the study is both fascinating and good. And it also directs attention at a major problem of the schools: to manipulate his language well—a major goal of education—the student seems likely to profit a great deal from learning how his language came to be.

BIBLIOGRAPHY

1. *The American College Dictionary*. New York: Random House, 1947 and later printings.
2. BAUGH, ALBERT C. *A History of English Language*. 2d ed. New York: Appleton-Century-Crofts, 1957.
3. *The Century Dictionary*. New York: Century Co., 1889.
4. CHOMSKY, NOAM A. *Syntactic Structures*. Janua Lingurum, Series Minor, No. 4, The Hague: Mouton & Co., 1957.
5. CRAIGIE, SIR WILLIAM, and HULBERT, JAMES R. (eds). *A Dictionary of American English on Historical Principles*. Chicago: University of Chicago Press, 1938.
6. CURME, G. O. *Parts of Speech and Accidence: A Grammar of the English Language*. Vol. 2. Boston: D. C. Heath & Co., 1953.
7. ———. *Syntax: A Grammar of English Usage*. Vol. 3. Boston: D. C. Heath & Co., 1931.
8. FRANCIS, W. NELSON. *The Structure of American English*. New York: Ronald Press, 1958.
9. *Funk and Wagnalls' Standard College Dictionary*, Text ed. New York: Harcourt, Brace & World, 1963 and later printings.
10. GLEASON, H. A. JR. "English Grammars" in his *Linguistics and English Grammar*, pp. 67-87. New York: Holt, Rinehart & Winston, 1965.
11. GURALNIK, DAVID B. *The Making of a New Dictionary*. Cleveland: World Publishing Co., 1953.
12. HILL, ARCHIBALD. *Introduction to Linguistic Structures: From Sound to Sentence in English*. New York: Harcourt, Brace & World, 1958.
13. JESPERSEN, J. O. H. *Essentials of English Grammar*. New York: Henry Holt & Co., 1933.

14. MARCKWARDT, ALBERT H. *American English*. New York: Oxford University Press, 1958.
15. MATHEWS, MITFORD M. (ed.). *Dictionary of Americanisms on Historical Principles*. Chicago: University of Chicago Press, 1951.
16. NIDA, EUGENE. *A Synopsis of English Syntax*. Norman, Okla.: Summer Institute of Linguistics, 1960.
17. *Oxford English Dictionary*. 10 vols. Oxford: Clarendon Press, 1884-1927 (one-volume supplement published in 1933).
18. PYLES, THOMAS. *The Origins and Development of the English Language*. New York: Harcourt, Brace & World, 1964.
19. ROBERTSON, STUART and CASSIDY, FREDERIC G. *The Development of Modern English*. 2d ed. New York: Prentice-Hall, 1954.
20. TRAGER, GEORGE L. and SMITH, HENRY LEE, JR. *An Outline of English Structure*. Studies in Linguistics, Occasional Papers, No. 3, reprinted. Washington: American Council of Learned Societies, 1957.
21. *Webster's Seventh New Collegiate Dictionary*. Text. ed. Springfield, Mass.: G. & C. Merriam Co., 1963 and later printings.
22. *Webster's New World Dictionary of the American Language*. College ed. Cleveland: World Publishing Co., 1953 and later printings.
23. *Webster's Third New International Dictionary of the English Language*. Springfield, Mass.: G. & C. Merriam Co., 1966.
24. WHITEHALL, HAROLD. "Introduction," *Webster's New World Dictionary of the American Language*. College ed. Cleveland: World Publishing Co., 1960.
25. WILSON, KENNETH G.; HENDRICKSON, R. H.; and TAYLOR, PETER ALAN. *Harbrace Guide to Dictionaries*. New York: Harcourt, Brace & World, 1963.
26. ZANDVOORT, R. W. *A Handbook of English Grammar*. London: Longmans, 1957.

CHAPTER V

Language and Composition:
Some "New" Rhetorical Perspectives

GENE L. PICHÉ

Introduction

In recent years, the subject of rhetoric, conceived as the art of effective expression, has been undergoing a major intellectual revival. The revival, no doubt, is part of a growing scientific interest in the study of language. But, equally as important, it reflects a new and humane preoccupation with problems of communicating truth and value in a period marked by clashing ideologies and by new tension in the struggle between tradition and change.

Coinciding with the revival of interest in rhetoric, there has been growing criticism of the teaching of the arts of language. Revisionism in English, sparked by publication less than a decade ago of *The National Interest and the Teaching of English* (17), has led to mounting frustration with the patchwork theory governing the school's teaching of composition. Intellectually and philosophically, a revived concept of rhetoric has seemed to offer a new and better rationale. Accordingly, in books and monographs, in national conferences and in special institutes for teachers, the "new" rhetoric has become part of the litany of "the new English."

As applied to the curriculum, the term "new" rhetoric signals new ambition and purpose more than it does an organized discipline. To be sure, the sources of a "new" rhetoric are impressive, ranging from a new interest in classical rhetoric to the most recent critical and scientific studies of language and communication. Nevertheless, what exists is a set of loosely related rhetorical perspectives—what Daniel Fogarty called "roots for a new rhetoric" (21)—rather than an immediately coherent body of knowledge. Ultimately, the development of a unified "new" or modern theory of rhetoric will depend on major tasks of redefinition and synthesis. At present, and particularly as applied to the teaching of composition in the schools, the work has only begun.

Accordingly, the present chapter is limited to reviewing representative sources or perspectives contributing to a new or revised theory. Although the relationship of that theory to instruction is considered, the intent is to survey newer sources of knowledge rather than to detail specific curricular applications. Functioning more as inventory than blueprint, the chapter begins by contrasting the "old" theory of rhetoric with the much reduced theory of "composition" inherited from the last century. It continues by contrasting that narrowly practical theory of composition with aspects of a newer macrorhetorical theory implied in modern studies of language and communication and in the critical theories of I.A. Richards, Kenneth Burke, and Richard Weaver.[1] From the larger domain of macrorhetoric, the chapter proceeds to summarize representative contributions to a new and developing microrhetoric of the English sentence and paragraph. It concludes with a discussion of new emphases in the rhetoric-composition curriculum, marked by recognition of the intimate relation of language and thought and by new respect for the personal and social correlates of composition as communication.

The Decline of Traditional Rhetoric

Formal study of the arts of language dates from the schools of Greece and Rome. In an essentially oral culture, rhetoric, the art of persuasion, was firmly established at the core of the ancient *trivium*. Its subject matter was defined within a series of separate divisions or canons. The first was *invention*, a division closely allied to dialectic or logic, which ordered the process of finding what might be said about a given subject to a given audience. Since the problem of knowledge was less a matter of new discovery than re-

---

1. I do not find the terms "macrorhetoric" or "microrhetoric" particularly pleasing choices. But if not pleasing, they do seem useful to distinguish between rhetorical theories bounded by concern for the formal texture or structure of words, sentences, and paragraphs in discourse (microrhetorics), and theories of larger rhetorical domain which attempt to take critical account of the interrelatedness of such variables as writer or speaker, his purpose or intent, the text, the audience, and the immediate or general historical context (macrorhetorics).

trieval of stored wisdom, the province of invention embraced a standard set of *topics* and *commonplaces* through which the orator worked to locate appropriate lines of argument. In conjunction with invention, the canon of *arrangement* described formulas for organizing the whole composition based on the divisions of the classical oration. The canon of *style* described the resources of language sound and rhythm and classified figures of speech and thought. The canons of *memory* and *delivery* completed the traditional divisions of the subject, drawing attention to voice and gesture and providing a mnemotechnical system for placing and holding received knowledge. Although the relative importance attached to each of its canons varied, the traditional study of rhetoric persevered in the schools until well into the nineteenth century.[2]

With the beginning of the modern period, the subject began a long process of decline, hastened by the rise of modern science and the progressive loosening of the grip of the classical languages on the curriculum. In the last half of the last century, textbook writers moved toward a deliberately "practical" theory of written composition. Rejecting the formalism of traditional rhetoric, their aim was to develop minimal skill in writing. The appearance of the first rhetorics of the English paragraph outlined the theory, describing rules for topic sentences and for achieving unity, coherence, and emphasis. The same textbooks, out of any social context, set the forms of discourse as description, narration, exposition, and argument.[3] Within those boundaries, the new composition-rhetoric developed an exclusive concern with matters of linguistic form. Long a part of traditional rhetoric, problems connecting to the nature of one's subject or to the relations between thought and its expression were largely gone. The office of a composition-rhetoric was to "[engage] upon the diction . . . without involving the subject under discussion (2:37)." Harvard, itself, led, by insisting on an entrance standard

2. For a discussion of traditional rhetorical theory and its place in the schools of antiquity as well as in the schools of the English Renaissance, see Clark (15, 16) and Baldwin (3). For an excellent historical analysis of major aspects of rhetorical theories, see Ehninger (18).

3. For an analysis of the principal lines of development in the rhetorical theory of the late nineteenth century, see Kitzhaber (30). For an account of the main lines of development in the study of rhetoric, composition, and grammar in the reform of the high school curriculum in the last century, see Piché (31).

of "correct spelling, punctuation, and expression (45:55)," and by admonishing teachers to avoid "that misused branch of study, Rhetoric" in favor of practical exercise and drill (1:421).

By the beginning of the present century, the dissipation of the "old" rhetoric was largely accomplished in the name of a radically utilitarian theory of written composition. Like grammar, it was viewed as an intellectually closed and exclusively preparatory subject. Although colleges grudgingly continued to augment the work of the schools, they had all but rejected rhetoric as a subject fit for advanced study or research. Taking stock of its status in 1936, Richards observed that rhetoric had "sunk so low that we would do better just to dismiss it to limbo than to trouble ourselves with it. . . . (36:3)"

Revitalization and Renewal: New Rhetorical Perspectives

But while interest in the subject lapsed among humanists, it was being revitalized by social scientists. As critic Kenneth Burke concluded:

> Precisely at a time when the term "rhetoric" had fallen into greatest neglect . . ., writers in the social sciences . . . were making good contributions to the New Rhetoric . . . in all those statements by anthropologists, ethnologists, individual and social psychologists, and the like, that bear upon the function of language as *addressed*, as direct and roundabout appeal to real or live audiences. . . . (13:43, 40).

What Burke observed has only accelerated. Today, man's language and communication behaviors provide a major area of study among scholars in more than a dozen fields. The very size of that contemporary intellectual investment resists summary. At best, one may point to some more or less typical strategies in studies of communication and language as preliminary sources for a new, scientific rhetoric.

STUDIES IN COMMUNICATION AND LANGUAGE

Since Aristotle, traditional rhetorics have emphasized the persuasive efficiency invested in the speaker, himself. Paralleling ancient theory, modern scholars have measured the persuasive effect of a communicator's avowed credibility or prestige. Typical of such experiments, work done by the late Carl Hovland and his associates at Yale both confirmed and refined traditional theory (24). Thus, their studies revealed that a greater measure of persuasive effect was registered on subjects receiving messages from high prestige sources. More interestingly, these initial effects of high prestige were dissipated over time, whereas a "sleeper effect" seemed to increase the impact of messages coming from low prestige sources.

Similarly, questions concerning the best arrangement of arguments are well within the province of traditional rhetoric. Writers and speakers must often choose to argue with or without explicit reference to opposing points of view. Does it make a difference? Researchers have turned up interesting, if ambiguous, answers. In still another group of studies done at Yale, both methods of presentation were reported to be about equally effective—but with different individuals (25). The single or one-sided presentation was most effective with individuals who were originally in favor of the proposition. For those initially opposed, a two-sided presentation was more effective. Moreover, the two-sided message was accompanied by an "immunization" effect. When later exposed to counter-persuasion, subjects showed greater resistance to opinion change than did those who had only received the one-sided communication.

An important body of modern study contributes to a "psychology of audiences" by describing the complex factors mediating responses to communication. For example, cognitive "balance" or "congruity" theories hypothesize a human psychic economy which resists introduction of inconsistent or contradictory opinions.[4] Other studies describe a more or less hierarchically ordered structure of underlying belief systems.[5] On the one hand, such theories point to the limits imposed on "meaning" by stereotypical cognitive operations; on the other, they contradict mechanistic assumptions which characterize audiences as passive and irrational receivers. With understanding, agreement grows that "man is both a rationalizing and rational animal," processing information with "a need to know, to understand, [and] to be competent" (41:270–71).

Traditional rhetoric classified oratory according to the major functions or purposes it served in generalized social contexts. Some-

4. For a summary of major aspects of "balance" or "consistency" theory, see Brown (8:549–609).

5. See, for instance, Rokeach (40).

what similarly, modern studies describing the interaction of language with aspects of communicative function, topic, and social setting contribute to the development of newer rhetorical theory.[6] Equally suggestive, recent work in the "anthropology of communication" invites comparative study of the distribution and significance of varied language functions in the total communicative economy of a culture or subculture (26, 27). Such studies further erode a homogenized ideal of linguistic "correctness" at the same time that they draw attention to the arbitrary limits of traditionally defined rhetorical forms and genres.

CRITICAL-INTERPRETIVE STUDIES OF MEANING, MOTIVE, AND VALUE

If scientific studies of communication and language comprise one set of sources for a new macrorhetoric, another appears in the critical-interpretive theories of I. A. Richards, Kenneth Burke, and Richard Weaver. As critics, all three writers have directed attention to the importance of an adequate theory of the interpretation of linguistic acts as defense against widespread verbal aggression and misunderstanding. Taken together, their critical theories constitute an impressive source for a new rhetoric granting special attention to problems in the interpretation of meaning, of motive, and of value.

Observing the low estate into which traditional rhetoric had fallen, Richards, British-American critic and teacher, called for a revival based on study of "the fundamental laws of the use of language. . . ." (36:7, 23). The province of a renewed study of rhetoric would be the study of "verbal understanding and mis-understanding" in all modes of utterance (36:23). For something over forty years, he has attempted to show what such a discipline might contribute to the interpretation of meaning in language.

As one remedy for misunderstanding, Richards has scored a "mosaic Usage Doctrine" which treats verbal messages as though they were made up of linguistic pieces of fixed shape and color with a right or good use for each piece (36:23). In conscious opposition to that doctrine, he has specified the ways in which the meanings of words shift in the changing contexts of language and experience.

6. For a summary of this research, see Ervin-Tripp (20).

Both as critic and as teacher, Richards has been most interested in improving communication by increasing understanding and comprehension. What he has meant is implied in his account of the responsibilities of readers to choose which meanings they will take seriously.

Understanding them [the meanings] is seeing how the varied possible meanings hang together, which of them depend upon what else, how and why the meanings which matter most to us form a part of our world —seeing thereby most clearly what our world is and what we are who are building it to live in (35:13).

Contributing to that understanding, Richards described four aspects or points of view from which nearly all articulate speech or writing may be regarded. They are (*a*) *sense* (what the speaker actually says), (*b*) *feeling* (his attitude toward what he is talking about), (*c*) *tone* (his attitude toward his hearers or readers) and (*d*) *intention* (his conscious or unconscious aim) (37:173–81). In any mode of communication, these "four kinds of meaning" meld or blend to effect a larger, balanced "total meaning." Still more recently, Richards has described another set of "speculative instruments" for comprehending which includes as aspects of meaning (*a*) *indicating*, (*c*) *realizing*, (*c*) *valuing*, (*d*) *influencing*, (*e*) *controlling* and (*f*) *purposing* (38). It is his theory that any full utterance performs all of these meaning functions at once and invites all of them in the listener or reader (38:27).

Thus, Richards' major contribution to a modern theory of rhetoric has been to chart directions for a disciplined inquiry into the principles of language meaning as those principles might contribute to the development of tools of understanding and interpretation. Pedagogically, the rhetoric Richards describes would be broader and deeper than the old rhetoric of pleadings and argument where "it is not the opponent's views which get demolished so much as other things of more importance to mankind" (38:166).

Burke's critical theories are distributed among nearly a dozen books and scores of shorter critical pieces. Like Richards, he has for over a quarter-century sought to grant new importance to the concept of rhetoric. Defining man as the animal who by nature responds to symbols, Burke offers an overarching concept of rhetoric which, he says, "is rooted in an essential function of language itself, a function that is wholly realistic and is constantly born anew; the use of language as a symbolic means of inducing cooperation in beings that by nature respond to symbols" (13:43).

The old rhetoric, with its stress on deliberate design, offered a monological concept of persuasion. For Burke, "identification" becomes the key term for a modern rhetoric, reflecting the fact that people unconsciously desire to identify themselves with one group or another. With emphasis on "identification," Burke broadens the range of rhetorical appeal, shifting the focus of the study from a grammar of persuasion to a general theory of cooperation based on symbolic action.

Basing his critical theory on the form of the drama, Burke has sought to uncover the essentially verbal or symbolic texture of motivation in all human relations. "Dramatistically," in any statement about human motives, he says:

> You must have some word that names the *act* (names what took place, in thought or deed), and another that names the *scene* (the background of the act, the situation in which it occured); also, you must indicate what person or kind of person (*agent*) performed the act, what means or instruments he used (*agency*), and the *purpose* (11:xvii).

Thus, the problem in interpreting linguistic acts is one of interpreting motives which, in effect, are simply those terms which are historically available for describing one's situation. One's names for his *act* and its *scene* and *purpose* are not simply the results of some interior set of "drives" but are themselves the terms shaping and conditioning his total experience. Thus, whether one says of the United States' involvement in Vietnam that it is an act of genocide or an act of moral defense against an evil and aggressive force, the difference in terms constitutes a difference in motives. Which is to say that, for Burke, motives are those verbal or symbolic screens through which men give form to their experience and their social relationships.

Beyond its critical-interpretive applications, Burke's dramatistic model contributes directly to a theory of rhetorical invention. In the introduction to *A Grammar of Motives*, Burke writes that his book "is concerned with the basic forms of thought which. . . are exemplified in the attributing of motives. These forms of thought . . . are equally present in systematically elaborated metaphysical

structures, in legal judgments, in poetry and fiction, in political
and scientific works, in news and in bits of gossip offered at random"
(11:xvii). Accordingly, Burke's "pentad" of dramatistic terms may
function as a set of consistent points for generating an interior
dialogue, preceding the act of writing or speaking. (One might begin
by asking *Who* am *I* in this particular context or *scene,* addressing
this topic? What is the real nature of my *act?* What is my ostensible
purpose? What *agencies* of language and style may be most instrumental, in this scene, with that purpose, etc.?) Further, the vocabulary of the drama carries with it an inescapable sense of audience,
leading through Burke's concept of "identification" to the search
for a common field of assumption and value between writer and
reader, speaker and listener.

Pedagogically then, Burke returns rhetoric to something of the
status of a formal discipline. The return is "formal" in its concern
for the underlying relatedness of linguistic forms and principles of
social order; it is "disciplinary" in its avowedly *preparatory* aim to
institutionalize a spirit of linguistic skepticism. Thus, in analyzing
human events dramatistically, Burke admonishes a deliberate coax-
ing forth of all of the relevant and competing views. In the resulting
jangle of partisan voices, "one hopes for ways whereby . . ., in
mutually correcting one another, [they] will lead toward a better
position than any one singly" (12:284). Such critical maneuvers
are designed to compel tentativeness. Their objective is "not to
outwit the opponent . . . but . . . in some degree to incorporate him,
to so act that his ways can help perfect one's own. . . ." (12:284). In
an age torn by conflict, Burke grants rhetoric new significance as
education for living. He offers a concept of the study based on
identification, seeking cooperation and avoiding the specious clarity
of antithesis—the clarity of an "Us-versus-Them alignment"
(10:372).

The late Richard Weaver, Professor of English at the University
of Chicago, contributed to the contemporary revival by returning
to a Platonic concept of rhetoric, defining it as "the intellectual love
of the Good . . . [which] at its truest seeks to perfect men by showing them better visions of themselves. . . ." (46:25). As teacher and
as critic, Weaver described a rhetoric based on honest examination
of alternatives which appealed through figurative language and

poetic association. So defined, the subject appears at the boundary of politics and literature with important claims on liberal education.

For Weaver, rhetoric was primarily concerned with discourse addressed to public questions of choice and avoidance, grounded in value and proceeding through the full "sermonic" language of tendency. Bringing rhetoric back to a firm union with dialectic, he called for instruction in formal logic and in what traditional rhetoricians had called the *topics* or regions of argument (6). In his own writing and teaching, he emphasized the topics of *genus*, *consequence, similitude* and *authority* as places in experience from which the substance of any argument might be drawn. Moreover, believing the link between language and value to be intimate, Weaver sought to classify these major regions of argument according to their relative capacity to clarify and extend men's visions of themselves.

STUDIES IN THE MICRORHETORIC OF THE SENTENCE AND PARAGRAPH

A number of scholars working within the boundaries imposed by the analysis of linguistic structures in written composition have contributed importantly to the development of new, microrhetorical theory. Employing the methods of modern linguistic analysis, the work of Francis Christensen, Kenneth Pike, Alton Becker, and Richard Young may be taken as representative of new interest and new study of the rhetoric of the English sentence and paragraph.

Rejecting traditional grammatical and rhetorical classifications of the sentence (simple, compound, complex or loose, periodic and balanced), Christensen of the University of Southern California has described a "generative" rhetoric of the sentence based on four major principles or characteristics of modern English prose.[7] The first principle assumes that composition is essentially a process of *addition*, a principle which shifts attention away from principal nouns and verbs to the manner in which they are added to by modifiers. Both *addition* and the principle of *direction of modification* are exhibited in cumulative sentences in which the main clause advances the discussion while the rest of the sentence points back to the main clause to modify or extend its meaning. Such

---

7. See Christensen (14: 1-22). Christensen has extended his "generative" principles from the sentence to the analysis of the paragraph, as well.

sentences, accumulating meaning by addition, evidence a "back-tracking" or "downshifting" direction of movement in the modification of the main clause. Moreover, the principle of *levels of generality* implies that the "downshifting" is most often in the direction of lower levels of abstraction. *Texture*, the fourth principle, contrasts bare, unmodified predications with those of sentences whose modification or texture is both dense and varied. In Christensen's examples which follow, the main clause provides preliminary predication with the texture of context and detail provided by the "backtracking" addition of modifiers. In the first example, meaning is extended or accumulated through a series of modifiers occurring in parallel or coordinate order. In the second, modifiers accumulate in a sequence of subordination (14:59, 12).

I

1 Lincoln's words still linger on the lips—
  2 eloquent and cunning, yes,
  2 vindictive and sarcastic in political debate,
  2 rippling and ribald in jokes,
  2 reverent in the half-formed utterance of prayer.

— Alistair Cooke —

II

1 A small Negro girl develops from the sheet of glare-frosted walk,
  2 walking barefooted,
    3 her brown legs striking and recoiling from the hot cement,
      4 her feet curling in,
        5 only the outer edges touching.

Christensen's "generative" rhetoric describes the cumulative sentence of modern prose as working in a direction opposite the traditional handbook descriptions of the periodic and balanced sentence. Rejecting their precast symmetry, it signals a less formal authorial voice, seeking and probing for its subject.

At the University of Michigan, Alton Becker and Richard Young (48) have applied principles derived from Kenneth Pike's tagmemic grammar to the analysis of the paragraph. Assuming an underlying structure or system of recurrencies in human behavior, Pike and others have quite self-consciously described a set of discovery procedures in conjunction with a system for analyzing variable-sized units of linguistic and other behavior events. Basic to tagmemic analysis is a distinction between *etic* and *emic* analytical perspectives. Paralleling the distinction between phonetic and phonemic analysis, an *etic* perspective provides an external, formal description in terms of an imposed set of descriptive categories. By contrast, an *emic* perspective affords a systemic view, yielding a description of the relations holding between the formally significant and functionally contrastive attributes of categories *discovered within the system* (33:37–72). For example, a paragraph might be defined *etically* as a set of one or more written English "sentences" formally marked off by an indentation. And *emic* definition, on the other hand, would pose a different kind of problem since to be adequate it would have to describe both the formal and the functional attributes contributing to the structual integrity of the paragraph. Ultimately, Becker and Young argue that written English paragraphs "are emically definable units—not just groups of sentences isolated by rather arbitrary indentations. . . ." (48:464).

Tagmemic descriptive procedures possess certain theoretical advantages for the analysis of extended discourse.[8] Developing from a modified "slot-and-filler" grammar, its procedures can be employed to describe contextually relative grammatical classes or units. Thus, in a simple English sentence, the grammatical relationship of "subject" is established by a limited number of grammatical forms. "Subject" identifies a slot in the structure of a sentence which can be filled by one or more of that set of substitutable forms. The concept of a *tagmeme*, then, includes both the slot and the class or set of those potentially interchangeable fillers. The concept is relative and may be applied to the partitioning of larger or smaller segments of recurring structure. In more traditional rhetorical terms, the cells of an argument or the terms of a syllogism are recurrent structures which might be described and partitioned into just such slot-and-filler classes.

Applying these concepts, Becker and Young have described two major patterns in English expository paragraphs. The first is composed of three functional slots labeled T (topic), R (restric-

---

8. It should be observed that still other aspects of tagmemic discovery procedures have been viewed as major contributions to a modern theory of rhetorical invention. See Pike (32) and English (19).

tion), and I (illustration). The T slot may be filled by one of a set of sentence types. The clearest example would be a simple propositional statement. In such a paragraph, the R slot is filled by a restatement or restriction of T, usually at a lower level of generality. Finally, the I slot is filled by one of a number of possible supporting or illustrative sentences, exhibiting such traditional rhetorical functions as support by example, analogy, comparison, etc. (48:464–66, 5:87). The paragraph below illustrates the TRI pattern with the I slot filled by sentences of exemplification.

(T) The Casual Style is not exactly new. (R) Originated in the early Twenties, it has been refined and improved and refined again by a relatively small band of writers, principally for the *New Yorker*, until now their mannerisms have become standards of sophistication. (I) Everybody is trying to join the club. Newspaper columnists have forsaken the beloved of the sports page for the Casual Style, and one of the quickest ways for an ad man to snag an award from other ad men is to give his copy the low-key, casual pitch; the copy shouldn't sing these days——it should whisper. Even Dr. Rudolph Flesch, who has been doing so much to teach people how to write like other people, is counseling his followers to use the Casual Style. Everywhere the ideal seems the same: be casual (47:87).

The second major pattern of expository paragraphs is described as two slots, P (problem) and S (solution). The P slot implies either a question or problem for which the S slot provides sentences functioning as solution or explanation. Often, the S slot itself reveals an embedded TRI structure. The following example illustrates the P and S pattern with a TIRI pattern embedded in the S slot.

(P) What in the beginning marked off the nascent American culture from that of Europe? (S-T) One thing I would suggest was poverty, poverty in a society already more egalitarian than that of Europe. (I) People came to America to get rich (among other reasons); they did not arrive rich. (R) Establishing their culture beachheads on the eastern coast, they had not the resources of time or of energy for the reproduction on the American shore of the elaborate cultural life that some of them had shared and all of them had heard of in Europe. (I) There was no demand for a Van Dyke, an Inigo Jones, a Milton in seventeenth-century America; no means of producing or sustaining such artists (7:89).

Expository paragraphs are not, of course, identically structured, but their differences and variations may be described as the result of processes of reordering, adding, deleting, and combining of just such paragraph tagmemes. In addition to rhetorical attributes, tagmemic analysis has pointed toward complex levels of graphic, lexical, grammatical and phonological signals contributing to the structural integrity of the paragraph.

In a number of ways, the theories of Christensen and the Michigan group are similar and complementary. Each begins by assuming an analogy between the structure of the sentence and the paragraph. But whereas Christensen approaches the problem from the point of view of the writer, tagmemic theorists have worked primarily from the point of view of the reader. Christensen has sought to apply his theories, normatively, to the immediate problems of instruction. Tagmemic theory seems to hold out the promise of equally important pedagogical applications, but it appears considerably more complex and, so far, limited to the construction of descriptive theory. Both approaches represent a departure from the deductive mold of traditional paragraph rhetoric. The work of Christensen, Pike, Becker, Young, and others represents a new inductive approach in the development of a microrhetoric for composition teaching.

New Purpose and New Directions in the Rhetoric-Composition Curriculum

The contributions of modern studies in language, in communication and criticism, to the development of a "new" rhetoric are rich and promising even though they do not yet offer any very coherent or intellectually unified theory. Nor is it easy to see precisely how the several dimensions of newer rhetorical theory might directly affect school programs. Even assuming the promise of some redefinition and reordering, we continue to face limits in our understanding of how to translate that theory into effective instructional programs. The very range of the potential "subject matter" as well as the gaps in our knowledge of appropriate instructional sequences and procedures make talk of "a new rhetoric for composition teaching" more than a little illusory.

Nonetheless, it is possible to point to certain broad trends in the teaching of rhetoric and composition in the schools which do seem to reflect new knowledge and new purpose. A new sense of purpose may come, for instance, with a growing recognition of the intimate relation between language and thought. Too often in the past, the teaching of composition has had little explicit rationale beyond providing a schedule of exercises for achieving linguistic and formal remediation. The school's hand-me-down rhetorical theory effectively divorced form and diction from relations with experience and knowledge. Today, armed by the findings of psychology and linguistics, teachers are becoming more and more conscious of the power of language to order thought and feeling. More than legislating a standard of "correctness," composition-teaching involves "teaching the calculus of thought . . . implicit in the combinatorial or productive power of language that is an invitation to take experience apart and put it together again in new ways" (9:105).

That growing awareness of the role of language in ordering thought is most clearly reflected in newer teaching strategies emphasizing the traditional rhetorical province of invention. To the extent that the teaching of composition accepts a limited managerial aim, writing is not really taught: it is simply assigned and "corrected." More recently, discussions of "inquiry" or "prewriting" have stressed the dialectical processes which must occur before words are put on paper. Moreover, attention to the prewriting or inventive process leads directly to a more active—or *interactive*—mode of instruction, featuring discussion and dialogue as integral parts of "composing." The problem becomes one of assisting the writer to order and conceptualize the "field" of his subject or proposition. Application of (*a*) Weaver's discussion of the topics of classical rhetoric, (*b*) Burke's system of dramatistic analysis, (*c*) tagmemic discovery procedures, and (*d*) experimentally developed "prewriting" programs (39) all point to new concern with ways of knowing, with ways in which student writers may engage in preliminary processing of knowledge, experience, and feeling.

Beyond the emphasis on developing a modern theory of rhetorical invention, a second, related trend in discussions of composition teaching emphasizes the important relationships holding between oral and written language development. The priority of the development of speaking and listening skills of youngsters accounts in large measure for the spread or lag in "linguistic age" between speaking and writing. One clear implication calls for more systematic attention to the oral language experiences of children in the lower schools. But in the secondary school, the interrelatedness of the two encoding systems also implies new emphases. Here, recognition of the shifting "styles" or "keys" of oral language may alert teachers to important questions of language function and variation. Thus, linguistically derived descriptions of speech functions (emotive, directive, referential, metalinguistic, poetic, phatic) and "keys" (intimate, casual, consultative, formal, oratorical) [9] contrast sharply with a traditional composition curriculum restricted to a more or less formal "key" and an essentially referential or expository function. Attempts to develop a new rhetoric of composition teaching which accounts for the diversity of language modalities builds on the observation that "The shape of style of mind is . . . the outcome of internalizing the [varied] functions inherent in the language we use" (9:107). Further, recognition of the extent to which language form and style vary with function and setting leads away from a socially stratified doctrine of correctness. Ultimately, recognition of the flexibility and interrelatedness of speech and writing may help students to respond with greater understanding and efficiency to the demands of changing personal and social contexts.

A final trend to be observed in a number of revisionist statements is the notion that instruction in rhetoric and composition, rather than simply developing "skills," serves unique individual and social ends. Individually, the act of composing is viewed as an existential process, limited and shaped by one's own perceptions as well as by the nature of language itself. The point of view is deliberately subjective, affirming that acts of speaking and writing, in addition to serving practical needs of communication, are "forms of self-actualization . . ., satisfying basic needs for self-affirmation. . . ." (9:107). Such a view tends to move instruction in rhetoric and composition out of the frame of a didactically structured set of drills and exercises toward the modes of inquiry and dialogue, grounded on a study of language itself. This is not to deny the usefulness of drills or exercises or the necessity for instruction which

9. For a discussion of speech functions, see Hymes (26) and Jakobson (28). For a discussion of variations in oral and written language "keys" or "styles," see Joos (29) and Gleason (22).

develops proficiency in and respect for the conventions of written and spoken English. Instead, it is to define those aims and procedures as instrumental aspects of a larger, more genuinely liberal ideal.

Socially, study of the nature and complexities of human communication emphasizes the fragility of the interpersonal process. Naive assumptions of rhetorical efficacy are replaced by the understanding that writers and speakers play, at best, for limited and marginal gains. Facing the complexity of the behavior and the very real limits of language and perception, modern theories of rhetoric tend to lower the barrier between writer and reader, speaker and listener. They tend, to move toward a "discussion rhetoric" in which a writer's purpose is altered in the transaction with a real or imagined audience. The emphasis shifts from a theory of specific advantage to a theory of mutual cooperation, "[drawing] attention away from the primitive level of verbal opposition to deeper levels where searching investigation is encouraged" (39).

Conclusion

These descriptions of new perspectives and new emphases in the rhetoric composition curriculum have been both abstract and elliptical. They describe no systematic body of theory or practice which might be either quickly or easily incorporated into school programs. At best, they point to signs of new interest and new resolve at one juncture in the schools' struggle between tradition and change. The traditional composition curriculum has been described as a legacy of an earlier period in the history of the schools which appears now to have been both intellectually and socially inadequate to the task. To apply Gilbert Ryle's distinction between knowing *how* and knowing *that* (42:25–61), instruction in composition has for too long been centered on knowing *how*, on mastering a limited set of mechanical and linguistic skills. The several perspectives characterizing the so-called new rhetoric contribute by extending the ways in which we may know both *how* and *that*. Thus, knowing *that* one's public language choices have consequences in the structure of self-identity makes of writing and speaking committed, deeply personal acts. Knowing *that* the very structures of language and thought are intimately linked effectively challenges a curriculum which assumes a "practical" division between thought and its expression. Finally, beyond knowing *how* and knowing *that*, a consistent theme marking the critical writings of the "new" rhetoric stresses the need for knowing *better*. In conjunction with shifting models or styles of teaching itself, that theme may help us to develop unabashedly valuative theories of public inquiry and dialogue. Such theories—such rhetorics—will begin with the understanding that communication which seeks honestly to address another embraces *compromise* grounded in *conscience*. More than legislating correctness, our objective might then appear to be the liberal pursuit of the rhetorical imagination necessary to free men and free institutions.

BIBLIOGRAPHY

1. ADAMS, CHARLES FRANCIS; GODKIN, E. L.; and NUTTER, GEORGE R. "Report of the Harvard Committee on Composition and Rhetoric." Report No. LXXI (1897). Harvard Library Special Collections.
2. BAIN, ALEXANDER. *On Teaching English*. New York: D. Appleton & Co., 1921.
3. BALDWIN, T. W. *William Shakespeare's Small Latine and Lesse Greeke*. 2 vols. Urbana: University of Illinois Press, 1944.
4. BECKER, ALTON L. "Symposium on the Paragraph," *College Composition and Communication*, XVII (May, 1966), 67-72.
5. ———. "A Tagmemic Approach to Paragraph Analysis," *College Composition and Communication*, XVII (December, 1965), 237-42.
6. BILSKY, MANUAL; HAZLETT, McCREA; STREETER, ROBERT; and WEAVER, RICHARD. "Looking for an Argument," *College English*, XIV (January, 153), 210-16.
7. BROGAN, DENNIS W. *America in the Modern World*. New Brunswick: Rutgers University Press, 1960.
8. BROWN, ROGER. *Social Psychology*. New York: The Free Press, 1965.
9. BRUNER, JEROME. *Toward a Theory of Instruction*. Cambridge: Harvard University Press, 1966.
10. BURKE, KENNETH. "Freedom and Authority in the Realm of the Poetic Imagination," in *Freedom and Authority in Our Time*, pp. 365-375. Edited by Lyman Bryson and others. Conference on Science, Philosophy and Religion in Their Relation to the Democratic Way of Life. New York: Harper & Brothers, 1953.
11. ———. *A Grammar of Motives*. New York: Prentice Hall, 1945.
12. ———. "Linguistic Approach to Problems of Education," in *Modern Philosophies and Education*, chap. vii. Edited by Nelson B. Henry. Fifty-fourth Yearbook of the National Society for the Study of Education, Part 1. Chicago: Distributed by University of Chicago Press, 1955.

PICHÉ   151

13. ———. *A Rhetoric of Motives*. New York: George Braziller, Inc., 1955.

14. CHRISTENSEN, FRANCIS. *Notes Toward a New Rhetoric*. New York: Harper & Row, 1967.

15. CLARK, DONALD LEMEN. *John Milton at St. Paul's School*. New York: Columbia University Press, 1948.

16. ———. *Rhetoric in Greco-Roman Education*. New York: Columbia University Press, 1967.

17. Committee on National Interest. *The National Interest and the Teaching of English*. Champaign, Ill.: National Council of Teachers of English, 1961.

18. EHNINGER, DOUGLAS. "On Systems of Rhetoric," *Philosophy and Rhetoric*, (Summer, 1968), 131–44.

19. ENGLISH, HUBERT M., JR. "Linguistic Theory as an Aid to Invention," *College Composition and Communication*, XV (October, 1964), 136–40.

20. ERVIN-TRIPP, SUSAN M. "An Analysis of the Interaction of Language, Topic and Listener," *American Anthropologist*, LXVI (December, 1964), 86-102.

21. FOGARTY, DANIEL. *Roots for a New Rhetoric*. New York: Bureau of Publications, Teachers College, Columbia University, 1959.

22. GLEASON, H. A., JR. *Linguistics and English Grammar*, chap. xv. New York: Holt, Rinehart & Winston, 1965.

23. GORRELL, ROBERT M. (ed.). *Rhetoric: Theories for Application*. Champaign, Illinois: National Council of Teachers of English, 1967.

24. HOVLAND, CARL I.; JANIS, IRVING L.; and KELLEY, HAROLD H. *Communication and Persuasion*. New Haven: Yale University Press, 1953.

25. HOVLAND, CARL I., and OTHERS. *The Order of Presentation in Persuasion*. New Haven: Yale University Press, 1957.

26. HYMES, DELL. "The Ethnography of Speaking." In *Anthropology and Human Behavior*, pp. 13–53. Edited by Thomas Gladwin and William C. Sturdevant. Washington, D.C.: Anthropological Society of Washington, 1962.

27. ———. "Models of the Interaction of Language and Social Setting." *Journal of Social Issues*, XXIII (April, 1967), 8–28.

28. JAKOBSON, ROMAN. "Closing Statement: Linguistics and Poetics." In *Style and Language*, pp. 356–377.

29. JOOS, MARTIN. *The Five Clocks*. New York: Harcourt, Brace & World, 1967.

30. KITZHABER, ALBERT R. "Rhetoric in American Colleges, 1850-1900." Unpublished Doctor's Dissertation, University of Washington, 1953.

31. PICHÉ, GENE L. "Revision and Reform in the Secondary School English Curriculum, 1870–1900." Unpublished Doctor's dissertation, University of Minnesota, 1967.

32. PIKE, KENNETH. "Language as Particle, Wave and Field," *Texas Quarterly*, II (Summer, 1959), 37–54.

33. ———. *Language in Relation to a Unified Theory of the Structure of Human Behavior.* 2d rev. ed. The Hague: Mouton & Co., 1967.

34. RAPOPORT, ANATOL. *Fights, Games and Debates.* Ann Arbor: University of Michigan Press, 1961.

35. RICHARDS, I. A. *How To Read a Page.* New York: W. W. Norton & Co., 1942.

36. ———. *The Philosophy of Rhetoric.* New York: Oxford University Press, 1936.

37. ———. *Practical Criticism.* New York: Harcourt, Brace & World, 1929.

38. ———. *Speculative Instruments.* Chicago: University of Chicago Press, 1955.

39. ROHMAN, D. GORDON and WLECKE, ALBERT O. *Pre-Writing: The Construction and Application of Models for Concept Formation in Writing.* U.S.O.E. Cooperative Research Project No. 2174. East Lansing: Michigan State University, 1964.

40. ROKEACH, MILTON. *Beliefs, Attitudes, and Values.* San Francisco: Jossey-Bass, Inc., 1968.

41. ———. "Images of the Consumer's Mind On and Off Madison Avenue," *ETC: A Review of General Semantics*, XXI (September, 1964), 261–73.

42. RYLE, GILBERT. *The Concept of Mind.* New York: Barnes and Noble, 1949.

43. SCHRAMM, WILBUR, (ed.). *The Science of Human Communication.* New York: Basic Books, 1963.

44. STEINMANN, MARTIN, JR. (ed.). *New Rhetorics.* New York: Charles Scribners' Sons, 1967.

45. *Twenty Years of School and College English.* Cambridge: Harvard University, 1896.

46. WEAVER, RICHARD. *The Ethnics of Rhetoric.* Chicago: Henry Regnery Co., 1953.

47. WHYTE, WILLIAM H. JR. "You Too Can Write the Casual Style," *Harpers Magazine*, October 1956, p. 87.

48. YOUNG, RICHARD E., and BECKER, ALTON L. "Toward a Modern Theory of Rhetoric: A Tagmemic Contribution," *Harvard Educational Review*, XXXIV (Fall, 1965), 450–68.

LEARNING AND LANGUAGE

The History of Language Instruction in the Schools

WALLACE W. DOUGLAS

The Nature and Status of
Language Instruction in Early America

THE UNCERTAIN POSITION OF LANGUAGE INSTRUCTION

Looked at dispassionately, if that is possible, the history of language instruction in United States schools can hardly be regarded as a great, or even a very considerable, example of the power of man's ingenuity, to say nothing of his wisdom. If English "grammar" did not get into the curriculum quite by accident, still it is hard to find in the apparent reasons for its presence any substantial evidence that much consideration was given either to the value or to the utility of having native-born speakers of English study the grammar of their language, whether to improve their own speech or to establish and control the forms of the language. In modern times, it is true, this question has been opened up, but though an answer (a negative one) seems to have been developed, it has had very little effect on school practice. Ambiguous in origin, tainted in use, "grammar" continues to occupy almost as dominant a part of the school day as it did when grammar schools were just that only; indeed for most people—pupils, teachers, and public alike—"grammar" probably defines "English," to the exclusion not merely of composition and literature but also of whatever might be thought to be meant by the child's fluency and essential literacy.

LANGUAGE INSTRUCTION IN COLONIAL TIMES

In the colonial period, instruction in the vernacular was certainly simple and seems also to have been reasonably utilitarian, consisting as it did of instruction in reading, (hand)writing, and spelling, to the end of fostering the religious, vocational, and governmental capacities of the community. This kind of instruction was carried on in dame schools and reading schools. Grammar, in the sense of the study of the system of a language, was reserved, as it was in England, for the grammar school, to which were sent children who were destined for the learned professions—the ministry and the law —and who, consequently, had to learn (or at least be instructed in) Latin, which was still considered, though inexactly, to be the language of the learned community and, insofar as the two were identical, also of the governmental apparatus. It seems likely that the purpose of this study was still, as anciently, the preservation of *latinitas;* that is to say, it was practical not theoretical, treating grammar as an art, not a science; and thus it helped to lay upon the schools of this country the dead hand of "language improvement" as the chief, if not the only, reason for grammatical studies.

THE ATTACK ON LATIN GRAMMAR

Assumptions of anti-Latinists.—Though its value as a social divider cannot ever have been exactly obscure, still the study of Latin grammar seems not to have had quite so secure a position in the school business of this country as might therefore be expected. In the first place, there was already established in the metropolitan countries, especially perhaps England, a fairly strong intellectual tradition (see the works of, for example, Comenius and Milton) which held that mastering Latin, whether by study of the grammar or otherwise, simply took too much time—time which might better be spent in moral development and the achievement of simple literacy in the vernacular. It should be noticed, however, that these reformers did not stand against the study of Latin as such, though indeed they seem to have had some feeling about approaching it through grammar. What they were against was the intrusion of Latin studies into the education of children whose social rôles could not conceivably demand its use. Of course they also argued that secular knowledge and affairs could and should be treated in the vernaculars; so to that extent they probably were also arguing against Latin and Greek as the learned languages. Since the Bible had been translated and since the business of the world was being conducted in the vernaculars, what need for Latin?

The authority of Locke: (*a*) Locke's Moralist's Position.—This tradition must have been very powerfully enforced by the authority of Locke's *Some Thoughts Concerning Education* (1693). In Locke's discussion, the social or sociological content of this controversy can be quite clearly seen. Locke starts from the moralist's assumption that it is not the languages only of Greece and Rome that are to be studied; the virtues of their brave, just, and wise men (that is, the values of Greek and Roman society) must be a part—indeed a major part—of schooling. It was "a strange value for words," he remarked acerbly that would confine education to the study of the classical languages, especially since, in fact, that hazard of the child's innocence and virtue would nearly always produce so little command of the language.

(*b*) Locke's definition of proper method in language studies.— But Locke's exact position on the place of studies in the learned languages and the appropriate method for pursuing such studies is somewhat ambiguous, though perhaps no more so than those that are held by many today. In part he seems to have objected merely to the method of teaching, which took so much time in "the grammatical flats and shallows"—the phrase is Milton's—that there was little time left for acquiring the tongue, to say nothing of inculcating what Sidney had called "the ending end of all earthly knowledge"— that is, virtuous action. Locke preferred something like the conversational or direct method that one knew as a refreshing reform in instruction in the modern languages some thirty years and more ago. Locke thought that Latin, like French and other languages of everyday use, could be "talked into" children by constant conversation: after all, the child learns English "without master, rule, or grammar"; why not also Latin, as Cicero did, he adds, as if by an afterthought so obvious as not to need argument.

Locke's comments on method suggest pretty strongly that his opposition to the classical languages was by no means unqualified. Latin, he says, is "absolutely necessary for a gentleman." What bothers him is the plight of the boy (girls, of course, were not of concern) whose father wasted his own money and his son's time by "setting him to learn the Roman language, when, at the same time, he designs him for a trade, wherein he, having no use of Latin, fails not to forget that little" which was whipped into him at school. It was ridiculous to Locke then, as it has been to others since, that not only gentlemen but even farmers and tradespeople should send their sons to a school—the grammar school—where "writing a good hand, and casting accounts," skills obviously necessary "to trade and commerce, and the business of the world," are forgotten in favor of wearisome efforts, year after year, to acquire a little Latin.

In Locke's enlightened view, such behavior was just one more illustration of the triumph of custom over reason. And to the extent (it is not much) that he is interested in discussing grammar at all, it is to lay down, in clear and distinct fashion, the precise limits of its usefulness. There is "more stir [by] a great deal" about grammar than needs be, he remarks sharply in one place. And he seems to have been convinced that grammar has no part in the mere *learning* of a language.

And I would fain have any one name to me that tongue, that any one can learn or speak as he should do, by the rules of grammar. Languages were made not by rules or art, but by accident, and the common use of people.

So Locke would have none of the notion that instruction in grammar has any place in the education of children, "to whom it does not at all belong," and who, at the age they generally get it, are only "tormented" and "perplexed" by it. His assumption is, of course, that most children grow up to be people concerned only with "the ordinary intercourse of society, and communication of thoughts in common life. . . ." For such people "the original way of learning a language by conversation not only serves well enough, but is to be preferred, as the most expedite, proper, and natural."

This so many of my readers must be forced to allow, as understand what I here say, and who conversing with others, understand them without having ever been taught the grammar of the English tongue: which I suppose is the case of incomparably the greatest part of Englishmen; of whom I have never yet known any one who learned his mother-tongue by rules.

(*c*) Locke's explanation of the place of grammar in language studies.—In the light of history, it is perhaps unfortunate that Locke did not let his argument stand at that, but instead went on to ask:

Is grammar then of no use? And have those who have taken so much pains in reducing several languages to rules and observations, who have writ so much about declensions and conjugations, about concords and syntaxis, lost their labour, and been learned to no purpose?

So plaintive a question, of course, demands but one answer. But even in that necessary affirmation of grammar's usefulness, Locke is very restrained. He concedes, though grudgingly it seems, that two sorts of people might need, or at least make use of, grammar. One sort is the scholars and others who "pique themselves upon their skill" in the dead ("which amongst us are called the learned") languages, and who "make them their study." Such people, who want to be "critically exact" in the languages, no doubt need careful study of the grammars.

The other group needing grammar is those "the greatest part of whose business in this world is to be done with their tongues, and with their pens." Here Locke introduces an idea that was to be of enormous importance in the development of the English curriculum in this country. That is the idea that the effectiveness of a communication depends on the "correctness' and propriety of its language-form. For the group he has in mind—and he means not professional authors but rather gentlemen in public positions (Aristotle's people of consequence)—Locke says that "it is convenient, if not necessary, that they should speak properly and correctly, whereby they may let their thoughts into other men's minds the more easily, and with the greater impression."

For a gentleman of this sort, it is not enough just to be understood. He must "understand his own country['s] speech nicely, and speak it properly, without shocking the ears of those it is addressed to with solecisms and offensive irregularities. And to this purpose, grammar is necessary. . . ."

On the whole, Locke seems to have thought that this need of grammatical knowledge was confined "to those only who would take pains in cultivating their language, and in perfecting their styles." He was, however, willing to have considered, presumably by others, the question of whether all gentlemen should not take such pains, "since the want of propriety and grammatical exactness is thought very misbecoming one of that rank, and usually draws on one guilty of such faults the censure of having had a lower breeding, and worse company than suits with his quality."

Thus was expressed another idea of very great importance; and it is to be noted, however regretfully, that it is one a good deal more firmly based in the reality of human behavior than is the one that ties communication effectiveness to the correctness and propriety of language forms.

Language Instruction in Nineteenth-Century Schools

THE NARROWED REFERENCE OF "GRAMMAR"

In any event, it has been the latter idea that has dominated the English curriculum in the United States; for three hundred years and more, children in this country have been marched through school to the utilitarianism of "Grammatica est recte scribendi, atque loquendi ars." In classical times and even in the Renaissance, that slogan must have carried a certain dignity and perhaps even a kind of opulence, for then *grammatica* had included in its reference not merely linguistic analysis but also literary and rhetorical studies and could therefore with some legitimacy be called the art of speaking and writing well (or correctly). But in the seventeenth and eighteenth centuries in this country, grammar seems to have been reduced to memorizing of rules and definitions, parsing, and correction of syntactical and (sometimes) stylistic flaws. Suggestions of the larger classical sense perhaps remained in the themes and declamations that students performed, in the selections from "good writers" that they studied in various fashions. But the subject of this essay is not the history of "English," rather it is the history of language instruction. And so far as that is concerned, for two centuries and more, the tool of the schoolmaster has been a grammar book that has differed little in form, and only as obviously necessary in content, from the school grammars that the ancient and medieval worlds had modeled on the *Techne grammatike* of Dionysius Thrax (2d. c. B.C.), in which he had epitomized Stoic and Alexandrian grammatical speculation and investigation.

THE CONTINUITY OF GRAMMATICAL INSTRUCTION

Thus the first main section of the Latin grammars treated *vox*, *litera*, and *syllaba*; similarly the first section of Lindley Murray's grammars did "the form and sound of letters, the combination of letters into syllables, and syllables into words." Where the Latin grammars had a second section on *partes orationis,* including the details of conjugation and declension, Murray had one on "the different sorts of words, their various modifications, and their derivation," the last being taken over from later Latin texts. Murray's third section, "on the union and right order of words in the formation of a sentence," perhaps shows the result of Priscian's addition of a full section, *de constructione;* the earlier grammars had treated syntax incidentally in the first two sections. Murray's fourth section, on "the just pronunciation and poetical construction of sentences," can perhaps be seen as a specialization of certain topics taken up in the third section of the early Latin grammars, concerning weaknesses and strengths in speech, along with others found in the later grammars.

THE SUPERFICIALITY OF REFORM

Early nineteenth-century reform.—In his *English Grammar in American Schools before 1850,*[1] R. L. Lyman described a revolution in the teaching of grammar that he saw as having occurred during the second quarter of the nineteenth century, reaching some sort of completion by 1850. Lyman's revolution involved nothing less than a shift from the ancient conception of grammar as an art to another that in some sense—so Lyman asserted—treated grammar as a science, specifically as a science of sentences (rather than of words, that is).

Looked at today, however, it is hard to find any signs of a radical overturn in the changes Lyman described. As so often in school matters, mere changes in procedure or practice (in "methods," to use the technical term) are confused with changes in substance. Lyman, it is true, criticized some of the essentials of the old grammar: its concentration on morphology, especially accidence, the idealist relation assumed between system and use. But in general his criticism went against mere teaching techniques: matters such as memorization, recitation, the ignoring of "practice." And he praised the new grammars (for example, Samuel Kirkham's, 1823, 1825) because they encouraged understanding and "immediate self-activity" by pupils in practicing principles as soon as acquired. But

1. This Ph.D. dissertation (University of Chicago, 1922) was also published as U.S. Office of Education Bulletin 1921, No. 12.

Charles Hoole had put forth the same complaints and remedies in his *Art of Teaching School,* which was published in England in 1660. And surely the use of visual (blackboards and slates) and oral (explanations by teachers) techniques of instruction did not, of necessity, require then a reexamination of content any more than various kinds of visual or oral projectors and schemes to increase teaching efficiency have done today.

But as a matter of fact, Lyman's revolution did include one technical change that might have entailed substantive consequences, for the teaching of "English" at least, if not necessarily for the teaching of English grammar. That was the introduction into school practice of "consecutive" writing. But this "constructive work" was treated as an adjunct to the teaching of grammar. The compositions became either sources of "data" for inductive or illustrative teaching of grammatical principles, or tests of children's abilities to practice what others were preaching, or means for identifying a class's needs in language to the end of assuring efficiency in instruction. (The last is a comparatively modern development, of course.) That the reformers had the authority of collegiate practice to support them does not improve the nature of their innovation. And that Lyman, writing in 1922, could find in it reason for praise is in itself evidence of the persistence, among American schoolmasters, of traditions and practices that were ancient when Quintilian set out to rationalize the rhetorical schools of Rome.

Grammar in the reorganization of the schools (1890–1920).— Indeed, in all the long history of the teaching of the mother tongue in this country, it is very hard to find signs of reform, let alone revolution. And this is so, incidentally, despite the fact that, for good portions of our history, the English taught in the schools has by no means been the native dialect, and in many cases not even the native language, of the children who were being asked to learn its grammar. It is true that the college-dominated (as it was said) Committee of Ten of the National Education Association (1894) recommended that children not be asked to do formal grammar and sentence analysis until age thirteen and then for no more than one school year; they also acknowledged that the study of formal grammar has only an indirect influence on speaking and writing. But their qualifications were attached to "formal grammar" (it would be interesting to know when that term got into the tradition), and they seem to have had no doubt that grammatical knowledge, if presented incidentally, in connection with committed errors or infelicities, would help children learn to use "good English," which, apparently, the Committee took to be a necessary and sufficient condition to a child's being able to "give expression to thoughts of his own."

The Committee of Fifteen (N.E.A., 1895) also admitted that knowledge of grammar was not a prerequisite to having "a good English style." But they recommended that, beginning with the second half of the fifth year, the school timetable should include a daily grammar lesson of twenty-five or thirty minutes, to be taught from a textbook. And so far as that goes, they had grammar even in the first four and a half grades, though it was grammar of the oral and functional sort, with the teacher "introducing the grammatical technique as it is needed to describe accurately the correct forms and usages violated."

"The high school has ceased to be mainly a preparatory school" is the opening sentence of *Reorganization of English in the Secondary Schools* (1917).[2] And in describing its "point of view," the Joint Committee noted that English is not a "formal subject," that mere "skill in the use and interpretation of symbols [words?]" is not "the sole end sought." "Only the specialist in language," they added, "can be induced to concentrate his attention upon the forms of speech and writing as objects of interest in themselves." But in the section on the aims of English, they asserted that expression depends on correctness in grammar and idiom. And when they came to outlining the work in English, the committee included grammar, under the heading of composition, as work "not to be neglected," though also not to be emphasized, in Grades VII through IX. The outline for Grade VIII contains the significant note that in grammar "it will facilitate the pupil's work in taking up a foreign language to emphasize nomenclature common to English and the language studied."

Modern reforms: (*a*) The Basic Issues Conference.—For all practical purposes, the curriculum of the American school was set for

2. This report was prepared by a committee representing the Commission on the Reorganization of Secondary Education (N.E.A.) and the National Council of Teachers of English and was published by the Office of Education, Bulletin 1917, No. 2.

two generations by the reports of these three committees; for English, the last one was especially significant. And it was not until 1958, the year after Sputnik, that the viability of this structure began to be questioned in any serious fashion. In that year, the Conference on Basic Issues in the Teaching of English asked (as one of its thirty-five "issues") not merely what kind of knowledge about the structure of English a student should have [in order to do what?], but also "how can such knowledge, at various levels [of the school?] be used to improve his ability to write well?" The moral imperative in "should have" is at least odd; the apparent refusal to recognize the child's speech is a bit of English department snobbery; and the second question in the "issue" certainly has some of the characteristics of a *petitio principii.* On the whole, then, so far as the teaching of language is concerned, the Basic Issues Conference rather retreated from the positions so hardly won by the great nineteenth-century reports. Or would it be more accurate to say that, for whatever reasons, the Conference did not choose to occupy the territory that its predecessors had left open for it?

This is not surprising, considering the composition of the Conference. There were twenty-eight members. Eighteen were from colleges and universities; at least eleven of these either were from eastern institutions or had strong classical leanings or both. Only four members were from schools (Greenwich, Jamaica, and New Trier High Schools, Germantown Friends School). Five others had some connection with the schools by reason of their interest in teacher preparation. There was only one linguist, a university man but fortunately one with school board experience, who was then in an English department whose interest in school affairs has been long and generally fruitful. Perhaps what is surprising is that the Conference got around to mentioning language at all.

(*b*) The Commission on English.—*Freedom and Discipline,* the Report of the Commission on English (College Entrance Examination Board, 1965), the next reform document that must be taken up, is like a grand reprise, a Wagnerian summation, of all the themes that this discourse has been built around. Perhaps more familiar than most with the schoolmaster's way of thinking, the writers of the report labored to balance the competing (and in many cases absolutely incompatible) assumptions and attitudes that, over the centuries, have gradually been drawn into the area of reference of the word "grammar." According to the Commission, "a child who speaks his language correctly can be said to know its grammar." There the Commission is recognizing the principles of modern ("positivistic") linguistic science. But in another place, the Commission recognizes the old habits and loyalties of teachers by referring to the fact that English teachers like to cultivate "socially acceptable spoken and written English," just as some professors rather like to imagine themselves "determining standards of acceptability." "Grammar study," according to the Commission, "is necessary for, or at least helpful in, the eradication of faults, and consequently it develops the power to read and write and speak well," though indeed it is "somewhat unrealistic" to suppose that grammar study "means power over the prestige dialect," or that "grammatical analysis exerts [any] appreciable control over usage."

Where these remarks leave the study of language in the schools is, indeed, a question to be asked. But for the moment what needs be noted is the extreme, the revolutionary ingenuity that the Commission exercised here. What they did was nothing less than, finally, after so many long centuries, to separate the roles of teacher and grammarian. Their argument allows to the grammarian all the purity and objectivity of the scientist. Not his to distinguish between good and bad, between *vitia* and *virtutes orationis*. For him only the dull task of recording mere facts. Meanwhile all the glamor that once went with grammar is transferred to the teacher, on whom devolves the rare, the rather awful privilege of making choices, of preserving standards, of inculcating a preference for the better over the worse.

Two Rationales for Language Instruction

On the whole, the schools in this country seem to be remaining faithful to the utilitarian view of language instruction. Teachers, curriculum planners, and textbook makers all want to have it that, though not every child *will* get ahead, still the responsibility of the schools is to make sure that the language of all children is "improved" enough so that any who do make it will be able to talk without calling attention to themselves among those who, by courtesy of the myths of our profession, speak "good English" because they already are among the ruling or at least the managing groups.

Put thus, this great organizing principle seems improbably crude; and it is surprising that it has persisted so long in the thinking of schoolmen. The persistence is the more surprising if it is remembered that another idea has been present to compete with the first since at least the publication of *Reorganization of English in the Secondary School* in 1917. There, to justify the amount of school time spent on English, the compiler of the report (James Fleming Hosic) said that "the relation of language to the expanding life is so close that to drop . . . speaking, writing, and reading at any point in the school program would be like ceasing to take food." Had Hosic and the members of the Joint Committee followed out the implications of the figure, (perhaps they did not even see them), they would have had to develop techniques to make the English classroom a place where children grow in and by using (not practicing the use of) their language.

But neither Hosic nor the Joint Committee seem to have noticed what they had said. And their operational recommendations follow the old assumption that school is a place where children study about a language that is rather better than their own, acquiring thereby the principles of "English" that will allow them to improve their own (necessarily inadequate) speech and writing. Indeed, I have been somewhat unfair. For the words deleted from Hosic's civilized and humane remark are "that to drop the systematic practice of." In the antithesis between "systematic practice" and the implications of taking food, there is embodied a radical contradiction between ends and means. On the one hand, the profession sets itself the end of encouraging the growth of children through English. On the other hand, the only means it has yet devised are derived from the techniques of teachers of the ancient dead languages ("which amongst us are called the learned"), and consist of "systematic practice" in the uses of English and more or less systematic study of one or another, or a mixture of several, of the grammars presenting English in an analytical and perhaps somewhat regularized form. The situation is in no way a happy one. And at the moment the best thing to be said is only that—perhaps as a result of the Dartmouth Conference—there is now a possibility that we can recognize the problem we have given ourselves.

CHAPTER VI

Language Acquisition and Development in Early Childhood

VERA P. JOHN
and
SARAH MOSKOVITZ

Introduction [1]

Children emerge as skillful speakers by the end of their preschool years. Their utterances tend to be grammatical, and in most instances their pronunciation of speech sounds is intelligible. Although the vocabulary of children ready to enter school varies widely, most children's social use of language is well developed, and some have started to discover the intellectual functions of language.

Throughout most of the twentieth century, students of language acquisition in preschool years have been content to describe the rate and sequence of this development. The linguist focused on the acquisition of sounds, while the acquisition of vocabulary was the domain of the psychologist. But theoretical work was lacking in both fields. In addition, the lack of effective interdisciplinary effort contributed to a somewhat pedestrian approach to the study of the exciting process of language acquisition.

Even when important theoretical contributions were made to a theory of language development, such as Piaget's early volume (94), Jakobson's contribution (52) to the study of phonological development, or Vygotsky's studies (125) of language and thought, the impact of these ideas was not reflected in theoretical controversies and imaginative research until the midcentury.

1. The preparation of this review was facilitated by an abundance of background information available as a result of research grants to the senior author (Ford Foundation Grant #67-435 and Office of Economic Opportunity Grant #2440). The assistance of Anne Eisenberg, Marshall Peller, and Pauline Papageorge is gratefully acknowledged by the authors.

Nevertheless, the study of language development has an honored position in the social and behavioral sciences. One indication of its status is the wealth of available reviews of the topic. Among the classical psychological reviews of this field are McCarthy's summaries (85). The linguistic literature was summarized in Leopold's (76) bibliography on child language, written in 1952.

During the 1950's, the field of language acquisition underwent a remarkable change. A new interest in systematic approaches, and in suggestive ideas about language development resulted in the study of the writings of developmental theorists such as Piaget, Bruner, and Vygotsky. It was in the context of the diversified collaborative efforts of psychologists and linguists that the new discipline of *psycholinguistics* emerged. In Boston, an outstanding group of scholars (which included among others Jakobson, Miller, Carroll, Chomsky, and Brown) joined together in the training of the first generation of psycholinguists, whose work represents a radical departure from the research on language during the first half of the century. More recent reviews prepared since the publication of the authoritative summaries by McCarthy and Leopold reflect the new interdisciplinary point of view of psycholinguistics.

The emphasis on theory also included a reexamination of Benjamin Lee Whorf's ideas. Although disagreeing with some of his notions of linguistic determination, sociologists and anthropologists developed a heightened interest in language. The result of this development was the beginning of *sociolinguistics*.

These new groups of interdisciplinary scholars were particularly concerned with the early grammatical development of young children, hence the multitude of research and reviews on this topic (1, 86, 112, 13).

The most comprehensive reviews of language development were written by Ervin, first in the Sixty-second Yearbook of the National Society for the Study of Education (39) and in a more recent article (37) in which she covers phonological, grammatical, and syntactical development. In view of the proficiency and availability of existing reviews, the authors have decided to complement them, and thus avoid unnecessary duplication. In addition, this paper is concerned with other areas which have not been treated as extensively—in particular those considered relevant to current debates surrounding classroom problems and practices.

This chapter will be divided into the following sections: (*a*) a discussion of differences in language skills as a function of social class; (*b*) an exploration of the role of language in learning and thought; and (*c*) a description of various preschool programs with a language focus.

The Social Context of Language Acquisition: Studies of Social Class Variations

Presently, the study of language acquisition in children is infused with dynamism born of controversy. The debate is particularly lively between the *nativists* (Chomsky, Lenneberg, McNeill and collaborators), who tend to impute innate language mechanisms to the young child,[2] and the *behaviorists* (Skinner, Staats, Jenkins and Palermo, Cofer and Sapon) whose stands differ on particulars although they all agree upon the central role of reinforcement in language learning.[3]

A fundamental role is given to the social environment in the theories of the behaviorists, but Chomsky and McNeill minimize its contribution. However these two groups of theorists do not always speak of the same aspects of language. By definition, Chomsky states that "all human languages share deep-seated properties of organization and structure. These properties—these linguistic universals—can be plausibly assumed to be innate mental endowment rather than the result of learning" (28:68). He restricts his discussion to the development of syntax. But those whose emphasis is upon the role of the social environment have drawn most of their empirical evidence from studies of vocabulary development and measurements of the rate of preverbal and verbal output. They have been

2. "In formal terms, then, we can describe the child's acquisition of language as a kind of theory construction. The child discovers the theory of his language with only small amounts of data from that language. Not only does his 'theory of the language' have an enormous predictive scope, but it also enables the child to reject a great deal of the very data on which the theory has been constructed (28:66)."

3. "I suggest that learning of inflectional and syntactical skills is akin to concept formation, and that its rate of occurrence may well be governed by such variables as number of instances, reinforcement contingencies, and all of the other variables pertinent to concept formation (29:198)."

impressed with the findings on children raised in institutions, with studies of birth-order differences, and with research on children raised in poverty, all of which show significant differences in verbal skills among children of varying early linguistic environments. In the following sections, a developmentally organized review of studies relating to the effects of social environment on language acquisition will be presented.

PRELINGUISTIC STAGE

The earliest vocalizations of infants are vowel-saturated; their cooing becomes interspersed with consonants by the age of five months. The six-months-old infant starts to babble, and it is at this age that the frequency and types of sounds uttered by deaf children become distinct from those of their hearing age-mates (74). The rate of vocalization has been increased in young infants by experimental manipulations. Rheingold (102) has shown that even two days of conditioning of three-months-old infants results in substantial increments in sound production. Rheingold has also examined the amount of talk directed to the young infant in family environments in contrast with institutional settings (101). The large difference in verbal output favoring the home may be one of the variables involved in the oft-repeated findings of the deleterious effects of institutions upon language development (15). In a systematic study comparing different conditions of stimulation and reinforcement, Weisberg (128) found that social stimulation contingent upon the child's vocalization was effective. These findings lend support to those who subscribe to a reinforcement model of learning.

Social class differences have also been shown to affect vocalizations. Irwin (51) has found that the number and frequency of sound productions differ from the age of eighteen months on, between middle and low-income children. In a subsequent study, Irwin tested the hypothesis that systematically reading stories to children between the ages of thirteen and thirty months would increase their phonetic production. He found a significant increase among those working-class children who belonged to the experimental group of the study.

Though these studies have often been quoted in support of a

learning approach to language development, Cazden (25) warns against an extension of these findings on vocalization behavior to verbal behavior, in view of the possible discontinuity between these aspects of development.

THE COMPREHENSION OF SPEECH

Fry (41) maintains that the ability to listen is influenced by the amount of speech the child hears and by the coupling of situational variations with speech variations. The testing of speech comprehension, however, without reliance upon overt speech is difficult. In a well-known study by Pasamanick and Knobloch (92) the authors, using the *Gesell Developmental Scale*, found significantly higher scores on verbal comprehension in a group of two-year-old Negro children than on verbal responsiveness. Similar conclusions were reached in a study of school-age children by Carson and Rabin (24), who also reported greater differences in verbal communication than in comprehension. In both of these studies the children were drawn from low-status homes.

In some studies there has been a confounding of effects between low-income status and membership in an ethnic group with speech patterns at variance with the Standard English of the white examiner. In a study of children's comprehension of teacher and peer speech, Peisach found "that Negro and lower-class children were penalized less by speech samples derived from children of similar background" (93:467). Baratz (3) has sharply criticized investigators who neglect dialect differences in their study of comprehension skills of Negro children.

SEMANTIC DEVELOPMENT

The preverbal infant perceives a verbal label as one of a multitude of attributes of an object (shape, weight, color, name). By the repeated association of seeing and touching the object and hearing the name of the object or person, the child acquires a bond between word and referent. The words first learned are embedded in a sentence (the verbal context), and their referents (the objects to be paired with the words) are surrounded by a multitude of extraneous features in the environment. Learning words requires selective attention—the inhibition of irrelevant aspects of the learning environment.

Although conditioning models have been proposed by some as a model of semantic development (see Jenkins and Palermo (53) for a particularly sophisticated approach), others have favored a more cognitive model. Briefly described, it consists of the continuous development and testing of tentative notions (hypotheses) about the meaning of words through verbal interaction with more verbally mature speakers.[4]

The developmental sequence characteristic of early semantic growth has often been described. The global communicative behavior of the infant—crying, kicking, pointing, pulling—is a precursor to what Skinner has called "mands"—attempts to elicit specific gratifying responses from the child's caretakers. Before his first birthday, the child also displays some passive command of words.

The first words of communicative effectiveness appear at age one, but precise estimates are difficult to obtain inasmuch as information is primarily derived from parental reports and diary studies.

The child's one-word utterances, or *holophrases*, have semantically and syntactically a different range than the single-word utterances of older children and adults.[5] First words tend to be nouns, verbs, and interjections. Their form is sometimes that of the repeated syllable. Lewis (79), in his discussion of the child's modification of the word "flower" to "fa-fa," illustrates how children's comprehension precedes production, a tendency which has been documented by other authors. During the second year of life the child's control of vocabulary expands rapidly; Smith (in 85:524) estimates that the average two-year-old has a vocabulary of 272 words.

Of great theoretical interest is the toddler's sudden demand for labels. The Sterns (115) describe how children between the ages of one and two point to objects and then wait to be told their names. Such active elicitation of names from older speakers lends

4. See Brown's description of reference games (17:313), Vygotsky's (125) discussion of word meaning acquisition and John and Goldstein (56).

5. Luria (81) reports a study by Rozegart-Pupko "who has shown that in the initial stage the word reflects not the object as a whole but only some major aspect of the object and this results in the 'diffuseness' or generalization of early verbal meanings to which many authors have referred (p.18)."

support to the theory of semantic acquisition favored by the authors, a process characterized by hypothesis development and testing.

The age at which significant differences in vocabulary performance among children of different socioeconomic groups appear has not been agreed upon, although many studies indicate that these differences have been established by age three. In a carefully designed study, Golden and Birns (42) found no differences among one and two-year-old welfare, low- and middle-status children on the verbal items of the *Cattell Infant Scale*. In a study of four- and five-year-old Negro children, Stodolsky (119) did find significant differences among similar groups of children on the *Peabody Picture Vocabulary Test*. Of particular interest is her finding of greater score variability among low-income than among middle-income children. In a study of ethnicity and social class, Lesser *et al.* (77) found interesting pattern differences among Chinese, Jewish, Negro, and Puerto Rican first-graders. Jewish children excelled in verbal skills, while Chinese children ranked first in space-conceptualization. The scores of middle-class children of all ethnic groups showed less variation from each other than did the somewhat lower scores of lower-class children, a trend which gave further support to other findings concerning variability in performance among low-income groups.

A number of other investigators have found social class differences in vocabulary skills among preschool and school-age children (120, 87, 72). Deutsch and associates (35) have reported that the effects of social class are cumulative; fifth-grade children, for instance, reveal greater differences in performance on language tasks than do first-grade children.

The consistency of results in these studies has given rise to generalizations such as the one by Williams and Naremore. They state that "limited verbal capabilities are often seen as the most evident deficit in preschool and school children from poverty and disadvantaged populations" (132:iv).

But these authors, together with many others, may err in proposing conclusions at this stage of our knowledge. The following considerations appear relevant in the discussion of this issue:

Heterogeneity.—Hylan Lewis (78) who has found sharply

varied child-rearing practices in the ghetto, suggests that it is inaccurate to conceptualize families in the Negro inner-city as representing a homogeneous population: culturally shaped variations lead to a great diversity among low-income groups in the United States.[6] Debilitating health conditions are another source of variability among low-income children;[7] in some studies, children in various stages of poor health are carefully excluded, while in others with different sampling strategies, they are unknowingly included.

Test construction.—In testing children from varied social backgrounds, the problem of representativeness of items in tapping verbal and nonverbal experiences presents itself. Baratz (3) has suggested that vocabulary tests such as the *Peabody Picture Vocabulary Test* are biased against Negro children. In a study of low-income children of kindergarten age, Thomas (122) found that only half of their spoken vocabulary overlapped with the vocabulary of school readers. In an item-analysis of the *PPVT*, John and Goldstein (56) found that urban four-year-olds failed to pass items such as "bush" and "nest," and they also had difficulty with experientially rare items, such as "kangaroo" and "caboose."

The coding skill of children drawn from diverse backgrounds was compared by Heider, Cazden, and Brown (46). They found that their subjects, who were drawn from two status groups, varied in style and effectiveness of coding. But when low-income children were directed to engage in a more effective style of information-conveying, they could do so. The authors raised the problem of whether cognitive and motivational variables may become confounded in some studies of social class differences.

6. Children are affected by the urban or rural setting of their home; ethnic differences in performance profiles have been shown by Lesser *et al.* Different language and cultural traditions are found by those who work with bilingual children. Recognizing these patterns, Stodolsky and Lesser favor maximum development of culturally specific skills, and, at the same time, greater equalization of opportunity and achievement of all groups.

7. In a review article Birch states: "In brief, though much of the information is incomplete, though certain aspects of the data are sparse, a serious consideration of available health information leaves little or no doubt that children who are economically and socially disadvantaged and in an ethnic group exposed to discrimination, are exposed to massively excessive risks for maldevelopment (9:30-31)." Pasamanick and Knobloch (92) have found minor brain damage, distractibility, and overactivity, as well as some visual and/or hearing impairment.

Motivation and class differences.—In discussing preschool intervention programs for disadvantaged children, Zigler and Butterfield
presented the following position: "performance on an intelligence
test is best conceptualized as reflecting three distinct factors: (*a*)
formal cognitive processes; (*b*) informational achievements which
reflect the content rather than the formal properties of cognition,
and (*c*) motivational factors which involve a wide range of personality variables" (134:2).[8]

Zigler and Butterfield reported an ingenious study in which
they tested preschool children at the beginning and at the end of a
nine-month intervention program. They developed methods for
obtaining an "ideal" as well as a "standard" estimate of intelligence
by varying the motivational components of the testing situation; a
ten-point increment in scores was obtained under the ideal condition. At the end of the program, the two sets of scores were closer,
and the authors concluded that their subjects "were better able to
use their intelligence in a standard testing situation." Although this
process has not been tried in vocabulary testing, it is possible that
a similar situation exists.

In short, it is likely that social class differences in vocabulary
performance are subject to variations as a function of test and motivational variables. In addition, because of the enormous *within-class*
variation, it is important to carefully evaluate groups of disadvantaged children in lieu of taking for granted the widespread belief
of their verbal limitations.

STUDIES OF SYNTAX

In most of the studies discussed thus far, the environmentalist
approach to language growth was stressed. The nativist position has
had particular impact upon those studying the acquisition of gram-

8. "A culturally deprived child may have an adequate storage and retrieval
system, a formal cognitive feature, to master quickly the correct answer to the
Binet vocabulary item 'What is a gown?' but may respond incorrectly because he has never heard the word 'gown' and thus has had no chance to
achieve this particular content or piece of knowledge. Alternatively, the role
of motivational factors can be seen in that instance in which the culturally
deprived child, whose experiences have led him to be fearful and wary, knows
what a gown is, but responds 'I don't know' in order to terminate as quickly
as possible the unpleasantness of interacting with a strange and demanding
adult (134:2)."

176 LANGUAGE ACQUISITION & DEVELOPMENT

mar in young children (18, 39, 112). There are a number of features of early grammatical acquisition which lend support to Chomsky's position—a position ascribing innate properties to language organization and structure. Lenneberg (74) cited young children's ability to rapidly acquire complex syntactical patterns in spite of environmental and physical handicaps. Brown and his co-workers (18) documented striking similarities in sequence of acquisition, regardless of large differences in the rate of grammatical acquisition. Brown, Cazden, and Bellugi also indicated that young children did not combine words randomly; their errors were those of omission and overgeneralization. In both instances, the children were thought to be in the process of developing patterns of their own instead of imitating adult patterns.

A study in grammatical development in very young children was conducted by Shipley, Smith and Gleitman (109); they compared the effectiveness of commands constructed to vary in syntactical complexity. Their subjects were toddlers, one group of which were at the *holophrastic* level of functioning (they spoke in one-word phrases), while the second group of subjects were at the more developed *telegraphic* stage (they were combining words, although omitting inflections and function words). Their findings were complex; the telegraphic children performed best when the commands were well-formed instead of telegraphic, while the less linguistically mature children responded best to one-word commands. The developmental strategies which the authors of this study used in attempting to account for the young child's skill in dealing with complex linguistic inputs were two-fold. They wrote of a filtering device; young children tuned out with nonsense words and highly complex sentences. In addition, the authors relied upon repetition in approaching the linguistic environment selectively.

The work of Brown and his associates is well known. Of particular concern are the comparisons they have made between middle-class white and low-income Negro children (18). One study relates to the development of inflection in these children roughly between ages two and three.[9] The data gathered from three longi-

9. The pattern discerned by Brown and his associates provides an interesting illustration of the role of overgeneralization. During the first period a particular feature, such as possessive plurals, was totally absent. During the next period of time the feature was produced occasionally, but with no errors

tudinal studies were compared with the protocols of eleven lower-
class Negro children from Roxbury. Cazden (26) concluded from
these comparisons:

> The overgeneralizations made by the two groups of children are
> strikingly similar. The Roxbury children not only make the same kind
> of errors; they even make them with many of the identical words. . . .
> To the extent that analogical errors indicate the rules in children's gram-
> mars, these data suggest that dialect differences do not make much
> difference at these early stages. It seems likely that the strategies or
> processes by which children learn that structure are also the same
> (26:17).

In the debate between environmentalists and nativists, one frequent question is: Can the acquisition of syntax be accelerated by
environmental intervention, and if so, what are the most effective
methods? Cazden (25) compared the effectiveness of *expansion*—
the response of adults to telegraphic sentences by completion—to
the effectiveness of *modeling*—the intervention characterized by
ample exposure to well-formed speech. She found that, contrary to
prediction, modeling is a more effective treatment than expansion.
This finding gives support to the notion that the richness-impov-
erishment dimension of the environment is a critical condition in
the development of syntax.

Comparative studies of syntactical development of preschool
children yield somewhat contradictory results. Osser (91) found
that low-income Negro children had a more limited range of syntactical structures than middle-class white children. The children's
syntax was analyzed by means of transformational grammar, and
dialect differences were minimized by a method of functional equivalence. In a study using a similar approach, Head Start Negro children were shown to perform within the expected developmental
range, according to Baratz and Povich (4). In a study of older
children, LaCivita, Kean, and Yamamoto (70) found that, contrary
to expectations, low- and high-income children performed equally
well on a task requiring syntactical sophistication. Lawton (73), on
the other hand, found social class differences in a British study;

---

of overgeneralization, and production increased markedly. During the last
period, the criterion of correctness (set by the researchers as 90 percent correct) was reached, and overgeneralizations decreased.

lower-class children used simpler syntactical structures. Loban (80) found a difference in the use of subordination to be related to social class. A recently completed bibliography, *Language and Poverty* (132), lists other studies in addition to those mentioned in this review.

Cazden proposed that *"the acquisition of grammar and the acquisition of vocabulary require different kinds of environmental assistance"* (27:12).

Although many research workers expected to find pervasive differences in grammatical skills as a function of social class to substantiate further the linguistic deficiency hypothesis, the differences which emerge are limited. At the earliest stages the guess advanced by Ervin-Tripp—namely, that "children in different dialect communities have identical grammars up to a point (though their parents do not). These might be rules which in fact disappear in later stages of development" (38:42)—seems to be supported by the limited amount of current evidence.

The interpretation of studies of sequential language in older children is particularly difficult in the case of the nonstandard speaker. Most research workers elicit speech from children in a single encounter and in a limited setting. However, Labov (68) has shown that the performance of nonstandard speakers varies according to tasks, settings, and motivation. Labov (69) concluded from a number of studies that he conducted that Negro children are frequently labeled as nonverbal, and that this labeling obscured the fact that they are proficient over a wide range of verbal skills. More carefully controlled studies of dialect variations are being conducted by Bailey (2), Stewart (118), Shuy (110), and Dillard (33), who have described some of the parameters of Negro nonstandard English. They have offered teachers many valuable suggestions for developing effective mastery of two dialects.

STUDIES OF VERBAL LEARNING

Are there differences in learning proficiency among children drawn from various socioeconomic backgrounds? Though many researchers have assumed on the basis of achievement-test results that low-income children will perform below others in learning tasks, there is increasing evidence that this is not the case. The most impressive findings have been reported by Rohwer (104) in a large-scale study of children ranging from preschool to high school age. Jensen (54), Rohwer, and their co-workers have found that on tasks such as digit-span, paired-associate, and serial learning, children drawn from low- and high-status groups performed equally well. Both groups profited from experimental conditions in which verbal and pictorial facilitation was included in the presentation of paired-associate items. (The implications of visual and verbal elaboration in learning will be discussed further in the next section of the chapter.) It is of interest that, while correlations between learning proficiency and intelligence tests were sizeable for middle-class children, these correlations were very low for low-income children. Rohwer argued that the laboratory conditions which facilitate attention and yield information about the adequacy of the child's performance contribute to the heightened performance of low-income children in contrast to their assessed proficiency in the classroom setting.

SUMMARY

Though the special features of the young child's verbal world have hardly been studied,[10] most authors ascribe an important role to parent-child dialogue in the development of language. Vocabulary development reflects most clearly the significant effects of verbal interaction in the home. Stodolsky (119) has shown that both the quality of the mother's language and her teaching style contribute to her child's verbal development as measured by vocabulary-test performance. Lesser (77) found that middle-class Jewish children excelled on verbal skills while children from other ethnic groups excelled on nonverbal tasks. This proficiency may be a reflection of the traditional emphasis among Jewish families on the "word."

A pervasive verbal deficit has been ascribed to low-income children. In this brief survey a more complex picture emerges. Low-income children equal their middle-income peers on certain tasks, even when the experimenter is geared toward a further documentation of differences. Labov (69), in studies with teen-agers, and Pasamanick and Knobloch (92), in work with very young children,

10. A notable exception is Horner's study (49).

have illustrated the difficulty involved in assessing accurately the varied verbal skills of children drawn from one subcultural group by the methods and expectations based upon the life-style of another group. Cross-cultural comparisons and comparisons across class lines are fraught with methodological and theoretical problems.

The Role of Language in Learning and Thought

INTRODUCTION

In his *Theory of Instruction* Bruner wrote of language: "Teaching is vastly facilitated by the medium of language, which ends by being not only the medium of exchange but *the* instrument the learner can use himself in bringing order into the environment" (21:6). The dual functions of language—communicative and intellective—have been emphasized by many theorists as crucial to learning. Piaget, however, viewed language as having secondary importance in the growth of intelligence. In an essay entitled, "Language and Thought from the Genetic Point of View," he stated that:

> Language is not enough to explain thought, because the structures that characterize thought have their roots in action and in sensorimotor mechanisms that are deeper than linguistics. It is also evident that the more the structures of thought are refined, the more language is necessary for the achievement of this elaboration. Language is thus a necessary but not a sufficient condition for the construction of logical operations (95:98).

The role of representations or schemata, the internal structures which are thought to be anchored in the motor behavior of the very young child, are emphasized by both Bruner and Piaget. It is of interest in beginning this discussion on the role of language to examine the relationship of words and acts in the life of the preschool child.

WORDS AND ACTS

The effects of words upon the actions of very young children have been studied by a number of Soviet investigators under the rubric of the "directive functions" of language. Some of the steps in the development of these functions are described by Luria: During the second year of life, most children have acquired a number of words; they will point to or hand someone an object when it is named. But when a twelve to fourteen-month-old is presented with two objects, his response when presented with a verbal request for one of these objects is influenced by the location of the other object. In Luria's words: "While the word easily directs behavior in a situation that lacks conflict, it loses its directive role if the immediate orientational reaction is evoked by a more closely located, or brighter, or more interesting object" (84:406). By the time they are three, some children have developed control over more complex actions, such as the ability to follow instructions formulated in conditional sentences (i.e., "when the light flashes, you will raise your hand"). Luria also describes how the initiation of a complex motor response, however difficult, is easier to bring about under verbal control than is its inhibition.

In an interesting addition to this series of experiments, subjects were taught to give themselves *self-commands*. Tikhomorov (123) has shown that three-year-old children can, if instructed, time their own verbal commands to the appearance of the signals given by the experimenter; such verbal self-commands are highly effective in their directive influence upon the child's motor behavior. This process starts during the preschool years, but continues, in different forms, to be of importance with older children and adults.

The role of verbalization in puzzle-assembly was investigated in an American study of four-year-olds. Stern and Lombard (116) found that practice accompanied by verbalization improved the children's performance with puzzles and formboards. Contrary to their expectations, however, practice with puzzle-assembly without verbalization was also effective. They pointed out in their discussions that both *verbal and non-verbal strategies* may well be involved in the solution of complex motor tasks.

WORDS AND PERCEPTION

The striking preoccupation of young children with the feel and appearance of objects, or with sounds made by animals and people, has interested developmental theorists (103). They have stressed the potency of perceptual qualities in determining the young child's orientation to his world.

One of the critical processes in perception is the differentiation between figure and ground. The object or design with figure characteristics holds the attention of the viewer in most instances. In two experiments with young children, Martsinovskaya and Abramayan have shown that verbal instructions can modify this relationship (reported in Luria [81]). Although adult instruction to the child to sequence his responses according to the background color was not effective in shifting the child's attention away from the figure, a modification in the experimental design brought about such a change. Abramayan found that by making speech commands more meaningful—that is, by giving a functional association to the background color—even three-year-old subjects could learn to reverse their attention and note background colors.

The Whorfian notion of linguistic determinism is of relevance to this discussion of words and perceptual attributes. Carroll and Casagrande's study (23)—an experimental comparison of Navajo-speaking and English-speaking children, all of whom lived on the Navajo reservation—is an example of a research project based on the Whorfian notion of language effects upon *perceptual salience*. The Navajo-speaking children matched objects according to shapes (the stimuli were chosen to represent those shapes which are signaled in Navajo verb-forms) while the English-speaking Navajo children chose color as a basis for matching. However, an additional control group of children from Massachusetts behaved similarly to their Navajo-speaking age-peers. The results were interpreted to indicate that language as well as nonlanguage influences (such as experience with educational toys) can both affect matching behavior.

Brown added an important elaboration to the notions of linguistic determinism by introducing the concept of codability.[11] The experimental investigations on codability by Brown and Lenneberg

11. "I will go further and propose that a perceptual category that is frequently utilized is more available than one less frequently utilized. When the Eskimo steps from his igloo in the morning, I expect him to see snow as falling into one or another of his single word-name categories. For the American who is only able to name these categories with a phrase (low codability) I do not expect such ready categorization of snows. If, however, the American were subjected to a discrimination learning experiment, if he were studying the Eskimo language, or if the perceptual structures were otherwise worth his while, he could see snow as the Eskimo does. It is proposed really that categories with shorter names (higher codability) are nearer the top of the cognitive deck—more likely to be used in ordinary perception, more available for expectancies and inventions (16:236)."

(19) and Lantz (71) were carried out with adults as subjects: color naming and color recognition were studied. The concept of codability is of particular importance to this discussion because of its relevance to the study of *semantic development* in children. Lantz found that codability scores (the ease with which the name of a color was successfully communicated) correlated to a low degree with success on a recognition task when the task was simple. However, a much higher correlation was obtained by substituting a more complex task in which four colors at a time were to be recognized.

One more study with adults illustrates further an emerging principle which ties all of these studies together. Naming can have a highly positive effect for certain tasks, while it has a negative effect in other tasks. Ranken (98) found that prior name-learning (where geometrical objects were used as stimuli) had a positive effect on a memory task, but that the same condition inhibited performance in a jigsaw-puzzle task. The author found support for his interpretation that *nominal* and *imaginal* representations differ in their properties.

Some work with children, such as that done by Whipple and Maier (129), illustrates trends similar to those found by Ranken. Many have commented on reciprocal relationships between verbal and nonverbal aspects of development in very young children. The relationship is not a simple one, however. It is possible that mutually enhancing as well as mutually inhibiting connections exist between different overt skills and covert representational processes. The antecedent variables of social and family life may have some role in shaping these connections. The findings of Lesser *et al.* (77) of differences in performance profiles in New York City first-grade pupils drawn from different ethnic communities include descriptions of the relative superiority of Chinese children in spatial tasks and a lack of such excellence in verbal tasks. This may be a reflection of a covert ordering of verbal and nonverbal representational processes. Koch's study (64) of five-and six-year old children indicates that firstborn children have greater proficiencies in verbal skills than children of other birth orders, while the latter-born excel in nonverbal tasks. She interpreted her birth-order findings to be related to the scope of intellectual stimulation which is available to first-born children.

Bruner characterizes the intellectual development of young children in three consecutive stages. He describes a progression that starts with *enactive* representation rooted in actions. The *iconic* stage, in which the child's perceptual processes and imagery are emphasized, follows. Finally, the child learns to rely upon words as a form of representation: this stage is called *symbolic*. The nature of interrelationships between enactive, iconic, and symbolic representations needs systematic exploration. The findings of Ranken and other researchers indicate that nominal and imaginal representations are both involved, even in the adult. Bruner's and Piaget's theoretical notions have stimulated much-needed debate; as yet, however, thinking about thought, and about thought and language, is primitive.

THE EFFECTIVENESS OF LANGUAGE IN LEARNING AND MEMORY

The developmental theorists' inferences about imagery, schemata, and covert processes have been discussed. Learning theorists reflect an experimental tradition in which speculation about the "black box" is distrusted. In spite of their differing stances, there is a growing overlap between the concepts of these two groups.

Labeling.—In studies of discrimination learning, the effectiveness of verbal responses has been conceptualized as adding to the distinctiveness of cues. The facilitating effects of naming have been shown by Spiker and his co-workers (114) in a well-designed series of studies. Children who had difficulty differentiating between a group of pen-drawn faces were taught to label them during pretraining; their subsequent performance excelled that of children who were given training in "attention." In addition, these investigators have shown that labels which are highly distinctive produce more effective performance in children than do labels (even nonsense words) which lack in distinctiveness. The role of self-verbalization, mentioned above in connection with the Soviet studies, was also found useful. Spiker reported that in all groups "many Ss invented and rehearsed their own verbal names for the stimuli and those who did so consistently learned better than those who did not" (114:71).

The developmental emergence of verbalization between the

ages of four and seven as an aid to learning has been studied by Tracy and Howard Kendler (60). Their focus was upon the mediating response, a crucial link in behavioral theory between simple and complex processes.[12]

The effectiveness of mediating responses is studied when children are faced with a task requiring a response to one of two cues—color or size. The child acquires the correct responses based on the first cue (i.e. color). He then is expected to shift either to the opposite color (white to black) and thus demonstrate a reversal shift, or to size, in a nonreversal shift. Verbalization of the relevant cue-dimension correlates highly with correct performance in reversal shift, as predicted by the investigators. Experimentally induced verbalizations are particularly effective with the four-year-old subjects; the older children are presumed to have learned to verbalize spontaneously.

Little attention was paid to the form of verbal responses in the work of the Kendlers and in the research of Spiker and his coworkers. It is useful, however, to differentiate between *naming*, or labeling, and the production of more complex utterances during learning and recall. The effectiveness of labeling was described by Cofer (29) as of particular significance in the identification, discrimination, and classification of elements. Studies relying upon sentence-produced (in contrast to single-label-produced) facilitation will be described below.

The role of labeling in *recall* is illustrated by a number of studies with children. Kurtz and Hovland (67) have emphasized the effectiveness of *overt* naming; subjects under this condition performed significantly better on a recognition task than did those who circled the names of the same objects without labeling them overtly. John (55) has indicated that the effectiveness of overt labeling is related to the magnification, through feedback, of the facilitating effects of language.[13]

12. "The mediator is a response, or series of responses which intercede between the external stimulus and the overt response to provide stimulation that influences the eventual course of behavior. These responses may be overt, but they are usually presumed to be covert (60:34)."

13. Brown describes, introspectively, a similar process—"how does one work at this task of delayed recognition? For myself, and for many subjects, it goes like this. When the color is removed the name can be retained, even

Sentence-produced facilitation.—In emphasizing codability, we stressed the manner in which the learner breaks up a perceptual dimension such as color into discretely labeled segments. By generating sentences, the learner can also link together spatially or temporally discrete aspects of the environment, and thus his language serves as a synthetic device.

The most interesting example of this aspect of language in learning is illustrated by Rohwer's programatic research (104) on sentence elaboration in paired-associate learning. In experiments with older school-age subjects, he has shown the effectiveness of sentence elaboration when compared with naming only the pairs of stimuli. After systematic examination of the sentence properties necessary for facilitating learning, Rohwer reported that ". . . facilitation was produced only by contextual strings that were both grammatical and meaningful. Furthermore, a form-class effect was obtained such that learning was most efficient with verb connectives, less (but not significantly so) with prepositions, and least with conjunctions" (104:296).

In a similar experiment with children ranging from two to seven years of age, Reese (99) found that verbal description of action, and visual depiction of such action, increased the learning of paired pictures.

It is in this context that Rohwer has been studying the role of elaborative processes in learning; he has found a highly consistent and marked effect of verbal and *visual* forms of elaboration. Positive effects of elaborative learning (as described above) were found among preschool children as well as among older children.

These findings may shed light on a recurrent controversy in the field of language and cognition. Deaf children have often served as subjects in studies aimed at assessing the efficacy of verbal mediation in learning and problem-solving. Oleron (89) and Furth (40) have shown that deaf children are deficient in their performance on a variety of tasks, such as *double-alteration* and *weight-conservation*. Usually this performance lag is ascribed to language handicap

---

rehearsed. Somehow, names are responsive to volition, in a way that images are not. Then you search around the perimeter of the wheel of colors, testing each chip against the name to see whether the two belong together. When the chip is found which best deserves the name, that is recognition (17:334)."

and is used as one argument for the importance of language mediation. But Furth argues that language has been exaggerated in its role; he believes that most contemporary theorists neglect nonverbal processes in their thinking about thought.

It is possible that psychologists, in their closeness to the workings of a highly technical society have failed to explore alternative representations of reality. On the other hand, the tutors of the deaf, whose goal it is to help the older deaf child bridge the gap between himself and hearing children, may excel in an intuitive understanding of visual elaboration, as shown by Rohwer in his studies.

THE ROLE OF LANGUAGE IN CLASSIFICATION

The child's grouping of events—recurrent sounds, similar objects, family rituals—into categories of alikeness is considered a critical developmental task. It is by means of implicit and explicit classifications that the child creates some order out of his fast-moving and overwhelmingly complex environment. Though classification is involved in simple perceptual and motor learning, the process gains significance when the child is confronted with multiple-dimensioned events. To ignore some attributes which are irrelevant to grouping, while observing systematic variations along other relevant dimensions, is the hard core of conceptual ordering.

Already, the young infant in his crib shows consistency in some of his preferences. He prefers moving objects to stationary ones; he attends selectively to complex designs (111); he is on his way to classification and abstraction.

But the acquisition of classificatory skills, in spite of the many promising beginnings that have been noted, is not a simple one.

Classificatory behavior is most often studied in the context of matching and sorting tasks; objects are chosen to vary along size, color, form, and functional dimensions. When four-year-olds are presented with objects which vary along a multiplicity of dimensions, they exhibit inconsistent behavior. Claparède's term for this approach is "incoherent coherence."

Vygotsky has described a progression in children's sorting behavior (125: ch. 5). The first stage consists of making "heaps." The child's basis of categorization seems arbitrary and often subjective. At a later stage, the child creates "complexes"—he now relies upon perceptually concrete and functional relationships. The final stage of "true concepts" requires the combination of synthesis and analysis, and most children have reached their adolescence before they can sort in this manner. Vygotsky stresses the critical role of language in this evolving process.

In a study of verbal concepts, Olver and Hornsby describe how the youngest subjects (six-year-olds) "group more often according to perceptible properties than older children. Their protocols are laced with the colors, sizes, shapes and places of things" (90:72). Older children pay closer attention to more abstract dimensions. But children are slow in developing nominal groupings of their own: "the self-directed use of linguistic terms for categorizing objects demonstrates a gradual course of development" (90:82).

Is language a necessary and sufficient condition for a high level of concept formation? Stodolsky in a study of five-year-old kindergarten children, found that a minimum amount of language (as measured by a receptive vocabulary test) is necessary for adequate performance on a sorting task. "But after a minimum level of language has been attained, there are still other factors which enter into determining the child's level of thought" (119:51). The importance of nonverbal thought processes has been indicated in various studies throughout this discussion.

INTERPRETIVE SUMMARY

The child's intellectual development is a continuous process, but the acquisition of many skills fundamental to systematic learning and schooling appears to accelerate at the end of the preschool period. White (130) describes this critical transition between the ages of five and seven. He summarizes the empirical findings and theoretical conjecture when he states that the building of the second 'cognitive' layer either begins, or is most marked, in the period from five to seven. Of particular significance to this discussion on the role of language in learning and thought are two of the transitions he describes: (a) The ability to maintain orientation toward invariant dimensions of stimuli in a surround of variance, and (b) the ability to string together internal representations of stimulus-response-consequences into sequences which, projected into the future, allow planning and, projected into the past, allow inference.

Although White's description of these transitions is couched in the language of learning theory, there are definite similarities between the trends he reports and those discussed in this section. The approach is descriptive in both attempts. Is it possible at this early stage of our knowledge to speak of underlying mechanisms?

The theorist whose work appears most relevant in this regard is Vygotsky. He advances two major hypotheses; he argues that "a prelinguistic phase in the development of thought and a preintellectual phase in the development of speech are clearly discernible" (125:41). He further states that "a connection originates, changes and grows in the course of the evolution of thinking and speech (p. 119)." The link between these two processes is reflected in his theory of the processes of word-meaning acquisition; "the meaning of a word represents such a close amalgam of thought and language that it is hard to tell whether it is a phenomenon of speech or a phenomenon of thought" (p. 120).

In an extension of Vygotsky's notions, John and Goldstein (56) suggest one common mechanism of relevance to semantic and conceptual development. Generalizing a word from one setting to another requires the discovery of irrelevant variations which accompany the essential constancy. (This notion is akin to White's first transition.) Speech invariance may be the basis for forming a hypothesis concerning a corresponding invariance in the referent, Brown (16) suggests. The process of *hypothesis-testing* (searching for significant invariances in the environment) is thought to be one common process in the development of language and thought.

In brief, we suggest a close linkage between verbal and non-verbal conceptual development during the preschool years, while we reject any simple notion of identity of language and thought.

Preschool Intervention Programs with a Language Focus

A new and dramatic emphasis upon the preschool years as a critical period in the development of cognition has characterized much of the thinking of psychologists and educators during the sixties. The two most influential volumes in this regard are *Intelligence and Experience* by Hunt (50), and Bloom's *The Stability and Change in Human Characteristics* (12). Bloom writes, "The effects of the environment appear to be greatest in the early and most rapid periods of development (p. 88)." Some of the theoretical and empirical considerations substantiating the singular importance of the early environment on intellectual development are presented in the previous section.

The new emphasis upon early childhood coincided with significant social and political movements focused upon the improvement of educational opportunities for the poor.[14] (The best-known outcome of these developments is Project Head Start, established in 1965.) The target populations of preschool compensatory programs begun during the sixties include low-income children from Negro, Puerto-Rican, Mexican-American, Indian, and southern white communities. These communities are characterized by discrimination, unemployment or seasonal employment, poor health, poor nutrition (even hunger in some parts of the country), poor housing, and limited educational opportunities and attainment. The literature on the poor abounds in detailed inventories of their inadequacies; few members of the advantaged communities are able to see strengths in the people of the ghettoes. Most compensatory programs aim at overcoming the deficiencies of children raised in poverty, and the design and execution of these programs are the products of professional research and planning.

Currently, there are new attempts in some of the nonwhite communities (Rough Rock Demonstration School on the Navajo Reservation, Ocean Hill-Brownsville in New York, and others) to develop compensatory programs based upon the educational ideology and experience of the minority people themselves. But these efforts toward community control and ethnic education are just beginning, and cannot be reported upon in any detail. Indeed, the scope and diversity of intervention programs preclude comprehensive treatment in the context of this reviewing effort. Our brief survey is limited to a discussion of theoretical assumptions and model characteristics of various preschool programs and to a summarization of some of the evaluative information on the effectiveness of these programs which have language as their focus.

PROGRAM DESCRIPTIONS

Language enrichment programs: Deutsch, Gray and Weikart.—

14. A comprehensive discussion of education for disadvantaged children is found in Gordon (43).

Before national attention was focused upon preschool education as a possible antidote to later school failure among the poor, Deutsch in New York (35), Gray in Tennessee (63), and Weikart in Michigan (126) each independently initiated preschool enrichment programs. While all three program innovators eschewed a single theoretical orientation, many programatic similarities characterized their work. Their approach predated Bruner's writings on instruction quoted above, but they, like Bruner, conceived of the role of language as a vehicle and tool of learning and thought.

Many specific innovations are included in these preschools although the daily program in these settings draws heavily upon traditional nursery-school objectives and practices. Some of the teaching aids and techniques for fostering language which have been developed by Deutsch and his co-workers include listening centers, the Alphabet Board, varied use of the Language Master, and language lottoes. The principles of programed instruction were employed in the development of some of these techniques. These innovations have been developed in the context of educational objectives stated as follows: "The proper task for early childhood education of disadvantaged children is the identification of stimulation lacks in their environment; the diagnosis of the areas of retardation in cognitive development of the children; the prescription of particular stimuli strategies and techniques for the presentation in order to accelerate the development of retarded functions; and the evaluation of the efficiency of the techniques used" (35:381).

Deutsch's work at the Institute for Developmental Studies is characterized by a closely intermeshed program of research and intervention aimed at identifying characteristic patterns of learning in disadvantaged children and at developing methods of specialized remediation. In Gray's work, an individualized approach to the child's language is stressed, and concrete and social reinforcements are often used in rewarding the child for producing patterned language.[15]

Weikart has characterized these preschools as "programs em-

15. Detailed description of program objectives and implementation is available for these carefully designed and evaluated programs. In addition to the specific sources by the program innovators, the reader is referred to Stendeler-Lavatelli (117). An Office of Education publication, Survey of Compensatory Programs," by D. G. Hawkridge et al. (45) includes a good description of the Deutsch and Weikart programs.

ploying structured nursery school methods"—their emphasis is upon specific cognitive and language outcomes. The basic approach has been incorporated in the work of others. Particularly noteworthy is the program of Hodges, McCandless and Spicker (48). While Deutsch, Gray, and Weikart have focused on young Negro children, Hodges and his co-workers in Indiana have worked with young white children raised in poverty. Their emphasis has also been upon the development of language skills.

The emphasis upon language in these programs has many roots. Of particular importance is the influence of the British sociolinguist, Basil Bernstein. The restricted code, as described by Bernstein (8), is the basis of some widely held assumptions about the language of low-income children and adults. He characterizes the speaker of this code as the one whose verbal exchanges are highly predictable; in contrast, a speaker of the elaborated code reflects his individual status by expanding and elaborating his meanings. Many educators have argued that lower-class individuals are limited by the restricted code and consequently are handicapped in their ability and skill in developing abstractions.[16] Although this is a popular stance, it raises many theoretical questions which are as yet unresolved (see previous section). Nevertheless, Deutsch, Gray, Weikart, and many other workers have attempted to effect, by means of intervention, both the overt verbal productions of low-income children and the use of productive language for purposes of abstraction.

Programs employing traditional nursery school methods.— While early-childhood educators recognize the importance of language in the development of children during their preschool years, their approach to fostering verbal skills differs from that of the "interventionists." They stress informal rather than formal teaching, although some formalized materials are used in many "traditional" classrooms. In their approach to intellectual development, the teacher takes cues from the children's own play activities and interests. He introduces language indirectly in the form of songs or rhymes. Verbal play grows out of the child's increasing knowledge of himself and his world through his play activities (62).

16. See, for example, the work of Hess and Shipman on maternal teaching styles and the effects of restricted language (47).

Programs of early stimulation for infants and toddlers.—The literature on the effects of social class background reveals no differences in the intellectual development of children of two years or younger (see our earlier discussion concerning the social context of language acquisition). Nevertheless, many workers believe that the quantity and quality of stimulation available to the very young child is causally linked to his later language and cognitive proficiency. Programs of early stimulation are based on this premise. Of particular interest is the work conducted at the Children's Center in Syracuse (22), an educationally oriented center for low-income children ranging in age from six-months to four years, and at the Infant Education Project of Washington, D.C. (108), a tutorial program for toddlers conducted in their homes. The former consists of a comprehensive program of research and intervention. To date, the results have been reported in fragments only, but the preliminary findings indicate a very promising approach for the care and development of young children of working mothers. Intellectual stimulation occurs in a setting of high adult-to-child ratio; cognitive learning is gamelike and accompanied by a warm, cuddling rapport between the children and their caretakers.

Songs, puzzles, walks, and books are used by the tutors in Washington in their enrichment work with toddlers. Siblings and parents are involved in the various phases of this innovative homebound program. The results of this intervention are presented below (see Table I); the findings of greatest theoretical interest are that the control children (those who were not subject to intervention) drop twenty points in their intelligence scores during a two-year period, while the experimental children maintain a slightly above-average score on the *Stanford-Binet* test.

Programs with a cognitive focus: the influence of Piaget.—While many programs have been successful in stimulating language development, particularly the growth of vocabulary in disadvantaged children, similar beneficial effects have not been reported in the development of verbal mediation.[17] The cognitive use of language and the development of skills in classification are stressed in the

17. Cynthia Deutsch (32) reports a failure in improved performance on a verbal mediation (Kendler concept-formation paradigm) while the experimental children improved in their scores on the *Illinois Test of Psycholinguistic Abiilties.*

TABLE 1. EVALUATION DATA ON PRESCHOOL INTERVENTION PROGRAMS

1. Deutsch, M., & Goldstein, L. Institute for Developmental Studies, New York University School of Education, New York. Project: Enriched Preschool Curriculum Early Childhood Project. Place: New York City. Reference: Hawkridge, D. G., et al. *A Study of Selected Exemplary Programs for the Education of Disadvantaged Children*, Part II. Final Report, U. S. Office of Education, Project No. 089013, 1968.

Groups or Waves	Type of Group	N	Binet				CMM					PPVT					ITPA				
			Pre	Post	Change	Diff.	N	Pre	Post	Change	Diff.	N	Pre	Post	Change	Diff.	N	Pre	Post	Change	Diff.
Wave 1 1962–63	E	32		102.2		10.0*			103.0		12.6*	31		90.4		10.7					
	C	12		92.2					90.4			12		79.7							
Wave 2 1963–64	E		93.0	99.0	6.0	9.0*		102.0	103.0	1.0	9.0*										
	C		92.0	90.0	−2.0			101.0	94.0	−7.0											
Wave 3 1964–65	E		92.0	101.0	9.0	8.0*															
	C		90.0	93.0	3.0																
Wave 4 1965–66	E		91.0	97.0	6.0	6.0*															
	C		89.0	91.0	2.0																
Wave 5 1966–67	E																				
	C																				
Wave 6 1967–68	E																				
	C																				

2. Gray, Susan, & Klaus, R. A. George Peabody College for Teachers, Nashville, Tenn. Project: Early Training Project for Disadvantaged Children. Place: City in the upper South. Reference: Klaus, R. A., & Gray, Susan W. "The Early Training Project for Disadvantaged Children: A Report after Five Years," *Monographs of the Society for Research in Child Development*, XXXIII (No. 4, Serial No. 120, 1968).

Groups or Waves	Type of Group	N	Binet Pre	Binet Post	Binet Change	Binet Diff.	CMM	Tests PPVT N	PPVT Pre	PPVT Post	PPVT Change	PPVT Diff.	ITPA N	ITPA Pre	ITPA Post	ITPA Change	ITPA Diff.
T₁: 10 week preschool over 3 summers and 3 yrs. wkly. meetings with a home visitor	E	19					Points at which results were significant:										
Sum. '62			87.6	102.0	14.4		Binet: Sum. '62 post-test		69.5	75.3	5.8						
Sum. '63			96.4	97.1	0.7		T₁ > T₂, T₃, T₄ at .05		79.0	78.4	-0.6						
Sum. '64				95.8			Sum. '63 post-test T₁ & T₂ > T₃ & T₄ at .05		81.2	83.0	1.8				21.1ᵃ		
T₂: 2 summers of special experiences and 2 yrs. meetings with a home visitor	E	19					PPVT: Sum. '62 post-test T₁ > T₂, T₃, T₄ at .05										
Sum. '63			94.8	97.5	2.7		ITPA: Sum. '64		69.6	83.6	14.0						
Sum. '64				96.6			T₁ & T₂ > T₃ & T₄ at .05		85.5	87.0	1.5				24.1		
T₃: local control group	C	18															
Sum. '62			85.4	88.2	2.8				66.4	65.8	-0.6						
Sum. '63			89.6	87.6	-2.0				69.3	64.0	-5.3						
Sum. '64				82.9					65.4	72.4	7.0				11.7		
T₄: control group 60 mi. away which could not interact with experimental group	C	24															
Sum. '62			86.9	88.2	1.3				74.0	62.9	-11.1						
Sum. '63			87.4	85.8	-1.6				70.2	65.5	-4.7						
Sum. '64				80.8					71.5	70.9	-0.6				8.3		

3. Spicker, H. H.; Hodges, W. L.; & McCandless, B. Indiana University. Project: A Diagnostically Based Curriculum for Psycho-Socially Deprived Preschool Mentally Retarded Children. Place: Bloomington, Indiana. Reference: Hawkridge, et al., op. cit.

<table>
<tr><th rowspan="3">Groups or Waves</th><th rowspan="3">Type of Group</th><th colspan="20">Tests</th></tr>
<tr><th colspan="5">Binet</th><th colspan="5">CMM</th><th colspan="5">PPVT</th><th colspan="5">ITPA</th></tr>
<tr><th>N</th><th>Pre</th><th>Post</th><th>Change</th><th>Diff</th><th>N</th><th>Pre</th><th>Post</th><th>Change</th><th>Diff</th><th>N</th><th>Pre</th><th>Post</th><th>Change</th><th>Diff</th><th>N</th><th>Pre</th><th>Post</th><th>Change</th><th>Diff</th></tr>
<tr><td>EPS: experimental groups (studies I, II and III combined)</td><td>E</td><td>42</td><td>73.6</td><td>90.4</td><td>16.8</td><td></td><td>42</td><td>84.0</td><td>94.4</td><td>10.4</td><td></td><td>42</td><td>64.7</td><td>91.4</td><td>26.6</td><td></td><td>26</td><td>46.6[b]</td><td>64.7</td><td>18.1</td><td></td></tr>
<tr><td>KC: kindergarten groups (I, II and III combined)</td><td>C$_1$</td><td>44</td><td>75.3</td><td>87.5</td><td>12.3</td><td></td><td>43</td><td>84.0</td><td>90.3</td><td>6.3</td><td></td><td>44</td><td>68.3</td><td>83.0</td><td>14.6</td><td></td><td>27</td><td>51.3</td><td>63.7</td><td>12.5</td><td></td></tr>
<tr><td>AHC: At home contrast groups (I, II and III combined)</td><td>C$_2$</td><td>56</td><td>74.2</td><td>78.3</td><td>4.1</td><td></td><td>42</td><td>82.4</td><td>82.9</td><td>0.5</td><td></td><td>56</td><td>65.2</td><td>75.3</td><td>10.1</td><td></td><td>27</td><td>50.5</td><td>57.3</td><td>6.8</td><td></td></tr>
<tr><td></td><td></td><td colspan="5">Significant differences: EPS>KC>AHC</td><td colspan="5">Significant differences: EPS>KC>AHC</td><td colspan="5">Significant differences: EPS>KC>AHC</td><td colspan="5">Significant differences: EPS>KC>AHC</td></tr>
</table>

4. Weikart, D. P.; Kami, Constance K.; & Radin, Norma L., Ypsilanti, Michigan. Project: Perry Preschool Project. Place: Ypsilanti Public Schools, Ypsilanti, Michigan. Reference: Hawkridge, et al., op. cit.

<table>
<tr><th rowspan="2"> </th><th rowspan="2"> </th><th colspan="5">Binet</th><th colspan="5">CMM</th><th colspan="5">PPVT</th><th colspan="5">ITPA</th></tr>
<tr><th>N</th><th>Pre</th><th>Post</th><th>Change</th><th>Diff</th><th>N</th><th>Pre</th><th>Post</th><th>Change</th><th>Diff</th><th>N</th><th>Pre</th><th>Post</th><th>Change</th><th>Diff</th><th>N</th><th>Pre</th><th>Post</th><th>Change</th><th>Diff</th></tr>
<tr><td>Combined Waves 0, 1, 2, 3, 4 for 2-yr. period</td><td>E</td><td>Pr 57
Ps 43</td><td>79.6</td><td>94.7</td><td>15.1</td><td>11.2†</td><td></td><td></td><td></td><td></td><td></td><td>Pr 57
Ps 43</td><td>67.1</td><td>81.4</td><td>14.3</td><td>18.5†</td><td>Pr 55
Ps 43</td><td>2.8</td><td>4.8</td><td>2.0</td><td>0.8†</td></tr>
<tr><td></td><td>C</td><td>Pr 65
Ps 49</td><td>78.5</td><td>83.5</td><td>5.0</td><td></td><td></td><td></td><td></td><td></td><td></td><td>Pr 60
Ps 49</td><td>62.2</td><td>62.9</td><td>0.7</td><td></td><td>Pr 65
Ps 47</td><td>2.6</td><td>4.0</td><td>1.3</td><td></td></tr>
</table>

(ITPA: in standard scores)

5. DiLorenzo, L. T., & Salter, Ruth. New York State Education Department, University of the State of New York. Project: An Evaluation Study of Prekindergarten Programs for Educationally Disadvantaged Children. Place: Selected sites in the state of New York. Reference: DiLorenzo, L. T., & Salter, Ruth. "An Evaluative Study of Prekindergarten Programs for Educationally Disadvantaged Children: Follow-up and Replication." Paper read at the 1968 Annual Meeting of the American Educational Research Association, New York, February, 1968.

Tests

Wave	Groups or Waves	Type of Group	Binet N	Binet Pre	Binet Post	Binet Change	Binet Diff	CMM N	CMM Pre	CMM Post	CMM Change	CMM Diff	PPVT N	PPVT Pre	PPVT Post	PPVT Change	PPVT Diff	ITPA N	ITPA Pre	ITPA Post	ITPA Change	ITPA Diff
Wave 1: 1965-66	Spring Valley: lang.-focused general enrich.	E	32	90.5	86.9	3.6†	0.5						34	30.4°	44.1	13.7*	2.0	31		57.3		5.2
		C	21	86.8	83.7	-3.1							21	30.4	42.1	11.7*		18		52.1		
	Long Beach: gen. enrich.	E	24	93.7	93.5	-0.2	1.8						26	31.5	43.5	12.1*	3.4	22		59.2		5.1
		C	28	94.7	92.7	-2.0							28	32.2	40.9	8.7*		24		54.1		
	Schnectady: reading skill	E	41	90.3	91.8	1.5	4.5*						41	33.5	48.6	15.1*	5.3*	40		61.0		8.6*
		C	53	88.8	85.8	-3.0*							52	32.0	41.9	9.8*		52		52.5		
	Mt. Vernon: 1/2 ERE & 1/2 Montessori	E	49	91.4	89.5	-1.9	0.1						48	27.4	41.7	14.3*	2.2	45		52.7		5.5
		C	37	88.5	86.7	-1.8							37	25.2	37.3	12.1*		35		47.2		
Wave 2: 1966-67	Spring Valley: lang.-focused general enrich.	E	27	90.6	96.5	6.0*	7.5*						27	34.0	45.0	11.0*	4.2†	27		63.8		6.9*
		C	24	91.0	89.5	-1.5							24	31.8	38.6	6.8*		23		56.9		
	Long Beach: gen. enrich.	E	28	87.3	86.9	-0.4	0.4						28	26.4	38.4	11.9*	0.9	27		56.5		0.3
		C	29	86.6	86.5	-0.1							27	25.3	36.4	11.0		28		56.2		
	Schnectady: reading skill	E	41	93.8	98.3	4.5*	8.4*						41	32.2	42.8	10.6*	0.0	41		59.2		1.0
		C	38	92.9	89.0	-3.9*							38	33.7	44.3	10.6*		38		58.2		
	Mt. Vernon: 1/2 ERE & 1/2 Montessori	E	48	95.5	97.2	1.6	2.9						47	34.8	44.9	10.1*	0.7	47		59.2		1.7
		C	23	93.2	92.0	-1.3							23	33.7	44.6	10.8*		23		57.5		
	Cortland: small discussion group	E	19	87.3	98.0	10.7*	10.9*						19	34.2	43.5	9.4*	0.7	19		68.5		5.1
		C	19	91.7	91.5	-0.2							19	34.1	42.8	8.7*		19		63.5		
	Cortland: pattern drill (Bereiter)	E	23	94.5	103.6	9.1*	9.3*						22	36.2	48.2	12.1*	3.4	23		67.9		4.4
		C	19	91.7	91.5	-0.2							19	34.1	42.8	8.7*		19		63.5		

6. **Karnes, Merle B.** Institute for Research on Exceptional Children, College of Education, University of Illinois. Project: Program to Determine the Effects of Various Preschool Intervention Programs on the Development of Disadvantaged Children. Place: University of Illinois. Reference: Karnes, Merle B. "A Research Program to Determine the Effects of Various Preschool Intervention Programs on the Development of Disadvantaged Children and the Strategic Age for Such Intervention." Paper read at the Convention of the American Educational Research Association, New York, February, 1968.

• Tests

Groups or Waves	Type of Group	Binet N	Pre	Post	Change	Diff.	CMM N	Pre	Post	Change	Diff.	PPVT N	Pre	Post	Change	Diff.	ITPA N	Pre	Post	Change	Diff.
Working with Mothers (children's age, 3 & 4)	E	13	91.3	98.8	7.5	7.5*+															
	C	13	95.5	95.5	0.0																
Ameliora-tion of lrng. defi-cits (age 3)	E	15	94.5	111.4	16.9	19.7‡												33.3	50.1	16.8	9.1†
	C	14	91.3	88.5	−2.8													34.1	33.9	7.7	
Traditional age, 4-4 to 5-0, 10/65-6/66	E	28	94.5	102.6	8.1*		For the one program interval reported, the Binet IQ scores for the Direct Verbal and Amelioration of Learning Deficits groups were significantly higher at the .05 level than the Traditional and Montessori groups on the post-tests. On the ITPA the Direct Verbal, Traditional, and Amelioration of Learning Deficits groups were significantly higher than the Montessori group.										26	48.0	59.2	11.2*	
Direct Ver-bal, age 4-4 to 5-0, 10/65-6/66	E	29	93.2	107.6	14.4*												29	46.2	59.1	12.9*	
Ameliora-tion of lrng. defi-cits, age 4-4 to 5-0	E	27	96.0	110.3	14.3*												27	49.2	63.2	14.0*	
Montessori, age 4-4 to 5-0, 10/65-6/66	E	16	94.1	99.6	5.5												16	45.8	52.8	7.0*	

7. Schaefer, E. S. National Institute of Mental Health, Chevy Chase, Maryland. <u>Project</u>: The Infant Education Research Project. <u>Place</u>: Washington, D. C. <u>Reference</u>: Hawkridge, *et al.*, *op. cit.*

Groups or Waves	Type of Group	Tests																			
		Binet					CMM					PPVT					ITPA				
		N	Pre	Post	Change	Diff.	N	Pre	Post	Change	Diff.	N	Pre	Post	Change	Diff.	N	Pre	Post	Change	Diff.
Children aged 14 mos. (state of project)	E	28	105[d]			−3															
	C	30	108																		
Children aged 36 mos. (end of project)	E	28		106		17†						28		87.1		10.9†					
	C	30		89								30		76.2							

[a] ITPA scores in this study are converted scores.
[b] ITPA scores are from Studies I and III of the program combined.
[c] PPVT scores in this study are raw scores, not I.Q.
[d] I.Q. scores at 14 months are from *Bayley Infant Scales of Developement.*
* Significant at .05 level.
† Significant at .01 level.
‡ Significant at .001 level.
+ One-tailed test.

NOTE: Some figures are rounded after subtraction of two-place decimals.
In parts 1 and 4 the difference is that between post scores.
In parts 5 and 6 the difference is that between the "change" values.

programatic objectives of various preschools, but frequently these objectives do not reflect a serious study and adaptation of the successive phases of such activity as described by Piaget and Vygotsky. Nevertheless, a few attempts have been made in this direction.

At the Oakland Children's center (75), a group of preschool children trained in cognitive activities as conceptualized by Piagetian psychologists improved in classificatory and seriation tasks, although no substantial improvement in intelligence scores was reported at the end of this twelve-week training program.

While environmentalists are highly optimistic about the effects of preschool upon the growth of intelligence, many Piagetian psychologists take a different view. Kohlberg (65) argues that the preschool child has a qualitatively different mode of thought from those above six, and that "the notion that academic intellectual instruction can remedy the cognitive-structural retardation of culturally disadvantaged children has little plausibility" (p. 1039).

Academically-oriented preschool: the Bereiter-Engelman program.—The limited achievements of preschool programs have motivated Bereiter and Engelman to develop a different approach. They broke completely with traditional nursery school methods, arguing that school time should be spent in directed cognitive pursuits.

The focus of their academically oriented program is the development of language, reading readiness, and arithmetic. Drawing upon Bernstein's notions of restricted and elaborated codes, these workers borrow their intervention methods from the pattern drills used by teachers of second languages. Their fundamental assumption is that children will learn to think by acquiring the logic of grammar. This assumption governs their choice of specific language goals, such as the acquisition of identity statements, negation, skill in polar opposites, the effective use of prepositions, and if-then deductions.

The specifics of this program of intervention are described by Bereiter and Engelman in their book: *Teaching Disadvantaged Children in Preschool* (6).

A number of communities have adopted the Bereiter program (see the foregoing tables), and have found it successful in developing certain desirable behavior. But many psychologists and educators have remained critical of this form of intervention. Stendler-Lavatelli asks, "Can one generalize that learning to speak certain sentences enables children to 'unpack' meaning from statements? . . . There are also questions as to whether such a program underestimates human intelligence. . . . [does] one become a logical thinker by manipulating statement patterns?" (117:370-71). Bereiter argues, on the other hand, that the achievement scores (particularly in reading) of the children who participated in his programs speak for themselves: "There is nothing left but to defend what was taught as being useful " (5:346).

Contingency management and verbal behavior.—A Skinnerian approach to the development of a verbal repertoire in young disadvantaged children has been developed by Stanley Sapon (107). He differentiates between (*a*) *receptive* language (or verbally controlled behavior), and (*b*) *productive* language, which he defines as verbally controlling behavior. Sapon's goal is the shaping of behaviors considered of importance in preschool settings (such as the children sitting and paying attention to the teacher). He uses varied methods of reinforcement to this end. Learning takes place in two settings: in a small tutorial room in which RABS (Requisite Antecedent Behaviors) are shaped, and then in the natural setting of the classroom. Although a detailed description of this approach is available, the quantitative findings have not been reported as yet.

Individualized instruction in the preschools.—Marion Blank (10, 11) and Solomon (11) argue that the deficiencies of low-income children in abstract thinking are insufficiently challenged or remedied in the group situation of the nursery school. Children can imitate the action of others or rely upon the clues offered by the teacher. It is often difficult to determine whether they are imitating a desired response or producing it independently. In addition, "the group situation severely limits the efficacy of its treatment" (10:1). As an alternative, Blank proposes a fifteen-to-twenty-minute tutorial program in addition to nursery school attendance. There are three types of activities that the author describes in great specificity: (*a*) development of cognitively directed perception, (*b*) improvement in coding process, and (*c*) growth in problem-solving abilities. The lessons require that the child rely upon language as his cognitive tool; the teacher elicits from the child the required language by a discriminate use of questions. The preliminary results of using this method of intervention show considerable gains in IQ scores. However, the group of subjects was quite small (11).

A different tutorial program was developed by the authors (57) several years ago. Based upon a specificity hypothesis stating that language has different levels (i.e. syntactic, semantic) and different functions (i.e. cognitive, communicative, emotive), methods of tutorial intervention were specified to bring about the growth of specific language skills. The prediction that a verbal mediation program of guided discovery would improve the children's use of conceptual verbalization without a corresponding growth in vocabulary was substantiated. Similarly, a story-based method of verbal interaction aimed at stimulating communicative competence and vocabulary growth revealed some gains in the predicted direction. But the reliability of the results of this program also suffers from the small number of subjects worked with to date.

PROGRAM EVALUATION

Do children profit from preschool intervention? Most workers express cautious optimism concerning the effectiveness of the new programs of compensatory education. While some of the most promising changes in children participating in Head Start programs are hard to quantify, most observers have agreed that constructive shifts in social behavior have taken place.

The focus of evaluative studies has been the intellectual and language performance of children. The most general findings are discussed in a report of the Research and Evaluation Division of Project Head Start (97): "It was found again and again that children who attend Head Start advance in measures of intelligence to significantly higher levels, . . . their scores show gains of about 10 points or more from the time they enter Head Start projects, and put them significantly above children of comparable backgrounds who were not Head Starters" (97:9). In this survey, we have limited the presentation of quantitative results to illustrating the types of findings reported by different workers whose approaches have been described above.

The most widely used language measures are the *Peabody Picture Vocabulary Test*, a receptive vocabulary measure which is easy to administer, and the *Illinois Test of Psycholinguistic Abilities*, a test which measures both receptive and productive skills. The *Stanford-Binet* test of intelligence and the *Columbia Mental Maturity Test* are used for assessing overall IQ; while the former has many different types of items, the latter is devoid of vocabulary and informational items.

It is difficult to present a comprehensive and accurate picture of program evaluation without a lengthy and technical exposition. Diversity in approaches, differences in evaluation methods (such as the choice of control groups, frequency of testing) complicate any effort toward uniformity in reporting. Consequently, the authors chose to limit themselves to an illustrative set of findings, urging the interested reader to search for further details in the original reports. A particular difficulty is the sketchiness of information currently available on follow-up studies.

The pioneers in enrichment (Deutsch, Gray and Weikart) have presented reports of consistent gains in intelligence scores among children enrolled in experimental programs. Of these workers, Weikart has been particularly effective in raising the language test scores as well as the general intelligence performance of experimental children in the various waves of his program. Currently, he is experimenting with a Bereiter program of intervention and has reported even more impressive gains. Observers have commented on the greater effectiveness of programs with children who are particularly low in test performance at the beginning of an intervention effort. In this respect, the findings of Spicker *et al.* in Bloomington, Indiana are of interest.

There is little systematic information available on the effectiveness of traditional nursery school programs in raising IQs. Several investigators have attempted, however, to compare the effectiveness of such an approach with more structured programs of intervention. Noteworthy is the evaluation program conducted by DiLorenzo of the New York State Department of Education (34). Different communities throughout the state were selected in which to implement various models of preschool intervention. Traditional nursery school methods with little emphasis on structured enrichment produced statistically insignificant intelligence gains. Even a Montessori program, which is characterized by the use of highly specific and programed materials, showed a similar pattern. In contrast, programs which stressed language, such as a Bereiter type of program in Cortland, or an enrichment (not academic) approach to language intervention chosen at Spring Valley, revealed demonstrable changes in tested performance. Although proponents of the Bereiter-Engelman approach maintain that these and similar findings (see 58) have clinched the debate in early education concerning preschool intervention, many unresolved problems remain.

EARLY EDUCATION: THE BEGINNING OF A DEBATE

Psychological and linguistic theories have thus far been of limited assistance to the educator in the development of lastingly successful programs of intervention. Although the importance of language as a tool of thought and as a socially effective medium of communication is well established, the precise role of language as a vehicle for strengthening pervasive intellectual growth is far from understood.

It has been argued that low-income children suffer from the absence of those classes of stimulation conducive to the development of certain intellectual skills. If this is indeed the case, it is reasonable that some proportion of their time in preschool should be spent on the strengthening of such skills. Preschool programs which have chosen specific goals (such as vocabulary growth or early reading) and have used highly specific programs of implementation (whether the academic preschool of Bereiter or the tutorial program of Blank), have achieved some success. None of these programs, however, has shown that these children once they are in regular elementary school continue to excel over children who have not been given specialized enrichment. Some have argued that the expectation that preschool education will produce permanent gains is unrealistic.[18]

The promise of educability for low-income children needs to be implemented with considerable care and realism. The relatively sheltered, though joyful, setting in which preschool children learn may prepare them poorly for life in ghetto schools. Preschool education without accompanying changes in ghetto schools can become a cruel joke instead of a constructive beginning.

18. See Kohlberg's discussion of this issue from the point of view of Piaget's cognitive-developmental theory (66).

Wolff and Stein (29) have shown that good teachers (some of whom were Head Start teachers) have been able to build upon the children's achievements in these programs. The inadequate teachers, on the other hand, seem to have contributed to the elimination of these early gains. The importance of motivational variables in children's intellectual development is highlighted in a study by Zigler described above. Of equal importance is the motivation of teachers to teach, as illustrated in Rosenthal and Jacobson's popular study, entitled *Pygmalion in the Classroom* (106). It is likely that most elementary teachers have neither the specialized training, the motivation, nor the support of personnel necessary to sustain the gains obtained by children in programs of early education.

We know very little about the way children learn in school. The emphasis upon outcomes, as presented in the accompanying table, is of superficial value to those concerned with the education of the poor. The contrasting approach, an emphasis upon the processes of learning, is just beginning in school settings. A desired outcome of such an approach is the development of effective sequencing of learning experiences, instead of the current widespread reliance upon educational fads. In our own survey, a recognition of the differential import of direct tuition in the acquisition of grammar in contrast with that of word meaning is an example of the utility of detailed studies of language acquisition, language teaching, and intellectual growth.

BIBLIOGRAPHY

1. *The Acquisition of Language.* Edited by Ursula Bellugi and Roger Brown. *Monographs of the Society for Research in Child Development,* XXIX (No. 1, Serial No. 92, 1964).
2. BAILEY, BERYL. "Some Basic Assumptions in the Teaching of Standard English to Speakers of Social Dialects." Paper presented at the Annual Convention of Teachers of English to Speakers of Other Languages, San Antonio, 1968.
3. BARATZ, JOAN. "Language and Cognitive Assessment of Negro Children; Assumptions and Research Needs." Paper presented at the American Psychological Association, San Francisco, 1968.
4. BARATZ, JOAN and POVICH, E. A. "Grammatical Construction in the Language of the Negro Preschool Child." Paper presented at American Speech and Hearing Association, November, 1966.
5. BEREITER, CARL. "A Nonpsychological Approach to Early Com-

pensatory Education." In *Social Class, Race, and Psychological Development*. Edited by Martin Deutsch, Irwin Katz, and Arthur R. Jensen. New York: Holt, Rinehart, & Winston, 1968.

6. BEREITER, CARL and ENGELMANN, SIEGFRIED. *Teaching Disadvantaged Children in the Preschool.* Englewood Cliffs, N.J.: Prentice-Hall, 1966.

7. BERLYNE, DANIEL E. "Soviet Research on Intellectual Processes in Children." In *Basic Cognitive Processes in Children*, pp. 168–83. Edited by Jerome Kagan and John C. Wright. *Monographs of the Society for Research in Child Development*, XXVIII (No. 2, Serial No. 86, 1963).

8. BERNSTEIN, BASIL. "Elaborated and Restricted Codes: Their Social Origins and Some Consequences," *American Anthropologist*, LXVI (December, 1964), Part 2, 55-69.

9. BIRCH, H. "Health and Education of Socially Disadvantaged Children." USOE Contract #6-10-240. Also used at Conference on Bio-Social Factors in the Development and Learning of Disadvantaged Children, Syracuse, N.Y., 1967, USOE Contract #6-10-243.

10. BLANK, MARION. "A Methodology for Fostering Abstract Thinking in Deprived Children." Paper presented at the Conference on Problems in the Teaching of Young Children, Toronto, March, 1968.

11. BLANK, MARION and SOLOMON, FRANCES. "A Tutorial Language Program to Develop Abstract Thinking in Socially Disadvantaged Preschool Children," *Child Development*, XXXIX (June, 1968), 379-90.

12. BLOOM, BENJAMIN S. *The Stability and Change in Human Characteristics.* New York: John Wiley & Sons, 1964.

13. BRAIN, M.D.S. "The Acquisition of Language in Infant and Child." In *The Learning of Language*. Edited by Carroll Read. In Press.

14. BRENT, S. B. and KLAMER, P. "The Naming and Conceptualization of Simple Geometric Figures: A Cross-Cultural Study." Paper presented at the meeting of the Society for Research in Child Development, New York, March, 1967.

15. BRODBECK, ARTHUR J. and IRWIN, ORVIS C. "The Speech Behavior of Infants without Families," *Child Development*, XVII (September, 1946), 145-56.

16. BROWN, ROGER W. *Words and Things.* Glencoe, Ill.: Free Press. 1958.

17. ———. *Social Psychology.* New York: Free Press, 1965.

18. BROWN, ROGER W.; CAZDEN, COURTNEY B.; and BELLUGI, URSULA. "The Child's Grammar from I to III." In *Minnesota Symposium on Child Psychology*. Edited by J. P. Hill. Minneapolis: University of Minnesota Press, forthcoming.

19. BROWN, ROGER W. and LENNEBERG, ERIC H. "A Study in Language

and Cognition," *Journal of Abnormal and Social Psychology*, XLIX (July, 1954), 454-62.

20. BRUNER, JEROME S. *Studies in Cognitive Growth*. New York: John Wiley & Sons, 1966.

21. ———. *Toward a Theory of Instruction*. Cambridge, Mass.: Belknap Press, 1966.

22. CALDWELL, B. M. and RICHMOND, J. B. "Programmed Day-care for the Very Young Child—A Preliminary Report," *Journal of Marriage and the Family*, XXVI (1964), 481-88.

23. CARROLL, JOHN B. and CASAGRANDE, JOSEPH B. "The Function of Language Classifications in Behavior." In *Readings in Social Psychology*, pp. 18-31. Edited by Eleanor E. Maccoby, Theodore M. Newcomb, and Eugene L. Hartley. New York: Holt, Rinehart, & Winston, 1958.

24. CARSON, ARNOLD S. and RABIN, A. I. "Verbal Comprehension and Communication in Negro and White Children," *Journal of Educational Psychology*, LI (April, 1960) 47-51.

25. CAZDEN, COURTNEY B. "Environmental Assistance to the Child's Acquisition of Grammar." Unpublished Doctor's dissertation, Harvard University, 1965.

26. ———. "The Acquisition of Noun and Verb Inflections." Unpublished paper, Harvard University, 1967.

27. ———. "Some Implications of Research on Language Development for Preschool Education." Chap. XI in *Early Education*. Edited by Robert D. Hess and Roberta Meyer Bear. Chicago: Aldine Publishing Co., 1968.

28. CHOMSKY, NOAM. "Language and the Mind," *Psychology Today*, I (No. 9, 1968), 48-51, 66-68.

29. COFER, CHARLES N. "The Role of Language in Human Problem-Solving." Paper read at the Conference on Human Problem-Solving Behavior, New York University, April, 1954.

30. DARLEY, FREDERIC L. and WINITZ, HARRIS. "Age of First Word: Review of Research," *Journal of Speech and Hearing Disorders*, XXVI (August, 1961), 272-90.

31. DEUTSCH, CYNTHIA. "Auditory Discrimination and Learning: Social Factors," *Merrill-Palmer Quarterly*, X (No. 3, 1964) 277-96.

32. ———. "Learning in the Disadvantaged." In *The Disadvantaged Child*. Edited by Martin Deutsch and Associates. New York: Basic Books, 1967.

33. DILLARD, JOSEPH L. "The Urban Language Study of the Center for Applied Linguistics," *Linguistic Reporter*, VIII (1967), 1-2.

34. DILORENZO, L. T. and SALTER, RUTH. "An Evaluative Study of Prekindergarten Programs for Educationally Disadvantaged Children: Follow-up and Replication." Paper read at the 1968 Annual Meeting of the American Educational Research Association, New York, 1968.

35. *The Disadvantaged Child.* Edited by Martin Deutsch and Associates. New York: Basic Books, 1967.
36. EELLS, KENNETH W. et al. *Intelligence and Cultural Differences.* Chicago: University of Chicago Press, 1951.
37. ERVIN-TRIPP, SUSAN. "Language Development." In *Review of Child Development Research,* II, 55-105. Edited by Martin L. Hoffman and Lois W. Hoffman. New York: Russell Sage Foundation, 1966.
38. ———. "Projected Activities," *Project Literacy Reports 6*, pp. 41-44. Ithaca: Cornell University Press, 1966. ERIC #ED-010-31a.
39. ERVIN-TRIPP, SUSAN and MILLER, W. "Language Development." In *Child Psychology.* Sixty-second Yearbook of the National Society for the Study of Education, Part I, pp. 108-43. Edited by H. W. Stevenson. Chicago: Distributed by University of Chicago Press, 1963.
40. FURTH, HANS G. *Thinking Without Language.* New York: Free Press, 1966.
41. FRY, DENNIS B. "The Development of the Phonological System in the Normal and the Deaf Child." In *The Genesis of Language,* pp. 187-207. Edited by Frank Smith and George A. Miller. Cambridge, Mass.: MIT Press, 1966.
42. GOLDEN, MARK and BIRNS, BEVERLY. "Social Class and Cognitive Development in Infancy," *Merrill-Palmer Quarterly,* XIV (April, 1968), 139-49.
43. GORDON, EDMUND W. "Programs of Compensatory Education." In *Social Class, Race and Psychological Development.* Edited by Martin Deutsch, Irwin Katz, and Arthur R. Jensen. New York: Holt, Rinehart, & Winston, 1968.
44. GUTTENBERG, MARCIA and ROSS, SYLVIA. "Perceptual vs. Movement Responses in the Learning of Verbal Symbolic Concepts by Deprived Children." Paper presented at annual meeting of the Eastern Psychological Association, Washington, D.C., April, 1968.
45. HAWKRIDGE, DAVID G.; CHALUPSKY, ALBERT B.; and ROBERTS, A. OSCAR H. *A Study of Selected Exemplary Programs for the Education of Disadvantaged Children,* Final Report, Project No. 089013, Contract No. OEC-0-8-089013-3515 (010), 1968. American Institutes for Research in the Behavioral Sciences, Palo Alto, California.
46. HEIDER, E.; CAZDEN, COURTNEY; and BROWN, ROGER. "Social Class Differences in the Effectiveness and Style of Children's Coding Ability." *Project Literacy Reports,* Cornell University, August, 1968.
47. HESS, ROBERT D. and SHIPMAN, VIRGINIA C. "Early Experience and the Socialization of Cognitive Modes in Children," *Child Development,* XXXVI (December, 1965), 869-86.
48. HODGES, W. L.; McCANDLESS, B. R.; and SPICKER, H. H. *The Development and Evaluation of a Diagnostically Based Curriculum for*

Preschool Psycho-Socially Deprived Children. Washington, D.C.: Bureau of Research of the Office of Education, December, 1967.

49. HORNER, VIVIAN. "The Verbal World of the Lower-Class Three-Year-Old: A Pilot Study in Linguistic Ecology." Unpublished Doctor's dissertation, University of Rochester, 1968.

50. HUNT, J. McVICKER. *Intelligence and Experience.* New York: Ronald Press Co., 1961.

51. IRWIN, ORVIS C. "Infant Speech: The Effect of Family Occupational Status and of Age on Use of Sound Types," *Journal of Speech and Hearing Disorders,* XIII (1948), 224-26.

52. JAKOBSON, R. *Kindersprache, Aphasie, und Allgemeine Lautgesetze.* Uppsala, Sweden: Almqvist & Wiksell, 1941.

53. JENKINS, JAMES J. and PALERMO, DAVID S. "Mediation Processes and the Acquisition of Linguistic Structure." In *The Acquisition of Language,* pp. 141-74. Edited by Ursula Bellugi and Roger Brown. *Monographs of the Society for Research in Child Development,* XXIX No. 1, Serial No. 92, 1964.

54. JENSEN, A. H. "Patterns of Mental Ability and Socio-economic Status." Paper presented at the annual meeting of the National Academy of Sciences, Washington, D.C., April 24, 1968.

55. JOHN, VERA P. "The Role of Language in Problem-Solving." Unpublished Ph.D. dissertation, University of Chicago, 1956.

56. JOHN, VERA P. and GOLDSTEIN, L. "The Social Context of Language Acquisition," *Merrill-Palmer Quarterly,* X (1964), 265-75.

57. JOHN, VERA P. and MOSKOVITZ, SARAH. *A Study of Language Change in Integrated and Homogeneous Classrooms.* Progress Report No. 2, OEO Grant #2440, 1968.

58. KARNES, MERLE B. "A Research Program to Determine the Effects of Various Preschool Intervention Programs on the Development of Disadvantaged Children and the Strategic Age for Such Intervention." Paper presented at the Convention of the American Educational Research Association, New York, 1968.

59. KENDLER, TRACY S. "Development of Mediating Responses in Children." In *Basic Cognitive Processes in Children,* pp. 33-48. Edited by John C. Wright and Jerome Kagan. *Monographs of the Society for Research in Child Development,* XXVIII No. 2, Serial No. 86, 1963.

60. KENDLER, TRACY S. and KENDLER, HOWARD H. "Reversal and Non-reversal Shifts in Kindergarten Children," *Journal of Experimental Psychology,* LVIII (July, 1959), 56-60.

61. KEZHERADZE, E. D. "The Role of the Word in Memorization, and Some Features of the Memory of the Child," *Voprosy Psikhol.,* 1960, No. 1, 78-85. Abstract in *The Genesis of Language, A Psycholinguistic Approach,* pp. 371-72. Edited by Frank Smith and George A. Miller. Cambridge, Mass.: MIT Press, 1966.

62. *A Kindergarten Curriculum Guide for Indian Children.* Kindergarten Training Project, Dilcon School, Winslow, Arizona, Summer, 1968.

63. KLAUS, R. A. and GRAY, SUSAN W. "The Early Training Project for Disadvantaged Children: A Report After Five Years," *Monographs of the Society for Research in Child Development,* XXXIII (No. 4, 1968).

64. KOCH, HELEN L. "The Relation of 'Primary Mental Abilities' in Five- and Six-Year-Olds to Sex of Children and Characteristics of His Siblings," *Child Development,* XXV (September, 1954), 209-23.

65. KOHLBERG, LAWRENCE. "Early Education: A Cognitive Developmental View," *Child Development,* XXXIX (December, 1968), 1013-62.

66. KOHLBERG, LAWRENCE; YAEGER, JUDY; and HJERTHOLM ELSE. "Private Speech: For Studies and a Review of Theories," *Child Development,* XXXIX (1968) 691-735.

67. KURTZ, KENNETH H. and HOVLAND, CARL I. "The Effect of Verbalization During Observation of Stimulus Objects upon Accuracy of Recognition and Recall," *Journal of Experimental Psychology,* XLV (March, 1953), 157-64.

68. LABOV, WILLIAM. "Phonological Correlates of Social Stratification." In *The Ethnography of Communication,* pp. 164-176. Edited by J.J. Gumperz and Dell Hymes. A special publication of *American Anthropologist,* LXVI (December, 964, Part 2).

69. ———. "The Non-standard Vernacular of the Negro Community: Some Practical Suggestions." Paper presented at the Seminar in English and Language Arts, Temple University, 1967.

70. LACIVITA, A.; KEAN, J. M.; and YAMAMOTO, K. "Socio-economic Status of Children and Acquisition of Grammar," *Journal of Educational Research,* LX (1967), 71-74.

71. LANTZ, DE LEE. "Color Naming and Color Recognition: A Study in the Psychology of Language." Unpublished dissertation, Harvard University, 1963.

72. LAWTON, DENIS. "Social Class Differences in Language Development; A Study of Some Samples of Written Work," *Language and Speech,* VI (1963), 120-43.

73. ———. "Social Class Language Differences in Group Discussions," *Language and Speech,* VII (1964), 183-204.

74. LENNEBERG, ERIC H. *Biological Foundations of Language.* New York: John Wiley & Sons, 1967.

75. LENROW, P. "Preschool Socialization and the Development of Competence." Berkeley: University of California, 1966. (Mimeographed)

76. LEOPOLD, WERNER F. *Bibliography of Child Language.* Evanston, Ill.: Northwestern University Press, 1952.

77. LESSER, GERALD S.; FIFER, GORDON; and CLARK, DONALD H. "Mental

Abilities of Children from Different Social-Class and Cultural Groups," *Monographs of the Society for Research in Child Development*, XXX (No. 4, Serial No. 102).

78. LEWIS, HYLAN. "Culture, Class and the Behavior of Low Income Families." Paper prepared for Conference on Lower Class Culture, New York, June, 1963.

79. LEWIS, M. M. *How Children Learn To Speak*. New York: Basic Books, 1959.

80. LOBAN, WALTER. "Language Proficiency and School Learning." In *Learning and the Educational Process*, pp. 113-31. Edited by J. D. Krumboltz. Chicago: Rand McNally & Co., 1965.

81. LURIA, ALEKSANDER R. *The Role of Speech in the Regulation of Normal and Abnormal Behavior*. New York: Pergamon Press, 1961.

82. ———. "Speech Development and the Formation of Mental Processes," *Psychological Science in the USSR*, I, 704-87. Washington, D.C.: U.S. Joint Publication Research Service, No. 11466, 1961.

83. ———. "The Regulative Function of Speech in Its Development and Dissolution." In *Verbal Behavior and Some Neurophysiological Implications*, pp. 405-23. Edited by Kurt Salzinger and Suzanne Salzinger. New York: Academic Press, 1967.

84. LURIA, ALEKSANDER R. and POLYAKVA, A. G. "Observations of the Development of the Voluntary Action in Early Childhood," *Proc. Acad. Pedag. Sci.*, 1959, Nos. 3 and 4. (Quoted in No. 83 above.)

85. McCARTHY, DOROTHY. "Language Development in Children." In *Manual of Child Psychology* (1946), pp. 476-581; 1954, pp. 492-630). Edited by Leonard Carmichael. New York: John Wiley & Sons, 1946, 1954.

86. McNEILL, DAVID. "Developmental Psycholinguistics." In *The Genesis of Language*, pp. 15-85. Edited by Frank Smith and George A. Miller. Cambridge, Mass.: MIT Press, 1966.

87. MILNER, ESTHER. "A Study of the Relationship between Reading Readiness in Grade One School Children and Patterns of Parent-Child Interaction," *Child Development*, XXII (June, 1951), 95-112.

88. MOWRER, ORVAL H. *Learning Theory and the Symbolic Process*. New York: John Wiley & Sons, 1960.

89. OLERON, P. *Recherches sur le developpement mental des sourdes-muets*. Paris: Centre national de la recherche scientifique, 1957.

90. OLVER, ROSE R. and HORNSBY, JOAN R. "On Equivalence." In *Studies in Cognitive Growth*, pp. 68-85. Edited by Jerome Bruner, et al. New York: John Wiley & Sons, 1966.

91. OSSER, HARRY. "The Syntactic Structures of Five-Year-Old Culturally Deprived Children." Paper presented at the Symposium on the Concept of Structure in Language and Thinking, Eastern Psychological Association Annual Meeting, New York, 1966.

92. PASAMANICK, BENJAMIN and KNOBLOCH, HILDA. "Early Language

Behavior in Negro Children and the Testing of Intelligence," *Journal of Abnormal and Social Psychology*, L (May, 1955), 401-2.

93. PEISACH, ESTELL C. "Children's Comprehension of Teacher and Peer Speech," *Child Development*, XXXVI (June, 1965), 467-80.

94. PIAGET, JEAN. *The Language and Thought of the Child*. London: Routledge and Kegan Paul, 1926.

95. ———. *Six Psychological Studies*. New York: Random House, 1967.

96. PREMACK, D. and SCHWARTZ, A. "Preparations for Discussing Behaviorism with Chimpanzees." In *The Genesis of Language*, pp. 295-347. Edited by Frank Smith and George A. Miller. Cambridge, Mass.: MIT Press, 1966.

97. *Project Head Start: Evaluation and Research, 1965-1967*. Division of Research and Evaluation, Project Head Start, Office of Economic Opportunity, Washington, D.C.

98. RANKIN, HOWARD B. "Language and Thinking: Positive and Negative Effects of Naming," *Science*, CXLI (July, 1963), 48-50.

99. REESE, HAYNE W. "Imagery in Paired-Associate Learning in Children," *Journal of Experimental Child Psychology*, II (September, 1965), 290-96.

100. *Research in Verbal Behavior and Some Neurophysiological Implications*. Edited by Kurt Salzinger and Suzanne Salzinger. New York: Academic Press, 1967.

101. RHEINGOLD, HARRIET. "Controlling the Infant's Exploratory Behavior." In *Determinants of Infant Behavior*, II, 171-78. Edited by B. M. Foss. New York: John Wiley & Sons, 1963.

102. RHEINGOLD, HARRIET; GEWIRTZ, JACOB L.; and ROSS, HELEN W. "Social Conditioning of Vocalizations in the Infant," *Journal of Comparative and Physiological Psychology*, LII (1959), 68-73.

103. RIESS, B. F. "Genetic Changes in Semantic Conditioning," *Journal of Experimental Psychology*, XXVI (1946), 143-52.

104. ROHWER, WILLIAM D., JR. Studies summarized in *Social Class Differences in the Role of Linguistic Structures in Paired-Associate Learning*. Final Report, November, 1967, Project No. 5-0605, Office of Education, OE 6-10-273.

105. ROHWER, WILLIAM D., JR.; LYNCH, STEVE; SUZUKI, NANCY; and LEVIN, JOEL R. "Verbal and Pictorial Facilitation of Paired-Associate Learning," *Journal of Experimental Child Psychology*, V (June, 1967), 294-302.

106. ROSENTHAL, ROBERT and JACOBSON, LENORE. *Pygmalion in the Classroom*. New York: Holt, Rinehart & Winston, 1968.

107. SAPON, STANLEY. "Engineering Verbal Behavior." Paper presented at the Conference on Problems in the Teaching of Young Children. Toronto, March, 1968.

108. SCHAEFER, EARL S. "Intellectual Stimulation of Culturally-Deprived

Infants." Mimeographed, 1965. Excerpted from Mental Health Grant Proposal No. MH-09224-01.

109. SHIPLEY, ELIZABETH F.; SMITH, CARLOTTA S.; and GLETIMAN, LILA R. "A Study in the Acquisition of Language—Free Responses to Commands." Unpublished manuscript, Eastern Pennsylvania Psychiatric Institute, 1968.

110. SHUY, R.; WOLFRAM, W.; and RILEY, W. *Linguistic Correlates of Speech Stratification in Detroit Speech.* Final Report, Cooperative Research Project 6, 1347, U.S. Office of Education, 1967.

111. SIGEL, I. E. "The Attainment of Concepts." In *Review of Child Development Research,* I, 209-49. Edited by Martin L. Hoffman and Lois N. Hoffman. New York: Russell Sage Foundation, 1964.

112. SLOBIN, DAN I. "Imitation and Grammatical Development in Children." In *Contemporary Issues in Developmental Psychology.* Edited by N. S. Endler, L. R. Boulter, and H. Osser. New York: Holt, Rinehart & Winston, 1967.

113. SOKHIN, F. A. Abstract in *The Genesis of Language, A Psycholinguistic Approach,* pp. 382-83. Edited by Frank Smith and George A. Miller. Cambridge, Mass.: MIT Press, 1966.

114. SPIKER, CHARLES C. "Verbal Factors in the Discrimination Learning of Children," In *Basic Cognitive Processes in Children,* pp. 53-69. Edited by John C. Wright and Jerome Kagan. *Monographs of the Society for Research in Child Development,* XXVIII (No. 2, Serial No. 86, 1963.)

115. STERN, C. and W. *Kindersprache.* Leipzig: J. A. Barth, 1928.

116. STERN, CAROLYN and LOMBARD, AVIMA. "The Effect of Verbalization on Young Children's Learning of a Manipulative Skill." Paper delivered at American Psychological Association, San Francisco, 1968.

117. STENDELER-LAVATELLI, CELIA. "Environmental Intervention in Infancy and Early Childhood." In *Social Class, Race and Psychological Development.* Edited by Martin Deutsch, Irwin Katz, and Arthur R. Jensen. New York: Holt, Rinehart, & Winston, 1968.

118. STEWART, WILLIAM. "Urban Negro Speech: Sociolinguistic Factors Affecting English Teaching." In *Social Dialects and Language Learning,* pp. 10-18. Edited by Roger Shuy. Champaign, Illinois: National Council of Teachers of English, 1964.

119. STODOLSKY, SUSAN. "Maternal Behavior and Language and Concept Formation in Negro Preschool Children: An Inquiry into Process." Unpublished Ph.D. dissertation. University of Chicago, 1965.

120. TEMPLIN, MILDRED C. *Certain Language Skills in Children: Their Development and Interrelationships.* Institute of Child Welfare Monograph Series, No. 26. Minneapolis: University of Minnesota Press, 1957.

214   LANGUAGE ACQUISITION & DEVELOPMENT

121. TEMPLIN, MILDRED C. "The Study of Articulation and Language Development During the Early School Years." In *The Genesis of Language*, pp. 173-80. Edited by Frank Smith and George A. Miller. Cambridge, Mass.: MIT Press, 1966.

122. THOMAS, D. R. "Oral Language, Sentence Structure, and Vocabulary of Kindergarten Children Living in Low Socio-Economic Urban Areas." Unpublished Doctor's dissertation, Wayne State University, 1962.

123. TIKHOMOROV, I. K. "On the Formation of Voluntary Movement in Children of Preschool Age." In *Problems of the Higher Nervous Activity of Normal and Abnormal Children*, II, 72-130. Edited by Aleksander R. Luria. Moscow: Acad. Pedag. Press, 1958 (in Russian). Quoted in translation in *Research in Verbal Behavior and Some Neurophysiological Implications*, Edited by Kurt Salzinger and Suzanne Salzinger. New York: Academic Press, 1967.

124. *Verbal Behavior and Learning.* Edited by N. Cofer and B. S. Musgrave. New York: McGraw-Hill Book Co., 1963.

125. VYGOTSKY, LEV G. *Thought and Language.* Edited and translated by Eugenia Hanfmann and Gertrude Vakar. Cambridge, Mass.: MIT Press, 1962.

126. WEIKART, DAVID P. *Preschool Intervention: A Preliminary Report of the Perry Preschool Project.* Ann Arbor, Michigan: Campus Publishers, 1967.

127. WEIR, RUTH H. "Some Questions on the Child's Learning of Phonology." In *The Genesis of Language*, pp. 153-68. Edited by Frank Smith and George A. Miller. Cambridge, Mass.: MIT Press, 1966.

128. WEISBERG, PAUL. "Social and Nonsocial Conditioning of Infant Vocalizations," *Child Development*, XXXIV (1963), 377-88.

129. WHIPPLE, CLIFFORD I. and MAIER, LOUISE J. "Perceptual-motor Maturation and Language Development in Young Children," *Perceptual and Motor Skills*, XXIII (December, 1966), 1208.

130. WHITE, SHELDON H. "Evidence for a Hierarchical Arrangement of Learning Processes." In *Advances in Child Development and Behavior*, II. Edited by Lewis P. Lipsitt and Charles C. Spiker. New York: Academic Press, 1965.

131. WHORF, BENJAMIN LEE. *Language, Thought, and Reality.* Cambridge, Mass.: MIT Press, 1956.

132. WILLIAMS, FREDERICK and NAREMORE, RITA C. *Language and Poverty: An Annotated Bibliography.* Institute for Research on Poverty, University of Wisconsin, n. d.

133. WOLFF, MAX, and STEIN, ANNIE. *Six Months Later—A Comparison of Children Who Had Head Start, Summer, 1965, with Their Classmates in Kindergarten.* Final Report, OEO Project 141-61, Study I.

134. ZIGLER, EDWARD and BUTTERFIELD, EARL C. "Motivational Aspects of Changes in IQ Test Performance of Culturally Deprived Nursery School Children," *Child Development*, XXXIX (1968), 1-14.

CHAPTER VII

Language Development in the School Years

Part I

LANGUAGE DEVELOPMENT: THE ELEMENTARY
SCHOOL YEARS

RICHARD E. HODGES

Introduction

The past decade has witnessed a burgeoning interest by educational researchers and practititioners in the language development of the elementary school child. With advances in linguistic theory, with the development of more sensitive techniques for analyzing child language, and with a renewed concern about the effectiveness of language instruction in the schools, Ervin and Miller's comment in 1963 that few structural analyses of the language of older children exist has been at least partially corrected (11).

Published overviews of investigations during the last quarter-century of children's language development demonstrate the marked changes that have occurred both in theory and methods of child language research (19, 4, 11, 12)—changes which sometimes made it difficult to compare the results of studies often based on different theories of language and employing different methodologies. Nonetheless, growing evidence does clarify the sequence of language development through the elementary school years. This section reviews selected contemporary studies of the language development of the elementary school child, roughly spanning ages six through twelve, with specific reference to both oral and written language production. Variations of language performance are similarly reviewed.

Oral and Written Language Trends

Phonological development.—Most children by school entrance age have control of the phonemic stock of their dialect, although misarticulations do continue to occur. Templin analyzed the articulations of spontaneously produced and repeated words of 480 boys and girls, ages three to eight, and found that three-year-olds have about 50 percent of the articulatory accuracy of eight-year-olds, while eight-year-olds achieved about 95 percent accuracy on the articulation measures Templin employed (30). Templin's findings, however, were not reported in terms of separate phonemes. By rearranging her data to permit analysis of phoneme articulation, Carroll showed that the only distinctive speech sounds not correctly articulated by at least 90 percent of Templin's sample population by age six were the fricatives /s/, /š/, /z/, /ž/, /ð/, and the affricative /č/, and the semivowel /hw/ (4).

The age at which individual children acquire general mastery of speech-sound articulation can vary considerably—an observation that tends to be obscured in normative studies. Templin's recent longitudinal investigation of the articulatory development of 436 boys and girls who were followed from prekindergarten through the fourth grade substantiates her earlier finding. Her longitudinal data, however, show that some children display functional articulatory control as early as age four and one-half, while some ten-year-olds still manifest certain misarticulations (31).

Wepman and Morency report somewhat similar relationships between misarticulation and age (32). Employing the concept of "age-appropriate misarticulation" in studying articulatory development, they call attention to a need to distinguish between developmental and pathological factors when observing the misarticulations of young children. From data obtained in a longitudinal study of 177 children followed from first through third grades, they unequivocally state that children who enter school with age-appropriate misarticulations are not hampered in general school learning—at least in the early grades. They reiterate the point that speech accuracy develops at its own rate, but in an expected order, for each individual. However, they also noted, as have others, that while developmentally caused misarticulations appear not to have significant effects upon school achievement, the ability to discriminate among speech sounds may (32, 6, 26)—a distinction of significance for spelling and reading instruction.

Morphological development.—The child's control of morphology proceeds, as do other language features, along a course of mastering the highly predictable and productive features toward the mastering of uncommon forms of limited distribution—for example, derivational suffixes and irregular inflections. The morphological "errors" of the beginning elementary school child quite clearly demonstrate his preference for the most generalizable patterns (2). His errors are in large part errors of analogy. On the other hand, the young child's inability to correctly employ uncommon forms in his own speech does not preclude his ability to comprehend them when used in the speech of others (20).

The elementary school years thus mark a time when the child gains mastery over most of the remaining morphological features, provided that adequate spoken language is available from which those features may be derived. The importance of accessibility of spoken language in morphological development is attested to by Cooper's study of the morphological abilities of both deaf and hearing subjects, ages seven to nineteen. Employing a paper and pencil test adapted from Berko, he found, as might be expected, that hearing subjects had strikingly superior scores. Moreover, the average scores of 19-year-old deaf subjects were below the average scores of hearing ten-year-olds, particularly in applying derivational suffixes (8).

Syntactic development.—Although the groundwork has been laid in early childhood for the full development of native language skills, that achievement requires the whole period of childhood and adolescence (5:69). Recognition of this fact underlies in part the growing interest in describing and analyzing the language of the elementary school child.

Contemporary studies of child grammar have usually attempted to classify children's syntactic constructions with reference to adult language norms, with the system of classification being determined by the grammar model the researcher chooses to employ. The next section of this chapter develops in some detail the use of transformational descriptions of language. In the present section, we shall focus on structural descriptions of child language development as depicted by the studies of Loban (17) and Strickland (29), bearing in mind that structural investigations have not distinguished between competence and performance.

Both researchers analyzed a syntactic element they termed the *phonological unit*—oral language samples which are segmented according to intonation patterns signaling the termination of some utterance. The following example from Loban (17:6) contains two phonological units which are marked by (#): "I'm going to get a boy| 'cause he hit me.# I'm going to beat him up and kick him in his nose|| and I'm going to get the girl, too.#"

The phonological unit is based on structural data. Loban, however, also employed semantic information and developed the *communication unit*, a group of words which cannot be further divided without a loss of essential meaning, which in Loban's study proved to be an independent clause with any of its modifiers. In the above example of the phonological unit, there are three communication units because the second phonological unit is a compound sentence.

Samples of child language then were analyzed at two levels. At Level I the frequency and variety of sentence types and their major construction were classified. These constructions included: (*a*) "fixed slots"(in traditional grammar such sentence elements as subjects, predicates, complements, and indirect objects); (*b*) "movables," or the adverbials of time, place, cause, and manner; and (*c*) "sentence connectors," the coordinating and subordinating conjunctions. At Level II the Level I constructions were examined in depth and the manner in which the respective "slots" and "movables" were constructed was noted—in particular, the use of noun and verb modifiers, or "satellites."

Strickland's cross-sectional study involved the analysis of 25 spontaneously produced phonological units obtained in an interview setting for each of 575 randomly selected children taken in approximately equal numbers from each of grades one through six. She found that the most commonly used pattern at all grade levels was the "1|2|4" pattern, consisting of subject, verb, and outer complement or direct object. Strickland further observed that ten sentence patterns used by older children did not appear at all in the speech of first-graders, although there was considerable overlap among the 25 predominant sentence patterns found at each grade level. Children at all grade levels were seen to employ adverbial expressions—

the movables—but the incidence of such expressions increased with advance in grade as well as did increased flexibility in how they were placed within a slot.

Strickland also compared the speech of a subsample of 15 first-graders and 15 fifth-graders in an attempt to provide a detailed analysis of growth of syntactic complexity. Although the small number of phonological units (750) that were analyzed limits her findings, progression toward mature speech is clearly identifiable. Fifth-graders consistently made greater use of "fillers" than did first-graders; indeed, the heavy use of long compound subject-predicate forms was found significantly to differentiate the speech of older children from that of the younger subjects.

Loban undertook a longitudinal study of the language development of 338 subjects from kindergarten through the first twelve years of school. His first report encompassed his analysis of the syntactic growth of children through the sixth grade. Language samples were obtained yearly by having individual subjects discuss a series of six still pictures shown to them. The communication units that were obtained were then given a two-level analysis in order to determine each subject's effectiveness in and control of language—(a) the Level I analysis providing evidence of an ability to use and vary English structural patterns, and (b) the Level II analysis indicating the dexterity with which children vary elements within these patterns. In addition to his analysis of the complete sample of 338 children, Loban also undertook an intensive comparative study of the language production of 30 children designated as exceptionally high, and 24 children designated as exceptionally low, in language ability.

As might be expected, all children at each succeeding year were found to say more, both in terms of number of communication units and the number of words within these units; but noticeable contrasts were identified between the high-ability and low-ability children. Although there were only negligible differences between groups at the first level of analysis (excepting noticeable differences in the use of linking verbs and partials), the dexterity with which elements within basic patterns were manipulated strikingly differentiated the high-ability group from the low-ability group. Moreover, Loban found that the frequency of use and the complexity of subordination varied according to general language proficiency as well as to socioeconomic status and chronological age. In addition, Loban provided evidence to question the commonly held view of the general linguistic superiority of girls (19:577). His findings indicated that boys in the low-ability group were least proficient, but the boys in the high-ability group excelled girls on the measures used.

Strickland and Loban were generally concerned with analyses of the oral language of children, although Loban did obtain samples of child writing from the third grade on for purposes of relating writing ability (rated on a five-point scale ranging from "superior" to "primitive") to achievement in reading, oral language, and other aspects of language. Other researchers, however, have looked expressly at contrasts between oral and written language development, as well as specifically at language development in the written mode. Riling's investigation of the oral and written language of fourth- and sixth-grade children represents one such study that employs the two-level structural analysis initiated by Strickland and Loban (25).

Riling was interested in determining the influences of such factors as intelligence, sex, socioeconomic status, parental education, and ethnic origin on the oral and written language of 300 fourth- and sixth-grade children in southeastern Oklahoma. From each subject, she obtained 25 oral and 25 written responses to a picture intended to stimulate narration; the responses then were analyzed in terms of their structural patterns and complexities.

Riling's findings further substantiate the developmental characteristics of child language, her sixth-grade subjects speaking with greater clarity than fourth-graders and writing longer, more complex sentences with greater variation than their younger counterparts. Of particular interest was Riling's observation that, even in fourth grade, some structural patterns which appeared in writing seldom appeared in speech, leading her to speculate that such differences result from the child's growing awareness of distinctions between oral and written communication.

As had Loban, Riling also observed in the high-ability group the general linguistic superiority of boys as compared to girls, while boys in the low-ability group were indeed "at the bottom of the heap" (25:87). She also noted differences in written language among

her subjects when differentiated in terms of rural and urban origins—
the former writing less, and doing so in shorter and more repetitious
syntactic patterns.

Hunt's study of the grammatical structures used in writing by
older children focused expressly on the written mode (13). However, unlike Riling, Strickland, and Loban (17:62), Hunt applied
transformational grammar techniques to distinguish levels of linguistic maturity. A detailed description is provided in Part II of this
chapter of both the methodology and findings of Hunt. The particular consequence of Hunt's study lies in its baseline data concerning the grammar of young writers—fourth-graders—compared with
older writers and in his observations of the development of skills
of individuals to consolidate sentences, reduce redundancies, and
to communicate through the written medium with increasing suc-
cinctness.

Hunt provided information about the written language abilities
of older elementary children. O'Donnell, Griffin, and Norris applied
Hunt's "T-unit" (a single independent predication together with
any subordinate clauses which may be grammatically related to it)
in the study of both the oral and written syntax of 180 children in
kindergarten and in Grades I, II, III, V, and VII (22). The investigators did not concern themselves with the full range of possible
grammatical structures and functions but selected for study main-
clause patterns and those structures dependent on sentence-combining transformations.

As had Hunt, they also observed that the length of the T-unit
increased grade by grade. But they also found that, though third-
graders used longer T-units in speech than in writing, the reverse
situation was true for the fifth-graders, suggesting that older children learn to control written expression with greater care than oral
language, an observation not unlike that of Riling (25). However,
the greatest advances in oral language development were found in
the earliest grades (kindergarten through first grade) and the later
grades (sixth and seventh), a finding which led the investigators to
speculate about the effectiveness of language instruction during the
middle elementary school years (22).

The development of grammatical control during the early school
years is further clarified by Slobin's study of the extent to which

and the manner in which children and adults comprehend negative and passive forms of basic sentences (28). Kindergarten, second-, fourth-, and sixth-grade children and a group of adults were presented with pictures and spoken sentences. For each picture-sentence pair, the subjects had to determine whether the sentence was true or false in reference to the picture. Four grammatical types of sentences were used which included (in presumed order of difficulty) kernel, negative, passive, and passive negative. Response times and errors were tabulated.

Contrary to prediction, the syntactically more complex passive sentences were simpler to evaluate than were the negative sentences. Moreover, this was true for both adults and children, although both response times and errors diminished with age, with a rapid change in response time between the ages of six to ten and a slowing down between ages ten and twelve. It could be inferred that grammatical control continues to improve fairly rapidly in the early school years, slowing down as mature levels of control are reached. Slobin's study demonstrates how, during the elementary school years, the child is involved in increasing skill in the manipulation of more complex and subtle features of the grammatical system.

The foregoing studies illustrate the increased efforts to describe child language in more precise and definitive ways. There can be little question but that language skills continue to develop throughout much of one's lifetime and that the elementary school years are important in the individual's growth toward linguistic maturity.

Whether or not the maturation process can be enhanced through explicit and systematic instruction in such linguistic devices as sentence combining transformations (13) has yet to be investigated substantively at the elementary school level. In one of the few such studies reported, Miller and Ney concluded that oral practice in sentence-combining did produce greater fluency and facility of writing among their fourth-grade subjects (21).

Language variations.—Studies of child language have, for the most part, assumed a model grammar, Standard English. That spoken language varies widely with reference to that model is noticeable by even the most casual language observer.

When language variations, either structural or functional, impede communication, there are likely to be adverse consequences for formal education since oral and written language are primary media of instruction (14). Conflicts between the child's linguistic system and the language of instruction not only can interfere with learning but, unfortunately, can also have social consequences. On both instructional and social grounds, language variations can be a major school problem (1, 27). The increasing literature concerning the language of the "disadvantaged child" is a visible commentary on the relevance of this problem (24, 7). In the main, examinations of language variations have been approached in terms of (a) the possible interrelationships between language and cognitive functioning and (b) their possible effects on spoken and written communication.

One theoretical position of current interest is that of Bernstein, who posits a relationship between social class speech systems, or codes, and orientations to abstract formulations (3,).[1] According to Bernstein, these codes can be described as *restricted* and *elaborated*, the former being characterized by its relatively simple syntax, redundancy, and high predictability, the latter being characterized by its complex syntax and low predictability. Because of the greater number of syntactic options that are possible, an elaborated code permits a greater range of possibilities in organizing experience.

Bernstein stipulates that neither code is necessarily better than the other in terms of its own possibilities. But the larger society may place different values on the kinds of experiences which the different codes may elicit, maintain, and reinforce. Further, although the middle-class person can and does use both codes, the individual from the lower class can be expected to be limited to a restricted code. And, because the language of instruction is typically that of the middle class—an elaborated code—it is crucial that the lower-class child be helped to possess, or at least be oriented toward, the elaborated code (3:164-65).

The attractiveness of Bernstein's approach as a means of accounting for differential learning behaviors among lower- and middle-class children establishes a potential for stereotyping the language capabilities of the lower-class child. It is, of course, apparent to the careful observer of child language that children do not fit so neatly into theoretical categories. Nonetheless, the possible consequences

1. For a comprehensive critique of Bernstein's view, see Lawton (16).

of such attempts for elementary school instruction are not to be lightly dismissed. It seems fair to note that to the extent to which language ability is a prerequisite to school learning, disparities with the model of the language used in the classroom can affect learning. Peisach, for example, found that fifth-graders' ability to fill in words systematically deleted from tapes of teacher and peer speech (the cloze procedure) is related to social class, suggesting that communication barriers may exist for lower-class children in middle-class classrooms (23).

Other effects of language variation on school learning have been reported by numerous investigators. Deutsch and his associates evaluated elements of expressive and receptive speech of Negro and white first- and fifth-grade children representative of three socioeconomic levels. The language measure included (a) total verbal output, (b) number of different words, (c) the number of nouns, verbs, adjectives, and adverbs, and (d) mean sentence length. Factor analysis revealed that language performance and intelligence test scores as measured by the nonverbal form of the *Lorge-Thorndike Intelligence Test* were significantly related, and that although intelligence test scores of advantaged children increased over time, fifth-grade disadvantaged children did relatively poorer on the tests than did their first-grade counterparts. The adverse effects of social disadvantage thus appear to become more pronounced with age, a "cumulative deficit," and are particularly noticeable in language measures among social classes (9, 10).[2]

In respect to usage differences, Loban further analyzed data from his longitudinal study (17), and classified what he determined were the most crucial and frequent oral language difficulties related to social dialect (18). From his stratified sample of 338 children, Loban selected four subgroups: 21 high-language-ability Caucasians, 21 low-language-ability Caucasians, 21 low-language-ability Negroes, and 50 randomly selected children. He then tabulated "errors" in the use of verbs, pronouns, and selected syntactic factors. Distinguishing between "errors" due to developmental factors and those of social dialect, he found that, over time, all children continued to have some difficulties in clarity and precision of expression, but the low-language-ability groups compounded these difficulties by con-

2. For a recent summary, see Whiteman and Deutsch (33).

tinued use of nonstandard speech patterns—for example, lack of agreement of subject and verb, double negatives, the omission of auxiliaries.

The relationship of language variations to instruction can be particularly important in the area of reading, where the language of instruction is most formalized. Labov suggests that phonological variations can have both grammatical and motivational consequences, the former in respect to such factors as "*r*-lessness" (*caught* for *court*), "*l*-lessness" (*toe* for *toll*), and simplification of consonant clusters (*pass* for *past* and *passed*), the latter in respect to the hyper-corrective teacher (14). Labov also calls attention to the influence of the informal vernacular of peers on the language behavior of the elementary school child (15).

Summary

The elementary school years are formative in the child's progression toward adult language norms. Although his basic grammar is ordinarily well established by school-entrance age, the immediately ensuing years contribute significantly to his ultimate potentiality to use the full range of linguistic possibilities which that grammar permits.

Emerging knowledge of the language of the elementary school child not only contributes to better understanding of general language development, but also provides curriculum-makers and teachers with data from which the language of instruction can be more efficiently matched to the language behavior of the child. Though language maturity appears to emerge in a fixed order, the rate of its development can vary widely both as a result of individual factors and of the influences of environment. The structuring of elementary school language programs which reflect what is known about language and the language user and which maximize the child's opportunities to ultimately develop a full range of linguistic capabilities is a challenge which has yet to be met.

BIBLIOGRAPHY

1. BAILEY, BERYL L. "Some Aspects of the Impact of Linguistics on Language Teaching in Disadvantaged Communities," *Elementary English*, XLV (May, 1968), 570–78, 626.

2. BERKO, JEAN. "The Child's Learning of English Morphology," *Word*, XIV (1958), 150–77.
3. BERNSTEIN, BASIL. "A Socio-Linguistic Approach to Social Learning." In *Penguin Survey of the Social Sciences*, 1965, pp. 144–68. Edited by Julius Gould. Baltimore, Maryland: Penguin Books, 1965.
4. CARROLL, JOHN B. "Language Development." In *Encyclopedia of Educational Research*, pp. 744–52. Edited by Chester W. Harris. New York: Macmillan Co., 1960.
5. ————. *Language and Thought.* Englewood Cliffs, N.J.: Prentice-Hall, 1964.
6. CAVOURES, DOROTHY G. "Phoneme Identification in Primary Reading and Spelling." Doctor's dissertation, Boston University School of Education, 1964.
7. CAZDEN, COURTNEY B. "Subcultural Differences in Child Language: An Inter-Disciplinary Review," *Merrill-Palmer Quarterly*, XII (July, 1966), 185–219.
8. COOPER, ROBERT L. "The Ability of Deaf and Hearing Children to Apply Morphological Rules." Doctor's dissertation, Columbia University, 1965.
9. DEUTSCH, MARTIN et al. *Communication of Information in the Elementary School Classroom.* Cooperative Research Project No. 908, 1964.
10. DEUTSCH, MARTIN. "The Role of Social Class in Language Development and Cognition," *American Journal of Orthopsychiatry*, XXXV (January, 1965), 78–88.
11. ERVIN, SUSAN M. and MILLER, WICK R. "Language Development." Chapter iii in *Child Psychology*. Sixty-second Yearbook of the National Society for the Study of Education, Part I, pp. 108-143. Edited by J. W. Stevenson. Chicago: University of Chicago Press, 1963.
12. ERVIN-TRIPP, SUSAN. "Language Development." In *Review of Child Development Research*, II, 55–105. Edited by Lois A. and Martin L. Hoffman. New York: Russell Sage Foundation, 1966.
13. HUNT, KELLOGG W. *Grammatical Structures Written at Three Grade Levels.* NCTE Research Report No. 3. Champaign, Ill.: National Council of Teachers of English, 1965.
14. LABOV, WILLIAM. "Some Sources of Reading Problems for Negro Speakers of Nonstandard English." In *New Directions in Elementary English*. Edited by Alexander Frazier. Champaign, Ill.: National Council of Teachers of English, 1967.
15. ————. "Stages in the Acquisition of Standard English." In *Social Dialects and Language Learning*, pp. 77–103. Edited by Roger Shuy. Champaign, Ill.: National Council of Teachers of English, 1965.
16. LAWTON, DENIS. *Social Class. Language, and Education.* London: Routledge & Kegan Paul, 1968.

17. LOBAN, WALTER D. *The Language of Elementary School Children.* NCTE Research Report No. 1. Champaign, Ill.: National Council of Teachers of English, 1963.

18. ———. *Problems in Oral English.* NCTE Research Report No. 5. Champaign, Ill.: National Council of Teachers of English, 1966.

19. McCARTHY, DOROTHEA. "Language Development in Children." Chapter ix in *Manual of Child Psychology.* 2d. ed., Edited by Leonard R. Carmichael. New York: John Wiley & Sons, 1954.

20. MENYUK, PAULA. "Children's Learning and Reproduction of Grammatical and Nongrammatical Phonological Sequences," *Child Development,* XXXIX (September, 1968), 849–59.

21. MILLER, BARBARA D. and NEY, JAMES W. "The Effect of Systematic Oral Exercises on the Writing of Fourth-Grade Students," *Research in the Teaching of English,* II (Spring, 1968), 44–61.

22. O'DONNELL, ROY C; GRIFFIN, WILLIAM J; and NORRIS, RAYMOND C. *Syntax of Kindergarten and Elementary School Children: A Transformational Analysis.* NCTE Research Report No. 8. Champaign, Ill.: National Council of Teachers of English, 1967.

23. PEISACH, ESTELLE C. "Children's Comprehension of Teacher and Peer Speech," *Child Development,* XXXVI (June, 1965), 467–80.

24. RAPH, J. B. "Language Development in Socially Disadvantaged Children," *Review of Educational Research,* XXXV (1965), 389–400.

25. RILING, MILDRED E. *Oral and Written Language of Children in Grades 4 and 6 Compared with the Language of Their Textbooks.* Cooperative Research Project No. 2410. Washington, D.C.: U.S. Department of Health, Education and Welfare, Office of Education, 1965.

26. SANDY, DON G. "Auditory Discrimination and Articulatory Proficiency of Kindergarten Children." Doctor's dissertation, Boston University School of Education, 1965.

27. SHUY, ROGER W. "Detroit Speech: Careless, Awkward, and Inconsistent, or Systematic, Graceful, and Regular?" *Elementary English,* XLV (May, 1968), 565–69.

28. SLOBIN, DAN I. "Grammatical Transformations and Sentence Comprehension in Childhood and Adulthood," *Journal of Verbal Learning and Verbal Behavior,* V (1966), 219–27.

29. STRICKLAND, RUTH G. *The Language of Elementary School Children: Its Relationship to the Language of Reading Textbooks and the Quality of Reading of Selected Children.* Bulletin of the School of Education, Indiana University, Vol. 38. Bloomington, Ind., 1962.

30. TEMPLIN, MILDRED C. *Certain Language Skills in Children: Their Development and Interrelationships.* Minneapolis: University of Minnesota Press, 1957.

31. ———. *Longitudinal Study Through the Fourth Grade of Language Skills of Children with Varying Speech Sound Articulation in Kin-*

dergarten. USOE Project H2220. Minneapolis: Institute of Child Development, University of Minnesota, January, 1968.

32. WEPMAN, JOSEPH M. and MORENCY, ANNE S. *School Achievement as Related to Developmental Speech Inaccuracy.* Unpublished report, Cooperative Research Project No. 2225, Office of Education, U.S. Department of Health, Education, and Welfare, July, 1967. University of Chicago.

33. WHITEMAN, MARTIN and DEUTSCH, MARTIN. "Social Disadvantage as Related to Intellectual and Language Development." *Social Class, Race, and Psychological Development,* pp. 86–114. Edited by Martin Deutsch, Irwin Katz, and Arthur R. Jensen. New York: Holt, Rinehart & Winston, 1968.

Part II

LANGUAGE DEVELOPMENT: THE SECONDARY SCHOOL YEARS

NATHAN S. BLOUNT

The discussion in this part of the chapter deals with the language development of young people in Grades VII through XII. The bulk of the research reported here deals with developments in syntax and morphology, although several of the studies treat oral expression and listening, or single out disadvantaged youth for attention. This discussion is presented under three major headings: normative studies, experimental and correlational studies, and development and dissemination.

Normative Studies

For a number of decades, studies in language development have tabulated (*a*) mean length of clauses; (*b*) mean length of sentences; (*c*) proportion of dependent clauses to main clauses; and (*d*) relative frequency of adjective, adverb, and noun clauses. McCarthy reviewed the literature reporting use of these measures and found that because of its objectivity and reliability, and ease of application, sentence length was the most widely used index of linguistic maturity. She reported that clause length does not increase between Grades IV and XII, and that, as children mature, their sentence length increases because they acquire the ability to add more subordinate clauses (20:492–630).

In recent decades, Loban, Strickland, and Hunt developed new quantitative measures for studying the development of sentence structure. Loban has used the "communication unit" (19:6–7); Strickland, the "phonological unit" (34); and Hunt, the "minimum terminable unit," or T-unit (10). Because the methodology and findings of Loban and Strickland are set forth in the first half of the present chapter, the focus of this part is often on the work of Hunt and other investigators who have used the T-unit.

Hunt first used T-unit analysis in the Cooperative Research Project (CRP) 1998. He defined T-unit as a shortened form for "minimal terminable unit," the shortest grammatically terminable unit into which a sentence can be segmented without leaving any fragments as residue (10:34). The number of T-units found in a single sentence can vary considerably. A young writer may set down an extremely long string of words, beginning with a capital letter and ending with a period. He would have only one sentence but many T-units. For example, here is a sentence written by an eighth-grader:

> If I had a million dollars I think that I would do many things but I would put most of the money in the bank and I would start on another job so people couldn't call me a lazy man.

Here is the same sentence segmented into T-units:

> If I had a million dollars I think that I would do many things / /
> but I would put most of the money in the bank / /
> and I would start on another job so people couldn't call me a lazy man. / /

Note that every T-unit has at least a main clause and, in addition, may have one or more subordinate clauses.

In CRP 1998, Hunt analyzed 1000 words of writing by fourth-, eighth-, and twelfth-grade students (total N=54) of average mental ability (90–110) as measured by the *California Test of Mental Maturity, Short Form*. Hunt found T-unit length a more valid index of maturity in writing than sentence length, clause length, or subordination radio. He found that T-units, single-clause and multi-clause, grew successively longer between Grades IV and XII, and that single-clause and multiclause T-units increased at about the same growth rate. Lengthening of single-clause T-units was accomplished by the addition of nonclause structures; lengthening of multiclause T-units was accomplished by the addition of both clause and non-clause structures. The major growth that Hunt found occurred in nominal structures. Nominals were expanded by noun clauses and nearclauses, and by the use of modifiers, some clausal but mostly nonclausal (10: *passim*).

In CRP 5-0313, Hunt had as his purposes (*a*) to refine and study further those quantitative syntactic measures which might serve as

significant indicators of chronological and mental maturity in writing, (b) to compare syntactic structures written by students of
superior mental ability in Grades IV and XII with structures
by students of average mental ability at the same grade levels, and
(c) to compare syntactic structures written by twelfth-grade students of average and superior mental ability with syntactic structures
written by skilled adults publishing in *Atlantic Monthly* and *Harper's Magazine*. The study reported five synopses of clause-to-sentence length factors—clause length, subordinate clause index, T-unit
length, main-clause coordination index, and sentence length—and
information on the frequency of subordinate clauses and complexity of nominals. Analyses were made for eighteen fourth-grade students, nine males and nine females of superior intelligence (130+,
CTMM, Short Form); and the data obtained were compared with
the scores for equal numbers of fourth-grade students of average
mental ability, the report cited above as CRP 1998. The same analyses and comparisons were made for eighteen twelfth graders of
superior intelligence and eighteen of average intelligence. Analyses of writing were also reported for nine skilled adults publishing in the *Atlantic* and for nine skilled adults publishing in *Harper's*.
Hunt reported his findings in two categories: procedural recommendations and further information about syntactic development.
In his procedural recommendations, Hunt stated that exclusion of
sentences containing direct discourse and of questions, answers, im-
peratives, and fragments did not make a significant difference in
the five synopses scores. The "subordinate-clause index" (clauses/
T-units) was more useful, though not more valid, than the "subordination ratio" (subordinate clauses/all clauses). The "main-clause
coordination index" (T-units/sentences) was found a useful index
for relating length of T-units to length of sentences. At least in the
early grades, T-unit length seemed a more valid index of maturity
than did sentence length. Giving information as to what older students did to make T-units and clauses longer, the complexity count
for nominals indicated the kind of inquiry which other investigators
might conduct. Among his findings on syntactic development, Hunt
reported that in the fourth grade, the T-unit length of superior students was significantly greater than it was for average students due
to a significantly larger frequency of adjective and adverb clauses.

The clause length of superior fourth-grade students did not differ from that of average students; the sentences of superior students were shorter than those of average students because superior students wrote fewer T-units per sentence. In the twelfth grade, it was not the number of subordinate clauses which distinguished students of superior IQ from students of average IQ. Superior students differed from average ones in length of T-unit and, more especially, in the length of their clauses. Superior twelfth graders were further ahead of average twelfth graders than the latter were ahead of average fourth graders. As represented by nonfiction articles published in the *Atlantic* and in *Harper's*, skilled adults were characterized by T-units longer than those written by secondary school students. Their T-unit length was greater, primarily, because their clause length was greater (11, 12).

Another investigation using the T-unit was conducted by O'Donnell, Griffin, and Norris. The emphases of this study were on identifying and quantifying grammatical structures and on defining the sequence of the acquisition and use of these structures. Speech samples were obtained from students in the kindergarten and Grades I, II, III, V, and VII. Using criteria similar to Hunt's, the investigators tabulated the responses on several indices. "Garbles" occurred much more often in speech than in writing. And when taking into account the total responses, the number of garbles tended to decline with increasing age. Although written responses were shorter than oral ones, total length of responses increased with age. T-unit length in speech was not significantly different from T-unit length in writing; however, an analysis of the structures revealed that students displayed much greater use of syntactic resources in writing than in speech. T-unit length and percentage of short T-units were sensitive measures of development toward maturity. An increasing use of syntactic resources was shown by the number of transforms per T-unit, a number which rose markedly in the speech samples and even more dramatically in the writing samples. The investigators concluded from these data that, although the use of syntactic resources in speech increases so that speech in the third grade is more mature than the newly learned writing skills, a shift in emphasis occurs by Grade V which causes writing to catch up with and to surpass skills in speech. The various types of transforms were examined and several of them appeared to reflect maturity quite well. Among these were adverbial infinitives; coordinations within T-units; the gerund phrase; nominals functioning as the object of a preposition; and modification of nouns by adjectives, participles, and prepositional phrases. Use of sentence patterns showed no major preference trends; even the younger children used all patterns. A reduction in incomplete clauses was apparent. First grade seemed to signal a spurt in speech development, as observed in use of adverbials, adverbial clauses, infinitives with subjects, nominals, and nominals as direct objects. Seventh grade showed another spurt in speech development in nearly all constructions: adverbial clauses, coordination, nominal function, noun clauses, and noun modification. Writing development improved markedly in Grade V and again in Grade VII in such uses as adverbial clauses, complex structures functioning as direct objects, coordination within T-units, genitive forms, and relative clauses. O'Donnell and his collaborators rejected total number of words and number of subordinate clauses as measures of maturity and concluded that the relative frequency of sentence-combining transformations was the most valid measure. However, they suggested that it is difficult to obtain the relative frequency of sentence-combining transformations, and that a good approximation is mean T-unit length (25).

The work of Labov with nonstandard vernacular of the urban ghettos indicated that the differences between this dialect and Standard English are greater on the surface than in the underlying grammatical structure. Competence of native speakers of the nonstandard vernacular indicated their ability to perceive, abstract, and reproduce the meaning of many standard forms which they did not produce themselves. Labov hypothesized that a single grammar can be constructed which can systematically account for the syntactic variation inhering in the speech of Ss (subjects) from the urban ghetto (16:66–84).

Beginning in 1952, Loban conducted a longitudinal study of children's language, kindergarten through Grade XII. In each of the thirteen years of the project, language samples were obtained. Loban's analyses of speech and writing samples were made using the "communication unit," a grammatically independent predication or an answer to a question lacking only the repetition of the question element. Taped oral interviews were conducted and a wide range of tests to measure listening ability, skill with written language, ability and growth in fluency in oral language, and so on were administered each year. Data indicated that students who developed proficiency in oral language also developed proficiency in listening, reading, and writing. From the data collected on students in Grades X, XI, and XII, Loban reported that students with high language proficiency used more optional and more accurate transformations in their sentence structures. These students used more adverbial clauses of cause, concession, and condition. They used relational words more accurately and more often. They employed more varied and flexible syntax than did students of lesser ability. Correlations suggested that students from above-average socioeconomic groups used nonstandard English less frequently, and developed language skills earlier and to a greater degree of competence than did students from below-average socioecemonic groups (18).

Several investigations examined the role of syntactic variables in sentence recall. On the basis of an experiment using 80 Ss, Mehler advanced the hypothesis that Ss analyze sentences into a semantic component plus syntactic corrections as they learn them and that this separation is one reason why it is generally easier to recall the general meaning of a message than its exact wording (22). Slobin, too, found an interaction between a syntactic component (affirmative-negative) and a semantic component (true-false) (32).

Experimental and Correlational Studies

Various correlational studies of the relationship of traditional grammar and writing ability conducted by such researchers as Asker (1), Boraas (4), Bradford (5), Catherwood (7), Hoyt (9), Rapeer (26), Robinson (28), and Segal and Barr (30) have suggested that traditional grammar as it has been taught has had little effect on the improvement of writing skills; and that traditional grammar has had little, if any, transfer value in developing writing ability.

Scholars formulating systematic analyses of language have often been unwilling to speculate on the uses of the new grammars in the secondary schools. However, some research has examined the impact of a study of structural and transformational grammars on language development as seen in writing.

Three investigators—Blake (3), Johnson (14), and O'Donnell (24)—found no evidence of the superiority of a structural approach over a traditional grammar approach in the teaching of writing. O'Donnell, using correlation analysis, found no basis for assuming that either knowledge of traditional grammar or knowledge of structural grammar would be regularly accompanied by excellence in written composition (24). A study by Lin failed to reveal any statistically significant differences between an experimental group receiving pattern practice (relying on structural grammar) and a control group (17). Klauser found that in seven months, in Grades VII and IX, structural grammar produced as good results as traditional grammar in effective writing (15).

Bateman and Zidonis assessed the effects of study of transformational grammar on the writing of ninth- and tenth-grade students over a two-year period. The pupils constituting the ninth-grade population (N=50) were assigned to two sections, taught by two teachers also assigned randomly. The experimental class studied the phrase structure component of transformational grammar in the first year of the experiment and transformational materials in the second. The exact treatment assigned the control group was not reported. Some 70,000 words of prose, written over a two-year period, were analyzed using an instrument which the investigators developed to assess the grammatical quality of the sentences in the sample. Bateman and Zidonis found that ninth- and tenth-grade students learned the principles of transformational grammar relatively easily and that knowledge of these principles enabled the student to increase significantly the proportion of well-formed sentences which he wrote. Analyses further tended to suggest that knowledge of transformational grammar enabled the student to increase sentence complexity without sacrificing sentence grammaticality. It was found that knowledge of transformational grammar enabled the student to reduce the occurrence of errors in his writing. Because almost half of the sentences written by ninth graders were malformed according to rigorous criteria of well-formedness, the investigators suggested that, while some linguists maintain that children have acquired virtually full command of English grammar at an early age, it is possible that the grammar of English is never fully mastered (2).

In a study of transformational sentence-combining, Mellon defined maturity of sentence structure in a statistical sense. He equated maturity with "syntactic fluency," the range of sentence types observed in representative samples of a student's writing. His hypothesis was that practice in transformational sentence-combining would enhance the normal growth of syntactic fluency. Three groups of seventh-grade students were given three different treatments during the course of a school year. One treatment was a series of sentence-combining problems; these were begun in January, after introductory material on base rules, kernel sentences, and simple transformations had been taught, and were continued through May. During the five months, 602 problems in transformational grammar were given to 100 students. The rationale for this treatment was "to direct a maximum of the student's attention to the way that content initially expressed in collections of separately represented kernel sentences may be collapsed into single statements" (23:32–33). A second group of 100 students, the control group, studied the usual curriculum which included 800 traditional exercises in phrasing sentences. A placebo group of forty-seven students received no direct instruction in grammar. In lieu of grammar, this placebo group studied literature and usage and received direct instruction in techniques for varying sentence structure. During the normal course of the year, all students wrote compositions in class. Ninety T-units written by each student during the first four weeks of school and another ninety T-unit sample written during the last four weeks of school provided the basic data for the dependent variable, syntactic fluency. Eleven tabulations were made which provided the basis for twelve factors of syntactic fluency: words per T-unit, subordination-coordination ratio, nominal clauses, nominal phrases, relative clauses, relative phrases, relative words, embedded kernel sentences, cluster frequency, mean cluster size, embedding frequency, and mean maximum depth level. The experimental group showed significant pre-post growth on all twelve measures, while the control group showed no significant growth. When compared to growth rates cited by Hunt, the experimental students gained the equivalent of three years in their use of noun clauses, noun phrases, relative clauses, and relative words. Although the experimental and control groups were similar in prewriting, analyses showed that the experimental group surpassed the control group on every measure in postwriting. The experimental group was significantly above the placebo group on eight of the twelve measures. Sex differences or school differences were not significant. There was some evidence to indicate that the better students gained more from the experimental treatment than did the poorer students.

Language development growing out of the use of three language modes, rather than out of a study of grammar, was the subject of an investigation by Tovatt and Miller (35). In this study, several kinds of stimuli were combined in an oral-aural-visual (OAV) approach in which the students practiced oral forms of language to improve writing. Intonation was applied to punctuation; oral discussion and criticism of what was to be written preceded actual writing; and oral sentence patterns were tested against written patterns. To facilitate the OAV approach, the students used a system of tape recorder and audio-active earphones. The authors compared OAV with a conventional method of teaching composition by randomly assigning thirty ninth-grade students to each method. The length of treatment for each group was one year. Five pretests and five posttests were given: STEP Reading, Writing, and Listening; Cooperative English Usage; and Modern Language Aptitude. In addition, five essays were collected during the year and were graded following the Educational Testing Service (ETS) rating form; and attitude scales were administered. During a second school year, eighty ninth-grade students used the OAV approach; and comparisons were made among the gains of students of high, medium, and low mental ability. The results of the first-year program showed significant differences on the three STEP tests and the Cooperative English Usage Test in favor of OAV students. The essays showed no changes in favor of OAV students; the attitude scales showed slight changes in favor of OAV students. The results from the second-year program with eighty new students showed that the high-ability students gained greatly in listening skills; and differences between ability groups were maintained in writing essays. The other tests showed significant but equivalent gains for each ability level (35).

Development and Dissemination

Squire and Applebee reported that in 1609 classes visited by their project staff, only 13.5 percent of the total time emphasized language. Relative emphasis on language dropped from 21.5 percent in Grade X to 8.4 percent in Grade XII. Relative emphasis on language study for terminal or non-college-bound students was slightly higher than 19.9 percent. The overwhelming majority of teachers used in the study viewed the fundamental concern of English instruction to be literature and composition rather than language. The overwhelming majority of programs in the study had been only indirectly influenced by modern linguistic scholarship (33).

Hawkins studied the structural-transformational foundations in representative language textbooks designed for use in English classes in the secondary school. He found that the most recent of these materials revealed dependency on the theories of structural linguistics and of generative-transformational grammars (8).

Materials incorporating the new grammars for use in the secondary school may be seen in the works of Roberts (27), Rogovin (29) Brown and White (6), and Jacobs and Rosenbaum (13).

Financed by Cooperative Research Project funds from the U.S. Office of Health, Education, and Welfare, a number of curriculum study centers around the nation developed curriculum materials utilizing recent grammars to foster language development in adolescents. Shugrue has described many of these materials (31). One example of development and dissemination activities, influenced in part by the work of Hunt and of Zidonis, can be seen in the Wisconsin English-Language-Arts Curriculum project under the direction of Robert C. Pooley. This center has produced a language program designed to serve two purposes: (a) to increase curiosity about language in general and the English language in particular, and (b) to help students use the English language more effectively. The proposed language curriculum begins with a listing of principles such as (a) study leading to language development should be spiraling and sequential from kindergarten through Grade XII; (b) the grammar taught should be eclectic; (c) experience with language should be acquired empirically; and so on. In kindergarten through Grade VI, it is envisioned that children should become aware of language processes through games, through observing word order in written and in oral discourse, from practicing verb forms in sentence patterns, and so on. In Grades VII through IX, various concepts and generalizations from structural and transformational grammars are to be taught to the end that students learn to generate varied sentences, in addition to acquiring the ability to classify words as parts of speech. In Grades X through XII, transformational grammar is to be used as the basis of sentence development to achieve "greater sophistication in syntactical structuring and manipulation commensurate with the varying abilities of high school students and the different grade levels" (36).

MacLeish reported the work of the Northern Illinois University Curriculum Center in developing instructional materials in structural and transformational grammars for the eleventh and twelfth grades and in investigating the effect of instruction in these materials upon student writing and attitude toward the study of linguistics. Data on the effect of instruction were inconclusive. However, MacLeish's research did suggest that structural and transformational grammar could be taught successfully in the secondary school by teachers trained in traditional grammar, both to students thoroughly indoctrinated in traditional grammar and to students who know little grammar. Knowledge of the grammars seemed to make students more sensitive to their language, both to its structure and to their own writing problems. The grammars provided teachers explicit and unambiguous ways to help students eliminate errors. They seemed to motivate both students and teachers to further English language study (21).

BIBLIOGRAPHY

1. ASKER, WILLIAM. "Does Knowledge of Formal Grammar Function?" *School and Society*, XVII (January, 1923), 109–11.
2. BATEMAN, DONALD and ZIDONIS, FRANK. *The Effect of A Study of Transformational Grammar on the Writing of Ninth and Tenth Graders*. NCTE Research Report No. 6. Champaign, Ill.: National Council of Teachers of English, 1966.
3. BLAKE, ROBERT W. "Linguistics and Punctuation," *English Record*, XV (October, 1964), 9–13.
4. BORAAS, JULIUS. "Formal English Grammar and the Practical Mastery of English." Doctor's dissertation. Department of Education, University of Minnesota, 1917.

5. BRADFORD, LELAND P. "Study of Certain Factors Affecting English Usage," *Journal of Educational Research*, XXXV (October, 1941), 109–18.

6. BROWN, MARSHALL L. and WHITE, ELMER. *A Grammar for English Sentences* (Books One and Two). Columbus, Ohio: Charles E. Merrill Books, 1966.

7. CATHERWOOD, CATHERINE. "A Study of Relationships Between A Knowledge of Rules and Ability to Correct Grammatical Errors and Between Identification of Sentences and Knowledge of Subject and Predicate." Master's thesis, University of Minnesota, 1932.

8. HAWKINS, JAMES PRESTON. "The 'New English Grammar," A Study of the Structural-Transformational Foundations in Materials Designed for Secondary Schools." Doctor's dissertation. Colorado State College, 1966.

9. HOYT, FRANKLIN S. "The Place of Grammar in the Elementary Curriculum," *Teachers College Record*, VII (November, 1906), 467–500.

10. HUNT, KELLOGG W. *Differences in Grammatical Structures Written at Three Grade Levels, The Structures To Be Analyzed by Transformational Methods*. Cooperative Research Project 1998. Tallahassee, Fla.: Florida State University and the Office of Education, U.S. Department of Health, Education, and Welfare, 1964.

11. ———. *Grammatical Structures Written at Three Grade Levels*. NCTE Research Report No. 3. Champaign, Ill.: National Council of Teachers of English, 1965.

12. ———. *Sentence Structures Used by Superior Students in Grades Four and Twelve, and by Superior Adults*. Cooperative Research Project No. 5-0313. Tallahassee, Fla.: Florida State University and the Cooperative Research Program of the Office of Education, U.S. Department of Health, Education, and Welfare, n. d.

13. JACOBS, RODERICK A. and ROSENBAUM, PETER S. *Grammar 1* and *Grammar 2*. Boston: Ginn & Co., 1967.

14. JOHNSON, FALK S. "Structural versus Non-Structural Teaching," *College Composition and Communication*, XI (December, 1960), 214–15.

15. KLAUSER, EVA L. "A Comparison of a Structural Approach and a Traditional Approach to the Teaching of Grammar in an Illinois Junior High School." Doctor's dissertation. University of Colorado, 1964.

16. LABOV, WILLIAM and COHEN, PAUL. "Systematic Relations of Standard and Non-Standard Rules in the Grammars of Negro Speakers." *Project Literacy Reports*, No. 8, pp. 66–84. Cornell University, 1967.

17. LIN, SAN-SU. *Pattern Practice on the Teaching of Standard English to Students with a Nonstandard Dialect*. Project No. 1339. Orangeburg, S.C.: Claflin University and the Office of Education, U.S. Department of Health, Education, and Welfare, 1965.

18. LOBAN, WALTER. *Language Ability: Grades Ten, Eleven, and*

Twelve. Project No. 2387. Berkeley: University of California and the Office of Education, U.S. Department of Health, Education, and Welfare, 1967.

19. ————. *The Language of Elementary School Children*. NCTE Research Report No. 1. Champaign, Ill.: National Council of Teachers of English, 1963.

20. McCarthy, Dorothea. "Language Development in Children." In *A Manual of Child Psychology*, 2d ed.; pp. 492–630. Edited by Leonard Carmichael. New York: John Wiley & Sons: 1954.

21. MacLeish, Andrew. *Materials and Methods for Teaching Structural and Generative Grammar to High School Students and Their Teachers*. Project No. H-144. Northern Illinois University and the Office of Education, U.S. Department of Health, Education, and Welfare, 1967.

22. Mehler, Jacques. "Some Effects of Grammatical Transformations on the Recall of English Sentences," *Journal of Verbal Learning and Verbal Behavior*, II (1963), 346–51.

23. Mellon, John C. *Transformational Sentence-Combining: A Method for Enhancing the Development of Syntactic Fluency in English Composition*. Cooperative Research Project No. 5-8418. Office of English Education and Laboratory for Research in Instruction, Graduate School of Education, Harvard University, Cambridge, Mass., and the Office of Education, U.S. Department of Health, Education, and Welfare, 1967.

24. O'Donnell, Roy C. *The Correlation of Awareness of Structural Relationships in English and Ability in Written Composition*. Cooperative Research Project No. 1524. Mount Olive, N.C.: Mount Olive Junior College and the Office of Education, U.S. Department of Health, Education, and Welfare, 1963.

25. O'Donnell, Roy C.; Griffin, William J.; and Norris, Raymond C. *Syntax of Kindergarten and Elementary School Children: A Transformational Analysis*. NCTE Research Report No. 8. Champaign, Ill.: National Council of Teachers of English, 1967.

26. Rapeer, Louis W. "The Problem of Formal Grammar in Elementary Education," *Journal of Educational Psychology*, IV (March, 1913), 125–37.

27. Roberts, Paul. *English Sentences*. New York: Harcourt, Brace, & World, 1962. See also *English Syntax*. New York: Harcourt, Brace, & World, 1964.

28. Robinson, Nora. "The Relation Between Knowledge of English Grammar and Ability in English Composition," *British Journal of Educational Psychology*, XXX (June, 1960), 184–86.

29. Rogovin, Syrell. *Modern English Sentence Structure*. New York: Random House-Singer, 1964.

30. Segal, David and Barr, Nora R. "Relation of Achievement in For-

mal Grammar to Achievement in Applied Grammar," *Journal of Educational Research*, XIV (December, 1926), 401-2.

31. SHUGRUE, MICHAEL F. "New Materials for the Teaching of English: The English Program of the USOE," *PMLA*, LXXXI (September, 1966), reprint.

32. SLOBIN, DAN I. "Grammatical Transformations and Sentence Comprehension in Childhood and Adulthood," *Journal of Verbal Learning and Verbal Behavior*, V (1966), 219-27.

33. SQUIRE, JAMES R. and APPLEBEE, ROGER K. *A Study of English Programs in Selected High Schools Which Consistently Educate Outstanding Students in English*. Cooperative Research Project No. 1994. Urbana, Ill.: University of Illinois and the Office of Education, U.S. Department of Health, Education, and Welfare, 1966.

34. STRICKLAND, RUTH G. *The Language of Elementary School Children: Its Relationship to the Language of Reading Textbooks and the Quality of Reading of Selected Children*. Bulletin of the School of Education, Indiana University, Vol. 38. Bloomington, Ind., 1962.

35. TOVATT, ANTHONY L. and MILLER, EBERT L. *Oral-Aural-Visual Stimuli Approach to Teaching Written Composition to 9th Grade Students*. Project No. 5-03892-12-1. Muncie, Ind.: Ball State University and the Office of Education, U.S. Department of Health, Education, and Welfare, 1967.

36. Wisconsin English-Language-Arts Curriculum Project, *Teaching the English Language in Wisconsin*. Experimental ed. Madison, Wis. Department of Public Instruction and the Cooperative Research Division of the U.S. Office of Education, 1967.

CHAPTER VIII

Contributions of Linguistics to Reading and Spelling

Part I

LINGUISTICS AND READING

SUMNER IVES
and
JOSEPHINE PIEKARZ IVES

Introduction

When one is relating two areas of instruction, it is usually best to consider first the fundamental objectives of the two areas, since a natural relationship may be suggested by these objectives. Linguistics is the systematic study of language and, more particularly, of the details of individual languages. English linguistics, of course, is the study of details of the English language. A language is a medium of communication, and the English language is such a medium. In a specific instance of communication (usually) someone uses forms of a particular language to express some message, and (usually) someone else perceives and interprets these forms and thereby understands the message. When the perception is visual rather than auditory, the process of interpretation is *reading*. In essence, then, certain courses in linguistics convey information about the forms of a language; courses in reading instruction teach the interpretation of such forms when they are manifested in a particular way—graphically rather than orally.

The preceding summary is greatly simplified, but it suggests the natural and essential relationship of the two instructional areas. At the same time, there is a difference between the two areas which is just as fundamental as this relationship, and this difference is also suggested by the objectives of the two areas. Linguistics deals with knowledge; research in linguistics accumulates information and develops theory based on this information; courses in linguistics convey this information and explain this theory. Reading instruction deals with performance; research in reading instruction studies a kind of behavior and looks for ways to guide this behavior more effectively; courses in reading instruction are largely expositions of methods. Since the behavior involves the recognition and interpretation of linguistic forms, the field of reading must assume that its information about the manifestation and import of these forms is both adequate and accurate. A student of language is primarily concerned with factual details; a teacher of reading is primarily concerned with pedagogical strategies. Both deal with linguistic forms as perceptible units that convey meaning.

Although the general relevance of linguistic information to reading is obvious, specific applications of the former to the latter require a closer examination of both. Regardless of theories about the connections between language and thought, and even without trying to reach a satisfactory definition of meaning, it is nevertheless clear that a language is a system which reflects thought and by means of which meaning can be communicated. A particular instance of verbal communication is usually called an *utterance*, and the use of utterances in communication is usually called *discourse*. These are therefore equivalent terms indicating different points of view toward what they identify and are appropriate to different contexts. Reading, then, is the reception of utterances, i.e., discourse, through the eyes rather than through the ears.

The representation of utterances for visual reception, in this discussion, will be called *writing*, whether the representation is by script, print, or other means. And writing will refer only to alphabetic writing—that is, representation by letters and marks of punctuation.

For purposes of description, it is convenient to divide a linguistic system (i.e., a language) into at least three subsystems—lexical, grammatical, and phonological. These are overlapping and interdependent components of the total system, not independent levels of the system. In any utterance longer than an involuntary exclamation, elements from all three component systems ordinarily appear. Speaking very generally, lexical items and grammatical signals are combined into meaningful structures, and these are manifested by units of the phonological system. When the utterance is written, this manifestation is by units of the orthographic system. The utterance is understood when the phonological or orthographic units are adequately recognized and, through them, the lexical and grammatical signals are adequately interpreted. Note that this summary does not specify the sizes of the phonological or the orthographic units which are the primary items in recognition. That is, it does not suggest that these units are of any particular length or character, or that they are the same for everyone. It may be that the primary unit of recognition in phonology is different from the corresponding unit in orthography. Nevertheless, primary signals of some kind are perceived and recognized. Also, it does not say that some words symbolize only lexical meaning, or only grammatical meaning. To do either is an over-simplification. Lexical and grammatical information is conveyed by means of linguistic forms which are represented by phonological or orthographic means.

The style and some other characteristics of spoken and written discourse are frequently different, but this difference will be ignored because the problem here is reading, which requires that something first be written. Aside from these differences, the lexical and grammatical information in an utterance is the same, whether it is spoken or written. Writing and speech are therefore different means for representing utterances that are otherwise the same, although the spoken form is likely to be richer in the actual signals of transmission. If this is so, the focus for primary attention is on the relationship between these two modes of representation. Other problems of recognition and interpretation are problems common to all use of language in communication, and improvement in them involves some increase in general command of the resources of the language, a matter that is not exclusively the responsibility of reading but of the total process of education. At the same time, when lexical and grammatical difficulties arise from dialectal differences, the reading teacher is likely to be the first teacher to encounter them in a crucial way.

Phoneme and Grapheme

If the critical difference (but not the only difference) between understanding what is spoken and understanding what is written results from the different modes of representation, then the next step is to examine the units of phonology and the units of orthography—what is commonly, though very loosely, known as the phoneme-grapheme relationship. Persons who are not well acquainted with linguistics are likely to refer to phonemes as sounds. To do so is an oversimplification which sometimes does no harm but which, if taken literally, can lead to serious error. The difference between phoneme and sound is like that between type and token. A phoneme is a designation of a contrast in a system of contrasts; a sound, in this context, is an event which manifests a phoneme, one of those which may manifest it.

A couple of illustrations will make this point clearer. When the word *pan* is pronounced, a sequence of three phonemes is manifested. The sounds which manifest each of the consonant phonemes are generally heard as the same regardless of the person speaking, provided, of course, he is a native speaker of English. However, there is considerable variety in the sounds which manifest the vowel in various parts of the United States, and in some sections there are even two short *a* phonemes, a fact that is not reflected in the spelling. The second illustration is the pronunciation of words like *here, fear,* and *beer.* In all dialects of American English, there is a contrast between the vowels of *bit* and *beat,* but this contrast is not consistently maintained in any region before an immediately following /r/ or corresponding phoneme that appears in its place i.e., regardless of whether /r/ is "lost" or not. One cannot, therefore, say that the vowel in *here, fear, beer,* etc., is either long *e* or short *i,* for the relevant contrast is not maintained in these words, and the phonetic quality often varies with the degree of stress given the word in an utterance. Similar statements can be made about other vowel contrasts before /r/ (or <r>). In fact, generalizations about sound and spelling which do not distinguish between vowels before /r/ and vowels before other consonants are ignoring a major fact about the pronunciation of English.

Illustrations such as these are neither few nor hard to find. They indicate a general fact about the relationship between phonology and orthography in American English. Despite claims to the contrary, attempts to devise a single phonemic system for all American

English have not been entirely successful. Some regions have different sets of phonemic contrasts than others have; some have different phonemes in the same words; and some manifest the same (or equivalent) phonemes with different phonetic qualities. The phonemic principle was developed for analyzing an internally consistent corpus, and attempts to extend it to a variety of dialects of the same language have resulted in the suppression or oversimplification of some phonological facts. Yet, a teacher cannot evade these facts, for they appear in her classroom.

In other words, with reference to phonology, there is no standard English that is typically used by most Americans (although some seem to think there is) [1] unless one extends the range of "standard" to include a considerable number of variations. A dialect, whether regional or social, is simply one of the existing manifestations of a linguistic system, and all such manifestations, including those that have the greatest prestige, are dialects. To say that someone speaks American English is really to say that he speaks a dialect of American English. On the phonemic level, the level that is relevant, these dialects are much more alike than unlike, but a considerable number of differences exist. Regional differences appear in the speech of persons of all social and educational levels. In addition, there are social differences wherever there are relatively homogeneous subcultures, which may be set off by residence, economic level, or even age. There are no "ethnic dialects," except as a result of ethnic separation from other groups.

The various social and regional dialects of a language are not random deviations. The major differences that are found in American English are not difficult to learn, for they can be described by general statements with a high level of consistency. The following are representative. In most dictionaries, different vowels are shown for *cot* and *caught*, and the words do have contrasting vowels in most of the country. But, in many areas, the vowels in question are not in contrast (i.e., are phonemically the same) in these words and in others. These sounds may be used, but they do not represent different phonemes. Also, their distribution, when they are phonemically distinct, is quite varied. They occur in different words in

1. See *Problems in Oral English* (13) and the review of this report by Virginia M. Burke (5).

different parts of the country. Once this general fact is understood, however, the local situation can be examined, and appropriate generalizations can be made. Another major source of differences is the occurrence of vowels before /r/ (or <r>). Instances have been given earlier, and the full situation in any region can be worked out by anyone who is able to test the various possibilities. The unabridged dictionaries have very good treatments of phonological variations, but one should look at the introductions as well as the entries.

This dialectal diversity in American English is relevant to reading instruction in three important areas—preparation of instructional materials, diagnosis of student difficulties, and, as a consequence of these, training of teachers. There is no fully comprehensive set of pronunciations which can be used as the basis for nationally valid statements about correspondences between sound and letter.[2] This statement does not imply that efforts to make such correspondences are useless, but it does suggest that at least some of the correspondences are not equally valid for all dialects.

For example, the same vowel phoneme occurs in *fool* and in *rude*, which illustrates the most common spellings for this vowel. In most American English, this vowel also occurs in *tune, duke,* and *nude* (after /t/, /d/, and /n/), but in a large part of the country, the vowel in these words is that in *cute*, the diphthong (or consonant plus vowel) that is sometimes called long *u*. To a more limited extent, this, or an equivalent complex sound, is also used in *suit, assume, lute,* and some others. It is obviously impossible to frame rules of phonics or spelling rules about these vocalic units which are applicable to the country as a whole, but since the variations are essentially systematic, they can be covered by a supplementary statement.

The customary rules of phonics have been attacked often, for some of them are hardly as accurate as they should be, entirely apart from the question of pedagogical efficiency. Such rules are in the area of information; whether to use them is in the area of strategy. The pedagogical usefulness of such rules cannot be

2. See *Phoneme-Grapheme Correspondence as Cues to Spelling Improvement* (II) and the reviews of this report by A. Hood Roberts (17) and David W. Reed (17).

properly determined until they are revised for accuracy, and a method based on them cannot be fully assessed until the rules have been adjusted for the locality in which they are to be tested. Such revision and adjustment are linguistic problems. Any method that is based on phonics is a linguistic method. The vital question is whether the linguistics is sound. At present, it is not.

The second problem raised by dialectal diversity is the diagnosis of student difficulties. When teachers and pupils have similar geographical and social backgrounds, they probably use the same phonemic system, have the same phonemic distributions, and manifest the phonemes with essentially the same phonetic qualities. They are therefore likely to interpret the instructional materials in the same way. However, teachers and pupils move, especially pupils. Moreover, especially in large cities, there are likely to be serious differences in speech among the various social groups contributing pupils to the same classes. Also, many teachers come from a social and educational background different from that of most pupils in their classes.

The implications for teachers training are obvious. Since it is hardly practical to publish different classroom materials for each region and social group—although in some instances this may be necessary—teachers should be able to observe the dialectal differences that cause trouble for individual pupils and attack the reason for the trouble rather than try to cope with the symptoms. This suggestion should not arouse excessive dismay. Teachers need not become dialectologists, for one can assume that publishers, once they see the need and can be assured of a market, will provide adequate guides to the use of their own materials. Teachers should, however, be able to make a few observations about local pronunciations and should be able to hear sounds independently of letters. For example, there is no /h/ in *this,* and the final sound in *missed* is /t/ not /d/. This proficiency could be attained in a properly taught one-semester course, if the rest of the training program did not contradict what was taught in this course.

Spelling Units

A fuller treatment of English spelling is given in the second part of this chapter, but some remarks about spelling units are needed here, if this discussion is to be reasonably comprehensive. The basic principle of alphabetic writing is that letters are used, rather than phonemes, as the primary signals which convey linguistic forms. Letters can, of course, be written in a variety of ways— lower case or capital, print or script, and so on. This range of manifestation is analogous to the range of sounds that manifest phonemes. In either instance, one does not deal with sameness but with equivalence, although "same" is used sometimes when "equivalent" is meant. Regional differences in spelling are trivial and will be ignored.

Obviously, there are more vowel and consonant phonemes in English than there are conventional letters to represent them. This fact makes a description of English spelling more complicated than a simple sound-letter correspondence. One necessary unit in describing spelling is the grapheme, which is a letter or letter combination that stands for a particular phoneme, at least in a particular instance. For example, both *sin* and *sing* have three phonemes, but the final phoneme in *sing* is spelled with two letters. This two-letter combination is therefore a grapheme. Sometimes, however, the designation of graphemes is not so simple. The assignment of the letter <u> to either the consonant or the vowel in *build* is necessarily arbitrary. Another kind of unit is the spelling pattern—a more or less generalized context which forms part of the visual signal. The most obvious instance is the occurrence of silent *e* in the sequence *VCE*, in which *V* represents a vowel letter, *C* a consonant grapheme (other than <dg> as in *edge*), and *E* represents silent *e*. Instances are *made, cede, ride, rode,* and *rude.* Both of these spelling devices invite further discussion, for their uses are not simple.

Generally speaking, the <ng> combination represents the velar nasal, as in *sing*, but this phoneme appears regularly before /k/, as in *think*, and in such words is usually spelled with <n>. Also, in most dialects, but not in all, *finger* has a /g/ that does not appear in *singer*. The grapheme <ch> usually represents /č/ in words surviving from Old English (*child*) and in words borrowed from early French (*chair*), but it also represents /k/ in many words derived from Greek (*chorus*), or /š/ in a few words recently borrowed from French (*chef*). Also, the grapheme <th> may represent a voiceless phoneme, as in *thin*, or a voiced phoneme, as in *then*, and in function words generally. In final position, <th> usually represents the voiceless phoneme, although *with* may be pronounced with either, and *smooth* has the voiced phoneme. The representation of the voiced phoneme in final position is <the>, as in *loathe*. In medial position, <th> customarily represents the voiced phoneme, but not in *ether*.

The examples for <th> introduce the importance of pattern, in this instance, of position in the word. A more subtle illustration of patterning is found in the interpretation of vowel letters before consonant clusters, for example, the sequence <ld>. In this context, the letters <i> and <o> ordinarily represent "long" vowels, as in *wild* and *cold*, but before <lt>, the letter <i> represents the short vowel as in *wilt*. These contexts do not affect interpretation of the letter <e> (*held* and *belt*). The letter <u> does not occur before <ld> and stands for a short vowel before <lt>. The letter <a> is here, as frequently, a special case. Before <ll> or <l> plus another consonant, it stands for neither long *a* nor short *a* (*call, scald, halt*), but note *calf* and *half*, which do not contain /l/ despite the spelling. Usually, the context preceding a vowel letter is not relevant to what the letter (or grapheme) stands for, but the context following it is frequently significant, as in the preceding instances. However, <w> preceding <a> is a relevant signal, as in *was, want*, and *water*. Close examination of English spelling shows a number of limited patterns such as those mentioned here.

The relations among stress, spelling, and pronunciation constitute another kind of patterning. When words are pronounced in isolation, as in a list, American English has a basically three-level system. Illustrations are *vacation, exercise*, and *secretary*. The effects of these levels are different. In fully unstressed syllables, some dialects have an *r*-vowel in all positions, but others do not have this vowel in final position, although it frequently occurs in others. Also, in final syllables, when the vowel letter is <y>, some dialects have something like short *i* and others have something like long *e*. This vowel remains when morphemes are added. Examples are *happy* and *happiness*. In other positions, and excluding the *r*-vowel some dialects have only one vowel phoneme, although the actual sound may vary; others have two—i.e., *sofas* and *watches* do not have the same second vowel. When, on the other hand, syllables have primary or secondary stress, this difference in stress does not correlate with a difference in phonemes, even though the phonetic qualities may differ. The difference in quality is the reason why some dictionaries refer to "half-long *a*," and so on. Thus, the first two vowels in *vacation* are the same phonemes, despite the differences in sound.

Another problem when associating sound and spelling is division into syllables. Most dictionaries indicate divisions in the spellings which show where a word may be divided at the end of a line, but these divisions do not consistently agree with phonological boundaries. Some examples are *pro-duce*, *prod-uct*, *knowl-edge*, *sum-mer*, and *bet-ter*. Sometimes these divisions are made at morpheme boundaries, sometimes between double consonants, and sometimes the division depends on whether the preceding vowel is long or not, although none of these is consistently a phonological boundary in all varieties of American English. In some instances, it is impossible to divide the spelling to agree with pronunciation. For instance, *situation* is usually pronounced "si chu way shun," or the consonant which ends the first syllable also begins the second. A similar difficulty is found in *gradual*, which is usually pronounced "gra ju wul." In both instances, there is a /w/ in the pronunciation that goes with the following vowel, but the only letter to represent it is the <u> which is part of the spelling for the preceding consonant.

Some reasons for English spelling habits can be found in the history of the language. Scholars generally assume that English writing was, at first, roughly phonemic. When alphabetic writing is first adopted, the associations of letters with sounds are likely to correspond, at least loosely, to the impressions of native speakers. But the earliest English had more vowel phonemes than the alphabet supplied, and there were some further complications in the consonants. It is clear that a reasonably firm spelling tradition, based on West Saxon, was established before the Norman Conquest, that this was broken down by the Conquest, that it was rebuilt, based on a different dialect, with considerable modification from French spelling customs, and that, after the beginning of printing, it became reasonably stabilized again. Although there have been some changes in spelling since then, the major development has been toward greater uniformity in the use of established customs.

During all this time, English phonology continued to change, and changes are still taking place. These changes have not been random but quite systematic, so that "rules" covering them have been formulated. One of them was a comprehensive shift affecting all the long vowels, so that the phonetic similarity between, say, short *e* and long *a* is now greater than that between short *e* and long *e*, although this was not previously the case.

Another factor has been the hospitality of the English to words from other languages. For example, *chief* was borrowed from French during the Middle Ages, but *chef* was borrowed more recently. The change in initial phonemes, not indicated in the spellings, reflects a consonant change that took place in the language of origin. Also, *dine* is an earlier borrowing from French, and *ravine* is a later borrowing from the same language. In this case, the difference in stressed vowels results from a change that took place in English, the vowel shift referred to earlier. Many words in English reflect spelling habits in other languages, especially those using a similar alphabet. Although theoretically one does not need data from history when making purely descriptive statements about a language, in this case a review of the history of English would provide clues for descriptive research and would make the results more understandable. No comprehensive and linguistically sound display of English spelling customs now exists, but some useful starts have been made.

The Teaching of Reading

So far as we know, the first books used to teach reading in English were the hornbook and, perhaps a little later, the battledore. The hornbook was a slab of wood on which was pasted a leaf of paper or parchment showing the alphabet, some simple syllables, and the Lord's Prayer. After the children were drilled on this material, they advanced to a real book, a prayer book or devotional manual called a primer. When reading was initiated, each word was spelled and pronounced in turn. People thought that the names of the letters were their sounds, that a child knew the sounds when he could name the letters, and that he could read when he could do this. As a result, letter names and speech sounds were frequently confused, a misunderstanding that persists. This procedure is known as the *ABC* or alphabetic method and prevailed when *The New England Primer*, spellers, and other similar materials were developed.

By the nineteenth century, however, elementary school teachers in the United States became dissatisfied with the teaching of reading and looked to Europe, especially Germany, for help. Two contrasting approaches were developed—the analytic and the synthetic. The analytic method started with the learning of whole words without reference to individual letters or sounds; the synthetic method started with the learning of individual sounds and letters which were then put together to form words.

Experimentation in the teaching of reading finally led to the basal reader, based on an eclectic method. In various forms, this method has dominated reading instruction in the United States for the past thirty to forty years. In it, a combination of techniques for words identification is presented: configurational clues, picture clues, contextual clues, word structure analysis, phonic analysis, and phonetic respelling. Stories are written, based on familiar interests of children at successive grade levels. The initial stories are written with short sentences, and the words for each level are selected according to frequency studies. The introduction and repetition of new words are controlled by formulas. The sequence of instruction starts with reading readiness skills consisting primarily of work in visual discrimination, auditory discrimination, left-to-right directional progression, and oral language development. The preprimer stage follows. Its purpose is to develop a sight vocabulary, a stock of fifty to a hundred words identified by means of configuration, picture, and meaning clues. In the primer stage, word structure and phonic analysis are introduced and then continued through the sixth grade, when the child is supposed to become an independent reader.

Workbooks for pupils and manuals for teachers are prepared to accompany the basal readers in each grade level. These manuals frequently do not supply all relevant information. For example, no basal reader series has ever identified or developed the application of specific picture clues, merely reminding the pupils to "look

at the picture." Many teachers have not used the supplementary
materials but merely have had their pupils read the stories, supply-
ing words which were not recognized. As a result, the difference
between promise and performance frequently has been considerable.

Linguists and Reading

Meanwhile, the study of language—linguistics—has been extremely active and productive in areas relevant to instruction in
reading, although many linguists are not interested in the practical
application of their findings. There is now a great deal of information about the nature of language, the details of English, and the
principles of language learning. Several persons, in both linguistics
and reading, have begun to apply this information to reading instruction. In general, the linguistic knowledge displayed by reading
specialists has been attacked, and the pedagogical strategies employed by the linguists have been questioned. Each side has been
diligent in defending its own realm and unwilling to accept relevant
findings in the other. As is usually the case, in the beginning the
debate was focused on current practices and was most visible in
attack and defense. As this is written, there seems to be some inclina-
tion to reexamine the total problem, from theoretical foundations
to classroom practices, and to look for information and strategy
where it is most likely to be found.

Critical statements and conclusions expressed by persons with
linguistic training include the following, some of which are certainly open to further investigation:

1. The first step in the process of reading is decoding the written message—that is, of reconstructing speech from written symbols. One understands the meaning only after decoding the symbols.
Hence, attention to meaning should be deferred until instruction in
this decoding has been well started, until the decoding of at least
some spelling patterns has become more or less automatic.

2. The first words that the child reads should be selected to
show consistent relationships between sound and spelling.

3. Phonemes are represented by graphemes; letters do not have
sounds, but stand for them. The distinction between letter and
sound must be made clear and maintained consistently.

4. Learning to read requires learning phoneme-grapheme relationships. It does not require learning sounds, for the pupil already knows the sounds of his own dialect. If, however, a particular child does not control a given phoneme, he should first be taught how to articulate and recognize the appropriate sound, or sounds, and then how to associate it with a grapheme.

5. The phoneme-grapheme relationships should be taught as parts of words and not in isolation, for, with few exceptions, that is how sounds and letters occur.

6. The introduction of sentence patterns, and, indeed, of all syntactic patterns, should be as carefully planned and controlled as the introduction of vocabulary. Although there has been an attempt to keep sentences short and to indicate sentence boundaries by devices other than punctuation, length and complexity do not always coincide, and the patterns of the short sentences are not always those that are common and natural.

7. Too little attention has been given to dialectal differences in the preparation of reading materials. Conventional materials ordinarily display a rather formal variety of written English, which many pupils find unfamiliar, and comments on sound and spelling assume much more uniformity in pronunciation than actually exists. When the dialectal problem is intensified by social as well as regional differences, it becomes much more acute. Teachers are frequently given no training in systematic phonology and such training is necessary.

8. Meaning is conveyed by the total combination of words and grammatical signals in an utterance, and is not easily grasped by exclusive attention to individual words. The sentence is the unit of grammar and hence of meaning, and individual words contribute components of meaning according to their uses in immediate sentences. Thus, a command of grammatical relationships is required, as well as a command of vocabulary.

9. Speech includes intonational signals which are not well represented in writing, including punctuation. In a spoken utterance, there is a pattern of pitch and stress levels and of vocal interruptions. Some words are pronounced differently in utterances than they are in a list. Thus, calling words in level sequence does not produce a natural utterance.

During the past half a dozen years, sets of reading materials have been developed which implement some of the preceding conclusions, and the term "linguistic approach" usually is applied to these programs. This is, of course, a rather narrow use of the term. Nevertheless, no such program has replaced the basal readers as the dominant type of instructional material.

The earliest of these programs was the one that finally appeared in amended form as *Let's Read: A Linguistic Approach*. In the mid-1930's, Leonard Bloomfield, working alone, prepared seventy-two lists of monosyllabic words in which no inconsistencies of spelling appeared. Reading exercises consisting of phrases and sentences using only these words were interspersed among the word lists. He later revised the materials, separating the lists into more manageable teaching units and adding to the exercises and stories. In 1939, Bloomfield and Clarence L. Barnhart formed a partnership to market the materials, but had little success. In 1958, Barnhart revised the materials and they were finally published in 1961, a dozen years after the death of Bloomfield (4). The total vocabulary includes 5,000 words, many of them having two or more syllables, which are distributed among 245 lessons. Having mastered this vocabulary, a child supposedly can read anything he wishes to. The lessons have been arranged into units suitable for classroom work and are now available in nine readers, together with workbooks and an *ABC* book for prereading use.

At the outset, the child sees no irregular spellings. He can rely on the correspondences between sound and spelling in the words presented to him. The emphasis is on learning these correspondences, and some nonsense syllables are provided so that the teacher can check the pupil's progress in mastering the spelling patterns. In time, words with irregular spellings are introduced. The most common are presented first, and they are grouped so as to facilitate learning. The emphasis throughout is on recognizing words from their spellings. There are no pictures to give help in following the story. Most pupils require one and a half to three years to complete the nine books in the series.

A more widely used program was developed under the guidance of C. C. Fries, following the publication of his *Linguistics and Reading* in 1962. This program, the *Merrill Linguistic Readers*, includes an alphabet book, six readers, and six practice books, all for the primary grades. The first phase of the program is devoted to direct teaching of the alphabet, both capital and lower-case letters. The first reading materials contain only language that the child presumably controls already. New words are introduced which conform to one of three major spelling patterns, as determined by Fries: CVC combinations, words ending in silent *e*, and words with vowel digraphs. Words from more common minor patterns follow. Emphasis is at all times on mastering spelling patterns rather than on memorizing words individually, but some irregularly spelled words are introduced as "sight words."

As the words are introduced, they are used in sentences illustrating practically all the basic patterns in English, and the sentences are used in stories which have continuity of content. There are no pictures, so the only clues are in printed words and punctuation. Spelling patterns are taught by means of minimal contrasts between words, not by correspondences between single letters and sounds. Unlike the Bloomfield method, this program places great emphasis on word meaning and cumulative meaning. The inclusion of some irregularly spelled words permits the use of natural, idiomatic English throughout the series.

Other reading programs based on the spelling pattern principle are *Read Along With Me*, by Allen and Allen (1); *The Basic Reading Series*, by Goldberg and Rasmussen (10); *Programmed Reading*, by Sullivan Associates (20); *Miami Linguistic Readers*, by Robinett (16); and the *Linguistic Science Readers*, by Stratemeyer and Smith (19).

A whole-sentence method of teaching reading was proposed by Carl LeFevre in 1964, in *Linguistics and the Teaching of Reading*. He stated, "no one can get meaning from the printed page without taking in whole language patterns at the sentence level, because these are the minimal meaning-bearing structures of most written communication (12:vii)." His method requires attention to intonation, sentence patterns, structure words, and morphological clues. He suggests that spelling patterns can be learned inductively as the pupil learns to write. He advises the sequential teaching of words according to their grammatical functions, including the use of certain words as markers.

Although some attention has been given to syntactic clues in the spelling-pattern type of reading material (e.g., the *Merrill Linguistic Readers* and the *Linguistic Science Readers* (19), no programs have been published so far (1968) which are primarily based on grammatical clues. In an informal way, the *Sounds of Language Readers* (14) incorporate a sentence approach (using literary materials) on the premises that "language is learned first in the ear, then in the eye," and that "sentence sounds are more important than individual word sounds in learning to read." The readers in this series are anthologies of poetry, stories, etc., selected for esthetic quality. The teacher first reads the selections to the pupils, who then memorize them and finally "read" them from the page.

Some applications of recent linguistic study are being made by Robert B. Ruddell. He does not discard the conventional basal reader but supplements it with exercises on language structures as meaning-conveying patterns. In the initial stages, he works with intonational patterns and punctuation, patterns of constructions, and manipulation of these patterns. In the second year, he introduces subordination and expansion, key structure words, and continuity in paragraphs. He has concluded that, after the second year:

. . . making provision for a high degree of consistency in grapheme-phoneme correspondences and placing special emphasis on language structure as related to meaning produced significantly higher Paragraph Meaning comprehension scores than did the program making provision for consistency in correspondences but placing no special emphasis on language structure as related to meaning (18:737).

Initial Teaching Alphabet (I.T.A)

The Initial Teaching Alphabet is a teaching medium rather than a method. Reasoning that the irregularities of English spelling were obstacles to the beginning reader, Sir James Pitman designed the I.T.A as a simpler and more reliable alphabet. It contains forty-four letters—all but <q> and <x> of the conventional twenty-six—and twenty augmentations designed to look like two familiar letters joined together. The I.T.A was developed in England and large-scale experimentation with it began there in 1961.

Reading materials are transliterated, using this alphabet, and these are used in the initial stages of reading instruction. The plan is for children to spend one year learning to read these materials and to write with this alphabet. Then they are to transfer to traditional orthography. The transfer is to be completed by the end of the third year. Reports from England are generally favorable (7). A number of small-scale experiments have been made in the United States, but the results have not been so favorable. The major United States experiment was conducted in Bethlehem, Pennsylvania, from 1963 to 1966, funded by a grant from the Fund for the Advancement of Education, and directed by Albert J. Mazurkiewicz (15).

In general, the reception of I.T.A in the United States has been lukewarm and its use limited and temporary. In part, this is due to a wait-and-see attitude, but published reports by those trying it have not been very encouraging. There are some obvious difficulties. For one thing, published I.T.A materials do not reflect dialectal differences in pronunciation, and some reflect British rather than American speech. Since the medium is based on a fit between letter and sound, this can be a serious handicap. In addition, most primary school teachers do not have a conscious knowledge of American English phonology, or even of their own speech habits, and hence are not prepared to cope with the materials or with dialectal variations in their classes. Until appropriate instruction is given to the teachers, I.T.A will be of limited value and of value to a limited number of children.

Conclusions

In recent years, others besides those immediately charged with training elementary teachers are showing concern over the teaching of reading. Studies made possible by the Carnegie Corporation have produced *The Torch Lighter: Tomorrow's Teacher of Reading*, 1961 (3); *The First R*, 1963 (2); and *Learning to Read: The Great Debate*, 1967 (6). During the 1964-65 school year, the United States Office of Education sponsored twenty-seven Grade I reading studies in different localities. Some of these studies were continued for a second year and some for a third year. In 1962 a Joint Committee on Linguistics and Reading was set up by the National Council of Teachers of English and the International Reading Association. And in 1965 the Center for Applied Linguistics agreed to compile and publish bibliographies and inventories of projects in reading and in English.

A survey of various studies indicates that success depends more on the teacher than on the method used. This conclusion suggests that no best method has been found, and that, for the present, efforts should be directed toward better and more comprehensive training for teachers and toward the accumulation of fundamental information basic to any method. It seems that basic research is still needed rather than competition among methods. The following conclusions seem to be indicated.

1. The fundamental linguistic data underlying all methods should be reexamined and, when necessary, corrected by reference to the findings of language scholars. Any research project accumulating such information should include at least one person from the appropriate branch of linguistics, or some member of the team should study with such a person.

2. The training of all teachers concerned with reading should include work in the phonological and grammatical systems of American English, including major dialectal variations, and in the representation of meaning by words and constructions.

3. In at least some instances, instructional material for beginning reading should be developed locally, especially when there are wide differences among social dialects. Material published for national use should be accompanied by manuals describing adaptations for local conditions.

4. The pedagogical efficiency of generalizations derived from linguistics should be tested on children. Effectiveness in the classroom does not always follow from logical design or strict accuracy. The study of linguistics is not a suitable replacement for customary training in the teaching of reading. Instead, it is a resource field, like learning theory or sociology, from which certain necessary and fundamental information is to be drawn. But this information should be adapted, tested, and evaluated by persons familiar with the difficulties that are encountered in classrooms and with how these are best overcome.

262   LINGUISTICS AND READING

BIBLIOGRAPHY

1. ALLEN, ROBERT L., and ALLEN, VIRGINIA F. *Read Along With Me*. New York: Bureau of Publications, Teachers College, Columbia University, 1964.
2. AUSTIN, MARY C., and MORRISON, COLEMAN. *The First R: The Harvard Report on Reading in Elementary Schools*. New York: Macmillan Co., 1963.
3. ———. *The Torch Lighters: Tomorrow's Teachers of Reading*. Cambridge, Mass.: Harvard University Press, 1961.
4. BLOOMFIELD, LEONARD, and BARNHART, CLARENCE L. *Let's Read*. Bronxville, N.Y.: C. L. Barnhart, Inc., 1963.
5. BURKE, VIRGINIA M. Review of Loban (13), *Elementary English*, XLIV (December, 1967), 913-19.
6. CHALL, JEANNE S. *Learning to Read: The Great Debate*. New York: McGraw-Hill Book Co., 1967.
7. DOWNING, J. A. *Evaluating the Initial Teaching Alphabet*. London: Cassell, 1967.
8. FRIES, CHARLES C. *Linguistics and Reading*. New York: Holt, Rinehart & Winston, 1962.
9. FRIES, CHARLES C.; WILSON, ROSEMARY G.; and RUDOLPH, MILDRED K. *Merrill Linguistic Readers, A Basic Program*. Columbus, Ohio: Charles E. Merrill Books, 1966.
10. GOLDBERG, LYNN, and RASMUSSEN, DONALD. *The Basic Reading Series*. Chicago: Science Research Associates, 1965.
11. HANNA, P. R.; HANNA, JEAN S.; HODGES, R. E.; and RUDORF, E. H. JR. *Phoneme-Grapheme Correspondences as Cues to Spelling Improvement*. U.S. Office of Education Research Program Monograph 16. Washington: Government Printing Office, 1966.
12. LEFEVRE, CARL A. *Linguistics and the Teaching of Reading*. New York: McGraw-Hill Book Co., 1964.
13. LOBAN, WALTER. *Problems in Oral English*. Champaign, Ill.: National Council of Teachers of English, 1966.
14. MARTIN, BILL, JR. *Sounds of Language Readers*. New York: Holt, Rinehart & Winston, 1966.
15. MAZURKIEWICZ, ALBERT J. *The Initial Teaching Alphabet in Reading Instruction*. (Lehigh-Bethlehem Evaluation-Demonstration Project on the Use of i. t. a.) Comprehensive Final Report, February, 1967.
16. ROBINETT, RALPH F. *Miami Linguistic Readers*. Miami: Board of Public Instruction, 1964.
17. Roundtable review of Hanna *et al. Phoneme—Grapheme Correspondences as Cues to Spelling Improvement* (11): A. Hood Roberts, "A Review by A Specialist in the Uses of Computers in Linguistics Research," pp. 201-7 and David W. Reed, "A Review by a Specialist

in Dialectology," pp. 207-15, *Research in the Teaching of English*, Fall, 1967.

18. RUDDELL, ROBERT B. "Reading Instruction in First Grade with Varying Emphasis on the Regularity of Grapheme-Phoneme Correspondences and the Relation of Language Structure to Meaning—Extended into Second Grade," *The Reading Teacher*, XX (May, 1967), 730-39.

19. STRATEMEYER, CLARA, and SMITH, HENRY LEE JR. *Linguistic Science Readers*. Evanston, Ill.: Harper & Row, 1963.

20. SULLIVAN ASSOCIATES. *Programmed Reading*. Manchester, Mo.: McGraw-Hill Book Co., 1963.

Part II

Linguistics and Spelling

RICHARD L. VENEZKY[1]

What Linguistics Can Contribute

The linguist, *qua* linguist, studies language in its various forms, accumulates inventories of phonological and grammatical units, constructs models for bundling these entities together, and speculates on the relationship of his models to nonverbal phenomena. But linguistics, however defined, is not education, nor is it psychology. Therefore, while the linguist can provide reliable data on the pronunciation of a language, the features of its writing system, and the relationship between speech and writing, he cannot, as a linguist, decide how such revelations should be deployed in the teaching of spelling. This latter task involves two major problems that the educator must solve. The first is that the linguist's descriptions are, in some sense, theories or inferences. That is, while he is describing language *habits*, he cannot observe them directly, but must infer them from observations of *behavior*. For example, the linguist observes that English words do not begin with /ŋ/ or /ž/, thus he infers that new words that begin with either of these two sounds would be perceived as non-English-like and would be difficult for English speakers to pronounce. However, the reactions of native English speakers to these sounds is not as predicted by the linguist, as a recent experiment has shown (3). Words beginning with /ž/ apparently are no more difficult to learn than words beginning with /ð/, /š/, or any other sound which occurs initially in English words.

The second problem is that the effectiveness of the methods selected for teaching spelling depends not just upon the linguistic

1. The preparation of this paper was supported by the Wisconsin Research and Development Center for Cognitive Learning, under a grant from the U.S. Office of Education.

264

nature of the spelling materials, but also upon the learning abilities
of the child, the teaching abilities of the teacher, and the school
setting. For example, initial /w/ in many areas has two spellings, as
in *wail* and *whale;* the first spelling (*w*) occurs approximately five
times more frequently than the second spelling (*wh*). But these
facts in no way predetermine how these spellings should be taught.
This decision depends upon the age of the children involved, the
words which are to be taught, and the relative efficiencies of different basic approaches to spelling. All of these decisions rest primarily
with the educator. The most important data which the linguist can
provide are those which relate to (*a*) pronunciation, (*b*) the writing
system, and (*c*) the relationship between speech and writing. Each
of these is discussed in the following pages.

Pronunciation

DIALECT DIFFERENCES

The nature of English pronunciation is discussed at various
places throughout this volume (see especially chaps. i and vii);
therefore only a sketch of those features important for spelling
will be discussed here. First among these is dialect differences.
American regional speech, primarily of the rural white, has been
studied for many years and considerable data are available (9, 10).[2]
Recently, studies of urban dialects, particularly of Negroes and
Mexican-Americans have been undertaken (11, 13). The dialect
differences brought out in these studies, in relation to spelling, can
be divided into four classes: (*a*) regular shifts without merger, (*b*)
regular shifts with merger, (*c*) irregular shifts, and (*d*) deletions.[3]

Regular shifts without merger.—These are shifts that generally
do not create differences in phonemic systems. For example, the
vowel + /r/ sequence in words like *ear* is realized as [ɪr] in Upper
Midwestern speech, but generally as [ɪə] in the South.[4] Thus, any

2. A short bibliography of materials on American English dialects can be
found in *Linguistics and English Linguistics* (12).

3. These differences are described in relation to Upper Midwestern speech
from which shifts or deletions are made. For a description of Upper Midwestern speech, see Allen (1).

4. This shift holds for both the Upper and Lower South. See Kurath and
McDavid (9:18-22).

266   LINGUISTICS AND SPELLING

pattern derived for Upper Midwestern [ɪr] holds for Southern [ɪə], with the substitution of [ɪə] for [ɪr]. (If [ɪə] occurs elsewhere in Southern speech then the pattern may change.) Such shifts should not, theoretically, cause additional spelling problems.

Regular shifts with merger.—In some urban speech, initial /θ/ shifts to /t/.[5] While the shift is regular, that is, all occurrences of /θ/ in one dialect are replaced by /t/ in the other dialect, spelling (but not reading) patterns are affected. For the /θ/ dialect, all occurrences of initial /θ/ are spelled *th*, and all occurrences of initial /t/ are spelled *t*. For the /t/ dialect, initial /θ/ does not exist, and initial /t/ is spelled either *t* or *th*, and nothing in the sounds or meanings of the words will help the speller discriminate the two patterns.

Irregular shifts.—Sometimes a single sound in one dialect may become two different sounds in another dialect. If this occurs without phonological or semantic conditioning, then new spelling patterns must be written for the second dialect. Such is the situation in the realization of Upper Midwestern /æ/ in Eastern New England. In some words, such as *glass* and *calves*, /a/ is used. In others, such as *hat* and *bag*, /æ/ is used.

Deletions.—A feature common to all urban dialects is the deletion of certain final consonants, especially in clusters like /ld/ and /nt/. Here, of course, fairly predictable spellings become unpredictable since silent letters result from the deletion.

SYLLABLE DIVISION

Syllables are generally not separated by clear pauses in free speech, except where unpronounceable consonant clusters occur, as in *wistful*, where /stf/ must be divided between the /t/ and the /f/. A word like *petal* can be pronounced with the /t/ ending the first syllable, or with it beginning the second, or with it forming a continuous link from one syllable peak to the next, as occurs in most fast speech. To establish spelling rules based upon particular syllable breaks for words like *petal* is to mislead both teachers and students. Unfortunately, what are represented as syllable breaks in a dictionary are not always based upon sound.[6]

5. I am ignoring the situations where the /t/ which replaces /θ/ is phonetically distinct from the /t/ at the beginning of *tin* and *ten*.

6. ". . . we especially need to recognize that the hyphenation and syllable-

English Orthography

THE WRITING SYSTEM

A theoretical basis for English orthography has been established through extensive research over the past ten years (14, 15, 16). Most important to this work is the view that English spelling is not simply a defective phonemic system for transcribing speech, but instead a more complex and more regular set of patterns in which both phonemic and morphemic elements share leading roles. The better known morphemic patterns include the noun plural marker -(e)s, the past tense marker -(e)d, and the various suffix patterns which cause vowel sound alternations.[7] Note that the noun plural spelling (and the various other morphemes which -(e)s can represent) stands for three distinct phonemes and all of these have distinct spellings which could have been employed: /s/: *cats*, /z/: *dogs*, /ɪz/: *judges*. Similarly, -(e)d could be /t/ as *walked*, /d/ as in *canned*, or /ɪd/ as in *mended*.

BASIC UNITS

The letters (graphemes) used to spell English comprise the 26 letters of the Roman alphabet.[8] The units which must be manipulated to relate sound to spelling, however, are not just the letters, but various letter combinations which function as single units, such as *th*, *ck*, *tch*, *oo*, and *ou;* all of these together are called spelling units. The most important spelling units are shown in Table 1.

The need for the classification *spelling unit* is best exemplified by the final *e* rule for single letter vowel spellings. If this rule is stated as follows: "A long vowel sound can be spelled by a single letter vowel, followed by a single consonant letter, and then a silent *e*," words like *axe*, *bathe*, and *writhe* appear to be exceptions. This pattern, however, is not based upon letters, but upon spelling

---

divisions set forth in our dictionaries is very largely arbitrary, and that they therefore do not, in fact cannot, have by the very nature of the situation, any absolute validity (6:55)."

7. For a detailed description of these patterns, viewed from the reading standpoint, see Venezky (15).

8. We might, following Francis (4:447), include the standard punctuation symbols plus certain suprasegmental features (capitals, etc.) as graphemes.

TABLE 1

THE MAJOR SPELLING UNITS

Consonant Units			Vowel Units	
Simple		Complex	Primary	Compound
b k s		ck	a	ai/ay oa
c l sh		dg	e	au/aw oe
ch m t		tch	i	ea oi/oy
d n th		x	o	ee oo
f p u			u	ei/ey ou/ow
g ph v			y	eu/ew ue
gh q w				ie ui
h r wh				
j rh y				
z				

units. The vowel spelling can be followed by a simple consonant spelling unit plus silent *e*. Complex spelling units—*x, dg, tch, ck*— either stand for two sounds (*x*) or are replacements for doubled consonants (*dg, tch, ck*). Spellings like *th, ch, sh*, and *ph* are simple spelling units since long vowel sounds can be spelled with single vowel letters standing before them (e.g., *bathe, cochineal, kosher, hyphen*); long vowel sounds can never be spelled with single vowel letters before the complex consonant units.

RELATIONAL UNITS AND MARKERS

Another feature of English orthography which current linguistic research has clarified is the distinction between *relational units* and *markers*. Relational units are those spelling units which relate directly to sound; markers are letters which indicate spelling-sound relationships, or preserve graphemic or morphemic patterns. Final *e* is a marker in *mate* since it indicates the long pronunciation of *a*. It is a dual marker in *rage*, indicating the pronunciations of both *a* and *g* (compare *rag*). In *love*, *e* preserves a pattern which forbids *v* to occur in final position; in *mouse, house*, and *moose* it indicates that the *s* is not a morphemic unit, that is, is not a plural or third singular indicator. In *guide* and *guest*, *u* is a marker, showing the /g/ pronunciation of *g*. All of these patterns relate as much to spelling as to reading; it is the task of the educator to decide if they can aid in the teaching of spelling, and if so, how.

Sound-Spelling Relationships

CLASSIFICATION

Sound-to-spelling patterns can best be classed for pedagogical purposes as (*a*) predictable, (*b*) unpredictable but frequent, and (*c*) unpredictable and rare. (The pitfalls inherent in using the terms "regular" and "irregular" to describe these patterns will be discussed shortly.)

PREDICTABLE PATTERNS

Predictable patterns divide into two sub-classes: invariant and variant. Invariant patterns, which are rare in the sound-spelling domain, are those which assign the same spelling to a particular sound (or sound sequence) regardless of its environment. /hw/, for those dialects which have this sequence, is invariably spelled *wh* as in *where* and *when*. When /ð/ and /θ/ occur, they are almost always spelled *th*. (The exceptions are proper names like *Matthew* and a few rare spellings like in *eighth* where /tθ/ is spelled *th*.) Except for *of* and a few double *v* spellings (*navvy, divvy*, etc.), /v/ is invariably spelled *v*. A few other consonant sounds have nearly invariant spellings, but no vowel sounds do.

Many sounds have variant spellings which can be predicted on the basis of either the environment of the sound or the meaning or form class of the word in which it occurs, Final /š/, for example, is almost always spelled *sh* as in *ash;* but initial /š/ can be *sh*, or *s* as in *sure* and *sugar*, or *ch* as in numerous French borrowings like *chalet* and *chef*.[9] (Medial /š/ is considerably less predictable.) Initial /m/ is always spelled *m*; final /m/ can be either *m*, or (in a small group of words) *mn*. This latter spelling can be predicted, however, from the pronunciation of compounds like *autumnal, columnal, damnation*, and *hymnal*. Initial /č/, except for *cello*, is spelled *ch*. Final /č/ is either *ch* or *tch; tch* occurs only after a short vowel sound which is spelled with a single letter, e.g., *batch, etch, itch, blotch, clutch. ch* occurs in all other circumstances, including vowel + /r/.[10]

9. Some rarer spellings are found in *pshaw* and *schist.*

10. The major exceptions to this pattern are *much, rich, such*, and *which*.

FREQUENT BUT UNPREDICTABLE PATTERNS

Many sounds have variant spellings which can not be predicted, but which occur frequently enough to merit special attention. An example of such a sound is final /o/ which may be *o* as in *go*, *ow* as in *low*, or *oe* as in *doe*.[11] The frequencies of occurrences of each of these spellings in the 20,000 most common words in English are: *o*: 140; *ow*: 7; *oe*: 12. This class is distinct from the class which follows because new words which are created for English would tend to have one of these spellings if it contained /o/.

RARE AND UNPREDICTABLE PATTERNS [12]

Unusual spellings which are limited to a small group of words fit into this class. Some well-known examples are the *f* spelling in *of*, the *au* spelling in *aunt*, and the *ct* spelling in *indict*. These are usually artifacts of isolated sound changes or the inheritances of scribal eccentricity, and while they provide ready offenders for pillorying in spelling-reform diatribes, they represent no serious threat to health and public safety.

The value of this tripart classification is that it separates spelling patterns according to the behaviors which we would expect good spellers to acquire. Predictable patterns, while they may require a concern for environment, are transferable to any word containing the sounds involved. Variant-predictable patterns require attention to such features as position, stress, or following sounds, but can still be transferred once the appropriate features are known. Unpredictable patterns cannot be transferred to new occurrences of the same sounds, but while one anticipates seeing certain frequent, unpredictable patterns in new words, one does not expect to see the rare, unpredictable patterns there. The difference between the two classes is, then, that the first occurs in an open-ended set of words and the second occurs in a closed set.

REGULAR VS. IRREGULAR

It should be obvious from the preceding discussion that the labels "regular" and "irregular" as applied to spelling patterns are quite

11. Rarer spellings are *ew* (*sew*), *eau* (*bureau*), and *ough* (*dough*).

12. Another title for this class is *hapax orthographica*.

misleading. "Regular" is commonly defined as the most frequently occurring correspondence,[13] yet this merges predictable patterns like initial and final /č/ with unpredictable patterns like medial /č/. That is, it fails to consider whether the variant spellings are predictable or not. Unfortunately, the term "regular" has become a shibboleth for a method of teaching spelling rather than a description for a rationally derived set of patterns.

Furthermore, the term is quite misleading in that the goal of spelling instruction is to teach correct spelling, not some probabilistic approximation to correct spelling. There are good reasons for teaching sound-spelling relationships, but the percent of regularity of isolated correspondences, no matter how "regular" is defined, is not sufficient. Notice that if a student were taught only the so-called regular spellings for each significant sound in English, he could be expected to spell correctly less than 41 percent of all English words.[14]

Spelling vs. Reading

While spelling patterns have some similarity to reading patterns, the differences are so great that the patterning from spelling to sound seldom mirrors that of sound to spelling. Assumptions about spelling, based upon the writings of linguists who were concerned primarily with reading, must be viewed with caution.[15] Some of the conflicts between reading patterns and spelling patterns are discussed below.

THE /W/ PATTERNS

For those areas of the country which pronounce initial *wh* as

13. In the Hanna studies (7, 8), the most frequent spelling for a sound is classed as the "regular" spelling for that sound, regardless of whether it represents 30 percent, 99 percent, or any other percentage of the spellings for a given sound.

14. If we begin with the 80 percent regularity figure mentioned above, and assume that there are four sounds in the average English word (and this is a low estimate), then the probability of spelling any word correctly is the product of the probabilities for the individual spellings in the word; .80 x .80 x .80 x .80, or .4096 (40.96 percent).

15. Bloomfield (2) wrote about reading, but never about spelling. Fries (5) proscribed sound-to-spelling concerns from *Linguistics and Reading* (see fn. 13, p. 171). Hall (6) developed his spelling patterns based upon reading, and mentions spelling only in a brief paragraph in the conclusions (p. 59).

/w/, the spelling of initial /w/ is unpredictable, although the reading patterns for initial *wh* and *w* are predictable, in that each is pronounced /w/.[16] The unpredictability of the spellings can be seen from the following examples:

whale	wail	whisk	wisp
wheel	week	whiskey	wisdom
whip	wipe	whistle	wistful

THE MEDIAL /t/ PATTERNS

In reading, *t* between vowel spellings is pronounced /t/ (e.g., *city*, *satin*), except in certain complex, but patterned environments, where it is /š/ or /č/ as in *nation* and *nature*. Medial *tt* is always pronounced /t/. Thus, from a reading standpoint the pronunciations of medial, intervocalic *t* and *tt* are predictable.

From a spelling standpoint, however, the correspondences for intervocalic /t/ cannot be predicted; either *t* or *tt* could occur. Observe, for example, the words shown below:

city	ditty	litany	gluttony
pity	witty	metal	glottal
satin	cotton	motor	latter

THE *th* PATTERNS

For reading, medial *th* spellings are generally unpredictable; they can be /θ/ as in *ether* or /ð/ as in *either*. (Some medial *th* patterns are predictable: *-the* and *-ther*, except for *ether*, are always /ð/.) From a spelling standpoint, as mentioned earlier, /ð/ and /θ/ are almost always spelled *th* (see under heading, "Sound-Spelling Relationships" in this chapter for the exceptions). Some matched pairs are:

apathy	swarthy	nothing	breathing
author	another	pithy	worthy
ether	either	zither	father

Conclusions

The linguist can provide for educators data on the pronunciation

16. The exceptions are the few *wh* words pronounced with initial /h/, e. g., *who*, *whoop*.

of English, the nature of the writing system, and the relationship between speech and writing. It is the educator's task, however, to determine which of the linguist's offerings can aid in the teaching of spelling, and how they should be used to achieve this end. A rational spelling program, regardless of its pedagogy, must be based upon the speech which the learner uses and not upon an idealized dialect, replete with synthetic syllable breaks and unreduced vowels. If sound-to-spelling relationships are to be used in the program (either overtly or covertly), they must be derived from sound linguistic work which recognizes the units and functions upon which English orthography is based. Rather than the probabilistic relationships inherent in the classes "regular" and "irregular", more pedagogically relevant relationships should be employed for classing sound-spelling patterns. Finally, spelling is not reading. Wholly new patterns must be derived, starting with sound and working towards spelling. This cannot be achieved through a simple reversal of spelling-to-sound patterns, but must come from careful and detailed analysis.

BIBLIOGRAPHY

1. ALLEN, HAROLD B. "Aspects of the Linguistic Geography of the Upper Midwest." In *Studies in Language and Linguistics in Honor of Charles C. Fries*, pp. 303-14. Edited by Albert H. Marckwardt. Ann Arbor: English Language Institute, University of Michigan, 1964.
2. BLOOMFIELD, LEONARD. *Language*. New York: Holt, Rinehart & Winston, 1933.
3. BRIÈRE, E. J.; CAMPBELL, R. N.; and SOEMARMO. "A Need for the Syllable in Contrastive Analyses," *Journal of Verbal Learning and Verbal Behavior*, VII (1968), 384-89.
4. FRANCIS, W. NELSON. *The Structure of American English*. New York: Ronald Press, 1958.
5. FRIES, CHARLES C. *Linguistics and Reading*. New York: Holt, Rinehart & Winston, 1962.
6. HALL, ROBERT A., JR. *Sound and Spelling in English*. Philadelphia: Chilton Co., 1961.
7. HANNA, PAUL R., and MOORE, JAMES T., JR. "Spelling—from Spoken Word to Written Symbol," *Elementary School Journal*, LIII (February, 1953), 329-37.
8. HANNA, PAUL R., et al. *Phoneme-Grapheme Correspondences as Cues to Spelling Improvement*. Washington, D.C.: U.S. Department of Health, Education, and Welfare, Office of Education, 1966.

9. KURATH, HANS, and McDAVID, RAVEN I., JR. *The Pronunciation of English in the Atlantic States.* Ann Arbor: University of Michigan Press, 1961.

10. KURATH, HANS *et al. Linguistic Atlas of New England.* 3 vols. Providence, R. I.: Brown University, 1939-43.

11. LABOV, WILLIAM. "Stages in the Acquisition of Standard English." In *Social Dialects and Language Learning.* Edited by Roger W. Shuy, Champaign, Ill.: National Council of Teachers of English, 1965, 77-103.

12. *Linguistics and English Linguistics.* Compiled by Harold B. Allen. New York: Appleton-Century-Crofts, 1966.

13. *Social Dialects and Language Learning.* Edited by Roger W. Shuy. Champaign, Ill.: National Council of Teachers of English, 1965.

14. VENEZKY, RICHARD L. *The Structure of English Orthography.* The Hague: Mouton & Co., 1969.

15. ———. "English Orthography: Its Graphical Structure and Its Relation to Sound," *Reading Research Quarterly,* II (Spring, 1967), 75-106.

16. WEIR, RUTH H., and VENEZKY, RICHARD L. "Rules to Aid in the Teaching of Reading." Final Report, Cooperative Research Project No. 2584 (Stanford University, 1965).

CHAPTER IX

Language and Thinking

RICHARD W. DETTERING *

As a Teacher's Concern

The topic of this chapter blends with other topics in this year-book. Still, in contrast to the phonological, structural, social, and historical facts about language, the relationship to thinking seems elusive. Linguistic performance, whether in speech or writing, audition or reading, tends to be observable and overt, palpable to the eye and ear, its occurrence usually acknowledged, its properties often measurable and predictable. Cognition, on the other hand, enjoys no such status as an object of agreement or scientific study. The subject at hand thus calls us to relate a part of human behavior which, although complex and mysterious, consists of data more or less evident to the senses of the public, with a part which, by its very nature, lies behind the scenes and can only be judged through introspection, inference, and speculation. This is only the first troublesome aspect of the inquiry.

Discussion of the human mind and its ideas has been until the last century the province of theologians, philosophers, and armchair psychologists, while the criticism and training of mouth-sounds and script-marks have been left to professional tutorial custody. In the Middle Ages the "seven liberal arts," as the backbone of the monastic curriculum, included grammar, rhetoric, logic, and arithmetic as *practical* skills to be taught to the literate elite, much as jousting and swordsmanship were taught to knights. Our contemporary school-master often teaches linguistic disciplines in a similar spirit. The final problem of the relationship of thought to symbolism thus re-

* Much acknowledgment is due to Frederick D. Beeman and David Griffiths, graduate students of San Francisco State College, for their contributions to this chapter.

mains in metaphysical dispute, while the etiquette of "proper usage" continues to be dispensed with unreflective confidence. Yet the educator often forgets that no approach to a symbol-based subject can be justified without assumptions and theories about the relation of language to thought.

There are many classroom problems which at least tacitly invoke some basic positions on how language involves cognition—or that *something* which is more than the sounds of speech. To make plain the relevance of the relationship between language and thought to the teacher's role, a few of these positions should be sketched.

INTIMACY BETWEEN THOUGHT AND LANGUAGE

In attempting to measure mental aptitudes and to raise academic achievement, the school works mainly with symbolic stimuli and responses. To rationalize such practice the educator must assume, (*a*) that thought and language are identical or at least mutually dependent and inseparable parts of one continuous process; or, (*b*) that, if separate, thought and language are so closely correlated that a modification of one is almost always followed by a modification of the other. The old definition that "A sentence is a group of words expressing a complete thought," springs from some such belief in the intimacy of cognition and verbalization.

MENTAL INDEPENDENCE FROM LANGUAGE

Oddly enough, the predominance of "intimacy" theories in the school has never banished the apparently contrary belief that mind is independent of language. The conviction (conceivably arising from our known ability to lie) that thinking is a deep, inner process which may or may not reflect itself in speech has for centuries stood beside the assumption of intimacy which it seems to deny. Without the least embarrassment, parents and teachers who have long prepared for the child's next verbal response with a sugar plum in one hand and a cane in the other have still proclaimed that what counts is "not what you say but what you believe." Unlike the intimacy theories which intersperse the spectrum from mentalism to behaviorism, the mental independence theories skew to the mentalistic end of the scale. Teachers and preachers have so hallowed the autonomy and secrecy of the mind that students have exploited the alibi, "I know the answer, but don't know how to say it," thus hoping to excuse their failure in test or classroom performance. Yet, the most common way to rate students is on the papers they turn in and not on the thoughts their minds are claimed to turn over.

MENTAL COMPARTMENTS

Although eighteenth-century "faculty psychology," which held the mind to be composed of separate powers, like reason, will, and instinct, has become obsolete, a belief that our cognitive abilities are segregated still persists. Indeed, some recent support of this view can be found in brain neurology and in a partial revival of "localization" theories of brain capacity. It is the school tradition rather than science, however, which gives this concept constantly renewed momentum. Foremost among these established symptoms is the policy of ability grouping in terms of subject matter, with low achievers in each field taking a remedial curriculum and high achievers an accelerated one. While measured achievement in various subjects reveals expected statistical imbalances for most children, the gross causes have not been isolated and shown to be genetic, or, for that matter, environmental. The assumption of inborn talents and deficiencies seems in any case to be a most unproven and dangerous one; it has the character of a "self-fulfilling prophecy" in that it directs counseling, selection, and student choice to make the lopsidedness even greater; once a student becomes stamped as stupid in mathematics and gifted in art, he and the school conspire to make the discrepancy even larger. The most notorious disagreement in modern times has been the debate over the "two-worlds theory" between C. P. Snow and F. R. Leavis. The question is whether scientists and artists are born or made, and, if made, are they made by a partisan education which has trained artists to be incompetent in science and scientists to be insensitive to art? Behind this issue is the hypothesis that training in, say, an aesthetic symbol system does or does not affect the ability to progress in a deductive symbol system (and vice versa). The school may have to learn that, notwithstanding its role in the education of countless "well rounded" geniuses, it has yielded to the professionalism of our time by teaching only one specialized language to many students and then concluding that they are only mediocre in their ability for all the others. If language conditions thinking, this might be the case; if not, not.

LINGUISTIC REIFICATION

The belief in cultural relativism has become a fad in modern academic and political thought, and adherence to it a mark of trans-cultural sophistication. The American school, long habituated to teaching a geography depicting the quaint, lovable customs of far-away folk, is well prepared to accept radical differences in the ways of other societies. It has not been so ready to accept a similar cultural relativism within its own society, however; and it is presently, sometimes with a touch of panic, beginning to realize and atone for the oversight. To an even less extent is there cognizance of the possibility that the language to which one is bred determines how he sees reality and forms his values. Each national language, according to this view, is supposed, in part, "to create" the objects and processes which its speakers take to be "real." In considering the new domestic anxieties of our schools, it is quite relevant to suggest that the latest efforts to teach "disadvantaged" students in their acquired patois may well imply that thinking is a function of language. For millions of unassimilated American youth, Standard English is not only an alien lingo; it does not even speak the same truths or refer to the same world as does the form of English they are accustomed to using. Here again we have another sample of the language-thought problem. The unresolved question is whether or not the introspected cognition is just an interior echo of the outside speech. Do we teach clear thinking by teaching clear symbolizing?

The above examples of theoretic-practical problems requiring the school to heed the language-thought relationship should at least suggest the complexity of the inquiry. Now we need to look at the background of hypotheses and research from which one may vindicate or disapprove the activities of the school in teaching language.

Conceptual and Investigative Contributions

Nowhere in speculation or inquiry has the shibboleth *interdisciplinary* had a more substantial reference than in the emerging study of linguistic-mental activity. To designate the combined enterprise, the term *psycholinguistics* has been used increasingly since 1954

(19). Yet, this term is far too narrow and fails to accredit the flow of contributions from anthropology, philosophy, logic, semantics, and cybernetics. In any case, this confluence of specialties has made the study of language both a more confusing and a more exciting intellectual venture.

Crisscrossing the variety of source disciplines lies another spectrum, that of basic assumptions and philosophic outlooks. There are divergent arbitrary modes of classification here too, but we shall use the one now most currently involved in linguistic forensics: the continuum ranging from rationalism to empiricism. The selection of this scale and the assignment of thinkers to different positions on it are bound to be somewhat arbitrary, especially as the intangible activity of thinking comes into play. But metaphysical arguments of ancient vintage are infiltrating constantly as linguistics, ironically enough, aspires more and more to become scientific.

THE RATIONALISTIC BIASES

Granting the sharp differences between various rationalistic theories, we can state their common position as one which stresses underlying cognition as the basis and compass of human language. The subservience of language to thinking is maintained in some form by all who take this stand. The implications are wide. They accent the innate and generic qualities of man and minimize the effects of the environment. They give credence not only to our conscious, but often to our unconscious mental structures and operations. They oppose the doctrine of linguistic relativism which has been a standby of the popular cultural relativism of our time. In so doing, they have resurrected traditional persuasions for the potency of reason and ideas, claims which have long been taken for granted in the Western school and home, as well as in much of oriental thought. They have shared the attitude that the relation of thinking to language is more a case of what thinking does to language than of what language does to thinking. We can now discuss a few of the more influential expressions of this perspective in modern linguistic circles.

Thought or reference theory.—One of the first books to give rise to an awareness of modern semantics was the 1930 edition of *The Meaning of Meaning* by C. K. Ogden and I. A. Richards (16). The analysis, though assuming introspection, was psychologically oriented, presenting the meaning situation as a triadic relationship between a symbol, a thought (or "reference"), and an object (or "referent"). The symbol never refers directly to the referent (the real object) but only to the thought (or reference)—to the mental representation of the external object. Although the authors contended that all perception is the occurrence of a sign situation and that thinking is a sign process, thus underscoring the pervasiveness of signs (or symbols) in human knowledge and understanding, their explication was still mentalistic with thoughts playing the pivotal role. Symbols stand for ideational entities which in turn refer to physical ones. The mediation of the mind is essential. This picture of semantic reference appears naive and inadequate today. It has long been rejected by the empirio-behaviorist schools for its claim that the very apex of the triangle where the "meaning of meaning" lies belongs to an inaccessible realm inside the head which prevents any scientific hypothesis from even arising. On the other hand, the linguistic rationalists find the notion of a simple thought or reference lacking that network of inner logic and grammar necessary to sustain the explicit character of grammatical expressions. Despite this shortcoming, the Ogden-Richards treatment, in addition to its pioneer importance, moves in the rationalist direction by affirming that it is ideas which give language its semantic sense.

Maturational grammar.—A singular approach to the relation of language and thought has been in progress for some years through the meticulous observations of the Swiss psychologist, Jean Piaget (17). His painstaking work with children has yielded a developmental interpretation of language achievement which emphasizes perceptual and conceptual activity as prerequisite to the emergence of speech. Before intelligible language is uttered the child passes through a series of stages in which he gradually externalizes himself as an object among other objects, begins to detach other bodies and motions from his own, arranges them in order of space and time, and finally—and most uniquely human—comes to substitute signs for things that are past or absent. A prelingual model of the adult world is thus built in advance as a cradle for acceptable utterances and awaits the perfection, through use and repetition, of grammatical formations which eventually parallel or approximate its preconstructed gestalts. In learning to talk, subordinate clause terms like "because," "despite," "however," "that," etc., become familiar and are often correctly used before the messages which contain them are grasped. In this regard, says Piaget, a kind of innate grammar precedes not only semantic intelligibility, but even logic itself. Though his case studies are few, Piaget believes his generalizations are universally valid; and thus he opposes the tenets of linguistic and cultural relativism. Controversial from the start, Piaget's developmental hypothesis suffers the criticism that he has overgeneralized from the language learning of the standard European family. So far as his specific observations, often rich with insight, contribute plausible evidence for his conclusions, he belongs with the genetic, rationalist school of linguistics.

Generative grammar.—While many analyses of the language-thought relationship are affiliated with rationalism, only in our own time has a potent and systematic school of linguistics swung an impressive group of authorities and students in this direction. This is the movement in which Noam Chomsky, supported by Morris Halle, P.M. Postal, J. A. Fodor, and others, has become the central figure, and which has reversed the empirical orientation prevailing from 1930 to 1958. Espousing a program of *generative grammar*, Chomsky is today the most original and formidable proponent of psycholinguistic rationalism, which has suddenly and unexpectedly ascended to defy and disconcert what had become an almost smothering gamesmanship of prejudiced behaviorism. The stream of Chomsky's writings [1] has partially or wholly convinced some leading empirical linguists and has moved others to highly defensive maneuvers. The general features of generative-transformational grammar have been explained in the prologue to section 1 and in chapter 1. The discussion here will be confined to the philosophical implications of the approach.

Generative grammarians contend that language capacity is a biological endowment. As such, it casts itself with remarkable flexibility and proliferation, having no evident connection with other forms of human intelligence. The ordinary child is able to use and diagnose language far beyond his exposure to it from parents, schools, or other environmental sources. Our natural languages,

1. Ranging from *Syntactic Structures* (5) to *Aspects of the Theory of Syntax* (4).

without more than colloquial instruction, empower a speaker to "generate" utterly new expressions which are both acceptable and grammatical. This ability to learn and process linguistic impulses is universal in our species.

An acute dispute occasioned by the generative grammarians comes from their distinction between linguistic "performance" and "competence." The "performance" of a language user signifies the sound and script-marks he actually emits when he speaks or writes, however elegant or unschooled his emission may be. Performance, Chomsky insists, is all the empirical or behaviorist linguist has to go on; vocal and script output is the sum of whatever he can regard as "language." This contingent and often crude vernacular corpus, nevertheless, cannot, through mere induction or experimental query, disclose the a priori lawfulness of languages. The need is for an ideal hypothesis on what the laws of language should (or must necessarily) be. This ideal for a language, entertained by an "ideal language user," is called "competence." Everyone who speaks and understands a natural language encloses within himself a little "ideal language user" and a "template" of the quintessential syntax. The basis of the criterion is built into his organism, not as a form of intelligence but as biological linguistic capacity.

Thus, the languages of the world differ mightily but they fit a common format. The format may be preconscious, unconscious, or so conscious that we can never objectify it, but must be there. Otherwise people would not have their ability to utter and to understand speech as we know it.

The average language user follows the laws of his language as he intuits whether or not any given construction is grammatical. According to Chomsky, the user applies a predeveloped model of competence behind the data to insure the success of his performance with the data. Performance itself needs a certain minimum of past performance to give acquaintance with and a certain momentum to the rules, but its full communicative maturity springs from innate language competence which is primed in childhood by only a fractional experience with the native tongue.

Chomsky and his rationalist allies have also distinguished between "surface structure" and "deep structure" analyses of language. Phonological components can be studied on the surface as part of performance. But the Chomsky school feels that most linguists have failed to see that the syntactic framework which makes sentences grammatical, transformed, and generated, lies under this surface. Up to a point, however, one can toy with actual utterances on the surface as a means of probing the deep syntactical determinants beneath it all.

Although Chomsky in his rationalism is perhaps the most philosophical of modern linguists, and holds out for an ultimate language reality that some critics regard as presumptuous and "metaphysical," his demand for scientific verification is as strong as that of the behaviorists. He says that any adequate linguistics must rest on both generative grammar *and* experimental tests. More than the Cartesians he so admires, he is willing to risk the submission of his theories to facts. While grammar in the deep sense is independent of meaning, it is still composed of orderly relationships from which vocal performances, including cognitive expressions, are but derivative symptoms. These symptoms, which are audible and measurable, must conform to the underlying theory of grammar if that theory is to stand up.

Likewise, it must be remembered that Chomsky's rationalism is not "mentalistic," at least in the traditional dualistic sense, but is biological and hereditary. Man's innate ability to handle complex languages is not due to what happened in childhood, with "its few months (or years) of experience," but "to millions of years of evolution or to principles of neural organization even more deeply grounded in physical law" (4:59). At the same time he reminds us that the empiricist can hold out "little hope that the structure of language can be learned by an organism initially uninformed as to its general character" (4:58). If this is so, then the human must learn his language because he is initially *in*formed—"informed" in the sense that the form is put in him by the act of procreation. Our power to learn and develop our language is thus at least innate. Exposure to the native tongue in childhood awakens this power, which, though constantly enhancing, remains largely unknown and perhaps unknowable to us. If there is no ambiguity in "language" or "theory of grammar" in Chomsky's schema, there is still an awesome one in "thinking," partly because the forms of thought may be called "thinking" by some people and the verbal expression of thought may be called "thinking" by others. While Chomsky is not clear on this point, the general tenor of his position indicates that an unconscious rationality precedes our symbolic endeavors, and that a rational "theory of grammar" is needed to make sense of what happens in talk or longhand. Reason is universal because thought is nativistic.

The apprehension of the skeptic is that Chomsky's "science" of language does not logically derive from authenticated linguistic data, but is a gratuitous, arbitrary contrivance of his own, which, as an attempt to make verbal performance intelligible, may be regarded as only one of an indefinite number of possible, competing explanatory systems. The nether-world of language has been largely unvisited. In being one of those who "has gotten there first," Chomsky runs a greater risk of error than those who stick close to what is familiar and secure. Even if his own world down under is fanciful, however, it may be that he is correct in arguing that some such world is necessary to make sense of the constantly baffling relationships of performed speech.

While detailed scientific confirmation of Chomsky's theory of a "language-reality" is still to be anticipated, a forceful general argument from biology has recently been presented by Eric H. Lenneburg (11). This specialist regards the remarkable human voice-team with its array of acoustic variables as our special biological birthright which has made us the most interdependent and communicative of all creatures. The extreme complexity of the simplest speech act involves a coordination of moving parts that puts our most sophisticated machines to shame. The overriding need in vocal utterance is the need for *system*, as the amount of random variation is otherwise incalculable. A high probability that some speech sounds will occur while others will not is thus built into our organisms. However diverse in kind and infinite in number our vocal emissions may be, their equiprobability must be merely apparent, as messages could not be sent or received did not an underlying order prevail. (This is one of the clear conclusions of modern cybernetics and "information theory.") Chomsky's position that deep-structure study of grammaticality, as a means for understanding language, surpasses surface-structure study of the phonological component is bound to find Lenneburg's outlook comforting. More research in these directions is continuing.

Syntactical semantics.—The promise of Chomsky's depth-sounding of syntactic *noumena* has only made the semantic (or meaning) dimension of language seem more appalling in its surface chaos. Naturally enough, there has been a call to establish rational order among linguistic meaning-units too, using a deep-level analysis; and this call has been obligingly heeded by another Chomsky follower, Jerold J. Katz (9). The whole reciprocal relationship between semantics and syntactics had already been mentioned by Chomsky as awaiting "a development of the theory of universal semantics." Katz's is a first attempt within technical linguistics to affix a rationalistic (and syntactical semantics) to Chomsky's generative grammar.

Katz tries to establish a theory for determining meaning by a technique of first breaking down a natural sentence (on the deep level) to its syntactic constituents, and then to its semantic constituents, aiming to exclude all extraneous potential meanings so as to discover at last the remaining "kernel meaning." This method results in a verbal atomism in which words or morphemes are the syntactic atoms, and eventually the semantic atoms. From the meaning of these atoms the semantic rules generate the meaning of larger units, such as the deep equivalents of phrases and sentences, the process being foolproof and rigorously logical. The purpose of the analysis is to do away with ambiguity; and this task requires detecting all the multiple meanings which are possible in the original pre-analyzed expression. Thus, in the sentence "There are many bachelors in New York," we must recognize for the word "bachelor" such legitimate lexical meanings as "a male fur seal without a mate during breeding time," "a knight serving under the standard of another knight," "a human who has the lowest academic degree," etc., before we arrive at the intended meaning of "an unmarried human male." According to Katz, "Semantic ambiguity . . . occurs when an underlying structure contains an ambiguous word or words that contribute its (their) multiple senses to the meaning of the whole sentence" (9:159). By achieving univocal meaning for each atomic particle of a given sentence, and by following the rules for combining these particles, the absolute meaning of a sentence is decided.

In overview, Katz's development falls back on Chomsky's theory

286

of "innate linguistic knowledge" as the source of meaning, and, in opposition to empiricism, dismisses "knowledge of the world" (1). His concept of language relies on how words get along with words, not on how they get along with things. The "creativity" of language, which is the most distinctive emphasis of generative grammar, is attributed not to the elasticity of speech in reporting the facts of life, but to its internal combinatorial mechanism. This attribution, while at least partly successful in a theory of syntax, is nonetheless more tenuous in a theory of semantics. While human psychological processes may be severely dominated by inborn linguistic capacity, their relation to the infinite varieties of experience is mediated by language which is fluid and metaphorical—more than Katz's generative semantics seems to allow.

*   *   *   *

These few examples of linguistic rationalism, while spanning forty years and representing different academic backgrounds, wear a common philosophic uniform. This is not the mentalism so well known in Platonic and Cartesian rationalism; rather it is linguistic universalism based on phylogenic universalism—in which the gift of tongues is granted equally to all normal men. As finally cultivated in generative grammar, *thinking* as the deep, biological operation of language exerts a control that approaches the awesome. Though naturalistic throughout, the latest stage of linguistic rationalism describes the language-thought phenomenon as structurally independent of the environment and the accidents of natural speech. Here is where the issue stays drawn, as we proceed to review the empirical biases, which express a contrary viewpoint.

THE EMPIRICAL BIASES

Like the rationalist orientation to the problem of language and thinking, the empiricist approach is characterized by a variety of claims, ranging from radical theories about the purely sensory origin of knowledge to emphases on the importance of the cultural environs in the acquisition of language. Whereas rationalistic linguistics gives great weight to the intrinsic nature of mental activity, empiricism focuses on the part played by incoming representations in affecting language structure—including those representations of the prevailing language itself. It must be realized that in its strongest aspect empirical linguistics does not hold that only the reference and meaning of speech is granted by extrinsic forces, but that the very grammar of language is imported from the cultural milieu. This contention paves the way to replace the linguistic universalism of the rationalists with a linguistic relativism, simply if it can be shown that the earth's languages differ in their most intimate syntactic patterns. Languages, for the empiricist, are systems of acquired habits, and not innate central processes. The source disciplines of the empirical biases are more diverse than those of rationalism for the obvious reason that the study of environmental determinants has a wider scope than the study of internal ones. The issue is directly joined within linguistics itself, and this we must now consider.

Linguistic empiricism.—Three or four decades ago the study of linguistics began to emerge as a distinct branch of the total scientific study of human behavior; as such, it would be expected to follow the dominant behaviorism of the era. As the chief expositor of this new linguistics, Leonard Bloomfield, in 1933 dispensed with inner cognition by defining the "meaning" of a linguistic form as "the situation in which the speaker utters it and the response which it calls forth in the hearer" (2). As Bloomfield and his early associates limited their analysis of speech to what was publicly observable, they founded modern "descriptive linguistics" as a discipline that avoided all reference to thinking or other introspective experiences. The role of the descriptive linguist is to accept the whole body of speech performance as data first to be analyzed into sounds and their variations, and then into their syntactic and semantic structures. The treatment of thinking did not include meaning, but only the semantic "pointing" of language forms to their respective referents. To consider meaning was to consider those utterances which have a "socially determined correspondence" with nonlinguistic phenomena.

The early efforts in descriptive linguistics were notable for their scientific dedication and their unsparing search for rigor. For some two decades, groups of linguistic behaviorists struggled with the vast mazes we call "natural languages," seeking correlations and inductive generalizations which would build up to a science. It was these efforts which Chomsky came to regard as failures, and which turned his own attempts towards creating a scientific linguistics in the direction of philosophy, logic, and mathematics. As a result, in the last fifteen years the polemics of the few remaining empirical linguists have been devoted to retaliatory criticism of generative grammar. A more recent and explicit counterattack against linguistic rationalism is that of Charles F. Hockett, one of the original Bloomfieldians, the title of whose book, *The State of the Art* (8), foreshadows the author's contention that linguistics is not only far from being a precise science, but is incapable of being "well defined" like a deductive system. Hockett distinguishes between formal systems and physical systems, the former characterizing the domain of symbolic competence and the latter, performance. Natural language, for Hockett, belongs with performance, and its grammaticality does not depend on a calculus (or "algorithm"). Hockett argues for "the openness of language"; language is more like football than like chess. If competence is more closed and rule-governed than performance, it merely indicates, contrary to Chomsky, that competence does not help us to understand performance. Language is "ill-defined"; it is generated by shading and metaphors, and by the semantic associations of experience, more than by any kind of logical rigor. Speech changes through time due to the trials and errors of living, to economical elisions and the editing of repetitions, to experiments in new combinations and word-orders, along with spontaneous and often poetic innovations. Hockett feels that rationalism has little to offer to the analysis of the ensuing data. He is for sticking by empirical linguistics in an improved empirical sense. In short, "analogy, blending and editing are the basic mechanisms for the generation of speech" (8:94). None of these mechanisms call for deep-structure analysis.

In such a neo-empirical perspective there is no need whatsoever for *thinking* to be given a privileged focus, not even in the Chomskian sense of innate language ability. While biological capacity is patently necessary for linguistic achievement, this capacity is a general capacity to symbolize freely, and not an intrinsic potential system of universal grammar. Though the critique of Chomsky still taunts the empirical endeavor, the continued failure of both the rationalist and empirical cadres to explain or predict so many anomalies of speech performance leaves the decision about them to a metaphysical option which a teacher of either persuasion may find consoling.

Operant behaviorism.—Quite expectedly, a sharp empirical conflict with linguistic rationalism has arisen from the ranks of behaviorist psychology so far as it is concerned with language. Such opposition has appeared from B. F. Skinner (18), who bears the mantle of Pavlov, Watson, and Hull in being the most influential behaviorist of his time. For Skinner, as for his predecessors, thinking is reduced to observable symbolic behavior, and language, as the most important part of that behavior, is in turn reduced to performance. Linguistic behavior consists of emitted responses called *operants* and for which no definite causal stimuli can be assigned. Like the early vocal noises of the infant, an operant response may begin accidentally, and then be repeated due to social reinforcement. With such reinforced (rewarded) continuance, speech begins to assume the patterns so evident in conversation. The originally undetected stimuli are replaced by deliberate ones, as a certain type of statement, question, or command provokes a certain type of reply. There is no need to infer some hidden dynamics of competence or mental laws. The speech of the human, although more complex, no more requires some inborn logical or grammatical tendency than the noises of the animal laboratory from which Skinner has drawn his guiding principles.

Chomsky criticized Skinner in an exhaustive review, finding his terminology vague to the point of uselessness and charging that his imported system was quite unable to provide any understanding of language. Thus, he writes that Skinner makes it "very clear that in his view reinforcement is a necessary condition for language learning and for the continued availability of linguistic responses in the adult." Chomsky continues:

However, the looseness of the term "reinforcement" as Skinner uses it . . . makes it entirely pointless to inquire into the truth or falsity of his claim. Examining the instances of what Skinner calls "reinforcement," we find that not even the requirement that a reinforcer be an identifiable stimulus is taken seriously.[2]

Despite such needling, Skinner's position rests on a manner of

2. See Noam Chomsky, Review of *Verbal Behavior* by B. F. Skinner, *Language* XXXV (1959), 37.

speaking which is convincing to many psychologists and educators. Perhaps the ultimate question is whether language acquisition results merely from a sufficient exposure to a language without ulterior incentives or from a minimum exposure accompanied by (the equivalents of) smiles or frowns. Perhaps the answer is "Both" but, if so, further answers are needed as to where one leaves off and the other begins.

There can be no satisfactory resolution of the debate at this time. A richer, encompassing behaviorism may well include many logical-grammatical determinants in its scope of causes—and this raises doubt as to whether we should still call it *behaviorism*. Similarly, a universal rationalism may well incorporate nonsymbolic or nongrammatical interferences in its linguistic purview—and this makes us wonder if it will not on doing so compromise its right to be labeled *rationalism*. All this triggers the suspicion that Chomskians and Skinnerians are talking past each other. In any case, we know that the status of thinking as an independent stream of internal phenomena is denied by the operant behaviorists and is affirmed by the generative grammarians—and this may be the only argument that would concern a teacher.

Ordinary language philosophy.—Much of modern philosophy has become the philosophy of language, for the first time in history. This unprecedented interest appeared most conspicuously in the twenties with the movement known as "logical positivism," centered in Vienna and Cambridge, which maintained that the perennial problems of philosophy would vanish if only the language in which they were framed was clarified and reformed. Knowledge, the logical positivists maintained, could not be generated by philosophy, but was the product of the senses or the sciences. The epistemology of rationalism was thus rejected, except for the information yielded by logic and mathematics which consists of "tautologies".—inferences in which the conclusions simply repeat explicitly what the premises state implicitly.

In subsequent years Ludwig Wittgenstein, a principal founder of logical positivism, modified his earlier position to initiate what is now known as "ordinary language philosophy" (21). According to this development, much of our thinking is part of certain "language games" which society has induced us to play. Thus we use sentences in which nouns like "time," "force," "motion," "intelligence," "abstraction," and "meaning" play pretend roles as though they were similar to the names of everyday things like rocks, trees, and birds. We mistakenly make commonplace statements of fact into our models for more "profound" statements about ultimate things. The most treacherous temptation is to group different experiences together under the names of a class, a universal, or an essence; and to proceed to think about this generality instead of thinking about the particular experience. In such ways our language traps us, and we must recognize that least of all do words have absolute meanings. They are idiomatic islands which have many connecting bridges with the rest of the archipelago of speech, but which still are governed by their own peculiarities of usage. To understand a subject or the "ideas" of another person, one must follow the explanatory language, which is like being guided by a partner in a dance; and of course this means a considerable, though by no means complete, coincidence between the language games of the sender and receiver. These acts of "following" and "using" language constitute at least a large part of what we call thinking. This concept precludes mentalist and rationalist accounts of cognition, because these accounts assign control to events inside the head and regard language as either expressing or being a universal system of thought.

Unlike the generative grammarians, the ordinary language philosophers do not seek and would not expect to find innate grammatical laws that clarify the verbal "bewitchments" to which we are so susceptible. Meanwhile, neutral educators may find each approach instructive and promising for a beginning linguistic enlightenment, without rushing to a final verdict on which position is more "correct."

Linguistic-relativity-determinism.—Another challenging theory favoring the view that thought is a product of language has sprung from a special development in anthropological linguistics, more technically called *metalinguistic*. The chief spokesman for this outlook was Benjamin Lee Whorf (20), who, in his studies under Edward Sapir, followed the hint that in different cultures the structure of the language is intimately connected with both the prevailing world view and the typical habits of thought. As Brown has interpreted this Whorf hypothesis, "The languages of the world are so many molds of varying shape into which infant minds are poured. The mold determines the cognitive cast of the adult" (3). For his most striking examples, Whorf used the speech of some American Indian cultures, finding that, in contrast to "standard average European" tongues, there is an entirely different repertoire of verbal equipment for representing both the world generally and objects or processes specifically. For example, while Western languages divide and apportion nature into distinct and bounded *objects* which move and relate in measureable ways, the Hopi and other Indians speak of *events:* Westerners say "The *light* (or *it*) flashed," but Hopi simply utter the equivalent of our verb "flash." Our subject-predicate grammar binds us to a world view in which objects remain what they are while they continue to do or not do certain things and lose or acquire certain properties, making it easy for an Aristotelian metaphysics of substance to become dominant.

The awkward label, "Linguistic-Relativity-Determinism," signifies the two complementary features of the Whorf hypothesis. While cultures are to be judged *relative* to their native tongues, the tongues still *determine* important parts of the culture—at least to a certain degree. There are no linguistic universals, but there are different grammars, syntaxes, and vocabularies for different societies. The liberation of thinking beyond a given culture requires an increase of the linguistic alternatives at one's command. By rejecting universalism, the Whorf hypothesis rejects rationalism. It nods towards empiricism by holding that the structure of language is learned rather than inborn, and that the interpretation of sense perceptions is individuated by social-lingual upbringing. At the same time, it rejects traditional sensory empiricism; it is not our eyes and ears, but language which fixes the form of our "reality." The educational implications of the Whorf hypothesis are very similar to those of popular semantics which is next discussed.

General semantics.—The linguistic movement which has prompted the most lively response from both the lay public and the public school has been the crusade of general semantics, which dates back to 1933 with the publication of Alfred Korzybski's *Science ad Sanity* (10). This work, although difficult and arrogant, became popular through the interpretations of S. I. Hayakawa, Stuart Chase, Wendell Johnson, Irving J. Lee, Anatol Rapoport, and numerous other writers whose books flooded the stands for many years. Korzybski proclaimed his position to be "non-Aristotelian," in that it rejected the ontological implications of traditional Indo-European language and sought a symbolic pattern more in harmony with twentieth-century science. In contrast to the Whorf hypothesis, general semantics holds that the aspiration of all languages is to reflect the reality around us *as it is*—independent of language and other subjective factors; and that the problems of intellectual falsehood and personal maladjustment ("unsanity") are in great part attributable to the inability of languages and our attitudes towards language to reflect this reality properly. General semantics has preached the values of an extensional as opposed to an intensional orientation; i.e., the virtue of responding to our environment as our nonverbal senses and our tested sciences dictate, rather than as our grammar and our semantic reactions tempt us. Among the evils of our inherited Western languages Korzybski included: the *is* of identity (e.g., to say "John is a criminal" fosters an illusion of some *criminality* in John's nature instead of merely mentioning that once in his youth John was convicted of robbing a store); the two-valued (either-or) orientation (e.g., the black-white, right-left, rich-poor, hot-cold, honest-dishonest, etc., dichotomies by which our speech tends to overlook the in-between classes and conditions of things); the passion for "allness" (e.g. the readiness to conclude that *all* x's are y's because most or even just some x's are y's—"All Republicans are conservative," "All unions resent capitalism," "All paranoids are dangerous," etc.). While many of these cognitive cautions have long been gospel to the critical scientist, along with the skeptical philosopher, Korzybski felt that the dangers in the modern world required that they be internalized from childhood as part of normal education. The role of general semantics, from the beginning, has been even more "therapeutic" than that of ordinary language philosophy. Sanity, for Korzybski, meant training from infancy in responding to sensations, and the subsequent learning of language that was anchored in sensory verifiability.

General semantics, on the other hand, has been close to the Whorf hypothesis in insisting that human beings do, in fact, respond more to the way their language presents their world than to their world itself. Whereas for Whorf this was just the way human beings were, for Korzybski it was always a pathology; and for this reason he constantly admonished his followers to get beneath language into the "silent level" of reality. Presymbolic or nonsymbolic thinking bears a fidelity to fact which is quickly trained out of us by our symbolic culture. Some of our linguistic upbringing, like the functional equations found in physics, has preserved the veracity of our beliefs because they have been grounded in observable events and have yielded correct statements about what comes next; but most of our verbiage has belied the reality around us. Our thinking processes are thus neurolinguistic processes, which are inextricably dependent upon our language habits. Korzybski's famous truism that "the word is not the thing" was constantly repeated in order to drill into the student the recognition that the symbol is not what it symbolizes. The resulting "semantic awareness" is a form of thinking too, but one that liberates us from the enslaved thinking to which so much of our language commits us. This position is contrary to Chomsky's intimation that our nativistic grammar is irrevocable and inescapable. General semantics clearly allows more freedom for language (performance) to determine thought than does generative grammar.

Total communicative involvement.—The most recent venture into communication to pass before the public grandstand has been the "pan-sensational" theory of Marshall McLuhan (13). Seemingly wild and far-fetched, McLuhan's argument that the sovereignty of the press has seen its days and is now yielding to a wholesale opening of all the senses, so far represented in television, has become widely acceptable to young people who sometimes admit that they do not fully understand him. The new media will have a comprehensive, "all-at-once" appeal to the audience; the "Gutenberg" eye-era is done for, and a new oral-aural-tactile era of symbolism is on its way in. Linear, step-by-step thinking is no longer for mass consumption; massive, simultaneous exposure is the rule of the day. McLuhan's most quoted statement, "The medium is the message," identifies the symbols with the world which the symbols disclose. Whatever truth lies in this argument serves to explain not only the sensory availability and excitement achieved in the psychedelic movement, but also the more passive and withdrawn affections of the new mystical and yoga disciplines now attracting many secondary and college students. The challenge to standard educational techniques is revolutionary. At the very least we must grant that the popularity of this stand cannot be wished away. If the sense it makes to many people is questionable, to others it appears to deserve the most careful consideration.

Regarding the problem of thinking, McLuhan reflects the most radical empiricism, and his views are more incompatible with the universal rationalism of Chomsky than any we have mentioned. In being the messages, the media are also the thinking that goes with the send-off and receipt of the messages. And the media are historically contingent upon the accidents of discovery, of economic and political ambition, and of blind societal developments. So then is thought. The vehicles of literacy, heretofore so predominant in Western institutions, begot the rich verbal culture of our immediate past, and created both the poetic and logical thinking for which it will be remembered. Nothing genetic or nativistic in man determines that his syntax will be that of rhymed couplets or of modern lightshows. The gratuitous impingement of environmental message systems and technologies is responsible for people thinking the way they do; and nothing more need be said.

* * * * *

This skimping over the empiricist approaches to language and thinking has omitted many names, some of which may turn out to be more memorable than those here mentioned. However, the foregoing samples cover enough variations of the empirical outlook to give the rationalist plenty to think about. As we scan the gamut of the foregoing views, extending from conventional linguistic empiricism to McLuhan's total sensory prehension, we can, in spite of the divergence of motive and interest, find two common questions aimed at the rationalist postion: First, does there exist a language-reason substructure which both potentializes and circumscribes the performance of cognitive speech? and, secondly, if such a substructure does exist, is it sufficiently potent and durable to withstand substantial modification and correction arising from both the linguistic and sensory environment? For the empiricist and behaviorist, thinking tends to be an acquired ability corresponding to the symbol systems which happen to be learned, and which may also be reinforced by extralinguistic stimuli. In any case, the answers are not all in. Meanwhile the educator can at least take a long look at the possibilities for education which lie within the continuance of the debate itself.

Classroom Considerations

Very few of the theoretical positions here presented will penetrate directly into the classroom or even into discussion between teachers themselves. Nevertheless, adherence to some philosophy of language and thinking is bound to betray itself no matter how "practical" and unphilosophical many teachers imagine themselves to be. This truth holds not only for the instructor of the obviously symbolic skills, like language and mathematics, but even for the instructor of such subjects as creative and industrial arts, physical education, and domestic science, in which nonverbal skills are taught. The abstract debates may be academically remote, but the justifications for the way the teacher teaches reach to the linguist, the philosopher, the psychologist, and the anthropologist, come what may.

It should be clear from this presentation that at this moment the power of the rationalist bias revolves around one central figure, Noam Chomsky, with his generative grammar. The empiricist biases, however, are distributed among a variety of spokesmen from different fields of knowledge. If the teacher finds the most telling insight of generative grammar to lie in its explanation of the language-acquisition process—of the combinatorial powers which allows sentences to be understood and used without prior exposure— he may also find in any one of the empiricist theories we have mentioned some good reasons for qualifying, limiting, or even suspending the claim of innate linguistic capacity.

Some last suggestions follow:

1. As the "school" of empirical linguistics is today as fluid as it asserts language to be, its message that every natural language is "loose" and "ill-defined" is one that can relax the teacher who is anxious from purist strictures. Thinking is, on the one hand, just the language ideal of formal systems and, on the other, simply the cumulus of actual usage. Empiricism stresses the latter as both more frequent and helpful in the mastery of a natural language, and the

teacher who knows that syntax guides all of speech may profit by learning that all of speech is not syntax.

2. If the theory of language dominates the debate between the linguistic empiricists and rationalists, the method of teaching it becomes paramount with the case of the operant behaviorists. However self-proliferating a minimal set of kernel sentences in a learned language may be, there must certainly be *some* reinforcements, defined independently of the pleasure in learning the language, that contribute to a student's motivation. The attempt to bring the mass of students into a standard pattern of middle-class English, for example, cannot rely on school models which lose out in competition with the more powerful models of the "uncouth" home and neighborhood; mere exposure and imitation will not suffice. The thinking expressed in such "substandard" speech tends to be denigrated by the school along with the speech, without even an effort to compare it with more "proper" usage. To stress and demonstrate the mutual translatability of such unapproved and approved dialects would seem to call, not only for exposure, but also for effective techniques of reward best suggested by behaviorism.

3. Direct pedagogical application of the insights of ordinary language philosophy might well tease and delight children into appreciating the "funniness" of our language. The bewilderments of thinking which accompany concepts of space, time, number, etc., can be shown to be linguistic in nature, along with common riddles, ambiguities, and puns. In later years a student may well utilize such playfulness to develop a critical attitude towards language. While the charm and humor of linguistic idiosyncrasies gain their effect against a background of grammatical consistency as stressed by the rationalists, they are themselves created through performance, as stressed by the empiricists and ordinary language philosophers.

4. The benefit to a student from realizing that some part of what is called the "different thinking" of alien people is due to peculiarities of their different language, can be achieved through the contributions of "metalinguistics." While "linguistic-relativity-determinism" at first suggests that our various language worlds are hermetic and mutually incommunicable, owing to their autonomous empirical development, further reflection reveals that some significant degree of translation is indeed possible, and that some universal language

conversion table may exist after all. Research on the diverse counting systems of scattered tribal cultures now leads us to believe that the attainment of higher numbers is lacking only when the need for it is lacking; and that when the need is present, almost any people, with their respective number bases, can generate the higher numbers just as well as we can. That this is so with all linguistic "inabilities" is not yet proven; and we are rather sure that no natural language can be exactly translated into another. Yet we have reason to think that rational interdependence between families of languages is quite possible to construct with only a certain degree of effort. The incompatibility of "world views" which linguistic differences appear to generate seems no greater than the incompatibilities arising within any given language—yet they may be of a different kind. As for the school, possibly the best position is to remain somewhat curious and searching. The possibility that the language-thought process of one culture can be, if not perfectly translated, at least adequately transfigured into that of another culture, permits the hope for ultimate communicative reconciliation around our planet.

5. The most widespread permeation of language-thought reform into the public school has been through the controversial general semantics movement, with conspicuous evidence of its growing popularity among elementary teachers.[3] Although Korzybski and Hayakawa warned of the dangers lying within the very structure of our Western languages, it has been their criticism of our "semantic reactions"—i.e., our responses to and attitudes towards language —that has been of most meaning to the teacher, who has been enabled to find many specific techniques for distinguishing words from things, for withholding unjustified generalities, for clarifying and discriminating between lower and higher levels of abstraction, and so on. Though such practices leave untouched the finer issues of rationalism and empiricism, they definitely imply a close tie-in between "sane" thinking and "sane" evaluations *in* and *about* language.

6. One influence that the future teacher, regardless of his convictions, cannot eschew, is the new electronic communicative environment. The fact of this environment is already with us, along

3. For example, in the period 1966-68, more than 2000 teachers requested instructional materials from the International Society for General Semantics.

with its first consequences, the child television watchers. The degree
to which our linear literacy of the past will be eventually replaced
remains uncertain, but a major occupation of the invading forces
has by now occurred. The teacher has still the option of how to
react to this historic change. The most conservative among them
are resisting, claiming that the victory of the tube spells not only the
end of spelling but the end of literacy and of the rational intellect.
The supposition behind this dread is that thinking is not only bound
to symbolism, but to the particular kind of written symbolism
which has formed our bibliographic tradition. At the other extreme
are those educators who welcome and use the new media to the
hilt. If they value the use of symbols they can argue that the new
simultaneous total messages are not only as symbolic as print but also
cultivate a revolutionary and dramatically organic kind of thinking
as well. McLuhan's position leaves "thinking" open to arbitrary
definition, but he does not equate training by the new media with
the end of cognitive man. Yet the "feel-thought" of psychedelic
art and music would seem related to the abandonment of literary
as well as mathematical expression. Whether the connection need
be so is a problem for study, and it may also be possible that our language of the past can now stand some inventiveness to reach out
in more embracing sensory directions. Something like this may be
required if the student is any longer to regard old-fashioned books
with respect.

If these pages have failed to yield answers to the serious teacher,
it is probably because the subject does not lend itself to the ready
formulation of meaningful questions. Yet the material and the concepts reviewed are most pervasive in an all-too-real occupational
environment for the teacher. Language about language—and symbols about symbols—is a favorite detachment of our age, constituting a powerful new self-consciousness for both individuals and institutions, much as the insights of Hegel, Marx, Darwin, and Freud
beckoned men to peer behind their own stage and discover that they
were not what they thought they were. So the nature of language,
which is part of ourselves, discloses information about ourselves and
our beliefs quite different from that which we conventionally intro-
spect. Indeed, introspection, supposedly a private and hidden activ-

ity, is likely as fettered by silent jargon as the average political speech is by noisy platitudes. Some perspective on the publicly performed speech may lead us to examine our "inner speech" as well. It is no doubt arduous for the teacher, like the average person, even to admit the possibility that his precious, unspoken cognitions may be aborted conversation or even muted oratory. This unexpected recognition, so firmly trained out of the student who is taught to verbalize a sharp distinction between words and thoughts, may, when revived for the adult teacher, become an important diagnostic lens for understanding that secretive, sensitive underworld where language and thinking blend to reflect experiences and express the maturing personality. When this happens, language and thinking are seen as inseparable aspects of both performance and competence in the classroom.

BIBLIOGRAPHY

1. BEEMAN, FREDERICK D. "Three Aspects of Syntax and Semantics in the Philosophy of Language." Unpublished Master's thesis, San Francisco State College, 1968.
2. BLOOMFIELD, LEONARD. *Language*. New York: Henry Holt & Co., 1933.
3. BROWN, ROGER. *Words and Things*. Glencoe, Ill.: The Free Press, 1958.
4. CHOMSKY, NOAM. *Aspects of the Theory of Syntax*. Cambridge, Mass.: M.I.T. Press, 1965.
5. ———. *Syntactic Structures*. The Hague: Mouton & Co., 1957.
6. CHAO, YUEN REN. *Language and Symbolic Systems*. Cambridge, England: Cambridge University Press, 1968.
7. HAYAKAWA, S. I. *Language in Thought and Action*. 2d ed. New York: Harcourt, Brace & World, 1963.
8. HOCKETT, CHARLES F. *The State of the Art*. The Hague: Mouton & Co., 1968.
9. KATZ, JEROLD J. *The Philosophy of Language*. New York: Harper & Row, 1968.
10. KORZYBSKI, ALFRED. *Science and Sanity*. 3d. ed. Lakeville: The International Non-Aristotelian Library Publishing Co. 1948.
11. LENNEBURG, ERIC H. *The Biological Foundations of Language*. New York: John Wiley & Sons, 1968.
12. McLUHAN, MARSHALL. *The Gutenberg Galaxy*. Toronto: University of Toronto Press, 1962.
13. ———. *Understanding Media*. New York: McGraw-Hill Book Co., 1964.

14. MILLER, GEORGE A. *Language and Communication.* New York: McGraw-Hill Book Co., 1951.
15. MORRIS, CHARLES. *Signs, Language, and Behavior.* New York: Prentice-Hall, 1946.
16. OGDEN, CHARLES K., and RICHARDS, I. A. *The Meaning of Meaning.* 3d. ed. New York: Harcourt, Brace & World, 1930.
17. PIAGET, JEAN. *The Child's Conception of the World.* Patterson: Littlefield, Adams & Co., 1960.
18. SKINNER, B. F. *Verbal Behavior.* New York: Appleton-Century-Crofts, 1957.
19. WELKER, DONALD E.; JENKINS, JAMES J.; SEBEOK, THOMAS A. "Language, Cognition, and Culture." In *Psycholinguistics, A Survey of Theory and Research Problems.* Supplement, *Journal of Abnormal and Social Psychology,* Vol. 49, October, 1954.
20. WHORF, BENJAMIN L. *Language, Thought and Reality.* Cambridge, Mass.: Technology Press, 1956.
21. WITTGENSTEIN, LUDWIG. *Philosophical Investigations.* Oxford: Blackwell, 1965.

CHAPTER X

Linguistics and Literature

SAMUEL R. LEVIN

Introduction

THE PROBLEM

Literature is language charged with a special function. The ordinary function of language is to convey information; the function of literature is, in addition, to please or to move. Literature thus poses certain problems for linguistics. Since the latter is designed, fundamentally, to deal with the ordinary function of language; it is not obvious that it is capable of dealing also with what, in general, we may call its esthetic function, which is usually conceded to fall within the purview of literary criticism. It would thus appear that in order to render an adequate account of literature one would need either a literary theory that assimilated linguistics or a linguistic theory that embodied literary criticism. These possibilities, however, although seemingly plausible, raise serious problems regarding the integrity of both linguistics and literary criticism in any such amalgamation. For it is by no means certain that the goals of each discipline would not be compromised if they should be made partners in such a combined enterprise. One is not speaking here of a procedure in which linguistics would perform a linguistic analysis on a literary text and then turn over its findings to literary criticism— or the reverse. This course of action, quite feasible, would not represent an integrated theory for dealing with the problem posed by literature; since the goals of both disciplines would not be at hand informing the entire analysis, the results of the separate procedures would not necessarily be of significance for one another. And if one should try to inform the analysis with the goals of both disciplines—use an integrated theory, in other words—the question would arise of whether the respective integrities of the two disciplines could be preserved.[1] In one form or another, the problem raised by the preceding considerations has figured in the entire development of linguistics as it relates to literature.

Survey of Some Historical Approaches to the Problem

CLASSICAL RHETORIC

Already in the development of classical rhetorical theories we see a response to this dual aspect of literature. On the one hand are detailed descriptions of the phonological, syntactic, and lexical devices of the literary language, culminating in the elaborate lists and definitions of the various kinds of trope, and, on the other, discussions of different literary genres, each suitable for certain themes and each associated with a certain style—grand, middle, plain. Although the notions of classical rhetoric are embedded in a highly elaborated taxonomic framework, there is no systematic theory of language underlying the description of literary linguistic devices. In fact, the linguistic data used in grammatical analysis are drawn almost exclusively from the literary language itself, thus precluding any possibility of ascertaining the literary character of the devices in some departure from the linguistic standard. In addition, grammatical studies of the period have a strongly normative cast, descriptive analysis for its own sake not yet being recognized as a desideratum (25:16). Against this background it is not surprising that the question of integrating the observations about literary devices into a comprehensive theory of language and literature is not raised. The various "rhetorics" and "poetics" of the classical period thus stand as storehouses of voluminous and valuable information and insights, but they do not provide a satisfactory account of the relation between language and literature. (One may say this in full recognition of the fact that centuries of research have not been able to achieve this same goal.)

The rhetorical tradition, for all its limitations, persisted with minor modifications through the Middle Ages, the Renaissance, and well into the modern period. Its hardiness can be attributed not only

1. For a discussion of this question see Juilland (12: 316 ff.); also Saporta (27: 82 ff.).

to the failure of succeeding ages to formulate anything better in the way of a linguistic theory of literature, but also to the comprehensiveness of the tradition (within its limits) and the obvious correctness of many of the principles it asserted. Both the virtues and the limitations of the tradition stem from the classical approach to rhetoric as constituting a fine art, quite on a par with music, poetry, and sculpture. The ancients were thus interested primarily in the effects produced by the literary devices and organizing principles of rhetoric and not so much in the linguistic means that made these effects possible.

Not until the eighteenth century did the influence of classical rhetoric begin to wane,[2] to be supplanted in the nineteenth century by two diverging attitudes—one with an emphasis (displayed most strikingly in the work of the comparative grammarians) on precise observation and description of concrete linguistic facts, to the virtual exclusion of questions concerning the function, esthetic or otherwise, of language; and the other, with an emphasis on the view that all uses of language constitute creative acts, thus providing a basis for conducting discussions of literary style in terms of man, his spirit, and his milieu.[3] These opposing attitudes underlie the two significant directions taken by stylistics, the modern avatar of rhetoric, in the twentieth century. One is represented in the work of Charles Bally, the other in that of Leo Spitzer (10:41ff.).

TWENTIETH CENTURY APPROACHES

Charles Bally.—Bally was a student of Ferdinand de Saussure, the Swiss linguist who in the early twentieth century was largely responsible for altering the course of language study. De Saussure is responsible for a number of important theoretical innovations, of which in the present context the most significant are his hypotheses (*a*) that it is just as necessary to study language synchronically, i.e., as a system, as it is to study it historically, and (*b*) that language—approached synchronically or diachronically—is best understood as a system, all the elements of which are related to each other (to

---

2. For a discussion of the reasons see Guiraud (10: 29 ff.).

3. The neogrammarian Karl Brugmann may be said to epitomize the first attitude; Wilhelm von Humboldt, with his conception of language as generative process, to provide the basis for the second.

speak redundantly). He also made a distinction between *langue*, the system, distributed in the collective consciousness, and *parole*, individual speech acts made possible by and interpretable through recourse to the *langue*. Language proceeds through the use of linguistic signs which have a psychological and a motor aspect. In the psychological phase a concept and a sound-image are united in the mind; in the motor phase this combination is vocally transmitted. These signs, in their network of relations (the *langue*), are deposited in the human brain, and it is by virtue of a common deposit that individuals are enabled to communicate with each other. It was against this theoretical background that Bally developed his brand of stylistics.[4]

Following De Saussure, Bally sees in language a vehicle for communicating our thoughts.[5] The information transmitted in the process is divided by Bally into two components: the notional, intellectual, or cognitive component and the component of feeling or emotion. Linguistics concentrates on the first component and stylistics on the second (remaining, however, a proper part of linguistics). Although at the extremes an utterance may comprise one of the components to the near or total exclusion of the other ("The earth turns"; "Oh!"), as a rule every utterance partakes of both. The linguistic features that express feelings or emotion are termed by Bally *affective*, or *expressive*, and it is these features that constitute the subject matter of stylistics. These expressive features occur at any and all levels of linguistic organization, from the phonological (including the level of intonation) to the lexical. Thus, even an utterance like "The earth turns" may, with an appropriate intonation—say, of incredulity or extreme conviction—comprise an expressive dimension.

Expressiveness is made possible because at every level of its organization the language offers to its user a choice among alterna-

---

4. Bally attended the three courses in general linguistics given by De Saussure, in 1906-07, 1908-09, and 1910-11. His earliest work on the subject, *Précis de stylistique* (2), which appeared in 1905, was thus a largely independent study. It is in the first edition of his *Traité de stylistique française* (3), which appeared in 1909, that one finds the influence of De Saussure's linguistic conceptions.

5. For Bally's views on stylistics, see his *Traité de stylistique française* (3) and *Le language et la vie* (1); cf. also Guiraud (10) and Ullmann (34).

tive ways of communicating his thoughts. The use of an archaic word, a metaphor, an unusual syntactic construction, an ellipsis, a formal or familiar variant—each of these represents a choice among possible alternatives. These forms thus assume their expressive value in function of a conscious or unconscious comparison made between them and the other available variants conveying the same notional content. Among the expressive forms Bally distinguishes two classes—the "natural" and the "evocative." Natural are those whose very physical structure is somehow apt for their designative function; thus, onomatopoetic and diminutive or hypocoristic forms. Expressiveness is evocative when the linguistic forms induce judgments about the social, geographic, or educational background of the speaker; thus, some forms are stilted or vulgar, some are urbane or provincial, others are cultured or illiterate. Also evocative are forms that derive from different professional or technical fields. In all these cases, of course, what is evoked is just these respective backgrounds. The task of stylistics, for Bally, then, is to investigate the reciprocal relations of the variant forms within the language system, to observe the effects produced by different variants, and to draw corresponding inferences about the temperament of the speaker and his social and other backgrounds.

For purposes of the present essay, the most important fact about Bally's stylistics is that it is not specially concerned with literature. For Bally, expressiveness is a pervasive element in all language. Literary language is just another variety of language, an esteemed one to be sure, but in all other respects like the varieties used for administrative purposes, for scientific purposes or for the discussion of sports. Moreover, since intonation is a prime conveyor of expressive features, it is the spoken and not the written language which should be the object of stylistic investigation. Bally distinguishes between the spontaneous expressive effects produced by the average speaker in the ordinary conduct of his affairs and the premeditated expressiveness of the writer aiming at an esthetic effect. In this connection he draws a corresponding distinction between the stylistics of a speaker and the style of a writer. But it is the former which is at the center of his interest. Bally's is a stylistics of ordinary speech.

Leo Spitzer.—For Leo Spitzer, on the other hand, the focus of stylistics was on the literary work. He was thus concerned with the style of a writer (29, 10, 34). Although trained in linguistics (Romance philology), Spitzer soon rebelled against what he regarded as its sterility and turned, beginning with his first publication (which dealt in particular with Rabelais), to the study of stylistic features in literature. Spitzer's method was to steep himself in the work being investigated until he became struck by a feature of its composition—a metaphor, a recurrence, an unusual construction, an aspect of organization. On the basis of this concrete feature, and using whatever knowledge, experience, and intuition he was able to bring to bear, he then sought a correlation with some psychological, intellectual, or emotional trait of the author. Having located this trait, he recurred again to the literary work for other linguistic forms or arrangements that were consistent with this trait, and so on. This back and forth movement was designed to determine the "psychological" etymon in the author, the etymon then being held to be reflected in the material forms of the work in question. In a study of *Don Quixote*, for example, Spitzer was struck first by the fact that the proper names occurred in variant forms; thus, Quixote was variously Quesada, Quixada, Quixana. This led him to hypothesize a linguistic perspectivism for Cervantes. Returning to the novel, he observed that different social and regional dialects were employed. This observation confirmed the hypothesis. A further stage in the analysis enabled Spitzer to see, in the midst of all the perspectivism—which comprehended also rational and illusionary views of reality—the God-like figure of Cervantes himself, controlling with a fixed, absolute power the strands of relativism in his novel.

Spitzer's stylistics is thus seen to be concerned with literature. Although he claimed a certain amount of rigor for his method, which he called that of the "philological circle," and which, as we have seen, was based in the first instance on linguistic facts, the ever-widening circles of his method led to conclusions which involved greater and greater reliance on intuition and literary sensitivity. Thus, the stage in his analysis of *Don Quixote* that established Cervantes as wielding his elements with a divine power, although culminating in an interesting critical conclusion, was not as firmly anchored in the linguistic facts as were the earlier stages. Although Spitzer is not susceptible to charges of impressionism (in his own view the emphasis on linguistic facts was one of the chief merits of his method), one may occasionally feel, as in the treatment of *Don Quixote*, that the critical judgments are not sufficiently supported by linguistic analysis. But this is part of a larger question, namely, what kinds of critical judgments it is possible to document with linguistic analysis. Spitzer's critical concerns were large, almost global ones. He wished to penetrate, by his method, into the psyche of a writer, and thence into the spirit of an epoch and the soul of a nation. Such goals can of course be realized in an irresponsible way—simply by asserting conclusions. Spitzer, however, wanted to be responsible; he wanted his conclusions to derive from verifiable linguistic observations. A great distance stretches, however, between the observation of a few isolated linguistic facts and such sweeping conclusions as those at which Spitzer customarily arrived. Whatever else may be needed to bridge the gap, it is certainly necessary to make use of a body of linguistic principles—a theory—much more sophisticated and thoroughgoing than that used by Spitzer, whose linguistics remained essentially that of the nineteenth-century philologists.

Russian Formalism.—Russian Formalism, with its extension as Prague School Structuralism, was a critical movement which flourished from 1915 to the early 1940's.[6] Although primarily, at least in its Russian phase, a development in literary criticism, it enjoyed the advantage of numbering among its members several eminent linguists. More than any comparable movement (except perhaps that of the New Critics) it sought to answer literary questions in terms of a thorough and exclusive analysis of literary language. Eschewing in the main such questions as the psychological state of the author, the genesis of the literary work, or its intellectual content, the analyses of the Formalists were centered squarely on the language event. This focus was justified by contentions that "poetry is verbal art," that "poetry . . . is simply an utterance oriented toward the mode of expression"; in other words, that in poetry the emphasis is on the medium of communication and not on its informational burden.

6. For the best discussion in English, see Erlich (8); representative readings may be found in the following collections: *Russian Formalist Criticism: Four Essays* (26), *Théorie de la littérature* (31), and *A Prague School Reader on Esthetics, Literary Structure, and Style* (23).

The Formalists' emphasis on the language of literature led them to formulate in precise fashion a number of specific problems and to provide for them original and, frequently, compelling answers. In the field of prosody they distinguished sharply between the abstract metrical scheme of a poem and its rhythm, the latter being for them the resultant of the demands made by the ordinary language dynamics of stress, quantity, and intonation as these were constrained by the periodic recurrences invoked by the meter. In studies of poetic euphony, detailed analyses were made of consonant and vowel repetition. Such studies were designed to show, on the phonological level, how in a poem the language is used in a way that is not typical, in a way that makes of a poem a language event *sui generis*, and by so doing induces the apprehender to a contemplation of its form. The process whereby this inducement was effected was explained in general as one in which the language was "de-automatized" from its normal function and made "perceptible" —as it were, palpable to the mind.

On the syntactic and semantic levels as well, this foregrounding of linguistic elements was analyzed and explained. Any unusual syntactic turn or pattern, by being unexpected, would call attention to itself *as a linguistic device* and thus result in a focus on the poem as object. Archaisms, neologisms, dialectal variants, and the various kinds of trope would produce the same result. Poetry thus induced the characteristic focus on the language event by strangeness or novelty, where this novelty took the form of departure from ordinary language usage, either in the way of artificial constraints like rhyme and meter or unwonted syntactic and semantic juxtapositions.[7]

From the foregoing it will be clear that the Formalists' conception of style, while focused on literature, was grounded in an awareness of the importance attached to the study of ordinary language— if only to explain the latter's function as a norm serving to validate the notion of poetic novelty. This awareness is especially marked in the case of the Prague School. In various pronouncements the claim is made, by Formalists and Structuralists, that *poetics*—the

7. The Formalists also made a number of striking observations on prose, distinguishing, for example, between the narrative material of a novel or tale and its plot, the latter being the characteristic artistic *arrangement* of the basic materials.

term used for their conception of literary theory—is an integral part of linguistics. It should be noted, however, that although linguistics can confirm the atypicality of certain sound patternings or syntactic and semantic arrangements, it provides no warrant for assigning to these configurations any special, say, an esthetic, function. On the other hand, literary criticism, although its stock in trade is precisely the consideration of these esthetic functions, presumably does not dispose of procedures for ascertaining whether a given linguistic arrangement adheres to or deviates from ordinary language usage. Bridging these difficulties, as was pointed out in the opening of this chapter, poses certain fundamental problems. Because of the unusual combination and close cooperation of linguists and literary critics embodied in the Slavic schools we have been discussing, they came closer to achieving a fruitful synthesis than perhaps any other comparable historical movement.

Developments in the United States

In the United States interest in linguistic approaches to literature, although developing relatively late, has grown remarkably in the last decade or so and now represents a burgeoning field of investigation. For purposes of discussing this development, it will be useful to describe a few of the theories and approaches that have been advanced for the analysis of language and then to consider some of the work in literary analysis that has derived from each of these linguistic approaches. Before doing so, however, a few words are in order about a noteworthy event that brought into focus a number of the views current at that time concerning the function of linguistics in the area of literary analysis.

INDIANA CONFERENCE ON STYLE

In 1958 the Conference on Style was held at Indiana University, the proceedings of which were subsequently published.[8] Invited to participate in the conference were leading representatives from a number of disciplines, most notably from linguistics, literary criticism, and psychology. The proceedings contain, in addition to some fifteen papers (and a half-dozen abstracts), a record of the discus-

8. Under the title *Style in Language,* edited by Thomas A. Sebeok (Cambridge, Mass., 1960).

LEVIN 311

sions, and the opening and closing statements of spokesmen from the three disciplines mentioned above.

The impact of the psychologists on the proceedings was perhaps of least significance. Numerically, they constituted the smallest group and, as has been pointed out elsewhere (16), they seemed least able to overcome the limitations of their discipline and project their techniques into areas of common concern. We may therefore turn to the contributions of the linguists and literary critics. Instead of detailing, or even summarizing, the contents of the individual papers (a procedure that would in any case take us beyond the confines set for the present discussion), we will examine the closing statements made by two of the most distinguished members participating in the conference—Roman Jakobson, representing linguistics, and René Wellek, representing literary criticism. In addition to representing high points in the conference generally, their two statements are notable for the opposing views they offered on the question of what role linguistics can or ought to play in the criticism of literature.

Jakobson is unequivocal. His motto is *Linguista sum: linguistici nihil a me alienum puto*, "I am a linguist: I regard nothing linguistic as foreign to me." Jakobson distinguishes the poetic function of language by first constructing a model of the language act. In such an act there is an *addresser* and an *addressee*, between whom a *message* is communicated. The message is about a *context*, i.e., a referent; it presupposes a *code* common to the addresser and the addressee and a *contact*, i.e., a channel open between them. Depending on whether the set, focus, or emphasis of the language act is on one or another of these six factors, Jakobson defines a characteristic linguistic function, each one corresponding to a different factor. Thus, to the context there corresponds the *referential* function, to the addresser the *emotive* function, and to the addressee the *conative* function. Corresponding to the contact or channel is the *phatic* function, to the code the *metalingual* function. It is when the set is to the message, that is, to the verbal (or written) communication as such, that we have the *poetic* function. According to Jakobson, the poetic function is thus one of the several functions of language. One therefore cannot study it apart from the study of language itself, and one cannot study language without considering the poetic function, since in addition to being manifested in literature, it appears in all kinds of language use—in slogans, paronomastic expressions, selective lexical or syntactic combinations, and so on.

In Jakobson's essay one finds a restatement and extension of many Formalist doctrines. This is not surprising inasmuch as he was responsible for a number of their conceptions. The essay is important not only for Jakobson's attempt to integrate poetics into a general linguistic framework, but also for the many interesting analyses that he gives in connection with the discussion of various literary problems, chiefly of poetry, and most particularly in the areas of prosody and euphony.

Wellek's statement consists largely of comments on the individual papers presented at the conference, but in the course of his remarks he had occasion to voice his views on the utility of linguistics in literary criticism. Unlike Jakobson, Wellek regards the role of linguistics as limited. He sees the problem of literary style as only one of the problems with which a theory of literature must deal. There are, in addition, such problems as a work of literature's fictionality, i.e., its private and proper reality, its setting in a tradition, and its esthetic dimension. All of these problems, according to Wellek, must be dealt with by a theory of literature, and linguistics, given its assumptions and goals, is inadequate for the task. Even in accounting for style, Wellek questions how far linguistics can be of assistance. He remarks on the emphasis placed by some of the conferees on style as a deviation from the expected. But he points out that frequently it is the commonplace expression that produces the esthetic effect and thus performs a stylistic function. In analyzing for style, therefore, devices must be judged against their contexts, first their linguistic context, and then the contexts of author, genre, and historical period. Wellek's overall view of the problem is expressed in his assertion, "Literary analysis begins where linguistic analysis stops." Once again, in this confrontation the issue at the heart of the problem of linguistics and literature is sharply drawn.

LINGUISTIC APPROACHES AND THE WORK IN LITERARY
ANALYSIS ASSOCIATED WITH THEM

In the development of linguistics in America during the last thirty or forty years, various theories and approaches have been advanced for the analysis of language. Deriving from each of these approaches have been a number of attempts to apply its principles to the analysis of literature. Therefore, it will prove useful to devote the following section of this essay to a consideration of these linguistic approaches and the work in literary analysis associated with each one.

Traditional grammar.—The first American linguistic approach requiring comment (we may say American even though it had counterparts in Europe) is that of descriptive grammar. But before discussing this grammar and its application to literature, it will perhaps be worthwhile to say a few words about the uses to which traditional grammar has been put in connection with literary analysis. Although, in a certain sense, traditional grammar may be regarded as a rather profound theory of language structure, what it provided for the person interested in elucidating literary works by its means was essentially a collection of grammatical labels and various notions of grammatical function. Its limitations derived chiefly from the fact that it did not aim at completeness (in the modern sense) and did not offer a systematic theoretical base. By its means one is enabled to label the parts of speech in a poem or novel, describe various sentence types and other syntactic structures, and so on. This procedure lends itself to making comparisons between the linguistic patterns in different works, different authors, and different periods. After these collations are made, however, the task of showing the relevance of the results to questions of literary significance arises. And here traditional grammar has little or nothing to offer. As we have seen, this problem is the fundamental and besetting problem of all linguistic approaches to literature, not just that of traditional grammar. Traditional grammar, however, in view of the limitations sketched above which apply to the scholarly works of men like Jespersen and Sweet (hence a fortiori to the diluted versions usually employed), is perhaps less able to overcome the problem than are other linguistic approaches.

Descriptive linguistics.—Descriptive (structural or Bloomfieldian) linguistics is characterized by its focus on the language event. Its approach is to language as a physical, not a mental, phenomenon. It is thus concerned not with a speaker's knowledge of his language, but with the product of that knowledge, namely, actual speech tokens. It is oriented toward the concrete, the observable, and, in a physicalist sense, the verifiable. The grammars that result from it are thus based on an analysis of actual linguistic utterances with no regard, at least in the doctrinaire version, for what the speaker producing those utterances might know about them in terms of grammatical relations implicit in the sentences, paraphrase relations between sentences, questions of grammatical well-formedness, and so on. It developed intensive and rigorous techniques for analyzing the phonology, the morphology, and, to a more limited extent, the syntax of a language—the raw material for these analyses consisting exclusively of a corpus of utterances.

Particularly in the area of phonology, the strong focus on the concrete facts of language led to the isolation and description of certain features that had previously been recognized in only a general and unsystematic way. These descriptive results, when carried over into the investigation of literature, particularly poetry, proved extremely fruitful. Thus, the application by Trager and Smith (33) of the phonemic principle to the so-called suprasegmental features— the dynamics of stress, pitch, and intonation—and their development of a precise if somewhat debated notation to describe these features, led some scholars, notably Archibald Hill, Seymour Chatman, and Smith himself, to reexamine English prosody in the light furnished by the new descriptive techniques. Using the Trager-Smith analysis and notation, it became possible to show the interplay between the abstract metrical scheme of the poem and the actual stress dynamics enjoined by the fact that the material of poetry is language. Systems of metrical scansion were of course available from the tradition; but the way in which the language imposed its own demands—of stress, pitch, and intonation contours—could also be registered by the description. The fact (recognized for a long time and described by Jespersen, by Jakobson, and other Formalists) that in poetry it is not the meter alone which is important but the tension set up between metrical regularity—at base a binary measure—and the varying dynamic features of the ordinary language as these are distributed in the syntax of a poem, was able to be presented and discussed in a much more explicit and satisfying framework with the availability of suprasegmental analysis. Within this framework "irregularities" like inverted feet, hovering accents, and the like, could be not merely noted; they could be explained as deviations occasioned by the linguistic demands. Chatman's book, *A Theory of Meter* (5), although it uses a type of suprasegmental analysis different from that of Trager and Smith, is a comprehensive study of the problem.[9]

The chief exhibit of descriptive linguistics in the field of syntax is immediate constituent analysis.[10] The major difference between this type of analysis and the traditional parsing of sentences lies in its use of formal procedures of substitution and expansion in place of the traditional reliance on meaning. A sentence is analyzed into its constituent elements at successive levels of its organization not by asking what kinds of functional or semantic relations the elements enter into, but by testing to see whether simpler elements may be substituted for them while preserving the grammatical status of the sentence. The element actually occurring in the sentence may then be viewed as an expansion of the simpler element and be analyzed as a constituent. This procedure is repeated at successive levels until the entire sentence is decomposed into its individual words (or, if desired, its morphemes), yielding in the process an analysis of the sentence into its immediate constituents at each level of its syntactic organization.

When this approach is applied to literary syntax, it is usually with a view to opening the way for literary criticism by a preliminary establishment of the syntactic relations—somewhat on the order of preparing the definitive text of a work, only at a higher level. The process, it must be admitted, did not, in most cases, yield results that were sharply at variance with those achieved by any careful reading of literature, but the technique of immediate constituents, usually applied in company with suprasegmental analysis, occasionally led to new readings or to a principled selection from among variant readings. Particularly was this true in the case of certain passages in poetry. Among those who made contributions along these lines were W. Nelson Francis (9:83-92), Sumner Ives (11:99-107), and Seymour Chatman (4).

Generative grammar.—A theory of language that has been very

9. Chatman's study is based on the suprasegmental analysis of Dwight Bolinger.

10. The fundamental statement is in Wells (35).

influential for the past ten years or so is that of generative (or transformational) grammar (7, 13, 6). Such a grammar is cast in the form of a series of rules whose purpose it is to enumerate just the set of grammatical sentences, with accompanying structural descriptions. Comprising the grammar are syntactic rules of two types (phrase-structure and transformation) as well as phonological and semantic rules. By including among the syntactic rules certain recursive mechanisms, a generative grammar can enumerate an infinite number of sentences.

One of the most important claims made in connection with the theory of generative grammar is that the purpose of a grammar is to account, primarily, not for a speaker's linguistic performance but, rather, for his linguistic competence, the latter being the body of tacit knowledge that a speaker has about his language and on the basis of which he actually produces and interprets sentences. Competence, according to this view, comprises a good deal more than what can be deduced from actual linguistic utterances; a corollary claim is that the explication of competence cannot be effected if the grammar is constructed exclusively on the basis of concrete linguistic data. The construction of the grammar may be guided by intuitions of various sorts which serve to prompt the selection of particular rules, their ordering, their arrangement, and so on. No circularity is involved here; the grammar makes explicit what is otherwise inchoate. The grammar is thus a formal theory to account for linguistic competence.

Under competence one understands such abilities of the native speaker as those (*a*) of producing or recognizing sentences that he may never previously have experienced (the formal analogue for this ability being the grammar's capacity to generate an infinite number of sentences), (*b*) of recognizing ambiguities of various types (anomaly, synonymy, paraphrase relations), and (*c*) of recognizing grammatical relations which do not appear as such in the actual structure of a sentence; e.g., that in imperative sentences there is an underlying subject, or that in comparative sentences the second term of the comparison is the subject of an implicit sentence. By way of explicating these abilities, generative grammar introduces a distinction between the deep and surface structures of a sentence where (*a*) the deep structure contains those aspects of grammatical and semantic relations which our competence tells us inhere in the sentence and (*b*) the surface structure contains those aspects which appear as such in the actually produced sentence. The grammar generates in the first place deep structures. Various transformation rules, of deletion, adjunction, and substitution then convert the deep structures into surface representations. Thus, a deep structure of a comparative sentence might be of the form *John is tall and Bill is tall*, containing also an element *-er than*, all provided with appropriate bracketing and labeling of the constituents. Similar representations in the grammar serve to explicate the other aspects of competence mentioned above.

It will be clear that, inasmuch as the purpose of a generative grammar is to enumerate all and only the grammatical sentences of a language, the construction of such a grammar focuses attention on various questions regarding the grammatical status of the sentences it generates. It is also the case that such a grammar, because it is generative (and because completely adequate grammars, of whatever type, are probably impossible of attainment), will generate many sentences (actually, an infinite number) whose grammatical status is open to question. The general area of grammaticalness, opened up strikingly by work on generative grammar, has provided an impetus for fresh investigation into literary language, chiefly poetry, where the occurrence of sequences whose grammatical status is questionable is fairly common. The fact that in poetry unusual syntactic and semantic collocations occur has been recognized by literary critics since antiquity. With the availability of a generative grammar, which is an explicit grammar, it has been possible to describe the actual linguistic processes involved in deviant sequences, ascertain what the deviance consists in linguistically, and on that basis suggest some correlation with the literary effect which such sequences induce (14, 15, 32).

Another aspect of generative grammar that has been applied in studies of literary language is the distinction between deep and surface structure. Thus, attempts have been made to show that certain effects produced by literary language, effects which do not lend themselves to explanation if one confines his examination to the language of the work itself, can be illuminated if recourse is had to the deep structure that underlies the passage in question. Sometimes

318   LINGUISTICS AND LITERATURE

it is the presence of additional linguistic matter in the deep structure
that is pointed to as responsible for a given literary effect. Other
times we may point to the various transformational processes inter-
vening between the deep and surface representations. Attempts have
also been made, chiefly by Richard Ohmann, to see in the different
kinds of transformations characterizing the grammatical patterns of
various writers so many indicia of literary styles (20, 21).

Because of its orientation toward linguistic competence, which
if not the seat of the esthetic experience is closer to it than are the
concrete facts of language, generative grammar would seem to provide one of the more promising avenues toward a satisfactory stylistics.

Computational stylistics.—Recently, computers have been pressed
into the service of stylistic analysis. In the main, however, the computer's function along these lines has been a limited one. The computer's ability to process huge amounts of data in a short time has
been exploited in the compilation of concordances, dictionaries,
bibliographies, and other similarly useful tools for literary research.
Striking use has also been made of computers in attribution studies,
in which extensive amounts of material are processed from the
known work of two or more candidates for the authorship of the
work in question, and the results, in terms of frequency counts,
word-class distributions, certain syntactic configurations, etc., are
then compared with similar features in the mooted work. Another
application of this sort is in the area of influence studies, where the
same general computational procedures are followed as for attribution decisions, but where the object of the investigation is to demonstrate an influence of one author on another. The same techniques
may be applied in attempts to ascertain the relative dating of various
literary texts, or in making decisions as to the genuine or spurious
character of works attributed to an author. From the foregoing
sketch, we see that in much of its application to literature the computer is used on problems that are peripheral to the main concerns
of literary criticism which, we may assume, focuses on the questions
"What is literature?" and "How does literature produce its characteristic effects?"

It is clear that the same techniques used in the peripheral studies
mentioned above can also be employed in an attempt to learn some-

thing of an individual author's style. Toward this end the computer makes available a large mass of data, processed in quantitative form, and thus provides an objective basis for making judgments about individual styles. The practitioners of this approach to style point to the objective nature of their evidence as representing a needed corrective to studies of style which proceed largely on the basis of subjective reactions to a literary text. In claiming this superiority for their method they are no doubt correct. It must be borne in mind, however, that the computer, although highly efficient at gathering all sorts of concrete information about the language of a literary work, is powerless to autonomously assign any value to the information it assembles. It provides us with an objective index to the writer's style, but the task of judging the esthetic or literary value of the style remains that of the human investigator (17, 18, 19).

Current Practice in the Schools

The following comments are based on a sampling of some of the materials currently being prepared for use in the schools and which deal with the teaching of literature.[11] Although the materials sampled would seem to be representative, it is quite possible that the sampling of additional or different material would lead to conclusion different from the ones arrived at in this brief survey.

The impression gained from an examination of *The Roberts English Series* (Books 3-6) is that, although poems (and other literary forms) are discussed from a linguistic point of view, the fact that the poems are *literary* texts and as such pose special problems for linguistic analysis is not seriously raised (24). By and large, a poem is treated simply as a corpus of linguistic material upon which analysis is to be performed. The linguistic analysis, moreover, is largely traditional, with here and there the use of a descriptive technique. There are exercises bearing on the phonological, syntactic, and semantic levels of the poem's composition, but there is little indication in these exercises that the elements examined at the various linguistic levels are functioning otherwise than they function in nonpoetic language.

11. In preparing the following section I was assisted greatly by Professor Marjorie B. Smiley, of Hunter College, who kindly made available to me the various materials on which it is based. The evaluation of them is my own.

In the Oregon materials (22) the description of the literature component emphasizes the importance of teaching literature as literature, not as a lesson in ethics, history, or life in general. The steps recommended for carrying out the program, however, amount essentially to the technique of close reading.

In a book published under the auspices of the Indiana center, (30) Blake's "A Poison Tree" is subjected to a close reading. The following quotation illustrates the authors' approach to the problem: "How might we describe the language used by the person in the poem? Are sentence structure, vocabulary, diction, and stanza form obstacles to understanding? Is the consciousness within the poem of comparable simplicity? Why, then, do you think the poet has chosen such simple poetic forms? The teacher should help the students recognize the sort of tension between the terrible experience within the poem and the almost childlike simplicity of the language which conveys it" (30:67). This statement is general enough, and sensitive enough to the kinds of problems posed by the language of poetry, to enable a teacher who commands any of the various linguistic approaches to literature to apply them in the attempt to reveal something of a poem's characteristic linguistic structure. It must be admitted, however, that the questions relating to such things as "consciousness" and "terrible experience," which are certainly of great importance to a thorough understanding of this and other poems, fall in general outside the limits of linguistic approaches to poetry as so far developed. Such approaches are concerned more with the arrangements of the linguistic elements in a poem than with their references. This follows from their concern with the esthetic rather than the cognitive dimension of poetry.

In the revised teacher's manual being prepared to accompany the volume *Creatures in Verse* (28), there are various hints concerning the teaching of literature, particularly poetry. Reference is made to different poetic conventions, including rhyme, rhythm, poetic forms, graphic indicators, and so on. In the comments on the language of poetry, reference is made to the analysis of words into roots and affixes, to onomatopoeia, and to the metaphoric extension of words' meanings.[12] These are all helpful hints, although traditional.

12. Professor Smiley, one of the authors, provided me with the *Manual*, which is due to appear shortly.

If the above sampling is representative, it would appear that instruction in the schools has not been very much affected by recent developments in the area of linguistic analysis of literature. This is perhaps not surprising when it is considered that such analysis is frequently limited to special aspects—largely formal—of poetry, and that it requires for its application a knowledge not only of linguistics but also of the special problems posed for linguistic analysis by the particular nature of literary texts. There is of course also the question of whether the results of such analysis, assuming they were to be achieved in the schools, would justify the effort and time expended in achieving them. The answer to the latter question would probably be determined in part by the type of students being taught.

BIBLIOGRAPHY

1. BALLY, CHARLES. *Le langage et la vie.* Paris: Payot, 1926.
2. ———. *Précis de stylistique.* Geneva: Eggiman, 1905.
3. ———. *Traité de stylistique française.* 3d ed. Paris: C. Klincksieck, 1951.
4. CHATMAN, SEYMOUR. "Linguistics, Poetics, and Interpretation: The Phonemic Dimension," *Quarterly Journal of Speech,* XLIII (1957), 248–56.
5. ———. *A Theory of Meter.* The Hague: Mouton & Co., 1965.
6. CHOMSKY, NOAM. *Aspects of the Theory of Syntax.* Cambridge, Mass.: M.I.T. Press, 1965.
7. ———. *Syntactic Structures.* The Hague: Mouton & Co., 1957.
8. ERLICH, VICTOR. *Russian Formalism: History—Doctrine.* 2d ed. The Hague: Mouton & Co., 1965.
9. FRANCIS, W. NELSON. "Syntax and Literary Interpretation." In Monograph Series No. 13, pp. 83-92, *Report of the Eleventh Annual Round Table Meeting on Linguistics and Language Studies.* Institute of Languages and Linguistics, Washington, D.C.: Georgetown University Press, 1962.
10. GUIRAUD, PIERRE. *La stylistique.* Paris: Presses Universitaires de France, 1967.
11. IVES, SUMNER. "Grammatical Analysis and Literary Criticism." In Monograph Series No. 13, pp. 99-107, *Report of the Eleventh Annual Round Table Meeting on Linguistics and Language Studies.* Institute of Languages and Linguistics, Washington, D.C.: Georgetown University Press, 1962.
12. JUILLAND, ALPHONSE G. Review of Charles Bruneau, *L'époque réaliste; premiére partie: Fin du romantisme et parnasse, Language,* XXX (1954), 313-38.

322   LINGUISTICS AND LITERATURE

13. KATZ, JERROLD J., and POSTAL, PAUL M. *An Integrated Theory of Linguistic Descriptions.* Cambridge, Mass.: M.I.T. Press, 1965.
14. LEVIN, SAMUEL R. "Deviation—Statistical and Determinate—in Poetic Language," *Lingua,* XII (1963), 276-90.
15. ———. "Internal and External Deviation in Poetry," *Word,* XXI (1965), 225-37.
16. MALKIEL, YAKOV. Review of *Style in Language.* Edited by Thomas A. Sebeok, *International Journal of American Linguistics,* XXVIII (1962), 271.
17. MILIC, LOUIS T. *A Quantitative Approach to the Style of Jonathan Swift.* The Hague: Mouton & Co., 1967.
18. ———. "Unconscious Ordering in the Prose of Swift." In *The Computer and Literary Style,* pp. 79-106. Edited by Jacob Leed. Kent, Ohio: Kent University Press, 1966.
19. ———. "Winged Words: Varieties of Computer Application to Literature," *Computers and the Humanities,* II (1967), 2-9.
20. OHMANN, RICHARD. "Generative Grammar and the Concept of Literary Style," *Word,* XX (1964), 423-39.
21. ———. "Literature as Sentences," *College English,* XXVII (1966), 261-67.
22. Oregon Curriculum Study Center. *A Curriculum in English, Grades 7-12.* Eugene, Ore.: University of Oregon Press, 1964.
23. *A Prague School Reader on Esthetics, Literary Structure, and Style.* Edited by Paul L. Garvin. Washington, D.C.: Georgetown University Press, 1964.
24. ROBERTS, PAUL. *The Roberts English Series,* Books 3—6. New York: Harcourt, Brace & World, 1966.
25. ROBINS, R. H. *Ancient and Medieval Grammatical Theory in Europe.* London, 1951.
26. *Russian Formalist Criticism: Four Essays.* Edited by Lee T. Lemon and Marion J. Reis. Lincoln, Neb.: University of Nebraska Press, 1965.
27. SAPORTA, SOL. "The Application of Linguistics to the Study of Poetic Language." In *Style in Language,* pp. 82-93. Edited by Thomas A. Sebeok. Cambridge, Mass.: M.I.T. Press, 1960.
28. SMILEY, MARJORIE B.; FREEDMAN, FLORENCE B.; and PATERNO, DOMENICA. *Creatures in Verse.* Macmillan Gateway Series. New York: Macmillan & Co., 1967.
29. SPITZER, LEO. *Linguistics and Literary Criticism: Essays in Stylistics.* Princeton, N.J.: Princeton University Press, 1948.
30. *Teaching Literature in Grades Seven Through Nine.* Indiana University English Curriculum Study Series. Edited by Edward B. Jenkinson and Jane Stouder Hawley. Bloomington: Indiana University Press, 1967.

31. *Théorie de la littérature.* Edited by Tzvetan Todorov. Paris: Editions de Seuil, 1965.

32. THORNE, JAMES PETER. "Stylistics and Generative Grammars," *Journal of Linguistics*, I (1965), 49-59.

33. TRAGER, GEORGE L., and SMITH, HENRY LEE. *An Outline of English Structure.* Studies in Linguistics, Occasional Papers 3. Norman, Okla.: Battenburg Press, 1951.

34. ULLMANN, STEPHEN. *Language and Style.* Oxford: Basil Blackwell, 1964.

35. WELLS, RULON S. "Immediate Constituents," *Language*, XXIII (1947), 81-117.

A Glance at the Past: A Look toward the Future

ALBERT H. MARCKWARDT

The chapters of this book have attempted to convey to the reader some idea of the dimensions of linguistic studies, the concerns and interests of those who work in the field, as well as the assumptions which underlie and the procedures which govern the discipline. Despite the best efforts of the contributors to this volume to discuss the assigned topics clearly and cogently, these matters are not always easily comprehended. In a way this is not surprising. Whenever any facet of human experience toward which we customarily take a pragmatic point of view is suddenly presented in terms of a rigorous, systematic discipline, we find ourselves quite unprepared for the basic questions which are raised about the nature of that experience and the ways in which it may be studied. In this sense the consideration of language does not differ from the consideration of the galaxies in the heavens (astronomy) or the recorded accounts of human experience (history). The induction into any science is a mind-stretching process; the novitiate is always disturbed by the fact that there are more questions than there seem to be answers, and the uncomfortable awareness that the answers are by no means definite or permanent. The result is often bewilderment and resentment. So it has been with the study of language, even among the members of the teaching profession, who must deal with it daily in the classroom on a practical and commonsense basis.

This helps to explain why it has taken so long for the systematic study of language, that is to say linguistics, to have the impact upon school curricula and classroom procedures which might normally have been expected. There is another way of looking at the matter, however, and that is in terms of the distinction between pure and applied science. There has always been a considerable time lag between any new development which is primarily theoretical and speculative and its practical application to one or another field of human endeavor. Charles C. Fries used to be fond of pointing out that although William Harvey described the circulation of the blood in 1628, thus rendering bleeding suspect as a form of medical treatment, George Washington was bled for pneumonia 171 years later. According to some, linguistics achieved the status of a systematic discipline in the middle of the eighteenth century with the work of the Port Royal grammarians in France; others would place it in Germany and Scandinavia in the early nineteenth, the time of the pioneer work in the historical and comparative study of language. At all events, the science is relatively new, and as in every other discipline, the amount of information available is multiplying so rapidly that the individual scholar in the field can no longer keep up with the entire output.

Moreover, the term *applied* is fundamental to our understanding of what may be done with the results of investigations into language structure and language learning in terms of their bearing upon school curricula, textbooks, and classroom procedures. Much has been said and written recently about the "New English" and about "linguistic methods" of teaching English. I am inclined to question the applicability of both terms. The newness of the New English seems somewhat different from that of physics or mathematics; it is a matter of emphasis rather than totally different subject matter, and this is not the first time that the emphasis has shifted. Furthermore, I would seriously question the propriety of the term "linguistic method." True enough, we may speak about and even hope for some influence of new concepts of language in textbooks and in the classroom, but this is a far cry from the direct teaching of a hitherto unknown or neglected body of subject matter. The impact of linguistics is likely to be greater in terms of the way the teacher and the textbook writer think about language than in any specific body of procedural gimmickry. As W. R. O'Donnell has written, "The applied linguist does not begin with a body of knowledge for which he must seek practical application, but rather with a collection of practical language problems towards the solution of which Linguistics proper may be expected to make some sort of contribution."

It will be helpful, moreover, to consider briefly the history of

English teaching in order to see what use has been made of linguistics in the past and to assess the present impact of the discipline. Only in the light of these shall we be able to make some reasonable projection for the future.

The initial impact of language studies upon English teaching was at the fairly pedestrian data-collecting level, but even so the task needed to be done. For some decades school textbooks had been totally unrealistic and inaccurate in their presentation of the actual usage of Standard English. They tried to be more correct than the language itself, unequivocally condemning forms and expressions which had become firmly established in the speech and writing of those who were carrying on the affairs of the English-speaking people. At the turn of the century and for some three decades thereafter, English language scholars busied themselves pointing out the broad gap between the language as portrayed in the school grammars and the actual facts of usage as reported in scholarly studies, dictionaries, and other reliable sources of linguistic information— and making surveys when the facts were not readily available.

Although this represented a fairly routine level of scholarly activity, it did have two important implications. It focused attention upon a justifiable descriptive function of grammar in contrast to the prevailing prescriptive concept and supplied an answer to the question of the source or basis of linguistic standards. The answer was that there could be no basis except usage itself, a point that had been made centuries ago by the poet Horace but had been overlooked in the interim. Finally, some doubt came to be felt about the appropriateness of the traditional grammatical approach to the English language, chiefly on the grounds that it was an excellent device for the description of Latin and Greek, languages which functioned with a heavy load of discrete inflectional suffixes, but somewhat less adaptable to English, which conveyed modification in meaning primarily through the devices of word order and function words.

These views met with heavy opposition at the outset, and their proponents were often accused either of incompetence in the use of the language themselves or of lacking any notion of linguistic nicety—or both. It must be confessed, however, that at times they were somewhat overzealous in the cause and tended to antagonize the opposition rather than to persuade it. Yet, in the course of time their efforts began to bear fruit. Some of the more obvious non-sensicalities with respect to the use of the language began to disappear from the grammar textbooks and composition manuals, but that was about where the matter ended. The response to the charge that the grammatical apparatus was in itself badly suited to the language was to teach less grammar rather than an improved version of it.

The development of structural linguistics in the 1930's gave the impetus for a second attempt to influence the nature of language instruction in the schools. This time attention was centered upon the grammatical description itself rather than the individual items of usage which were its surface manifestation. The frequent complaint that the study of traditional grammar had not proved an effective means of improving the language command of the student was answered with the assertion that this would not be the case if a grammar which described the language more accurately and effectively were employed. The controversy remained in the theoretical realm for some time, but gradually in the 1950's some linguistically oriented textbooks began to appear. Among these were Paul Roberts' *Patterns of English*, Harold Whitehall's *Structural Essentials of English*, and Lloyd and Warfel's *American English in Its Cultural Setting*, the last two, however, being designed for college rather than school use. It is fair to say that all of them had a measurable degree of success whenever they came into the hands of teachers who were properly equipped to use them. Unfortunately such teachers were few in number.

This very fact led to the next major development in the attempt to apply the fruits of linguistic knowledge to the classroom. By this time, which is to say the mid-1950's, a marked change in the teaching of the modern foreign languages had already occurred. It had begun with our entry into World War II, when this country suddenly found itself without persons with an expert knowledge or competence in the host of Asian, African, and eastern European languages required for a successful prosecution of the war effort. In this situation the discipline of linguistics proved to be of immense value. Persons trained in it set about analyzing these little-known languages, developed teaching materials for them, and working under highly favorable conditions in terms of class size and contact hours, proceeded to teach them in a most effective manner. The Army, impressed with the success of the endeavor, applied the same regimen to its teaching of the more common Western European languages.

After the war there was a regression with respect to the school and college teaching of languages, but again an awareness of the national need came to the fore, culminating in the inclusion of foreign-language study in the National Defense Education Act, passed in the era of immediate post-Sputnik shock. Again the linguists figured prominently in the development of new textbooks, different classroom procedures, and the adaptation of instruction to the electronic media of the language laboratory. It was immediately apparent, however, that the success of their efforts depended heavily upon the inclusion of an applied linguistics component in the training of new teachers and the retraining of those already in service. Summer institutes were organized for the latter; some changes in teacher-education programs were established for the former. That these efforts have met with some success is indicated by the recent survey of modern foreign language instruction in the high schools conducted by the Educational Testing Service.

The parallel between this situation and instruction in the teaching of the native language was immediately apparent. When, in 1964, the National Defense Education Act was broadened to include English, language training was generally provided in the institutes organized for teachers of English. Even before this, the Commission on English of the College Entrance Examination Board had supported some twenty institutes for teachers of English in the summer of 1962. Each institute included one graduate level course in the English language, presented in a linguistically oriented fashion. Nor should one overlook the fact that the teaching of English as a foreign language, as it is carried on in our binational centers abroad and for the benefit of foreign university students in this country, had already been deeply influenced by the linguists. At any rate, for the past five years there have been some eighty to one hundred NDEA summer institutes for teachers of English every year, along with some full-year programs, affecting possibly between twenty and twenty-five thousand teachers, most of whom were presumably exposed to some linguistics. It is true that in some instances a little knowledge is a dangerous thing, but at the very least this wide exposure has brought about a receptivity to ideas about language than might not have developed otherwise.

The preservice training of teachers has changed somewhat more slowly, but the *Guidelines for the Preparation of Teachers of English,* prepared under the combined auspices of the Modern Language Association, the National Council of Teachers of English, and the National Association of State Directors of Teacher Education and Certification, and published in 1967, calls for "a well-balanced descriptive and historical knowledge of the English language" on the part of the teacher candidate. Under this rubric, the following specifications are to be found:

1. He should have some knowledge of phonology, morphology and syntax; the sources and development of the English vocabulary; semantics; and social, regional, and functional varieties of English usage.
2. He should be acquainted with methods of preparation and uses of dictionaries and grammars.
3. He should be well-grounded in one grammatical system and have a working acquaintance with at least one other system.
4. He should have studied basic principles of language learning in order to apply his knowledge at various grade levels to the problems of those learning to speak, listen, read, and write to a variety of audiences.
5. He should have an understanding of the respective domains of linguistics and rhetoric, and of the range of choice available within the structure of the language.

Admittedly these are guidelines, statements of what the profession would like to see established rather than anything that exists at the present time. Yet in terms of the awesome responsibility of English teachers for developing language competence in their pupils, they are not unreasonable. The omission of any one of the five elements would be difficult to justify. Moreover, a year's course in the history and structure of English, in the hands of a skilled and knowledgeable teacher, could achieve the stated goals. Particularly noteworthy here is the third statement, calling for an acquaintance with two grammatical systems. The purpose should be obvious; namely, to prevent a total commitment to any one "school" of linguistics, and assuring at least a degree of eclecticism and sophistication.

The development of linguistically oriented curricula follows a pattern similar to that of the training of teachers: a number of sporadic local efforts early in the 1950's succeeded by large-scale activity on the part of the U.S. Office of Education. Notable among the early efforts were projects in Portland, Oregon and Westport, Connecticut. In both systems highly able linguistic specialists were brought in as consultants; they worked with the local teachers, developing courses of study and teacher's guides which incorporated the results of recent research on language. In each instance the results were impressive.

Late in 1961 the U.S. Office of Education inaugurated a large-scale curriculum development program which was first known as Project English. Under its aegis a number of curriculum study centers were established at colleges and universities throughout the country, some twenty-five all told. In some of them language was the primary focus. At the University of Minnesota, for example, Stanley B. Kegler prepared thirty-one resource units in language for the junior and senior high schools. At the Universities of Oregon and Nebraska there were strong language components in programs which included literature and composition as well. Since new curricula could not be considered in the abstract, the study centers soon found themselves undertaking research in the growth of language in children and in the relative teaching effectiveness of different grammatical approaches. The Bateman-Zidonis study, *The Effect of a Study of Transformational Grammar on the Writing of Ninth and Tenth Graders*, has already been described in one of the earlier chapters of this volume. Another kind of project, equally significant for an understanding of language and language teaching, is Paul Olson's *A Longitudinal Study of the Syntax and Content of Children's Compositions (Grades 2-6)*, designed to measure the effectiveness of materials developed at the University of Nebraska. In short, the increased involvement of hundreds of English teachers and trained linguists in the development of curricula and the preparation of teaching materials in the period between 1961 and 1965 strikes one as little short of miraculous.

Finally, some of these materials are finding their way into print, and in doing so they have stimulated the production of other linguistically based textbooks. In 1968, Holt, Rinehart and Winston

MARCKWARDT 331

began to publish *The Oregon Curriculum, A Sequential Program in English,* which had been prepared under the general direction of Professor Albert R. Kitzhaber, director of the Curriculum Study Center at the University of Oregon. Two other linguistically based series of textbooks, prepared independently of the study centers, have appeared recently. These are: *The Roberts English Series,* published by Harcourt, Brace and World, bearing the subtitle, *A Linguistic Program Extending from Grade 3 through 9.* The series is all-inclusive in that it covers reading, spelling, literature, and composition as well as language. Linguistically it is based on the premise that transformational grammar "will establish itself as the theoretical background for the grammar taught in all schools at all levels."

Holt, Rinehart and Winston has also published a series of textbooks in which Professor Neil Postman figures as the principal author, collaborating with a number of other writers to produce texts with such titles as *Discovering Your Language, Exploring Your Language, Uses of Language,* and so forth. In addition to being linguistically oriented, they approach the study of English inductively, providing an opportunity for students to arrive by their own inquiries at valid generalizations about the language.

There would be little purpose in extending this survey of textbooks. It is sufficient to make the point that linguistically based materials are now available, while ten years ago there were few, and fifteen years ago virtually none. In fact, it begins to seem as if every major publisher and some minor ones have succeeded in snaring someone who can pass as a linguistic consultant. In some instances, moreover, especially with materials originally developed at the curriculum study centers, the books which are published represent the best efforts of a group of people working together, and they have the advantage of having been revised on the basis of classroom trial.

Within the past five years a new problem has arisen, or at least it has assumed larger proportions than it previously had, that is, English for the disadvantaged. This has resulted in a flurry of research for the purpose of describing in detail the various dialects, not only of the urban poor but those in the mountain country and the coal fields as well. The chief purpose is to determine the difference between these dialects and Standard English, thus identifying the points of greatest difficulty for the pupils in their learning of the standard language. Several projects are under way in such cities as New York, Chicago, Los Angeles, Philadelphia, Detroit, Washington, and Pittsburgh. The research is merely a first step, preparatory to developing curricula and teaching materials, but it has resulted in a number of impressive publications. Among these are *The Social Stratification of English in New York City* by William Labov, and *Conversations in a Negro American Dialect*, transcribed and edited by Bengt Loman, a Swedish scholar who did the field work for this study in Washington, D.C. Both government and foundations have supported the research; the next step is the development and field trial of teaching materials.

Already two widely held conclusions have emerged from this work. The first is that dialects of English at the lower end of the social scale do not necessarily reveal a linguistic impoverishment, but rather that each dialect has a structural system of its own, capable at times of subtleties of expression fully equal to but different from those of Standard English. The second relates to educational goals; namely, that the student should be permitted to retain his native dialect for use in those familiar and homely situations where it is the natural means of communication, but that he should be taught the standard language as a second dialect, as a vehicle for wider use. There is not complete agreement on the second point, but it is more widely held than the two polar views, one of which is the laissez-faire attitude of "leave your language alone," and the other insisting upon Standard English as a total replacement for the pupil's natural mode of speech. In connection with all this there has arisen the mistaken view that the teaching of Standard English to speakers of a nonstandard variety is equivalent or analogous to teaching English as a foreign language. This is clearly not the case. There are a number of similarities in teaching strategies and method which may be employed, but the learning situation is quite different.

So much for the present. The final questions are what the future holds in store for the development of linguistic studies and the potential of such new developments for use in the English classroom.

The presentation of linguistics in this book has been couched largely in terms of a conflict between structural and transformational grammar. Even now they are not at all the only modes of linguistic study. We must reckon as well with tagmemic and with stratificational grammar. The second is somewhat new, but the first has been widely used in describing a number of the Central and South American languages. In addition, we must also take into account the neo-Firthian linguistics in England and glossematics, which created considerable interest in continental Europe a decade or more ago.

Admittedly, this discourages those teachers and schools administrators who ardently wish that the linguists might be able to agree on one approach and have done with it. Such agreement is not likely to occur in any discipline that is alive. Inquiring minds will inevitably strike out in new directions, and in the course of time these too may be expected to make their contributions to the solution of practical educational problems, not necessarily displacing everything that has gone before, but supplementing and combining with it.

There are signs of increased activity in a number of the subfields of linguistic studies. Research in dialects, especially social dialects, has already been mentioned. The grammar of Standard English, especially its syntax and the relationship between the syntactic and semantic components, is being explored more thoroughly than it has been in the past. The history of the English language is being reconsidered in the light of new approaches to the contemporary language.

Another significant development is to be found in the interdisciplinary relationships of linguistics. More than four decades ago, work in anthropological linguistics was well under way as a consequence of the interest in the languages of so-called primitive peoples, which was just another way of saying that they had not adopted Western European culture. But the languages were found to be anything but primitive or simple in their structure. In the early 1950's the psychologists and linguists combined forces and developed psycholinguistics, a cross-disciplinary approach to matters connected with language learning and with cognition. The study of sounds cannot be separated from the work of the physiologist and neurophysiologist on the productive side nor from that of the physicist on the receptive or acoustic side. Since language is a social phenomenon, the emergence of sociolinguistics is surprising only in that it has been so very recent. The preceding chapter dealt with the application of linguistics to the study of literature. The philosophers have always been concerned with linguistic problems; the mathematicians are beginning to be concerned. Each of these interdisciplinary pursuits has benefited the linguist in giving him a broader view of the ramifications of his subject and in eliciting insights that he as linguist qua linguist might not have been aware of.

Another question which is rapidly arising is that of the usefulness of technology—of electronic devices. The computer is capable of saving the investigator untold hours formerly spent in sorting, classifying, and locating data, and this is by no means all that can be said for computational linguistics. The advantages of more sophisticated and accurate methods of recording and reproducing speech are obvious. The potential of these methods in the English classroom has not been realized to the extent that it has been in the teaching of foreign languages, but experimental work is under way. The least that can be said is that we are still on the threshold of an exciting period of discovery and development; and that the centrality of language to the human experience, human activity, and improved understanding demands a greater awareness of the relevance of its systematic study to the school program and the extension of such study into fields now only imperfectly explored.

INDEX

Index

Abercrombie, David, 104
Academies (learned), origin and influence of, 89-91
Alexander, Henry, 72
Allen, Harold B., 72
Allen, Robert L. and Virginia F., 258
American English: development of, 95; dialectical diversity in, 247-50; see also Language
American speakers of English, history of, since the settlements, 112-13
Anglo-Saxon language, modern English traced from, 110-12
Applebee, Roger K., 238
Atwood, E. Bagby, 81
Asker, William, 234

Bailey, Beryl, 178
Bailey, Nathaniel, 126, 127
Bally, Charles, 304, 305, 306
Baratz, Joan, 171, 174, 177
Barnhart, Clarence L., 257
Barr, Nora R., 234
Basal readers, nature of, 254-55
Basic Issues Conference, recommendations of, 163-64
Bateman, Donald R., 58, 59, 235, 336
Becker, Alton L., 142, 143, 144, 146
Bereiter, Carl, 200, 203, 204; quoted 201
Berko, Jean, 217
Bernstein, Basil, 104, 192, 223
Birns, Beverly, 173
Blake, Robert W., 235
Blank, Marion, 201, 204
Bloch, Bernard, 40
Bloom, Benjamin S., 189
Bloomfield, Leonard, 40-41, 81, 121, 257, 258, 287, 288, 313
Boraas, Julius, 234
Borrowing of speech, conditions leading to, 113-15
Bradford, Leland P., 234
British Received Pronunciation, use of, 94

British Standard English, changes in, since eighteenth century, 92; see also Standard English
Brown, Marshall L., 238
Brown, Roger W., 174, 176, 189; quoted, 182
Bruner, Jerome S., 167, 184, 191; quoted, 180
Burke, Kenneth, 134, 138, 139, 141, 147; quoted, 136, 140
Butterfield, Earl C., quoted (with Zigler), 175

Carroll, John B., 168
Carson, Arnold S., 171
Casagrande, Joseph B., 182
Catherwood, Catherine, 234
Cazden, Courtney B., 171, 174, 176, 178; quoted, 177
Chase, Stuart, 292
Chatman, Seymour, 314, 315
Chomsky, Noam, 44, 52, 125, 168, 176, 281, 282, 283, 284, 285, 287, 288, 294, 295, 296; quoted 169, 289
Christensen, Francis, 142, 143, 146
Classical rhetoric, approach of, to literary-linguistic problem, 303-4; see also Rhetoric
Classification, role of language in, 187
Codability, relevance of, to semantic development in child, 182-83
Code switching: difficulties involved in, in U.S., 35; explanation of, 34
Cofer, Charles N., 169, 185
Cognition and language, controversy in field of, 186-87
College Entrance Examination Board, Commission on English of, 328
Collegiate dictionaries, evaluation of, 129
Committee of Fifteen (N.E.A.), recommendations of, 163
Committee of Ten (N.E.A.), recommendations of, 162-63
Communication and language, studies of, 136-37

337

CONSTITUTION AND BY-LAWS
OF
THE NATIONAL SOCIETY FOR THE STUDY OF EDUCATION

(As adopted May, 1944, and amended June, 1945, February, 1949, September, 1962 and February, 1968)

ARTICLE I

NAME

The name of this corporation shall be "The National Society for the Study of Education," an Illinois corporation not for profit.

ARTICLE II

PURPOSES

Its purposes are to carry on the investigation of educational problems, to publish the results of same, and to promote their discussion.

The corporation also has such powers as are now, or may hereafter be, granted by the General Not For Profit Corporation Act of the State of Illinois.

ARTICLE III

OFFICES

The corporation shall have and continuously maintain in this state a registered office and a registered agent whose office is identical with such registered office, and may have other offices within or without the State of Illinois as the Board of Directors may from time to time determine.

ARTICLE IV

MEMBERSHIP

Section 1. *Classes.* There shall be two classes of members—active and honorary. The qualifications and rights of the members of such classes shall be as follows:

(*a*) Any person who is desirous of promoting the purposes of this corporation is eligible to active membership and shall become such on payment of dues as prescribed.

(*b*) Active members shall be entitled to vote, to participate in discussion, and, subject to the conditions set forth in Article V, to hold office.

(*c*) Honorary members shall be entitled to all the privileges of active members, with the exception of voting and holding office, and shall be exempt from the payment of dues. A person may be elected to honorary membership by vote of the active members of the corporation on nomination by the Board of Directors.

(*d*) Any active member of the Society may, at any time after reaching the age of sixty, become a life member on payment of the aggregate amount of the regular annual dues for the period of life expectancy, as determined by standard actuarial tables, such membership to entitle the member to receive all yearbooks and to enjoy all other privileges of active membership in the Society for the lifetime of the member.

Section 2. *Termination of Membership.*

(*a*) The Board of Directors by affirmative vote of two-thirds of the members of the Board may suspend or expel a member for cause after appropriate hearing.

(*b*) Termination of membership for nonpayment of dues shall become effective as provided in Article XIV.

Section 3. *Reinstatement.* The Board of Directors may by the affirmation vote of two-thirds of the members of the Board reinstate a former member whose membership was previously terminated for cause other than nonpayment of dues.

Section 4. *Transfer of Membership.* Membership in this corporation is not transferable or assignable.

ARTICLE V

BOARD OF DIRECTORS

Section 1. *General Powers.* The business and affairs of the corporation shall be managed by its Board of Directors. It shall appoint the Chairman and Vice-Chairman of the Board of Directors, the Secretary-Treasurer, and Members of the Council. It may appoint a member to fill any vacancy on the Board until such vacancy shall have been filled by election as provided in Section 3 of this Article.

Section 2. *Number, Tenure, and Qualifications.* The Board of Directors shall consist of seven members, namely, six to be elected by the members of the corporation, and the Secretary-Treasurer to be the seventh member. Only active members who have contributed to the Yearbook shall be eligible for election to serve as directors. A member who has been elected for a full term of three years as director and has not attended at least two-thirds of the meetings duly called and held during that term shall not be eligible for election again before the fifth annual election after the expiration of the term for which he was first elected. No member who has been elected for two full terms as director in immediate succession shall be elected a director for a term next succeeding. This provision shall not apply to the Secretary-Treasurer who is appointed by the Board of Directors. Each director shall hold office for the term for which he is elected or appointed and until his successor shall have been selected and qualified. Directors need not be residents of Illinois.

Section 3. *Election.*

(*a*) The directors named in the Articles of Incorporation shall hold office until their successors shall have been duly selected and shall have qualified. Thereafter, two directors shall be elected annually to serve three years, beginning March first after their election. If, at the time of any annual election, a vacancy exists in the Board of Directors, a director shall be elected at such election to fill such vacancy.

(*b*) Elections of directors shall be held by ballots sent by United States mail as follows: A nominating ballot together with a list of members eligible to be directors shall be mailed by the Secretary-Treasurer to all active members of the corporation in October. From such list, the active members shall nominate on such ballot one eligible member for each of the two regular terms and for any vacancy to be filled and return such ballots to the office of the Secretary-Treasurer within twenty-one days after said date of mailing by the Secretary-Treasurer. The Secretary-Treasurer shall prepare an election ballot and place thereon in alphabetical order the names of persons equal to three times the number of offices to be filled, these persons to be those who received the highest number of votes on the nominating ballot, provided, however, that not more than one person connected with a given institution or agency shall be named on such final ballot, the person so named to be the one receiving the highest vote on the nominating ballot. Such election ballot shall be mailed by the Secretary-Treasurer to all active members in November next succeeding. The active members shall vote thereon for one member for each such office. Election ballots must be in the office of the Secretary-Treasurer within twenty-one days after the said date of mailing by the Secretary-Treasurer. The ballots shall be counted by the Secretary-Treasurer, or by an election committee, if any, appointed by the Board. The two members receiving the highest number of votes shall be declared elected for the regular term and the member or members receiving the next highest number of votes shall be declared elected for any vacancy or vacancies to be filled.

Section 4. *Regular Meetings.* A regular annual meeting of the Board of Directors shall be held, without other notice than this by-law, at the same place and as nearly as possible on the same date as the annual meeting of the corporation. The Board of Directors may provide the time and place, either within or without the State of Illinois, for the holding of additional regular meetings of the Board.

Section 5. *Special Meetings.* Special meetings of the Board of Directors may be called by or at the request of the Chairman or a majority of the directors. Such special meetings shall be held at the office of the corporation unless a majority of the directors agree upon a different place for such meetings.

Section 6. *Notice.* Notice of any special meeting of the Board of Directors shall be given at least fifteen days previously thereto by written notice delivered personally or mailed to each director at his business address, or by telegram. If mailed, such notice shall be deemed to be delivered when deposited in the United States mail in a sealed envelope so addressed, with postage thereon prepaid. If notice be given by telegram, such notice shall be deemed to be delivered when the telegram is delivered to the telegraph company. Any director may waive notice of any meeting. The attendance of a director at any meeting shall constitute a waiver of notice of such meeting, except where a director attends a meeting for the express purpose of objecting to the transaction of any business because the meeting is not lawfully called or convened. Neither the business to be transacted at, nor the purpose of, any regular or special meeting of the Board need be specified in the notice or waiver of notice of such meeting.

Section 7. *Quorum.* A majority of the Board of Directors shall constitute a quorum for the transaction of business at any meeting of the Board, provided, that if less than a majority of the directors are present at said meeting, a majority of the directors present may adjourn the meeting from time to time without further notice.

Section 8. *Manner of Acting.* The act of the majority of the directors present at a meeting at which a quorum is present shall be the act of the Board of Directors, except where otherwise provided by law or by these by-laws.

ARTICLE VI

THE COUNCIL

Section 1. *Appointment.* The Council shall consist of the Board of Directors, the Chairmen of the corporation's Yearbook and Research Committees, and such other active members of the corporation as the Board of Directors may appoint.

Section 2. *Duties.* The duties of the Council shall be to further the objects of the corporation by assisting the Board of Directors in planning and carrying forward the educational undertakings of the corporation.

ARTICLE VII

OFFICERS

Section 1. *Officers.* The officers of the corporation shall be a Chairman of the Board of Directors, a Vice-Chairman of the Board of Directors, and a Secretary-Treasurer. The Board of Directors, by resolution, may create additional offices. Any two or more offices may be held by the same person, except the offices of Chairman and Secretary-Treasurer.

Section 2. *Election and Term of Office.* The officers of the corporation shall be elected annually by the Board of Directors at the annual regular meeting of the Board of Directors, provided, however, that the Secretary-Treasurer may be elected for a term longer than one year. If the election of officers shall not be held at such meeting, such election shall be held as soon thereafter as conveniently may be. Vacancies may be filled or new offices created and filled at any meeting of the Board of Directors. Each officer shall hold office until his successor shall have been duly elected and shall have qualified or until his death or until he shall resign or shall have been removed in the manner hereinafter provided.

Section 3. *Removal.* Any officer or agent elected or appointed by the Board of Directors may be removed by the Board of Directors whenever in its judgment the best interests of the corporation would be served thereby, but such removal shall be without prejudice to the contract rights, if any, of the person so removed.

Section 4. *Chairman of the Board of Directors.* The Chairman of the Board of Directors shall be the principal officer of the corporation. He shall preside at all meetings of the members of the Board of Directors, shall perform all duties incident to the office of chairman of the Board of Directors and such other duties as may be prescribed by the Board of Directors from time to time.

Section 5. *Vice-Chairman of the Board of Directors.* In the absence of the Chairman of the Board of Directors or in the event of his inability or refusal to act, the Vice-Chairman of the Board of Directors shall perform the duties of the Chairman of the Board of Directors, and when so acting, shall have all the powers of and be subject to all the restrictions upon the Chairman of the Board of Directors. Any Vice-Chairman of the Board of Directors shall perform such other duties as from time to time may be assigned to him by the Board of Directors.

Section 6. *Secretary-Treasurer.* The Secretary-Treasurer shall be the managing executive officer of the corporation. He shall: (a) keep the minutes of the meetings of the members and of the Board of Directors in one or more books provided for that purpose; (b) see that all notices are duly given in accordance with the provisions of these by-laws or as required by law; (c) be custodian of the corporate records and of the seal of the corporation and see that the seal of the corporation is affixed to all documents, the execution of which on behalf of the corporation under its seal is duly authorized in accordance with the provisions of these by-laws; (d) keep a register of the postoffice address of each member as furnished to the secretary-treasurer by such member; (e) in general perform all duties incident to the office of secretary and such other duties as from time to time may be assigned to him by the Chairman of the Board of Directors or by the Board of Directors. He shall also: (1) have charge and custody of and be responsible for all funds and securities of the corporation; receive and give receipts for moneys due and payable to the corporation from any source whatsoever, and deposit all such moneys in the name of the corporation in such banks, trust companies or other depositories as shall be selected in accordance with the provisions of Article XI of these by-laws; (2) in general perform all the duties incident to the office of Treasurer and such other duties as from time to time may be assigned to him by the Chairman of the Board of Directors or by the Board of Directors. The Secretary-Treasurer shall give a bond for the faithful discharge of his duties in such sum and with such surety or sureties as the Board of Directors shall determine, said bond to be placed in the custody of the Chairman of the Board of Directors.

ARTICLE VIII

COMMITTEES

The Board of Directors, by appropriate resolution duly passed, may create and appoint such committees for such purposes and periods of time as it may deem advisable.

ARTICLE IX

PUBLICATIONS

Section 1. The corporation shall publish *The Yearbook of the National Society for the Study of Education,* such supplements thereto, and such other materials as the Board of Directors may provide for.

Section 2. *Names of Members.* The names of the active and honorary members shall be printed in the Yearbook or, at the direction of the Board of Directors, may be published in a special list.

ARTICLE X

ANNUAL MEETINGS

The corporation shall hold its annual meetings at the time and place of the Annual Meeting of the American Association of School Administrators of the National Education Association. Other meetings may be held when authorized by the corporation or by the Board of Directors.

ARTICLE XI

CONTRACTS, CHECKS, DEPOSITS, AND GIFTS

Section 1. *Contracts.* The Board of Directors may authorize any officer or officers, agent or agents of the corporation, in addition to the officers so authorized by these by-laws to enter into any contract or execute and deliver any instrument in the name of and on behalf of the corporation and such authority may be general or confined to specific instances.

Section. 2. *Checks, drafts, etc.* All checks, drafts, or other orders for the payment of money, notes, or other evidences of indebtedness issued in the name of the corporation, shall be signed by such officer or officers, agent or agents of the corporation and in such manner as shall from time to time be determined by resolution of the Board of Directors. In the absence of such determination of the Board of Directors, such instruments shall be signed by the Secretary-Treasurer.

Section 3. *Deposits.* All funds of the corporation shall be deposited from time to time to the credit of the corporation in such banks, trust companies, or other depositories as the Board of Directors may select.

Section 4. *Gifts.* The Board of Directors may accept on behalf of the corporation any contribution, gift, bequest, or device for the general purposes or for any special purpose of the corporation.

Section 5. *Dissolution.* In case of dissolution of the National Society for the Study of Education (incorporated under the GENERAL NOT FOR PROFIT CORPORATION ACT of the State of Illinois), the Board of Directors shall, after paying or making provision for the payment of all liabilities of the Corporation, dispose of all assets of the Corporation to such organization or organizations organized and operated exclusively for charitable, educational, or scientific purposes as shall at the time qualify as an exempt organization or organizations under Section 561 (C) (3) of the Internal Revenue Code of 1954 (or the corresponding provision of any future United States Internal Revenue Law), as the Board of Directors shall determine.

Article XII
BOOKS AND RECORDS

The corporation shall keep correct and complete books and records of account and shall also keep minutes of the proceedings of its members, Board of Directors, and committees having any of the authority of the Board of Directors, and shall keep at the registered or principal office a record giving the names and addresses of the members entitled to vote. All books and records of the corporation may be inspected by any member or his agent or attorney for any proper purpose at any reasonable time.

Article XIII
FISCAL YEAR

The fiscal year of the corporation shall begin on the first day of July in each year and end on the last day of June of the following year.

Article XIV
DUES

Section 1. *Annual Dues.* The annual dues for active members of the Society shall be determined by vote of the Board of Directors at a regular meeting duly called and held.

Section 2. *Election Fee.* An election fee of $1.00 shall be paid in advance by each applicant for active membership.

Section 3. *Payment of Dues.* Dues for each calendar year shall be payable in advance on or before the first day of January of that year. Notice of dues for the ensuing year shall be mailed to members at the time set for mailing the primary ballots.

Section 4. *Default and Termination of Membership.* Annual membership shall terminate automatically for those members whose dues remain unpaid after the first day of January of each year. Members so in default will be reinstated on payment of the annual dues plus a reinstatement fee of fifty cents.

ARTICLE XV

SEAL

The Board of Directors shall provide a corporate seal which shall be in the form of a circle and shall have inscribed thereon the name of the corporation and the words "Corporate Seal, Illinois."

ARTICLE XVI

WAIVER OF NOTICE

Whenever any notice whatever is required to be given under the provision of the General Not For Profit Corporation Act of Illinois or under the provisions of the Articles of Incorporation or the by-laws of the corporation, a waiver thereof in writing signed by the person or persons entitled to such notice, whether before or after the time stated therein, shall be deemed equivalent to the giving of such notice.

ARTICLE XVII

AMENDMENTS

Section 1. *Amendments by Directors.* The constitution and by-laws may be altered or amended at any meeting of the Board of Directors duly called and held, provided that affirmative vote of at least five directors shall be required for such action.

Section 2. *Amendments by Members.* By petition of twenty-five or more active members duly filed with the Secretary-Treasurer, a proposal to amend the constitution and by-laws shall be submitted to all active members by United States mail together with ballots on which the members shall vote for or against the proposal. Such ballots shall be returned by United States mail to the office of the Secretary-Treasurer within twenty-one days after date of mailing of the proposal and ballots by the Secretary-Treasurer. The Secretary-Treasurer or a committee appointed by the Board of Directors for that purpose shall count the ballots and advise the members of the result. A vote in favor of such proposal by two-thirds of the members voting thereon shall be required for adoption of such amendment.

MINUTES OF THE ANNUAL MEETING OF THE SOCIETY

The 1969 annual meeting of the Society was held in the American Room of the Traymore Hotel in Atlantic City at 2:30 P.M., Sunday, February 16, with William C. Kvaraceus presiding and with some three hundred members and friends present.

The annual meeting has been often devoted to presentations of Parts I and II of the yearbook. However, since Part II, *Educational Evaluation*, had been presented in Los Angeles on February 8, only Part I, *The United States and International Education*, was presented at the annual meeting.

The programs of both meetings follow:

PROGRAM OF THE ATLANTIC CITY MEETING

Joint Meeting of the National Society for the Study of Education and the American Association of School Administrators

Sunday, February 16, 2:30 P.M.
American Room, Traymore Hotel

Presiding: William C. Kvaraceus, Chairman, Department of Education, Clark University; Chairman of the Board of Directors of the National Society

Presentation of

The United States and International Education

(Part I of the Society's Sixty-eighth Yearbook)

Introducing the Yearbook

Harold G. Shane, University Professor of Education, Indiana University

Critique of the Yearbook

William W. Brickman, Professor of Educational History and Comparative Education, University of Pennsylvania
Henry I. Willett, Superintendent of Schools, Richmond, Virginia

Informal Discussion

Mr. Kvaraceus, Mr. Shane, Mr. Brickman, Mr. Willett, and audience

Joint Meeting of the National Society for the Study
of Education and the American Educational Research Association

Saturday, February 8, 9:30 A.M.
Los Angeles, Calif.

Presiding: John I. Goodlad, Professor and Dean, School of Education,
University of California—Los Angeles

Presentation of

Educational Evaluation: New Roles, New Means

(Part II of the Society's Sixty-eighth Yearbook)

Introduction

John I. Goodlad

Discussion of the Yearbook

Ralph W. Tyler, Director Emeritus, Center for Advanced Studies
in the Behavioral Sciences

Informal Discussion

Mr. Goodlad, Mr. Tyler and audience

SYNOPSIS OF THE PROCEEDINGS OF THE BOARD OF DIRECTORS OF THE SOCIETY FOR 1969

I. Meeting of Feburary 16, 1969

The Board of Directors of the National Society met at 9:00 A.M. on February 16, in the Dennis Hotel with the following members present: William C. Kvaraceus (Chairman), Ralph W. Tyler (Vice-Chairman), Robert J. Havighurst, Paul A. Witty, and Herman G. Richey (Secretary). On invitation of the Board, Harold G. Shane, elected to membership on the Board for a three-year term beginning March 1, 1969 also attended the meeting.

1. The Secretary reported that the election of members of the Board of Directors held in November and December had resulted in the election of N.L. Gage and Harold G. Shane, each for a term of three years beginning March 1, 1969.

2. Officers of the Board of Directors for the year beginning March 1, 1969 were elected as follows: Ralph W. Tyler, Chairman; Robert J. Havighurst, Vice-Chairman; and Herman G. Richey, Secretary.

3. The Secretary reported that the sale of Yearbooks continued to be satisfactory; that membership was at an all-time high; and that rising costs were threatening but had not as yet seriously endangered the Society's financial position.

4. It was voted to present the Sixty-ninth Yearbook, Part II (*Linguistics in School Programs*) at the Atlantic City meeting on February 15, 1970 and to arrange for the presentation of Part I (*Mathematics Education*) at the March (1970) meeting of the American Educational Research Association in Minneapolis.

5. The Board expressed the Society's thanks to the American Educational Research Association for co-sponsoring the very successful meeting in Los Angeles at which Ralph W. Tyler presented the Sixty-eighth Yearbook, Part II (*Educational Evaluation: New Roles, New Means.*)

6. Progress reports were presented for the following authorized yearbooks: *Mathematics Education* (Edward G. Begle), *Linquistics in School Programs* (Albert H. Marckwardt), *The Curriculum* (Robert M. McClure), *Leaders in Education* (Robert J. Havighurst), and *Educational Philosophy* (Lawrence G. Thomas).

7. The Board examined the memorandum prepared by Ruth Strang on early childhood learning, reviewed other memoranda on the subject, and discussed Mr. Havighurst's report on conferences and correspondence with Robert Hess and others on the same subject. The Board voted to place all materials in the hands of Harold G. Shane who was asked to prepare, with the assistance of a committee to be appointed, a proposal for discussion at the next meeting of the Board.

8. Mr. Kvaraceus reported on an exploratory meeting of a small

group of sociologists held at Cambridge on January 29, 1969. A report of the Committee is included in the official copy of these minutes. It was voted to allow expenses for a small number of specialists to be invited by Mr. Kvaraceus to further develop the proposal for a yearbook in educational sociology.

9. Other suggested topics and proposals for yearbooks (Humanities and the Arts, Education and Creativity, Teacher Education, Instruction, Media of Instruction, etc.) were discussed and referred to interested Board members for further study.

10. Mr. Havighurst presented a proposal for the establishment of a seven-man Joint Commission on Research in Leadership in Education. The Commission would consist of three members selected by the National Society, three appointed by Phi Delta Kappa, and William Gebbard, Director of Research Services for Phi Delta Kappa. The Board approved the proposal and the tentative arrangements as approved by Mr. Havighurst.

II. MEETING OF JUNE 29-30, 1969

The Board of Directors met at 2:30 P.M. on June 29, 1969 at the Center for Continuing Education (Chicago) with the following members present: Ralph W. Tyler (Chairman), Robert J. Havighurst (Vice-Chairman), N. L. Gage, Harold G. Shane, and Herman G. Richey (Secretary).

1. The Secretary presented the "Report of the Treasurer of the Society for 1968-69." (See page xv.) Attention was called to the fact that the lower income figures for 1968-69 (as compared with those for 1967-68) were the result of the payment after July 1 of royalties heretofore received before that date.

2. The Secretary reported that arrangements had been or were being made for the presentation of Part II (*Linguistics in School Programs*) in Atlantic City and of Part I (*Mathematics Education*) at the annual meeting (1970) of the American Educational Research Association in Minneapolis.

3. Progress reports on yearbooks in preparation were made for *Mathematics Education* (1970), *Linguistics in School Programs* (1970), *Curriculum* (1971), *Leaders in Education* (1971), and *Philosophy of Education* (1972).

4. The Board approved the proposal for a yearbook on early learning (working title: "Education in Early Childhood").

5. The discussion of the proposed yearbook on educational sociology was deferred until Mr. Kvaraceus could be present.

6. Earlier suggestions for and memoranda on a proposed yearbook on educational psychology were reviewed by Mr. Gage who also outlined what he conceived the nature of such a volume should be. The

Board asked Mr. Gage to obtain whatever assistance that might be needed and to prepare a tentative proposal to be discussed at the February meeting.

7. Other topics, briefly considered were Communications, Humanities and the Arts, Instruction, Education for Creativity, Materials for Childrens' Learning, and Learning Experiments-Applications to Education. Further discussion of these topics was deferred to a subsequent meeting.

8. Mr. Havighurst reported on the activities of the Joint Commission on Research in Leadership in Education.

REPORT OF THE TREASURER OF THE SOCIETY

1968-69

RECEIPTS AND DISBURSEMENTS

Receipts:

Membership Dues	$ 40,119.13
Sale of yearbooks*	48,377.01*
Interest and dividends	3,073.65
Miscellaneous	679.24
Total	**$ 92,249.03**

* Owing to unavoidable circumstances, the University of Chicago could not process the payment of royalty in the amount of $8,779.00 for the fourth quarter. For comparison with other years, sales of yearbooks amounted to $57,156.01 and the total receipts amounted to $101,028.03.

Disbursements:

Yearbooks:

Manufacturing	$ 39,606.00
Reprinting	20,218.47
Preparation	786.91
Meetings of Board and Society	1,520.39

Secretary's Office:

Editorial, secretarial, and clerical	21,688.94
Supplies	3,736.25
Equipment	68.51
Telephone and telegraph	276.00

Miscellaneous:

Bank charges	83.35
Refunds and transfers (commercial orders)	913.01
Insurance	292.00
Other	28.60
Total	**$ 89,218.43**

Excess receipts over disbursements	$ 3,030.60
Checking account, June 30, 1968	345.49
Checking account, June 30, 1969	3,376.09

STATEMENT OF CASH AND SECURITIES
As of June 30, 1969

Cash:

University National Bank, Chicago, Ill.
Checking account . . . . $ 3,376.09
Savings account 2,522.79
Hyde Park Savings and Loan Assn. 15,000.00
Chicago Federal Savings and Loan Assn. 10,000.00
Home Federal Savings and Loan Assn. 10,000.00
Telegraph Savings and Loan Assn. 10,000.00
Hyde Park Bank and Trust Co. 15,000.00

Securities:

38 shares, First National Bank of Boston, capital stock. . . .   1,063.97
U.S. government Bonds ("H"), dated March 1, 1967. . . .   15,000.00
Royalty withheld 8,779.00

Total assets . . . .$ 90,758.83

Charges against current assets:

Annual dues paid for 1970. . . . .   277.00
Life membership fund 8,000.00
Reprinting (on order and chargeable to 1968-69). . . . Est. 20,000.00

Total . . . .$ 28,277.00

Unencumbered assets . . . .$ 62,481.83

MEMBERS OF THE NATIONAL SOCIETY FOR THE STUDY OF EDUCATION

[This list includes all persons enrolled November 1, 1969, whether for 1969 or 1970. An asterisk (*) indicates Life Members of the Society.]

Aarestad, Amanda B., 1887 Gilmore Ave., Winona, Minn.
Aaron, Ira Edward, Col. of Educ., University of Georgia, Athens, Ga.
Aarons, Marjorie, 8 Mary Anna Drive, Fitchburg, Mass.
Abbott, Frank C., Colorado Comm. on Higher Education, Denver, Colo.
Abbott, Samuel Lee, Jr., Plymouth State College, Plymouth, N.H.
Abel, Frederick P., Western Illinois University, Macomb, Ill.
Abel, Harold, Sch. of Educ., University of Oregon, Eugene, Oreg.
Abelson, Harold H., Sch. of Educ., City University, New York, N.Y.
Abercrombie, Mrs. Charlotte, 1121 N. Waverly Pl., Milwaukee, Wis.
Ables, Jack B., East Aurora Jr. High School, East Aurora, N.Y.
Abraham, Willard, Arizona State University, Temple, Ariz.
Abrahamson, David A., 131 Livingston St., Brooklyn, N.Y.
Abrahamson, Edward, Prin., Flower Hill School, Huntington, N.Y.
Abrahamson, Stephen, Sch. of Med., Univ. of So. Calif., Los Angeles, Calif.
Abramowitz, Mortimer J., 345 Lakeville Rd., Great Neck, N.Y.
Accetta, M. A., 2053 Swallow Hill Road, Pittsburgh, Pa.
Achilles, Charles M., Box 317 B, Rt. #1, Geneva, N.Y.
Ackerlund, George C., Southern Illinois Univ., Edwardsville, Ill.
Ackerman, Thomas J., Univ. of Florida, Gainesville, Fla.
Ackley, James F., 1150 S. Pasadena Rd., Pasadena, Calif.
Adair, Mary R., Asst. Prof. of Spec. Educ., University Park, Pa.
Adams, Don, University of Pittsburgh, Pittsburgh, Pa.
Adams, Ernest L., Michigan State University, East Lansing, Mich.
Adams, Fern B., Office of Co. Supt. of Schls., Los Angeles, Calif.
Adams, James A., 1106 S. State St., Tahlequah, Okla.
Adams, Mrs. Ruth R., Sch. of Educ., New York City College, New York, N.Y.
Adatto, Albert, 228—165th Ave., N.E., Bellevue, Wash.
Adelberg, Arthur J., Supt. of Schls., Elmburst, Ill.
* Adell, James C., 16723 Fernway Rd., Shaker Heights, Ohio
Aden, Robert C., Middle Tennessee St. Univ., Murfreesboro, Tenn.
Adler, Mrs. Leona K., 101 Central Park W., New York, N.Y.
Adler, Manfred, John Carroll University, Cleveland, Ohio
Adler, Norman A., 51 West 52nd St., New York, N.Y.
Adolphsen, Louis J., Hinsdale Senior High School, Hinsdale, Ill.
Ahlers, Shirley, Texas Tech. Univ., Lubbock, Tex.
Ahrendt, Kenneth M., 2166 Dollarton Hwy., North Vancouver, B.C., Canada
Ahrnsbrak, Henry C., 425 Berwyn Dr., Madison, Wis.
Aiken, Warren R., 2323 Farleigh Road, Columbus, Ohio
Airasian, Peter W., Cath. Educ. Res. Cent., Boston Col., Chestnut Hill, Mass.
Akemann, Mrs. Rhea, Marion Community Schools, Marion, Ind.
Akins, Harold S., 1300 High St., Wichita, Kans.
Alagna, Agostino A., 478 W. 26th St., Chicago, Ill.
Alberg, Gary L., 1990 Lakeaires Blvd., White Bear Lake, Minn.
Albrecht, Milton C., State Univ. of New York, Buffalo, N.Y.
Albright, Frank S., 1 N. Campus Drive, Canton, Mo.

xvii

Alcock, Wayne T., Dillond Univ., New Orleans, La.
Alexander, Burton F., Petersburg High School, Petersburg, Va.
Alexander, Elenora, Rm. 234, 1300 Capital Ave., Houston, Texas
Alexander, William M., Col. of Educ., Univ. of Florida, Gainesville, Fla.
Alkin, Marvin C., University of California, Los Angeles, Calif.
Allen, Annabelle, 286 Main St., New Canaan, Conn.
Allen, David, 8437 Truxton Ave., Los Angeles, Calif.
Allen, D. Ian, Simon Fraser University, Burnaby 2, B.C., Canada
Allen, Dwight W., Sch. of Educ., Univ. of Mass., Amherst, Mass.
Allen, Edward E., Akron Central Schools, Akron, N.Y.
Allen, Graham, Coburg Teachers College, Coburg, Melbourne, Australia
Allen, H. Don, Nova Scotia Teachers College, Truro, Nova Scotia, Canada
Allen, Mrs. Irene A., R.F.D. 1, Swanton, Vt.
Allen, James Robert, 1249 Lake Ave., Fort Wayne, Ind.
Allen, John E., 306 Arbour Dr., Newark, Del.
Allen, Ross L., State Univ. College, Cortland, N.Y.
Allen, Sylvia D., P.O. Box 14, Woodbridge, Va.
Allen, Warren G., State Teachers College, Minot, N.Dak.
Allison, John J., 200 Bloomfield Ave., West Hartford, Conn.
Allman, Reva White, Alabama State College, Montgomery, Ala.
Alm, Richard S., Dept. of Educ., University of Hawaii, Honolulu, Hawaii
Almen, Rev. Dr. Louis, 231 Madison Ave., New York, N.Y.
Almcrantz, Mrs. Georgia, 402 Brown Circle, Knox, Ind.
Almroth, Frank S., 20 Hilltop Ter., Wayne, N.J.
Alper, Arthur E., Col. of Educ., Univ. of Ga., Athens, Ga.
Alprin, Stanley I., Cleveland State University, Cleveland, Ohio
Al-Rubaiy, Abdul Amir, Kent State University, Kent, Ohio
Alt, Pauline M., Central Connecticut State College, New Britain, Conn.
Althaus, Rosemary, Sch. of Educ., Winthrop College, Rock Hill, S.C.
Altman, Harold, 12006 Stanwood Dr., Los Angeles, Calif.
Altman, Herbert H., 832 Ocean Ave., Brooklyn, N.Y.
Amacher, Mrs. Walter, 7471 Mudbrook St., N.W., Massillon, Ohio
Amar, Wesley F., Waller High School, Chicago, Ill.
Ambrose, Edna V., 2124 N.E. 7th Ter., Gainesville, Fla.
Amershek, Kathleen, Col. of Educ., Univ. of Maryland, College Park, Md.
Ames, John L., Queens College, Kissena Blvd., Flushing, N.Y.
Amioka, Shiro, University of Hawaii, Honolulu, Hawaii
Anastasiow, Nicholas J., Univ. School, By Pass #46, Bloomington, Ind.
Anders, Mrs. Elizabeth M., 3601 Palm Dr., Riviera Beach, Fla.
Anderson, Donald G., Oakland Public Schls., 1025 Second Ave., Oakland, Calif.
Anderson, Donald L., 4708 Winthrop Drive, Ft. Worth, Tex.
Anderson, Doyle R., 935 Lewis Ave., St. Joseph, Mich.
Anderson, Edmond C., Sequoyah Junior High School, Dallas, Tex.
Anderson, Ernest M., Kansas State Col., Pittsburg, Kan.
Anderson, G. Lester, Pa. State Univ., University Park, Pa.
Anderson, Harold, 1531 W. Mourilaine, Ft. Collins, Colo.
Anderson, Harold A., North Park College, Chicago, Ill.
*Anderson, Howard R., Houghton Mifflin Co., Boston, Mass.
Anderson, Isabel C., Sch. of Educ., Temple University, Philadelphia, Pa.
Anderson, J. Paul, Col. of Educ., Univ. of Maryland, College Park, Md.
Anderson, James Wendell, St. Cloud State Col., St. Cloud, Minn.
Anderson, Kenneth E., Sch. of Educ., Univ. of Kansas, Lawrence, Kans.
Anderson, Lester W., Sch. of Educ., Univ. of Michigan, Ann Arbor, Mich.
Anderson, Linnea M., 2103 S. Franklin, Apt. D, Kirksville, Mo.
Anderson, Philip S., Wisconsin State University, River Falls, Wis.
Anderson, Robert Henry, Grad. Sch. of Educ., Harvard Univ., Cambridge, Mass.
Anderson, Ruth, 2569—7th Ave., Apt. 24 I, New York, N.Y.
Anderson, Stuart A., 3408 W. Third Ave., McHenry, Ill.
Anderson, Vernon E., Col. of Educ., University of Maryland, College Park, Md.
Anderson, William J., P.O. Box 288, Georgetown, Tex.
Andree, R. G., Southern Illinois University, Edwardsville, Ill.

Andregg, Neal B., 2553 Richmond Hill Rd., Augusta, Ga.
Andrews, Clay S., Dept. of Educ., San Jose State College, San Jose, Calif.
Andrews, Esther, 1937 N. Wilton Pl., Hollywood, Calif.
Andrews, Richard L., 2402-156th Ave., S.E., Bellevue, Wash.
Andrews, Sam D., Bowling Green State University, Bowling Green, Ohio
Andrews, Stella F., 544 Washington Ave., Pleasantville, N.Y.
Andrisek, John R., 119 Meadow Dr., Berea, Ohio
Angelini, Arrigo L., University of Sao Paulo, Sao Paulo, Brazil
Angell, George W., State University College, Plattsburg, N.Y.
Angelo, Rev. Mark V., St. Bonaventure Univ., St. Bonaventure, N.Y.
Angle, Philip H., Central Bucks School, Doylestown, Pa.
*Annis, Helen W., 6711 Conway Ave., Takoma Park, Md.
Ansel, James O., Western Michigan University, Kalamazoo, Mich.
Anselm, Karl R., 1666 Morgan St., Mountain View, Calif.
Anthony, Sally M., San Diego State Col., San Diego, Calif.
Antoine, Tamlin C., P.O. Box 1647, Taipei, Taiwan, Rep. of China
Anton, Anne S., 12435 Debby St., North Hollywood, Calif.
Antonelli, Luiz K., Queens College, Flushing, N.Y.
Apel, J. Dale, Kansas State Univ., Manhattan, Kans.
Apple, Joe A., San Diego State College, San Diego, Calif.
Apple, Michael W., 784 Columbus St., Apt. 7R, New York, N.Y.
Appleton, David, Supt. of Schools, Pine St., North Conway, N.H.
Arcarese, Lawrence C., State Univ. Col. of Arts & Sci., Plattsburgh, N.Y.
Archer, Marguerite P., 137 Highbrook Ave., Pelham, N.Y.
Arends, Wade B., 439 Wildwood, Park Forest, Ill.
Arfield, John W., 720 Shady Ave., Pittsburgh, Pa.
Armistead, Roy B., 9234 Queenston Dr., St. Louis, Mo.
Armstrong, Betty W., Univ. of Cincinnati, Cincinnati, Ohio
Armstrong, Mrs. Carmen L., R.F.D. No. 2, 5 Points Rd., Sycamore, Ill.
Armstrong, James L., 17552 Parthenia St., Northridge, Calif.
Armstrong, Mrs. Jenny R., Univ. of Wisconsin, Madison, Wis.
Armstrong, J. Niel, Sch. of Educ., Agric. & Tech. College, Greensboro, N.C.
Arnaud, E. E., Our Lady of the Lake College, San Antonio, Tex.
* Arnesen, Arthur E., 35 Hillside Drive, Salt Lake City, Utah
Arnoff, Melvin, 4325 Groveland Rd., University Heights, Ohio
Arnold, Gala, 740 "J" Ave., Coronado, Calif.
Arnold, J. E., Box 8540, University Station, Knoxville, Tenn.
Arnold, Marshall, 301 S. Water St., Henderson, Ky.
Arnold, Phyllis D., 628 Patterson Ave., San Antonio, Tex.
Arnold, Shirley L., 54 Kehr St., Buffalo, N.Y.
Arnsdorf, Val E., Sch. of Educ., Univ. of Delaware, Newark, Del.
Arnstein, George E., 2500 Virginia Ave. N.W., Washington, D.C.
Aromi, Eugene J., Univ. of So. Alabama, Mobile, Ala.
Arthur, Douglas C., Petaluma City Schools, Petaluma, Calif.
Arveson, Raymond G., 3178 Oakes Drive, Hayward, Calif.
Arvin, Charles L., Crawfordsville Community Schools, Crawfordsville, Ind.
Ashburn, Arnold G., Mississippi Southern College, Hattiesburg, Miss.
Ashe, Robert W., Dept. of Educ., Arizona State University, Tempe, Ariz.
Asher, William, Dept. of Educ., Purdue Univ., Lafayette, Ind.
Ashley, Rubelle, 906 Searles Rd., Toledo, Ohio
Askins, Billy E., Box 4234, Texas Tech. College, Lubbock, Tex.
Aspridy, Chrisoula, 2986 Lyell Rd., Rochester, N.Y.
Atkins, Thurston A., Teachers Col., Columbia Univ., New York, N.Y.
Atkinson, Gene, Col. of Educ., Univ. of Houston, Houston, Tex.
Atkinson, William N., Jackson Junior College, Jackson, Mich.
Aubin, Albert E., 2336 Glendon Ave., Los Angeles, Calif.
Auble, Donavon, Western Col. for Women, Oxford, Ohio
Aubry, A. J., L. B. Landry School, New Orleans, La.
Ause, Orval L., 8108-48th Ave. So., Seattle, Wash.
Austin, Carole, Baptist Col., Charleston, S.C.
Austin, David B., Richmond College, Staten Island, New York

Austin, Martha Lou, Univ. of South Florida, Tampa, Fla.
Austin, Mary C., Col. of Educ., Univ. of Hawaii, Honolulu, Hawaii
Austin, Roy S., State University College, Potsdam, N.Y.
Ausubel, David P., City University of New York, New York, N.Y.
Avant, Dorothea B., 8637 S. Michigan Ave., Chicago, Ill.
Avegno, T. Sylvia, 907 Castle Pt. Terrace, Hoboken, N.J.
Avinger, W. H., Abilene Christian College, Abilene, Texas
Ayer, Joseph C., 4200 Manchester Road, Middletown, Ohio
Azzarelli, Joseph J., New York University, Washington Sq., New York, N.Y.

Babcock, William E., 131 W. Nittany Ave., State College, Pa.
Babel, John, Jr., Ohio State Univ., Columbus, Ohio
Bach, Jacob O., Southern Illinois University, Carbondale, Ill.
Bachman, Ralph V., South High School, Salt Lake City, Utah
Backus, Thomas A., 570—115th Ave., Treasure Island, Fla.
Bacon, William P., Sch. of Educ., Univ. of the Pacific, Stockton, Calif.
Bacsalmasi, Stephen, York Cent. Dist. H.S. Brd., Richmond Hill, Ont., Canada
Baer, Campion, Capuchin Sem. of St. Mary, Crown Point, Ind.
Bagott, Nancy, 835 N. Sixth Ave., Tucson, Ariz.
Bahlke, Susan J., 2101 Philo Road, Urbana, Ill.
Bahn, Lorene A., 2843 Lomita Circle, Springfield, Mo.
Bahner, Joel H., Box 9177, APO, New York, N.Y.
Bahner, John M., 5335 Far Hills Ave., Dayton, Ohio
Bahrenburg, Erma M., 27 Ninth St., Carle Place, L.I., N.Y.
Baich, Henry, University of Portland, Portland, Ore.
Bailer, Joseph R., Dept. of Educ., Western Maryland College, Westminster, Md.
Bailey, Lucile, 119 E. University Dr., Tempe, Arizona
Bajek, Michalina, 1634 Neil Ave., Columbus, Ohio
Bajek, Robert S., 3830 S. Scoville, Berwyn, Ill.
Bajwa, Ranjit Singh, 2235 Georgetown Blvd., Ann Arbor, Mich.
Baker, Arthur F., 10 Ditson Place, Methuen, Mass.
Baker, Charles, R. #1, Carson City, Mich.
Baker, Earlene, 43 Barnes St., Providence, R.I.
Baker, Eugene H., 1402 N. Harvard, Arlington Hghts., Ill.
Baker, Harry J., 2241 Q Via Puerta, Laguna Hills, Calif.
Baker, I. D., Greenville College, Greenville, Ill.
Baker, John E., Col. of Educ. & Nurs., Univ. of Vermont, Burlington, Vt.
Baker, Lillian Mrs. 20257 Allentown Dr., Woodland Hills, Calif.
Baker, Rebecca, Southern Illinois University, Carbondale, Ill.
Baker, Robert C., Bemidji State College, Bemidji, Minn.
Baker, Robert E., Sch. of Educ., George Washington Univ., Washington, D.C.
Baker, William E., 11247 Dempsey Ave., Granada Hills, Calif.
Baldauf, R., 122 Forest Ave., Oak Park, Ill.
Baldwin, Alan L., Redwood City Sch. Dist., Redwood City, Calif.
Baldwin, Rollin, 924 West End Ave., New York, N.Y.
Balian, Arthur, 6804 W. Dickinson St., Milwaukee, Wis.
Ball, George G., Univ. of Northern Iowa, Cedar Falls, Iowa
Ballantine, Francis A., San Diego State College, San Diego, Calif.
Ballantine, Harden Parke, 303 W. 2nd St., Bloomington, Ind.
Ballou, Stephen V., Div. of Educ., Fresno State College, Fresno, Calif.
Balow, Irving H., Dept. of Educ., Univ. of Calif., Riverside, Calif.
Balser, Paul, Forest Hills H.S., 67-01—110th St., Forest Hills, N.Y.
Balzer, David M., Col. of Educ., University of Toledo, Toledo, Ohio
Bank, Adrianne, 4949 Ethel Ave., Sherman Oaks, Calif.
Banks, Marie, State University College, Plattsburgh, N.Y.
Banner, Carolyn Ann, 216 E. Ashley, Jefferson City, Mo.
Bany, Mary, 411 N. Third St., Alhambra, Calif.
Baratta, Anthony N., Sch. of Educ., Fordham University, New York, N.Y.
Barbaree, Frank, P.O. Box 547, Jackson, Ala.
Barbe, Richard H., Sch. of Educ., University of Delaware, Newark, Del.
Barbe, Walter B., 803 Church St., Honesdale, Pa.

Barber, Anson Burette, 17 Cushing St., Hingham, Mass.
Barber, Grant W., 1251 Shipman St., Birmingham, Mich.
Barber, Richard L., Col. of Arts & Sci., Univ. of Louisville, Louisville, Ky.
Barclay, Doris, 5151 State College Dr., Los Angeles, Calif.
Bard, George, 922A Maxwell Terrace, Bloomington, Ind.
Bardellini, Justin M., 337 Menlo Court, Walnut Creek, Calif.
Barden, Michael W., Sch. of Educ., Boston Univ., Westwood, Mass.
Bardsley, Frederick G., 4 Eldorado Road, Chelmsford, Mass.
Barkley, Margaret V., Arizona State University, Tempe, Ariz.
Barlow, Melvin L., Sch. of Educ., Univ. of California, Los Angeles, Calif.
Barnard, J. Darrell, 16 Links Drive, Great Neck, N.Y.
Barnard, W. Robert, Evans Chem. Lab., 88 W. 18th Ave., Columbus, Ohio
Barnes, Cyrus W., Beachlake, Pa.
Barnes, Fred P., Col. of Educ., University of Illinois, Urbana, Ill.
Barnes, O. Dennis, 2016 S. Third St., Alhambra, Calif.
Barney, Angelo T., 818 Black Rd., Joliet, Ill.
Barr, Charlotte A., Chicago State College, Chicago, Ill.
Barr, Dixon A., Sch. of Educ., East. Kentucky State Col., Richmond, Ky.
Barratt, Thomas K., Supt., Warren County Sch. Dist., Warren, Pa.
Barrett, George M., 152 Philcris Dr., Dover, Del.
Barron, Donald, 240 W. 22nd St., Deer Park, N.Y.
Barron, William E., University of Texas, Austin, Tex.
Barros, Raymond, Catholic University of Valparaiso, Valparaiso, Chile
Barry, Florence G., 5956 Race Ave., Chicago, Ill.
Bartel, Fred C., 125 Audubon Road, Frankfort, Ky.
Bartelt, Kenneth C., 205 E. 10th St., Muscatine, Iowa
Barter, Alice K., 8547 W. 102nd St., Palos Hills, Ill.
Bartlett, Fernand E., 740 Westcott St., Syracuse, N.Y.
Barlett, Robert C., 2105 S. 23rd Ave., Broadview, Ill.
Bartley, Imon D., Southwest Missouri State College, Springfield, Mo.
Barton, Carl L., Superintendent, Community Cons. Sch. Dist. 70, Freeburg, Ill.
Barton, George E., Jr., 1010 Short St., New Orleans, La.
Bartoo, Eugene, 34 Ellis Ave., Springville, N.Y.
Batha, Robert, Chester Junior-Senior High School, Chester, Calif.
Batinich, Mary Ellen, 9215 S. Troy Ave., Chicago, Ill.
Batten, James W., Box 2455, East. Carolina College, Greenville, N.C.
Battle, J. A., University of South Florida, Tampa, Fla.
Battle, John A., 11 Jones St., New Hyde Park, N.Y.
Battles, John J., 12 Ellis Ave., Ossining, N.Y.
Bauer, Edith B., Brigham Young University, Provo, Utah
Bauer, Norman J., 28 Westview Crescent, Geneseo, N.Y.
Bauman, Reemt R., Col. of Educ., Univ. of Toledo, Toledo, Ohio
Baumann, Max, 3800 Washington Ave., Baltimore, Md.
Baumgartner, Reuben A., Senior High School, Freeport, Ill.
Baumgartner, Rolla W., 7500 Air Base Group, A P O, N.Y. 09218
Bauthues, Donald J., 219 5th Ave., N.E. No. 29, Puyallup, Wash.
Baxel, George H., 1776 Raritan Rd., Scotch Plains, N.J.
Baxter, Eugenia, 629 Fourth St., Monongahela, Pa.
Baxter, Marlin B., Moline Public Schools, 1619 Eleventh Ave., Moline, Ill.
Bayless, Kathleen M., 95 Clairehaven Drive, Hudson, Ohio
Beach, Lowell W., 3606 Univ. H.S., Univ. of Michigan, Ann Arbor, Mich.
Beach, Mary L., 412 Delaware Drive, Westerville, Ohio
Beall, David C., Dir., Pupil Personnel Serv., Mentor, Ohio
Beamer, George C., North Texas State College, Denton, Tex.
Beamer, Rufus W., Virginia Polytechnic Inst., Blacksburg, Va.
Bear, David E., 12 Ramona Pl., Godfrey, Ill.
Beard, Richard L., 1812 Meadowbrook Hgts. Rd., Charlottesville, Va.
Beaton, Daniel W., 225 Vista Del Parque, Hollywood Riviera, Calif.
Beattie, George W., P.O. Box 100, Aptos, Calif.
Beatty, Charles J., 13011 Bellevue St., Beltsville, Md.
Beatty, Walcott H., 209 Kensington Way, San Francisco, Calif.

Beaubier, Edward Wm., 5631 El Parque St., Long Beach, Calif.
Beauchamp, George A., Sch. of Educ., Northwestern University, Evanston, Ill.
Beauchamp, Marian Z., 107 Century Drive, Syracuse, N.Y.
Beaumont, Urville J., Tenney High School, Methuen, Mass.
Bebb, Randall R., Univ. of No. Iowa, Cedar Falls, Iowa
Bebell, Clifford S., Southern Colorado State Col., Pueblo, Colo.
Beck, Hubert Park, Sch. of Educ., City College, 523 W. 121st St., New York, N.Y.
Beck, John M., 5832 Stony Island Ave., Chicago, Ill.
Beck, Norman W., Supt., Monroe County Schls., Waterloo, Ill.
Beck, Robert H., 233 Burton Hall, University of Minnesota, Minneapolis, Minn.
Becker, Harry A., Superintendent of Schools, Norwalk, Conn.
Becker, Millie A., 7637 S. Loomis Blvd., Chicago, Ill.
Bedell, Ralph, 701 Lewis Hall, Univ. of Missouri, Columbia, Mo.
Beebe, Nelson, Jr., Pennsville Memorial High School, Pennsville, N.J.
Beeching, Robert B., 1461 W. Shaw, Fresno, Calif.
Beery, Cleo C., La Verne College, La Verne, Calif.
Beery, John R., Sch. of Educ., University of Miami, Coral Gables, Fla.
Behnke, Donald J., 60 Everit Ave., Hewlett, N.Y.
Behrens, Herman D., 811 S. Johnson St., Ada, Ohio
*Behrens, Minnie S., Pomeroy, Iowa
Beighley, Archie F., Dept. of Educ., Winona State Col., Winona, Minn.
Beitler, Roger T., 2676 Walnut Blvd., Ashtabula, Ohio
Belcastro, Frank P., Univ. of San Diego, San Diego, Calif.
Belcher, Eddie W., Louisville Public Schls., 506 W. Hill St., Louisville, Ky.
Belgum, Loretta E., San Francisco State College, San Francisco, Calif.
Bell, Keith A., 22906—72 Pl., W., Mountlake Terrace, Wash.
Bell, Mary Anne. 118 N. Mozart St., Chicago, Ill.
Bell, Mildred, Harding College, Searcy, Ark.
Bell, Robert M., 2819 W. Sherwin Ave., Chicago, Ill.
Bell, Robert W., Wells Lane, Stony Brook, N.Y.
Bell, Wilmer V., 702 Kingston Rd., Baltimore, Md.
Bellack, Arno A., Tchrs. Col., Columbia University, New York, N.Y.
Belville, Donald H., 5925 Holly Glen Drive, Toledo, Ohio
Bemis, James Richard, 5243 Tango Ave., Yorba Linda, Calif.
Benben, John S., 7 Victoria Rd., Ardsley, N.Y.
Benda, Harold, Educ. Dept., West Chester State College, West Chester, Pa.
Bender, Kenneth R., University of Mississippi, University, Miss.
Bender, Martin L., 384 Prospect Ave., Hackensack, N.J.
Bender, Ralph E., Ohio State University, Columbus, Ohio
Benito, Sabado S., Off. of Soc. Sci., Wiley College, Marshall, Tex.
Benner, Robert D., Dept. of Elem. Educ., Colorado State Col., Greeley, Colo.
Bennett, Dale E., Col. of Educ., Univ. of Ill., Urbana, Ill.
Bennett, Lloyd M., Texas Woman's University, Denton, Tex.
Bennett, Robert N., Greene Central School, Greene, N.Y.
Bennett, Roger V., 6736 Melrose Drive, McLean, Va.
Bennett, William R., Mt. Vernon Nazarene Col., Mt. Vernon, Ohio
Bennie, William A., Univ. of Texas, Austin, Tex.
Benson, Paul A., 1705 Campus Road, Toledo, Ohio
Bentley, Caryl B., Rt. 1, Co. T, Sun Prairie, Wis.
Bentley, Harold, Northern Essex Community Col., Haverhill, Mass.
Bentley, Mrs. Harriett P., 2985 Wooster Rd., Rocky River, Ohio
Bentley, Robert, 1535 Walton Ave., Bronx, N.Y.
Bentzen, Mary M., 26740 Latigo Shore Drive, Malibu, Calif.
Benvenuto, Arthur, 158 Garden Pkwy., Henrietta, N.Y.
Benz, Marion H., S-4493 So. Buffalo St., Orchard Park, N.Y.
Berg, Arthur D., Music Consult., Dearborn Pub. Schools, Dearborn, Mich.
Berg, Dorothy D., 5924 N. Forest Glen Ave., Chicago, Ill.
Berg, Selmer H., 1216 Running Springs Rd., Walnut Creek, Calif.
Berger, Allen, University of Alberta, Edmonton, Alba., Canada
Bergeson, Clarence O., State University College, Geneseo, N.Y.

Bergeson, John B., 2415 Skyline St., Kalamazoo, Mich.
Berghoefer, Clara M., 1434 Punahou St., Honolulu, Hawaii
Berkihiser, Frances, Evangel College, Springfield, Mo.
Berkowitz, Edward, 2 Loretta Dr., Syosset, L.I., N.Y.
Berkowitz, Howard, State University College, Oneonta, N.Y.
Berlin, Pearl, University of Massachusetts, Amherst, Mass.
Berlin, Robert S., 383 Grand St., New York, N.Y.
Bernal, Leslie C., 10 Ditson Pl., Methuen, Mass.
Bernard, Donald H., 134 Paulison Ave., Ridgefield Park, N.J.
Bernard, Harold W., 1985 S.W. Warwick Ave., Portland, Oreg.
Bernd, John M., 824 Ellis St., Stevens Point, Wis.
Bernert, Roman A., S.J., Marquette Univ., Milwaukee, Wis.
Bernhoft, Otto L., Prin., South H.S., Fargo, N.D.
Berning, Norbert J., 204 W. Sunset Pl., DeKalb, Ill.
Bernstein, Abbot A., 104 Edwards Rd., Clifton, N.J.
Bernstein, Abraham, Dept. of Educ., Brooklyn College, Brooklyn, N.Y.
Berry, Henry W., Ft. Valley State Col., Fort Valley, Ga.
Berson, Minnie P., 1001 Spring St., Apt. 405, Silver Spring, Md.
Bertness, Henry J., 2909 N. 29th St., Tacoma, Wash.
Bertolaet, Frederick W., Univ. of Mich., Ann Arbor, Mich.
Bertolli, Robert L., 44 A St. Paul Street, Brookline, Mass.
Bertrand, John R., Berry College, Mt. Berry, Ga.
Besselsen, Gilbert, 2242 Elliott S.E., Grand Rapids, Mich.
Best, Mrs. Drusilla, 1148—8th Ave., S.W., Fairbault, Minn.
Bettelheim, Bruno 1365 E. 60th St., Chicago, Ill.
Bettina, Al, Eastern New Mexico University, Portales, N.Mex.
Betts, Emmett A., Sch. of Educ., University of Miami, Coral Gables, Fla.
Bettwy, Leroy J., 827 Fruithurst Dr., Pittsburgh, Pa.
Beyer, Fred C., Superintendent of County Schools, Modesto, Calif.
Beynon, Robert P., Devel. & Resch., Bowling Green Univ., Bowling Green, Ohio
Bezanson, Clyde O., 2410 Hillside Rd., White Bear Lake, Minn.
Bhola, H.S., UNESCO/Undp, Mwanza, Tanzania, East Africa
Bickert, Roderick N., Supt. of Schools, Mason City, Iowa
Bidwell, Wilma W., 1400 Washington Ave., Albany, N.Y.
*Bigelow, M. A., Litchfield, Conn.
Bigelow, Roy G., 404 S. 37th Ave., Hattiesburg, Miss.
Biggs, Sarah Dorothy, 804 Court, Fulton, Mo.
Biggy, Mary Virginia, 16 Park Ln., Concord, Mass.
Billups, Mrs. Clairene B., 2409 Tidewater Dr., Norfolk, Va.
Binford, George H., Central High School, Charlotte Courthouse, Va.
Binford, Linwood T., J. Andrew Bowler School, Richmond, Va.
Bingham, William C., Rutgers University, New Brunswick, N.J.
Binkley, Marvin Edward, 1000 Noelton Ln., Nashville, Tenn.
Birch, Jack W., 2704 C.L., Univ. of Pittsburgh, Pittsburgh, Pa.
Bird, Barbara R., 541 Sligh Blvd., N.E., Grand Rapids, Mich.
Bird, Charles A., 23 Fraser Pl., Hastings on Hudson, N.Y.
Birdsell, Don F., Supt. of Schools, Wheaton, Ill.
Bishop, Clifford L., Univ. of Iowa, Cedar Falls, Iowa
Bishop, Martha D., Dept. of Educ., Winthrop College, Rock Hill, S.C.
Bissell, Norman E., 295 Erkenbrecker Ave., Cincinnati, Ohio
Bizinkauskas, 424 North Cary St., Brockton, Mass.
Bjork, Alton J., Dept. of Educ., Illinois State University, Normal, Ill.
Black, Donald B., Univ. of Calgary, Calgary 44, Alberta, Canada
Black, Hugh C., Dept. of Educ., Univ. of California, Davis, Calif.
Black, Leo P., State Dept. of Educ., State Office Bldg., Denver, Colo.
Black, Mrs. Marian W., Sch. of Educ., Florida State Univ., Tallahassee, Fla.
Black, Millard H., 10031 Vecino Lane, La Habra, Calif.
Blackhurst, A. Edward, University of Kentucky, Lexington, Ky.
Blackledge, Mrs. Helen V., Southern Heights Sch., Fort Wayne, Ind.
Blackman, Charles A., 1962 Pawnee Trail, Okemos, Mich.
Blackshear, John S., 3933 Wisteria Ln., S.W., Atlanta, Georgia

Blackwell Leslie, Western Wash. State Col., Bellingham, Wash.
Blackwell, Lewis F., Jr., Box 1026, University, Ala.
Blackwell, Sara, N.Y. State Col. of H.E., Cornell Univ., Ithaca, N.Y.
Blaine, Russell K., 1816 Park Ave., S.E., Cedar Rapids, Iowa
Blake, Duane L., Colorado State Univ., Fort Collins, Colo.
Blakely, Richard F., Iona College, New Rochelle, N.Y.
Blanchard, Robert W., 22 Valley Rd., Montclair, N.J.
Blanchard, Walter J., Rhode Island Col., Warwick, R.I.
Blanco, Carlomagno J., Univ. of Toledo, Toledo, Ohio
Blaney, Mrs. Rose Marie, Shelter Rock School, Manhasset, N.Y.
Blankenship, A. H., Educational Research Council, Cleveland, Ohio
Blanton, Roy R., Jr., Appalachian St. Univ., Boone, N.C.
Blaser, John W., Wahtonka High School, The Dalles, Ore.
Blessington, John P., Whitby School, Greenwich, Conn.
Bleyer, John F., Seton Hill Col., Greensburg, Pa.
Blezien, Stephen S., 5762 N. Kercheval, Chicago, Ill.
Bliesmer, Emery P., Read. Ctr., Pennsylvania State Univ., University Park, Pa.
Bligh, Harold F., 81 Lincoln Ave., Ardsley, N.Y.
Blocher, R. Banks, P.O. Box 446, South Harwich, Mass.
Block, Elaine C., Hunter College, New York, N.Y.
Blomenberg, Gilbert, 345 North 2nd St., Seward, Nebr.
Blomgren, Glen H., Fresno State College, Fresno, Calif.
Blommers, Paul, East Hall, State University of Iowa, Iowa City, Iowa
Bloom, Herbert C., 3481 Sheridan Ave., Miami Beach, Fla.
Blough, John A., 2840 Proctor Drive, Columbus, Ohio
Blum, Mrs. Joanne L., Point Park Junior College, Pittsburgh, Pa.
Blythe, L. Ross, 108 Green Acres, Valparaiso, Ind.
Boario, Dora A., 422 Third St., Leechburg, Pa.
Bock, R. Darrell, Dept. of Educ., Univ. of Chicago, Chicago, Ill.
Bodkin, Raymond C., Box 196, Stanley, Va.
Boeck, Clarence H., 18 Arthur Ave., S.E. #12, Minneapolis, Minn.
Boeck, Marjorie A., 5101 Ewing Ave. South, Minneapolis, Minn.
Boeck, Robert W., 4090 Geddes Rd., Ann Arbor, Mich.
Boenig, Robert W., State Univ. Col., Fredonia, N.Y.
Boger, D. L., Morehouse College, Atlanta, Ga.
Boggess, Violet F., 2445 New Milford Rd., Atwater, Ohio
Bogle, Frank P., Superintendent of Schools, Millville, N.J.
Bogren, Mrs. Nadine, 1702 Wiggins Ave., Saskatoon, Sask., Canada
Boisclair, Cecile, University of Montreal, Montreal, Que., Canada
Boldt, Frederick J., 3704 Duffy Way, Bonita, Calif.
Bolin, Mrs. Phyllis W., 605 N.W. 18th St., W. Lauderdale, Fla.
Bolton, Dale L., Dept. of Educ., Univ. of Washington, Seattle, Wash.
Boltuck, Charles J., St., Cloud State Col., St. Cloud, Minn.
Bonar, Hugh S., Lewis College, Joliet, Ill.
Bond, Barbara, Univ. of South Carolina, Columbia, S.C.
Bond, George W., 3 Julia Ave., New Paltz, N.Y.
Bond, Horace M., Sch. of Educ., Atlanta University, Atlanta, Ga.
Bondy, Elmer G., Pasadena Ind. Schl. Dist., Pasadena, Tex.
Bonk, Edward C., North Texas University, Denton, Tex.
Booker, Ann, 849 E. 215th St., Bronx, N.Y.
*Booker, Ivan A., N.E.A. Mem. Div., 1201 Sixteenth St., N.W., Washington, D.C.
Boos, Robert W., 1335 Waukegan Rd., Glenview, Ill.
Booth, Delores C., 6604 Tremont St., Oakland, Calif.
Borden, Miles B., Amityville Pub. Schools, Amityville, N.Y.
Borders, Frances R., 3617 Raymond St., Chevy Chase, Md.
Borg, Robert L., Scott Hall, University of Minnesota, Minneapolis, Minn.
Borg, Walter R., 342 Mangrove Way, Walnut Greek, Calif.
Bortz, A. G., Lansing Sch. Bd. of Educ. (MSU), Lansing, Mich.
Bosch, Albert C., 500 W. 235th St., New York, N.Y.
Bosch, Gerald, 228 Ellen Ave., State College, Pa.
Bosco, J. Anthony, S.U.N.Y., 1400 Western Ave., Albany, N.Y.

MEMBERS OF THE NATIONAL SOCIETY   XXV

Bosco, James, Western Michigan University, Kalamazoo, Mich.
Bossard, Grace, Route 3, Box 6, Seaford, Del.
Bossier, Antonia M., 1661 No. Roman St., New Orleans, La.
Bossing, Nelson L., 1668 W. Glendale Ave., Apt. 520, Phoenix, Ariz.
Bouchard, John B., State Univ. Col., Fredonia, N.Y.
Boula, James A., 316 S. 2nd St., Springfield, Ill.
Boulac, Brian Michael, University of Notre Dame, Notre Dame, Ind.
Bouseman, John W., Cent. Y.M.C.A. Comm. Col., Chicago, Ill.
Bowen, James J., 619 S. Russell St., Monterey Park, Calif.
Bower, Robert K., 1905 E. Loma Alta Dr., Altadena, Calif.
Bowers, A. Eugene, Fayette County Schools, Fayetteville, Ga.
Bowers, Norman D., Sch. of Educ., Northwestern Univ., Evanston, Ill.
Bowers, Victor L., Southwest Texas State College, San Marcos, Tex.
Bowman, Howard A., Box 3307, Terminal Annex, Los Angeles, Calif.
Bowman, Orrin H., 66 Creekview Drive, Rochester, N.Y.
Boyajy, Robert J., 10 North Drive, Livingston, N.J.
Boyd, Laurence E., Sch. of Educ., Atlanta University, Atlanta, Ga.
Boyd, Robert D., Dept. of Educ., Univ. of Wisconsin, Madison, Wis.
Boyd, Robert M., Col. of Educ., Ohio University, Athens, Ohio
Boyer, Francis J., Northern Illinois University, DeKalb, Ill.
Boykin, Leander L., Florida A. & M. University, Tallahassee, Fla.
Boyle, William J., 620 W. Clairmont Ave., Eau Claire, Wis.
Boynton, Paul M., Connecticut State Dept. of Educ., Hartford, Conn.
Bozzelli, Albert, 70 Park Ave., West Caldwell, N.J.
Braam, L. S., Sch. of Educ., Syracuse University, Syracuse, N.Y.
Bracewell, George, Southern Illinois University, Carbondale, Ill.
Brackbill, A. L., Jr., Millersville State College, Millersville, Pa.
Bradford, James L., 1692 Northwest Blvd., Columbus, Ohio
Bradley, Mrs. George W., East Tenn. State Univ., Jonhson City, Tenn.
Bradley, Mrs. Howard R., 2147 Blue Hills Rd., Manhattan, Kans.
Bradtmueller, Weldon G., Northern Ill. Univ., DeKalb, Ill.
Brady, Florence A., 15A Troy Drive, Springfield, N.J.
Brady, Francis X., Elmira College, Elmira, N.Y.
Brady, John C., Bemidji State College, Bemidji, Minn.
Brain, George B., Col. of Educ., Washington State Univ., Pullman, Wash.
Brainard, Lois, San Jose State College, San Jose, Calif.
Bramwell, John R., Univ. of Oregon, Eugene, Oreg.
Brandinger, Mrs. Alice, 19 Carnation Pl., Trenton, N.J.
Brandt, Willard J., University of Wisconsin-Milwaukee, Milwaukee, Wis.
Brannan, Phyllis J., 1414 E. 59th St., Int. House, Chicago, Ill.
Brantley, Mabel, 623 N. First St., DeKalb, Ill.
Brantley, Mrs. Sybil, 108 Lomaland Dr., West Monroe, La.
Braswell, Robert H., Box 652, Orangeburg, S.C.
Brauer, Walter L., Washington H.S., Milwaukee, Wis.
Braun, Frank R., Col. of Educ., University of Minnesota, Minneapolis, Minn.
Braun, Frederick G., Col. of Educ., Univ. of Hawaii, Honolulu, Hawaii
Braun, Gertrude E., West Conn. State Col., Danbury, Conn.
Braun, Irma D., 228 Ocean Blvd., Atlantic Highlands, N.J.
Braun, Mary Ann R., 709 S. Race St., Urbana, Ill.
Braun, Ray H., 101 N. McCullough St., Urbana, Ill.
Bravo, Anna, 32 Beach Hill St., Ft. Salonga, N.Y.
Bredesen, Dorothy A., 644 "D" St., N.E., Washington, D.C.
Breeding, Clifford C., 2708 Bridal Wreath Ln., Dallas, Tex.
Breen, John F., 124 Smith St., Freeport, N.Y.
Bregman, Sydell, 17 Bodnarik Rd., Edison, N.J.
Breihan, Edna, 1512 Briggs St., Lockport, Ill.
Brenner, Anton, East. Mich. Univ., Ypsilanti, Mich.
Brereton, Matthew J., 22 Oakland Ter., Newark, N.J.
Bresina, Bertha M., 8308 E. Highland Ave., Scottsdale, Ariz.
Breslin, Frederick D., Glassboro State College, Glassboro, N.J.
Bretsch, Howard S., Sch. of Ed., Univ. of Rochester, Rochester, N.Y.

Bretz, Frank H., 1909 Arlington Ave., Columbus, Ohio
Brewster, Maurice A., Jr., Memorial Univ., St. John's Newfoundland
Brewton, Raymond E., Supt. of County Schools, Palo Pinto, Tex.
Brickman, Benjamin, Dept. of Educ., Brooklyn College, Brooklyn, N.Y.
Brickman, William W., University of Pennsylvania, Philadelphia, Pa.
Bridgers, Raymond B., R.D. 2, Broadway Rd., Oswego, N.Y.
Bridges, C. M., Col. of Educ., University of Florida, Gainesville, Fla.
Bridges, Lonnie H., Box 10194, Southern University, Baton Rouge, La.
Bridges, Raymond H., Box 10194, Southern University, Baton Rouge, La.
Bridgham, Robert G., Sch. of Ed., Stanford Univ., Palo Alto, Calif.
Briggs, Albert A., Dunbar Vocational High School, Chicago, Ill.
Briggs, Joseph M., 1710½ Cherry St., Fremont, Ohio
Bright, John H., 628 Cuesta Ave., San Mateo, Calif.
* Bright, Orville T., 516½ Prospect Ave., Lake Bluff, Ill.
Brill, Donald M., 5420 Maher Ave., Madison, Wis.
Brim, Burl, West Texas State University, Canyon, Tex.
Brimhall, Mrs. Alice, 111 Monticello Ave., Piedmont, Calif.
Briner, Conrad, 1221 Cambridge Ave., Claremont, Calif.
Brink, William G., Sch. of Educ., Northwestern University, Evanston, Ill.
Brinkman, J. Warren, Kansas State Tchrs. College, Emporia, Kans.
Brinkmann, E. H., So. Illinois Univ., Edwardsville, Ill.
Brinkmeier, Oria A., 2384 Valentine, St. Paul, Minn.
Briscoe, Laurel A., 1520 Cedar Ridge Dr., N.E., Albuquerque, N.Mex.
Brish, William M., Supt., Washington Co. Schools, Hagerstown, Md.
Brislawn, J., 28th & Lilac St., Longview, Wash.
*Bristow, William H., 70 Exeter St., Forest Hills, N.Y.
Britt, Laurence V., S.J., John Carroll Univ., Cleveland, Ohio
Brittain, Clay V., 1810 Panda Ln., McLean, Va.
Britton, Edward C., Sacramento State Col., Sacramento, Calif.
Broadbent, Frank W., 6401 Allison Ave., Des Moines, Iowa
Brody, Erness B., 32 Shady Brook Lane, Princeton, N.J.
Brody, Seymour, 38 Burnett Terr., Maplewood, N.J.
Broening, Angela M., 3700 N. Charles St., Baltimore, Md.
Bromwich, Rose M., 13507 Hart St., Van Nuys, Calif.
Bronson, Homer D., Chico State College, Chico, Calif.
Bronson, Moses L., 290 Ninth Ave., New York, N.Y.
Brookins, Jack E., 1323 Bayview, North Bend, Ore.
Brooks, B. Marian, City College, 135th and Convent, New York, N.Y
Brostoff, Theodore M., 10474 Santa Monica Blvd., Los Angeles, Calif.
Brother Adelbert James, Manhattan College, New York, N.Y.
Brother Charles Roe, F.S.C., 1515 Jackson, River Forest, Ill.
Brother Cosmas Herlihy, St. Francis College, Brooklyn, N.Y.
Brother Joseph Brusnahan, F.S.C., 650 E. Parkway So., Memphis, Tenn.
Brother Leo Gilskey, 414 N. Forest Ave., Oak Park, Ill.
Brother Leonard Coutney, St. Mary's College, Winona, Minn.
Brother Stephen Walsh, St. Edward's University, Austin, Tex.
Brother U. Cassian, St. Mary's Col., St. Mary's, Calif.
Brottman, Marvin A., 8926 Bellefort, Morton Grove, Ill.
Brousseau, Sandy E., 43 Carlos Ct., Walnut Creek, Calif.
Brown, Aaron, 1468 President St., Brooklyn, N.Y.
Brown, Bryon B., Baylor Univ., Waco, Tex.
Brown, Carol L., 1701 W. Pensacola, Apt. 121, Tallahassee, Fla.
Brown, Carol S., 1400 N. Magnolia, Lansing, Mich.
Brown, Chester J., Col. of Educ., University of Arizona, Tucson, Ariz.
Brown, Cynthiana Ellen, 6644 Wildlife Rd., Malibu, Calif.
Brown, Douglas H., Pine Wood Dr., Contoocook, N.H.
Brown, Douglas M., Superintendent of Schools, Shorewood, Wis.
Brown, Mrs. Edith F., 2821 N. 2nd St., Harrisburg, Pa.
Brown, Francis A., 2821 N. 2nd St., Harrisburg, Pa.
Brown, George W., Superintendent of Schools, Webster Groves, Mo.
Brown, Gerald W., California State College, Hayward, Calif.

Brown, Gertrude E., 2835 Milan St., New Orleans, La.
Brown, Gordon L., 1012 Darrow Ave., Evanston, Ill.
Brown, Howard L., Schl. Admin. Center, 49 E. College Ave., Springfield, Ohio
Brown, Jeremy, Castleton State Col., Castleton, Vt.
Brown, Kenneth B., University of Missouri, Columbia, Mo.
Brown, Kenneth R., California Tchrs. Assn., 1705 Murchison Dr., Burlingame, Calif.
Brown, Lawrence D., Sch. of Educ., Indiana University, Bloomington, Ind.
Brown, Linda, 1515 No. Cherry St., Chico, Calif.
Brown, Marion R., 404 Riverside Dr., New York, N.Y.
Brown, Mrs. Marjorie D., 4455 West 64th St., Los Angeles, Calif.
Brown, Marjorie M., University of Minnesota, St. Paul, Minn.
Brown, Max C., Johannesburg-Lewiston Area Schls., Johannesburg, Mich.
Brown, Nellie-Leigh, Charlottesville Public Schls., Charlottesville, Va.
Brown, Pauline, 25800 Hillary St., Hayward, Calif.
Brown, Perry, Lock Haven State College, Lock Haven, Pa.
Brown, Robert S., 702 N. Grandview, Stillwater, Okla.
Brown, Roy A., Asst. Supt., Bethlehem Area Schools, Bethlehem, Pa.
Brown, Ruby J., 412 Steward Ave., Jackson, Mich.
Brown, Sara M., So. Connecticut State Col., New Haven, Conn.
Brown, Rev. Syl, St. Mary's Col., Winona, Minn.
Brown, Thomas J., Hofstra Univ., Hempstead, N.Y.
Brown, Virginia H., 1 Lafayette Plaisance, Detroit, Mich.
Brown, Warren M., Supt. of Schools, Ferguson, Mo.
Brownell, Samuel M., Yale Univ. & Univ. of Conn., New Haven, Conn.
Brownell, William A., 701 Spruce St., Berkeley, Calif.
Browning, Mrs. Linda, 5335 Far Hills Ave., Dayton, Ohio
Browning, Roy W., Topeka Public Schools, Topeka, Kans.
Brownlee, Geraldine D., 6937 S. Crandon Ave., Chicago, Ill.
Brownstein, Jewell, Dept. of Educ., Univ. of Louisville, Louisville, Ky.
Browy, Marjorie J., California State College, Los Angeles, Calif.
Broz, Joseph R., 3402 Clarendon Rd., Cleveland, Ohio
Brubaker, Leonard A., 409 Marian Ave., Normal, Ill.
Bruce, William C., 9205 Jackson Park Blvd., Wauwatosa, Wis.
Brumbaugh, W. Donald, University of Utah, Salt Lake City, Utah
Brunnelle, Paul E., Prin., Winthrop High School, Winthrop, Me.
Brunetti, Frank A., 36 C. Escondido Village, Stanford, Calif.
Bruning, Charles R., University of Minnesota, Minneapolis, Minn.
Brunk, Jason W., Col. of Educ., Ohio Univ., Athens, Ohio
Brunner, Edward F., 847 El Prado, Lake City, Fla.
Bruno, Gordon A., Darien H.S., Darien, Conn.
Brunson, Mrs. Dewitt, P.O. Box 484, Orangeburg, S.C.
Brunsvold, Perley O., Mankato State Col., Mankato, Minn.
Bryan, Ray J., 220 Curtiss Hall, Iowa State Univ., Ames, Iowa
Bryant, B. Carleton, 810 Clear Lake Ave., West Palm Beach, Fla.
Bryant, Ira B., Kashmere Gardens High Sch., Houston, Tex.
Bryner, James R., 185 Salisbury Dr., Saskatoon, Sask., Canada
Buchanan, Alfred K., 80 Grove St., Plantsville, Conn.
Buchanan, M. Marcia, Campus View House, 526 Bloomington, Ind.
Buchanan, Paul G., 61 Rosemary St., Buffalo, N.Y.
Buck, James E., Oregon College of Educ., Monmouth, Oreg.
Buckley, J. L., Superintendent of Schools, Lockhart, Tex.
Buckley, Richard Dale, Sch. of Educ., Wisconsin State University, Oshkosh, Wis.
Buckner, John D., 4246 W. North Market St., St. Louis, Mo.
Buckner, William N., 2643—15th St., N.W., Washington, D.C.
Budd, Mrs. Edith M., 3227 Parker Ave., West Palm Beach, Fla.
Bueker, Armin H., Superintendent of Schools, Marshall, Mo.
Buelke, John A., Western Michigan University, Kalamazoo, Mich.
Bulla, Helen M., Asst. Prin., Waterford Twsp. H.S., Pontiac, Mich.
Bullock, Portia C., 408 Tea St., N.W., Washington, D.C.
Bullock, William J., Superintendent of Schools, Kannapolis, N.C.

Bunda, Mary Anne, 301 W. Green, Champaign, Ill.
Bunger, Marianne, Alaska Methodist University, Anchorage, Alaska
Bunker, James G., Supt., Novato Unified Sch. Dist., Novato, Calif.
Bunnell, Mrs. Constance O., Mamaroneck High School, Mamaroneck, N.Y.
Bunnell, Robert A., Ford Foundation, 320 E. 43rd St., New York, N.Y.
Bunning, Madeline, Univ. of the Pacific, Stockton, Calif.
Buntrock, Richard M., West Bend Pub. Schools, West Bend, Wis.
Buol, Mary Steudler, 91 Ten Acre Rd., New Britain, Conn.
Burch, Charles H., 1803 McDonald Dr., Champaign, Ill.
Burch, Mary J., 1123 Old Hillsborough Rd., RFD 4, Chapel Hill, N.C.
Burchell, Helen R., Univ. of Pennsylvania, Philadelphia, Pa.
Burdick, Alger E., St. Col. of Arkansas, Conway, Ark.
Burdick, Richard L., Educ. Dept., Carroll College, Waukesha, Wis.
Burg, Mrs. Mary, 2259 Wolfangle Rd., Cincinnati, Ohio
Burgdorf, Otto P., 36-12—210th St., Bayside, N.Y.
Burke, Carolyn L., 52 Portage, Highland Park, Mich.
Burke, Doyle K., Newport Spec. Sch. Dist., Newport, Ark.
Burke, Eileen M., 48 Bayberry Rd., Trenton, N.J.
* Burke, Gladys, 244 Outlook, Youngstown, Ohio
Burke, Henry R., 197 Ridgewood Ave., Glen Ridge, N.J.
Burke, Paul J., 1 Lookout Pl., Ardsley, N.Y.
Burke, Thomas O., 424 Bayberry Dr., Plantation, Fla.
Burke, Thomas S., 3171 W. 83rd St., Chicago, Ill.
Burkett, Lowell A., 1510 H. St. N.W., Washington, D.C.
Burks, Herbert M., Jr., 122 Kensington Rd., E. Lansing, Mich.
Burks, John B., Jersey City State College, Jersey City, N.J.
Burnham, Robert A., 1805 Carle Drive, Urbana, Ill.
Burns, Constance M., University of Bridgeport, Bridgeport, Conn.
Burns, Cranford H., Box 1549, Mobile, Ala.
Burns, Mrs. Doris, 115 W. 86th St., Apt. 6F, New York, N.Y.
Burns, Hobert W., San Jose State Col., San Jose, Calif.
Burns, James W., 2115 Waite Ave., Kalamazoo, Mich.
Burns, Mildred L., MacDonald College, Quebec, Canada
Burr, Elbert W., Monsanto Chemical Co., Lindbergh and Olive, St. Louis, Mo.
Burrell, E. William, Ocean Ave., Newport, R.I.
Burrough, Rudolph V., 526 Kirby, Shreveport, La.
Burrows, Alvina Treut, 117 Nassau Ave., Manhasset, N.Y.
Bursuk, Laura, 11 Harbor Lane, Glen Head, L.I., N.Y.
Burt, Lucile, Lincoln School, 338 Forest Ave., Fond du Lac, Wis.
Burton, Jane, R.R. #3, North Manchester, Ind.
Bushnell, Allan C., 309 South St., New Providence, N.J.
Buss, Dennis C., 70 John F. Kennedy Blvd., Somerset, N.J.
Buswell, Guy T., 1836 Thousand Oaks Blvd., Berkeley, Calif.
Butler, Mrs. B. LaConyea, Spelman College, Atlanta, Ga.
Butler, E. Frank, Contra Costa College, San Pablo, Calif.
Butler, Laurence, 630 Leonard St., Ashland, Oreg.
Butler, Lester G., 468 E. Lincoln Ave., Columbus, Ohio
Butler, Marjorie, Div. of Ed., State Univ. Col., New Paltz, N.Y.
Butler, Paul W., 721 Australian Ave., W. Palm Beach, Fla.
Butler, Thomas M., 1428 W. Riverview St., Decatur, Ill.
Butts, David P., University of Texas, Austin, Tex.
Butts, Franklin A., 54 N. Hamilton St., Poughkeepsie, N.Y.
Butts, Gordon K., Southern Illinois University, Carbondale, Ill.
Butts, R. Freeman, Tchrs. Col., Columbia University, New York, N.Y.
Buyse, R., Sch. of Educ., University of Louvain, Tournai, Belgium
Buzard, Judith, 52 E. 14th Ave., Columbus, Ohio
Byers, Joe L., Michigan State Univ., East Lansing, Mich.
Byram, Harold M., Sch. of Educ., Michigan State Univ., East Lansing, Mich.
Byrne, John, Dist. Supt., Chicago Board of Education, Chicago, Ill.
Byrne, Richard Hill, Col. of Educ., Univ. of Maryland, College Park, Md.

Caccavo, Emil, 123 Willow St., Roslyn Heights, N.Y.
Cadd, Ayrles W., Box 17, Shandon, Calif.
Cady, Henry L., Ohio State University, Columbus, Ohio
Cafiero, Albert J., Supt., Oradell Pub. Schools, Oradell, N.J.
Cafone, Harold C., Dept. of Educ., Oakland Univ., Rochester, Mich.
Cahan, Mrs. Ruth, 1916 Overland Ave., Los Angeles, Calif.
Cahraman, Thomas P., 35550 Bella Vista Dr., Yucaipa, Calif.
Cain, E. J., University of Nevada, Reno, Nev.
Cain, Lee C., Georgia Southern Branch, Statesboro, Ga.
Cain, Ralph W., Sutton Hall, University of Texas, Austin, Tex.
Caird, Florence B., Joyce Kilmer School, Chicago, Ill.
Caldwell, Cleon C., 2917 Noble Ave., Bakersfield, Calif.
Caldwell, Herbert M., 2568 St. Andrews Drive, Glendale, Calif.
Cali, Anthony J., 28 Malden Circle, Wyandanch, N.Y.
Califf, Stanley N., Chapman College, Orange, Calif.
Calip, Rev. Osmundo A., St. John's University, Jamaica, N.Y.
Call, Mrs. Ardell, Utah Education Association, Salt Lake City, Utah
Callahan, William T., 131 Jericho Turnpike, Jericho, N.Y.
Callan, John H., McQuaid Hall, Seton Hall Univ., South Orange, N.J.
Callas, Eliza E., 7080 Oregon Ave., N.W., Washington, D.C.
Callaway, A. Byron, Col. of Educ., Univ. of Georgia, Athens, Ga.
Calmes, Robert E., 5216 Mission Hill Dr., Tucson, Ariz.
Calvert, Lloyd, Supt. of Schools, Windsor, Conn.
Calvin, Thomas H., State Educ. Dept., State Univ. of N.Y., Albany, N.Y.
Cameron, Don C., 350 E. 700 S., St. George, Utah
Campbell, Clyde M., Michigan State University, East Lansing, Mich.
Campbell, E. G., Col. of Educ., Univ. of Maryland, College Park, Md.
Campbell, Roald F., Sch. of Educ., University of Chicago, Chicago, Ill.
Campbell, Ronald T., 23644 Edward, Dearborn, Mich.
Campos, Mrs. M. A. Pourchet, Caixa Postal 30.F86, Sao Paulo, S. P., Brazil
Canar, Donald A., Central YMCA Schls., 211 W. Wacker Dr., Chicago, Ill.
Candoli, Italo C., 315 Bryant Ave., Worthington, Ohio
Canfield, John M., Superintendent of Schools, West Plains, Mo.
Cannon, Wendell, Univ. of So. California, Los Angeles, Calif.
Cantlon, R. Jerry, Illinois State University, Normal, Ill.
Capehart, Bertis E., 120 Squire Hill Rd., Upper Montclair, N.J.
Capocy, John S., 4628 Seeley St., Downers Grove, Ill.
Cappa, Dan, California State Col., Los Angeles, Calif.
Cappelluzzo, Emma M., University of Massachusetts, Amherst, Mass.
Capps, Lelon R., Bailey Hall, University of Kansas, Lawrence, Kans.
Capps, Mrs. Marian P., Virginia State College, Norfolk, Va.
Capri, Walter P., 2339 Chateau Way, Livermore, Calif.
Carder, W. Ray, Hillsboro High School, Hillsboro, Oreg.
Cardina, Philip J., Box 269, R.D. 2, Farmingdale, N.J.
Cardinale, Anthony, Dir., Dependents Educ., Dept. of Defense, Washington, D.C.
Cardozo, Joseph A., Box 9958, Baton Rouge, La.
Cardwell, Robert H., Tyson Junior High School, Knoxville, Tenn.
Carey, Clarence B., Dir., Jones Commercial H.S., Chicago, Ill.
Carey, E. Neil, 142 Michael's Way, Ellicott City, Md.
Carey, Jess Wendell, Park College, Parkville, Mo.
Carey, Justin P., 105 Lyncroft Rd., New Rochelle, N.Y.
Carlin, James B., Reading Center, Murray St. Univ., Murray, Ky.
Carline, Donald E., 365 Seminole, Boulder, Colo.
Carlisle, John C., Col. of Educ., Utah State Univ., Logan, Utah
Carlson, Alma Jane, 81 Manito Ave., Oakland, N.J.
Carlson, Mrs. Evelyn F., 6899 N. Wildwood, Chicago, Ill.
Carlson, F. Roy, Mt. Ida Junior College, Newton Centre, Mass.
Carlson, Robert A., No. 901—640 Main St., Saskatoon, Sask., Canada
Carlson, Mrs. Ruth K., 1718 LeRoy Ave., Berkeley, Calif.
Carlson, Thorston R., 415 Monte Vista Lane, Santa Rosa, Calif.

Carman, Beatrice D., 223 Chapel Dr., Tallahassee, Fla.
Carmichael, John H., Essex County Col., Newark, N.J.
Carne, Vernon E., 1383 Dorothy Dr., Decatur, Ga.
Carnochan, John L., Jr., Route 5, Frederick, Md.
Carpenter, Aaron C., P.O. Box 387, Grambling, La.
Carpenter, James L., 206 S. 19th Ave., Maywood, Ill.
Carpenter, John A., Univ. of Southern Calif., Los Angeles, Calif.
Carpenter, N. H., Superintendent, City Schools, Elkin, N.C.
Carr, Carolyn Jane, 1409 N. Walnut Grove Ave., Rosemead, Calif.
Carr, Julian W., 1410 Terrace Drive, St. Paul, Minn.
Carriere, Robert H., 57 Theroux Dr., Chicopee, Mass.
Carrington, Joel A., Univ. of Maryland, College Park, Md.
Carroll, Clifford, Gonzaga University, Spokane, Wash.
Carroll, John B., Educational Testing Service, Princeton, N.J.
Carroll, Margaret L., 208 Fairmont Rd., DeKalb, Ill.
Carruth, Edwin Ronald, University of Southern Mississippi, McComb, Miss.
Carsello, Carmen J., University of Illinois Circle Campus, Chicago, Ill.
Carstater, Eugene D., Bur. of Naval Personnel, Washington, D.C.
Carter, Burdellis L., 6437 Lupine Dr., Indianapolis, Ind.
Carter, Harold D., Sch. of Educ., University of California, Berkeley, Calif.
Carter, Heather L., Univ. of Texas, Austin, Tex.
Carter, James S., North High School, Phoenix, Ariz.
Carter, Dr. Lamore J., Grambling Col., Grambling, La.
Carter, Margaret Ann, Wayne State University, Detroit, Mich.
Carter, Richard C., Box E, Glendale, Oreg.
Carter, Sims, 214 Spalding Dr., Beverly Hills, Calif.
Carter, Susan C., 10634 Eggleston Ave., Chicago, Ill.
Carter, Thomas D., Alamo Hgts. Indep. Sch. Dist., San Antonio, Tex.
Carter, Vincent, San Jose State College, San Jose, Calif.
Cartwright, William H., Duke University, Durham, N.C.
Caruso, George E., Town Hall, 333 Washington St., Brookline, Mass.
Case, Charles W., 400 Kendrick Rd., Apt. 820, Rochester, N.Y.
Caselli, Robert E., 1614 S. Phillips Ave., Sioux Falls, S.Dak.
Casey, Barbara A., 700 Seventh St., Apt. 220, Washington, D.C.
Casey, John J., 197 Nebraska Ave., Hamilton Square, N.J.
Casey, Neal E., 7607 Kirwin Lane, San Jose, Calif.
* Cash, Christine B., Arkansas Baptist College, Little Rock, Ark.
Caskey, Helen C., Tchrs. Col., University of Cincinnati, Cincinnati, Ohio
Casper, T. A., Suite 14, 2707 Seventh St., E.. Saskatoon, Sask., Canada
Cassidy, Rosalind, University of California, 405 Hilgard Ave., Los Angeles, Calif.
Castaneda, Alberta M., U. of Texas, Austin, Tex.
Castrale, Remo, Supt. of Schools, Johnston City, Ill.
Catlin, Dorothy M., 440 S. Beverly Lane, Arlington Heights, Calif.
Catrambone, Anthony Ronald, 106 S. Landis Ave., Vineland, N.J.
Caughran, Alex M., 93 N. Main St., Orono, Me.
Caulfield, Patrick J., Dept. of Educ., St. Peter's College, Jersey City, N.J.
Cawein, Paul E., 2032 Belmont Rd., N.W., Apt. 600, Washington, D.C.
Cawrse, Robert C., 26927 Osborn Rd., Bayvillage, Ohio
* Cayco, Florentino, President, Arellano University, Manila, Philippines
Cecco, Mrs. Josephine L., Springfield College, Springfield, Mass.
Cecil, Eddie D., Div. of Educ., Benedict College, Columbia, S.C.
Center, Benjamin, 1653 Roseview Drive, Columbus, Ohio
Chaffee, Pamila, 8920 Canby Ave., Northridge, Calif.
Chall, Jeanne, Grad. Sch. of Educ., Harvard University, Cambridge, Mass.
Chambers, William M., 2113 Chambers, N.W., Albuquerque, N.Mex.
Champagne, R. P., Holy Savior Central High School, Lockport, La.
Champoux, Mrs. Ellen M., 301 Mendenhall St., Apt. 2, Greenboro, N.C.
Chandler, Herbert E., 1304 Fairlane, Lawrence, Kans.
Chang, Alvin K., 3642 S. Court St., Palo Alto, Calif.
* Chang, Jen-chi, 323 Arpieka Ave., St. Augustine, Fla.
Chang, Mrs. Lynette Y.C., Univ. of Victoria, Victoria, B.C., Canada

Channell, W. R., Argentine High School, Kansas City, Kans.
Chansky, Norman M., Temple University, Philadelphia, Pa.
Chao, Sankey C., 154 Redwood Ave., Wayne, N.J.
Chaplin, Charles C., 265 Hawthorne St., Brooklyn, N.Y.
Chapline, Elaine Burns, Queens Col., Flushing, N.Y.
Charles, Ramon L., 327 Nickell Rd., Topeka, Kan.
Charlton, Huey E., 3785 Wisteria Lane, S.W., Atlanta, Ga.
Charters, Alexander N., Syracuse University, Syracuse, N.Y.
Chase, Francis S., Dept. of Educ., Univ. of Chicago, Chicago, Ill.
Chase, Naomi C., University of Minnesota, Minneapolis, Minn.
Chasnoff, Robert, Newark State College, Union, N.J.
Chatfield, Walter L., 1437 Hunter Ave., Columbus, Ohio
Chatwin, Jerry M., 2312-27th St., Santa Monica, Calif.
Chavez, Phillip G., 1148 Navajo, Barstow, Calif.
Chavis, James S., Box 25, McLain, Miss.
Chay, Josephine S., 1669 Makuakane Place, Honolulu, Hawaii
Cheatham, Alflorence, Dist. Supt., Dist. 19, Chicago, Ill.
Cheers, Arlynne Lake, Grambling College, Grambling, La.
Chen, Kuan-Yu, Central Conn. St. Col., New Britain, Conn.
Chern, Mrs. Nona E., 492 Concord Rd., Broomall, Pa.
Chiavaro, John, Newfane Cent. Sch., Newfane, N.Y.
Chidekel, Samuel J., Madison Sch., Chicago, Ill.
Chidester, Charles B., 8646 Linden St., Munster, Ind.
Childs, James N., Lincoln Elem. Sch., Rt. 4, Riverwood, Minn.
Childs, Vernon C., 1514 South 14th St., Manitowoc, Wis.
Christensen, Viktor Albert, 5130 Leon Court, Riverside, Calif.
Christenson, Bernice M., 5045 Alta Canyada Rd., La Canada, Calif.
Christina, Robert J., 122 Smalley Rd., Syracuse, N.Y.
Christine, Ray O., Arizona State University, Tempe, Ariz.
Christoplos, Florence, 6410 Sandy Street, Laurel, Md.
Chuck, Harry C., 265 Kanoelam Dr., Hilo, Hawaii
Chudler, Albert A., Intern. Sch. of Kuala Lumpur, Kuala Lumpur, Malaysia
Chung, Yong Hwan, Dept. of Educ., Wiley College, Marshall, Tex.
Church, John, Dept. of Educ., 721 Capitol Mall, Sacramento, Calif.
Churchill, Donald W., Bemidji State College, Bemidji, Minn.
Cianciolo, Patricia J., Michigan State University, East Lansing, Mich.
Cicchelli, Jerry J., Prin., Oradell Public School, Oradell, N.J.
Ciccoricco, Edward A., 48 Clark St., Brockport, N.Y.
Ciklamini, Joseph, 921 Carnegie Ave., Plainfield, N.J.
Ciminillo, Lewis, Col. of Educ., Indiana University, Bloomington, Ind.
Cioffi, Joseph M., 652 Doriskill Ct., River Vale, N.J.
Clague, W. Donald, La Verne Col., La Verne, Calif.
Clanin, Edgar E., 309 Highland Dr., West Lafayette, Ind.
Clare, Mrs. Elizabeth Rae, 949 N. Alfred St., Los Angeles, Calif.
Clark, Angeline, 493 Pittsfield Drive, Worthington, Ohio
Clark, Charles W., P.O. Box 254, Rogue River, Oreg.
Clark, David L., 1243 Matlock Rd., Bloomington, Ind.
Clark, Elmer J., Col. of Educ., Southern Illinois Univ., Carbondale, Ill.
Clark, Franklin B., Dist. Supt. of Schools, Athens, N.Y.
Clark, H. Robert, 430 No. Michigan Ave., Chicago, Ill.
Clark, John Francis, 1848 Iroquois St., Long Beach, Calif.
Clark, Leonard H., 240 Van Nostrand Ave., Jersey City, N.J.
Clark, Lewis E., Supt., Coquille Sch. Dist. #8, Coquille, Ore
Clark, Maurice P., Supt. of Schools, Western Springs, Ill.
Clark, Max R., Supt. of Schools, 142 Main St., Calmar, Iowa
Clark, Moses, Alabama State College, Montgomery, Ala.
Clark, Raymond M., Michigan State University, East Lansing, Mich.
Clark, Richard M., State University of N.Y., Albany, N.Y.
Clark, Richard McCallum, Schl. of Educ., S.U.N.Y., Albany, N.Y.
Clark, Sidney L., 855 Bronson Rd., Fairfield, Conn.
Clark, Stephen C., OSD/ARPA, RDFV-V, APO, San Francisco, Calif.

Clark, Thomas Hall, 1316 W. Ritchie, Enid, Okla.
Clark, Woodrow Wilson, 101 W. Leake St., Clinton, Miss.
Clarke, Juno-Ann, San Francisco State Col., San Francisco, Calif.
Clarke, Stanley C. T., 11615—78th Ave., Edmonton, Alba., Canada
Clarkston, Emmerine A., 8216 Eberhart Ave., Chicago, Ill.
Classon, Miss Marion E., 19 Nantes Rd., Parsippany, N.J.
Claxton, Norman L., So. Junior High Schl., Bloomfield, N.J.
Clayton, Thomas E., #2 Road West, Manlius, N.Y.
Clegg, Ambrose A., Jr. Tri-Univ. Proj., Univ. of Wash., Seattle, Wash.
Cleland, Donald L., Sch. of Educ., Univ. of Pittsburgh, Pittsburgh, Pa.
Clifford, Mrs. Miriam, 920 Monmouth Ave., Durham, N.C.
Clift, Virgil A., Sch. of Educ., New York University, New York, N.Y.
Cline, Marion, Jr., Univ. of Texas, El Paso, Tex.
Clinton, Robert, Jr., 3002 McElroy, Austin, Tex.
Clopper, Elizabeth, Brd. of Educ., Anne Arundel Cnty., Annapolis, Md.
Clouser, John J., 901 Graceland St., Des Plaines, Ill.
Clouthier, Raymond P., St. Norbert College, West DePere, Wis.
Clymer, Theodore Wm., 1588 Northrop St., St. Paul, Minn.
Cobb, Beatrice M., Cambell Shore Rd., Gray, Maine
Cobb, Joseph L., 2706 Baynard Blvd., Wilmington, Del.
Cobban, Margaret R., 424 Victoria St., Glassboro, N.J.
Coblentz, Dwight O., 615 N. School St., Normal, Ill.
Cobley, Herbert F., Superintendent of Schools, Nazareth, Pa.
Cobun, Frank E., State University College, New Paltz, N.Y.
Cochi, Oscar R., 471 Manse Ln., Rochester, N.Y.
Cochran, Alton W., Supt. of Schools, Charlestown, Ind.
Cochran, John R., Kalamazoo Public Schools, 1220 Howard St., Kalamazoo, Mich.
Cochran, Russell T., 19815 Larbert, Saugus, Calif.
Code, Allen L., 208 S. Third St., Seneca, S.C.
Coen, Alban Wasson, II, Central Michigan University, Mt. Pleasant, Mich.
Cofell, William L., St. John's University, Collegeville, Minn.
Coffee, James M., 5903 Woodside Drive, Jacksonville, Fla.
Coffey, Thomas F., 5900 N. Glenwood Ave., Chicago, Ill.
Coffey, Warren C., 7416 East Parkway, Sacramento, Calif.
Coffman, Phillip, 4618 Secor, Toledo, Ohio
Cogswell, Mark E., Northern State College, Aberdeen, S.Dak.
Cohen, Edward G., 558 E. Parr Ave., Long Beach, N.Y.
Cohen, George, 8 Etheride Pl., Park Ridge, N.J.
Cohen, Hyman Z., 744 Henry Rd., Far Rockaway, N.Y.
Cohen, Jerome, Barry College, Miami, Fla.
Cohen, Samuel J., 9 Coventry Rd., Syosset, N.Y.
Cohler, Milton J., 3450 N. Lake Shore Drive, Chicago, Ill.
Coker, William F., Portland Sr. High Sch., Portland, Tenn.
Colbath, Edwin H., 97-16 118th St., Richmond Hill, N.Y.
Colburn, A. B., Cascade Senior High School, Everett, Wash.
Colclazer, Gloria L., 18209 Ludlow St., Northridge, Calif.
Cole, Glenn A., University of Arkansas, Fayetteville, Ark.
Cole, James C., 1946 Mira Flores, Turlock, Calif.
Cole, James E., University of Utah, Salt Lake City, Utah
Coleman, Alwin B., Sch. of Educ., West. Mich. Univ., Kalamazoo, Mich.
Coleman, Mary E., 3122 Valley Lane, Falls Church, Va.
Coleman, Mary Elisabeth, University of Pennsylvania, Philadelphia, Pa.
Colla, Frances S., 49 Regina St., Trumbull, Conn.
Collier, Mrs. Anna K., 903 Fourth St., Liverpool, N.Y.
Collier, Calhoun C., Michigan State University, East Lansing, Mich.
Collier, Richard E., 4822 Eades St., Rockville, Md.
Collings, Miller R., 9201 W. Outer Dr., Detroit, Mich.
Collins, F. Ethel, Box 536, Presidential Way, Guilderland, N.Y.
Collins, Helen C., 1203 Gilpin Ave., Wilmington, Del.
Collins, Mary Lucille, Beaubien Sch., 5025 N. Laramie Ave., Chicago, Ill.
Collins, Paul W., R. #5, Box 221C, Ocala, Fla.

Collins, Mrs. Ray, 3101 W. Carson, Torrance, Calif.
Collins, Robert E., State Dept. of Education, St. Paul, Minn.
Collins, Ted, 1023 Oakdale St., West Covina, Calif.
Collison, Sidney B., 410 New London Road, Newark, Del.
Colman, John E., C.M., Sch. of Educ., St. John's University, Jamaica, N.Y.
Combs, Lawrence, 1595 Yearling Drive, Florissant, Md.
Combs, W. E., Florida A. & M. University, Tallahassee, Fla.
Comer, J. M., Box 820, Rt. 2, Collinsville, Ill.
Conan, Mrs. Beatrice, 2063—74th St., Brooklyn, N.Y.
Conaway, John O., 431 S. Brown, Terre Haute, Ind.
Condra, James B., Birmingham-Southern College, Birmingham, Ala.
Congleston, Joseph W., Jr., E. Carolina Univ., Greenville, N.C.
Congreve, Willard J., 807 S. 6th St.W., Newton, Iowa
Conley, Jack, Prin., Elementary School, Culver City, Calif.
Conley, William H., Sacred Heart University, Bridgeport, Conn.
Conner, John W., University High School, Univ. of Iowa, Iowa City, Ia.
Conner, Orval, 305 E. McGuffey Hall, Miami U., Oxford, Ohio
Connor, E. Faye, Huntington College Library, Huntington, Ind.
Connor, William H., Washington Univ. Grad. Inst. of Education, St. Louis, Mo.
Conry, Rev. Thomas P., S.J., John Carroll Univ., Cleveland, Ohio
Conte, Anthony F., 1000 Spruce St., Trenton, N.J.
Converse, David T., State Univ. Col., Buffalo, N.Y.
Conway, Marie M., Jefferson Court No. 31, 4925 Saul St., Philadelphia, Pa.
Cook, William J., 385 Winnetka Ave., Winnetka, Ill.
Cookingham, Frank, Michigan State University, East Lansing, Mich.
Cool, Dwight W., 6840 W. 32nd Pl., Wheat Ridge, Colo.
Cooley, Max L., Box 44, Newton, Utah
Cooley, Robert L., Supt., Dunkirk Public Schools, Dunkirk, N.Y.
Cooling, Elizabeth, 600 Mt. Pleasant Ave., Providence, R.I.
Cooper, Bernice L., Baldwin Hall, Univ. of Georgia, Athens, Ga.
Cooper, Dian Annise, 500 E. 33rd St., Chicago, Ill.
Cooper, George H., 8946 Bennett Ave., Chicago, Ill.
Cooper, J. David, 1610 Dorchester Dr., Bloomington, Ind.
Cooper, John H., 63 Lucero St., Thousand Oaks, Calif.
Cooper, Joyce, University of Florida, Gainesville, Fla.
Cooper, Shawn, Psychology Dept., Brown Univ., Providence, R.I.
Cooper, Thelma, 55 Knolls Crescent-(9k), Riverdale, N.Y.
Cooperman, Saul, Box 147B, Skillman, N.J.
Copeland, Harlan G., Sch. of Educ., Syracuse Univ., Syracuse, N.Y.
Coplein, Leonard E., Haddon Township Bd. of Educ., Westmont, N.J.
Corbin, Joseph W., 2700 Warwick Lane, Modesto, Calif.
Cordasco, Frank M., Montclair State Col., Upper Montclair, N.J.
Corey, Stephen M., University of Miami, Coral Gables, Fla.
Corley, Clifford L., Oregon College of Education, Monmouth, Oreg.
Corman, Bernard R., 705-11025—82nd Ave., Edmonton, Alba., Canada
Cornell, Francis G., 7 Holland Ave., White Plains, N.Y.
Cornish, Robert L., Arkansas University, Fayetteville, Ark.
Corona, Bert C., 426 Locust St., Modesto, Calif.
Corrozi, John F., Col. of Educ., Univ. of Delaware, Newark, Del.
Cortage, Cecelia, 2053 Illinois Ave., Santa Rosa, Calif.
Cory, N. Durward, 908 W. North St., Muncie, Ind.
Cosentino, Bruno, 6 Glenside Dr., New City, N.Y.
Cosper, Cecil, Box 107, West. Carolina Univ., Cullowhee, N.C.
Coster, John K., North Carolina State University, Raleigh, N.C.
Cotner, Janet, Scott, Foresman & Co., Collingswood, N.J.
Cotter, Katharine C., Boston Col., Chestnut Hill, Mass.
Cotton, Janie West, Univ. of Minn., Minneapolis, Minn.
Cottone, Sebastian Charles, School Planning Dept., Philadelphia, Pa.
Couch, Paul E., Arkansas St. University, State College, Ark.
Couche, Martha E., Rust College, Holly Springs, Miss.
Coughlan, Robert J., Sch. of Educ., Northwestern Univ., Evanston, Ill.

Coulter, Myron L., Sch. of Educ., West. Michigan Univ., Kalamazoo, Mich.
* Courtis, S. A., 22445 Cupertino Rd., Cupertino, Calif.
Courtney, Robert W., Box 198, Middlebush, N.J.
Covert, Warren O., Western Illinois University, Macomb, Ill.
Cowan, William P., 118 Chapel Hill Drive, Brentwood, N.Y.
Coward, Gertrude O., Charlotte-Mecklenburg Bd. of Educ., Charlotte, N.C.
Cowen, Persis H., 333 W. Calif. #208, Pasadena, Calif.
Cowgill, Robt. G., Col. of Educ., Fla. Tech. Univ., Orlando Park, Fla.
Cowles, Clifton V., Jr., Div. of Music, Ark. St. Univ., State College, Ark.
Cowles, James D., 104 Leon Drive, Williamsburg Va.
Cowles, Milly, Sch. of Educ., Univ. of South Carolina, Columbia, S.C.
Cox, Edwin A., Superintendent of Schools, North Parade, Stratford, Conn.
Cox, Hugh F., 17012 Grovemont St., Santa Ana, Calif.
Cox, John A., 735 N. Allen St., State College, Pa.
Cox, Robert A., University of Pittsburgh, Pittsburgh, Pa.
Cozine, June E., Col. of Educ., Kansas State Univ., Manhattan, Kans.
* Craig, Gerald S., 8 Paseo Redondo, Tucson, Ariz.
Craig, James C., 9403 Crosby Rd., Silver Spring, Md.
Craig, Jimmie M., 11512 Fuerte Farms Rd., El Cajon, Calif.
Craig, Robert C., Michigan State University, East Lansing, Mich.
Craig, William S., Central Wash. State College, Ellensburg, Wash.
Crane, Donald C., 67 Payson Lane, Piscataway, N.J.
Crarey, Hugh W., 9150 S. Cregier Ave., Chicago, Ill.
Craton, Edward J., 1777 Glenwood Ct., Bakersfield, Calif.
Craver, Samuel Mock, 717 E. Thach Ave., Auburn, Ala.
Crawford, Dorothy M., 212 W. Washington St., Ottawa, Ill.
Crawford, Leslie W., Ohio Univ., Athens, Ohio
Crawford, T. James, Sch. of Business, Indiana University, Bloomington, Ind.
Creason, M. Frank, 9101 Grant Lane, Overland Park, Kans.
Creighton, Samuel L., 1517 Secor Rd. #134, Toledo, Ohio
Cresci, Gerald D., 1171 Los Molinos Way, Sacramento, Calif.
Crescimbeni, Joseph, Jacksonville University, Jacksonville, Fla.
Crespy, H. Victor, 94 Broad St., Freehold, N.J.
Creswell, Mrs. Rowena C., 305 Montclair Ave., So., College Station, Tex.
Crews, Alton C., Rt. 1, Due West Road, Marietta, Ga.
Crews, Roy L., Aurora College, Aurora, Ill.
Crim, Kenneth, 15 N. Main St., Dayton, Ohio
Criscuolo, Nicholas P., Read. Spec., Pub. Schools, New Haven, Conn.
Crocker, Richard F., Jr., Superintendent of Schools, Caribou, Maine
Crohn, Burrill L., 944 Third Ave., New York, N.Y.
Cromartie, Sue W., Col. of Educ., University of Georgia, Athens, Ga.
Crombe, William A., 1087 Webster Rd., Webster, N.Y.
Cron, Celeste Maia, 801 Gull Ave., San Mateo, Calif.
Cronin, Rev. Robert E., 3245 Rio St., Apt. 811, Falls Church, Va.
Crook, Robert B., Queens Col., Flushing, N.Y.
Crooks, Judith, 128 N. Carolina Ave. SE, Washington, D.C.
Cross, Donald A., Bathurst Tchrs. Col., Bathurst, N.S.W., Australia
Crossland, Mrs. Kathryn M., 3326 Pinafore Drive, Durham, N.C.
Crossley, J. K., 44 Eglinton Ave. W., Toronto 310, Ontario, Canada
Crosson, Robert Henry, 2747 West 35th Ave., Denver, Colo.
*Crow, Lester D., 5300 Washington St., Hollywood, Fla.
Crowell, R. A., Col. of Educ., University of Arizona, Tucson, Ariz.
Crowley, Mary C., 7 Boone Lane, Dearborn, Mich.
Crowley, Robert J., 7 Charles St., Hamilton, N.Y.
Croy, Hazel, California State College, Fullerton, Calif.
Cruckson, Fred A., 72 S. Portland St., Fond du Lac, Wis.
Crum, Clyde E., Div. of Educ., San Diego State College, San Diego, Calif.
Culbertson, Jack A., Ohio State University, Columbus, Ohio
Culhane, Joseph W., 3405 Crimson King Court, Lexington, Ky.
Cumbee, Carroll F., Apt. D-4, Trojan Arms Apt., Troy, Ala.
Cummings, C. Thomas, Canajoharie Central Schools, Canajoharie, N.Y.

Cummings, Mabel Anna, 6044 Linden St., Brooklyn, N.Y.
Cummings, Reta Gines, 14802 Newport Ave. 18C, Santa Ana, Calif.
Cummings, Susan N., Arizona State University, Tempe, Ariz.
Cummins, L. Ross, Dept. of Educ. & Psych., Bates Col., Lewiston, Me.
Cummins, Lester L., 3512 S. 263rd St., Kent, Wash.
Cunningham, Donald J., 2020 East Third St., Bloomington, Ind.
Cunningham, George S., 4 Glenwood St., Orono, Me.
Cunningham, Luvern L., Dean of Educ., Ohio State Univ., Columbus, Ohio
Cunningham, Myron, Col. of Educ., University of Florida, Gainesville, Fla.
Cupp, Gene R., 1704 N. Park Ave., Canton, Ohio
Curley, Ann, 1920 Grand View Ave., Irwin, Pa.
Currey, Ralph B., State Dept. of Education, Charleston, W.Va.
Currie, Craig H., 346-2nd Ave., S.W., Cedar Rapids, Iowa
Currie, Robert J., Col. of Educ., University of Idaho, Moscow, Idaho
Currier, Mrs. Lynor O., 1925 Harwood Rd., Annapolis, Md.
Curry, John F., Box 6765, North Texas State College, Denton, Tex.
Curry, Laura June, 352 San Antonio Blvd., C-4, Norfolk, Va.
Curtin, James T., 4140 Lindell Blvd., St. Louis, Mo.
Curtin, John T., 21761 Mauer Dr., St. Clair Shores, Mich.
Curtis, Delores M., University of Hawaii, Honolulu, Hawaii
Curtis, E. Louise, Macalester College, St. Paul, Minn.
Curtis, Francis H., Univ. of Scranton, Scranton, Pa.
Curtis, James E., 325 Conifer Ln., Santa Cruz, Calif.
Curtis, James P., University of Alabama, University, Ala.
Curtis, Theodore, Warwick School Dept., Warwick, R.I.
Cusick, Ralph, 6721 N. Newgard, Chicago, Ill.

Daddazio, Arthur H., 41 Brady Ave., Newburgh, N.Y.
Daeufer, Carl Joseph, Box 59, Saipan, Mariana Isls.
D'Agostino, Nicholas E., Wolcott High School, Wolcott, Conn.
Dahl, John A., California State College, Los Angeles, Calif.
Dahlberg, E. John, Jr., P.O. Box 3631, Agana, Guam
Dale, Arbie Myron, Sch. of Commerce, New York University, New York, N.Y.
Dale, Edgar, Sch. of Educ., Ohio State University, Columbus, Ohio
D'Alessio, Theodore, 10 Gaston St., W. Orange, N.J.
Dal Santo, John, 917 Washington St., Mendota, Ill.
Daly, Edmund B., 1839 N. Richmond St., Chicago, Ill.
Daly, Francis M., Jr., Eastern Michigan University, Ypsilanti, Mich.
Dandoy, Maxine A., Fresno State College, Fresno, Calif.
Daniel, George T., N. 319 Locust Rd., Spokane, Wash.
Daniel, Dr. Kathryn B., 83 Nob Hill, Columbia, S.C.
Daniel, Sheldon C., 3459 Sea Grape Drive, Sarasota, Fla.
Daniels, Paul R., 520 "N" St. S.W., Apt. S-131, Washington, D.C.
Danielson, Paul J., Col. of Educ., University of Arizona, Tucson, Ariz.
Danzy, Richard L., Woodlawn Experimental Schls., 7420 Ingleside, Chicago, Ill.
Darcy, Natalie T., Dept. of Educ., Brooklyn College, Brooklyn, N.Y.
Darling, Dennis E., 501 N. Clarendon, Kalamazoo, Mich.
Darr, George F., 155 Rodeo Rd., Glendora, Calif.
Darrow, Helen F., 162 N. Carmelina Ave., Los Angeles, Calif.
D'Ascoli, Louis N., 5 Hughes Ter., Yonkers, N.Y.
Daubek, Gerald G., Univ. of Kentucky Ext., Fort Knox, Ky.
Davenport, William R., Campbellsville College, Campbellsville, Ky.
Davey, Mrs. Elizabeth P., 5748 Harper Ave., Chicago, Ill.
Davidson, Mrs. Evelyn K., Dept. of Educ., Kent State University, Kent, Ohio
Davidson, Terrence R., University of Michigan, Ann Arbor, Mich.
Davie, Lynn, 1815 University Ave., Madison, Wis.
Davies, Daniel R., Croft Consult. Serv., Tucson, Ariz.
Davies, Don, NCTEPS (NEA), 1201—16th St., N.W., Washington, D.C.
Davies, J. Leonard, Bur. of Educ. Resch., Univ. of Iowa, Iowa City, Iowa
Davies, Lillian S., Illinois State University, Normal, Ill.
Davis, Ann E., 525 N.W. Armstrong Way, Corvallis, Oreg.

Davis, Curtis, 1605 Park Ave., San Jose, Calif.
Davis, David Carson, 1045 E St., Apt. 4, Lincoln, Nebr.
Davis, David E., Supr., Tyrrell Co. Public Schools, Columbia, N.C.
Davis, Donald E., University of Minnesota, Minneapolis, Minn.
Davis, Donald Jack, P.O. Box 11504, St. Louis, Mo.
Davis, Dwight E., 6726 S. Washington Ave., Lansing, Mich.
Davis, Dwight M., 505 Glenview Dr., Des Moines, Iowa
Davis, Mrs. Eldred D., Knoxville College, Knoxville, Tenn.
Davis, Frederick B., 3700 Walnut St., Philadelphia, Pa.
Davis, Guy C., Trinidad State Junior College, Trinidad, Colo.
Davis, H. Curtis, 1605 Park Ave., San Jose, Calif.
Davis, Harold S., 21934 River Oaks Dr., Rocky River, Ohio
Davis, Hazel Grubbs, Queens Col., City Univ. of N.Y., Flushing, N.Y.
Davis, J. Clark, Col. of Educ., University of Nevada, Reno, Nev.
Davis, J. Sanford, Box 646, Madison, Conn.
Davis, Joseph H., 8300 Jackson St., St. Louis, Mo.
Davis, Marianna W., 156 Aberdeen Ave., Columbia, S.C.
Davis, Milton J., 725 West 18th St., North Chicago, Ill.
Davis, O. L., Jr., Col. of Educ., Univ. of Texas, Austin, Tex.
Davis, Paul Ford, Morehead State Univ., Morehead, Ky.
Davis, Ron W., 223 Hillcrest Cir., Chapel Hill, N.C.
Davoren, David, Superintendent of Schools, Milford, Mass.
Dawkins, M. B., 1110 Izard St., Little Rock, Ark.
Dawkins, Sue, 17 E. 14th Ave., Columbus, Ohio
Dawson, Kenneth E., P.O. Box 31, Lawrenceville, Va.
Dawson, W. Read, Baylor University, Waco, Tex.
Day, James F., Dept. of Educ., Univ. of Texas, El Paso, Tex.
Day, Marjorie S., 7626 Stetson Ave., Los Angeles, Calif.
Deady, John E., Supt. of Schools, Springfield, Mass.
Deam, Calvin W., Sch. of Educ., Boston University, Boston, Mass.
Dease, E. Richard, 413 Lorraine Rd., Wheaton, Ill.
DeBernardis, Amo, 6049 S. W. Luradel, Portland, Oreg.
Debin, Louis, 83-37—247th St., Bellerose, N.Y.
DeBoer, Dorothy L., 3930 W. Southport Ave., Chicago, Ill.
Debus, Raymond L., 7 Brooks St., Lane Cove, New South Wales, Australia
Deever, Merwin, Col. of Educ., Arizona State University, Tempe, Ariz.
DeGrow, Gerald S., 509 Stanton St., Port Huron, Mich.
Dejnozka, Edward L., 49 Rockleigh Drive, Trenton, N.J.
DeKock, Henry C., Col. of Educ., State Univ. of Iowa, Iowa City, Iowa
Della Penta, A. H., Superintendent of Schools, Lodi, N.J.
Deller, W. McGregor, Superintendent of Schools, Fairport, N.Y.
Delmonaco, Thomas M., 44 Lanewood Ave., Framingham Centre, Mass.
Delon, Floyd G., 302 Natl. Old Line Bldg., Little Rock, Ark.
DeLong, Arthur R., Grand Valley State College, Allendale, Mich.
Demerio, William D., Hollywood Park, Liverpool, N.Y.
Demming, John A., Bldg. S-502, 6th St., N., West Palm Beach, Fla.
DeMoraes, Maria P. Tito, WHO Reg. Off., 8 Scherfigsvej, Copenhagen, Denmark
Dempsey, Richard A., P.O. Box 1167, Darien, Conn.
Denemark, George W., University of Kentucky, Lexington, Ky.
Denham, Lynne S., 2111 E. Broadway, Logansport, Ind.
De Nio, James, 308 Gates Manor Dr., Rochester, N.Y.
Denning, Mrs. Bernadine, 5057 Woodward, Rm. 1338, Detroit, Mich.
Dennis, David M., Western New Mexico-Tchr. Educ. Center, Silver City, N.Mex.
Dennis, Donald Albert, 19533 Haynes St., Reseda, Calif.
Dennis, Ronald T., Northwestern State College, Natchitoches, La.
Deno, Stanley L., Col. of Educ., Univ. of Delaware, Newark, Del.
Denova, Charles C., 420 N. Prospect, Redondo Beach, Calif.
Denson, Lucille D., Braemar House, Hollywood Pk., Liverpool, N.Y.
De Nye, Julius B., Jr., 1100 W. 107th Pl., Chicago, Ill.
De Ortega, Eneida Santizo, Calle Real 6101, Betania-Panama, Rep. of Panama
DePaul, Frank J., 2727 North Long Ave., Chicago, Ill.

Derby, Orlo Lee, State Univ. Col., Brockport, N.Y.
DeRidder, Lawrence M., Col. of Educ., Univ. of Tennessee, Knoxville, Tenn.
DeRoche, Edward F., Marquette Univ., Milwaukee, Wis.
DeSantis, Joseph P., 204 Orchard St., Dowagiac, Mich.
Desimowich, Donald M., Route 3, Box 30, Hartland, Wis.
Desjarlais, Lionel P., 1684 Rhodes Ct., Ottawa 8, Ont., Canada
DeStefano, Anthony J., 48 Lenox Ave., Hicksville, N.Y.
Detrick, Frederick M., 10 Sheldon Rd., Pemberton, N.J.
Dettre, John Richard, Univ. of New Mexico, Albuquerque, N. Mex.
Detwiller, Harry G., George Washington Univ., Washington, D.C.
Deutschman, Mrs. Marilyn L., 201 St. Pauls Ave., Jersey City, N.J.
De Vaughn, J. E., Georgia State College, Atlanta, Ga.
DeVault, M. Vere, University of Wisconsin, Madison, Wis.
De Velez, Esther Arvelo, Univ. of Puerto Rico, Rio Piedras, P.R.
Devenport, Claude N., 2810 Leeway Drive, Apt. 3, Columbia, Mo.
Devens, John S., Columbia College, Columbia, S.C.
Devine, Thomas Gerald, 8 Rambler Road, Jamaica Plain, Mass.
Devor, J. W., 6309 E. Holbert Rd., Bethesda, Md.
DeVries, Ted, Ball State University, Muncie, Ind.
DeWalt, Homer C., Supt. of Schools, Diocese of Erie, Erie, Pa.
Deyell, J. Douglas, Provincial Teachers College, North Bay, Ont., Canada
Dickens, Hugh L., Wm. Carey College, Hattiesburg, Miss.
Dickey, Otis M., Superintendent of Schools, Oak Park, Mich.
Dickmeyer, Mrs. K. H., 200 8th Ave., S.E., Fairfax, Minn.
*Diederich, A. F., St. Norbert College, West DePere, Wis.
Diederich, Paul B., Educ. Testing Serv., Princeton, N.J.
Diedrich, Richard C., 155 Knox Dr., West Lafayette, Ind.
Diefenderfer, Omie T., 828 Third St., Fullerton, Pa.
Diehl, T. Handley, Miami University, Oxford, Ohio
Diener, Russell E., 1034 Novara St., San Diego, Calif.
Dierzen, Mrs. Verda, Comm. Consol. Sch. Dist., Woodstock, Ill.
Dieterle, Louise E., 10700 S. Avenue F, Chicago, Ill.
Dietz, Elisabeth H., 1093 Northern Blvd., Baldwin, N.Y.
Diffley, Jerome, St. Bernard College, St. Bernard, Ala.
Diggs, Eugene A., Supt., Sch. Dist. No. 110, Overland Park, Kans.
DiGiammarino, Frank, Lexington Public Schools, Lexington, Mass.
DiLeonarde, Joseph H., 6309 N. Cicero Ave., Chicago, Ill.
DiLieto, Ray Marie, 4 Bayberry Lane, Westport, Conn.
Dillehay, James A., Bowling Green State Univ., Bowling Green, Ohio
Dillman, Duane H., 139 Pelham Rd., Philadelphia, Pa.
Dillon, Jesse D., Jr., 850 Cranbrook Dr., Liftwood Estates, Wilmington, Del.
DiLuglio, Domenic R., 1849 Warwick Ave., Warwick, R.I.
Dimitroff, Lillian, 1525 Brummel St., Evanston, Ill.
Dimond, Ray A., Jr., 4034 E. Cambridge, Phoenix, Ariz.
Dimond, Stanley E., 2012 Shadford Rd., Ann Arbor, Mich.
Di Muccio, Virginia, Hanford Elem. Schl., Hanford, Calif.
DiNardo, V. James, Massachusetts State College, Bridgewater, Mass.
DiPasquale, Vincent C., 330 Oak Grove, Apt. 801, Minneapolis, Minn.
Disberger, Jay, Box 268, Haven, Kans.
Disko, Michael, 16 Briarwood Dr., Athens, Ohio
Distin, Leslie, Supt. of Schls., Johnson City, N.Y.
Dittemore, Ron, 707 W. Market St., Savannah, Mo.
Dittmer, Daniel G., 1647 Francis Hammond Pkwy., Alexandria, Va.
Dittmer, Jane E., Kouts High School, Kouts, Ind.
Dixon, Glendora M., 3969 Dakota Rd., S.E., Salem, Oreg.
Dixon, James E., 27146 Elias St., Saugus, Calif.
Dixon, James T., 13 Lake Rd., Huntington Station, L.I., N.Y.
Dixon, W. Robert, University of Michigan, Ann Arbor, Mich.
Dodd, John M., Eastern Montana College, Billings, Mont.
Dodds, A. Gordon, Superintendent of Schools, Edwardsville, Ill.
Dodge, Norman B., 523 S. Oneida Way, Denver, Colo.

Dodson, Dan W., New York University, Washington Sq., New York, N.Y.
Dodson, Edwin S., Col. of Educ., University of Nevada, Reno, Nev.
Dohemann, H. Warren, San Francisco State Col., San Francisco, Calif.
Doherty, Benton H., 403 Washington, Park Ridge, Ill.
Dohmann, C. William, 640 Main St., El Segundo, Calif.
Doll, Ronald C., 17 Rossmore Ter., Livingston, N.J.
Domian, O. E., 6801 Olympia, Golden Valley, Minn.
Donahoe, Thomas J., 74 Fallston St., Springfield, Mass.
Donatelli, Rosemary V., Loyola University, Chicago, Ill.
Donnelly, Peter J., Jersey City State Col., Jersey City, N.J.
Donnersberger, Anne, 2309 W. 91st St., Chicago, Ill.
Donoghue, Mildred R., California State College, Fullerton, Calif.
Donovan, Charles F., Sch. of Educ., Boston College, Chestnut Hill, Mass.
Donovan, Daniel E., C.M., St. John's Prep. Sch., Brooklyn, N.Y.
Donovan, David, 6095 Harkson, E. Lansing, Mich.
Doody, Louise E., 191 Dedham St., Newton Highlands, Mass.
Dooley, Bobby J., 1725 Cardinal Rd., Milledgeville, Ga.
Doria, Helen D., 3144 Ridge Rd., Highland, Ind.
Dorricott, H. J., Western State College, Gunnison, Colo.
Doss, Jesse Paul, 12631 Fletcher Dr., Garden Grove, Calif.
Dotson, John M., 154 Jones Dr., Pocatello, Idaho
Douglass, Harl R., Col. of Educ., University of Colorado, Boulder, Colo.
Douglass, Malcolm P., Claremont Grad. Sch., Claremont, Calif.
Dow, John A., 2597 W. Calimyrna, Fresno, Calif.
Downey, Richard D., Evergreen Terrace 173-7, Carbondale, Ill.
Downing, Carl, Central State Col., Edmond, Okla.
Doyle, Andrew McCormick, 1106 Bellerive Blvd., St. Louis, Mo.
Doyle, David W., 75 Koenig Rd., Tonawanda, N.Y.
Doyle, E. A., Jesuit High School, New Orleans, La.
Doyle, James Francis, 1751 Noble Drive, N.E., Atlanta, Ga.
Doyle, Jean, 511 E. High St., Lexington, Ky.
Doyle, Walter, University of Notre Dame, Notre Dame, Ind.
Drag, Francis L., California Western Univ., San Diego, Calif.
Dragositz, Anna, Educational Testing Service, Princeton, N.J.
Drake, Thelbert L., Univ. of Connecticut, Storrs, Conn.
Drechsel, Lionel C., 2009 Fillmore, Ogden, Utah
*Dreikurs, Rudolph, 6 N. Michigan Ave., Chicago, Ill.
Dreisbach, Dodson E., Gibraltar, Pa.
Dressel, Paul L., Michigan State University, East Lansing, Mich.
Drew, Alfred S., Purdue University, Lafayette, Ind.
Drew, Robert E., Community Unit School Dist. 303, St. Charles, Ill.
Drexel, Karl O., 1005 Escobar St., Martinez, Calif.
Driver, Cecil E., Vandenberg Elem. School, APO, New York, N.Y.
Dropkin, Stanley, Queens College, Flushing, N.Y.
Drucker, Howard, 3393 Southwood Dr., San Luis Obispo, Calif.
Drummond, Harold D., Univ. of New Mexico, Albuquerque, N.Mex.
Drummond, William H., 623 S. Decatur, Olympia, Wash.
DuBois, Helen, Medical Center, Maple Ave. Ext., Glen Cove, N.Y.
Ducanis, Alex J., 230 N. Craig, Apt. 703, Pittsburgh, Pa.
Duckers, Ronald L., 320 Jon Court, Des Plaines, Ill.
Duckworth, Alice, 100 Reef Rd., Fairfield, Conn.
Dudley, James, Col. of Educ., Univ. of Maryland, College Park, Md.
Duff, Franklin L., Bur. of Instr. Res., Univ. of Illinois, Urbana, Ill.
Duffett, John W., 341 Bellefield Ave., Pittsburgh, Pa.
Duffey, Robert V., 9225 Limestone Pl., College Park, Md.
Dufford, William E., Box 651, Orangeburg, S.C.
Duffy, Bernard A., Seton Hall University, South Orange, N.J.
Duffy, Gerald G., 357 Michigan St. Univ., E. Lansing, Mich.
Duggan, John M., Vassar Col., Poughkeepsie, N.Y.
Duke, Ralph L., Sch. of Educ., University of Delaware, Newark, Del.
Dumler, Marvin J., Concordia Teachers College, River Forest, Ill.

Dunbar, Donald A., Mt. Lebanon Sch. Dist., Pittsburgh, Pa.
Duncan, Ernest R., Sch. of Educ., Rutgers Univ., New Brunswick, N.J.
Duncan, J. A., Agric. Hall, University of Wisconsin, Madison, Wis.
Duncan, William B., Miami Edison Senior High School, Miami, Fla.
Dunham, Ralph E., 2113 White Oaks Dr., Alexandria, Va.
Dunkel, Harold B., Dept. of Educ., University of Chicago, Chicago, Ill.
Dunkeld, Colin G., 414 W. Ells, Champaign, Ill.
Dunkle, Maurice Albert, Superintendent, Calver Co. Schls., Prince Frederick, Md.
Dunlap, William H., Hempfield Area Schl. Dist., Greensburg, Pa.
Dunn, Mary S., Chicago State College, Chicago, Ill.
Dunnell, John P., 1004 Wenonah, Oak Park, Ill.
Dunning, Frances E., 125 Owre Hall, Univ. of Minnesota, Minneapolis, Minn.
Durant, Adrian J., Jr., 1115 Holiday Park Dr., Champaign, Ill.
Durante, Spencer E., 2219 Senior Dr., Charlotte, N.C.
Durflinger, Glenn W., 5665 Cielo Ave., Goleta, Calif.
Durkee, Frank M., Box 911, Harrisburg, Pa.
Durost, Walter N., RFD # 2, Box 120, Dover, N.H.
Durr, William K., Col. of Educ., Michigan State Univ., East Lansing, Mich.
Durrell, Donald D., Boston University, 332 Bay State Rd., Boston, Mass.
Dussault, Gilles, 926 Ave. de Bourgogne, Quebec 10, Quebec, Canada
Duthler, B. Thomas, 3444 Drummond Rd., Toledo, Ohio
Dutro, Richard F., Lakewood Public Schools, Lakewood, Ohio
Dutton, Wilbur H., 1913 Greenfield Ave., Los Angeles, Calif.
DuVall, Lloyd A., 30 Mountain Rise, Fairport, N.Y.
Dwyer, Roy E., P.O. Box 343, Thonotasassa, Fla.
Dyer, Frank E., Supt., Delano Jt. Union High School, Delano, Calif.
Dygert, Marian, 1930 Sylvan Ave., Grand Rapids, Mich.
Dyke, Elwood E., Southport Elem. Sch., 723—76th St., Kenosha, Wis.
Dykes, Mrs. Alma, 9755 Cincinnati-Columbus Rd., Cincinnati, Ohio
Dyson, R. E., 202 Northlawn Ave., East Lansing, Mich.
Dziuban, Charles D., 101 Femrite Dr., Madison, Wis.

Eaddy, Edward Allen, Superintendent of Schools, Georgetown, S.C.
Earles, Lucius C., Jr., 123 Peabody St., N.W., Washington, D.C.
Eash, Maurice J., Univ. of Ill. (Circle Campus), Chicago, Ill.
Easterly, Ambrose, Harper Col. Library, Palatine, Ill.
Eastman, Kermit L., Dist. Admin. Bldg., 13th Av. & 7th St.S., St. Cloud, Minn.
Eaton, Albert G., Saybrook School, Ashtabula, Ohio
Eaton, Edward J., 4042 N.W. 35th Ave., Fort Lauderdale, Fla.
Ebel, Robert L., Michigan State University, East Lansing, Mich.
Eberle, August William, Indiana Univ., Bloomington, Ind.
Eberman, Paul W., 1801 John F. Kennedy Blvd., Philadelphia, Pa.
Eboch, Sidney C., Dept. of Educ., Ohio State Univ., Columbus, Ohio
Echevarris, Major Ramon L., Inter. Amer. University, APO, New York, N.Y.
Eckert, Edwin K., Supt., Lutheran Schools, Chicago, Ill.
Eckert, Ruth E., Col. of Educ., University of Minnesota, Minneapolis, Minn.
Eckhardt, John W., 2600 Elm St., Bakersfield, Calif.
Eddins, William N., P.O. Box 9036, Crestline Heights Br., Birmingham, Ala.
Edelfelt, Roy A., 1201 - 16th St. N.W., Washington, D.C.
Edelmann, Anne M., 7614 Garden Rd., Cheltenham, Pa.
Edelstein, David S., Connecticut State College, Yonkers, N.Y.
Eden, Donald F., Adams State College, Alamosa, Colo.
Edick, Helen M., 125 Terry Rd., Hartford, Conn.
Edinger, Lois V., University of North Carolina, Greensboro, N.C.
Edmundson, W. Dean, Detroit Public Schls., 12021 Evanston, Detroit, Mich.
Edson, William H., 206 Burton Hall, Univ. of Minnesota, Minneapolis, Minn.
Edstrom, A. E., Senior High School, 1001 State Hwy., Hopkins, Minn.
Edwards, Andrew S., Georgia Southern College, Statesboro, Ga.
Edwards, Arthur U., Eastern Illinois University, Charleston, Ill.
Edwards, Carlos R., Boys High School, Brooklyn, N.Y.
Edwards, Charles, Illinois State Univ., Normal, Ill.

Edwards, Gerald F., 3075 - 14 Ave., Marion, Iowa
Edwards, Joseph O., Jr., 251 - 13th St., Arcata, Calif.
Edwards, T. Bentley, Sch. of Educ., Univ. of California, Berkeley, Calif.
Egan, Gerard V., 79 Ward Pl., South Orange, N.J.
Egelston, Elwood, Jr., Illinois State University, Normal, Ill.
Egge, Donald E., 325 N.E. 10th St., Newport, Oreg.
Eggerding, Roland F., Lutheran High School, South, St. Louis, Mo.
Eherenman, William C., Wisconsin State University, Platteville, Wis.
Ehlers, Henry J., Duluth Branch, University of Minnesota, Duluth, Minn.
Ehrlich, Emanuel, 92 Joyce Rd., East Chester, N.Y.
Eibler, Herbert J., University of Michigan, Ann Arbor, Mich.
Eicher, Charles E., 936 N. Summit, Madison, S. Dak.
Eichholz, G. C., Educ. Research, Inc., Tampa, Fla.
Eidell, Terry L., CAESA, Univ. of Oregon, Eugene, Oreg.
Eikaas, Alf T., Kjolsdalen, Nordfjord, Norway
Einolf, W. L., Birchrunville, Pa.
Eisenstein, Herbert S., Pennsylvania State University, Middletown, Pa.
Eiserer, Paul E., Tchrs. Col., Columbia University, New York, N.Y.
Eisner, Elliot W., Stanford University, Stanford, Calif.
Eiszler, Charles F., Jr., 714 Superior Ave., N.W., Cleveland, Ohio
Eke, Verne M., 954 S. Carondelet St., Los Angeles, Calif.
Eko, Ewa U., 2000 L St. N.W., Suite 606, Washington, D.C.
Elder, Rachel A., Tolman Hall, University of California, Berkeley, Calif.
Elder, Richard D., Child Study Cent., Kent State Univ., Kent, Ohio
Eldridge, M. L., Spring Branch Elem. Sch., Houston, Tex.
Elie, Marie-Therese, 2920 Boulevard Rosemont, Montreal 36, Quebec, Canada
Elkins, Keith, 7330 Pershing Blvd., University City, Mo.
Elland, A. H., Hutchinson Junior College, 1300 Plum Hutchinson, Kans.
Elle, Martin J., Southern Oregon College, Ashland, Oreg.
Ellenburg, Fred C., Rt. #1, Grove Lakes, Statesboro, Ga.
Ellerbrook, Louis William, Box 4628, S.F.A. Sta., Nacogdoches, Tex.
Ellery, Marilynne, Ohio Northern University, Ada, Ohio
Ellingson, Mark, Rochester Institute of Technology, Rochester, N.Y.
Elliott, Arthur H., Simon Fraser University, Burnaby 2, B.C., Canada
Elliott, David L., Sch. of Educ., Univ. of California, Berkeley, Calif.
Ellis, Mrs. Celia Diamond, 1125 S. LaJolla Ave., Los Angeles, Calif.
Ellis, Frederick E., Western Washington State Col., Bellingham, Wash.
Ellis, Gerald W., Birmingham Pub. Schs., Birmingham, Mich.
Ellis, G. W., Drew Junior High School, 1055 N.W. 52nd St., Miami, Fla.
Ellis, John F., Simon Fraser University, Burnaby, B.C., Canada
Ellis, Joseph R., Northern Illinois University, DeKalb, Ill.
Ellis, Robert L., 1125 S. LaJolla Ave., Los Angeles, Calif.
Ellison, Alfred, New York University, Washington Sq., New York, N.Y.
Ellison, F. Robert, 1354 Laurel St., Casper, Wyo.
Ellison, Jack L., Francis W. Parker Sch., Chicago, Ill.
Ellner, Carolyn Lipton, 426 S. McCadden Pl., Los Angeles, Calif.
Ellson, Douglas G., Indiana University, Bloomington, Ind.
Ellwein, Mrs. Ileane, 2905 S. Jefferson St., Sioux Falls, S. Dak.
Elstein, Arthur J., Olin Health Center, MSU, E. Lansing, Mich.
Emans, Robert, 29 W. Woodruff Ave., Columbus, Ohio
Emery, Harriet E., 15200 McLain Ave., Allen Park, Mich.
Emeson, David L., 210 - 5th Ave. N.E., Independence, Iowa
Emmet, Thomas A., 5440 Cass Ave., Suite 412, Detroit, Mich.
Emmons, Jean F., Col. of Educ., Ohio State University, Columbus, Ohio
Ende, Russell S., Northern Illinois University, DeKalb, Ill.
Endres, Mary P., Purdue University, Lafayette, Ind.
Endres, Richard J., 707 Salisbury Rd., Columbus, Ohio
Engelhardt, Jack E., 1500 Maywood Ave., Ann Arbor, Mich.
Engelhardt, Nickolaus L., Jr., Purdy Station, N.Y.
Engle, Shirley H., Sch. of Educ., Indiana University, Bloomington, Ind.
Engler, David, McGraw-Hill Book Co., New York, N.Y.

English, John W., Superintendent of Schools, Southfield, Mich.
English, Marvin D., National College of Education, Evanston, Ill.
Enoch, June E., Manchester College, North Manchester, Ind.
Entwisle, Doris, Johns Hopkins University, Baltimore, Md.
Eraut, Michael R., University of Sussex, Brighton, Sussex, England
Erbe, Wesley A., Col. of Educ., Univ. of Iowa, Iowa City, Iowa
Erdman, Robert L., Univ. of Utah, Salt Lake City, Utah
Erickson, Harley E., University of North Iowa, Cedar Falls, Iowa
Erickson, L. W., Sch. of Educ., Univ. of California, Los Angeles, Calif.
Erickson, Ralph J., Virginia Union University, Richmond, Va.
Erickson, Ralph W., 105 Third Ave., Columbus, Miss.
Erickson, Wayne C., 266 Orrin St., Winona, Minn.
Ersted, Ruth, State Department of Education, St. Paul, Minn.
Ervin, John B., 5933 Enright St., St. Louis, Mo.
Ervin, William B., 1 Midland Pl., Newark, N.J.
Erxleben, Arnold C., 157 Bemis Dr., Seward, Nebr.
Erzen, Richard G., 931 Bartlett Terr., Libertyville, Ill.
Eson, Morris E., State University of New York, Albany, N.Y.
Essig, Lester Clay, Jr., Utah State University, Logan, Utah
Estes, Kenneth A., 1722 Woodhurst Ave., Bowling Green, Ky.
Estes, Sidney H., Urban Lab. in Educ., Atlanta, Ga.
Estle, Glen L., 1000 Pfingsten Rd., Northbrook, Ill.
Estvan, Frank J., Col. of Educ., Wayne State Univ., Detroit, Mich.
Etheridge, Robert F., Miami University, Oxford, Ohio
Etscovitz, Lionel, 5 Shaw Pl., Lexington, Mass.
Ettinger, Mrs. Bernadette C., 474 Brooklyn Blvd., Brightwaters, L.I., N.Y.
Eurich, Alvin C., Acad. for Educ. Dev., 437 Madison Ave., New York, N.Y.
Evans, Edgar Ernest, Alabama State College, Montgomery, Ala.
Evans, Harley, Jr., 35952 Matoma Dr., Eastlake, Ohio
Evans, J. Bernard, 3163 Warrington Rd., Shaker Heights, Ohio
Evans, Orlynn R., F-15 So. Campus Court, Lafayette, Ind.
Evans, Ralph F., Fresno State College, Fresno, Calif.
Evans, Rupert N., Col. of Educ., Univ. of Illinois, Urbana, Ill.
Evans, Warren D., 34 E. Winding Rd., Mechanicsburg, Pa.
Eve, Arthur W., Schl. of Educ., Univ. of Mass., Amherst, Mass.
Even, Mary Jane, 1815 University Ave., Madison, Wis.
Evenson, Warren L., 1528 S. Douglas St., Springfield, Ill.
Evertts, Eldonna L., N.C.T.E., Champaign, Ill.
* Ewigleben, Mrs. Muriel, 3727 Weisser Park Ave., Ft. Wayne, Ind.
Ewing, Parmer L., Dept. of Educ. Admin., So. Ill. Univ., Carbondale, Ill.
Eyster, Elvin S., Dept. of Bus. Educ., Indiana Univ., Bloomington, Ind.

Facok, John, Tchrs. Col., Columbia Univ., New York, N.Y.
Fadden, Joseph A., Marywood College, Scranton, Pa.
Faddis, Mrs. Gabrielle J., Col. of Educ., Temple University, Philadelphia, Pa.
Failor, Harvey A., 13800 Ford Road, Dearborn, Mich.
Fair, Jean E., Wayne State University, Detroit, Mich.
Fairbanks, Gar, Supt. of Schools, Rocky Hill, Conn.
Falk, Alma M., 1330 New Hampshire Ave., N.W., Washington, D.C.
Falk, Philip H., 3721 Council Crest, Madison, Wis.
Fallon, Berlie J., Dept. of Educ., Texas Technological Col., Lubbock, Tex.
Fanslow, W. V., R.F.D. 3, Amherst, Mass.
Farber, Bernard E., Brady Elementary School, Detroit, Mich.
Farber, Irvin J., 10823 Kelvin Ave., Philadelphia, Pa.
Fargen, J. Jerome, Catherine Spalding College, Louisville, Ky.
Farley, Gilbert J., Belmont Abbey Col., Belmont, N.C.
Farmer, Geraldine, University of Alberta, Edmonton, Alba., Canada
Farrell, Anne B., 342-74th St., Brooklyn, N.Y.
Farrell, Joseph I., 109 Cornell Ave., Hawthorne, N.J.
Farrell, Mathew C., University of Scranton, Scranton, Pa.
Farris, Dan C., 954 N. Atherton, State College, Pa.

Fasan, Walter R., 3401 West 65th Pl., Chicago, Ill.
Faust, Claire Edward, 206 Floral Ave., Mankato, Minn.
Fawcett, Claude W., Sch. of Educ., Univ. of California, Los Angeles, Calif.
Fawley, Paul C., Dept. of Educ., University of Utah, Salt Lake City, Utah
Fay, Leo C., Sch. of Educ., Indiana University, Bloomington, Ind.
Fay, Robert S., Schl. of Educ., Boston Univ., Boston, Mass.
Fearn, Leif, San Diego State Col., San Diego, Calif.
Fee, Edward M., Bok Technical High School, Philadelphia, Pa.
Feely, Robert W., 10117 Albany Ave., Evergreen Park, Ill.
Feingold, S. Norman, 1640 Rhode Island Ave., N.W., Washington, D.C.
Felsenthal, Mrs. Norman, 422 Waldron Ave., West Lafayette, Ind.
Feltner, Bill D., Inst. of Higher Educ., Univ. of Georgia, Athens, Ga.
Fenderson, Julia K., Culver City Unified Schools, Culver City, Calif.
Fennema, Elizabeth H., 121 N. Allen, Madison, Wis.
Fenollosa, George M., Houghton Mifflin Co., 110 Tremont St., Boston, Mass.
Fenske, Arthur S., 435 Liberty St., Belmont, Wis.
Feringer, F. R., Western Washington State College, Bellingham, Wash.
Ferris, Donald, 1316 N. Salisbury St., West Lafayette, Ind.
Ferris, Francis X, Spencerport, N.Y.
Ferry, Richard E., 236 Delmar, Decatur, Ill.
Fesperman, Mrs. Kathleen C., Newberry College, Newberry, S.C.
Feuerbach, F. Kenneth, Hammond High School, Hammond, Ind.
Feuers, Mrs. Stelle, Pierce College, Woodland Hills, Calif.
Ficek, Daniel E., 315 Arno, S.E., Albuquerque, N.Mex.
Fiedler, E. L., Superintendent of Schools, Abilene, Kans.
Field, Robert L., 1506 Jackson St., Oshkosh, Wis.
Fields, Ralph R., Tchrs. Col., Columbia University, New York, N.Y.
Fielstra, Clarence, Sch. of Educ., Univ. of California, Los Angeles, Calif.
Fielstra, Helen, San Fernando Valley State College, Northridge, Calif.
Fieman, Marvin E., 305 S. Arnaz Dr., Los Angeles, Calif.
Figurel, J. Allen, Indiana University, N.W. Campus, Gary, Ind.
Filbeck, Orval, Abilene Christian College, Abilene, Tex.
Filbeck, Robert W., Lincoln Job Corps Center, Lincoln, Nebr.
Fillbrandt, James R., 601 Taylor, Bakersfield, Calif.
Fillmer, Henry T., University of Florida, Gainesville, Fla.
Filosa, Mary G., 32 Ross Hall Blvd., No., Piscataway, N.J.
Fina, Robert P., 2625 Chew St., Allentown, Pa.
Finch, F. H., Col. of Educ., Univ. of Illinois, Urbana, Ill.
Finder, Morris, State University of N.Y., Albany, N.Y.
Findlay, Stephen W., Delbarton School, Morristown, N.J.
Findley, Dale, 1639 S. Sixth St., Terre Haute, Ind.
Findley, Warren G., Col. of Educ., University of Georgia, Athens, Ga.
Findley, William H., Jr., 111 Curtiss Pkwy., Miami Springs, Fla.
Fink, Abel K., State University College, 1300 Elmwood Ave., Buffalo, N.Y.
Fink, Herbert J., Tuley High School, 1313 N. Claremont Ave., Chicago, Ill.
Fink, Martin B., 3713 Merridan Dr., Concord, Calif.
Finstein, Milton W., Div. of Educ., Indiana Univ., Gary, Ind.
Finster, Virginia, 2203 Mocking Bird Drive, Baytown, Tex.
Finucan, J. Thomas, Assumption High School, Wisconsin Rapids, Wis.
Firth, Gerald R., University of Alabama, Tuscaloosa, Ala.
Fischer, John H., Tchrs. Col., Columbia University, New York, N.Y.
Fischer, Louis, San Fernando Valley State College, Northridge, Calif.
Fischler, Abraham S., 5000 Taylor St., Ft. Lauderdale, Fla.
Fischoff, Ephraim, 15 Riverview Pl., Lynchburg, Va.
Fish, Lawrence D., NWREL, 710 S.W. 2nd Ave., Portland, Oreg.
Fishback, Woodson W., Southern Illinois University, Carbondale, Ill.
Fishco, Daniel T., Southern Ill. University, Carbondale, Ill.
Fishell, Kenneth N., Syracuse University, Syracuse, N.Y.
Fisher, Betty G., 49 E. College Ave., Springfield, Ohio
Fisher, Carol M., R.R. # 2, 5747 Detrick-Jordan Rd., Springfield, Ohio
Fisher, George, Ohio State University, Columbus, Ohio

Fisher, Ijourie Stocks, Miami-Dade Junior College, Miami, Fla.
Fisher, Lawrence A., Col. of Medicine, Univ. of Illinois, Chicago, Ill.
Fisher, Robert D., 4930 Sharon Ave., Columbus, Ohio
* Fisher, Mrs. Welthy H., Literacy Village, P.O. Singar Nagar, Lucknow, U.P., India
Fisher, Welthy H., 50 W. 67th St., New York, N.Y.
Fishler, Edward, 72 Hedgerow Lane, Commack, L.I., N.Y.
Fisk, Robert S., State University of New York, Buffalo, N.Y.
Fitzgerald, William F., 5835 Kimbark Ave., Chicago, Ill.
Fitzpatrick, E. D., Illinois State University, Normal, Ill.
Flagg, E. Alma, 44 Stengel Ave., Newark, N.J.
Flamand, Ruth K., 72 Goldenridge Dr., Levittown, Pa.
Flanagan, John C., P.O. Box 1113, Palo Alto, Calif.
Flanders, Ned A., Sch. of Educ., Univ. of Mich., Ann Arbor, Mich.
Fleck, Henrietta, H.E. Dept., New York Univ., Washington Sq., New York, N.Y.
Fleckles, David E., San Jose Unified Schl. Dist., San Jose, Calif.
Fleming, Elyse S., Western Reserve University, Cleveland, Ohio
Fleming, Harold D., 2020 Birchmont Dr., Bemidji, Minn.
Fleming, Robert S., Virginia Commonwealth Univ., Richmond, Va.
Fletcher, Ruby J., University of Utah, Salt Lake City, Utah
Fliegel, Norris E., 98 Riverside Dr., New York, N.Y.
Fliegler, Louis A., Dept. of Spec. Educ., Kent State Univ., Kent, Ohio
Fligor, R. J., Southern Illinois University, Carbondale, Ill.
Flint, Jack M., Kansas City Community Junior College, Kansas City, Kans.
Flodin, Raymond, P.O. Box 213, 24 W. Spring St., Oxford, Ohio
Flores, Vetal, 2818 Southland Blvd., San Angelo, Tex.
Flower, George E., Ontario Inst. for Studies in Educ., Toronto, Ont., Canada
Flowers, Anne, Box 3231, Columbia, S.C.
Flug, Eugene R. F., Stout State University, Menomonie, Wis.
Fluitt, John L., Col. of Educ., Louisiana State Univ., New Orleans, La.
Fochs, John S., 1732 Wauwatosa Ave., Wauwatosa, Wis.
Focht, James R., Educ. Dept., Salisbury State Col., Salisbury, Md.
Fogg, William E., Long Beach State College, Long Beach, Calif.
Foley, Robert L., 2901 S. Parkway, Chicago, Ill.
Fonacier, Andres M., Laoag, Ilocos Norte, Philippines
Foord, James, University of Manchester, Manchester, England
Foran, Mary Ellen, 6301 N. Sheridan Rd., Chicago, Ill.
Foran, William L., 1007 Alberta, Oceanside, Calif.
Forbes, Beverly A., Univ. of Washington, Renton, Wash.
Forbing, Shirley E., California State College, Long Beach, Calif.
Force, Dewey G., Jr., Pattee Hall, Univ. of Minnesota, Minneapolis, Minn.
Force, William R., 1875 Scully Drive, Mt. Pleasant, Mich.
Ford, Gervais W., San Jose State College, San Jose, Calif.
Ford, Harry J., 19009 E. Badillo St., Covina, Calif.
Ford, John, 315 Ashbourne Rd., Elkins Park, Pa.
Ford, Luther L., P.O. Box 805, Grambling, La.
Ford, Roxana R., Sch. of Home Econ., Univ. of Minnesota, St. Paul, Minn.
Forer, Ruth K., 6013 Greenbush Ave., Van Nuys, Calif.
Foresi, Joseph, Jr., 29-C Hasbrouck Apt., Ithaca, N.Y.
Forrester, Carl M., Lake Park H.S., 6 N. 600 Medina Rd., Roselle, Ill.
Fortess, Lillian, 96 Bay State Rd., Boston, Mass.
Fortin, John E., Murray State University, Murray, Ky.
Fosback, Alta B., P.O. Box 443, Carlton, Oreg.
Foshay, Arthur W., Tchrs. Col., Columbia University, New York, N.Y.
Fossett, Barbara, Box 323, Churchville, N.Y.
Fossieck, Theodore H., The Milne Sch., State Univ. of New York, Albany, N.Y.
Foster, E. M., Fresno State Col., 4021 Mt. Vernon Ave., Bakersfield, Calif.
Foster, Gordon, Merrick Hall, Univ. of Miami, Coral Gables, Fla.
Fournier, Rev. Edmond A., 241 Pearson Ave., Ferndale, Mich.
Fowler, William, Ontario Inst. for Stud. in Educ., Toronto, Ont., Canada
Fowler, Wilton R., Jr., 1120 Forest Oaks, Hurst, Tex.

Fowlkes, John Guy, 204 Educ. Bldg., Univ. of Wisconsin, Madison, Wis.
Fox, Marion W., 3200 Atlantic Ave., Atlantic City, N.J.
Fox, Robert S., 102 Univ. Sch., University of Michigan, Ann Arbor, Mich.
Frain, Thomas J., 1931 Brunswick Ave., Trenton, N.J.
France, Harold S., Memorial Schl., Grant Ave., Maywood, N.J.
Francis, Ida L., Public Schools, Somerville, N.J.
Francis, Rodney I., 16 London Dr., W. Wollongong, N.S.W., Australia
Frandsen, Arden N., Utah State University, Logan, Utah
Frankland, Elizabeth M., 512 Algoma Blvd., Oshkosh, Wis.
Franklin, Arthur J., Univ. of So. Louisiana, Lafayette, La.
Franklin, Ruby Holden, Roosevelt University, 430 S. Michigan Ave., Chicago, Ill.
Franson, Arthur H., 50 N. Spring, LaGrange, Ill.
Franz, Evelyn B., Dept. of Educ., Trenton State College, Trenton, N.J.
Franzen, William L., Col. of Educ., Univ. of Toledo, Toledo, Ohio
Frase, H. Weldon. 1635 Hutchinson, S.E., Grand Rapids, Mich.
Fraser, Dorothy McClure, Hunter College, New York, N.Y.
Fraser, Hugh W., 502 Browncroft Blvd., Rochester, N.Y.
Fraser, Rosemary, Miami University, Oxford, Ohio
Frater, Dorothy, 632 W. Prospect Ave., State College, Pa.
Frazier, Andrew J., 303 Biddle Ave., Harrison, Ohio
Fred, Bernhart G., 108 McCormick Dr., DeKalb, Ill.
Frederick, William C., Shoreline School District, Seattle, Wash.
Frederickson, Wade, State Dep. of Educ., Santa Fe, N. Mex.
Fredman, Norman, 76-07 168th St., Flushing, N.Y.
Fredrick, James R., Arizona State College, Flagstaff, Ariz.
Freeberg, Howard, 207 Sixth Ave. East, West Fargo, N.Dak.
Freeman, Daniel M., R.D. 1, W. Springfield, Pa.
Freeman, Donald, 831 Crown Blvd., East Lansing, Mich.
Freeman, Kenneth H., 3308 59th St., Lubbock, Tex.
Freeman, Robert P., 406 Hollywood Ave., Hampton, Va.
Freeman, Ruges Richmond, Jr., 8027 Bennett Ave., St. Louis, Mo.
Fremont, Herbert, Queens College, Flushing, N.Y.
French, Henry P., 2 Bedford Way, Pittsford, N.Y.
French, William M., Muhlenberg College, Allentown, Pa.
Frerichs, Allen H., Northern Illinois University, DeKalb, Ill.
Fretwell, Elbert K., Jr., Pres., State Univ. Col., Buffalo, N.Y.
Freund, Evelyn, 5954 Guilford, Detroit, Mich.
Frick, Herman L., Florida State University, Tallahassee, Fla.
Frick, Ralph, 6940 Roswell Rd. N.W., Atlanta, Ga.
Fridlund, John V., 414 N. Elm St., Itasca, Ill.
Frieberg, Carter N., Loyola University, 820 N. Michigan Ave., Chicago, Ill.
Friedhoff, Walter H., Illinois State University, Normal, Ill.
Friedrich, Kurt, San Diego State College, San Diego, Calif.
Frisk, Jack L., Supt. of Schools, Yakima, Wash.
Froehlich, Gustave J., Bur. of Inst. Res., Univ. of Illinois, Urbana, Ill.
Frohnhoefer, Joseph J., Jr., State Univ. Col. at Buffalo, Buffalo, N.Y.
Froling, Raymond S., Nether Providence Sch. Dist., Wallingford, Pa.
Frost, Ralph J., Jr., Maine Twp. High School East, Park Ridge, Ill.
Frye, Richard M., Purdue University, Lafayette, Ind.
Fryer, Thomas W., Jr., Miami-Dade Junior College, Miami, Fla.
Fuglaar, Ollie B., Louisiana State University, Baton Rouge, La.
Full, Harold, 870 United Nations Plaza, New York, N.Y.
Fullagar, William A., Box 40, Mendon, N.Y.
Fuller, R. Buckminster, Southern Illinois University, Carbondale, Ill.
Fullerton, Craig K., 2712 North 52nd St., Omaha, Nebr.
Fultz, Mrs. Jane N., Col. of Educ., Univ. of Hawaii, Honolulu, Hawaii
Funderburk, Earl C., Fairfax County Schools, Fairfax, Va.
Furey, Mary Z., 7926 Jackson Rd., Alexandria, Va.
Furlow, Mrs. Florine D., 2968 Collier Dr., N.W., Atlanta, Ga.
Furst, Philip W., 790 Riverside Dr., New York, N.Y.
Futch, Olivia, Woman's College, Furman University, Greenville, S.C.

Gaetano, Mary Ann, 2648 Eaton Rd., University Hts., Ohio
Gage, George J., Univ. of California, Los, Angeles, Calif.
Gage, N. L., Sch. of Educ., Stanford University, Stanford, Calif.
Gaines, Berthera E., 4208 S. Galvez St., New Orleans, La.
Gaines, John C., State University of Tennessee, Nashville, Tenn.
Gaiter, Worrell G., Florida A. & M. University, Tallahassee, Fla.
Galbreath, Dorothy J., 3001 South Parkway, Chicago, Ill.
Gale, Ann V., 403 Jackson Ave., Glencoe, Ill.
Gale, Frederick, 20820 River Rd., Haney, B.C., Canada
Gall, Morris, Educ. Direction, Inc., Westport, Conn.
Gallicchio, Francis A., 325 College Ave., Mt. Pleasant, Pa.
Gallington, Ralph O., Florida State University, Tallahassee, Fla.
Galtere, Gordon R., Rt. 206, Red Lion, Vincentown, N.J.
Gaman, Vivian C., Yeshiva Univ., New York, N.Y.
Gambert, Charles A., 24 Bennett Village Terr., Buffalo, N.Y.
Gambino, Vincent, Dept. of Educ., Roosevelt University, Chicago, Ill.
Gamelin, Francis C., 2359-29th St., Rock Island, Ill.
Gandy, Frances C., 2597 Avery Ave., Memphis, Tenn.
Gandy, Thomas W., Berry Col., Mt. Berry, Ga.
Gannon, John T., Supt. of Schools, Eagle Grove, Iowa
Gans, Leo, 4300 West 62nd St., Indianapolis, Ind.
Gansberg, Lucille, 2255-C Goodrich St., Sacramento, Calif.
Gantz, Ralph M., Superintendent of Schools, New Britain, Conn.
Garbe, Lester, 2110 W. Marne Ave., Milwaukee, Wis.
Garbee, Frederick E., State Dept. of Educ., Los Angeles, Calif.
Garbel, Marianne, 6732 Crandon Ave., Chicago, Ill.
Garber, M. Delott, Central Connecticut State College, New Britain, Conn.
Gardiner, Robert J., Asst. Prin., Bakersfield H.S., Bakersfield, Calif.
Gardner, Harrison, 1007 Ravinia, West Lafayette, Ind.
Garetto, Lawrence A., 5162 Walnut Ave., Chino, Calif.
Garfinkel, Alan, Dept. of Educ., Okla. St. Univ., Stillwater, Okla.
Garinger, Elmer H., 2625 Briarcliff Pl., Charlotte, N.C.
Garland, Colden G., 223 Varinna Dr., Rochester, N.Y.
Garlich, Marvin O., 8901 McVicker Ave., Morton Grove, Ill.
Garoutte, Bill Charles, Univ. of California Medical Center, San Francisco, Calif.
Garrett, Charles G., 2130 Tarpon Road, Naples, Fla.
Garrison, C. B., Supt. of Schools, Pine Bluff, Ark.
Garrison, Harry L., 4802 E. Mercer Way, Mercer Island, Wash.
Garrison, Martin B., Supt. of Schools, University City, Mo.
Garrity, William J., Jr., 45 Gaynos Dr., Bridgeport, Conn.
Gartrell, Callie, P.O. Box 33, Cheboygan, Mich.
Garvey, Reba, 12700 Fairhill Rd., Cleveland, Ohio
Gaston, Don, Couns., New Rochelle High School, New Rochelle, N.Y.
*Gates, Arthur I., Tchrs. Col., Columbia University, New York, N.Y.
Gates, James O., Jr., Northwest Missouri St. Col., Maryvillle, Mo.
Gatti, Ora J., 20 Irving St., Worcester, Mass.
Gaudette, R. Dean, Eastern Washington St. Col., Cheney, Wash.
Gauerke, Warren E., 316 Merriweather Rd., Grosse Pointe Farms, Mich.
Gaunt, W. F., Sch. Dist. of Affton, 8309 Mackenzie Rd., Affton, Mo.
Gauvey, Ralph E., Roger Williams Jr. Col., Providence, R.I.
Gavin, Ann M., 617 Broad St., Bldg. 10 #9, East Weymouth, Mass.
Gayheart, S. Jack, 315 S. Locust St., Apt. 4, Oxford, Ohio
Gaynor, Alan K., 358 Alex. Colony East, Columbus, Ohio
Gayo, Francisco, Box 526, Eigenmann Hall, Bloomington, Ind.
Gazelle, Hazel N., 60 N. Auburn Ave., Sierra Madre, Calif.
Geckler, Jack W., Asst. Supt., Oak Ridge Schools, Oak Ridge, Tenn.
Geeslin, Robert H., 204 N. Orange St., Madison, Fla.
Geigle, Ralph C., Superintendent of Schools, Reading, Pa.
Geiken, Lloyd A., Prin., Shorewood High School, Shorewood, Wis.
Geiss, Doris T., 117 Southern Blvd., Albany, N.Y.
Geitgey, Richard, 1026 Menlo Circle, Ashland, Ohio

Gelerinter, Alfred, Sch. Psych., Rochester City Schools, Rochester, N.Y.
Geller, Joshua S., 20539 Blackstone, Detroit, Mich.
Gellman, William, Jewish Vocational Service Library, Chicago, Ill.
Geng, George, Glassboro State College, Glassboro, N.J.
Gentry, George H., Box 663, Baytown, Tex.
George, Howard A., Northwest Missouri State College, Maryville, Mo.
George, John E., Sch. of Educ., Univ. of South Carolina, Columbia, S.C.
Georgiades, William, Univ. of Southern California, Los Angeles, Calif.
Georgiady, Nicholas P., 110 W. Bull Run Dr., Oxford, Ohio
Gephart, Woodrow W., Supt. of Schools, Jefferson, Ohio
Geraty, T. S., 7422 Hancock Ave., Takoma Park, Md.
Gerber, Wayne J., Bethel College, Mishawaka, Ind.
Gerhardt, Frank, 2437 Lamberton, Cleveland Hghts., Ohio
Gerlach, Vernon S., Arizona State University, Tempe, Ariz.
Gerletti, John D., 1901 Mission St., South Pasadena, Calif.
Gerlock, D. E., Dept. of Educ., Valdosta State College, Valdosta, Ga.
Gernet, Herbert F., 414 Park Ave., Leonia, N.J.
Gerut, Ronald B., 9636 N. Kenton Ave., Skokie, Ill.
Gesler, Harriet L., 70 Agnes Dr., Manchester, Conn.
Gest, Mrs. Viola S., P.O. Box 254, Seguin, Tex.
Getz, Howard E., Westbrook Addn., Morton, Ill.
Getzels, J. W., Dept. of Educ., University of Chicago, Chicago, Ill.
Geyer, John J., Sch. of Educ., Rutgers Univ., New Brunswick, N.J.
Ghalib, Hanna, P. O. Box 4638, Beirut, Lebanon
Gialas, George J., 1150 Wayland Ave., Cornwells Heights, Pa.
Gibbons, Constance M., 74 Franklin Ave., Oakville, Conn.
Gibbs, Edward Delmar, Univ. of Puget Sound, Tacoma, Wash.
Gibbs, Edward, III, 1145 Clinton Ter., South Plainfield, N.J.
Gibbs, Gloria Stanley, 501 East 32nd St., Chicago, Ill.
Gibbs, John Donald, 1147 S. Ash St., Moses Lake, Wash.
Gibbs, Wesley, Superintendent, Dist. No. 68, 9300 N. Kenton, Skokie, Ill.
Gibert, James M., Randolph-Macon Woman's Col., Lynchburg, Va.
Gibson, Charles H., Eastern Kentucky Univ., Richmond, Ky.
Gibson, Mrs. Kathryn Snell, Prairie View A & M College, Prairie View, Tex.
Gibson, R. Oliver, State University of New York, Buffalo, N.Y.
Giesecke, G. Ernst, Provost, University of Toledo, Toledo, Ohio
Giesy, John P., 1017 Blanchard, Flint, Mich.
Gilbert, Daniel, 8446 Major, Morton Grove, Ill.
Gilbert, Mrs. Doris Wilcox, 1044 Euclid Ave., Berkeley, Calif.
Gilbert, Floyd O., Minnesota State College, St. Cloud, Minn.
Gilbert, Harry B., Dept. of Educ., Fordham University, Bronx, N.Y.
Gilbert, Jerome H., 815 Ashbury, El Cerrito, Calif.
Gilbert, John H., Dept. of Educ., Monmouth College, West Long Branch, N.J.
Gilbert, William B., Onondaga Central School, Nedrow, N.Y.
Giles, LeRoy H., University of Dubuque, Dubuque, Iowa
Gili, Joe D., West Washington High School, Campbellsburg, Ind.
Gilk, Edwin John, P.O. Box 642, Columbia Falls, Mont.
Gilkey, Richard W., 5516 S.W. Seymour St., Portland, Oreg.
Gill, Margaret, Mills College, Oakland, Calif.
Gilland, Thomas M., 504 S. Washington St., Greencastle, Pa.
Gillette, B. Frank, Superintendent of Schools, Los Gatos, Calif.
Gillis, Ruby, 6300 Grand River Ave., Detroit, Mich.
Gilmore, Douglas M., Central Michigan University, Mt. Pleasant, Mich.
Gimble, Mrs. Vernon S., 707 N. Main St., Cheboygan, Mich.
Gingerich, Julia B., 1408 Lewis, Des Moines, Iowa
Giroux, Robert J., Clarke Col., Dubuque, Iowa
Gittler, Joseph B., Yeshiva Univ., New York, N.Y.
Glaess, Herman L., Concordia Teachers College, Seward, Nebr.
Glaser, Robert, Res. & Dev. Cent., Univ. of Pittsburgh, Pittsburgh, Pa.
Glasman, Naftaly S., 404 Peach Grove Lane, Santa Barbara, Calif.
Glasow, Ogden L., P.O. Box 143, Macomb, Ill.

Glass, Olive Jewell, 3910 Latimer St., Dallas, Tex.
Glassman, Milton R., 520 Silver Oaks Dr., Kent, Ohio
Glatt, Charles A., Sch. of Educ., Ohio State Univ., Columbus, Ohio
Glendenning, Donald E., 6 Johnson Ave., Charlottetown, P.E.I., Canada
Glicken, Irwin J., 2135 W. Walters, Northbrook, Ill.
Glock, Marvin D., Stone Hall, Cornell University, Ithaca, N.Y.
Glogau, Arthur H., Oregon College of Education, Monmouth, Oreg.
Glover, Robert H., Mutual Plaza, Durham, N.C.
Gobetz, Wallace, 540 East 22nd St., Brooklyn, N.Y.
Goble, Robert I., McGuffey No. 301, Miami University, Oxford, Ohio
Godden, Albert I., Old Dominion Col., Norfolk, Va.
Godfrey, Mary E., Pennsylvania State University, University Park, Pa.
Goebel, E. J., Supt., Archdiocese of Milwaukee, Milwaukee, Wis.
Goff, Robert J., Univ. of Massachusetts, Amherst, Mass.
Gold, Charles E., 1418 E. Colton Ave., Redlands, Calif.
Gold, Louis L., P.O. Box 171, Marion Center, Pa.
Gold, Milton J., Hunter College, 695 Park Ave., New York, N.Y.
Goldberg, Miriam L., Tchrs. Col., Columbia University, New York, N.Y.
Goldberg, Nathan, 75-47—196th St., Flushing, N.Y.
Goldhammer, Keith, 2929 Highland Way, Corvallis, Oreg.
Goldman, Bert A., Sch. of Educ., Univ. of North Carolina, Greensboro, N.C.
Goldman, Harvey, Col. of Educ., Univ. of Maryland, College Park, Md.
Goldman, Samuel, Sch. of Educ., Syracuse University, Syracuse, N.Y.
Goldner, Ralph H., Sch. of Educ., New York University, New York, N.Y.
Goldstein, Herbert, Yeshiva University, 55 Fifth Ave., New York, N.Y.
Goldstein, Sanford G., 115 Woodgate Terr., Rochester, N.Y.
Goltry, Keith, Dept. of Educ., Parsons College, Fairfield, Iowa
Gomberg, Adeline W., Beaver College, Glenside, Pa.
Gomes, Lawrence A., Jr., 4 Vincent Ave., Belmont, Mass.
Gonzalez, Alice M., University of Puerto Rico, Rio Piedras, Puerto Rico
Goo, Frederick J. K., c/o Bur. of Indian Affairs Sch., Barrow, Alaska
Good, Richard M., 12521 Eastbourne Dr., Silver Spring, Md.
Good, Warren R., 1604 Stony Run Dr., Northwood, Wilmington, Del.
Goodlad, John I., Sch. of Educ., Univ. of California, Los Angeles, Calif.
Goodman, John O., University of Connecticut, Storrs, Conn.
Goodman, Kenneth S., Wayne State Univ., Detroit, Mich.
Goodpaster, Robert L., University of Kentucky-Ashland Center, Ashland, Ky.
Goodside, Samuel, 504 Beach 139th St., Belle Harbor, L.I., N.Y.
Goodwin, William L., 14 Mt. Pleasant St., Winchester, Mass.
Googins, Duane G., 2964—116th Ave., N.W., Coon Rapids, Minn.
Goolsby, Thomas M., Res. and Dev. Cen., Univ. of Georgia, Athens, Ga.
Goossen, Carl V., 108 Burton Hall, Univ. of Minnesota, Minneapolis, Minn.
Gordon, Bill K., Marshall Univ., Huntington, W. Va.
Gordon, Mrs. Catherine J., 326 Wellesley Rd., Philadelphia, Pa.
Gordon, Irving, 3374 Curtis Dr., Hillcrest Heights, Md.
Gordon, Ted E., 317 N. Lucerne, Los Angeles, Calif.
Gordon, William M., Sch. of Educ., Miami University, Oxford, Ohio
Gore, Jeffrey B., 5795-A N. Meadows Blvd., Columbus, Ohio
Gorham, Marion, Elem. Prin., Emerson School, Concord, Mass.
Gorman, Anna M., Col. of Educ., University of Kentucky, Lexington, Ky.
Gorman, William J., 219-40—93rd Ave., Queens Village, N.Y.
Gormley, Charles L., Dept. of Educ., Alabama College, Montevallo, Ala.
Gorn, Janice L., 60 E. 12th St., New York, N.Y.
Gorth, William P., 15 Brae Burn Rd., S. Deerfield, Mass.
Gorton, Harry B., 224 Orange St., Northumberland, Pa.
Gotsch, Richard E., 8701 Mackenzie Rd., St. Louis, Mo.
Gott, John W., 305 High St., Pullman, Wash.
Gottenid, Allan J., Comm. on Educ., ELCT, P.O. Box 412, Arusha, Tanzania
Gotts, Ernest A., U. of Texas, Austin, Tex.
Gough, Jessie P., LaGrange College, LaGrange, Ga.

Gould, Norman M., Supt., Madera County Schools, Madera, Calif.
Gow, James S., 4519 Middle Rd., Allison Park, Pa.
Gowan, John Curtis, San Fernando Valley State Col., Northridge, Calif.
Gowin, Dixie B., Stone Hall, Cornell Univ., Ithaca, N.Y.
Graber, Eldon W., Freeman Jr. College, Freeman, S. Dak.
Grabowski, A. A., 2512 Southport Ave., Chicago, Ill.
Grady, Gertrude A., 65 Yeaman St., Revere, Mass.
Graef, Ardelle, 1232 S. Dewey St., Eau Claire, Wis.
Graff, Orin B., Col. of Educ., University of Tennessee, Knoxville, Tenn.
Grahm, Milton L., Cambridge School of Business, Boston, Mass.
Granskog, Dorothy, Knox Col., Galesburg, Ill.
Grant, Eugene B., Northern Illinois University, DeKalb, Ill.
Grant, Geraldine R., 701 Locust Ave., Long Beach, Calif.
Grant, Sydney R., Florida State Univ., Tallahassee, Fla.
* Grant, Wayman R. F., Booker T. Washington Junior High School, Mobile, Ala.
Grau, R. T., Clinton Public Schls., Box 110, Clinton, Iowa
Graves, Jack A., P.O. Box 671, Turlock, Calif.
Graves, Linwood D., 115 Leathers Circle, N.W., Atlanta, Ga.
Graves, William, 907 Poplar Rd., Starkville, Miss.
Gray, Dorothy, Dept. of Educ., Queens College, Flushing, N.Y.
Gray, George T., c/o 303 N. Hillcrest Dr. S.W., Marietta, Ga.
Gray, Mary Jane, Loyola University, 820 N. Michigan, Chicago, Ill.
Gray, Ronald F., Canadian Nazarene Col., Winnipeg, Manitoba, Canada
Graybeal, William S., 1330 Massachusetts Ave., N.W., Washington, D.C.
Graye, Mytrolene L., 25 W. 132nd St., New York, N.Y.
Grayson, William H., Jr., 21-71—34th Ave., Long Island City, N.Y.
Green, Donald Ross, 680 Dry Creek Rd., Monterey, Calif.
Green, Gertrude B., 100 W. Hickory Grove Rd., Bloomfield Hills, Mich.
Green, John A., Central Washington St. Col., Ellensburg, Wash.
Green, Ronald F., Sch. of Educ., Indiana Univ., Bloomington, Ind.
Greenberg, Gilda M., University of Tennessee, Nashville, Tenn.
Greenberg, Mrs. Judith W., Sch. of Educ., City College, New York, N.Y.
Greenblatt, Edward L., 211 Calle de Arboles, Redondo Beach, Calif.
Greene, Bert I., 1111 Grant St., Ypsilanti, Mich.
Greene, Charles E., P.O. Box 185, East Side Sta., Santa Cruz, Calif.
Greene, Frank P., 707 Sumner Ave., Syracuse, N.Y.
Greene, Mrs. Maxine, 1080—5th Ave., New York, N.Y.
Greene, Mrs. Minnie S., 1121 Chestnut St., San Marcos, Tex.
Greenfield, Curtis O., 345 W. Windsor Ave., Phoenix, Ariz.
Greenlaw, Marilyn J., 1804 Hamilton Rd., Okemos, Mich.
Greenman, Margaret H., P.O. Box 56, Goreville, Ill.
Greenwood, Edward D., Menninger Clinic, Box 829, Topeka, Kans.
Greenwood, Joann, Simon Fraser Univ., No. Vancouver, B.C., Canada
Greer, Evelyn, Fayette County Schls., 400 Lafayette Dr., Lexington, Ky.
Greer, Mrs. Shirley J., 8441 E. Hubbell St., Scottsdale, Ariz.
Gregg, Russell T., Sch. of Educ., University of Wisconsin, Madison, Wis.
Greif, Ivo P., Illinois State University, Normal, Ill.
Greivell, Richard H., Trust Terr. of the Pac. Is., Ponape, E. Caroline Is.
Grenda, Ted T., Box 189, Stone Ridge, N.Y.
Grennell, Robert L., State University College, Fredonia, N.Y.
Griffin, Gary A., 1255 New Hampshire Ave., N.W., Washington, D.C.
Griffing, Barry L., State Office Bldg., 217 W. First St., Los Angeles, Calif.
Griffith, William S., Dept. of Educ., Univ. of Chicago, Chicago, Ill.
Griffiths, Daniel E., 54 Clarendon Rd., Scarsdale, N.Y.
Griffiths, John A., Superintendent of Schools, Monongahela, Pa.
Griffiths, Ruth, Massachusetts State College, Worcester, Mass.
Grimes, Wellington V., 4 Liberty Sq., Boston, Mass.
* Grizzell, E. Duncan, 640 Maxwelton Ct., Lexington, Ky.
Grobman, Hulda, Juniper Lane, Piscataway, N.J.
Groff, Warren H., 721 Highland Ave., Jenkintown, Pa.
Gromacki, Chester P., 1000 N. Lemon St., Fullerton, Calif.

Gronlund, Norman E., Col. of Educ., University of Illinois, Urbana, Ill.
Grose, Robert F., Amherst College, Amherst, Mass.
Gross, Lydia E., State Col., Lock Haven, Pa.
Gross, Neal, Grad. Sch. of Educ., Harvard University, Cambridge, Mass.
Gross, Robert D., 123 Ninth Ave., Iron River, Mich.
Grossman, Ruth H., Sch. of Educ., City College of N.Y., New York, N.Y.
Grossnickle, Foster E., 1116 Melbourne Ave., Melbourne, Fla.
Grosswald, Jules, 21st St. and the Parkway, Philadelphia, Pa.
Grover, Burton L., Western Washington St. Col., Bellingham, Wash.
Groves, Vernon T., Olivet Nazarene College, Kankakee, Ill.
Gruber, Frederick C., Grad. Sch. of Educ., Univ. of Pa., Philadelphia, Pa.
Grudell, Regina C., 45 Chadwick Rd., Teaneck, N.J.
Guba, Egon G., NISEC, Indiana Univ., Bloomington, Ind.
Guckenheimer, S. N., Heath Area Vocational School, Heath, Ohio
Guditus, Charles W., Schl. of Educ., Lehigh Univ., Bethlehem, Pa.
Guilbault, Georges, Box 160, Ste. Anne, Man., Canada
Guild, Joann, 6139 Flores Ave., Los Angeles, Calif.
Guilford, Jerome O., 705 Searles Rd., Toledo, Ohio
Gunn, Jack G., 103 N. 14th Ave., Laurel, Miss.
Gunther, John F., 3 Cek Ct., Sayville, L.I., N.Y.
Gurr, John E., P.O. Box 56, Bethel, Alaska
Guss, Carolyn, Indiana Univ., Bloomington, Ind.
Gussner, William S., Superintendent of Schools, Jamestown, N.Dak.
Gustafson, A. M., Alice Vail Junior High Sch., 5350 E. 16th St., Tucson, Ariz.
Gustafson, Alma L., 1211 North 5th St., East Grand Forks, Minn.
Gutcher, G. Dale, Colo. St. Univ., Fort Collins, Colo.
Gwynn, J. Minor, 514 North St., Chapel Hill. N.C.
Gyuro, Steven J., Col. of Educ., Univ. of Ky., Lexington, Ky.

Haage, Catherine M., College of New Rochelle, New Rochelle, N.Y.
Haas. Richard J., Jr., 119 Stubbs Dr., Trotwood, Ohio
Haberbosch, John F., Dept. of Educ., State Offices Bldg., Denver, Colo.
Haberman, Martin, Dept. of Educ., Rutgers Univ., New Brunswick, N.J.
Hack, Walter G., Ohio State University, Columbus, Ohio
Hacking, Eleanor, 34 Hamlet St., Fairhaven, Mass.
Hackney, Ben H., Jr., 4618 Walker Rd., Charlotte, N.C.
Hadden, John F., Rt. # 2, Cranbury, N.J.
Haddock, Thomas T., 7232 N. 12th Ave., Phoenix, Ariz.
Haffner, Hyman, 6229 Nicholson St., Pittsburgh, Pa.
Hagen, Donald E., 13028 Root Rd., Columbia Station, Ohio
Hagen, Elizabeth, Tchrs. Col., Columbia University, New York, N.Y.
Hager, Walter E., 4625 S. Chelsea Ln., Bethesda, Md.
Haggerson, Nelson L., 132 W. Balboa Dr., Tempe, Ariz.
Hagglund, Oliver C., Gustavus Adolphus College, St. Peter, Minn.
Hagstrom, Ellis A., 1330 Christmas Lane, N.E., Atlanta, Ga.
Hahn, Albert R., Veterans' Administration Hospital, Phoenix, Ariz.
Hahn, L. Donald, Western Illinois University, Macomb, Ill.
Haight, Wilbur T., 314 S. DuPont Blvd., Milford, Del.
Haimowitz, Clement, Box 134, Hillsboro Rd., Belle Mead, N.Y.
Hale, Gifford G., Sch. of Educ., Florida State University, Tallahassee, Fla.
Hale, R. Nelson, State Teachers College. Slippery Rock, Pa.
Hales, Russell G., University of Utah, Salt Lake City, Utah
Haley, Elizabeth M., 843 Marshall Dr., Palo Alto, Calif.
Halfter, Mrs. Irma Theobald, 222 N. Grove Ave., Oak Park, Ill.
Hall, Barbara C., 2 Knollcrest Court, Normal, Ill.
Hall, J. Floyd, 301 S. Harvey, Oak Park, Ill.
Hall, James A., Superintendent of Schools, Port Washington, N.Y.
Hall, John E., Jackson State College, Jackson. Miss.
Hall, John W., 7½ University Ave., Canton, N.Y.
Hall, Joseph I., 3333 Elston Ave., Chicago, Ill.
Hall, Keith A., Pennsylvania State Univ., University Park, Pa.

Hall, Morris E., Box 343, SFA Station, Nacogdoches, Tex.
Hall, Robert H., Gulf Coast Junior College, Panama City, Fla.
Hall, Walter J., Jr., Haverford Senior High School, Havertown, Pa.
Hall, William Frank, 125 E. Lincoln St., Phoenix, Ariz.
Hall, William H., 291 E. 1st St., Corning, N.Y.
Hall, William P., 19300 Watkins Mill Road, Gaithersburg, Md.
Hallenbeck, Edwin F., Roger Williams Junior College, Providence, R.I.
Hallgren, Ragnar F., Box 297, R.D. 1, Mount Joy, Pa.
Halliday, Laura A., Court House, Stroudsburg, Pa.
Halligan, W. W., Jr., Converse College, Spartanburg, S.C.
Halliwell, Joseph W., 17 Mary Drive, Woodcliff Lake, N.J.
Halpern, Aaron, Clifton Senior High School, Clifton, N.J.
Hamann, H. A., 2000 Harrison St., Glenview, Ill.
Hamblen, Charles P., The Norwich Free Academy, Norwich, Conn.
Hamilton, Gene E., Sunny Hollow Elem. Schl., Minneapolis, Minn.
Hamilton, Herbert M., Sch. of Bus. Adm., Miami Univ., Oxford, Ohio
Hamilton, H. J., 7 Highgate Ave. Box 42, Buffalo, N.Y.
Hamilton, Lester L., Charleston Cnty. Schl. Dist., Charleston, S.C.
Hammel, John A., 1275 Cook Rd., Grosse Pointe Woods, Mich.
Hammer, Eugene L., Dept. of Educ., Wilkes College, Wilkes-Barre, Pa.
Hammer, Viola, Redwood City Schools, Redwood City, Calif.
Hammock, Robert C., Grad. Schl. of Educ., Univ. of Pa., Philadelphia, Pa.
Hammond, Granville S., USAID-Educ.-New Delhi, Dept. of State, Washington, D.C.
Hampton, Bill R., Ferguson Florissant Schl. Dist., Ferguson, Mo.
Hancock, Emily, Florida Southern College, Lakeland, Fla.
Handle, Christa, 1 Berlin 15, Bayerische Str. 3, Germany
Handley, W. Harold, Granite School District, Salt Lake City, Utah
Hanigan, Levin B., Superintendent, Echobrook School, Mountainside, N.J.
Hanisits, Richard M., 8623 S. Kilpatrick Ave., Chicago, Ill.
Hanitchak, John J., Sch. of Educ., Indiana Univ., Bloomington, Ind.
Hanna, Alvis N., Prin., John Tyler School, Tyler, Tex.
Hannemann, Charles E., 5820 S.W. 51st Terr., Miami, Fla.
Hannifin, Mrs. Blanche B., 5259 Strohm Ave., North Hollywood, Calif.
Hannon, Elizabeth F., 1432 S. Crescent Ave., Park Ridge, Ill.
Hannon, Joseph P., 25 E. Chestnut St., Chicago, Ill.
Hansen, Calvin G., 550 Mountain View, Moab, Utah
Hansen, Dorothy Gregg, 722 Ivanhoe Rd., Tallahassee, Fla.
Hansen, G. G., Superintendent of County Schools, Aurora, Nebr.
Hansen, Helge E., 15735 Andover Dr., Dearborn, Mich.
Hansen, Henry R., Sacramento State College, Sacramento, Calif.
Hansen, Maxine M., Wis. State Univ., Whitewater, Wis.
Hansen, R. G., 2075 St. Johns Ave., Highland Park, Ill.
Hansen, Robert E., Cherry Hill High School, Cherry Hill, N.J.
Hansen, Stewart R., St. John's University, Collegeville, Minn.
Hanson, Donald L., 1709 Cherry Lane, Cedar Falls, Iowa
Hanson, Eddie, Jr., Rt. No. 1, Box 1432, Auburn, Calif.
Hanson, Ellis G., 3810 Bel Aire Rd., Des Moines, Iowa
Hanson, Gordon C., Wichita State Univ., Wichita, Kans.
Hanson, Ralph A., 1505 North La Brea, Inglewood, Calif.
Hanson, Wesley L., 3021 Washburn Pl., Minneapolis, Minn.
Hanuska, Julius P., 550 Edith Ave., Johnstown, Pa.
Happy, Kenneth F., 79 Rugar St., Plattsburg, N.Y.
Harckham, Laura D., 240 New Hempstead Rd., New City, N.Y.
Hardesty, Cecil D., 6401 Linda Vista Rd., San Diego, Calif.
Harding, James, Prin., Dunbar Elementary School, Dickinson, Tex.
Harding, Lowry W., Arps Hall, Ohio State University, Columbus, Ohio
Harding, Merle D., 421 Irving St., Beatrice, Nebr.
Hardt, Annanelle, Ariz. St. Univ., Tempe, Ariz.
Hardy, J. Garrick, Alabama State College, Montgomery, Ala.
Hargett, Earl F., 111 W. Brookwood Dr., Valdosta, Ga.

Harlow, James G., Pres., West Virginia Univ., Morgantown, W.Va.
Harmon, Ruth E., 1720 Commonwealth Ave., West Newton, Mass.
Harnack, Robert S., Sch. of Educ., State Univ. Col., Buffalo, N.Y.
Harner, Robert W., Rt. 2, Box 288C, Rigrish Rd., Sciotoville, Ohio
Harney, Paul J., University of San Francisco, San Francisco, Calif.
Harootunian, Berj, Sch. of Educ., Syracuse Univ., Syracuse, N.Y.
Harper, Ray G., Michigan State Univ., East Lansing, Mich.
Harring, L. Richard, 3425 W. Mich. Univ., Kalamazoo, Mich.
Harrington, Edmund Ross, 309 Ave. E., Redondo Beach, Calif.
Harrington, Johns H., 1515 Greenbriar Rd., Glendale, Calif.
Harris, Albert J., 345 E. Grand St., Mt. Vernon, N.Y.
Harris, Ben M., 325 Sutton Hall, University of Texas, Austin, Tex.
Harris, C. W., P.O. Box 1510, Deland, Fla.
Harris, Claude C., 501 S. 30th St., Muskogee, Okla.
Harris, Dale B., Burrowes Bldg., Pennsylvania State Univ., University Park, Pa.
Harris, Eugene, Capitol Area Vocational School, Baton Rouge, La.
Harris, Fred E., Baldwin-Wallace College, Berea, Ohio
Harris, James M., 3045 E. Buckingham, Fresno, Calif.
Harris, Janet D., 130 Boylston St., Chestnut Hill, Mass.
Harris, Larry A., Dept. of Educ., Univ. of N. Dak., Grand Forks, N. Dak.
Harris, Lewis E., 3752 N. Hight St., Columbus, Ohio
Harris, Mary Jo, Educ. Dept., Univ. of South. Alabama, Mobile, Ala.
Harris, Raymond P., 15 Westerly Lane, Thornwood, N.Y.
Harris, Robert B., Bryan Adams High School, Dallas, Tex.
Harris, Theodore L., Dept. of Educ., Univ. of Puget Sound, Tacoma, Wash.
Harris, Yeuell Y., U.S. Office of Educ., Washington, D.C.
Harrison, C. Barker, 6143 Haddington St., Memphis, Tenn.
Harrison, Edward N., Park Terrace Apts., Jefferson City, Tenn.
Harrison, James P., 200 S. Providence Rd., Wallingford, Pa.
Harry, David P., Jr., 1659 Compton Rd., Cleveland Heights, Ohio
Harsanyi, Mrs. Audrey, Pennsylvania State University, University Park, Pa.
Harshbarger, Lawrence H., Educ. Dept., Ball State Univ., Muncie, Ind.
Hart, Mrs. Lawrence W., P.O. Box 14, Rock Falls, Ill.
Hart, Mary A., 28 McKesson Hill Rd., Chappaqua, N.Y.
Hart, Ruth M. R., 1100 Douglas Ave., Minneapolis, Minn.
Harting, Roger D., 4711 Orchard Ln., Columbia, Mo.
Hartjen, Raymond H., 160 N. Craig St., Pittsburgh, Pa.
Hartley, Harold V., Jr., Clarion State Col., Clarion, Pa.
Hartley, James R., Univ. Extn., University of California, Riverside, Calif.
Hartsell, Horace C., Univ. of Texas, Dental Branch, Houston, Tex.
Hartsig, Barbara A., California State College, Fullerton, Calif.
Hartstein, Jacob I., Kingsborough Community College, Brooklyn, N.Y.
Hartung, Maurice L., Dept. of Educ., University of Chicago, Chicago, Ill.
Hartwell, Mrs. Lois, Northern State Col., Aberdeen, S.Dak.
Harvey, Jasper, 1801 Lavaca, Apt. 25, Austin, Tex.
Harvey, Leonard, 258 Riverside Drive, New York, N.Y.
Harvey, Valerien, Univ. Laval, Quebec, Canada
Harwell, John Earl, Nicholls State Col., Thibodaux, La.
Hasenpflug, Thomas R., 600 Hunt Rd., Jamestown, N.Y.
Hash, Mrs. Virginia, State College of Iowa, Cedar Falls, Iowa
Haskew, Laurence D., Col. of Educ., University of Texas, Austin, Tex.
Haskins, Esther N., Box 4798, Carmel, Calif.
Hasman, Richard H., 61 Oakwood Ave., Farmingdale, N.Y.
Hastie, Reid, University of Minnesota, Minneapolis, Minn.
Hastings, Glen R., Dept. of Educ., State Col. of Iowa, Cedar Falls, Iowa
Hastings, Howard H., 255 W. Vermont, Villa Park, Ill.
Hastings, J. Thomas, Educ. Bldg., University of Illinois, Urbana, Ill.
Hatalsan, John W., 4184 Palisades Rd., San Diego, Calif.
Hatashita, Elizabeth S., 6510 Cielo Drive, San Diego, Calif.
Hatch, J. Cordell, Pennsylvania State University, University Park, Pa.
Hatch, Terrance E., Col. of Educ., Utah State University, Logan, Utah

Hatfield, Donald M., Dept. of Educ., University of California, Berkeley, Calif.
Haubrich, Vernon F., Sch. of Educ., Univ. of Wisconsin, Madison, Wis.
Hauer, Nelson A., Louisiana State University, Baton Rouge, La.
Haupt, Leonard R., 2801 Glenview Rd., Glenview, Ill.
Hauptfuehrer, Helen, 159 Norris Gym, Univ. of Minn., Minneapolis, Minn.
Hauschild, Mrs. J. R., 20528 Rhoda St., Woodland Hills, Calif.
* Havighurst, Robert J., Dept. of Educ., University of Chicago, Chicago, Ill.
Hawkins, Edwin L., Horace Mann High School, Little Rock, Ark.
Hawkins, Lee E., 322 S. Jordan, Bloomington, Ind.
Hawkinson, Mabel J., 11 Gregory St., Oswego, N.Y.
Hawley, Leslie R., 94 Walden Dr., RFD #1, Lakeview, Erie Co., N.Y.
Hawley, Ray C., Superintendent of County Schools, Ottawa, Ill.
Haws, J. C., Brd. of Educ. Office, Cnty. Court Hse., Brigham City, Utah
Hayden, Alice H., Miller Hall, University of Washington, Seattle, Wash.
Hayden, James R., 166 William St., New Bedford, Mass.
Hayden, Mary Lee Griffith, 3449 Longview Ave., Bloomington, Ind.
Hayes, Allen P., 757 McKinley Ave., Auburn, Ala.
Hayes, Glenn E., California State College, Long Beach, Calif.
Hayes, Gordon M., Consult., State Dept. of Educ., Sacramento, Calif.
Hayes, Hathia, 460 Morton Ave., Athens, Ga.
Hayes, Paul C., Supt. of Schools, 457 Sawyer Ct., Grove City, Ohio
Hayes, Robert B., Dept. of Pub. Instr., Harrisburg, Pa.
Haynes, Hubert Ray, 108 E. Tilden Dr., Brownsburg, Ind.
Hays, Albert Z., Abilene Christian College, Abilene, Tex.
Hays, Harry N., Supv. Prin., West Branch Area Sch. Dist., Morrisdale, Pa.
Hays, Warren S., 3218 N. Reno Ave., Tucson, Ariz.
Hayward, W. George, 357A Dorchester Dr., Lakewood, N.J.
Hazell, Joseph W., 866 Gooding Dr., Albany, Calif.
Hazleton, Edward W., Bogan High School, Chicago, Ill.
Headd, Pearl Walker, Tuskegee Institute, Ala.
Headley, Quentin, Univ. of Delaware, Newark, Del.
Headley, Ross A., 80 Hauppauge Dr., Commack, N.Y.
Heagney, Genevieve, Towson State Col., Baltimore, Md.
Heald, James E., 4277 Tacoma Blvd., Okemos, Mich.
Healy, Winston, Jr., Punahou Schl., 1601 Punahou St., Honolulu, Hawaii
Heathers, Glen, University of Pittsburgh, Pittsburgh, Pa.
Heavenridge, Glen G., 5844 Gilman St., Garden City, Mich.
Hebeler, Jean R., University of Maryland, College Park, Md.
Heck, Theodore, St. Meinrad Seminary, St. Meinrad, Ind.
Hedden, George W., 1435 Twinridge Rd., Santa Barbara, Calif.
Hedges, William D., 5454 Beacon, Pittsburgh, Pa.
Heding, Howard W., Col. of Educ., Univ. of Missouri, Columbia, Mo.
Heger, Herbert K., 649 Springridge Dr., Lexington, Ky.
Hegman, M. Marian, 332 South Ave., Medina, N.Y.
Heim, Dennis, 5151 State College Dr., Los Angeles, Calif.
Heimann, Therese M., 2330 W. Lapham St., Milwaukee, Wis.
Heimberger, Mary J., Falk Lab Sch., Univ. of Pittsburgh, Pittsburgh, Pa.
Hein, William J., Mills College, Oakland, Calif.
Heintz, Kenneth G., 315 Windermere Blvd., Buffalo, N.Y.
Heinz, John A., California State Polytechnic College, San Luis Obispo, Calif.
Heise, Margaret A., 5361 Princeton Ave., Westminster, Calif.
Heisler, Florence, Dept. of Educ., Brooklyn College, Brooklyn, N.Y.
Heisner, H. Fred, Redlands Unified Sch. Dist., Redlands, Calif.
Heist, Paul H., 4606 Tolman Hall, Univ. of California, Berkeley, Calif.
Held, John T., 426 College Ave., Gettysburg, Pa.
Helge, Erich E., 1118 Sunrise Dr., Seward, Nebr.
Heller, Melvin P., Dept. of Educ., Loyola University, Chicago, Ill.
Hellerich, Mahlon H., Wartburg College, Waverly, Iowa
* Helms, W. T., 1109 Roosevelt Ave., Richmond, Calif.
Helser, David C., 2738 Dover Dr., Troy, Mich.
Heltibridle, Mary E., 39 Sullivan St., Mansfield, Pa.

Heming, Hilton P., 12 Leonard Ave., Plattsburgh, N.Y.
Hemink, Lyle H., 4134 Trailing Dr., Williamsville, N.Y.
Hencley, Stephen P., 1505 Indian Hills Dr., Salt Lake City, Utah
Henderson, Edward, New York University, Washington Sq., New York, N.Y.
Henderson, Robert A., Col. of Educ., University of Illinois, Urbana, Ill.
Hendrick, Irving G., University of California, Riverside, Calif.
Hendrix, Holbert H., Nevada Southern Univ., Las Vegas, Nev.
Hendrix, Jon R., 835 N. Rensselaer, Griffith, Ind.
Hengesbach, Robert W., 7886 Munson Rd., Mentor, Ohio
Hengoed, James, Boston University, Boston, Mass.
Henion, Ethel S., 435 N. Central Ave., Ramsey, N.J.
Henle, R. J., Georgetown Univ., Washington, D.C.
Henry, Bailey Ray, Supt. of Schools, Farmington, Mo.
Henry, George H., Alison Hall, Univ. of Delaware, Newark, Del.
Hephner, Thomas A., Ohio State University, Columbus, Ohio
Herber, Harold L., 209 N. Manlius St., Fayetteville, N.Y.
Herbst, Leonard A., 3550 Crestmoor Dr., San Bruno, Calif.
Herge, Henry C., 12 South Dr., East Brunswick, N.J.
Herget, George H., 2619 N.W. 11th Ave., Gainesville, Fla.
Herman, James A., 4325 Virgusell Circle, Carmichael, Calif.
Herman, Wayne L., Jr., Col. of Educ., Univ. of Maryland, College Park, Md.
Hermanowicz, Henry J., Illinois State University, Normal, Ill.
Herr, Ross, 3452 W. Drummond Pl., Chicago, Ill.
Herr, William A., 536 W. Maple St., Hazleton, Pa.
Herrington, Mrs. Evelyn F., Texas A. & I. Univ., Kingsville, Tex.
Herrmann, D. J., College of William and Mary, Williamsburg, Va.
Herrscher, Barton R., RELCV- Mutual Plaza, Durham, N.C.
Hershberger, James K., 215 N. Whiteoak St., Kutztown, Pa.
Hershey, Gerald L., Sch. of Bus., Indiana University, Bloomington, Ind.
Hertling, James E., 921 Tulip Tree House, Bloomington, Ind.
* Hertzler, Silas, 1618 So. 8th St., Goshen, Ind.
Herz, Mort, 1864 Pattiz Ave., Long Beach, Calif.
Hesla, Orden E., Mankato State College, Mankato, Minn.
Heslep, Thomas R., Superintendent of Schools, Altoona, Pa.
Hess, Clarke F., Marshall College, Huntington, W.Va.
Hess, Glenn C., 44 W. Wheeling St., Washington, Pa.
Hesse, Alexander N., 90 Salisbury Ave., Garden City, L.I., N.Y.
Hetrick, Dr. J. B., Dept. of Educ., Edinboro State Col., Edinboro, Pa.
Hetzel, Walter L., Superintendent of Schools, Ames, Iowa
Heuer, Josephine C., 8444 Edna St., St. Louis, Mo.
Heusner, William W., Michigan State University, East Lansing, Mich.
Hickey, Bernard, 7 Digren Rd., Natick, Mass.
Hickey, Howard, Michigan State University, East Lansing, Mich.
Hickman, Lauren C., Nation's Schools, Chicago, Ill.
Hickner, Marybelle R., Stout State Univ., Menomonie, Wis.
Hicks, Mrs. Aline Black, 812 Lexington St., Norfolk, Va.
Hicks, Samuel I., Inst. of Educ., Ahmadu Bello Univ., Zaria, Nigeria
Hicks, William R., Southern University, Baton Rouge, La.
Hidy, Mrs. Elizabeth Willson, Box 287, Gila Bend, Ariz.
Hiebert, Noble C., 504 Madison Ave., Plainfield, N.J.
Hieronymus, Albert N., East Hall, State Univ. of Iowa, Iowa City, Iowa
Hiers, Mrs. Turner M., 1501 S.E. 15th St., Ft. Lauderdale, Fla.
Higdon, Claude J., 1106 S. Harvard Blvd., Los Angeles, Calif.
Higgins, F. Edward, 9524 S. Keeler Ave., Oak Lawn, Ill.
Highbarger, Mrs. Claire, 1045 N. Quentin Rd., Palatine, Ill.
Hightower, Emory A., 14 W. 64th St., New York, N.Y.
Hilgard, Ernest R., Dept. of Psych., Stanford University, Stanford, Calif.
Hill, Alberta D., White Hall, W.S.U., Pullman, Wash.
Hill, Charles E., 529 Fifth St., S.W., Rochester, Minn.
Hill, George E., Dept. of Educ., Ohio University, Athens, Ohio
Hill, Joseph K., Downstate Medical Center, Brooklyn, N.Y.

Hill, Katherine E., Press 23, New York Univ., Washington Sq., New York, N.Y.
Hill, Norman J., 49 S. Lake Ave., Bergen, N.Y.
Hill, Richard, 2206 Haddington Road, St. Paul, Minn.
Hill, Suzanne D., Louisiana State University, New Orleans, La.
Hillerich, Robert L., 950 Huber Lane, Glenview, Ill.
Hillson, Maurie, 1208 Emerson Ave., Teaneck, N.J.
Himes, Jack E., 6718 Callaghan Rd. #202, San Antonio, Tex.
Hinds, Charles F., Murray State University Library, Murray, Ky.
Hinds, Jean, 3401 S. 39th St., Milwaukee, Wis.
Hinds, Lillian Ruth, 13855 Superior Rd., Cleveland, Ohio
Hindsman, Edwin, S.W. Educ. Dev. Corp., Commodore Perry Hotel, Austin, Tex.
Hineline, Edna C., Fac. of Educ., Macdonald College, Quebec, Canada
Hines, Vynce A., 1220 S.W. Ninth Rd., Gainesville, Fla.
Hintz, Edward R., Westwood Heights Schools, Flint, Mich.
Hipkins, Wendell C., 1311 Delaware Ave., S.W., Washington, D.C.
Hirsch, Mrs. Gloria T., 13121 Addison St., Sherman Oaks, Calif.
Hirst, Wilma E., 3458 Green Valley Rd., Cheyenne, Wyo.
Hitchcock, Catharine, 1837 E. Erie Ave., Lorain, Ohio
Hites, Christopher, 302 Portola Rd., Portola Valley, Calif.
Hitt, Harold H., 4206 Sylvan Oaks, San Antonio, Tex.
Hittinger, Martha S., 12417 E. Beverly Dr., Whittier, Calif.
Hittle, David R., 201 S. 16th St., Escanaba, Mich.
Ho, Thomas C. K., 72 Distler Ave., West Caldwell, N.J.
Ho, Wai Ching, Educ. Research Council, Rockefeller Bldg., Cleveland, Ohio
Hoagland, Robert M., 627 Houseman, La Canada, Calif.
Hoak, Duane C., 1031 Newbury St., Toledo, Ohio
Hobbie, Katherine E., State University College, Oneonta, N.Y.
Hobbs, Billy S., White House High School, White House, Tenn.
Hobbs, Earl W., Renton Sch. Dist., 1525 Fourth Ave., N., Renton, Wash.
Hobbs, Walter R., Roger Williams College, Providence, R.I.
Hochstetler, Ruth, 225 S. Nichols, Muncie, Ind.
Hock, Louise E., Sch. of Educ., New York Univ., New York, N.Y.
Hockwalt, Ronald W., 1563 Hobert Dr., Camarillo, Calif.
Hodge, Harry F., P.O. Box 940, State University, Ark.
Hodge, William Carey, McKendree College, Lebanon, Ill.
Hodges, David Julian, 185 Hall St., Apt. 507, Brooklyn, N.Y.
Hodges, James G., 3856 Kenard Court, Columbus, Ohio
Hodges, Lawrence W., University of Montana, Missoula, Mont.
Hodges, Richard E., Grad. Sch. of Educ., Univ. of Chicago, Chicago, Ill.
Hodges, Ruth Hall, Morris Brown College, Atlanta, Ga.
Hodgins, George W., Paramus High School, Paramus, N.J.
Hodnett, Ruth Germann, Scott, Foresman & Co., Chicago, Ill.
Hoeffner, Karl, Prin., Wm. Hawley Atwell Junior High School, Dallas, Tex.
Hoekstra, S. Robert, RR 1, Box 77H, Grayslake, Ill.
Hoerauf, William E., 19990 Beaufait, Harper Woods, Mich.
Hoffman, Carl B., Abington Sch. Dist., Abington, Pa.
Hofstrand, John M., USAID/HR, Santo Domingo, Dominican Rep.
Hohl, George W., Superintendent of Schools, Waterloo, Iowa
Holbrook, Steven T., Northwestern Univ., Evanston, Ill.
Holda, Frederick W., 26 Hampden Rd., Monson, Mass.
* Holden, A. John, Jr., 19-A Charlesbank Rd., Newton, Mass.
Holliday, Jay N., 10224 N. Wellen Ln., Spokane, Wash.
Hollis, Loye Y., Col. of Educ., University of Houston, Houston, Tex.
Holloway, George E., Jr., 64 Main St., Pittsfield, N.H.
Holm, Joy A., 424 W. Union, Edwardsville, Ill.
Holman, W. Earl, Jackson High School, 544 Wildwood Ave., Jackson, Mich.
Holmes, Augusta, 9001 S. Cottage Grove, Chicago, Ill.
Holmes, Daniel L., Willett School, Attleboro, Mass.
Holmes, Emma E., 17621 E. 17th St., Tustin, Calif.
Holmes, Robert W., Windham College, Putney, Vt.

Holmquist, Emily, Indiana Univ. School of Nursing, Indianapolis, Ind.
Holt, Charles C., 807 S. 1st St., Maywood, Ill.
Holton, Samuel M., University of North Carolina, Chapel Hill, N.C.
Homer, Francis R., 4800 Conshohocken Ave., Philadelphia, Pa.
Honel, Milton F., 167 E. Jackson, Elmhurst, Ill.
Honeychuck, Joseph M., 2808 Parker Ave., Silver Spring, Md.
Hood, Edwin M., 19 Seneca Ave., White Plains, N.Y.
Hood, Evans C., Superintendent of Schools, Palestine, Tex.
Hood, W. R., 2627—29th St., S.W., Calgary, Alba., Canada
Hooker, Clifford P., University of Minnesota, Minneapolis, Minn.
Hooper, George J., 3631 S. Yorktown, Tulsa, Okla.
Hoops, Robert C., 76 Branch Ave., Red Bank, N.J.
Hoover, Erna B., Tennessee A. & I. State Univ., Nashville, Tenn.
Hoover, Louis H., 2304 Tenth Ave. So., Broadview, Ill.
Hopkins, Everett P., 1520 Pinecrest Rd., Durham, N.C.
Hopkins, Theresa, 226 N. Buchanan, Edwardsville, Ill.
Hopmann, Robert P., Concordia Teachers College, River Forest, Ill.
Hoppock, Anne, State Department of Education, Trenton, N.J.
Horn, Ernest W., Indiana University, Bloomington, Ind.
Horn, Margaret, Concordia College, St. Paul, Minn.
Horn, Thomas D., Sutton Hall, University of Texas, Austin, Tex.
Hornback, Mrs. May, Rt. 1, Old Sauk Rd., Middleton, Wis.
Hornbeck, William J., 3335 Wood Terr., Los Angeles, Calif.
Hornburg, Mabel C., 118 Champlain Ave., Ticonderoga, N.Y.
Hornick, Sandra Jo, 1937 Courtland Drive, Kent, Ohio
Horning, Leora N., University of Nebraska, Lincoln, Nebr.
Horns, Virginia, 1934 A Shades Cliff Terr., Birmingham, Ala.
Horrocks, John E., Ohio State University, Columbus, Ohio
Horsman, Ralph D., Supt., Mt. Lebanon Public Schools, Pittsburgh, Pa.
Horvat, John, Schl. of Educ., Indiana U., Bloomington, Ind.
Horwich, Frances R., 400 E. Randolph St., Chicago, Ill.
Hosford, Marion H., Trenton State College, Trenton, N.J.
Hoskins, Charles W., 503 Sioux Lane, San Jose, Calif.
Hoskins, Glen C., Dept. of Educ., Southern Methodist Univ., Dallas, Tex.
Hotchkiss, James M., Sch. of Educ., University of Oregon, Eugene, Oreg.
Houck, William R., 550 Dauphin, P.O. Box 129, Mobile, Ala.
Hough, John M., Jr., Mars Hill College, Mars Hill, N.C.
Hough, Robert E., Arthur L. Johnson Regional High School, Clark, N.J.
Houghton, Charlene J., 7401 S.W. 72nd Ct., Miami, Fla.
Houghton, John J., Superintendent of Schools, Ferndale, Mich.
Houlahan, F. J., Catholic University of America, Washington, D.C.
Houle, Cyril O., Dept. of Educ., University of Chicago, Chicago, Ill.
Hounshell, Paul B., Univ. of North Carolina, Chapel Hill, N.C.
Householder, Daniel L., Sch. of Tech., Purdue University, Lafayette, Ind.
Houston, James J., Jr., Patterson State Col., Wayne, N.J.
Houston, John, Superintendent of Schools, Medford, Mass.
Houston, W. Robert, Col. of Educ., Mich. State University, East Lansing, Mich.
Houts, Earl, Westminster College, New Wilmington, Pa.
Hovet, Kenneth O., University of Maryland, College Park, Md.
Howard, Alexander H., Jr., Central Washington State Col., Ellensburg, Wash.
Howard, Bobby R., Auburn Univ., Georgetown, S.C.
Howard, Daniel D., Pestalozzi-Froebel Tchrs. College, Chicago, Ill.
Howard, Elizabeth Z., Col. of Educ., Univ. of Rochester, Rochester, N.Y.
Howard, Glenn W., Queens College, Flushing, N.Y.
Howard, Harry, Box 765, Hillsborough, N.C.
Howard, Herbert, Prin., R. B. Walter Elem. School, Tioga, Pa.
Howd, M. Curtis, 200 Winthrop Rd., Muncie, Ind.
Howe, Robert W., Assoc. Prof., Ohio State University, Columbus, Ohio
Howe, Walter A., 6840 Eastern Ave., N.W., Washington, D.C.
Howell, Wallace J., Penfield Senior High School, Penfield, N.Y.
Howitt, Lillian, Winthrop Jr. High Schl., Brooklyn, N.Y.

Howlett, Dorn, R.D. 1, Edinboro, Pa.
Howsam, Robert B., University of Houston, Houston, Tex.
Hoye, Almon G., Marshall Univ. H.S., Minneapolis, Minn.
Hoyle, Anne M., 3900 Hamilton St., L-103, Hyattsville, Md.
Hoyle, Dorothy, Temple University, Philadelphia, Pa.
Hoyt, Cyril J., Burton Hall, Univ. of Minnesota, Minneapolis, Minn.
Hrabi, James S., Dept. of Educ., 10820—98th Ave., Edmonton, Alba., Canada
Hrynyk, Nicholas P., 11010—142nd St., Edmonton, Alba., Canada
Hubbard, Ben, Illinois State University, Normal, Ill.
Huber, H. Ronald, 315 W. State St., Doylestown, Pa.
Hubert, Frank W. R., Texas A. & M. Univ., College Station, Tex.
Huck, Charlotte S., Ohio State University, Columbus, Ohio
Huckins, Wesley, 2309 Randy Drive, Kettering, Ohio
Hudson, Bertha J., 7251 S. Euclid Ave., Chicago, Ill.
Hudson, Bruce M., 2892 Robb Circle, Lakewood, Colo.
Hudson, Douglas, 3981 Greenmont Drive, Warren, Ohio
Hudson, L. P., 1225 Oakwood St., Bedfort, Va.
Hudson, Robert I., University of Manitoba, Winnipeg, Manitoba, Canada
Hudson, Wilburn, Cordova High School, Cordova, Ala.
Huebner, Dwayne E., Tchrs. Col., Columbia University, New York, N.Y.
Huebner, Mildred H., So. Connecticut State Col., New Haven, Conn.
Huehn, Kermith S., Superintendent of County Schools, Eldora, Iowa
Huelsman, Charles B., Jr., 74 S. Roosevelt Rd., Columbus, Ohio
Huff, Jack F., 9030 Glorieta Ct., Elk Grove, Calif.
Hug, John W., 2090 Frank Rd., Columbus, Ohio
Hughes, Carolyn Sue, 415 Catalina Ave., Wooster, Ohio
Hughes, John, 534 Michigan Ave., Evanston, Ill.
Hughes, Larry W., 4046 Towanda Trail, Knoxville, Tenn.
Hughes, McDonald, 1732—32nd Ave., Tuscaloosa, Ala.
Hughes, Thomas G., Ventura College, Ventura, Calif.
Hughes, Thomas M., 990 Brower Rd., Memphis, Tenn.
Hughes, Vergil H., San Jose State College, San Jose, Calif.
Hughes, Msgr. William A., Supt., Diocese of Youngstown, Youngstown, Ohio
Hughson, Arthur, 131 East 21st St., Brooklyn, N.Y.
Hulbert, Dolores S., 16301 Lassen St., Sepulveda, Calif.
Hull, J. H., Supt. of Schools, Torrance, Calif.
Hult, Esther M., Dept. of Educ., State College of Iowa, Cedar Falls, Iowa
Hulteen, Curtis D., 519 Whitney, Kewanee, Ill.
Humelsine, Martha, Roberts Wesleyan College, North Chili, N.Y.
Humes, Cornelia Z., Cedar Crest Col., Northampton, Pa.
Humphrey, Charles F., 6001 Berkeley Dr., Berkeley, Mo.
Humphrey, G. C., 316 Fraser Dr. East, Mesa, Ariz.
Humphries, Jack W., Sam Houston St. Univ., Huntsville, Tex.
Hunkins, Francis P., University of Washington, Seattle, Wash.
Hunsicker, C. L., Mansfield State College, Mansfield, Pa.
Hunt, Dorothy D., 2000 East 46th St., N., Kansas City, Mo.
Hunt, Herold C., Grad. Sch. of Educ., Harvard University, Cambridge, Mass.
Hunter, Eugenia, Woman's Col., Univ. of North Carolina, Greensboro, N.C.
Hunter, James Jamison, Jr., 6240 Cresthaven Dr., La Mesa, Calif.
Hunter, Richard D., Prin., Washington Jr. High School, Olympia, Wash.
Hunter, Robert W., Grambling College, Grambling, La.
*Huntington, Albert H., 2535 Kentland Dr., St. Louis, Mo.
Huntington, John F., Miami Univ., Oxford, Ohio
Hupper, Richard D., 765 Depot Rd., Gurnee, Ill.
Hurd, Blair E., 8015 South Lake Circle, Loomis, Calif.
Hurd, Paul DeH., Sch. of Educ., Stanford University, Stanford, Calif.
Hurt, E. L., Jr., Gragg Junior High School, Memphis, Tenn.
Hurt, Mary Lee, Div. of Voc. & Tech. Educ., Washington, D.C.
Husk, William L., Dept. of Educ., Univ. of Louisville, Louisville, Ky.
Husmann, John L., 256 Ash St., Crystal Lake, Ill.

Huss, Francis C., 4655 Parker Rd., Florissant, Mo.
Husson, Chesley H., Husson College, 157 Park St., Bangor, Maine
Husted, Inez M., P.O. Box 1165, Kingston, Pa.
Husted, Vernon L., Supt., Armstrong Twp. High School, Armstrong, Ill.
Hutchison, James M., 26904 Grayslake Rd., Palos Verdes Peninsula, Calif.
Hutson, Percival W., University of Pittsburgh, Pittsburgh, Pa.
Hutto, Jerome A., Los Angeles State College, Los Angeles, Calif.
Hutton, Duane E., Sch. of Educ., Syracuse University, Syracuse, N.Y.
Hutton, Harry K., Pennsylvania State University, University Park, Pa.
Hyde, Sandra, 8113 Dawson Drive, S.E., Warren, Ohio
Hyder, Charles M., Univ. of Chattanooga, Chatanooga, Tenn.
Hyer, Anna L., 7613 Wiley Dr., Lorton, Va.
Hyman, Ronald Terry, 15 Oakbrook Pl., Somerset, N.J.
Hyram, George H., 4092 Fieldstone Dr., Florissant, Mo.

Iannacone, George, Supt. of Schools, Palisades Park, N.J.
Iannaccone, Laurence, Linstead Court, Weston, Ont., Canada
Igo, Robert V., Pennsylvania State University, University Park, Pa.
Ihrman, Donald L., Superintendent of Schools, Holland, Mich.
Ilowit, Roy, C. W. Post College, Greenvale, L.I., N.Y.
Imbriano, Louis A., Revere Public Schools, Revere, Mass.
Imes, Orley B., 3985 La Cresenta Rd., El Sobrante, Calif.
Imhoff, Myrtle M., 5151 State Col. Blvd., Los Angeles, Calif.
Imura, Harry S., University of California, Berkeley, Calif.
Inabnit, Darrell J., Sacramento State College, Sacramento, Calif.
Incardona, Joseph S., 325 Busti Ave., Buffalo, N.Y.
Ingebritson, Kasper I., 2790 Sunny Grove Ave., Arcata, Calif.
Ingle, Robert, 5321 N. Hollywood, Whitefish Bay, Wis.
Ingram, Margaret H., East Carolina College, Greenville, N.C.
Ingrelli, Anthony V., University of Wisconsin-Milwaukee, Milwaukee, Wis.
Inlow, Gail M., Sch. of Educ., Northwestern University, Evanston, Ill.
Inskeep, James E., Jr., San Diego State College, San Diego, Calif.
Ireland, Robert Stanton, Old Orchard Lane, Boxborough, Mass.
Irizarry, Casandra Rivera de, 1628 Arenida Central, Caparra Terr., P.R.
Irsfeld, H. L., Superintendent of Schools, Mineral Wells, Tex.
Irving, James Lee, 5713 Ogontz Ave., Philadelphia, Pa.
Irwin, Alice M., Dept. of Spec. Classes, Public Schls., New Bedford, Mass.
Irwin, Mrs. Norma J., 404 H Educ. Bldg., Kent State University, Kent, Ohio
Isaacs, Ann F., Natl. Assn. Gifted Children, Cincinnati, Ohio
Isacksen, Roy O., Hazel Pk. Jr. H.S., 1140 White Bear Ave., St. Paul, Minn.
Isenberg, Robert M., 3117 Helsel Dr. Silver Spring, Md.
Isert, Rev. Louis F., 1600 Webster St., N.E., Washington, D.C.
Israel, Benjamin L., 2560 Linden Blvd., Brooklyn, N.Y.
Ives, Josephine Piekarz, New York University, New York, N.Y.
Ivie, Claude M., Div. of Curric., State Dept. of Educ., Atlanta, Ga.
Ivins, George H., Roosevelt Univ., 430 S. Michigan Ave., Chicago, Ill.
Ivins, Wilson H., Col. of Educ., Univ. of New Mexico, Albuquerque, N.Mex.
Izard, John F., 9 Abelia Court, Bundoora, Vic. 3083, Australia
Izzo, Raymond J., 12 Girard Rd., Winchester, Mass.

Jacklin, William, 411 E. 17th St., Lombard, Ill.
Jackson, Bryant H., Illinois State University, Normal, Ill.
Jackson, Philip W., Dept. of Educ., Univ. of Chicago, Chicago, Ill.
Jackson, Ronald B., 5 Gibson Rd., Lexington, Mass.
Jackson, Thomas A., Florida A. & M. Univ., Tallahassee, Fla.
Jacobs, J., 26141 Schoolcraft Rd., Detroit, Mich.
Jacobs, John F., 12299 Univ. Stat., Gainesville, Fla.
Jacobs, Robert, American Embassy, APO San Francisco, Calif.
Jaeger, Alan Warren, 10220 Dale Dr., San Jose, Calif.
Jaeger, Eloise M., 158 Morris Gym, Univ. of Minnesota, Minneapolis, Minn.
Jaeger, Herman F., Box 10, Grandview, Wash.

Jaffarian, Sara, 251 Waltham St., Lexington, Mass.
Jahns, Irwin R., Florida State Univ., Tallahassee, Fla.
James, C. Rodney, 1687 Guilford Rd., Columbus, Ohio
James, Carl A., Superintendent of Schools, Emporia, Kans.
James, Jo Nell, Northwestern St. Col. of La., Natchitoches, La.
* James, Preston E., Dept. of Geog., Syracuse University, Syracuse, N.Y.
James, Ronald G., 230 E. Eagle St., Findlay, Ohio
James, W. Raymond, 9 Bugbee Rd., Oneonta, N.Y.
Jameson, Sanford C., Reg. Dir., Col. Entr. Exam. Brd., Evanston, Ill.
Jansen, Udo H., Tchrs. Col., Univ. of Nebraska, Lincoln, Nebr.
*Jansen, William, 900 Palmer Rd., Bronxville, N.Y.
Jansic, Anthony F., Educ. Clinic, City College of New York, New York, N.Y.
Jardine, Alex, 2105—19th Ave., Greeley, Colo.
Jarrell, George R., P.O. Box 3283, Charleston, S.C.
Jarvie, Lawrence L., Pres., Fashion Inst. of Tech., New York, N.Y.
Jarvis, Mrs. Elizabeth O., Bayview House, R.R. 2, Hamilton, Ont., Canada
Jarvis, Galen M., 9040 Kostner Rd., Skokie, Ill.
Jaski, Ernest, 10438 S. Hamilton, Chicago, Ill.
Jason, Hilliard, Col. of Med., Michigan State Univ., East Lansing, Mich.
Jaspen, Nathan, New York University, New York, N.Y.
Jeffers, Jay W., 931 Franklin Ave., Las Vegas, Nev.
Jeffries, Thomas S., Sch. of Educ., Univ. of Louisville, Louisville, Ky.
Jelinek, James J., Col. of Educ., Arizona State University, Tempe, Ariz.
Jellins, Miriam H., 2849 Dale Creek Dr., N.W., Atlanta, Ga.
Jenkins, Clara Barnes, St. Paul's College, Lawrenceville, Va.
Jenkins, David S., Supt., Anne Arundel County Schools, Annapolis, Md.
Jenkins, Ernest W., 811 W. 2nd St., Pittsburgh, Kans.
Jenkins, James J., University of Minnesota, Minneapolis, Minn.
Jenkins, Jerry Allen, Sch. of Educ., Indiana State Univ., Terre Haute, Ind.
Jenkins, Offa Lou, Marshall University, Huntington, W.Va.
Jenkins, Walter D., 712 Cactus Ln., Las Vegas, Nev.
Jenness, L. S., Forest View High School, Arlington Heights, Ill.
Jensen, Arthur M., Tuttle School, 1042—18th Ave., Minneapolis, Minn.
Jensen, Arthur R., University of California, Berkeley, Calif.
Jensen, Esther M., University of Wisconsin, Milwaukee, Wis.
Jensen, Gale E., 3055 Lakewood Dr., Ann Arbor, Mich.
Jensen, Grant W., Kern Jt. Union H.S. Dist., Bakersfield, Calif.
Jenson, Dean, Bowling Green State University, Bowling Green, Ohio
Jenson, T. J., 1024 Lyn Rd., Bowling Green, Ohio
Jess, C. Donald, Superintendent of Schools, Bergenfield, N.J.
Jetton, Clyde T., 720 Amherst, Abilene, Tex.
Jewell, R. Ewart, Superintendent of Schools, 547 Wall St., Bend, Oreg.
Jewett, Mary Jane, 9 Lincoln Place, New Platz, N.Y.
Jex, Frank B., Dept. of Educ. Psych., Univ. of Utah, Salt Lake City, Utah
Jinks, Elsie H., 1597 Lochmoor Blvd., Grosse Pointe Woods, Mich.
Jobe, (Robinson), Helen M., 3710 Gulf of Mex., Sarasota, Fla.
Jobe, Mrs. Mildred, Moffat County High School, Craig, Colo.
Johns, Edward B., Dept. of P.E., University of California, Los Angeles, Calif.
Johns, Jerry L., 251 S. Marshall St., Pontiac, Mich.
Johns, John P., 822 Park Ave., Baltimore, Md..
Johns, O. D., Col. of Educ., Univ. of Oklahoma, Norman, Okla.
Johnsen, E. Peter, 1003 W. 29th Terr., Lawrence, Kans.
Johnson, Mrs. Andrew L., 101 E. 14th Ave., Apt. L, Columbus, Ohio
Johnson, B. Lamar, Sch. of Educ., Univ. of California, Los Angeles, Calif.
Johnson, Claudine, 112-39—175th St., Jamaica, N.Y.
Johnson, Dale A., 1318 Gibbs Ave., St. Paul Minn.
Johnson, Dale L., Dept. of Psych., University of Houston, Houston, Tex.
Johnson, Mrs. Dorothea N., 317 Whitman Blvd., Elyria, Ohio
Johnson, Dorothy E., Calumet Campus, Purdue Univ., Hammond, Ind.
Johnson, Douglas A., 341 Claydon Way, Sacramento, Calif.
Johnson, Einar O., 3254 48th Ave. South, Minneapolis, Minn.

Johnson, Eleanor M., Box 360, Middletown, Conn.
Johnson, Forbes R., 122 Evans St., Iowa City, Ia.
Johnson, Frank R., Brd. of Educ., Granville Ave., Margate City, N.J.
Johnson, G. Orville, Col. of Educ., Ohio State University, Columbus, Ohio
Johnson, George L., Lincoln University of Missouri, Jefferson City, Mo.
Johnson, Harry C., Duluth Branch, Univ. of Minnesota, Duluth, Minn.
Johnson, Homer M., 301 Acalanes Dr., Apt. 57, Sunnyvale, Calif.
Johnson, Jerry G., Asst. Supt. of Schls., Alexander County, McClure, Ill.
Johnson, J. O., Central Jr. H.S., Rochester, Minn.
Johnson, Joan C., 1440 Holiday Blvd., Merritt Island, Fla.
Johnson, John L., 805 S. Crouse Ave., Syracuse, N.Y.
Johnson, Leonard E., Prin., Bugbee Sch., West Hartford, Conn.
Johnson, Lois V., California State Col., Los Angeles, Calif.
Johnson, Margaret E., Alpine School District, American Fork, Utah
Johnson, Mrs. Marjorie Seddon, 61 Grove Ave., Flourtown, Pa.
Johnson, Olive Lucille, 1925 Thornwood Ave., Wilmette, Ill.
Johnson, Paul E., Livonia Public Schools, Livonia, Mich.
Johnson, Paul O., Salem H.S., Geremonty Dr., Salem, N.H.
Johnson, Philip E., 53 Front St., Bath, Maine
Johnson, Robert L., 9333 W. Lincoln Ave., West Allis, Wis.
Johnson, Robert Leonard, 2500 South 118th St., West Allis, Wis.
Johnson, Robert O., Port Washington Public Schls., Port Washington, N.Y.
Johnson, Roger E., 218 Park Ridge Ave., Temple Terrace, Fla.
* Johnson, Roy Ivan, 2333 Southwest Eighth Dr., Gainesville, Fla.
Johnson, Simon O., 2001 S.W. 5th Pl., Ocala, Fla.
Johnson, Theodore D., 5236 N. Bernard St., Chicago, Ill.
Johnson, Valdimar K., University of Victoria, Victoria, B.C., Canada
Johnson, Walter F., Col. of Educ., Michigan State Univ., East Lansing, Mich.
Johnson, Walter R., Libertyville High School, Libertyville, Ill.
Johnston, Aaron M., Col. of Educ., Univ. of Tennessee, Knoxville, Tenn.
Johnston, Edgar G., 2301 Vinewood Ave., Ann Arbor, Mich.
Johnston, Lillian B., 538 W. Vernon Ave., Phoenix, Ariz.
Johnston, William R., 1241 Satinwood Lane, Whitewater, Wis.
Jones, Annie Lee, University of North Carolina, Chapel Hill, N.C.
Jones, Clyde A., University of Connecticut, Storrs, Conn.
Jones, Daisy M., Sch. of Educ., Arizona State University, Tempe, Ariz.
Jones, Delores C., 4415 Havelock Rd., Lanham, Md.
Jones, Dilys M., 305 Roxbury Rd., Shippensburg, Pa.
Jones, Donald W., 508 W. North St., Muncie, Ind.
Jones, Earl, Tex. A&M Univ. Bldg., College Station, Tex.
Jones, Elvet Glyn, Western Washington State Col., Bellingham, Wash.
Jones, Harvey E., 104 Lee Avenue, Tahlequah, Okla.
Jones, Henry W., Western Washington State College, Bellingham, Wash.
Jones, Howard Robert, State University of Iowa, Iowa City, Iowa
Jones, Jack J., Supt. of Schools, Borrego Springs, Calif.
Jones, Janie L., Southeastern St. Col., Durant, Okla.
Jones, John E., University of Oregon, Eugene, Oreg.
Jones, Kenneth G., State University College, Oswego, N.Y.
Jones, Lloyd Meredith, State University of New York, Farmingdale, N.Y.
Jones, Nevin, Prin., Model School, Box 67, Shannon, Ga.
Jones, Olwen M., Fox Run Lane, Greenwich, Conn.
Jones, Richard N., Carroll Rd., Monkton, Md.
Jones, Richard V., Jr., Stanislaus State College, Turlock, Calif.
Jones, Robert William, Lincoln Community High School, Lincoln, Ill.
Jones, Roger H., 216 Bell Court East, Lexington, Ky.
Jones, Ruth G., 3938 Walnut Ave., Lynwood, Calif.
Jones, Vyron Lloyd, 5901 S. Wahoo Dr., Terre Haute, Ind.
Jones, Wendell P., Sch. of Educ., Univ. of California, Los Angeles, Calif.
Jones, William E., California State College, Hayward, Calif.
Joneson, Della, 1040 State St., Ottawa, Ill.
Jongsma, Eugene A., 2639 E. Second St., Bloomington, Ind.

Jonsson, Harold, Div. of Educ., San Francisco State Col., San Francisco, Calif.
Jordan, A. B., 5811 Riverview Blvd., St. Louis, Mo.
Jordan, Benjamin W., Educ. Bldg., Wayne State Univ., Detroit, Mich.
Joselyn, Edwin G., 4068 Hampshire Ave., N., Minneapolis, Minn.
Joy, Donald M., Light & Life Press, Winona, Ind.
Joynt, Denis, University of Papua and New Guinea, Boroko, Papua
Juan, K. C., Fisk University, Nashville, Tenn.
Judenfriend, Harold, 41-25 Kissena Blvd., Flushing, N.Y.
Julstrom, Eva, 7647 Colfax Ave., Chicago, Ill.
June, Elmer D., 619 Bamford Rd., Cherry Hill, N.J.
Junge, Charlotte W., Col. of Educ., Wayne University, Detroit, Mich.
Junker, Margaret, 9138 S. Claremont Ave., Chicago, Ill.
Jurjevich, J. C., Jr., 1844 74th Ave., Elmwood Park, Ill.
Justman, Joseph, Sch. of Educ., Fordham Univ., New York, N.Y.
Juvancic, William A., Eli Whitney Elem. Sch., Chicago, Ill.

* Karr, Mrs. Galeta M., 7050 Ridge Ave., Chicago, Ill.
Kabrud, Margaret J., Univ. of North Dakota, Ellendale Cent., Ellendale, N.Dak.
Kacik, Terrence D., Rt. 18, Cedar Hill Rd., Pottstown, Pa.
Kaffer, Roger L., St. Charles Borromeo Seminary, Lockport, Ill.
Kahn, Albert S., Sch. of Educ., Boston University, Boston, Mass.
Kahnk, Donald L., 720 East Ninth St., Fremont, Nebr.
Kahrs, Mary V., Mankato State College, Mankato, Minn.
Kairies, Eugene B., Jr., 947- 17th Ave. S.E. Minneapolis, Minn.
Kaiser, Eldor, 543 Iles Park Pl., Springfield, Ill.
Kalina, David L., P.O. Box 134, Shenorock, N.Y.
Kalish, Thomas F., 813 Walworth, Kingsford, Mich.
Kallenbach, W. Warren, San Jose State College, San Jose, Calif.
Kalme, Albert P., West Virginia State Col., Institute, W.Va.
Kamil, Irving, 885 Bolton Ave., Bronx, N.Y.
Kandyba, Bernard S., 9403 N. Parkside Dr., Des Plaines, Ill.
Kane, Dermott P., 1300 West 97 Pl., Chicago, Ill.
Kane, Elmer R., 7530 Maryland Ave., Clayton, Mo.
Kane, James L., Stratford School, Garden City, L.I., N.Y.
Kantor, Bernard R., 117 S. Poinsettia Pl., Los Angeles, Calif.
Kaplan, Lawrence, Rutgers Univ., St. Univ. of N.J., New Brunswick, N.J.
Kaplan, Louis, 3710 W. 230th, Torrance, Calif.
Karlin, Robert, Dept. of Educ., Queens College, Flushing, N.Y.
Karlsen, Bjorn, 7252 Bennett Valley Rd., Santa Rosa, Calif.
Karr, Johnston T., 300 W. 59th Ave., Merrillville, Ind.
Kasdon, Lawrence M., 13 W. 13th St., New York, N.Y.
Kashuba, Michael, 1535 Township Line Rd., Willow Grove, Pa.
Kass, Corrine E., 5801 Camino Esplendora, Tucson, Ariz.
Kata, Joseph J., Redbank Valley Joint Schools, New Bethlehem, Pa.
Katenkamp, Theodore W., Jr., 9128 Bengal Rd., Randallstown, Md.
Katz, Joseph, University of British Columbia, Vancouver, B.C., Canada
Kauffman, Merle M., Col. of Educ., Bradley University, Peoria, Ill.
Kaufman, Martin, 5610 Shoalwood Ave., Austin, Tex.
Kaulfers, Walter V., University of Illinois, Urbana, Ill.
Kaur, Amrit, Dept. Educ. Res., Punjabi U., Patiale, Punjab, India
Kavanaugh, J. Keith, 1639 So. Maple Ave., Berwyn, Ill.
Kean, John M., Univ. of Wisconsin, Madison, Wis.
Keane, John M., 4148 W. 82nd Pl., Chicago, Ill.
Kearl, Jennie W., State Department of Education, Salt Lake City, Utah
Kearney, Rev. George G., 15785A Foothills Rd., Morgan Hill, Calif.
Keating, Frederic, 25 Lucile Dr., Sayville, N.Y.
Keck, Winston B., Westfield State College, Westfield, Mass.
Keefer, Daryle E., Southern Illinois University, Carbondale, Ill.
Keeling, Kenneth E., Morton East High School, Cicero, Ill.
Keesling, James W., 1521 Yale St., Santa Monica, Calif.
Kehas, Chris D., Claremont Graduate School, Claremont, Calif.

Keislar, Evan R., University of California, Los Angeles, Calif.
Keithley, Perry G., 2202 Deane Dr., Pullman, Wash,
Keleher, Gregory C., St. Bernard College, St. Bernard, Ala.
*Keliher, Alice V., Box 307, Peterborough, N.H.
Kelleher, William J., Hirsch High School, Chicago, Ill.
* Keller, Franklin J., 333 E. Mosholu Pkwy., New York, N.Y.
Keller, Horace T., Glassboro State College, Glassboro, N.J.
Keller, Robert J., Col. of Educ., Univ. of Minnesota, Minneapolis, Minn.
Kelley, Claude, West Virginia University, Morgantown, W. Va.
Kelley, H. Paul, University of Texas, Austin, Tex.
Kelley, Robert, S.U.N.Y. at Albany, 1400 Washington Ave., Albany, N.Y.
Kelley, William F., S.J., Creighton Univ., Omaha, Nebr.
Kelly, Dean, 175 Tamarack Dr., Berea, Ohio
Kelly, Edward J., 2109 Buena Vista Dr., Greeley, Colo.
Kelly, Edward L., East 103 Orion Dr., Pullman, Wash.
Kelly, James A., Teachers College, Columbia University, New York, N.Y.
Kelly, James A., 101 Borromeo Ave., Placentia, Calif.
Kelly, John W., 27 Earle Pl., New Rochelle, N.Y.
Kelly, Preston W., Holt, Rinehart & Winston, Inc., New York, N.Y.
Kelly, Shaun, Jr., 55 Fifth Ave., Rm. 1535, New York, N.Y.
Kelly, William F., University of Rhode Island, Kingston, R.I.
Kelsey, Roger R., Educ. Annex, University of Maryland, College Park, Md.
Kemper, Lawrence B., 4837 Oakwood Lane, La Canada, Calif.
Kennedy, Anna Helen, 101 N. Grand Ave., Pasadena, Calif.
Kennedy, Clephane A., Benjamin Franklin University, Washington, D.C.
Kenney, Helen J., Dept. of Educ., Northeastern Univ., Boston, Mass.
Kentner, Harold M., Rochester Institute of Technology, Rochester, N.Y.
Keohane, Robert E., Shimer College, Mt. Carroll, Ill.
Kephart, Ruby Grey, 1807 Milton, Lima, Ohio
Kepner, Henry S., Jr., University School, Iowa City, Iowa
Kerns, LeRoy, Lab. Sch., Colorado State College, Greeley, Colo.
Kerr, Everett F., Superintendent of Schools, Blue Island, Ill.
Kerr, Margaret, 7558 Drexel Dr., University City, Mo.
Kerr, R. D., 113 Hill Hall, Univ. of Missouri, Columbia, Mo.
Keske, Eldora E., 2329 Chalet Gardens Rd., Madison, Wis.
Kessler Clifton L., 4008 Edgerock Drive, Austin, Tex.
Kester, Scott W., Oklahoma Baptist Univ., Shawnee, Okla.
Kherlopian, Richard H., Univ. of South Carolina, Columbia, S.C.
Khouri, John W., Superintendent of Schools, Bethlehem, Pa.
Kicklighter, Ray S., Resch. Physicist, Eastman Kodak, Rochester, N.Y.
Kidder, Frederick E., Univ. of P.R., San Juan, Puerto Rico
Kidder, William W., 216 Walton Ave., South Orange, N.J.
Kilbourn, Mrs. Robert W., 4902 Argyle St., Dearborn, Mich.
Kilburn, H. Parley, Evening Div., Bakersfield College, Bakersfield, Calif.
Killam, Jacqueline R., 860 Third St., No. 14, Santa Monica, Calif.
Kilpatrick, Arnold R., Pres., Northwestern State Col., Natchitoches, La.
Kilpatrick, Joel Fred, Western Carolina College, Cullowhee, N.C.
Kimberly, Mrs. Marian, 33 Southern Way, Princeton, N.J.
Kincheloe, James B., University of Kentucky, Lexington, Ky.
Kindy, Harold G., 110 Bleecker St., New York, N.Y.
King, A. Richard, Univ. of Victoria, Victoria, B.C., Canada
King, Charles T., Millburn Twp. Pub. Schls., Millburn, N.J.
King, Mrs. June, Box 39, Prince Frederick, Md.
King, Kent H., 103 Thayer Ave., Mankato, Minn.
King, Lloyd H., Sch. of Educ., Univ. of the Pacific, Stockton, Calif.
King, Louise M., Univ. of Portland, Milwaukie, Oreg.
King, Robert N., 15 Quade St., Glens Falls, N.Y.
King, Thomas C., Sch. of Educ., University of Miami, Coral Gables, Fla.
Kingsley, Iva Marie, Box 157, Bellmont Rur. Sta., Flagstaff, Ariz.
Kinkade, Jerry B., R.R. #2, Eldorado, Ill.
Kinlin, J. F., 44 Eglinton Ave., W., Toronto, Ont., Canada

Kinsellar, Frances M., Rye St., Broad Brook, Conn.
*Kinsman, Kephas A., 2177-0 Via Puerta, Laguna Hills, Calif.
Kinzer, John R., 5756 East 6th St., Tucson, Ariz.
Kirby, Inabell T., 2002 E. Main St., Decatur, Ill.
Kirchhaefer, Esther, Illinois State University, Normal, Ill.
Kirchman, Mrs. Rose, Jamaica High School, Jamaica, N.Y.
Kirk, Samuel A., Col. of Educ., Univ. of Arizona, Tucson, Ariz.
Kirkland, Eleanor R., 8707 Mohawk Way, Fair Oaks, Calif.
Kirkland, J. Bryant, North Carolina State College, Raleigh, N.C.
Kirkman, Ralph E., R. #4, Murfreesboro, Tenn.
Kirkwood, James J., Ball State Univ., Muncie, Ind.
Kirsch, Victor, Commack Public Schools, Commack, N.Y.
Kise, Leonard, Northern Illinois Univ., DeKalb, Ill.
Kiser, Chester, State University of New York, Buffalo, N.Y.
Kissinger, Doris C., 34 Roosevelt St., Glen Head, L.I., N.Y.
* Kitch, Donald E., 520 Messina Hall, Sacramento, Calif.
Kitson, Elizabeth W. P., 9411 Jamaica Dr., Miami, Fla.
Kittell, Jack E., Col. of Educ., University of Washington, Seattle, Wash.
Kittleson, Howard, Kansas St. Univ., Manhattan, Kans.
Kitts, Harry W., Dept. of Agric. Educ., Univ. of Minn., St. Paul, Minn.
Kizer, George A., Iowa State Univ., Ames, Iowa
Kjarsgaard, Donald R., 3600 Lakeway Dr., Bellingham, Wash.
Klahn, Richard P., Des Moines Indep. Comm. Sch. Dist., Des Moines, Iowa
Klaus, Catherine R., 111½ N. Vine, West Union, Iowa
Klausmeier, Herbert J., Sch. of Educ., University of Wisconsin, Madison, Wis.
Kleffner, John H., Assoc. Supt. of Cath. Schools, Oklahoma City, Okla.
Klein, Howard A., Col. of Educ., Univ. of Sask., Saskatoon, Sask., Canada
Klein, M. Francis, 928-23rd St., Santa Monica, Calif.
Klein, Philip, 1520 Spruce St., Philadelphia, Pa.
Klein, Richard K., Department of Public Instruction, Bismarck, N.Dak.
Klein, Russel, 4975 Whiteaker St., Eugene, Oreg.
Kleis, Russell J., Michigan State University, East Lansing, Mich.
Klevan, Albert, 45 W. Bayberry Rd., Clemont, N.Y.
Kleyensteuber, Carl J., Northland College, Ashland, Wis.
Klinckmann, Evelyn, San Francisco Col. for Women, San Francisco, Calif.
Kline, Charles E., Purdue University, Lafayette, Ind.
Kline, Francis F., 1643 Elmwood Ct., Oshkosh, Wis.
Kline, Robert D., 12078 Golden Gate Ave., N.E., Albuquerque, N. Mex.
Kling, Martin, Grad. Sch. of Educ., Rutgers State Univ., New Brunswick, N.J.
Klingstedt, Joe Lars, 5411 40th St., Lubbock, Tex.
Klohr, Paul R., 420 Walhalla Rd., Columbus, Ohio
Klopf, Gordon J., Bank Street Col. of Educ., New York, N.Y.
Klopfer, Leopold E., University of Pittsburgh, Pittsburgh, Pa.
Knape, Clifford S., 1024 North 18-A St., Waco, Tex.
Knapp, Frederick C., 272 Rochelle Park, Tonawanda, N.Y.
Knapp, William D., 6800 Schoolway, Greendale, Wis.
Knauer, Thomas E., 1410 Central Ave., Deerfield, Ill.
Knepp, A. Christine, 1782 Roberts Lane N.E., Warren, Ohio
Knight, Octavia B., North Carolina College, Durham, N.C.
Knight, Reginald R., 4338 Heather Rd., Long Beach, Calif.
Knirk, Frederick G., 161 Brookside Lane, Fayetteville, N.Y.
Knoblock, Peter, 805 S. Crouse Ave., Syracuse, N.Y.
Knolle, Lawrence M., Chatham College, Pittsburgh, Pa.
Knope, Mrs. Perle, Madison Public Schools, Madison, Wis.
Knorr, Amy Jean, University of Arizona, Tucson, Ariz.
Knowlden, Gayle E., 3003 Laurel Ave., Manhattan Beach, Calif.
Knox, Carl S., 2017 Louisiana St., Lawrence, Kans.
Knox, Stanley C., St. Cloud State College, St. Cloud, Minn.
Koch, Mrs. Sylvia L., 539 N. Highland Ave., Los Angeles, Calif.
Kocum, Eleanor G., Thackery Lane Rd. No. 1, Mendham, N.J.
Koehler, Everette E., The King's College, Briarcliff Manor, N.Y.

Koehring, Dorothy, Univ. of N. Iowa Field Serv., Cedar Falls, Iowa
Koenig, Vernon H., 11878 Ridgecrest Dr., Riverside, Calif.
Koeppe, Richard P., Asst. Supt., Denver Public Schools, Denver, Colo.
Koerber, Walter F., Scarborough Board of Education, Scarborough, Ont., Canada
Koerner, Warren A., 4608 West 106th St., Oak Lawn, Ill.
Koester, George A., San Diego State College, San Diego, Calif.
Koff, Robert H., 1044 Vernier Pl., Stanford, Calif.
Kohake, Cletus, St. Benedict's Col. Library, Atchison, Kans.
Kohler, Lewis T., 7659 Whitsett Ave., N. Hollywood, Calif.
Kohlmann, Eleanor L., 169 MacKay Hall, Iowa State University, Ames, Iowa
Kohn, Martin, 35 West 92nd St., New York, N.Y.
Kohrs, E. V., Gillette, Wyo.
Kokras, Nocolaos, Elia-Gonnon, Parissa, Greece
Kolakowski, Donald, 5719 S. Kimbark Ave., Chicago, Ill.
Kollar, Theodore H., Paterson Cath. Reg. H.S., Paterson, N.J.
Konecny, Frank J., 101 S. Rita St., Waco, Tex.
Konishi, Walter K., San Jose State College, San Jose, Calif.
Konrad, Abram G., Tabor College, Hillsboro, Kans.
Konsh, Adeline, 7 East 14th St., New York, N.Y.
Konstantinos, K. K., Lenape Regional High School, Medford, N.J.
Kontos, George, Jr., 351 N.E. Chambers Ct., Newport, Oreg.
Koontz, David, West Virginia State College, Institute, W. Va.
Koos, Leonard V., Route 2, Newago, Mich.
Kopan, Andrew T., 1228 Ashland Ave., River Forest, Ill.
Kopel, David, Chicago St. Col. 6800 Stewart Ave., Chicago, Ill.
Koppenhaver, Albert H., Calif. State Col., Long Beach, Calif.
Korella, Lynell, 6212 Lewis Dr., S.W., Calgary, 10, Alberta, Canada
Korntheuer, Gerhard A., St. Johns College, Winfield, Kan.
Kovach, Gaza, Pocahontas High School, Pocahontas, Va.
Kowitz, George T., Dept. of Educ. Psych., Univ. of Oklahoma, Norman, Okla.
Koyanagi, Elliot Y., 2630 Dekist St., Bloomington, Ind.
Kozma, Ernest J., 8081 Worthington Park Dr., Strongsville, Ohio
Krafft, Larry J., 739 Roslyn St., Glenside, Pa.
Kraft, Dennis, Northern State Col., Aberdeen, S. Dak.
Kraft, Milton Edward, Earlham College, Richmond, Ind.
Kramer, William A., 3558 S. Jefferson Ave., St. Louis, Mo.
Kratz, Gerald B., Huron Valley Schools, Milford, Mich.
Krauf, Philip E., 40 E. 84th St., New York, N.Y.
Kraus, Howard F., 512 Alameda de las Pulgas, Belmont, Calif.
Krause, Frank, 5120 Southgreen Dr., Indianapolis, Ind.
Kravetz, Nathan, 555 Kappock St., Riverdale, N.Y.
Kravetz, Sol, 11545 Duque Dr., Studio City, Calif.
Kravitz, Bernard, 4098 Union Bay Circle, N.E., Seattle, Wash.
Kravitz, Jerry, 986 Van Buren St., Baldwin, N.Y.
Krawitz, E. Harris, 6503 N. Le Mal, Lincolnwood, Ill.
Kreinheder, Adeline E., Muhlenberg Col., Allentown, Pa.
Kreismer, Clifford R., Clara E. Coleman Sch., 100 Pinelynn Rd., Glen Rock, N.J.
Kreitlow, Burton W., Route #1, Mazonmanie, Wis.
Kress, Roy A., 800 Moredon Rd., Meadowbrook, Pa.
Krich, Percy, Dept. of Educ., Queens College, Flushing, N.Y.
Krippner, Stanley C., Dept. of Psychiatry, Maimonides Hosp., Brooklyn, N.Y.
Krolikowski, W. P., Loyola University, Chicago, Ill.
Kroman, Nathan, University of Saskatchewan, Saskatoon, Sask., Canada
Kropp, John P., 12455 Russell Ave., Chino, Calif.
Kropp, Russell P., Florida State University, Tallahassee, Fla.
Krueger, Louise W., 1520 Laburnum Ave., Chico, Calif.
Krug, Edward, Dept. of Educ., University of Wisconsin, Madison, Wis.
Kruppa, Richard A., 1150 Louisiana Ave., Perrysburg, Ohio
Kruszynski, Eugene S., San Francisco State College, San Francisco, Calif.
Krzesinski, Daniel J., R.D. 1, Attica, N.Y.

Kubalek, Josef, Usenory 198, O Praha-Zapad, C S S R, Czech.
Kubik, Edmund J., 9741 S. Leavitt St., Chicago, Ill.
Kuhn, Donald K., 8520 Mackenzie Rd., St. Louis, Mo.
Kuhn, Doris Y., Univ. of Houston, Houston, Tex.
Kuhn, Joseph A., 99 Buffalo Ave., Long Beach, N.Y.
Kuhnen, Mrs. Mildred, 2106 Park Ave., Chico, Calif.
Kulberg, Janet M., 149 Cedar St., Bangor, Maine
Kullman, N. E., Jr., 153 Murray Ave., Delmar, N.Y.
Kumpf, Carl H., Superintendent of Schools, Clark, N.J.
Kunimoto, Mrs. Tadako, 734—16th Ave., Honolulu, Hawaii
Kuntz, Allen H., 72 Lombardy St., Lancaster, N.Y.
Kunzler, William J., 34 Overbrook Dr., Kirksville, Mo.
Kurtz, John J., Inst. for Child Study, Univ. of Maryland, College Park, Md.
Kusler, Gerald E., E. Lansing High Schl., E. Lansing, Mich.
Kusmik, Cornell J., 7400 Augusta St., River Forest, Ill.
Kutz, Frederick B., Newark High School, Newark, Del.
Kvaraceus, William C., Clark University, Worcester, Mass.
Kyle, Helen F., Rhode Island College, Providence, R.I.
Kynard, Alfred T., Prairie View A. & M. College, Prairie View, Tex.
Kysilka, Marcella L., Univ. of Tex., Austin, Tex.

Labatte, Henry, 40 College St., Toronto, Ontario, Canada
LaBay, Michael J., Col. of Educ., University of Toledo, Toledo, Ohio
Lacey, Archie L., Hunter Col., City University of N.Y., New York, N.Y.
Lache, Sheldon, University of Connecticut, Storrs, Conn.
Lacivita, James, 1206 A. Boxwood Dr., Mt. Prospect, Ill.
Lackey, Kenneth E., 809 Lockett Rd., St. Louis, Mo.
Ladd, Edward T., Emory University, Atlanta, Ga.
Ladd, Eleanor M., Col. of Educ., University of Georgia, Athens, Ga.
Ladd, Paul, Wooster High School, Wooster, Ohio
LaDue, Donald C., Elem. Educ. Dept., Temple University, Philadelphia, Pa.
LaFauci, Horatio M., 871 Commonwealth Ave., Boston, Mass.
Lafferty, Charles W., Supt. of Schools, Fairbanks, Alaska
Lafferty, Henry M., East Texas State Univ., Commerce, Tex.
LaForce, Charles L., 426 Malden Ave., LaGrange Park, Ill.
Lafranchi, W. E., Stabley Library, State College, Indiana, Pa.
LaGrone, Herbert F., Sch. of Educ., Texas Christian Univ., Fort Worth, Tex.
Lahaderne, Henrietta M., IDEA, 1100 Glendon Ave., Los Angeles, Calif.
Laird, Albert W., Western Ky. Univ., Bowling Green, Ky.
Lake, Doris S., State Univ. Col., Oneonta, N.Y.
Lambert, Pierre D., Sch. of Educ., Boston College, Chestnut Hill, Mass.
Lambert, Roger H., 1409 H Spartan Village, E. Lansing, Mich.
Lambert, Ronald T., University of Minnesota, Minneapolis, Minn.
Lampard, Dorothy M., Univ. of Letherbridge, Letherbridge, Alba., Canada
Lampshire, Richard H., Drake University, Des Moines, Iowa
Lamson, William E., 4850 E. Melissa St., Tucson, Ariz.
Lane, Frank T., USAID, Rio de Janiero/SUN, APO New York, NY.
Lane, Mrs. Mary B., 10 Lundy's Lane, San Mateo, Calif.
Lane, Vera J., P.O. Box 44064-Louisiana St. Dept. of Educ., Baton Rouge, La.
Lang, Mrs. Pauline R., Southern Connecticut State Col., New Haven, Conn.
Lange, Paul W., 2304 Linden Dr., Valparaiso, Ind.
Lange, Phil C., Tchrs. Col., Columbia University, New York, N.Y.
Langeveld, M. J., Prins Hendriklaan 6, Bilthoven, Holland
Langland, Lois E., 4021 Olive Hill Dr., Claremont, Calif.
Langley, Elizabeth M., 4937 W. Wellington Ave., Chicago, Ill.
Langman, Muriel P., 2111 Delafield Dr., Ann Arbor, Mich.
Langston, Genevieve R., Eureka College, Eureka, Ill.
Langston, Roderick G., 1451 S. Loma Verde St., Monterey Park, Calif.
Lanham, Frank W., 3212 Charing Cross, Ann Arbor, Mich.
Lanier, Ruby, Route No. 2, Box 619, Hickory, N.C.
Lanning, Frank W., Northern Illinois University, DeKalb, Ill.

Lano, Richard L., University of California, Los Angeles, Calif.
Lansing, Marvin G., 122 Mappa St., Eau Claire, Wis.
Lansu, Walter J., 6036 Metropolitan Plaza, Los Angeles, Calif.
Lantz, James S., 413 Burr Oak St., Albion, Mich.
Lantz, Ralph G., Box 278, Warrington, Pa.
Lapp, Diane, 1235 Eigenmann Hall, Bloomington, Ind.
Larkin, Lewis B., 15818 Westbrook, Detroit, Mich.
Larkins, William J., 32000 Chagrin Blvd., Cleveland, Ohio
Larmee, Roy A., Cntr. for Educ. Admn., Ohio State Univ., Columbus, Ohio
Larsen, Arthur Hoff, Illinois State University, Normal, Ill.
Larson, Eleanore E., Col. of Educ., Univ. of Rochester, Rochester, N.Y.
Larson, L. C., Audio-Visual Center, Indiana University, Bloomington, Ind.
Larson, Shirley G., Univ. of Minn. St. Paul, Minn.
Larson, Vera M., 13601 N.E. Fremont St., Portland, Oreg.
Lashingter, Donald R., Syracuse Univ., Syracuse, N.Y.
Laska, John, Sutton Hall, Univ. of Texas, Austin, Tex.
Lassanske, Paul A., 4389 Hodgson Rd., St. Paul, Minn.
Lathrop, Irvin T., California State College, Long Beach, Calif.
Lattimer, Everett C., Magee Rd., Glenmont, N.Y.
Laudico, Minerva G., Centro Escolar University, Manila, Philippines
Lauria, Joseph L., 6401 Shoup Ave., Canoga Park, Calif.
Laurier, Blaise V., Les Clercs de Saint-Viateur, Montreal, Quebec, Canada
Lavenburg, F. M., Public Schls., 155 Broad St., Bloomfield, N.J.
Lavenburg, Jack, 2185 Seventeenth Ct., W., Eugene, Oreg.
Laverty, John A., 5944 S. Washtenaw Ave., Chicago, Ill.
Lawhead, Victor B., Ball State University, Muncie, Ind.
Lawler, Marcella R., Tchrs. Col., Columbia University, New York, N.Y.
Lawrence, Clayton G., Marion College, Marion, Ind.
Lawrence, Richard E., Univ. of New Mexico, Albuquerque, N.Mex.
Lawrence, Ruth E., 627 Grove St., Denton, Tex.
Lawrie, Jack D., 1274 Duane Rd., Chattanooga, Tenn.
Lawski, A. J., Edsel Ford High School, 20601 Rotunda Dr., Dearborn, Mich.
Lawson, James R., Dept. of Educ., Trust Terr. Govt., Ponape, E. Caroline Islands
Layton, Donald H., University of California, Los Angeles, Calif.
Lazar, Alfred L., Schl. of Educ., Calif. St. Col. at Long Beach, Long Beach, Calif.
Lazow, Alfred, 2631 W. Berwyn Ave., Chicago, Ill.
Leavitt, Jerome E., Col. of Educ., Univ. of Arizona, Tucson, Ariz.
Lebofsky, Arthur E., Rd. #1, Box 814, June Rd., Chester, N.Y.
Lechiara, Francis J., 1400 Miller Rd., Coral Gables, Fla.
Lee, Annabel, Univ. of Puget Sound, Tacoma, Wash.
Lee, Della, Asst. Prin., Public School, Bronx, N.Y.
Lee, Ernest C., Prin., Beaufort H.S., Beaufort, Victoria, Australia
Lee, Harold Fletcher, Box 38, Lincoln University, Jefferson City, Mo.
Lee, Howard D., Atwater School, Shorewood, Wis.
Lee, J. Murray, Southern Illinois University, Carbondale, Ill.
Lee, James Michael, University of Notre Dame, Notre Dame, Ind.
Lee, John J., Col. of Educ., Wayne State University, Detroit, Mich.
Lee, William B., U.S.D.E.S.E.A., APO New York, N.Y.
Lee, William C., Fairleigh Dickinson University, Rutherford, N.J.
Leeds, Donald S., Northeastern University, Boston, Mass.
Leeds, Willard L., Univ. of Wisc., Madison, Wis.
Leese, Joseph, State Univ. Col., Albany, N.Y.
Lefever, David Welty, Sch. of Educ., Univ. of California, Los Angeles, Calif.
* Lefforge, Roxy, 1945 Fruit St., Huntington, Ind.
Lehman, Lloyd W., 926 Ferdinand, Forest Park, Ill.
Lehmann, Irvin J., Michigan State University, East Lansing, Mich.
Lehmkuhl, Carlton B., 4 Wilogreen Rd., Natick, Mass.
Lehsten, Nelson G., Sch. of Educ., Univ. of Michigan, Ann Arbor, Mich.
Leib, Joseph A., 240 Sinclair Pl., Westfield, N.J.
Leibert, Robert E., 1005 W. Gregory Ave., Kansas City, Mo.

Leibik, Leon J., 204 Dodge Ave., Evanston, Ill.
Leigh, Robert K., Box 2501, University, Ala.
Leinster, Carolyn J., P.O. Box 126, Keuka Park, N.Y.
Leitch, John J., Jr., Admin. Off., Wheeler Rd., Central Islip, N.Y.
Lembo, John M., 77 N. Duke St., Millersville, Pa.
Lennon, Joseph L., Providence College, Providence, R.I.
Lennon, Lawrence J., 310 N. Webster Ave., Scranton, Pa.
Lennox, Robert S., P.O. Box 2486, Davidson, N.C.
Leonard, Lloyd L., Dept. of Educ., Northern Illinois Univ., DeKalb, Ill.
Leonard, William P., Univ. of Pittsburgh, Pittsburgh, Pa.
Lepera, Alfred G., 254 Franklin St., Newton, Mass.
LePere, Jean M., Michigan State University, East Lansing, Mich.
Lepore, Albert R., 2614 Lancaster Rd., Hayward, Calif.
Lesniak, Robert J., 314 W. Oak St., Palmyra, Pa.
Lester, J. William, Superintendent, Diocesan Schls., Fort Wayne, Ind.
Leverson, Leonard O., 201 W. Newhall Ave., Waukesha, Wis.
Levin, Alvin I., 12336 Addison St., North Hollywood, Calif.
Levin, J. Joseph, 221 N. Cuyler Ave., Oak Park, Ill.
Levine, Daniel U., Sch. of Educ., Univ. of Missouri, Kansas City, Mo.
Levine, Murray, 74 Colonial Circle, Buffalo, N.Y.
Levine, Stanley L., 1627 Anita Ln., Newport Beach, Calif.
Levinson, Leo, Clarkston Sch. Dist. No. 1, New City, N.Y.
Levit, Martin, Sch. of Educ., University of Missouri, Kansas City, Mo.
Levy, Nathalie, 506 Mississippi Ave., Bogalusa, La.
Lewis, Arthur J., Col. of Educ., Univ. of Fla., Gainesville, Fla.
Lewis, Edward R., 5293 Greenridge Rd., Castro Valley, Calif.
Lewis, Elizabeth V., P.O. Box 1833, University, Ala.
Lewis, Eva P., Box 296, Grambling, La.
Lewis, Maurice S., Col. of Educ., Arizona State University, Tempe, Ariz.
Lewis, P. Helen, 1634 Neil Ave., Box 84, Columbus, Ohio
Lewis, Philip, 6900 S. Crandon Ave., Chicago, Ill.
Lewis, Robert, 915 N. Union St., Natchez, Miss.
Lewis, Roland B., Eastern Washington State College, Cheney, Wash.
Lewis, William, Millikin Univ. Library, Decatur, Ill.
Licata, William, State Univ. Col., Buffalo, N.Y.
Licthy, E. A., Illinois State University, Normal, Ill.
Lieb, L. V., Dept. of Educ., State University College, Oswego, N.Y.
Lieberman, Ann, 13040 Hartland St., North Hollywood, Calif.
Lieberman, Marcus, 5835 Kimbark Ave., Chicago, Ill.
Lien, Ronald L., Mankato State College, Mankato, Minn.
Lietwiler, Helena K., 5907 Aberdeen Rd., Bethesda, Md.
Liggett, Donald R., Grinnell College, Grinnell, Ia.
Liggitt, William A., 703 St. Marks Ave., Westheld, N.J.
Light, Alfred B., 480 Glen St., Glens Falls, N.Y.
Light, Judy A., 5930 Howe St., Pittsburgh, Pa.
Lighthall, Frederick, Dept. of Educ., Univ. of Chicago, Chicago, Ill.
Ligon, Mary Gilbert, Hofstra College, Hempstead, N.Y.
Liljenlad, Maynard T., Barstow Schl., Barstow, Calif.
* Lincoln, Edward A., Thompson St., Halifax, Mass.
Lind, Arthur E., 1422 Johnston Ave., Richland, Wash.
Lind, Marshall L., P.O. Box 557, Kodiak, Alaska
Lindberg, Lucile, Queens College, Flushing, N.Y.
Lindbloom, Dwight, 1636 Hewitt St., St. Paul, Minn.
Lindeman, Richard H., Tchrs. Col., Columbia University, New York, N.Y.
Lindemer, George Charles, Seton Hall University, South Orange, N.J.
Lindgren, Henry C., 1975-15th Ave., San Francisco, Calif.
Lindly, Charles, 809 South St., Rapid City, S. Dak.
Lindman, Mrs. Margaret R., Prin., College Hill School, Skokie, Ill.
Lindvall, C. Mauritz, Sch. of Educ., University of Pittsburgh, Pittsburgh, Pa.
Linehan, Mrs. Louise W., 4 Bolton Pl., Fair Lawn, N.J.
Linn, Frank J., S.E. Mo. State College, Cape Girardeau, Mo.

Linson, Marvin G., 933 Fulton St., Aurora, Colo.
Linstrum, Dick, 2156 Sierra Way, San Luis Obispo, Calif.
Lipham, James M., Dept. of Educ., University of Wisconsin, Madison, Wis.
Lipscomb, William A., Box 249, Eureka, Nev.
Lissovoy, Vladimir de, Pennsylvania State Univ., University Park, Pa.
Litherland, Bennett H., 2705-34th St., Rock Island, Ill.
Litin, Mrs. Annette, 5302 N. Granite Reef Rd., Scottsdale, Ariz.
Litsinger, Dolores A., San Fernando Valley State College, Northridge, Calif.
Little, J. Kenneth, Bascom Hall, University of Wisconsin, Madison, Wis.
Little, Sara, Presbyterian Sch. of Christian Education, Richmond, Va.
Littlefield, Roy S., Superintendent of Schools, Dell, Ark.
Litton, H. John, Jr., Crystal Sprgs Dr., Rt. 4, Falcon Ranche, Lexington, S.C.
Litwin, Mrs. Zelda, Responsive Environment Program, Brooklyn, N.Y.
Litzky, Leo, 11 Pomona Ave., Newark, N.J.
Livingston, Thomas B., Box 4060, Texas Tech. Station, Lubbock, Tex.
Livo, Mrs. Norma J., 11960 W. 22nd Pl., Denver, Colo.
Llewellyn, Ardelle A., San Francisco State College, San Francisco, Calif.
*Lloyd, Francis V., Jr., 5834 Stony Island Ave., Chicago, Ill.
Lloyd-Jones, Esther M., 430 West 116th St., New York, N.Y.
Lobdell, Lawrence O., Springfield Coll., Springfield, Mass.
Locke, William W., 1317 Pine St., Kingsport, Tenn.
Lockett, B. T., 1848 Tiger Flowers Dr., N.W., Atlanta, Ga.
Lockett, Mortimer W., 904 Cumberland Dr., Woodbridge, Va.
Lockwood, William L., 215 Harbor St., Glencoe, Ill.
Lofgren, Marie Luise S., 5068 Cocoa Palm Way, Fair Oaks, Calif.
Logan, Lillian May, Brandon Univ., Brandon, Manitoba, Canada
Logdeser, Mrs. Thomas, 11616 Woodview Blvd., Parma Heights, Ohio
Lohman, Maurice A., Tchrs. Col., Columbia University, New York, N.Y.
Lohmann, Victor L., St. Cloud St. Col., St. Cloud, Minn.
Lohse, Arnold W., 3595 Stillwater Rd., St. Paul, Minn.
Lola, Justita O., Bicol Teachers College, Legaspi, Albay, Philippines
Lomax, James L., 808 S. Loombs, Valdosta, Ga.
London, Jack, 2328 Derby St., Berkeley, Calif.
Long, Isabelle, 4343 Harriet Ave., S., Minneapolis, Minn.
Longsdorf, Homer, 413 Leslie, Lansing, Mich.
Lonsdale, Mrs. Maxine deLappe, 1405 Campbell Lane, Sacramento, Calif.
Lonsdale, Richard C., 220 Palmer Ave., North Tarrytown, N.Y.
Lonsway, Rev. Francis A., O.F.M., Bellarmine Col., Louisville, Ky.
Looby, Thomas F., 241 S. Ocean Ave., Patchogue, N.Y.
Loomis, Arthur K., 917 W. Bonita Ave., Claremont, Calif.
Loomis, William G., 684 Illinois Ave., N.E., Salem, Oreg.
Loop, Alfred B., P.O. Box 896, Bellingham, Wash.
Loree, M. Ray, Box 742, University of Alabama, University, Ala.
Lorenz, Donald W., Concordia H. S., Portland, Oreg.
Loudon, Mrs. Mary Lou, 1408 Stephens Ave., Baton Rouge, La.
Loughlin, Leo J., 257 Rolfe Rd., DeKalb, Ill.
Loughrea, Mildred K., 659 City Hall, St. Paul, Minn.
Love, Virginia H., 1515 W. Washington, Sherman, Tex.
Lovely, Edward C., Trumbull High School, Trumbull, Conn.
Lovette, Joanne P., 88 Rt. 119 South, Indiana, Pa.
Lowe, A. J., University of South Florida, Tampa, Fla.
Lowe, Mary G., Dept. of H.E., University of Utah, Salt Lake City, Utah
Lowe, R. N., Sch. of Educ., University of Oregon, Eugene, Oreg.
Lowe, Viola C., 1512 S. Gamon Rd., Wheaton, Ill.
Lowe, William T., 328 Hopeman, University of Rochester, Rochester, N.Y.
Lower, William J., Art Dept., Troy State Univ., Troy, Ala.
Lowery, Zeb A., Rutherford County Schools, Rutherford, N.C.
Lowes, Ruth, 2004 Seventh Ave., Canyon, Tex.
Lowey, Warren G., Box 64, Setauket, L.I., N.Y.
Lowther, Malcolm A., Sch. of Educ., Univ. of Michigan, Ann Arbor, Mich.
Lowther, William L., Supt. of Schools, Boonton, N.J.

Lubell, Richard M., 2 Stoddard Pl., Brooklyn, N.Y.
Lubin, Harry, Supt. of Schools, Bellmawr, N.J.
Lucas, J. H., 2006 Fayetteville St., Durham, N.C.
Lucas, Robert E., Fort Morgan High School, Fort Morgan, Colo.
Lucash, Benjamin, 9801 Montour St., Philadelphia, Pa.
Lucietto, Lena, 5835 Kimbark Ave., Chicago, Ill.
Lucio, William H., Sch. of Educ., University of California, Los Angeles, Calif.
Lucito, Leonard J., Apt. 704, 700 Seventh St., S.W., Washington, D.C.
Luddeke, Nancy, 848 Yorkhaven Rd., Cincinnati, Ohio
Ludeman, Ruth, Augsburg College, Minneapolis, Minn.
Ludwig, Lois K., 2644 S.E. 51st Ave., Portland, Oreg.
Luebke, Martin F., 1704 W. Jackson St., Springfield, Ill.
Luetkemeyer, Joseph F., 7002 St. Annes Ave., Lanham, Md.
Luhmann, Philip, 1407 E. 54th St., Chicago, Ill.
Luker, Arno Henry, Colorado State College, Greeley, Colo.
Lund, S. E. Torsten, 45-B Tolman Hall, Univ. of California, Berkeley, Calif.
Lunde, Mrs. Josephine, 505 Oxford, Grand Forks, N.Dak.
Lundin, Stephen C., 3405 N. Cleveland #5, St. Paul, Minn.
Lunney, Gerald H., L. I. Univ., Greenvale, N.Y.
LuPone, O. J., 4520 Culbertson, LaMesa, Calif.
Lyman, Francis J., Washington Schl., 735 Washington Rd., Pittsburgh, Pa.
Lynch, Florence M., 8338 S. Kedvale Ave., Chicago, Ill.
Lynch, James M., Superintendent of Schools, Rt. No. 9, East Brunswick, N.J.
Lynch, John C., DePaul University, Chicago, Ill.
Lynch, Patrick D., Pa. State Univ., University Park, Pa.
Lyons, Mrs. Cora E., P.O. Box 133, Amboy, Ill.
Lyons, John H., 17 Colton Rd., Somers, Conn.
Lyons, Paul R., 300-11 Diamond Village, Gainesville, Fla.

Maag, Raymond E., 122 W. Franklin Ave., Minneapolis, Minn.
MacArthur, Austin J., Schl. Three, 230 Joralemon St., Belleville, N.Y.
MacConnell, John C., Muhlenberg College, Allentown, Pa.
MacDonald, Donald V., University of Scranton, Scranton, Pa.
Macdonald, Leland S., 5609—19th St., N., Arlington, Va.
MacDonald, M. Gertrude, 78 Sheffield Rd., Melrose, Mass.
MacGown, Paul C., 3128 N. Ash St., Spokane, Wash.
Mack, Esther, San Jose State College, San Jose, Calif.
* MacKay, James L., 3737 Fredericksburg Rd., San Antonio, Tex.
MacKay, Vera A., Col. of Educ., Univ. of British Columbia, Vancouver, B.C.
MacKay, William R., 124 Underhill Rd., Bellingham, Wash.
Mackenzie, Donald M., White House, Park College, Parkville, Mo.
MacKenzie, Elbridge G., Anderson College, Anderson, Ind.
Mackenzie, Gordon N., Tchrs. Col., Columbia University, New York, N.Y.
Mackintosh, Helen K., 215 Wolfe St., Alexandria, Va.
MacLean, Effie, Saskatoon Pub. Sch. Brd., Saskatoon, Sask., Canada
MacLeay, Ian A., P.O. Box 560, Lennoxville, Quebec, Canada
MacLeod, James J., 6300 Grand River, Detroit, Mich.
MacMillan, Robert W., Univ. of R.I., Kingston, R.I.
MacNaughton, Elizabeth A., 2990 Richmond Ave., Houston, Tex.
MacRae, Douglas G., Fulton County Board of Educ., Atlanta, Ga.
Madding, Jane B., 9431-47th Dr. NE, Marysville, Wash.
Maddox, Mrs. Clifford R., 525 Enid Ave., Dayton, Ohio
Madeja, Stanley S., 6838 Pershing Ave., University City, Mo.
Mader, Charles E., Univ. of Ill.-Chicago Circle, Chicago, Ill.
Madonna, Mrs. Shirley M., 47-27—215th St., Bayside, N.Y.
Madore, Normand William, Illinois State University, Normal, Ill.
Magary, James F., Sch. of Educ., Univ. of So. California, Los Angeles, Calif.
Magee, Eunice H., P.O. Box 445, College Station, Hammond, La.
Maginnis, Maria, 20522 Parthenia St., Canoga Park, Calif.
Magoon, Thomas M., 1316 Canyon Rd., Silver Spring, Md.
Magram, P. Theodore, 88 E. Mohawk St., Oswego, N.Y.

Mahan, H. James, 200 Westview Ave., Columbus, Ohio
Mahar, Robert J., Col. of Educ., Temple University, Philadelphia, Pa.
Maher, Alan E., Unqua School, Massapequa, N.Y.
Maher, Trafford P., St. Louis University, 15 N. Grand Blvd., St. Louis, Mo.
Mahler, Clarence A., Chico St. Col., Chico, Calif.
Mahon, Bruce R., Mount Royal Junior College, Calgary 2, Alba., Canada
Mailey, James H., Supt. of Schools, Midland, Tex.
Mailliard, Mrs. Margaret E., 221 E. 49th St., Chicago, Ill.
Mains, Mrs. Susie T., 29 West St., Barre, Vt.
Major, Suzanne T., 222 Capri Terr., Wheeling, Ill.
Maloof, Mitchell, 63 Main St., Williamstown, Mass.
Manchester, Frank S., Radnor School Dist., Wayne, Pa.
Mandel, E. Jules, 20918 Calimali Rd., Woodland Hills, Calif.
Mangum, G. C., P.O. Box 494, Darlington, S.C.
Manion, Richard T., Prin., Noah Wallace School, Farmington, Conn.
Manley, Francis J., Frontier Central Sch., Bay View Rd., Hamburg, N.Y.
Mann, Edward L., Jr., P.O. Box 188, Great Barrington, Mass.
Mann, James W., Roosevelt University, Chicago, Ill.
Mann, Jesse A., Georgetown Univ., Washington, D.C.
Mann, Sidney J., Syracuse City Schools, Syracuse, N.Y.
Mann, Mrs. Thelma T., 949 Hunakai St., Honolulu, Hawaii
Mann, Vernal S., Box 266, State College, Miss.
Mannan, Golam, Indiana Univ., Northwest, Gary, Ind.
Manning, Doris E., University of Arizona, Tucson, Ariz.
Mannos, Nicholas T., Niles Twp. High School West, Skokie, Ill.
Manoil, Adolph, Sch. of Educ., Boston University, Boston, Mass.
Manone, Carl, 34 Kirkline Ave., Hellertown, Pa.
Manuel, Herschel T., University of Texas, Austin, Tex.
Mapel, Seldon B., Jr., 1919 Mercedes Rd., Denton, Tex.
Marazzi, Maureen, 10 Plaza St., Brooklyn, N.Y.
Marburger, Carl L., Dept. of Educ., 225 W. State St., Trenton, N.J.
Marc-Aurele, Paul, 455, 80 Rue Est, Charlesbourg, Quebec 7, Canada
Marchie, Howard E., 26 Norman St., Springfield, Mass.
Marcus, Marie, Louisiana State University, New Orleans, La.
Margarones, John J., 210 College St., Lewiston, Maine
Margolis, Henry, 2030 S. Taylor Rd., Cleveland Heights, Ohio
Mark, Arthur, 6 Cross Brook Ln., Westport, Conn.
Markarian, Robert E., Springfield College, Springfield, Mass.
Marks, Claude H., Univ. of Tex., Austin, Tex.
Marks, Merle B., University of So. California, Los Angeles, Calif.
Marks, Ralph M., 641 N.E. 26th Ave., Ocala, Fla.
Marksberry, Mary Lee, Sch. of Educ., Univ. of Missouri, Kansas City, Mo.
Marksheffel, Ned D., Oregon State University, Corvallis, Oreg.
Markus, Frank 1420 Heights Blvd., Winona, Minn.
Marquand, Richard L., Michigan State Univ., East Lansing, Mich.
Marquardt, Robert L., Thiokol Chemical Corp., Ogden, Utah
Marquis, Francis N., 4712 Elzo Lane, Kettering, Ohio
Marquis, R. L., Jr., Box 5282, North Texas Sta., Denton, Tex.
Marsden, W. Ware, Okla. St. Univ., Zuck Addition, Stillwater, Okla.
Marsh, Mrs. Augusta B., 252 Bronner St., Prichard, Ala.
Marshall, Beth, 1325 S. Orange, Fullerton, Calif.
Marshall, Daniel W., Filene Center, Tufts University, Medford, Mass.
Marshall, Thomas O., 17 Mill Rd., Durham, N.H.
Marshall, Wayne P., 704 East 36th St., Kearney, Nebr.
Marso, Ronald N., Bowling Green State Univ., Bowling Green, Ohio
Marston, Mrs. Marjorie, 860 Lake Shore Dr., Chicago, Ill.
Martin, C. Keith, Col. of Educ., Univ. of Md., College Park, Md.
Martin, Edwin D., 2341 Quenby, Houston, Tex.
Martin, F. Gerald, Sacred Heart Seminary, Detroit, Mich.
Martin, Jackson J., 509 Irene Pl., Cheney, Wash.
Martin, Kathryn J., 2208 Fairhill Ave., Glenside, Pa.

Martin, Mavis D., SWCEL, 117 Richmond, N.E., Albuquerque, N.Mex.
Martin, R. Lee, State Univ. Col., Oswego, N.Y.
Martin, Robert M., University of Hawaii, Honolulu, Hawaii
Martin, Ruth G., 206 Parkview Dr., Marietta, Ga.
Martin, William R., 320 N.W. 19th Ave., Fort Lauderdale, Fla.
Martini, Miss Angiolina A., 1555 Oxford St., Berkeley, Calif.
Martinson, John S., 7 Rustic Lane, S.W., Tacoma, Wash.
Martire, Harriette A., St. Joseph College, West Hartford, Conn.
Martorana, Sabastian V., State University of New York, Albany, N.Y.
Marx, George L., Col. of Educ., University of Maryland, College Park, Md.
Marzolf, Stanley S., Illinois State University, Normal, Ill.
Marzullo, Santo P., Manpower Training Center, Rochester, N.Y.
Masem, Paul W., University of South Carolina, Columbia, S.C.
Masia, Bertram B., Dept. of Educ., Western Reserve Univ., Cleveland, Ohio
Masiko, Peter, Miami-Dade Junior College, Miami, Fla.
Mason, John M., Michigan State University, East Lansing, Mich.
Masoner, Paul H., University of Pittsburgh, Pittsburgh, Pa.
Massey, William J., 4906 Roland Ave., Baltimore, Md.
Massialas, Byron G., University of Michigan, Ann Arbor, Mich.
Massingill, Richard A., 15905 Harrison, Livonia, Mich.
Mathiott, James E., 3165 Ramona, Palo Alto, Calif.
Mathis, Claude, Sch. of Educ., Northwestern University, Evanston, Ill.
Matovich, Mike, 4332 Ivy St., East Chicago, Ind.
Matthew, Eunice Sophia, 340 Riverside Dr., New York, N.Y.
Matthews, James W., Star Rt. 3, McGrath Rd., Fairbanks, Alaska
Matthews, William P., 1114 N. Centennial, High Point, N.C.
Mattila, Ruth Hughes, P.O. Box 872, Las Vegas, N.Mex.
Mattox, Daniel V., Jr., Schl. of Educ., Ind. Univ. of Pa., Indiana, Pa.
Matwijcow, Peter, 12 Cardigan Rd., Hamilton Sq., Trenton, N.J.
Matzner, G. C., Eastern Illinois University, Charleston, Ill.
Mauk, Gertrude, Box 312, Garden City, Mich.
Maurer, Marion V., 148 Ann St., Apt. 23, Clarendon Hills, Ill.
Maurer, Robert L., California State Polytechnic College, Pomona, Calif.
Mauth, Leslie J., Ball State University, Muncie, Ind.
Maw, Wallace H., Sch. of Educ., University of Delaware, Newark, Del.
Mawter, Paul T., Wollongong Teachers Col., Wollongong, N.S.W., Australia
Maxcy, Horace P., Michigan State University, East Lansing, Mich.
Maxwell, Celia V., 316 Houston Dr., Morgantown, W. Va.
Maxwell, Ida E., 9 Chester Creek Rd., Cheyney, Pa.
May, Charles R., 431 S. 55th St., Lincoln, Nebr.
May, John B., State Teachers College, Salisbury, Md.
May, Robert E., Emerson Vocational High School, Buffalo, N.Y.
Mayer, Lewis F., 4275 W. 196th St., Fairview Park, Ohio
Mayer, Ronald W., 275 Vernon St., San Francisco, Calif.
Mayhew, Lewis B., 945 Valdez Pl., Stanford, Calif.
Maynard, Glenn, Kent State University, Kent, Ohio
Mayo, Samuel T., Sch. of Educ., Loyola University, Chicago, Ill.
Mayor, John R., AAAS, 1515 Massachusetts Ave., N.W., Washington, D.C.
Mazyck, Harold E., Jr., 2007 Chelsea Lane, Greensboro, N.C.
McAllister, David, Kathmandu, State Dept., Washington, D.C.
McArthur, L. C., Jr., Drawer 1180, Sumter, S.C.
McAuliffe, M. Eileen, 5649 N. Kolmar Ave., Chicago, Ill.
McBirney, Ruth, Boise St., Col. Library, Boise, Idaho
McBride, James H., 1246 Riverside Drive, Huron, Ohio
McBride, Ralph, Supt., Buckley-Loda Unit #8, Loda, Ill.
McBride, Richard L., 3221 Ave. S., Birmingham, Ala.
McBride, William B., Ohio State University, Columbus, Ohio
McBurney, Mrs. Doris, 1641 West 105th St., Chicago, Ill.
McCaffery, James F., Asst. Prin., Abington H.S., Abington, Pa.
McCahon, David M., 2300 Pittock St., Pittsburgh, Pa.
McCaig, Thomas E., 3447 W. Pierce Ave., Chicago, Ill.

McCain, Paul M., Arkansas College, Batesville, Ark.
McCall, Charlotte L., 320 N.E. 54th St. Apt. 4, Miami, Fla.
McCann, Lewis E., 18637 San Fernando Mission Blvd., Northridge, Calif.
McCann, Thomas W., 19 Jeffery Pl., Trumbull, Conn.
McCarthy, Joseph F. X., 641 Forest Ave., Larchmont, N.Y.
McCarthy, Joseph J., 9531 S. Kostner, Oak Lawn, Ill.
McCartney, Hilda, 2916 Redwood Ave., Costa Mesa, Calif.
McCarty, Henry R., 206 Ebony Ave., Imperial Beach, Calif.
McCaslin, James J., 5916 N. Crittenden, Indianapolis, Ind.
McCaul, Robert L., Col. of Educ., University of Chicago, Chicago, Ill.
McClanahan, L. D., 86 W. State St., Athens, Ohio
McClard, Donavon, San Diego State College, San Diego, Calif.
McCleary, Lloyd E., University of Illinois, Urbana, Ill.
McClellan, James E., 70 Greentree Dr., Doylestown, Pa.
McClelland, Denis A., Y.M.C.A., 36 College St., Toronto 2, Ont., Canada
McClendon, Patricia R., Winthrop College, Rock Hill, S.C.
McClintock, Eugene, Kaskaskia College, Shattuc Rd., Centralia, Ill.
McClintock, James A., Drew University, Madison, N.J.
McClure, Donald E., 1905 Harding Dr., Urbana, Ill.
McClure, L. Morris, Col. of Educ., Univ. of Maryland, College Park, Md.
McClure, Nancy, Col. of Educ., Univ. of Kentucky, Lexington. Ky.
McClure, Robert M., 3314 Tennyson St., N.W., Washington, D.C.
McClurkin, W. D., Peabody College, Nashville, Tenn.
McClusky, Howard Yale, Elem. Sch., University of Michigan, Ann Arbor, Mich.
McCollum, Elinor C., 619 Ridge Ave., Evanston, Ill.
McCollum, Robert E., Col. of Educ., Temple Univ., Philadelphia, Pa.
McConnell, Emma, Vassar College, Poughkeepsie, N.Y.
McConnell, Gaither, Cen. for Tchr. Educ., Tulane Univ., New Orleans. La.
McConnell, Thomas R., Center for Study of Higher Educ., Berkeley, Calif.
McCook, T. Joseph, 1408 W. Friendly Ave., Greensboro, N.C.
McCormick, Ethel M., Lehigh Univ., Bethlehem, Pa.
McCormick, Felix J., Tchrs. Col., Columbia University, New York, N.Y.
McCormick, Robert W., Ohio State University, Columbus, Ohio
McCowan, Richard J., 2466 W. Oakfield Dr., Grand Island, N.Y.
McCoy, Noel H., 1905 Sabine, Apt. 102, Austin, Tex.
McCracken, Oliver, Jr., Superintendent of Schools, Skokie, Ill.
McCuaig, Susannah, Col. of Educ., U. of Maryland, College Park, Md.
McCue, Robert E., 2308 N. Hazelwood Ave., Davenport, Iowa
McCuen, John T., 1340 Loretta Dr., Glendale, Calif.
McCullough, Constance M., 80 Vincente Rd., Berkeley, Calif.
McCuskey, Dorothy, Western Michigan University, Kalamazoo, Mich.
McCutcheon, Nancy Sue, Sch. of Educ., Univ. of South Carolina, Columbia, S.C.
McDaniel, Ernest D., Educ. Resch. Cent., Purdue Univ., Lafayette, Ind.
McDaniel, Marjorie C., Indiana State University, Terre Haute, Ind.
McDaniels, Garry L., 8830 Pincy Branch Rd., Silver Spring, Md.
McDavit, H. W., South Orange-Maplewood Public Schools, South Orange, N.J.
McDiarmid, Garnet Leo, 102 Bloor St. West, Toronto, Ont., Canada
McDonald, Donald, Texas Technological College, Lubbock, Tex.
McDonald, L. R., Woodruff Senior High School, Peoria, Ill.
McDonough, Fred J., McKinley Schl., 65 Yeaman St., Revere, Mass.
McDougle, Larry G., 522 Center St., Findlay, Ohio
McDowell, John B., 11 Blvd. of Allies, Pittsburgh, Pa.
McDowell, Thelma B., 773 Chestnut Ridge Rd., Morgantown, W. Va.
McElhinney, James, 3816 Brook Dr., Muncie, Ind.
McElroy, Louis A., Technical-Vocational School, Gary, Ind.
McEwen, Gordon B., 13602 E. Walnut, Whittier, Calif.
McFarland, John W., Sch. of Educ., Univ. of Texas, El Paso, Tex.
McFarren, G. Allen, 11 Willow Lane Ct., Tonawanda, N.Y.
McFeaters, Margaret M., 608 Brown's Lane, Pittsburgh, Pa.
McGary, Carroll R., 125 Stroudwater St., Westbrook, Maine
McGavern, John H., University of Hartford, Hartford, Conn.

McGee, Ralph G., 1526 Washington Ave., Wilmette, Ill.
McGee, Robert T., Asst. Supt. Pennsbury School Dist., Fallsington, Pa.
McGeoch, Dorothy M., Tchrs. Col., Columbia University, New York, N.Y.
McGinnis, Frederick A., Wilberforce University, P.O. Box 22, Wilberforce, Ohio
McGinnis, James H., Knoxville College, Knoxville, Tenn.
McGivney, Joseph, Syracuse Univ., Fayetteville, N.Y.
McGlasson, Maurice A., Sch. of Educ., Indiana University, Bloomington, Ind.
McGrath, J. H., Dept. of Ed. Admin., Illinois State Univ., Normal, Ill.
McGrath, John W., Superintendent of Schools, Belmont, Mass.
McGraw, Mrs. Robert, 108 Grannis Rd., Orange, Conn.
McGregor, Louis, Wayland Baptist College, Plainview, Texas
McGroarty, Rosemary, Queens College Teacher Corps, Flushing, N.Y.
McGuire, George K., 7211 Merrill Ave., Chicago, Ill.
McGuire, J. Carson, Col. of Educ., University of Texas, Austin, Tex.
McHugh, Walter J., California State College, Hayward, Calif.
McInerney, George K., 88-19—211th St., Jamaica, N.Y.
McIntyre, Margaret, George Washington Univ., Washington, D.C.
McIsaac, Don, University of Wisconsin, Madison, Wis.
McKay, Jean W., Board of Education, Manassas, Va.
McKean, Robert C., Col. of Educ., University of Colorado, Boulder, Colo.
McKee, Paul J., 3106 Elmwood Ave. Apt. 10, Rochester, N.Y.
McKelpin, Joseph P., 620 Peachtree St., N.E., Atlanta, Ga.
McKelvey, Troy V., State Univ. of N.Y. at Buffalo, N.Y.
McKenna, Charles D., Sch. Dist. of the City of Ladue, St. Louis, Mo.
McKenna, John J., Jr., Brd. of Educ., Greenvillage Rd., Madison, N.J.
McKenney, James L., Grad. Sch. of Business, Harvard Univ., Boston, Mass.
McKenzie, Robert M., 2031 Poyntz, Manhattan, Kans.
McKercher, Mrs. Berneth N., 1600 Dryden Rd., Metamora, Mich.
McKinney, Carolyn, 3540 Merrick Crt. Lexington, Ky.
McKinney, Lorella A., State Univ. Col., New Paltz, N.Y.
McKnight, Eloise, Dept. of Educ., St. Univ. Col., New Paltz, N.Y.
McKnight, Philip C., 250 No. Terrace Dr., Wichita, Kans.
McKown, George W., 2603 S. Forest Ave., Palatine, Ill.
McKoy, Judith B., Hunter College, New York, N.Y.
McKune, Esther J., State Univ. Col., Oneonta, N.Y.
McLain, William T., P.O. Box 86, Newark, Del.
McLaughlin, Eleanor T., Albion College, Albion, Mich.
McLaughlin, Frances, Ida V. Moffett Schl. of Nursing, Birmingham, Ala.
McLaughlin, Kenneth F., 871 N. Madison, Arlington, Va.
McLaughlin, Rita E., 126 University Rd., Brookline, Mass.
McLees, Mrs. Martha P., Univ. of South Carolina, Columbia, S.C.
McLellan, Keith A., 113 Heaslip St., Wollongong 2500, N.S.W., Australia
McLendon, Jonathan C., Col. of Educ., Univ. of Georgia, Athens, Ga.
McMahan, John Julia, Keene State College, Keene, New Hampshire
McMahon, Charles W., 22218 Gregory, Dearborn, Mich.
McMahon, Frances E., University of Missouri, Columbia, Mo.
McManus, William E., Supt. Catholic Schls, 430 N. Michigan, Chicago, Ill.
McMaster, Blanche E., 102 Hull St., Bristol, Conn.
McMillen, Leland A., Winona St. Col., Winona, Minn.
McNally, Harold J., 7132 N. Crossway Rd., Fox Point, Wis.
McNeil, Don C., Dept. of Spec. Educ., University of Texas, Austin, Tex.
McNeill, Charles A., Sch. of Educ., University of S.C., Columbia, S.C.
McNutt, C. R., 116 Ridge Rd., Woodbridge, Va.
McPhee, Roderick F., Punahou Schl., Honolulu, Hawaii
McPherson, Virgil L., Adams State College, Alamosa, Colo.
* McPherson, W. N., Darke County Superintendent of Schools, Greenville, Ohio
McSwain, E. T., University of North Carolina, Greensboro, N.C.
McSweeney, Maryellen, Mich. St. Univ., E. Lansing, Mich.
McTeer, Blanche R., 803 Lafayette St., Beaufort, S.C.
McWilliams, Elma A., William Carey College, Hattiesburg, Miss.
* Mead, Arthur R., 1719 N.W. 6th Ave., Gainesville, Fla.

Meade, David W., 722 W. 5th, Red Wing, Minn.
Meaders, O. Donald, Col. of Educ., Michigan State Univ., East Lansing, Mich.
Mease, Clyde D., Superintendent of Schools, Humboldt, Iowa
Medeiros, Joseph V., Superintendent of Schools, New London, Conn.
Medler, Byron W., Sch. of Educ., No. Texas St. Univ., Denton, Tex.
Mednick, Martha T., 6428 Bannockburre Dr., Bethesda, Md.
Medsker, Leland L., Ctr., Study of Higher Educ., Univ. of Calif., Berkeley, Calif.
Medsker, Nancy D., 611 Jerome St., Marshalltown, Iowa
Medved, A. A., Cherry Lawn School, Darien, Conn.
Meeks, Heber J., 12931 Morene St., Poway, Calif.
Meer, Samuel J., 631 Lafayette Ave., Mt. Vernon, N.Y.
Megiveron, Gene Erwin, 3170 Angelus Dr., Pontiac, Mich.
Megonegal, E. Russell, 464 Granite Ter., Springfield, Pa.
Mehrens, William, Michigan State Univ., East Lansing, Mich.
Meier, Frederick A., State Col. at Salem, Salem, Mass.
Meier, Mrs. Paralee B., 13 Woodside Ln., Chico, Calif.
Meier, Willard H., Dept. of Educ., La Sierra Col., Riverside, Calif.
Meinke, Dean L., Col. of Educ., University of Toledo, Toledo, Ohio
Meiselman, Max S., 87-56 Francis Lewis Blvd., Queens Village, N.Y.
Meissner, Harley W., 13 Devonshire, Pleasant Ridge, Mich.
Melberg, Merritt E., 1222 W. 22nd St., Cedar Falls, Iowa
Melbo, Irving R., University of Southern California, Los Angeles, Calif.
Melby, Ernest O., Michigan State University, East Lansing, Mich.
Mellott, Malcolm E., Col. of Educ., Temple University, Philadelphia, Pa.
Mellott, Virginia T., 335 E. Granville Rd., Worthington, Ohio
Melnick, Curtis C., Supt., Dist. 14, Chicago Public Schls., Chicago, Ill.
Melnik, Amelia, Col. of Educ., University of Arizona. Tucson, Ariz.
Melton, Arthur W., Dept. of Psychol., Univ. of Michigan, Ann Arbor, Mich.
Melvin, Keith L., Peru State College, Peru, Nebr.
Mendel, Mrs. Dolores M., Paterson State College, Wayne, N.J.
* Mendoza, Romulo Y., 17 Iba, Sta. Mesa Heights, Quezon City, Philippines
Menge, Joseph W., Wayne University, Detroit, Mich.
Menosky, Dorothy, Wayne St. Univ., Detroit, Mich.
Merchant, Vasant V., 308 W. Forest Ave., Flagstaff, Ariz.
Meredith, Cameron W., Southern Illinois Univ., Edwardsville, Ill.
Merenda, Peter F., 258 Negansett Ave., Warwick, R.I.
Merideth, Howard V., Central Sch. Dist. No. 2, Syosset, L.I., N.Y.
Merigis, Harry, Eastern Illinois University, Charleston, Ill.
Merkhofer, Beatrice E., Chicago State College, Chicago, Ill.
Merryman, Edward P., Ball State Univ., Muncie, Ind.
Merryman, John E., Col. of Educ., Indiana University, Indiana, Pa.
Mersand, Joseph, Jamaica High Sch., 168th St. and Gothic Dr., Jamaica, N.Y.
Merwin, Jack C., Col. of Educ., Univ. of Minn., Minneapolis, Minn.
Mescher, C. Harold, 1702 Julianne Dr., Marion, Ill.
Mestdagh, William A., 1640 Vernier Rd., Grosse Pointe Woods, Mich.
Metfessel, Newton S., Univ. of Southern California, Los Angeles, Calif.
Metzner, William, 1121 Welsh Rd., Philadelphia, Pa.
Meyer, Ammon B., Route 1, Fredericksburg, Pa.
Meyer, Goldye W., Univ. of Bridgeport, Bridgeport, Conn.
Meyer, Lorraine V., 2940 N. 124th St., Apt. #4, Wauwatosa, Wis.
Meyer, Mrs. Marie, Douglass Col., Rutgers Univ., New Brunswick, N.J.
Meyer, Richard C., East. Texas State University, Commerce, Tex.
Meyer, Warren G., 5829 Portland Ave., So., Minneapolis, Minn.
Meyer, William T., Adams State College, Alamosa, Colo.
Meyerhoff, Herman, 5400 E. Pomona Blvd., Los Angeles, Calif.
Meyers, Howard E., Peru State Col., Peru, Nebr.
Meyers, Max B., 324 E. 59th St., Brooklyn, N.Y.
Meyers, Robert E., Middlebury High School, Middlebury, Ind.
Meyers, Russell W., 5835 Kimbark Ave., Chicago, Ill.
Michael, Calvin B., Col. of Educ., East. Mich., Univ., Ypsilanti, Mich.
Michael, Lloyd S., Evanston Township High School, Evanston, Ill.

Michael, William B., Sch. of Educ., Univ. of So. California, Los Angeles, Calif.
Michaelis, John U., Sch. of Educ., Univ. of California, Berkeley, Calif.
Michaels, Melvin L., Highland Park High School, Highland Park, N.J.
Micheels, William J., Stout State University, Menomonie, Wis.
Michie, James K., Superintendent of Schools, St. Cloud, Minn.
Mickelsen, John K., 106 Jackson Dr., Liverpool, N.Y.
Mickelson, John M., Sch. of Educ., Temple University, Philadelphia, Pa.
Middledorf, Carl W., St. Peter's Lutheran School, East Detroit, Mich.
Middleton, C. A., State College of Iowa, Cedar Falls, Iowa
Midjaas, Carl L., 12408 Via Catherina, Grand Blanc, Mich.
Milchus, Norman J., 20504 Williamsburg Rd., Dearborn Heights, Mich.
Miles, F. Mike, 424 Oakland Ave., Iowa City, Iowa
Milheim, Robert P., Wright State Univ., Dayton, Ohio
Milhollan, Frank E., 6003—85th Pl., Hyattsville, Md.
Millar, Allen R., Southern State Tchrs. College, Springfield, S.Dak.
Miller, Arthur L., 5625 Rosa Ave., St. Louis, Mo.
Miller, Benjamin, 251 Ft. Washington Ave., New York, N.Y.
Miller, C. Earl, Jr., 157 Eldridge Ave., Mill Valley, Calif.
Miller, Carroll H., Dept. of Educ., Northern Illinois Univ., DeKalb, Ill.
Miller, Carroll L., Howard University, Washington, D.C.
Miller, Eliza Beth, Catskill High School, Catskill, N.Y.
Miller, Ethel B., 337 Kishwaukee Dr., Sycamore, Ill.
Miller, G. Dean, State Dept. of Educ., St. Paul, Minn.
Miller, G. Harold, 1600 N. Morris, Gastonia, N.C.
Miller, George E., Univ. of Illinois Col. of Medicine, Chicago, Ill.
Miller, George R., University of Pittsburgh, Pittsburgh, Pa.
Miller, Harold E., Eastern Mennonite Col., Harrisonburg, Va.
Miller, Mrs. Helen H., 1471 Westhaven Rd., San Marino, Calif.
Miller, Henry, Sch. of Educ., City College of New York, New York, N.Y.
Miller, Herbert R., 1229 Larrabee St., Los Angeles, Calif.
Miller, Holbert M., 1026 Washington St., Iowa City, Iowa
Miller, Howard G., North Carolina State College, Raleigh, N.C.
Miller, Ingrid O., Edina-Morningside Senior High School, Edina, Minn.
Miller, Ira E., Eastern Mennonite College, Harrisonburg, Va.
Miller, Jack W., Box 35, Peabody College, Nashville, Tenn.
Miller, Jacob W., Brooke Rd., Savbrooke Park, Pottstown, Pa.
Miller, John L., Supt. of Schools, Great Neck, N.Y.
Miller, Leon F., Northwest Missouri State College, Maryville, Mo.
Miller, Lyle L., Col. of Educ., University of Wyoming, Laramie, Wyo.
Miller, Mrs. Marian B., Dept. of Pub. Instr., Dover, Del.
Miller, N. A., Jr., Watauga High School, Boone, N.C.
Miller, Norman N., Superintendent of Schools, Tyrone, Pa.
Miller, Olimpia V., Fordham Univ., Redding, Conn.
Miller, Paul A., 230 E. Ninth St., Cincinnati, Ohio
Miller, Richard I., Col. of Educ., University of Kentucky, Lexington, Ky.
Miller, Robert F., 7106 Farralone Ave., Canoga Park, Calif.
Miller, Ross, West Georgia College, Carrollton, Ga.
Miller, Texton R., North Carolina State University, Raleigh, N.C.
Milling, Euleas, 231 Spring St., N.W., Concord, N.C.
Mills, Boyd C., Eastern Washington State Col., Cheney, Wash.
Mills, Donna M., 530 Taft Place, Gary, Ind.
Mills, Forrest L., Racine Public Library, Racine, Wis.
Mills, Henry C., Provost, St. John's Univ., Jamaica, N.Y.
Mills, Patricia, Miami University, Oxford, Ohio
Mills, Ruth I., Concord College, Athens, W.Va.
Mills, William H., Sch. of Educ., Univ. of Michigan, Ann Arbor, Mich.
Milner, Ernest J., Sch. of Educ., Syracuse University, Syracuse, N.Y.
Mimaki, James M., 11224 Huston St., North Hollywood, Calif.
Mims, Samuel, Bethany Bible College, Santa Cruz, Calif.
Mincy, Homer F., 100 Wildwood Dr., Oak Ridge, Tenn.
Miniclier, Gordon E., 1965 Laurel Ave., St. Paul, Minn.

Mininberg, Elliot I., 7-13 Washington Square, New York, N.Y.
Minkler, F. W., 15 Oakburn Crest, Willowdale, Ont., Canada
Minkoff, Sol., 601 N. Eastwood, Mt. Prospect, Ill.
Minnis, Roy B., 7889 E. Kenyon Ave., Denver, Colo.
Minock, Mrs. Daniel F., 5520 Donna Ave, Tarzana, Calif.
Mirenda, Joseph J., 1627 N. Humboldt Ave., Milwaukee, Wis.
Misner, Paul J., Western Michigan Univ., Kalamazoo, Mich.
Misun, John, 5555 S. Nicholson Ave., Cudahy, Wis.
Mitby, Norman P., 211 N. Carroll St., Madison, Wis.
Mitchell, Addie S., Dept. of Eng., Morehouse College, Atlanta, Ga.
Mitchell, Donald P., 5166 Tilden St., N.W., Washington, D.C.
Mitchell, Guy Clifford, Sch. of Educ., Baylor University, Waco, Tex.
Mitchell, Virginia L., Indiana State Univ., Terre Haute, Ind.
Mitzel, Harold E., 928 S. Sparks St., State College, Pa.
Miyasato, Albert H., 297 Puiwa Rd., Honolulu, Hawaii
Mobley, Frank, Dept. of Educ., Louisiana College, Pineville, La.
Moe, Alden J., Dept. of Educ., Clarke College, Dubuque, Iowa
Moffatt, Maurice P., 210 Valencia Blvd., Largo, Fla.
Mohr, Raymond E., 2050 S. 108th St., Milwaukee, Wis.
Molenkamp, Alice, 5 Homeside Lane, White Plains, N.Y.
Molloy, Eugene J., Superintendent, Catholic Schools, Brooklyn, N.Y.
Monell, Ira H., 2714 Augusta Blvd., Chicago, Ill.
Monfort, Jay, 143 Hillcrest Rd., Berkeley, Calif.
Monke, Mrs. Edgar W., High Point High School, Beltsville, Md.
Monnin, Lloyd N., 4733 W. National Rd., Springfield, Ohio
Monroe, Bruce Perry, 640 Sea Breeze Dr., Seal Beach, Calif.
Monroe, Mrs. Helen V., 1253 Lake Breeze, Oshkosh, Wis.
Montgomery, Wanda, 1223 Rose Vista Ct 7, St. Paul, Minn.
Montor, Karel, 732 Cottonwood Dr., Severna Park, Md.
Monts, Elizabeth A., Home Ec. Dept., Univ. of Wisconsin, Madison, Wis.
Moody, Lamar, 1100 Bridle Park Rd., Rt. 3, Box 303, Starkville, Miss.
Moore, Barry E., 103 William Dr., Normal, Ill.
Moore, C. Fletcher, Box 186, Elon College, N.C.
Moore, Harold E., Col. of Educ., Arizona State University, Tempe, Ariz.
Moore, Robert Ezra, 20 Tapia Dr., San Francisco, Calif.
Moore, Wilhelmina E., C. D. Hine Library, State Office Bldg., Hartford, Conn.
Moore, William J., 372 High St., Richmond, Ky.
Moorefield, Thomas E., Off. of Educ., 400 Maryland Ave., Washington, D.C.
Moorhead, Sylvester A., Sch. of Educ., Univ. of Mississippi, University, Miss.
Moray, Joseph, San Francisco State College, San Francisco, Calif.
Morden, Frederick P., Dept. of Educ., Univ. of Mich., Ann Arbor, Mich.
Morehouse, Charles O., 601 S. Howard St., Kimball, Nebr.
Moreland, Kenneth O., 107 William Dr., Normal, Ill.
Moretz, Elmo E., Grad. Sch. of Educ., Eastern Kentucky Univ., Richmond, Ky.
Morford, John A., John Carroll University, Cleveland, Ohio
Morgan, Donald L., 20 Graham Ave., Brookeville, Pa.
Morgan, Lorraine Lee, 6909 Meade St., Pittsburgh, Pa.
Morgan, Muriel, Newark State College, Union, N.J.
Morgan, Roland R., Superintendent, Mooresville City Schls., Mooresville, N.C.
Morgenroth, Edwin C., 714 W. California Blvd., Pasadena, Calif.
Morgenstern, Anne, 2037 Oliver Way, Merrick, L.I., N.Y.
Morley, Franklin P., 101 Arthur Ave., Webster Groves, Mo.
Morris, Earl W., Rt. 5, East Lake Drive, Edwardsville, Ill.
Morris, Gregory A., 811 Maple St., West Mifflin, Pa.
Morris, James D., Col. of Educ., Univ. of Hawaii, Honolulu, Hawaii
Morris, James L., 675 Omar Circle, Yellow Springs, Ohio
Morris, Rev. John E., Diocesan Schls., Paterson, N.J.
Morris, M. B., 1133 Westridge, Abilene, Tex.
Morris, Mrs. Marjorie S., 16225 Moorpark, Encino, Calif.
Morris, William P., Somerset Lake, R.R. 1, Nashville, Ind.
Morrison, D. A., East York Bd. of Educ., Toronto, Ont., Canada

* Morrison, J. Cayce, 580 North Bank Ln., Lake Forest, Ill.
Morrison, Leger R., 16 Brown St., Warren, R.I.
Morrow, Richard G., 502 State St., Madison, Wis.
Morrow, Robert O., Dept. of Psych., State College of Ark., Conway, Ark.
Morse, William C., 2010 Penncraft Ct., Ann Arbor, Mich.
Morton, R. Clark, 210 Drummond St., Warrensburg, Mo.
Mosbo, Alvin O., Colorado State College, Greeley, Colo.
Moseley, S. Meredith, 424 N.W. 15th Way, Fort Lauderdale, Fla.
Moser, Robert P., 316 Master Hall, Univ. of Wis., Madison, Wis.
Moser, William G., 95 Concord Rd., Chester, Pa.
Moses, Doris E., Essex Co., Col. Library, Newark, N.J.
Moses, Elizabeth, 7483 Countrybrook Dr., Indianapolis, Ind.
Mosher, Frank Kenneth, Sadaquada Apt., Whitesboro, N.Y.
Moss, Theodore C., 88 Sixth Ave., Oswego, N.Y.
Mother C. Welch, San Francisco College for Women, San Francisco, Calif.
Mother Margaret Burke, Barat Col. of the Sacred Heart, Lake Forest, Ill.
Mother Mary Aimee Rossi, San Diego Col. for Women, San Diego, Calif.
Mother Mary Dennis, Rosemont College, Rosemont, Pa.
Mother M. Gonzaga, Blessed Sacrament College, Cornwells Heights, Pa.
Mother Rose Alice, 2675 Larpenteur Ave. East, St. Paul, Minn.
Mott, Edward B., R.F.D., Richmondville, N.Y.
Motyka, Agnes L., 6311 Utah Ave., N.W., Washington, D.C.
Muck, Mrs. Ruth E. S., 1091 Stony Point Rd., Grand Island, N.Y.
Muck, Webster C., Bethel Col., St. Paul, Minn.
Muckenhirn, Erma F., Dept. of Educ., East. Mich. Univ., Ypsilanti, Mich.
Muellen, T. K., 3606 Spruell Dr., Silver Spring, Md.
Mueller, Richard J., Northern Illinois University, DeKalb, Ill.
Mueller, Siegfried G., 5429 Sawyer, Chicago, Ill.
Mueller, Van D., Col. of Educ., Univ. of Minn., Minneapolis, Minn.
Mullen, Norman, Superintendent of Schools, Woodsville, N.H.
Muller, Philippe H., University of Neuchatel, Neuchatel, Switzerland
Mulliner, John H., 645 Abbotsford Rd., Kenilworth, Ill.
Mumford, Kennedy A., 14845 Robinson St., Miami, Fla.
Muns, Arthur C., Northern Illinois Univ., DeKalb, Ill.
Munshaw, Carroll, 555 Byron St., Plymouth, Mich.
Muntyan, Milosh, Michigan State University, East Lansing, Mich.
Murdick, Olin J., Superintendent, Diocesan Schools, Saginaw, Mich.
Murdock, Mrs. Ruth, Andrews University, Berrien Springs, Mich.
Murfin, Don L., Prin., South H.S., Bakersfield, Calif.
Murphy, Anne P., 480 S. Jersey St., Denver, Colo.
Murphy, Daniel A., Seton Hall University, South Orange, N.J.
Murphy, Dennis K., Grinnell College, Grinnell, Iowa
Murphy, Forrest W., 201 S. Hickory St., Aberdeen, Miss.
Murphy, John E., Clifton H. S., 333 Colfax Ave., Clifton, N.J.
Murphy, Kenneth B., Jersey City State Col., Jersey City, N.J.
Murphy, Loretta M., 415 Larkin Ave., Joliet, Ill.
Murphy, William F., 37 High St., Milford, Mass.
Murray, Joseph A., Jr., Cranston School Dept., Cranston, R.I.
Murray, William J., 1 Bay View Pl., South Boston, Mass.
Musgrave, Ray S., Univ. of Southern Mississippi, Hattiesburg, Miss.
Musick, James E., University of California, Los Angeles, Calif.
Myer, Marshall E., Col. of Educ., Univ. of Tenn., Knoxville, Tenn.
Myers, Donald A., 1100 Glendon Ave., Los Angeles, Calif.
Myers, Donald W., State Univ. Coll., Brockport, N.Y.
Myers, G. T., Superintendent of Schools, Lancaster, S.C.
Myers, Garry C., Ed., Highlights for Children, Honesdale, Pa.

Nacke, Phil L., Univ. of Brit. Columbia, Vancouver, B. C., Canada
Nadler, Leonard, Col. of Educ., Univ. of Md., College Park, Md.
Nafziger, Mary K., Goshen College, Goshen, Ind.
Nagel, Wilma I., Dept. of Educ., Univ. of Rhode Island, Kingston, R.I.

Nagy, Richard, North Junior High School, Bloomfield, N.J.
Nahshon, Samuel, Hebrew Teachers College, Brookline, Mass.
Nairus, John P., Cleveland Public Schools, Cleveland, Ohio
Nakashima, Mitsugi, P.O. Box 155, Kaumakani, Kanai, Hawaii
Nally, Thomas P., University of Rhode Island, Kingston, R.I.
Nance, Mrs. Afton Dill, State Educ. Bldg., 721 Capitol Ave., Sacramento, Calif.
Nance, Helen M., Illinois State University, Normal, Ill.
Narkis, William F., 1046 S. 22nd Ave., Bellwood, Ill.
Nash, Philip C., 3336 Sycamore Pl., Carmel, Calif.
Naslund, Robert A., Sch. of Educ., Univ. of So. California, Los Angeles, Calif.
Nason, Doris E., University of Connecticut, Storrs, Conn.
Nasser, Sheffield T., 6801 Pennywell Dr., Nashville, Tenn.
Nasstrom, Roy R., Jr., Col. of Educ., U. of Ky., Lexington, Ky.
Nattress, LeRoy W., 430 N. Mich. Ave., Chicago, Ill.
Nault, William H., Field Enterprises Educational Corp., Chicago, Ill.
Naus, Grant H., 374 "D" Ave., Coronado, Calif.
Naylor, Marilyn, 233 W. Cascade, River Falls, Wis.
Neal, Ellis H., Superintendent of Schools, Pendleton, Oreg.
Neale, Daniel C., Col. of Educ., University of Minnesota, Minneapolis, Minn.
Nearhoff, Orrin, 2745 Bennett Ave., Des Moines, Iowa
Nearing, Mrs. Jewell, 9050 S. Parnell, Chicago, Ill.
Nebel, Dale, Colorado State College, Greeley, Colo.
Nelson, Avis, 4618 Russell Ave., No. Minneapolis, Minn.
Nelson, Carl B., New York State University College, Cortland, N.Y.
Nelson, Clifford L., Univ. of Maryland, College Park, Md.
Nelson, Edith I., 380 Claremont Ave., Montclair, N.J.
Nelson, Ethel C., 692 Des Plaines Ave., Des Plaines, Ill.
Nelson, Florence A., Univ. of South Carolina, 825 Sumter St., Columbia, S.C.
Nelson, Frank G., R. 2, Box 169-0, Pullman, Wash.
Nelson, Jack L., State Univ. Col., Buffalo, N.Y.
Nelson, Janice Ann, 8350 Olentangy River Rd., Worthington, Ohio
Nelson, John M., Dept. of Educ., Purdue University, Lafayette, Ind.
Nelson, Kenneth G., Shore Acres, Dunkirk, N.Y.
Nelson, Lois Ney, 7 Lakeview Dr., Daly City, Calif.
Nelson, Margaret B., 223 N. 13th St., La Crosse, Wis.
Nelson, Orville W., Stout State College, Menomonie, Wis.
Nelson, Owen N., 2521 E. 2nd St., Bloomington, Ind.
Nelson, Quentin D., 5050 N. Mozart St., Chicago, Ill.
Nelson, Sylvia, 415 W. 8th St., Topeka, Kans.
Nelson, Torlef, University of Hawaii, Honolulu, Hawaii
Nelum, J. Nathaniel, Div. of Educ., Bishop College, Dallas, Tex.
Nemzek, Claude L., Educ. Dept., Univ. of Detroit, Detroit, Mich.
Nerbovig, Marcella, Northern Illinois University, DeKalb, Ill.
Nesbitt, William O., University of Houston, Houston, Tex.
Nesi, Carmella, 906 Peace St., Pelham Manor, N.Y.
Neuman, Donald B., Univ. of Wis. Milwaukee, Milwaukee, Wis.
Neuner, Elsie Flint, 2 Atlas Place, Mt. Vernon, N.Y.
Neville, Donald, Child Study Center, Peabody College, Nashville, Tenn.
Neville, Richard F., Col. of Educ., University of Maryland, College Park, Md.
Nevin, Mrs. Virginia L., 418 Franklin St., Fayetteville, N.Y.
Newburn, H. K., Col. of Educ., Arizona State University, Tempe, Ariz.
Newbury, David N., Curric Cood., H.P. Sch. Dist., Hazel Park, Mich.
Newcomer, Charles A., Lock Haven State Col., Lock Haven, Pa.
Newman, David, Sch. Psych., Oceanside, N.Y.
Newman, Herbert M., Educ. Dept., Brooklyn College, Brooklyn, N.Y.
Newman, Wilfred, West High School, Rochester, N.Y.
Newmann, John, The Ford Foundation, 320 E. 43rd St., New York, N.Y.
Newsom, Herman A., P.O. Box 5243, North Texas Station, Denton, Tex.
Newton, Kathryn L., 42 13th Ave., Columbus, Ohio
Newton, W. L., Florida State University, Tallahassee, Fla.
Nicholas, William T., 2205 Monte Vista Ave., Modesto, Calif.

Nichols, David L., University of Maine, Orono, Me.
Nichols, Edith J., 2655 Littleton Rd., El Cajon, Calif.
Nichols, Richard J., 1209 Maple Hill Rd., Scotch Plains, N.J.
Nicholson, Jon M., 312 Nevada, Northfield, Minn.
Nicholson, Lawrence E., Psych. Dept., Harris Tchrs. Col., St. Louis, Mo.
Nicholson, Robert A., Anderson Col., Anderson, Ind.
Nicholson, Sarah Alice, 1009 E. Hatton St., Pensacola, Fla.
Nicklas, Martin, Jefferson Jr. H. S., Pittsburgh, Pa.
Nicolari, Richard F., Willis Schl., Ansonia, Conn.
Niehaus, Philip C., Sch. of Educ., Duquesne University, Pittsburgh, Pa.
Niemeyer, John H., Bank Street College of Education, New York, N.Y.
Nigg, William J., Superintendent of Schools, Mankato, Minn.
Niland, William P., 417 Candleberry Rd., Walnut Creek, Calif.
Nimroth, William T., 1011 Wood Bridge, Ann Arbor, Mich.
Nixon, Clifford L., Penbrooke State College, Penbrooke, N.C.
Nixon, John Erskine, Sch. of Educ., Stanford University, Stanford, Calif.
Noar, Gertrude, 500 E. 77th St., New York, N.Y.
Noe, Samuel V., 506 West Hill St., Louisville, Ky.
Nolan, Barbara B., Psychology Dept., S.U.N.Y., Geneseo, N.Y.
Nolde, Randall L., 312 E. Main, Barrington, Ill.
Noll, Frances E., 1810 Taylor St., N.W., Washington, D.C.
Noll, Victor H., Col. of Educ., Michigan State Univ., East Lansing, Mich.
Noon, Elizabeth F., F. A. Owen Publishing Co., Dansville, N.Y.
Norcross, Claude E., 301 E. Lucard, Taft, Calif.
Norman, Ralph Paul, 18395 Clemison Ave., Saratoga, Calif.
Norman, Robert H., 315—4th Ave., N.W., Faribault, Minn.
Norris, Mrs. Dorothy G., 1907 Dumaine St., New Orleans, La.
Norris, Ralph C., 112-116—11th St., Des Moines, Iowa
North, Stewart D., 502 State St., Madison, Wis.
Northey, Ethel M., 1309 Orange St., Muscatine, Iowa
Northrup, Sunbeam Ann, 1816 Queens Lane, Arlington, Va.
Norton, Chauncey E., 31 Decker Rd., R.D. 1, Newfield, N.J.
Norton, Frank Edgar, Jr., 225 Fairway Dr., Wharton, Tex.
Norton, Robert E., Univ. of Arkansas, Fayetteville, Ark.
Novak, Benjamin J., Frankford High School, Philadelphia, Pa.
Novotney, Jerrold M., 1100 Glendon Ave., Los Angeles, Calif.
Now, Herbert O., State Dept. of Educ., Findlay, Ohio
Noyes, M. Elliot, Great Neck No. Senior High School, Great Neck, N.Y.
Nunnally, Nancy, 5916 Monticello Ave., Cincinnati, Ohio
Nussel, Edward J., Col. of Educ., Univ. of Toledo, Toledo, Ohio
Nutter, H. E., Norman Hall, University of Florida, Gainesville, Fla.
*Nutterville, Catherine, 1101 Third St., S.W., Washington, D.C.
Nutting, William C., 4653 Fortuna Way, Salt Lake City, Utah
Nuzum, Lawrence H., Marshall University, Huntington, W.Va.
Nye, Robert E., Sch. of Music, University of Oregon, Eugene, Oreg.
Nygaard, Joseph M., Butler University, Indianapolis, Ind.
Nystrand, Raphael O., Ohio State Univ., Columbus, Ohio

Oakland, Thomas D., 2702 Greenlawn Pkwy., Austin, Tex.
Oaks, Ruth E., B-104 Haverford Villa, Haverford, Pa.
Oberholtzer, Kenneth E., Superintendent of Schools, Denver, Colo.
Obourn, L. C., Superintendent of Schools, East Rochester, N.Y.
O'Brien, Cyril C., P.O. Box 666, Edmonton, Alba., Canada
O'Connor, John D., Maple Park, Ill.
O'Connor, Mrs. Marguerite O., Maple Park, Ill.
O'Connor, P. D., 103 Addison Rd., Manly 2095, N.S.W., Australia
O'Donnell, Lewis B., State University of New York, Oswego, N.Y.
Oehring, Esther A., Southern Oregon College, Ashland, Oreg.
Oen, Urban T., 4465 Kenneth, Okemos, Mich.
O'Fallon, O. K., Sch. of Educ., Kansas State University, Manhattan, Kans.
O'Farrell, John J., Loyola University, 7101 W. 80th St., Los Angeles, Calif.

O'Hare, Mary Rita, 212 Hollywood Ave., Tuckahoe, N.Y.
O'Hearn, George T., 202 Warren Ct., Green Bay, Wis.
Ohlsen, Merle M., Indiana State Univ., Terre Haute, Ind.
Ohs, Phyllis D., 727 Crestline, Kamloops, B. C., Canada
Ojeman, Ralph H., Educ. Research Council, Rockefeller Bldg., Cleveland, Ohio
O'Kane, Robert M., 306 Nut Bush Circle, Jamestown, N.C.
O'Keefe, Kathleen, 5441 Sanger Ave., Alexandria, Va.
Okula, Frederick S., 90 Mattatuck Rd., Bristol, Conn.
Olander, Herbert T., University of Pittsburgh, Pittsburgh, Pa.
* Oldham, Mrs. Birdie V., 621 W. 2nd St., Lakeland, Fla.
O'Leary, Francis V., 5480 S. Cornell Ave., Chicago, Ill.
Olicker, Isidore I., 85-17—143rd St., Jamaica, N.Y.
Olivas, Romeo A., 412 Brookview Ct., Oxford, Ohio
Oliver, Tommy, Willard Schl., Ada, Okla.
Oliver, T. S., Federal City Col., Washington, D.C.
Ollenburger, Alvin, 2613 Jean Duluth Rd., Duluth, Minn.
Olmsted, M. D., State University College, Oneonta, N.Y.
Olphert, Warwick B., Univ. of New England, Armidale, N.S.W., Australia
Olsen, Clarence R., The Univ. of Conn., Storrs, Conn.
Olsen, David E., 7866 Mulberry Rd., Chesterland, Ohio
Olsen, Eugene A., Purdue University, Lafayette, Ind.
Olsen, Hans C., Jr., University of Missouri, St. Louis, Mo.
Olson, Boyd E., P.O. Box 226, Singapore, Rep. of Singapore
Olson, Gerald Victor, 8610 W. 19th St., Phoenix, Ariz.
Olson, LeRoy C., 329 Nichols Ave., McDaniels Crest, Wilmington, Del.
Olson, Manley E., Col. of Educ., Univ. of Minnesota, Minneapolis, Minn.
Olson, R. A., Ball State University, Muncie, Ind.
Olson, Richard F., Western Pub. Educ. Co., Ossining, N.Y.
* Olson, Willard C., Sch. of Educ., University of Michigan, Ann Arbor, Mich.
Olson, William L., 1945 Sharondale Ave., St. Paul, Minn.
O'Malley, Mrs. Martha R., 44 Glenview Dr., Belleville, Ill.
O'Mara, J. Francis, 29 Snowling Rd., Uxbridge, Mass.
O'Neill, John H., 1039 W. Vine St., Springfield, Ill.
O'Neill, John J., Boston State College, Boston, Mass.
O'Neill, Patrick J., Superintendent, Diocesan Schools, Fall River, Mass.
O'Piela, Joan M., Res. & Dev., Detroit Pub. Schools, Detroit, Mich.
Oppenheimer, E. H., 3760 N. Pine Grove, Chicago, Ill.
Oppleman, Dan L., P.O. Box 182, Cedar Falls, Iowa
Ore, Malvern L., 903 East 52nd St., Chicago, Ill.
Ore, Stanley H., Jr., 2221 Emmers Dr., Appleton, Wis.
O'Reilly, Robert C., University of Nebraska at Omaha, Omaha, Nebr.
Orlovich, Joseph Jr., 206 S. Reed St., Joliet, Ill.
O'Rourke, Joseph, 3197 Gerbert Rd., Columbus, Ohio
Orr, Charles W., 137 Oakmont Circle, Durham, N.C.
Orr, Louise, 925 Crockett St., Amarillo, Tex.
Orton, Don A., Lesley College, Cambridge, Mass.
Orton, Kenneth D., Tchrs, Col., University of Nebraska, Lincoln, Nebr.
Osborn, Wayland W., 2701 Hickman Rd., Des Moines, Iowa
Osibov, Henry, University of Oregon, Eugene, Oreg.
Ostrander, Raymond H., 15 Winter St., Weston, Mass.
Ostwalt, Jay H., P.O. Box 387, Davidson. N.C.
Osuch, A. E., 6636 N. Odell, Chicago, Ill.
Oswalt, William W., Jr., 9 Berger St., Emmaus, Pa.
Otomo, Aiko, 3085 Felix St., Honolulu, Hawaii
O'Toole, James J., Cleveland Hghts. High Schl., Cleveland Heights, Ohio
Ott, Elizabeth, 4615 Laurel Canyon Dr., Austin, Tex.
Otto, Henry J., University of Texas, Austin, Tex.
Otts, John, University of South Carolina, Columbia, S.C.
Ouellette, Helen C., College of St. Rose, Albany, N.Y.
Overfield, Ruth, State Educ. Bldg., 721 Capitol Ave., Sacramento, Calif.
*Overstreet, George Thomas, 811 S. Frances St., Terrell, Tex.

Owen, John M., Psych. Dept., State University College, Potsdam, N.Y.
Owings, Ralph S., Univ. of Southern Mississippi, Hattiesburg, Miss.

Pace, C. Robert, Sch. of Educ., University of California, Los Angeles, Calif.
Page, Ellis B., Bur. of Educ. Res., Univ. of Connecticut, Storrs, Conn.
Pagel, Betty Lou, 304 E. 5th Ave., Cheyenne, Wyo.
Painter, Fred B., Superintendent, Brighton School Dist. No. 1, Rochester, N.Y.
Palisi, Anthony T., Seton Hall Univ., 181 Stanton, Rahway, N.J.
Palisi, Marino A., 300 Woodland Ave., Point Pleasant Beach, N.J.
Palladino, Joseph R., State College, Framingham, Mass.
Pallesen, Lorraine Sysel, 2727 Royal Ct., Lincoln, Nebr.
Palliser, Guy C., P.O. Box 30-632, Lower Hutt, New Zealand
Palmatier, Robert A., Jr., Col. of Educ., U. of Georgia, Athens, Ga.
Palmer, Albert, San Joaquin Delta College, Stockton, Calif.
Palmer, Anne M. H., 22277 Cass Ave., Woodland Hills, Calif.
Palmer, Dale H., Univ. of Washington, Seattle, Wash.
Palmer, Frank J., 208 Church St., North Syracuse, N.Y.
Palmer, James Bey, Illinois State University, Normal, Ill.
Palmer, John C., Tufts University, Medford, Mass.
Paltridge, James G., 2632 Tamalipas Ave., El Cerrito, Calif.
Panos, Robert J., 900 W. Minnehaha Pkwy., Minneapolis, Minn.
Papanek, Ernst, 1 West 64th St., New York, N.Y.
Papke, Ross R., Wisconsin State Univ., Richland Center, Wis.
Paradis, Edward E., Univ. of Minn., Minneapolis, Minn.
Parelius, Allen M., St. Louis University, St. Louis, Mo.
Parisho, Eugenia B., Lab. School, Univ. of North. Iowa, Cedar Falls, Iowa
Park, Mary Frances, Educ. Dept., Sam Houston State Col., Huntsville, Tex.
Park, Maxwell G., 44 Clayton Ave., Cortland, N.Y.
Parker, Don H., Emlimar, Big Sur, Calif.
Parker, Emma W., Cath. Univ. of Amer., Washington, D.C.
Parker, Glenn C., Harrisburg Schools, Harrisburg, Pa.
Parker, Jack F., University of Oklahoma, Norman, Okla.
Parker, James R., 210 Thornbrook Rd., DeKalb, Ill.
Parker, Jesse J., Louisiana State University, Baton Rouge, La.
Parker, Mrs. Lilla C., Box 464-A, Donnan Road, Macon, Ga.
Parker, Virjean, W. Va. Univ., Morgantown, W. Va.
Parkinson, Daniel S., 409 W. Vine St., Oxford, Ohio
Parr, Kenneth E., Box 1348 c/o Tapline, Beirut, Lebanon
Parrett, Betty J., 3024 South Shore Dr., Albany, Oreg.
Parry, O. Meredith, William Penn Senior High School, York, Pa.
Parsey, John M., 305 Droste Circle, East Lansing, Mich.
Parsley, Kenneth M., 214 St. Ives Dr., Severna Park, Md.
Parsons, Brooks A., Superintendent of Schools, Norwood, Ohio
Parsons, David R., Alexander Mackie Col., Paddington, N.S.W., Australia
Pascoe, David D., LaMesa Spring Valley Sch. Dist., LaMesa, Calif.
Passow, Aaron Harry, Teachers College, Columbia University, New York, N.Y.
Paster, Julius, 867 Barbara Dr., Teaneck, N.J.
Patch, Robert B., 4 Carleton Dr., Glens Falls, N.Y.
Pate, Mrs. Jimmie H., 11619 S. Bishop, Chicago, Ill.
Pate, Mildred, 1806 East 6th St., Greenville, N.C.
Paterson, John J., 377 Lawnview Dr., Morgantown, W.Va.
Paton, William, Superintendent of Schools, Oconomowoc, Wis.
Patrick, Robert B., 433 W. Park Ave., State College, Pa.
Patrick, T. L., Tulane Univ., New Orleans, La.
Patten, W. George, 2250 W. Roosevelt Blvd., Milwaukee, Wis.
Patterson, Gerald E., 6815 S.W. 63 St., Miami, Fla.
Patterson, Gordon E., New Mexico Highlands Univ., Las Vegas, N.Mex.
Patterson, Harold D., 3736 Crestbrook Rd., Birmingham, Ala.
Patteson, Charles, Lynchburg Col., Lynchburg, Va.

Patton, Earl D., Superintendent of Schools, Culver City, Calif.
Patty, Delbert L., 1412B Anthony St., Columbia, Mo.
Paul, Marvin S., 4750 W. Glenlake Ave., Chicago, Ill.
Paul, Warren I., 2203 Indiana Ave., Columbus, Ohio
Paulsen, Gaige B., 36 Fairview Ave., Athens, Ohio
Paulson, Casper F., Jr., Oregon College of Education, Monmouth, Oreg.
Paulston, Rolland G., University of Pittsburgh, Pittsburgh, Pa.
Pautz, Wilmer A., Wisconsin State University, Eau Claire, Wis.
Paxson, Robert C., Troy State College, Troy, Ala.
Paxton, Mrs. J. Hall, 1405 Pine St., Apt. 606, St. Louis, Mo.
Payne, David L., 131 Juanita St., Columbus, Miss.
Payne, LaVeta M., P.O. Box 591, Pierson and Suhrie Dr., Collegedale, Tenn.
Payne, William V., Tuskegee Institute, Tuskegee Institute, Ala.
Paynovitch, Nicholas, 921 W. Las Lomitas, Tucson, Ariz.
Payzant, Thomas W., 30 Glenn Circle, Philadelphia, Pa.
Paziotopoulos, James A., St. Constantine School, Oak Park, Ill.
Pearson, Guelda, 8907 Lemont Rd., Downers Grove, Ill.
Pearson, James R., Dade Co. Public Schools, Miami, Fla.
Pearson, Lois, State University College, Buffalo, N.Y.
Peccolo, Charles M., 2840 Nevada St., Manhattan, Kans.
Peck, Austin, State Univ. Col., Potsdam, N.Y.
Peckenpaugh, Donald H., 6 So. 36th Ave. East, Duluth, Minn.
Peddicord, Paul W., Univ. of Southern Miss., Hattiesburg, Miss.
Pederson, Arne K., Pacific Lutheran University, Tacoma, Wash.
Pederson, Clara A., Dept. of Educ., Univ. of North Dakota, Grand Forks, N.Dak.
Pederson, Otis, 1203 Pioneer Pkwy., Arlington, Tex.
Pedvin, Ruth E., 9150 Roberds St., Alta Loma, Calif.
Peirce, Leonard D., Olympia Public Schools, Olympia, Wash.
Pella, Milton O., Wisconsin High School, Univ. of Wisconsin, Madison, Wis.
Pellegrin, Lionel, 945 E. River Oaks Dr., Baton Rouge, La.
Pelton, Frank M., Dept. of Educ., Univ. of Rhode Island, Kingston, R.I.
Peltz, Seamen, 6650 S. Ellis Ave., Chicago, Ill.
Pendarvis, S. T., McNeese State College, Lake Charles, La.
Penn, Floy L., 2675 Strathmore Lane, Bethel Park, Pa.
Penniman, Blanche L., Bergenfield High School, Bergenfield, N.J.
Pentecost, Percy M., 540 Coconut St., Satellite Beach, Fla.
Perdew, Philip W., Sch. of Educ., University of Denver, Denver, Colo.
Perkins, Frederick D., Alto High School, Alto, La.
Perry, Arthur V., Superintendent of Schools, Batavia, Ill.
Perry, Clarence R., Shady Lane, Dover, Mass.
Perry, Harold J., 1040 Park Ave., West Highland Park, Ill.
Perry, James Olden, 3602 S. MacGregor Way, Houston, Tex.
Perry, T. Edward, Chagrin River Rd., Gates Mills, Ohio
Perryman, Lucile C., 330 Third Ave., New York, N.Y.
Persing, Thomas E., Wyomissing Area Schls., Wyomissing, Pa.
Pescosolido, John R., Central Connecticut State College, New Britain, Conn.
Peters, Donald L., Pennsylvania St. Univ., University Park, Pa.
Peters, J. L., Sr., 3505 Rangeley Dr., Flint, Mich.
Peters, Jon S., 41705 Covington, Fremont, Calif.
Peters, Mary Magdalene, 1366 Lafayette Rd., Claremont, Calif.
Petersen, Clarence E., 19 Fulton St., Redwood City, Calif.
Petersen, Dorothy G., Trenton State College, Trenton, N.J.
Petersen, Dwain F., 108 E. Glencrest Dr., Mankato, Minn.
Peterson, Barbara A., 38 Crest Road West, Rolling Hills, Calif.
Peterson, Bernadine H., University of Wisconsin, Madison, Wis.
Peterson, Donald W., 4708—25th Ave., Rock Island, Ill.
Peterson, Donovan, Amer. Embassy, Tegucigueka, Honduras, Central Amer.
Peterson, Douglas W., 1402 Henry St., Ann Arbor, Mich.
Peterson, J. Vincent, 2910 S. Woodmont, South Bend, Ind.
Peterson, Mrs. Leona, 341 Poplar Ave., Elmhurst, Ill.
Peterson, Miriam E., 5422 Wayne Ave., Chicago, Ill.

Pethick, Wayne M., 6136 Northwest Hwy., Chicago, Ill.
Petor, Andrew P., 728 Hulton Rd., Oakmont, Pa.
Petrequin, Gaynor, 3905 S.E. 91st Ave., Portland, Oreg.
Pett, Dennis W., 4228 Saratoga Drive, Bloomington, Ind.
Pettersch, Carl A., 200 Southern Blvd., Danbury, Conn.
Pettiss, J. O., Dept. of Educ., Louisiana State University, Baton Rouge, La.
Petty, Mary Clare, Col. of Educ., University of Oklahoma, Norman, Okla.
Petty, Michael A., Palpa 2440/Capital Federal, Argentina
Petty, Olan L., Box 6906, Col. Sta., Duke University, Durham, N.C.
Petty, Walter T., Sch. of Educ., State Univ. of New York, Buffalo, N.Y.
Pewitt, Edith M., North Texas State Univ., Denton, Tex.
Pezzoli, Jean A., Peace Corp Training Center, Hilo, Hawaii
Pezzullo, Thomas J., 268 Greenville Ave., Johnston, R.I.
Pfeifer, Michael F. CM, 2233 N. Kenmore, Chicago, Ill.
Phay, John E., Bur. of Educ. Res., University of Mississippi, University, Miss.
Phelan, William F., 201 Sunrise Hwy., Patchogue, N.Y.
Phelps, H. Vaughn, 8727 Shamrock Rd., Omaha, Nebr.
Phelps, Harold R., Illinois State University, Normal, Ill.
Phelps, Roger P., 718 Barnes Ave., Baldwin, L.I., N.Y.
Phillips, Cecil K., University of Northern Iowa, Cedar Falls, Iowa
Phillips, Don O., 1158 S. Harris Ave., Columbus, Ohio
Phillips, James A., Jr., Col. of Educ., Kent State University, Kent, Ohio
Phillips, James E., 1446 E. Maryland Ave., St. Paul, Minn.
Phillips, Leonard W., Nevada Southern Univ., Las Vegas, Nev.
Phillips, Paul, Supt. of Schools, 520 W. Palmer St., Morrisville, Pa.
Phillips, Richard C., Univ. of North Carolina, Chapel Hill, N.C.
Phillips, Thomas Arthur, 1536 S. Sixth St., Terre Haute, Ind.
Philp, William A., 440 Williams Ave., Natchitoches, La.
Phleger, John V., Superintendent of Schools, Geneseo, Ill.
Phoenix, William D., 8561 Holmes Rd., Kansas City, Mo.
Piche, Gene L., Univ. of Minnesota, Minneapolis, Minn.
Pickett, Paul C., Upper Iowa University, Fayette, Iowa
Pickett, Vernon R., 2411 Brookland Ave., N.E., Cedar Rapids, Iowa
Pickrel, Glenn E., Supt. of Schools, Dists. 58 and 99, Downers Grove, Ill.
Pierce, Arthur N., Supt. of Schools, Hanover, N.H.
Pierce, R. Kenneth, Rte. 463 and Fines St., Lansdale, Pa.
Pierce, Truman M., Sch. of Educ., Auburn University, Auburn, Ala.
Pierleoni, Robert G., 21 Nova Ln., Rochester, N.Y.
Piggush, Kenneth J., 324 Sauganash, Park Forest, Ill.
Pike, Earl O., Jr., 2194 16th Ave. W., Eugene, Oreg.
Pikunas, Justin, Psych. Dept., University of Detroit, Detroit, Mich.
Piland, Joseph C., Bronk Road, Plainfield, Ill.
Ping, Charles J., Tusculum College, Greeneville, Tenn.
Pinkham, Mrs. Rossalie G., Southern Connecticut State College, New Haven, Conn.
Pino, Charles E., 74 Eastern Ave., Revere, Mass.
Pins, Arnulf M., 345 E. 46th St., New York, N.Y.
Pitkin, Royce, Goddard College, Plainfield, Vt.
Pitman, John C., 88 Chestnut St., Camden, Maine
Pittman, Dewitt Kennieth, 6700 Monroe Rd., Charlotte, N.C.
Piucci, Virginio, Rhode Island Col., Providence, R.I.
Pletcher, James D., Niagara County Community College, Niagara Falls, N.Y.
Pletcher, Paul R., Jr., 3001 Floravista Ct., Riverside, Calif.
Pletsch, Douglas H., University of Guelf, Guelf, Ont., Canada
Plimpton, Blair, Superintendent of Schools, 400 S. Western Ave., Park Ridge, Ill.
Pliska, Stanley Robert, 1041 S. Lexan Cr., Norfolk, Va.
Plumb, Valworth R., University of Minnesota, Duluth Branch, Duluth, Minn.
Poche, Margaret Una, 3861 Virgil Blvd., New Orleans, La.
Pocket, Delmar B., 738 Cherokee Court, Murfeesboro, Tenn.
Poehler, W. A., Concordia College, St. Paul, Minn.
Poelker, Msgr. Gerard L., Supt., Diocesan Schls., Jefferson City, Mo.
Pogue, E. Graham, Ball State University, Muncie, Ind.

Pohek, Marguerite V., 13 Coolidge Ave., Glen Head, N.Y.
Pohlmann, Neil A., Bowling Green State University, Bowling Green, Ohio
Poindexter, Robert C., 9740 S. 50th Ct., Oaklawn, Ill.
Pole, E. John, Ball State University, Muncie, Ind.
Polglase, Robert J., 5 Upper Warren Way, Warren, N.J.
Pollach, Samuel, California State College, Long Beach, Calif.
Pollack, Allan, 3534 Thurmond St., Columbia, S. C.
Pollard, William, Jr., 403 E. 2nd St., Metropolis, Ill.
Pollert, Irene E., 700 N. Alabama, Indianapolis, Ind.
Pollock, Marion B., Calif. State Col. L.B., So. Pasadena, Calif.
Polmantier, Paul C., University of Missouri, Columbia, Mo.
Pond, Millard Z., Superintendent of Schools, Dist. No. 4, Eugene, Oreg.
Pool, Harbison, Oberlin Col., Oberlin, Ohio
Poole, Albert E., 214 N. Washington Cir., Lake Forest, Ill.
Pope, Allen, 1407 Missoula Ave., Helena, Mont.
Pope, Madaline, Rt. 3, Box 544, Courtland, Ohio
Popper, Samuel H., Burton Hall, University of Minnesota, Minneapolis, Minn.
Portee, Richard C., 2941 Michigan, Chicago, Ill.
Porter, Donald A., Edmonton Public Schools, Edmonton, Alba., Canada
Porter, LeRoy E., 560 Hayannis Dr., Sunnyvale, Calif.
Porter, M. Roseamonde, MTEC, Ponape, East. Caroline Islands
Porter, R. H., The Steck Co., P.O. Box 2028, Austin, Tex.
Porter, William E., Pulaski High School, Pulaski, Va.
Porter, Willis P., Sch. of Educ., Indiana University, Bloomington, Ind.
Posch, Peter, Bauernfeldgasse 7/1 A-1190, Wien, Europe
Potell, Herbert, New Utrecht High School, Brooklyn, N.Y.
Potts, John F., Voorhees Junior College, Denmark, S.C.
Poulos, Thomas H., Michigan School for the Deaf, Flint, Mich.
Poulter, James R., Superintendent of Schools, Anamosa, Iowa
Pounds, Ralph L., Tchrs. Col., University of Cincinnati, Cincinnati, Ohio
Powell, Mrs. Ruth Marie, 1601 Lock Rd., Nashville, Tenn.
Powers, Francis P., State College, Fitchburg, Mass.
Powers, Fred R., 619 Cleveland Ave., Amherst, Ohio
Powers, Philander, Ventura College, 4667 Telegraph Rd., Ventura, Calif.
Pozdal, Marvin D., 224 Pasture Lane, Muncie, Ind.
Prasch, John, 8224 S. Hazelwood Dr., Lincoln, Nebr.
Pratt, Anna M., 105 Colton Ave., San Carlos, Calif.
Preil, Joseph J., 189 Shelley Ave., Elizabeth, N.J.
Prentice, Justus A., Board of Coop. Educ'l Serv., Buffalo, N.Y.
Preseren, Herman J., Wake Forest College, Winston-Salem, N.C.
Pressman, Florence, 3080 Broadway, New York, N.Y.
Preston, Albert P., Prin., Washington High School, Norfolk, Va.
Preston, Ralph C., Sch. of Educ., University of Pennsylvania, Philadelphia, Pa.
Prestwood, Elwood L., 426 Righters Mill Rd., Gladwyne, Pa.
Pricco, Ernest, Melrose Park School, Melrose Park, Ill.
Price, Louis E., University of New Mexico, Albuquerque, N.Mex.
Price, Randel K., University of Missouri, Columbia, Mo.
Price, Robert Diddams, 7819 Pinemeadow Lane, Cincinnati, Ohio
Price, Robert R., Agric. Hall, Oklahoma State Univ., Stillwater, Okla.
Price, Uberto, Appalachian State College, Boone, N.C.
Pridgen, Mrs. Ennie Mae, 1507 Russell St., Charlotte, N.C.
Priestley, Mabel, Directorate, USDESEA, APO, New York, N.Y.
Prince, Mrs. Virginia Faye, P.O. Box 4015, St. Louis, Mo.
Pritzkau, Philo T., Univ. of Conn., Storrs, Conn.
Procunier, Robert W., 999 Kedzie Ave., Flossmoor, Ill.
Prokop, Manfred F., Univ. of Alberta, Edmonton, Alberta, Canada
Prokop, Polly, Rt. 1, Archer Ave., Lemont, Ill.
Propsting, Mrs. M., 44 Henrietta St., Waverley, N.S.W., Australia
Protheroe, Donald W., 154 Chambers Bldg., University Park, Pa.
Prutzman, Stuart E., 135 Alum St., Lehighton, Pa.
Pryor, Guy C., Our Lady of the Lake Col., San Antonio, Tex.

Przewlocki, Lester E., Supt. of Schools, Dist. No. 4, Addison, Ill.
Puffer, Richard J., 4401—6th St., S.W., P.O. Box 1689, Cedar Rapids, Iowa
Pugmire, Dorothy Jean, 468 E. Fourth St. No., Logan, Utah
Purdy, Ralph D., 927 Silyoer Lane, Oxford, Ohio
Purifoy, Cecil E., Jr., Univ. of Tenn., Knoxville, Tenn.
Puryear, Royal W., Fla. Memorial Col., Miami, Fla.
Putnam, John F., Office of Education, Dept. of H.E.W., Washington, D.C.
Pyfer, Jean L., 503 Fess, Bloomington, Ind.

Quall, Alvin B., Whitworth College, Spokane, Wash.
Quanbeck, Martin, Augsburg College, Minneapolis, Minn.
Quaranta, Joseph J., 3198 Kenney Rd., Columbus, Ohio
Quatraro, John A., 25 Harrison Ave., Delmar, N.Y.
Queen, Bernard, Marshall University, Huntington, W.Va.
Queensland, Kenneth, Supt. of Schools, Blue Earth, Minn.
Quick, Henry E., 293 Main St., Box 279, Oswego, Tioga County, N.Y.
Quick, Maryalice, 806 Grand Ave., Rochester, N.Y.
Quick, Otho J., Northern Illinos University, DeKalb, Ill.
Quilling, Joan I., Owen Hall, Michigan State Univ., East Lansing, Mich.
Quinn, Villa H., State Department of Education, Augusta, Maine
Quintero, Angel G., Secretary of Education, Rio Piedras, Puerto Rico
Quish, Bernard A., 4343 W. Wrightwood Ave., Chicago, Ill.

Rabin, Bernard, Bowling Green State University, Bowling Green, Ohio
Rachford, George R., Col. of Grad. Studies, Univ. of Omaha, Omaha, Nebr.
Rackauskas, John A., 6558 S. Rockwell St., Chicago, Ill.
Racky, Donald J., Lane Technical High School, Chicago, Ill.
Radcliffe, David H., 516 N. Jackson St., Danville, Ill.
Radebaugh, Byron F., Northern Illinois University, DeKalb, Ill.
Rademaker, Dean B., Superintendent of Schools, Virginia, Ill.
Rader, William D., 240 Laurel Ave., Wilmette, Ill.
Rafalides, Madeline B., Jersey City State College, Jersey City, N.J.
Raffone, Alexander M., Woodbridge Public Schools, Woodbridge, Conn.
Ragan, William Burk, University of Oklahoma, Norman, Okla.
Ragsdale, Ted R., Southern Ill. Univ., Carbondale, Ill.
Rahn, James E., Concordia Academy, St. Paul, Minn.
Railton, Esther P., California State Col., Hayward, Calif.
Raine, Douglas, Rt. 6, Box 296, Tucson, Ariz.
Rakow, Ernest A., Cath. Educ. Research Ctr., Boston Col., Chestnut Hill, Mass.
Ramer, Earl M., University of Tennessee, Knoxville, Tenn.
Ramey, Mrs. Beatrix B., Dept. of Educ., Appalachian State Univ., Boone, N.C.
Ramig, Clifford L., 11859 Canfield Ct., Cincinnati, Ohio
Ramirez, Judith, UCLA, Moore Hall, 244, Los Angeles, Calif.
Ramos, John P., Jr., 117 Green Ave., Madison, N.J.
Ramos, Rafael E., 69 Bomb Sq., Loring AFB, Maine
Ramsay, James G., 2 Washington Square Village, New York, N.Y.
Ramsey, Imogene, 257 Sunset Ave., Richmond, Ky.
Ramseyer, Lloyd L., Blufften College, Blufften, Ohio
Randall, Edwin H., Western State College, Gunnison, Colo.
Randall, Robert S., S.W. Educ'l Devel. Lab., Austin, Tex.
Rank, Ben, 1721 Brook Ave. S.E., Minneapolis, Minn.
Rankin, Earl F., Jr., 3921 Lynncrest Dr., Fort Worth, Tex.
Rankin, Eugene L., 36 Yellowstone Dr., W. Henrietta, N.Y.
Rankin, Marjorie E., Drexel Inst. of Tech., Philadelphia, Pa.
Rankine, Frederick C., 548 Squires St., Fredericton, New Brunswick, Canada
Rappaport, David, 2747 Coyle Ave., Chicago, Ill.
Rarick, David L., 202 E. 13th St., Columbus, Ohio
Rasmussen, Elmer M., Dana College, Blair, Nebr.
Rasmussen, H. L., 427 S.W. Bade Ave., College Place, Wash.
Rasmussen, L. V., 514 Vinnedge Ride, Tallahassee, Fla.
Rausch, Richard G., "Rescue," 120 Main St., Danbury, Conn.

Rawson, Kenneth O., Superintendent of Schools, Clintonville, Wis.
Ray, Lanie L., 1118 Marlowe, Montgomery, Ala.
Ray, Rolland, State University of Iowa, Iowa City, Iowa
Razik, Taher A., State University of New York, Buffalo, N.Y.
Rea, Robert E., 8001 National Bridge St., St. Louis, Mo.
Reavis, Peyton, 125 E. Prince Rd., Tucson, Ariz.
Reddin, Estoy, Dept. of Educ., Lehigh University, Bethlehem, Pa.
* Reddy, Anne L., P.O. Box 64, Runnymede, Bluffton, S.C.
Rediger, Milo A., Taylor University, Upland, Ind.
Reed, Harold J., 1200 N. Nash St. #230, Arlington, Va.
Reed, John L., 122 White St., Saratoga Springs, N.Y.
Reese, Clyde, State College of Arkansas, Conway, Ark.
Reeve, Roscoe E., U. of N.C., Chapel Hill, N.C.
Reeves, Emily D., Centre College of Kentucky, Danville, Ky.
Reeves, Glenn D., Saginaw Public Schools, Saginaw, Tex.
Reeves, Louis H., 905 Thorndale Drive, Ottawa, Ont., Canada
Regier, Margaret, Roosevelt Univ., 430 S. Michigan Ave., Chicago, Ill.
Regner, Olga W., 116 South 4th St., Darby, Pa.
Rehage, Kenneth J., Dept. of Educ., University of Chicago, Chicago, Ill.
Reichert, Conrad A., Andrews Univ., Berrien Springs, Mich.
Reid, Clarence E., Jr., 8740 Skyview, Beaumont, Tex.
Reid, Leon L., Rt. 2, Box 221, McDonald, Pa.
Reilley, Albert G., 28 Long Ave., Framingham, Mass.
Reiner, Kenneth, 3191 S. Evelyn Way, Denver, Colo.
Reiner, William B., Hunter College, 695 Park Ave., New York, N.Y.
Reinhardt, Adina Marie, Col. of Nursing, U. of Utah, Salt Lake City, Utah
*Reinhardt, Emma, Pittsfield, Ill.
Reinking, Wayne W., 1105 St. Louis, Edwardsville, Ill.
Reinstein, Barry J., Univ. of South Carolina, Columbia, S.C.
Reisboard, Richard J., 5500 S.W., 77th Ct., Miami, Fla.
Reisen, Seymour, 120 E. 184th St., Bronx, N.Y.
Reisman, Diana J., 223 N. Highland Ave., Merion Station, Pa.
Reiss, William, 2156 Birchwood Ave., Eugene, Oreg.
Reiter, Anne, 155 West 68th St., New York, N.Y.
Reitz, Donald J., Loyola College, 4501 N. Charles St., Baltimore, Md.
Reitz, Louis M., St. Thomas Seminary, 7101 Brownsboro Rd., Louisville, Ky.
Reller, Theodore L., Sch. of Educ., Univ. of California, Berkeley, Calif.
Rempel, Peter J., Rte. 1, P.O. Box 977, Sequim, Wash.
Renard, John N., Oxnard Evening High School, Oxnard, Calif.
Renfrow, O. W., Thornton Township High School, Harvey, Ill.
Rennels, Max R., 506 N. Cotton Ave., Bloomington, Ind.
Renouf, Edna M., 116 Yale Square, Swarthmore. Pa.
Rentsch, George J., 80 Main St. W., Rochester, N.Y.
Replogle, V. L., Metcalf School, Normal, Ill.
Reschly, Daniel J., 77 Greenacres Rd., Eugene, Oreg.
Restaino, Lillian, Fordham Univ. at Lincoln Center, New York, N.Y.
Reuter, George S., Jr., P.O. Box 862, Cherokee, Iowa
Reuwsaat, Emily A., Bloomsburg State College, Bloomsburg, Pa.
Revie, Virgil A., California State Col., Long Beach, Calif.
Rex, Ronald G., Michigan State University, East Lansing, Mich.
Reyna, L. J., 227 Beacon St., Boston, Mass.
Reynolds, James Walton, Box 7998, University of Texas, Austin, Tex.
Reynolds, Lee, 113 Woodland Dr., Boone, N.C.
Reynolds, M. C., University of Minnesota, Minneapolis, Minn.
Rhoads, Philip A., 3908 Klausmier Rd., Baltimore, Md.
Rhodes, Gladys L., State University College, Geneseo. N.Y.
Rhodes, Patricia Hertert, Rt. 2, Box 343, Sonora, Calif.
Ricciardi, Richard S., Dept. of Education. 100 Reef Rd., Fairfield, Conn.
Rice, Arthur H., R.R. 3, 3705 Cameron, Bloomington, Ind.
Rice, David, Indiana State University, Evansville, Ind.
Rice, Dick C., 120 Houck Ave., Centerbury, Ohio

Rice, Eric D., 759 W. Hwy. 80, El Centro, Calif.
Rice, James A., University of Houston, Houston, Tex.
Rice, John E., Jenkintown High School, Jenkintown, Pa.
Rice, Robert K., 4820 Campanile Dr., San Diego, Calif.
Rice, Roy C., Arizona State University, Tempe, Ariz.
Rice, Theodore D., 17158 Hubbell, Detroit, Mich.
Richards, Eugene R., 8912 S. McVickers, Oaklawn, Ill.
Richards, H. L., P.O. Box 326, Grambling, La.
Richards, James J., 8200-7 Kennedy Blvd. East, No. Bergen, N.J.
Richardson, Canute M., Paine College, Augusta, Ga.
Richardson, Edwin W., 1800 Grand Ave., Des Moines, Iowa
Richardson, Orvin T., Ball State University, Muncie, Ind.
Richardson, Thomas H., 852 Valley Rd., Upper Montclair, N.J.
Richardson, William R., University of North Carolina, Chapel Hill, N.C.
Richey, Herman G., Dept. of Educ., University of Chicago, Chicago, Ill.
Richey, Robert W., Sch. of Educ., Indiana University, Bloomington, Ind.
Richmond, George S., Crestview Village, 30th & Frederick, St. Joseph, Mo.
Richter, Charles O., Public Schools, 7 Whiting Lane, West Hartford, Conn.
Riedel, Mark T., 210 S. Edgewood, LaGrange, Ill.
Riederer, L. A., 2160 Cameron St., Regina, Sask., Canada
Riehm, Carl L., 7402 Fenwood Ct., Manassas, Va.
Riese, Harlan C., 511 North Ave., East, Missoula, Mont.
*Riethmiller, M. Gorton, Olivet College, Olivet, Mich.
Riggle, Earl L., 180 Highland Dr., New Concord, Ohio
Riggs, William J., 716 Clover Ct., Cheney, Wash.
Rigney, Mrs. Margaret G., Hunter College, Park Ave. and 68th St., New York,N.Y.
Rigney, Raymond P., 31 East 50th St., New York, N.Y.
Rikkola, V. John, Horace Mann Training Schl., Salem, Mass.
Riley, Garland G., 115 Kishwaukee Lane, DeKalb, Ill.
Ringler, Leonore, New York Univ., New York, N.Y.
Ringler, Mrs. Norma, 3721 Lytle Rd., Shaker Heights, Ohio
Rinsland, Roland Del, 100 W. 73rd St., New York, N.Y.
Riordan, Eugene, Queen of Apostles College, Dedham, Mass.
Ripper, Eleanor S., Geneva College, Beaver Falls, Pa.
Rippey, Robert M., 18845 Hood Ave., Homewood, Ill.
Ripple, Richard E., Stone Hall, Cornell University, Ithaca, N.Y.
Risinger, Robert G., Col. of Educ., University of Maryland, College Park, Md.
Risinger, Mrs. Rosalie C., Essex County Voc. & Tech. H.S., Newark, N.J.
Risk, Thomas M., 622 Gilbert Ave., Eau Claire, Wis.
Ritchie, Harold L., Superintendent of Schools, West Paterson, N.J.
Ritter, William E., 2910 E. State St., Sharon, Pa.
Rittschoff, Louis W., 240 Kenwood Dr., Thiensville, Wis.
Rivard, Thomas L., Superintendent of Schools, Chelmsford, Mass.
Rivlin, Harry N., 302 Broadway, New York, N.Y.
Roaden, Arliss, Dept. of Education, Ohio State University, Columbus, Ohio
Roark, Bill, Wayland Academy, Beaver Dam, Wis.
Robarts, James R., Florida State University, Tallahassee, Fla.
Robbins, Edward L., 7346 Shamrock Dr., Indianapolis, Ind.
Robbins, Edward T., 602 Larkwood Dr., San Antonio, Tex.
Robbins, Jerry H., Sch. of Educ., Univ. of Miss., Oxford, Miss.
Robeck, Mildred C., 452 Venado Dr., Santa Barbara, Calif.
Roberson, James A., 2925 S. Perkins Rd., Memphis, Tenn.
Roberts, Dodd Edward, University of Maine, Orono, Maine
Roberts, Jack D., Dept. of Educ., Queens College, Flushing, N.Y.
Roberts, Maurice, 920 Tanglewood Dr., Cary, N.C.
Roberts, R. Ray, 3309 Rocky Mount Rd., Fairfax, Va.
Robertson, Anne McK., Tchrs. Col., Columbia University, New York, N.Y.
Robertson, Jean E., University of Alberta, Edmonton, Alba., Canada
Robertson, Robert L., 315 East Main St., Springfield, Ky.

Robinson, Alice, Board of Educ., 115 E. Church St., Frederick, Md.
Robinson, Cliff, Chico State College, Chico, Calif.
Robinson, H. Alan, Hofstra Univ., Hempstead, L.I., N.Y.
Robinson, Herbert B., California State Col., Long Beach, Calif.
Robinson, John D., 106 S. Overhill Dr., Bloomington, Ind.
Robinson, Lucille T., 603 Buena Vista, Redlands, Calif.
Robinson, Phil C., 1367 Joliet Pl., Detroit, Mich.
Robinson, Robert S., Jr., Eastern Michigan Univ., Ypsilanti, Mich.
Robinson, Russell D., Univ. of Wis.-Milwaukee, Milwaukee, Wis.
Robinson, Thomas L., Alabama St. Col., Montgomery, Ala.
Robinson, Walter J., Northwestern State College, Natchitoches, La.
Robinson, Walter K., New England College, Henniker, N.H.
Robison, W. L., Norfolk City Schools, Norfolk, Va.
Roche, Lawrence A., Duquesne University, Pittsburgh, Pa.
Rochfort, George B., Jr., RFD #1, Cedar Point Rd., Durham, N.H.
Rockwell, Perry J., Jr., Wisconsin State Univ., Platteville, Wis.
Roden, Aubrey H., State Univ. of New York, Buffalo, N.Y.
Rodgers, John O., 4115 Honeycomb Cir., Austin, Tex.
Rodgers, Margaret, Lamar State College of Technology, Beaumont, Tex.
Rodgers, Paul R., 255 W. Vermont St., Villa Park, Ill.
Rodney, Clare, Long Beach State College, Long Beach, Calif.
Roe, Anne, 5151 E. Holmes St., Tucson, Ariz.
Roelke, Patricia L., 329 S. Highland, Bloomington, Ind.
Roenigk, Elsie Mae, 121 Oak Ridge Dr., Butler, Pa.
Roeper, George A., City and Country School, Bloomfield Hills, Mich.
Roff, Mrs. Rosella Zuber, 4410 S. 148th St., Seattle, Wash.
Rogers, Martha E., Div. of Nurse Educ., N.Y.U., New York, N.Y.
Rogers, Virgil M., 3810 Birchwood Rd., Falls Church, Va.
Rogowski, Richard A., 2421 Pearsall Pkwy., Waukegan, Ill.
Rohan, William, E. G. Foreman High School, Chicago, Ill.
Rolleta, Vincent M., 35 Clearview Dr., Spencerport, N.Y.
Rolfe, Howard C., 5160 Atherton, Long Beach, Calif.
Roller, Lawrence W., King George County Public Schls., King George, Va.
Rollins, William B., Jr., 7772 Otto St., Downey, Calif.
Rolloff, John A., University of Arkansas, Fayetteville, Ark.
Romano, Louis, Michigan State University, East Lansing, Mich.
Romano, Louis A., 227—65th St., West New York, N.J.
Rome, Samuel, 9852 Cerritos Ave., Anaheim, Calif.
Romoser, Richard C., Clarion State College, Clarion, Pa.
Rondinella, Orestes R., 48 Sheridan Ave., West Orange, N.J.
Roose, Jack L., Ulster County Boces, New Paltz, N.Y.
Root, Edward L., Maryland Fellow-Univ. of Md., Cumberland, Md.
Rorison, Margaret L., University of S.C., Columbia, S.C.
Rosamilia, M. T., 183 Union Ave., Belleville, N.J.
Roschy, Bertha B., 204 Greenwell Dr., Hampton, Va.
Rose, Gale W., Schl. of Educ., N.Y. Univ., New York, N.Y.
Rose, Mrs. Ruth R., 908 S.W. 18th Ct., Fort Lauderdale, Fla.
Rosebrock, Allan F., State Dept. of Educ., 175 W. State St., Trenton, N.J.
Rosen, Carl L., 1165 Falstaff Dr., Roswell, Ga.
Rosen, Sidney, Col. of Educ., University of Illinois, Urbana, Ill.
Rosenbaum, Wyatt I., 2645 Chesapeake Lane, Northbrook, Ill.
Rosenberg, Donald A., Supt., Lutheran Schools, Wausau, Wis.
Rosenberg, Max, 5057 Woodward Ave., Detroit, Mich.
Rosenberger, Russell S., Dept. of Educ., Gettysburg Col., Gettysburg, Pa.
Rosenbluh, Benjamin J., Central High School, Bridgeport, Conn.
Rosenblum, Beth W., 2185 LeMoine Ave., Ft. Lee, N.J.
Rosenman, I. S., Rm. 710-65 Court St., Brooklyn, N.Y.
Rosenthal, Alan G., 18 Homeside Lane, White Plains, N.Y.
Rosenthal, Alice M., S.U.N.Y., Buffalo, N.Y.
Rosenthal, Lester, 94 Stirling Ave., Freeport, N.Y.
Rosenthal, Samuel, 5213 N. Moody Ave., Chicago, Ill.

Rosenzweig, Celia, 6239 N. Leavitt St., Chicago, Ill.
Rosewell, Paul T., Iowa State Univ., Ames, Iowa
Rosin, Bill, Box 2096, Eastern New Mexico Univ., Portales, N.Mex.
Ross, Mrs. Alice M., 1446 Wilbraham Rd., Springfield, Mass.
Ross, Robert D., Auburn Community College, Auburn, N.Y.
Rossi, Mary Jean, University of Miami, Miami, Fla.
Rossien, Saul, 107 Eton Rd., Yardley, Pa.
Rossmiller, Richard A., 5806 Cable Ave., Madison, Wis.
Roth, Mrs. Frances, 21598 Ellacott Pkwy., Cleveland, Ohio
Roth, Lois H., 5209 Brentwood Dr., Lacey, Wash.
Rothenberg, William, Jr., 1 S. Broadway, Hastings-on-Hudson, N.Y.
Rothenberger, Otis J., 1517 Pennsylvania St., Allentown, Pa.
Rothstein, Jerome H., San Francisco State College, San Francisco, Calif.
Rothwell, Angus B., Coord. Council for Higher Educ., Madison, Wis.
Roueche, John E., RELCV—Mutual Plaza, Durham, N.C.
Rousseau, Joseph, P.O. Box 340, Wabush, Newfoundland and Labrador, Canada
Rousseve, Numa Joseph, Xavier University, New Orleans, La.
Row, Howard E., State Dept. of Pub. Instr., Dover, Del.
Rowley, Judge Kernan, Morris Brown College, Atlanta, Ga.
Rozendaal, Julia, University of North. Iowa, Cedar Falls, Iowa
Rozran, Andrea Rice, 4248 N. Hazel, Chicago, Ill.
Rubadeau, Duane O., State University College, Geneseo, N.Y.
Ruch, Mary A. R., R.F.D. No. 1, Tower City, Pa.
Rucinski, Philip R., Wisconsin State Univ., Oshkosh, Wis.
Rucker, Chauncy N., Rockridge Apts., Baxter Rd., Storrs, Conn.
Rucker, W. Ray, 8655 Pomerado Rd., San Diego, Calif.
Rudman, Herbert C., Col. of Educ., Michigan State Univ., East Lansing, Mich.
Rueff, Charles M., Jr., 626 S. Sixth St., McComb, Miss.
Ruggles, Stanford D., 96 Lochatong Rd., Trenton, N.J.
Rummel, J. Francis, Sch. of Educ., Univ. of Montana, Missoula, Mont.
Rumpf, Edwin L., 1805 Rupert St., McLean, Va.
Runbeck, Junet E., Bethel College, St. Paul, Minn.
Runyan, Charles S., Marshall University, Huntington, W.Va.
Rusch, Reuben R., State University of New York, Albany, N.Y.
Rusche, Philip J., 118 Edgemere Rd., W. Roxbury, Mass..
Russel, John H., Col. of Educ., Univ. of Toledo, Toledo, Ohio
Russell, Mrs. Audrey B., Admin. Bldg., 228 W. Franklin St., Elkhart, Ind.
Russell, David L., Dept. of Psych., Ohio University, Athens, Ohio
Russell, Elder H., P.O. Box 4313, Phoenix, Ariz.
Russell, Irene, Lock Haven State College, Lock Haven, Pa.
* Russell, John Dale, R.R. 10, Russell Rd., Bloomington, Ind.
Russell, William J., Pelham Memorial High School, Pelham, N.Y.
Russo, Anthony J., Dept. of Public Schools, 211 Veazie St., Providence, R.I.
Russum, Elizabeth H., 925 Rockford Rd., Birmingham, Ala.
Rutherford, William L., 1812 Cedar Ridge Dr., Austin, Tex.
Rutledge, James A., Univ. High School, Univ. of Nebraska, Lincoln, Nebr.
Ryan, Carl J., 220 W. Liberty St., Cincinnati, Ohio
Ryan, Kevin, Univ. of Chicago, Chicago, Ill.
Ryan, Melnyk M., 220 Orville St., Fairborn, Ohio
Rzepka, Louis, S.U.N.Y., College at Cortland, Cortland, N.Y.

Sack, Saul, Grad. Sch. of Educ., Univ. of Pennsylvania, Philadelphia, Pa.
Safford, George R., 3640 Scenic Dr., Redding, Calif.
Sage, Daniel D., Syracuse University, Syracuse, N.Y.
Sager, Kenneth, Lawrence University, Appleton, Wis.
Salatino, A. P., S.U.N.Y., Geneseo, N.Y.
Sales, M. Vance, Arkansas State University, State University, Ark.
Salett, Stanley J., 225 W. State St., Trenton, N.J.
Salinger, Herbert E., 1273 Sylvaner, St. Helena, Calif.
Salisbury, C. Jackson, 410 Conshohocken St. Rd., Narberth, Pa.
Sallee, Mrs. Mozelle T., 4401 North Ave., Richmond, Va.

Salmon, Hanford A., 310 Stratford St., Syracuse, N.Y.
Salmons, George B., State College, Plymouth, N.H.
* Salser, G Alden, 516 E. Estelle, Wichita, Kans.
Salten, David G., 41 Park Ave., New York, N.Y.
Saltzman, Irving J., Dept. of Psych., Indiana Univ., Bloomington, Ind.
Sam, Norman H., Lehigh University, Bethlehem, Pa.
Samlin, John R., 840 Cheryl Lane, Kankakee, Ill.
Sample, William J., 3022 Cedarbrook Court, Vineland, N.J.
Samson, Gordon E., Cleveland State University, Cleveland, Ohio
Sand, Ole, Natl. Educ. Assn., 1201 Sixteenth St., N.W., Washington, D.C.
Sandahl, David G., Hufford Jr. H.S., Joliet, Ill.
Sandel, Lenore, 33 Sherman Avenue, Rockville Centre, N.Y.
Sander, Paul J., 3139 E. Monterosa, Phoenix, Ariz.
Sanders, Mrs. Ruby, P.O. Box 1956, Waco, Tex.
Sandilos, Peter C., Superintendent of Schools, West Long Branch, N.J.
Sandin, Robert T., University of Toledo, Toledo, Ohio
Sandow, Lyn A., Grolier Incorporated, New York, N.Y.
Sands, Miss Billie L., Michigan State Univ., East Lansing, Mich.
Sangster, Cecil Henry, 1248 Cross Cres. S.W., Calgary, Alba., Canada
Santigian, M. Marty, 4596 E. Fredora, Fresno, Calif.
Sardo, Arlene A., 34 Braemar House, Liverpool, N.Y.
Sartain, Harry W., Falk Lab. Schls., Univ. of Pittsburgh, Pittsburgh, Pa.
Saterlie, Mary E., 1710 Kurtz Avenue, Lutherville, Md.
Sauer, Lois E., 753 Houston Mill Road, Atlanta, Georgia
Saunders, Margaret C., 701 Wheeling Ave., Muncie, Ind.
Sause, Edwin F., Jr., 484 Cary Avenue, Staten Island, N.Y.
Sauter, Joyce H., 1041 Catalpa Road, Arcadia, Calif.
Sauvain, Walter H., Dept. of Educ., Bucknell Univ., Lewisburg, Pa.
Savage, Kent B., Fairview Senior High School, Berkeley, Mo.
Savage, Mary E., 114 Middleton Pl., Bronxville, N.Y.
Sax, Gilbert, University of Washington, Seattle, Wash.
Saxe, Richard W., Univ. of Toledo, Toledo, Ohio
Saylor, Charles F., 535 Kathryn St., New Wilmington, Pa.
Saylor, J. Galen, University of Nebraska, Lincoln, Nebr.
Scales, Eldridge E., 795 Peachtree St., Atlanta, Ga.
Scanlan, William J., Highland Park Sr. High School, St. Paul, Minn.
Scanlon, Kathryn I., Fordham Univ., Lincoln Center Campus, New York, N.Y.
Scarnato, Samuel A., P.O. Box 869, Wilmington, Del.
Schaadt, Mrs. Lucy G., Cedar Crest College, Allentown, Pa.
Schaefer, Alan E., 900 Crestfield Ave., Libertyville, Ill.
Schaefer, Wilbert S., 194 Hillside Ave., Mineola, L.I., N.Y.
Schaeffer, Norma C., 10700 S. Hamlin, Chicago, Ill.
Schaffer, Phyllis J., Room 922, Eigenmann Center, Bloomington, Ind.
Schaibly, Colon L., Waukegan Township High School, Waukegan, Ill.
Schall, William E., 1472 Deerwood Ct., Cincinnati, Ohio
Scharf, Louis, 350 Sterling St., Brooklyn, N.Y.
Schasteen, Joyce W., 2500 Spruce St., Bakersfield, Calif.
Schauerman, Sam, Jr., 22806 Eriel Ave., Torrance, Calif.
Schell, Very Rev. Joseph O., John Carroll Univ., Cleveland, Ohio
Schell, Leo M., Col. of Educ., Kansas State Univ., Manhattan, Kans.
Schenke, Lahron H., 301 Chamberlin Dr., Charleston, Ill.
Scherer, Frank H., Rutgers University, New Brunswick, N.J.
Schiller, Clarke E., 863 Garland Dr., Palo Alto, Calif.
Schiller, Leroy, Mankato State College, Mankato, Minn.
Schilling, Paul M., Superintendent of Schools, LaGrange Park, Ill.
Schleif, Mabel E., 110 Forest Ave., Vermillion, S. Dak.
Schlenker, Alma H., 1450 Westgate Dr., Bethlehem, Pa.
Schlessinger, Fred R., 1399 LaRochelle Dr., Columbus, Ohio
Schlosser, Alvin, 144-15 41st Ave., Flushing, N.Y.
Schmidt, Florence M., 5925 Canterbury Dr., Culver City, Calif.
Schmidt, L. G. H., J. J. Cahill Mem. Sch., Mascot, N.S.W., Australia

Schmidt, Lyle D., 3320 Edgemere Ave., N.E., Minneapolis, Minn.
Schmidt, Ralph L. W., 568 Magnolia Wood Dr., Baton Rouge, La.
Schmidt, William S., County Superintendent of Schools, Upper Marlboro, Md.
Schnabel, Robert V., 6902 S. Calhoun St., Fort Wayne, Ind.
Schneider, Albert A., Superintendent of Schools, Albuquerque, N.Mex.
Schneider, Arthur J., Webster Cent. School, Webster, N.Y.
Schneider, Byron J., 3416 Humboldt Ave. So., Minneapolis, Minn.
Schneider, Erwin H., Univ. of Iowa, Iowa City, Iowa
Schneider, Raymond C., University of Washington, Seattle, Wash.
Schneider, Samuel, 315 West 70th St., New York, N.Y.
Schnell, Fred, 2724 Highland Terrace, Sheboygan, Wis.
Schnell, Rodolph L., Univ. of Calgary, Calgary, Alba., Canada
Schnepf, Virginia, 718 Normal Ave., Normal, Ill.
Schneyer, J. Wesley, 7454 Ruskin Rd., Philadelphia, Pa.
Schnitzen, Joseph P., University of Houston, Houston, Tex.
Schoeller, Arthur W., 8626 W. Lawrence Ave., Milwaukee, Wis.
Scholl, Margaret, 1206 Marshall Lane, Austin, Tex.
Scholl, Paul A., Univ. of Connecticut, Storrs, Conn.
Schollmeyer, Fred C., Dade County Public Schools, Miami, Fla.
Schooler, Virgil E., 209 S. Hillsdale Dr., Bloomington, Ind.
Schooling, Herbert W., Col. of Educ., Univ. of Missouri, Columbia, Mo.
Schor, Theodore, 149 N. Fifth Ave., Highland Park, N.J.
Schorow, Mitchell, 50 N. Medical Dr., Salt Lake City, Utah
Schott, Marion S., Central Missouri State College, Warrensburg, Mo.
Schowe, Ben M., Jr., 500 Morse Rd., Columbus, Ohio
Schreiber, Daniel, 7 Peter Cooper Rd., New York, N.Y.
Schroeder, Carl N., 39 Othoridge Rd., Lutherville, Md.
Schroeder, Marie L., 3125 N. Spangler St., Philadelphia, Pa.
Schroeder, W. P., State Polytechnic College, San Luis Obispo, Calif.
Schuller, Charles F., Michigan State University, East Lansing, Mich.
Schulman, Milton, 660 Locust St., Mt. Vernon, N.Y.
Schulte, Emerita S., Dept. of English, Ball St. Univ., Muncie, Ind.
Shultz, Kenneth M., 847 New England Ave., Centerville, Ohio
Schumann, Victor, 1537 Cedar Lane, Waukesha, Wis.
Schwanholt, Dana B., Valparaiso University, Valparaiso, Ind.
Schwartz, Alfred, Drake University, Des Moines, Iowa
Schwartz, Judy Iris, 330 E. 46th St., Apt. 1C, New York, N.Y.
Schwartz, Melvin, 9 Stonegate Rd., Ossining, N.Y.
Schwartz, William, 467 W. Cross St., Westbury, L.I., N.Y.
Schwartz, William P., 273 Ave. P., Brooklyn, N.Y.
Schwarz, Peggy M., 25 Cornell St., Scarsdale, N.Y.
Schwarzenberger, Alfred J., Sault Sainte Marie, Mich.
Schwebel, Milton, Sch. of Educ., New York University, New York, N.Y.
Schweitzer, Thomas F., 89-19 218 St., Queens Village, L.I., N.Y.
Schwyhart, Keith, Earlham College, Richmond, Ind.
Sciranka, Paul G., 323 Monte Vista Ave., Oakland, Calif.
Scobel, Thomas B., Gen. Motors Inst., 1700 W. 3rd Ave., Flint, Mich.
Scobey, Mary-Margaret, San Francisco State College, San Francisco, Calif.
Scofield, Alice Gill, San Jose State College, San Jose, Calif.
Scofield, J. Woodleigh, 4 Fontlee Lane, Fontana, Calif.
Scoggins, James A., 1912 E. Gadsden St., Pensacola, Fla.
Scott, Guy, 1521 N. Webster, Liberal, Kans.
Scott, Hugh M., 370 Olin Health Ctr., MSU, E. Lansing, Mich.
Scott, Loren L., Idaho State University, Pocatello, Idaho
Scott, Robert C., Drawer 829, Florence, S.C.
Scott, Thomas B., University of Tennessee, Knoxville, Tenn.
Scott, Waldo I., 1100 Clove Ave., Apt. 5G, Staten Island, N.Y.
Scribner, Jay D., University of California, Los Angeles, Calif.
Scritchfield, Floyd C., Univ. of Nev., Las Vegas, Nev.
Seagoe, May V., Sch. of Educ., University of California, Los Angeles, Calif.
Seaquist, Robert G., Schl. of Educ., Univ. of Ala., University, Ala.

Searles, Warren B., Queens Col., Flushing, N.Y.
Sears, Jesse B., 40 Tevis Pl., Palo Alto, Calif.
Seaton, Donald F., Superintendent of Schools, Boone, Iowa
*Seay, Maurice F., W. Mich. Univ., Kalamazoo, Mich.
Sebaly, A. L., Western Michigan Universty, Kalamazoo, Mich.
Sebolt, Alberta P., Resource Learning Lab-Title 111, Sturbridge, Mass.
See, Harold W., Col. of Educ., Univ. of Bridgeport, Bridgeport, Conn.
Seelye, Margaret R., 335 W. Drummond, Bourbonnais, Ill.
Segal, Marilyn, The Pre-School, Hollywood, Fla.
Seidman, Eric, University of Maryland, College Park, Md.
Seifert, George G., Bowling Green State Univ., Bowling Green, Ohio
Selden, Edward H., Dept. of Psych., Wisconsin State Univ., River Falls, Wis.
Self, David W., Univ. of Alabama, University, Ala.
Sellery, Austin Roy, 5021 Rolling Hills Pl., El Cavon, Calif.
Seltzer, Richard W., 639 Redlion Rd., Huntingdon Valley, Pa.
Seltzer, Ronald, 4004 Bleckley Rd., Lincoln, Nebr.
Selzer, Edwin, 67-30 167th St., Flushing, N.Y.
Semmel, Melvyn I., University of Michigan, Ann Arbor, Mich.
Semple, Stuart W. 1603 Larch St., Halifax, N.S., Canada
Semrow, Joseph J., North Central Association, Chicago, Ill.
Sentman, Everett E., United Educators, Inc., Lake Bluff, Ill.
Severino, D. Alexander, Alisal H.S., Salinas, Calif.
Severson, John E., 11 Chalon Cir., Salinas, Calif.
Seyfert, Warren C., 5607 Gloster Rd., Washington, D.C.
Shaddick, Bryan A., 1023 Lincoln St., Hobart, Ind.
Shafer, Robert E., Arizona State University, Tempe, Ariz.
Shafran, Lillian, 711 E. 11th St., New York, N.Y.
Shane, Estelle, 1425 Chautauqua, Pacific Palisades, Calif.
Shane, Harold G., Sch. of Educ., Indiana University, Bloomington, Ind.
Shane, James, 5941 Fuller Ct., Riverside, Calif.
Shank, Lloyd L., Superintendent of Schools, Arkansas City, Kans.
Shankman, Florence, Temple University, Philadelphia, Pa.
Shapiro, Benjamin, Rutgers Univ., New Brunswick, N.J.
Shaplin, Judson T., Washington University, St. Louis, Mo.
Sharp, George M., Lakewood Terr., New Milford, Conn.
Shaw, Frances, 4717 Central Ave., Indianapolis, Ind.
Shaw, M. Luelle, 1126 N.W. Eighth Ave., Miami, Fla.
Shaw, Nancy E., 2530 First St., Melbourne, Fla.
Shaw, Robert C., Superintendent of Schools, Columbia, Mo.
Shea, James, 59 Old Farm Road, Levittown, N.Y.
Shear, Twyla M., 212 Educ. Bldg., University Park, Pa.
Sheely, Richard L., Lancaster City Schools, Lancaster, Ohio
Sheldon, Muriel Inez, Los Angeles City Board of Educ., Los Angeles, Calif.
Sheldon, William Denley, 508 University Pl., Syracuse, N.Y.
Shelton, Nollie W., 328 Blowing Rock Rd., Boone, N.C.
Shepard, Loraine V., Antioch Col., Yellow Springs, Ohio
Shepard, Samuel, Jr., 4633 Moffitt Ave., St. Louis, Mo.
Shepard, Stanley, 24-A Lowell St., Cambridge, Mass.
Sheppard, Lawrence E., 1322 S. 58th St., Richmond, Calif.
Sherer, Harry, 2158 Fielding Rd., Riverside, Calif.
Sheridan, Alton, NEA, 1201 Sixteenth St., N.W., Washington, D.C.
Sheridan, William C., 333 Washington St., Brookline, Mass.
Sherk, John K., Jr., 6112 Summit St., Kansas City, Mo.
Sherman, C. A., 121 Bauman Ave., Pittsburgh, Pa.
Sherman, Mrs. Helene, 350 Central Park West, New York, N.Y.
Sherman, Mrs. Twyla, Col. of Educ., Wichita State Univ., Wichita, Kans.
Sherwood, Virgil, Radford College, Radford, Va.
Sherwyn, Fred, State Dept. of Educ., Cupertino, Calif.
Shier, John B., 200 Elm High Dr., Edgerton, Wis.
Shimel, W. A., Univ. Ext., Univ. of Wis., Rhinelander, Wis.

Shinol, Julian W., 2405 Bird Dr., Wesleyville, Pa.
Shnayer, Sidney W., Chico State College, Chico, Calif.
Shoemaker, A. T., Box 584, Vidalia, La.
Shoemaker, Marjorie P., Bowling Green State Univ., Bowling Green, Ohio
Shohen, Samuel S., 229 Friends Lane, Westbury, L.I., N.Y.
Sholund, Milford, Gospel Light Press, 725 E. Colorado, Glendale, Calif.
Shope, Nathaniel H., Appalachian State Univ., Boone, N.C.
Shores, J. Harlan, University of Illinois, Urbana, Ill.
Short, Edmund C., University of Toledo, Toledo, Ohio
Short, Robert Allen, 15510—112th St., Bothell, Wash.
Showalter, Miriam R., Roosevelt University, Chicago, Ill.
Showkeir, James R., 1909 Penbrook Lane, Flint, Mich.
Shroff, Piroja, California Col. of Arts & Crafts, Oakland, Calif.
Shulman, Lee S., Col. of Educ., Michigan State Univ., East Lansing, Mich.
* Shuman, Elsie, 805 S. Florence St., Kirksville, Mo.
* Sias, A. B., Route 3, Box 459B, Orlando, Fla.
Sidden, Curtis A., P.O. Box 385, Pickens, S.C.
Siegel, Martin, 154 1st St., New Providence, N.J.
Siegner, C. Vernon, Peru State College, Box 75, Peru, Nebr.
Sieving, Eldor C., Concordia Teachers College, River Forest, Ill.
Siewers, Karl, 2301 Estes Ave., Chicago, Ill.
Sigwalt, J. Q., Box 351, Republic, Pa.
Silberman, Charles E., Fortune-Time/Life Bldg., New York, N.Y.
Silva, J. Winston, California State Dept. of Educ., Sacramento, Calif.
Silvaroli, Nicholas J., Arizona State University, Tempe, Ariz.
Silvern, Leonard C., Educ. & Trng. Consults. Co., Los Angeles, Calif.
Simmons, Eleanor L., Fall River Elem. School, McArthur, Calif.
Simmons, M. Lindsay, 1 Lexington Dr., Urbana, Ill.
Simmons, Muriel H., 304—22nd Ave. North, Nashville, Tenn.
Simmons, Virginia Lee, Indianapolis Public Schools, Indianapolis, Ind.
Simms, Naomi, 333 College Ct., Kent, Ohio
Simon, Dan, Superintendent of Schools, East Chicago, Ind.
Simon, Herman, 3510 Bergenline Ave., Union City, N.J.
Simon, Murray, Rockland Community Coll., Suffern, N.Y.
Simons, Herbert D., 46 Shepard St., Cambridge, Mass.
Simpkins, Katherine W., P.O. Box 88, Chesapeake, Ohio
Simpson, Mrs. Anne E., Bethel Park Senior High School, Bethel Park, Pa.
Simpson, Mrs. Elizabeth A., 5627 Blackstone Ave., Chicago, Ill.
Simpson, Frederick W., University of Tulsa, Tulsa, Okla.
Simpson, Mrs. Hazel D., Col. of Educ., University of Georgia, Athens, Ga.
Simpson, Raymond J., San Francisco State College, San Francisco, Calif.
Sims, Harold W., 9423 Harvard Ave., Chicago, Ill.
Sims, Stephen B., Leonia Public Schools, Leonia, N.J.
Sincock, William R., Allegheny College, Meadville, Pa.
Singe, Anthony L., 1138 McQuade Ave., Utica, N.Y.
Singer, Harry, Div. of Soc. Sci., Univ. of California, Riverside, Calif.
Singletary, James Daniel, USAID/Education, APO San Francisco, Calif. 96243
Singleton, Ira C., Silver Burdett Co., Morristown, N.J.
Singleton, John, University of Pittsburgh, Pittsburgh, Pa.
Singleton, Stanton J., Col. of Educ., University of Georgia, Athens, Ga.
Sipay, Edward R., 16 Belmonte Lane, Elnora, N.Y.
Sipe, H. Craig, State Univ. of New York, Albany, N.Y.
Sirchio, Joseph J., Chicago Voc. H.S., Chicago, Ill.
Sires, Ely, 9245 N. Waverly Dr., Milwaukee, Wis.
Sister Alice Huber SSJ, Mt. St. Joseph Col., Buffalo, N.Y.
Sister Angela Schreiber, 354 Buttles Ave., Columbus, Ohio
Sister Ann Augusta, 400 The Fenway, Boston, Mass.
Sister Ann Mary Gullan, Mount Senario College, Ladysmith, Wis.
Sister Anna Marie (Weinreis), Presentation College, Aberdeen, S.Dak.
Sister Anne Martina (Ganser), St. Joseph's Col., Crookston, Minn.
Sister Dorothy Marie Riordan, College of St. Elizabeth, Convent Station, N.J.

Sister Fides Huber, College of St. Catherine, St. Paul, Minn.
Sister Helen Thompson, Clarke College, Dubuque, Iowa
Sister James Claudia, Siena Heights College, Adrian, Mich.
Sister James Edward, Brescia College, Owensboro, Ky.
Sister John Vianney Coyle, St. Francis Convent, Graymoor, Garrison, N.Y.
Sister Josephine Concannon, Boston College, Chestnut Hill, Mass.
Sister Julia Ford, 444 Centre St., Milton, Mass.
Sister Laurina Kaiser, Mount Mary Col., Yankton, S. Dak.
Sister Margaret Mary, R.S.M., Gwynedd-Mercy College, Gwynedd Valley, Pa.
Sister Margaret Mary, Monsignor O'Brien High School, Kalamazoo, Mich.
Sister Marie Claudia, Barry College, Miami Shores, Fla.
Sister Marie Gabrielle, Annhurst Col., Woodstock, Conn.
Sister Marilyn Hofer, Marian Col., Indianapolis, Ind.
Sister Maris Stella Ross, Dept. of Educ. Rm. 213, New Orleans, La.
Sister Mary Agnes Hennessey, Mount Mercy College, Cedar Rapids, Iowa
Sister Mary Albertus, Mount St. Vincent Univ., Halifax, Canada
Sister Mary Alma, St. Mary's College, Notre Dame, Ind.
Sister M. Arilda, St. Francis Col., Ft. Wayne, Ind.
Sister Mary Basil, Good Counsel College, White Plains, N.Y.
Sister Mary Bernice, Our Lady of the Elms, Akron, Ohio
Sister Mary Bonita, The Felician Col., Chicago, Ill.
Sister M. Brideen Long, Holy Family College, Manitowoc, Wis.
Sister M. Camille Kliebhan, Cardinal Stritch College, Milwaukee, Wis.
Sister Mary Charles, Molloy Catholic College for Women, Rockville Centre, N.Y.
Sister M. Christopher, 5801 Smith Ave., Baltimore, Md.
Sister Mary Chrysostom, College of Our Lady of the Elms, Chicopee, Mass.
Sister Mary Clarissa, Dominican College of Blauvelt, Blauvelt, N.Y.
Sister Mary David, College of St. Benedict, St. Joseph, Minn.
Sister Mary de Lourdes, Saint Joseph College, West Hartford, Conn.
Sister Mary Dorothy, Queen of Apostles Col. Library, Harrimon, N.Y.
Sister M. Edith Brotz, Marian Col., Fond du Lac, Wis.
Sister Mary Edward, 1229 Mt. Loretto Ave., Dubuque, Iowa
Sister Mary Edwina, 5286 South Park Ave., Hamburg, N.Y.
Sister Mary Fidelia, Immaculata College, Bartlett, Ill.
Sister Mary Fidelma, Marylhurst College, Marylhurst, Oreg.
Sister M. Francis Regis, 444 Centre St., Milton, Mass.
Sister Mary Gabrieline, Marygrove College, Detroit, Mich.
Sister Mary Gabrielle, Nazareth College, Nazareth, Mich.
Sister M. Gregory, Marymount Col., Palo Verdes Estates, Calif.
Sister M. Harriet Sanborn, Aquinas College, Grand Rapids, Mich.
Sister Mary Helen, Dominican Col., Racine, Wis.
Sister Mary Hugh, Fontbonne College, St. Louis, Mo.
Sister M. Iona Taylor, Assumption Grotto Convent, Detroit, Mich.
Sister Mary Irmina Saelinger, Villa Madonna College, Covington, Ky.
Sister Mary Joanne, Marycrest College, Davenport, Iowa
Sister Mary Judith, Dept. of Educ., Briar Cliff College, Sioux City, Iowa
Sister Mary Lawrence, Mary Manse College, Toledo, Ohio
Sister Mary Leo, Immaculata College, Immaculata, Pa.
Sister Mary Luke Reiland, 20 S. 6th Ave., Highland Park, N.J.
Sister Mary Madeleine, Russell Col., Burlingame, Calif.
Sister M. Margarita, Rosary College, River Forest, Ill.
Sister Mary Martin, Mercyhurst Col. Library, Erie, Pa.
Sister M. Matthew, Sacred Heart Dominican College, Houston, Tex.
Sister Mary Mercita, St. Mary College, Xavier, Kans.
Sister M. Merici, Educ. Dept., Ursuline College, Louisville, Ky.
Sister M. Merle, St. Matthia School, Chicago, Ill.
Sister M. Michaela, 211 N. Otsego, Gaylord, Mich.
Sister Mary Paul, Mt. Mercy College, Pittsburgh, Pa.
Sister Mary Priscilla, Notre Dame College, Cleveland, Ohio
Sister Mary Rachel, 309 Brooks St., Bridgeport, Conn.
Sister Mary Raymial, 10216 South Vernon Ave., Chicago, Ill.

Sister Mary of St. Michael, College of the Holy Names, Oakland, Calif.
Sister Mary Stephanie, Mt. St. Mary College, Hooksett, N.Y.
Sister Mary Theodine Sebold, Viterbo College, La Crosse, Wis.
Sister Mary Trinita Meehan, Ind. Univ., Bloomington, Ind.
Sister Mary Vianney, St. Xavier College, 103rd and Central Park, Chicago, Ill.
Sister Mary Warin, Notre Dame of Dallas, Irving, Tex.
Sister Mildred Clare, Nazareth College, Nazareth, Ky.
Sister Miriam Richard, St. James Convent, Elkins Park, Pa.
Sister Muriel Hogan, Ottumwa Heights College, Ottumwa, Iowa
Sister Patrick Mary, 501 E. 163rd St., Calumet City, Ill.
Sister Regina Clare, Mt. St. Mary's College, Los Angeles, Calif.
Sister Rita Donahue, Notre Dame College, Staten Island, N.Y.
Sister Rose Matthew, Marygrove College, Detroit, Mich.
Sister Rosemarie Julie, Educ. Dept., College of Notre Dame, Belmont, Calif.
Sister Rosemary Hufker, Notre Dame Col., St. Louis, Mo.
Skaggs, Darcy A., 3699 N. Holly Ave., Baldwin Park, Calif.
Skalski, John M., Sch. of Educ., Fordham University, New York, N.Y.
Skarzinski, Jo., 205 Virginia Ave., Pittsburgh, Pa.
Skatzes, D. H., Box 125, Old Washington, Ohio
Skilton, John E., 793 Sycamore, Dr., Southhampton, Pa.
Skinner, Halver M., Montana State College, Bozeman, Mont.
Skinner, Richard C., Clarion State College, Clarion, Pa.
Skinner, William S., Arizona State University, Scottsdale, Ariz.
Skogsberg, Alfred H., Bloomfield Junior High School, Bloomfield, N.J.
Skrocki, Patricia M., 409 Espanola Ave., Parchment, Mich.
Sletten, Vernon, Sch. of Educ., Univ. of Montana, Missoula, Mont.
Sliepcevich, Elena M., 2000 N. St. N.W. #301, Washington, D.C.
Sligo, Joseph R., 102 N. Lancaster St., Athens, Ohio
Slobetz, Frank, St. Cloud State College, St. Cloud, Minn.
Slocum, Terry S., Jane Stenson Schl., Skokie, Ill.
Slocum, Thomas J., 11 S. Cagwin, Joliet, Ill.
*Smallenberg, Harry W., Supt. of Schools, L. A. Co., L.A., Calif.
Smart, Barbara C., Public Schools, Palmer, Alaska
Smedstad, Alton O., Superintendent, Elem. Schools, Hillsboro, Oreg.
Smelser, Rex H., 501 Broad St., Lake Charles, La.
Smith, Alvin H., St. Andrews Presbyterian College, Laurinburg, N.C.
Smith, Anne M., 1873 Mark Twain St., Palo Alto, Calif.
Smith, Ara K., 609 Lafayette St., Michigan City, Ind.
Smith, B. Othanel, Col. of Educ., University of Illinois, Urbana, Ill.
Smith, Burnell R., 650 S. 15th St., Marion, Iowa
Smith, Calvert H., 8813 S. Eggleston, Chicago, Ill.
Smith, Calvin M., Jr., Columbus Public Schls., Columbus, Ohio
Smith, Cleovis C., 4801 Tremont St., Dallas, Tex.
Smith, Clodus R., 9203 St. Andrews Pl., College Park, Md.
Smith, David C., Michigan State University, East Lansing, Mich.
Smith, Earl P., 122 Sims Road, Syracuse, N.Y.
Smith, E. Brooks, Wayne State University, Detroit, Mich.
Smith, Edward C., 990 Grove St., Evanston, Ill.
Smith, Emmitt D., Box 745, West Texas Station, Canyon, Tex.
Smith, Garmon B., Furman Univ., Greenville, S.C.
Smith, Gary F., 400 E. Market St., Salem, Ind.
Smith, Gary R., 3514 Arrowvale Dr., Orchard Lake, Mich.
Smith, Gerald R., 411 Audubon Dr., Bloomington, Ind.
Smith, Hannis S., State Office Annex, 117 University Ave., St. Paul, Minn.
Smith, Harry E., The Har Schl., Princeton, N.J.
Smith, Herbert A., Colorado State University, Fort Collins, Colo.
Smith, Hester M., 26 Holmes Rd., Rochester, N.Y.
Smith, Hilda C., Dept. of Educ., Loyola University, New Orleans, La.
Smith, Inez L., N.Y.U., 100 Bleecker St., New York, N.Y.
Smith, James B., 221 S. Missouri, Belleville, Ill.

Smith, James J., Jr., New York Urban League, Albany, N.Y.
Smith, James O., 684 Van Ave., Shelbyville, Ind.
Smith, John W., 10001 Princeton Ave., Chicago, Ill.
Smith, Joseph M., 83 Apple Hill, Wethersfield, Conn.
Smith, Kenneth E., Grad. Sch. of Educ., Univ. of Chicago, Chicago, Ill.
Smith, Lawrence J., Central Michigan University, Mt. Pleasant, Mich.
Smith, Leslie F., 705 N. Killingsworth, Portland, Oreg.
Smith, Lewis B., University of Idaho, Moscow, Idaho
Smith, Lloyd N., Dept. of Educ., Indiana State University, Terre Haute, Ind.
Smith, Mark H., 682 Riverview Dr., Columbus, Ohio
Smith, Mary Alice, State College, Lock Haven, Pa.
Smith, Melvin, Lockport Twp. H.S., Lockport, Ill.
Smith, Menrie M., Rte. 4, Hamilton, Ala.
Smith, Nila Banton, 800 W. First St., Los Angeles, Calif.
Smith, Paul E., P.O. Box 11, Boulder, Colo.
Smith, Paul M., 1001 Maple, Wasco, Calif.
Smith, Philip John, Box 63, Post Office, South Perth, W. Australia
Smith Richard N., 4214-43rd St., Des Moines, Iowa
Smith, Robert L., The Sidwell Friends Schl., Washington, D.C.
Smith, Robert M., Pennsylvania State Univ., University Park, Pa.
Smith, Russell F. W., 9 Bursley Pl., White Plains, N.Y.
Smith, Sisera, 115 South 54th St., Philadelphia, Pa.
* Smith, Stephen E., East Texas Baptist College, Marshall, Tex.
Smith, W. Holmes, El Camino Col., Torrance, Calif.
Smolens, Richard, 69 Wooleys, Great Neck, N.Y.
Snead, William E., 1021 Farnway Ln., St. Louis, Mo.
Snearline, Paul A., 815 Market St., Lewisburg, Pa.
Snider, Donald A., 2680 Fayette, Mountain View, Calif.
Snider, Glenn R., Col. of Educ., University of Oklahoma, Norman, Okla.
Snider, Hervon Leroy, Sch. of Educ., University of Idaho, Moscow, Idaho
Sniderman, Sam M., Ann Arbor Brd of Educ., 1220 Wells, Ann Arbor, Mich.
Snyder, Agnes, 50 Central Ter., Clifton Park, Wilmington, Del.
Snyder, Darl E., 424 S. Sixth Ave., La Grange, Ill.
Snyder, Harvey B., Pasadena College, 1539 E. Howard St., Pasadena, Calif.
Snyder, Helen I., 1020 W. Beaver Ave., State College, Pa.
Snyder, Jerome R., 1114 Mogford St., Midland, Tex.
Snyder, Marjorie Sims, Col. of Educ., Indiana St. Univ., Terre Haute, Ind.
Snyder, Robert D., Superintendent of Schools, Wayzata, Minn.
Snyder, Ruth C., 110 Laurelton Rd., Rochester, N.Y.
Soares, Anthony T., 290 Lawrence Rd., Trumbull, Conn.
Sobin, Gloria A., 370 Seymour Ave., Derby, Conn.
Soderberg, L. O., Educ. Dept., Univ. of R.I., Kingston, R.I.
Soeberg, Dorothy D., 4034 Calle Ariana, Cyprus Shore, San Clemente, Calif.
Sokol, John N., 455 Park Ave., Leonia, N.J.
Solomon, Benjamin, Indust. Cntr., Univ. of Chicago, Chicago, Ill.
Solomon, Ruth H., 91 N. Allen St., Albany, N.Y.
Somers, Mary Louise, Sch. of SSA, Univ. of Chicago, Chicago, Ill.
Sommer, Maynard E., 1348 Romona Dr., Camarillo, Calif.
Sommers, George, 8300 W. 30½ St., St. Louis Park, Minn.
Sommers, Mildred, Board of Educ., 290 W. Michigan Ave., Jackson, Mich.
Sommers, Wesley S., 820 Sixth St., Menomonie, Wis.
Sonntag, Ida May, 5101 Norwich Rd., Toledo, Ohio
Sonstegard, Manford A., Southern Illinois Univ., Edwardsville, Ill.
Sorbo, Paul J., Jr., Board of Education, Windsor, Conn.
Sorensen, Edwin, P.O. Box 210, Northport, N.Y.
Sorenson, A. Garth, Moore Hall, University of California, Los Angeles, Calif.
Sorenson, Helmer E., Okla. St. Univ., Stillwater, Okla.
Sorenson, Mrs. Virginia, 105 N. Division Ave., Grand Rapids, Mich.
Sorenson, Wayne L., Hayward Unified Sch. Dist., Hayward, Calif.
Sosulski, Michael C., Dutchess Comm. Col., Poughkeepsie, N.Y.
Soucy, Leo A., Dist. Supt. of Schools, Auburn, N.Y.

Southall, George A., RD. 2, Kirkville, N.Y.
Southall, Maycie K., Box 867, Peabody Col., Nashville, Tenn.
Sowards, George W., Florida State Univ., Tallahassee, Fla.
Spalke, E. Pauline, P.O. Box 405, Salem Depot, N.H.
Sparling, Joseph J., Old Oxford Rd., Chapel Hill, N.C.
Spaulding, Robert L., Duke University, Durham, N.C.
Spaulding, Seth J., UNESCO, Place de Fontenory, Paris VII, France
Spear, William G., 7233 W. Lunt Ave., Chicago, Ill.
Spears, Louise, Eigenmann Center, Univ. of Ind., Bloomington, Ind.
Spears, Sol, El Marino School, Culver City, Calif.
Speciale, Anna Gloria, 120 Soundview Ave., Plains, N.Y.
Speer, Hugh W., University of Missouri, Kansas City, Mo.
Speicher, A. Dean, 8008 Kennedy Ave., Highland, Ind.
Speights, Mrs. R. M., Limestone College, Gaffney, S.C.
Spence, Joseph R., Clarion State College, Clarion, Pa.
Spence, Ralph B., 355 Beechwood Dr., Athens, Ga.
Spencer, Doris U., Johnson State College, Johnson, Vt.
Spencer, Edward M., Fresno State College, Fresno, Calif.
Spencer, Elizabeth F., Ball State University, Muncie, Ind.
Spencer, James E., P.O. Box 813, Danville, Calif.
Sperber, Robert I., 21 Lowell Rd., Brookline, Mass.
Spielman, Lester A., 2970 N. Lake Shore Dr., Chicago, Ill.
Spigle, Irving S., Park Forest Pub. Schools, Park Forest, Ill.
Spinks, Sam Hattiesburg Pub. Schls., Hattiesburg, Miss.
Spinner, Arnold, New York University, New York, N.Y.
Spinola. A. R., Superintendent, Denville School Dist. No. 1, Denville, N.J.
Spiro, Mrs. David (Molly), 68 Vernon Dr., Pittsburgh, Pa.
Spitzer, Lillian K., IDEA, 1100 Glendon Ave., Los Angeles, Calif.
Spiva, Dorothy, 81 W. Dodridge St., Columbus, Ohio
Springman, John H., 1215 Waukegan Rd., Glenview, Ill.
Squire, James R., Ginn & Co., Boston, Mass.
Stadthaus, Alice, 6499 Kenview Dr., Cincinnati, Ohio
Stafford, H. D., P.O. Box 21, Murrayville, B.C., Canada
Staggs, Jack, Sam Houston State Col., Huntsville, Tex.
Stahl, Albert F., Bloomfield Hills, Mich.
Stahlecker, Lotar V., Kent State University, Kent, Ohio
Stahly, Harold L., 8343 Manchester Dr., Grand Blanc, Mich.
Staidl, Doris J., 1 East Gilman, Madison, Wis.
Staiger, Ralph C., 701 Dallam Rd., Newark, Del.
Staiger, Roger P., Dept. of Chem., Ursinus College, Collegeville, Pa.
Stalnaker, John M., 569 Briar Lane, Northfield, Ill.
Stang, Genevieve E., 730 First St., Apt. H, Bowling Green, Ohio
Stanley, Calvin, Texas Southern University, Houston, Tex.
Stanojevic, Patricia S. B., PH3, 240 Wellesley St. E., Toronto, Ont., Canada
Stansbury, George W., Jr., 4484 Janice Lee Dr., Okemos, Mich.
Stanton, Hy, 8340 S.W. 131st St., Miami, Fla.
Stanton, William A., Purdue University, Lafeyette, Ind.
Starner, Norman Dean, Wyalusing Valley Joint High School, Wyalusing, Pa.
Starnes, Thomas A., Atlanta Public Schools, Atlanta, Ga.
Starr, Fay H., M. W. Regional Educ. Lab., St. Ann, Ill.
Stathopulos, Peter H., 320 Second Ave., Phoenixville, Pa.
Statler, Charles R., Univ. of South Carolina, Columbia, S.C.
Stauffer, Arthur L., Jr., State Univ. Col., Fredonia, N.Y.
Stauffer, Russell G., University of Delaware, Newark, Del.
Staven, LaVier L., 1304 MacArthur Rd., Hays, Kans.
Steadman, E. R., 277 Columbia, Elmhurst, Ill.
Steege, Barbara, Concordia Theological Sem. Libr., Springfield, Ill.
Steele, Joe Milan, 1016 W. William St., Champaign, Ill.
Steele, Lysle Hugh, P.O. Box 914, Beloit, Wis.
Steele, Marilyn H., 510 Mott Foundation Bldg., Flint, Mich.

Steensma, Geraldine J., Covenant Col., Lookout Mountain, Tenn.
Steer, Donald R., University of Michigan, Ann Arbor, Mich.
Steeves, Frank L., Dept. of Educ., Marquette Univ., Milwaukee, Wis.
Steg, Doreen E., 1616 Hepburn Dr., Villanova, Pa.
Stegall, Alma Lirline, Virginia State College, Petersburg, Va.
Steger, Robert I., 530 S. Tenth Ave., LaGrange, Ill.
Steigelman, Vivian R., 1440 Navallier, El Cerrito, Calif.
Stein, Michael W., Western Jr. H.S., Greenwich, Conn.
Stein, Rita F., Ind. Schl. of Nursing, Indianapolis, Ind.
Steinberg, Paul M., Hebrew Union Col., New York, N.Y.
Steinberg, Warren L., 2737 Dunleer Pl., Los Angeles, Calif.
Steiner, Harry, 5 Belaire Dr., Roseland, N.J.
Steinhagen, Margaret J., 107 McKendree Ave., Annapolis, Md.
Steinhauer, Charlotte H., 1560—75th St., Downers Grove, Ill.
Steininger, Earl W., 535 West 5th St., Dubuque, Iowa
Stell, Samuel C., Robeson County Bd. of Educ., Lumberton, N.C.
Stephens, E. R., Univ. of Iowa, Iowa City, Iowa
Stephens, Kenton, Oak Park Schools, Oak Park, Ill.
Stephenson, Alan R., 11227 Plymouth Ave., Cleveland, Ohio
Sterling, A. M., 1017 Garner Ave., Schenectady, N.Y.
Sternberg, William N., Public Sch. 114, 1155 Cromwell Ave., New York, N.Y.
Sterner, William S., Rutgers Univ., Newark, N.J.
Stetson, Ethel A., 47 Westchester Ave., North Babylon, N.Y.
Stevens, J. H., 916 Carter Hill Rd., Montgomery, Ala.
Stewart, Alan D., St. Educ. Dept., 480 Madison Ave., Albany, N.Y.
Stewart, Clinton, E., Schl. of Educ., Baylor Univ., Waco, Tex.
Stewart, Frederick H., 600 E. St. Rd., Trevose, Pa.
Stewart, James T., Delgado Institute, New Orleans, La.
Stewart, Joyce, 5330 H. Ballones Dr., Austin, Tex.
Stewart, Lawrence H., University of California, Berkeley, Calif.
Stickler, W. Hugh, Florida State University, Tallahassee, Fla.
Stickley, William T., 2107 Adelbert Rd., Cleveland, Ohio
Stiemke, Eugenia A., Valparaiso University, Valparaiso, Ind.
Stier, Lealand D., P.O. Box 247, Saratoga, Calif.
Stiles, Grace E., Box 502, Farmington, Maine
Stirzaker, Norbert A., 766 Palmetto, Spartanburg, S.C.
Stitt, J. Howard, Northern Arizona University, Flagstaff, Ariz.
Stitt, Sam C., Superintendent of Schools, Ellinwood, Kans.
Stivers, Stephen N., 3731 University Way, N.E., Seattle, Wash.
Stoddard, George D., 434 E. 87th St., New York, N.Y.
Stofega, Michael E., 271 State St., Perth Amboy, N.J.
Stoffler, James A., Colorado State College, Greeley, Colo.
Stoia, George, 234 Conover Rd., Pittsburgh, Pa.
Stokes, Maurice S., Savannah State College, Savannah, Ga.
Stolee, Michael J., 6618 San Vincente Ave., Coral Gables, Fla.
Stolurow, Lawrence M., 110 Pleasant St., Lexington, Mass.
Stone, Curtis C., Kent State University, Kent, Ohio
Stone, Franklin D., Univ. of Iowa, Iowa City, Iowa
Stone, George P., Union College, Lincoln, Nebr.
Stone, Howard L., 1732 Wauwatosa Ave., Wauwatosa, Wis.
Stone, James C., University of California, Berkeley, Calif.
Stone, Paul T., Huntingdon College, Montgomery, Ala.
Stonehocker, D. Doyle, 1515 Oakdale St., Burlington, Iowa
Stoneking, Lewis W., Parsons College, Fairfield, Iowa
Stoner, Lee H., Sch. of Educ., Indiana Univ., Bloomington, Ind.
Stoops, John A., Dept. of Educ., Lehigh University, Bethlehem, Pa.
Stordahl, Kalmer E., Northern Michigan Univ., Marquette, Mich.
Storen, Helen F., 114 Morningside Dr., New York, N.Y.
Storlie, Theodore R., 1400 W. Maple Ave., Downers Grove, Ill.
Storm, Jerome F., 432 S. 21st St., Richmond, Ind.
Stormer, Donald L., Rt. # 1, Waunakee, Wis.

Stottler, Richard H., University of Maryland, College Park, Md.
Stoughton, Robert W., State Department of Education, Hartford, Conn.
Stoumbis, George C., Col. of Educ., Univ. of Utah, Salt Lake City, Utah
Strahler, Violet R., 5340 Brendonwood Ln., Dayton, Ohio
Strain, John P., Dept. of Educ., Texas Tech. Col., Lubbock, Tex.
Strain, Mrs. Sibyl M., 2236 Los Lunas St., Pasadena, Calif.
Strand, Helen A., Luther College, Decorah, Iowa
Strand, William H., Sch. of Educ., Stanford University, Stanford, Calif.
Strang, Ruth M., 1904 N. Jones Ave., Wantagh, L.I., New York
Strathairn, Pamela L., Women's Phy. Ed. Dept., Stanford Univ., Stanford, Calif.
Straub, Raymond R., Jr., 1120 S. Gay St., Phoenixville, Pa.
Strauss, John F., Jr., 14004-119th Ave. N.E., Kirkland, Wash.
Strawn, Aimee W., Chicago State Col., South, Chicago, Ill.
Strayer, George D., Jr. Col. of Educ., University of Washington, Seattle, Wash.
Strebel, Jane D., Bd. of Educ., 807 N.E. Broadway, Minneapolis, Minn.
Street, William Paul, Univ. of Kentucky, Lexington, Ky.
Streich, William H., Farmington Pub. Schools, Farmington, Conn.
Streitmatter, Kenneth D., Saipan, Marianas Islands
Strem, Bruce E., 109 Marykay Rd., Timonium, Md.
Streng, Alice, University of Wisconsin-Milwaukee, Milwaukee, Wis.
Strickland, C. G., Sch. of Educ., Baylor University, Waco, Tex.
Strickland, J. D., 3302 Conner Dr., Canyon, Tex.
Stringfellow, Mrs. Jackie R., 1833 Second St., S.E., Moultrie, Ga.
Strohbehn, Earl F., 12151 Mellowood Dr., Saratoga, Calif.
Strole, Lois E., R.R. No. 2, West Terre Haute, Ind.
Stromberg, Francis I., Oklahoma State University, Stillwater, Okla.
Strowbridge, Edwin D., Oregon State University, Corvallis, Oreg.
Stuart, Alden T., St. Andrews Rd., Southampton, N.Y.
Stuart, Chipman G., Col. of Educ., Univ. of Okla., Norman, Okla.
Stuber, George, Clayton School Dist., 7530 Maryland Ave., Clayton, Mo.
Stuck, Dean L., Col. of Educ., Southern Ill. Univ., Carbondale, Ill.
Stuenkel, Walter W., Concordia College, Milwaukee, Wis.
Stull, Lorren L., Arps Hall, Ohio St. Univ., Columbus, Ohio
Sturge, Harry H., 91 Victor St., Plainview, N.Y.
Stutzman, Carl R., 2130 Aaron Way, Sacramento, Calif.
Sudyk, James Edward, 830 Williams Way, Mountain View, Calif.
Suess, Alan R., M. Golden Labs., Purdue Univ., Lafayette, Ind.
Sugarman, Alan, Ramapo Cent. Sch. Dist. No. 2, Spring Valley, N.Y.
Sugden, W. E., Superintendent of Schools, 7776 Lake St., River Forest, Ill.
Suhd, Melvin, 8501 Tampa, Northridge, Calif.
Suhr, Virtus W., Northern Illinois University, DeKalb, Ill.
Suiter, Phil E., Chesapeake High School, Chesapeake, Ohio
Sullivan, Dorothy D., University of Maryland, College Park, Md.
Sullivan, Edmund V., 102 Bloor St., W., Toronto, Ont., Canada
Sullivan, Floyd W., 1015 Lena St., N.W., Atlanta, Ga.
Sullivan, Joanna, Fairleigh Dickensen Univ., Hellertown, Pa.
Sullivan, John J., Roosevelt Sch. Dist., Phoenix, Ariz.
Sullivan, Mona Lee R., 1302 Brooklawn Rd., N.E., Atlanta, Ga.
Sullivan, Robert E., Notre Dame Col., Cotabato City, Philippines
Sullivan, Ruth E., 306 Bayswater, Salem Harbour, Andalusia, Pa.
Sullivan, Stephen P., 3532 Herschel View, Cincinnati, Ohio
Sulzer, Edward Stanton, Southern Illinois University, Carbondale, Ill.
Sundquist, Ralph R., Jr., Hartford Seminary Foundation, Hartford, Conn.
Sunzeri, Adeline V., 6142 Afton Pl., Hollywood, Calif.
Supworth, Flora D., Miami-Dade Jr. Col., Coral Gables, Fla.
Susskind, Edwin G., 150-14th St., Buffalo, N.Y.
Sutherland, Angus W., Public Schools, Detroit, Mich.
Sutherland, Jack W., San Jose State College, San Jose, Calif.
Sutherland, Margaret, Col. of Educ., University of California, Davis, Calif.
Sutton, Elizabeth W., 800 Fourth St., S.W., Washington, D.C.

Sutton, Kenneth R., Dept. of Educ., Univ. of N. Mex., Albuquerque, N. Mex.
Swalm, James, Reading Center, Rutgers Univ., Piscataway, N.J.
Swann, Mrs. A. Ruth, 2713 Mapleton Ave., Norfolk, Va.
Swanson, Gordon I., Dept. of Agric. Educ., Univ. of Minnesota, St. Paul, Minn.
Swanson, Herbert L., El Camino Col., Torrance, Calif.
Swarr, Philip C., 2A Phelps Dr., Homer, N.Y.
Swartout, Sherwin G., State Univ. Col., Brockport, N.Y.
Swartzmiller, Jean, 90 Ridge Ave., North Plainfield, N.J.
Sweany, H. Paul, Michigan State University, East Lansing, Mich.
Sweeney, Christopher J., Youngstown St. Univ., Youngstown, Ohio
Swenson, Esther J., Box 1942, University, Ala.
Swertfeger, Floyd F., Route 3, Box 16, Farmville, Va.
Swindall, Wellington, Palmdale School, 3000 E. Wier Ave., Phoenix, Ariz.
Swindel, Mrs. Mabel A., Three Rivers Jr. Col., Poplar Bluff, Mo.
Syvinski, Henry B., Villanova University, Villanova, Pa.

Tadena, Tomas P., Univ. of the Philippines, Quezon City, Philippines
*Tag, Herbert G., Univ. of Conn., Storrs, Conn.
Tajima, Yuri, 1918 N. Bissell, Chicago, Ill.
Tallen, Rachel R., Psych. Dept., Indiana Univ., Bloomington, Ind.
*Tallman, Russell W., Jewell, Iowa
Tamashunas, Edward, 2220 Park Ave., Bridgeport, Conn.
Tambe, Naren, Box 1393, Durham, N.C.
Tannenbaum, Bernard M., 3600 N. Lake Shore Dr., Chicago, Ill.
Tanner, B. William, 650 S. Detroit Ave., Toledo, Ohio
Tanner, Daniel, Rutgers University, New Brunswick, N.J.
Tanner, Wilbur H., Northwestern State University, Alva, Okla.
Tant, Norman, Morehead State College, Morehead, Ky.
Taplette, Owinda W., N. O. Public Schools, New Orleans, La.
Tarver, K. E., John P. Odom School, 3445 Fannett Rd., Beaumont, Tex.
Tashow, Horst, P.O. Box 268, Bend, Oreg.
Tate, Virginia, 2228 Eighth St. Cr., Charleston, Ill.
Tauber, Ann, 16401 Knollwood Dr., Granada Hills, Calif.
Taylor, Azella, 18 Vista Rd., Ellensburg, Wash.
Taylor, Barr, Murray State Col., Murray, Ky.
Taylor, Mrs. Emily C., Mayo Elementary School, Edgewater, Md.
Taylor, Faith, 10427 Montrose Ave., Bethesda, Md.
Taylor, James I., Miami-Dade Jr. Col., Coral Gables, Fla.
Taylor, John M., 9905 S.W. 196th St., Miami, Fla.
Taylor, Kenneth I., Madison Public Schools, Madison, Wis.
Taylor, Marvin, Div. of Educ., Queens College, Flushing, N.Y.
Taylor, Marvin J., St. Paul School of Theology, Kansas City, Mo.
Taylor, Mrs. Mary C., Box 164, Rt. No. 1, New Lenox, Ill.
Taylor, Peter A., Fac. of Educ., Univ. of Manitoba, Winnepeg, Man., Canada
Taylor, Robert E., 1840 Milden Rd., Columbus, Ohio
Taylor, Wayne, 160 Kenberry, East Lansing, Mich.
Taylor, Zina Lee, 407 Waltham, Hammond, Ind.
Teare, Benjamin R., Jr., Carnegie-Mellon Univ., Schenley Park, Pa.
Tedeschi, Anthony, P.O. Box 216, Falls Village, Conn.
Telego, Gene, Ashland College, Ashland, Ohio
Telford, Charles W., San Jose State College, San Jose, Calif.
Temp, George E., Educ. Test. Service, Berkeley, Calif.
Tempero, Howard E., Teachers Col., University of Nebraska, Lincoln, Nebr.
Temple, F. L., Box 2185, University, Ala.
Templin, Mildred C., Inst. of Child Welfare, Univ. of Minnesota, Minneapolis, Minn.
Tenny, John W., 239 E. 12 Mile Rd., Royal Oak, Mich.
Terlaje, Shirley A., P.O. Box 1719, Agana, Guam
Tetz, Henry E., Oregon College of Education, Monmouth, Oreg.
Thelen, L. J., University of Massachusetts, Amherst, Mass.
Theus, Robert, Box 123, Kearney St. Col., Kearney, Nebr.

Thevaos, Deno G., 575 Westview Ave., State College, Pa.
Thomann, Don F., Dept. of Educ., Ripon College, Ripon, Wis.
Thomas, A. M., Can. Assn. for Adult Educ., Toronto, Ont., Canada
Thomas, David C., Ottawa Univ., Ottawa, Kans.
Thomas, Granville S., Superintendent of Schools, Salem, N.J.
Thomas, J. Alan, University of Chicago, Chicago, Ill.
Thomas, James E., Supt. of Schools, Bristol, Tenn.
Thomas, John I., 204 Capri Rd., Las Cruces, N. Mex.
Thomas, T. M., 45 Potter Pl., Springfield, Mass.
Thomas, Virginia F., Iowa State Univ., Ames, Iowa
Thomas, Wade F., Santa Monica City College, Santa Monica, Calif.
Thompson, Mrs. Alberta S., Dept. of H.E., Kent State Univ., Kent, Ohio
Thompson, Anton, Long Beach Public Schls., 715 Locust Ave., Long Beach,
    Calif.
Thompson, Barry B., Waco Independent School Dist., Waco, Tex.
Thompson, Bertha Boya, Western Col. for Women, Oxford, Ohio
Thompson, Charles H., Grad. Sch., Howard University, Washington, D.C.
Thompson, Elton N., Calif. State Col., San Bernadino, Calif.
Thompson, Franklin J., South Pasadena High School, South Pasadena, Calif.
Thompson, Fred R., Col. of Educ., Univ. of Maryland, College Park, Md.
Thompson, Gary, 821 Harley Dr., Columbus, Ohio
Thompson, Helen M., Thompson Reading Clinic, Orange, Calif.
Thompson, James H., 35 Pleasantview Dr., Athens, Ohio
Thompson, John D., P.O. Drawer 877, Seminole Public Schools, Seminole, Tex.
Thompson, John F., 1483 Carver St., Madison, Wis.
Thompson, Lloyd R., 5018 N. Geer Rd., Turlock, Calif.
Thompson, Margaret M., San Fernando State Col., Northridge, Calif.
Thompson, O. E., University of California, Davis, Calif.
Thompson, Olive L., 1541 Iroquois Ave., Long Beach, Calif.
Thompson, Ralph H., Western Washington State Col., Bellingham, Wash.
Thompson, Ray, North Carolina College, Durham, N.C.
Thompson, Mrs. Sheilah, 930 Whitchurch St., North Vancouver, B.C., Canada
Thoms, Denis, Campus View # 124, Bloomington, Ind.
Thomsen, Ronald W., Box 361, Sidney, Mont.
Thomson, Procter, Pitzer Hall, Claremont Men's College, Claremont, Calif.
Thomson, Scott C., 2508 Benvenue #204, Berkeley, Calif.
Thorn, Elizabeth, Provincial Teachers College, North Bay, Ont., Canada
Thorndike, Robert L., Tchrs. Col., Columbia University, New York, N.Y.
Thornsley, Jerome R., 764 Laurel Ave., Pomona, Calif.
Thornton, James W., Jr., San Jose State College, San Jose, Calif.
Throne, Elsie M., 306 Lincoln Ave., Avon-by-the-Sea, N.J.
Thuemmel, William L., 1313D University Village, E. Lansing, Mich.
Thursby, Marilyn P., 3435 Mogadore Rd., Mogadore, Ohio
Thursby, Mrs. Ruth E., 3628 Taft St., Riverside, Calif.
Thyberg, Clifford S., 1717 W. Merced Ave., West Covina, Calif.
Tidrow, Joe, Dept. of Educ. and Phil., Texas Tech. College, Lubbock, Tex.
Tidwell, Robert E., 1602 Alaca Pl., Tuscaloosa, Ala.
Tiedeman, Herman R., Illinois State University, Normal, Ill.
Tielke, Elton F., Univ. Park Elem. Schl., Dallas, Tex.
Tiffany, Betty Jane, 305 E. Church St., Ridgecrest, Calif.
Tiffany, Burton C., Supt. of Schools, Chula Vista, Calif.
Tikansigh, Ancel J., 117 Lidster Ave., Grass Valley, Calif.
Tillan, Lynn, 417 Hillsboro Pkwy., Syracuse, N.Y.
Tillman, Rodney, George Washington University, Washington, D.C.
Timberlake, Walter B., 319 W. Dayton, Yellow Springs Rd., Fairborn, Ohio
Timmons, F. Alan, 1700 Octavia St., San Francisco, Calif.
Tinari, Charles, Shackamaxon School, Scotch Plains, N.J.
Tingle, Mary J., Col. of Educ., University of Georgia, Athens, Ga.
Tink, Albert K., 18 Wendall Pl., DeKalb, Ill.
Tinker, Miles A., P.O. Box 3193, Santa Barbara, Calif.
Tinney, James J., Supt. of Schools, Rutland, Vt.

Tinsley, Drew, 3909 Roland Blvd., St. Louis, Mo.
Tipton, Elis May, 865-B Lighthouse Ave., Pacific Grove, Calif.
Tira, Daniel E., Ohio St. Univ., Columbus, Ohio
Tisdall, William J., University of Kentucky, Lexington, Ky.
Tittle, Carol K., 133 W. 94th St., New York, N.Y.
Todd, Edward S., 20 Hearthstone Rd., Pittsford, N.Y.
Todd, G. Raymond, R.D. No. 3, Bethlehem, Pa.
Todd, Karen, 2402 Woodmere Dr., Cleveland Heights, Ohio
Todd, Neal F., 128 Main St., Ware, Mass.
Todd, Thomas W., 311 Belmont Ave., Elyria, Ill.
Toepfer, Conrad F., Jr., State Univ. Col., Buffalo, N.Y.
Toles, Caesar F., Bishop Junior College, 4527 Crozier St., Dallas, Tex.
Tolleson, Sherwell K., Box 146A, T.T.U., Cookeville, Tenn.
Tom, Chow Loy, 47 W. Brighton Rd., Columbus, Ohio
Tomaszewski, Raymond J., 333 Richard Ter., S.E., Grand Rapids, Mich.
Tomecek, Carolyn L., 747 N. Wabash, Chicago, Ill.
Toops, Herbert A., 1430 Cambridge Blvd., Columbus, Ohio
Toporowski, Theodore T., Danbury State College, Danbury, Conn.
Topp, Robert F., Col. of Educ., Northern Illinois University, DeKalb, Ill.
Torchia, Joseph, Millersville State Col., Millersville, Pa.
Torkelson, Gerald M., 408 Miller, Univ. of Washington, Seattle, Wash.
Torrance, E. Paul, University of Georgia, Athens, Ga.
Tothill, Herbert, Eastern Michigan University, Ypsilanti, Mich.
Totten, W. Fred, Mott Sci. Bldg., 1401 E. Court St., Flint, Mich.
Toussaint, Isabella H., 1670 River Rd., Beaver, Pa.
Towers, Richard L., Pickens County Schl. Dist. A, Pickens, S.C.
Townsend, Richard G., 2553 E. 76th St., Chicago, Ill.
Trachtman, Gilbert M., Sch. of Educ., New York Univ., New York, N.Y.
Tracy, Elaine M., St. Olaf College, Northfield, Minn.
Tracy, Neal H., University of North Carolina, Chapel Hill, N.C.
Traeger, Carl, 375 N. Eagle St., Oshkosh, Wis.
Traiber, Frank, USAID Mission, Guatemala, State Dept., Washington, D.C.
Tramondo, Anthony, White Plains High School, White Plains, N.Y.
Travelstead, Chester C., Col. of Educ., Univ. of New Mexico, Albuquerque, N.M.
Travers, John F., Boston College, Chestnut Hill, Mass.
Travers, Kenneth J., Col. of Educ., Univ. of Ill., Urbana, Ill.
Travis, Vaud A., Dept. of Educ., Northeastern State College, Tahlequa, Okla.
Travis, Vaud A., Jr., Central Piedmont Community Col., Charlotte, N.C.
Traxler, Arthur E., 6825 S.W. 59th St. Miami, Fla.
Treece, Marion B., Southern Illinois University, Carbondale, Ill.
Treffinger, Donald J., 1010 N. Salisbury, W. Lafayette, Ind.
Tremont, Joseph J., 22 Fletcher St., Ayer, Mass.
Trigg, Harold L., State Board of Educ., Greensboro, N.C.
Triggs, Frances, Mountain Home, N.C.
Trippe, Matthew J., University of Michigan, Ann Arbor, Mich.
Trout, Douglas G., Tusculum College, Greenville, Tenn.
Trout, Len L., 2000 Royal Dr., Reno, Nev.
Trow, William Clark, Sch. of Educ., University of Michigan, Ann Arbor, Mich.
Troyer, Maurice E., Syracuse Univ., Syracuse, N.Y.
Truckey, George R., 1424 Price Drive, Cape Girardeau, Mo.
Truher, Helen Burke, 245 Hillside Rd., South Pasadena, Calif.
Trumble, Verna J., 42 West St., Johnson City, N.Y.
Trump, J. Lloyd, Nat. Assoc. Sec. Sch. Prin., Washington, D.C.
Truncellito, Louis, 6129 Leesburg Pike, Falls Church, Va.
Trusty, Francis M., 8605 Wimbledon Dr., Knoxville, Tenn.
Tuchman, Maurice S., Hebrew Col., Brookline, Mass.
Tucker, Jan L., 3780 Starr King Circle, Palo Alto, Calif.
Tucker, Sylvia B., 30929 Rue Langlois, Palos Verdes, Pen, Calif.
Tupper, Frank B., 389 Congress St., Portland, Maine
Turansky, Isadore, Western Michigan University, Kalamazoo, Mich.

Turchan, Donald G., 1026 White Dr., New Castle, Ind.
Turck, Merton J., Jr., Tennessee Polytechnic Inst., Cookeville, Tenn.
Turner, Delia F., 3310 Edgemont, Tucson, Ariz.
Turner, Harold E., Univ. of Missouri, St. Louis, Mo.
Turner, Howard, Col. of Educ., Univ. of S.W. Louisiana, Lafayette, La.
Turney, David T., Sch. of Educ., Indiana State Univ., Terre Haute, Ind.
Turnquist, Carl H., Detroit Pub. Schls., 5057 Woodward Ave., Detroit, Mich.
Tuseth, Alice A., 6410—37th Ave. No., Minneapolis, Minn.
Tuttle, Edwin A., Jr., State Univ. Col., New Paltz, N.Y.
Twombly, John J., Sch. of Educ., State Univ. of N.Y., Albany, N.Y.
Tydings, R. N., Hobbs Municipal Schools, Hobbs, N.Mex.
Tyer, Harold L., 111 Chelsea Circle, Statesboro, Ga.
Tyler, Fred T., University of Victoria, Victoria, B.C., Canada
Tyler, I. Keith, Ohio State University, Columbus, Ohio
Tyler, Louise L., University of California, Los Angeles, Calif.
Tyler, Priscilla, Univ. of Missouri, Kansas City, Mo.
Tyler, Ralph W., 5825 Dorchester Ave., Chicago, Ill.
Tyler, Robert, Educ. Dept., Southwestern State College, Weatherford, Okla.
Tyrrell, Francis M., Immaculate Conception Seminary, Huntington, N.Y.
Tystad, Edna, Thoreau Public Schools, Thoreau, N.M.

Ubben, Gerald S., Teachers Col., Univ. of Nebraska, Lincoln, Nebr.
Uhl, Norman P., 407 Landerwood Lane, Chapel Hill, N.C.
Uhlir, Richard F., 800½ W. White St., Champaign, Ill.
Umansky, Harlan L., Emerson High School, Union City, N.J.
Umholtz, Mrs. Anne K., 292 N. Fifth Ave., Highland Park, N.J.
Umstattd, James G., Sutton Hall, University of Texas, Austin, Tex.
Underwood, Mrs. Anna, Box 72, Southard, Okla.
Underwood, Bertha M., Alabama State Col., Montgomery, Ala.
Underwood, Mrs. Frances A., 5900 Hilltop Rd., Pensacola, Fla.
Underwood, Helen B., School of Voc. Nurs., Napa, Calif.
Underwood, Mary Hope, R. 2, Chapel Dr. 29, Whitewater, Wis.
Underwood, William J., 304 Lakeview, Lee's Summit, Mo.
Unger, Mrs. Dorothy Holberg, 99 Lawton Rd., Riverside, Ill.
Unruh, Adolph, 151 N. Bemiston, Clayton, Mo.
Urbach, Floyd, Univ. of Nebraska, Waverly, Nebr.
Urdang, Miriam E., Queens College, Flushing, N.Y.
Usitalo, Richard J., 2015 Clairemont Cir., Olympia, Wash.
Utley, Quentin, 136 E.S. Temple, Salt Lake City, Utah

Vail, Edward O., Los Angeles City Schools, Los Angeles, Calif.
Valdez, Barbara M., Harmon Johnson Schl., Sacramento, Calif.
Van Auken, Robert A., Superintendent of Schools, North Olmsted, Ohio
Van Bruggen, John A., 1590 Innes St., N.E., Grand Rapids, Mich.
Vance, Douglas S., Mesa Public Schools, Mesa, Ariz.
Vanderhoof, C. David, Superintendent of Schools, Little Silver, N.J.
Vander Horck, Karl J., 644 Leicester, Duluth, Minn.
Vander Linde, Louis F., 3344 Pall Dr., Warren, Mich.
Vander Meer, A. W., 627 W. Hamilton, State College, Pa.
Van de Roovaart, Elizabeth G., 203 East 113th St., Chicago, Ill.
Vanderpool, J. Alden, 1736 Escalante Way, Burlingame, Calif.
Vander Werf, Lester S., Long Island Univ., Brookville, N.Y.
Van Dongen, Richard D., 1008 La Poblana Rd. N.W., Albuquerque, N. Mex.
Van Every, Donald F., 19265 Linville Ave., Grosse Pointe Woods, Mich.
Van Hoy, Neal E., 8308 E. Clarendon Ave., Scottsdale, Ariz.
Van Istendal, Theodore G., Spartan Village, East Lansing, Mich.
Van Loo, Eleanor, South Macomb Com. College, Detroit, Mich.
Van Pelt, Jacob J., 721 N. Juanita St., LaHabra, Calif.
Van Wagenen, Marvin J., 1729 Irving Ave., South, Minneapolis, Minn.
Van Zanten, Mrs. Hazel, 4754 Curwood, S.E., Grand Rapids, Mich.
Van Zwoll, James A., Col. of Educ., University of Maryland, College Park, Md.

Varn, Guy L., Supt. of Schools, 1616 Richland St., Columbia, S.C.
Varner, Charles S., Supt. of Schools, Runnells, Iowa
Varner, Leo P., Bakersfield Cntr., Fresno State Col., Bakersfield, Calif.
Varty, Jonathan W., 149 Brixton Rd., Garden City, N.Y.
Vasey, Hamilton G., 346 Second Ave., S.W., Cedar Rapids, Iowa
Vaughan, W. Donald, R. D., Pipersville, Pa.
Vaughn, C. A., Jr., Howey Academy, Howey-in-the-Hills, Fla.
Vaught, Maxine H., 1415 Crestwood Dr., Fayetteville, Ark.
Vayhinger, Harold P., Ohio Northern Univ., Ada, Ohio
Veltman, Peter, 600 College Ave., Wheaton, Ill.
Venditto, John G., Warwick Sch. Dept., Warwick, R.I.
Vergiels, John M., Col. of Educ., Univ. of Nevada, Las Vegas, Nev.
Verill, John E., University of Minnesota, Duluth, Minn.
Verseput, Robert Frank, 8 South St., Dover, N.J.
Vial, Lynda W., 6522 Pennsylvania Ave., Kansas City, Mo.
Vigilante, Nicholas J., Frostburg St. Col., Frostburg, Md.
Vikner, Carl F., Gustavus Adolphus College, St. Peter, Minn.
Vinicombe, Harry W., Jr., 2445 Lyttonsville Rd., Silver Spring, Md.
Vint, Virginia H., 910 Snyder Drive, Bloomington, Ill.
Vlahakos, Irene J., Cent. Connecticut State Col., New Britain, Conn.
Vlcek, Charles, Central Washington State College, Ellensburg, Wash.
Voelker, Paul Henry, 552 N. Neville St., Pittsburgh, Pa.
Vogel, Francis X., 5500 N. St. Louis, Chicago, Ill.
Voigt, Harry R., St. Paul's College, Concordia, Mo.
Voigt, Virginia E., 9 East Clark Pl., South Orange, N.J.
Volante, William, 220 W. Jersey St., Elizabeth, N.J.
Vonk, Paul K., 5355 Timber Trail, N.E., Atlanta, Ga.
Vopni, Sylvia, Univ. of Washington, Col. of Educ., Seattle, Wash.
Voris, George A., R.D. No. 1, Goodyear Lake, Oneonta, N.Y.
Voss, Burton E., Univ. High Sch., University of Michigan, Ann Arbor, Mich.
Votaw, M. JoAnne, 1634 Neil Ave., Columbus, Ohio
Voth, John A., Univ. of Missouri, Columbia, Mo.
Vroon, John W., 2376 Glenmont Circle, Silver Spring, Md.

Wade, D. E., Col. of Educ., Univ. of Houston, Houston, Tex.
Wagner, Robert W., Ohio State University, Columbus, Ohio
Wagstaff, Lonnie H., 1965-1 Belcher Dr., Columbus, Ohio
Wagstaff, Robert F., Box 541, LeClaire, Iowa
Waimon, Morton D., Illinois State University, Normal, Ill.
Waine, Sidney I., 34 Thomas Dr., Hauppauge, N.Y.
Wainscott, Carlton O., 3607 Fleetwood, Austin, Tex.
Walby, Grace S., 700 Elgin Ave., Winnipeg 4, Man., Canada
Waldron, James S., New Slocum Hgts. Syracuse, N.Y.
Waldron, Margaret L., Ayrshire, Iowa
Walker, Charles L., P.O. Box 114, Jonas Ridge, N.C.
Walker, Clare C., Univ. of Guam, Agana, Guam
Walker, Decker, Apt. 67F-Escondido Village, Stanford, Calif.
Walker, K. P., Superintendent of Schools, Jackson, Miss.
Walker, W. Del, Superintendent Jefferson County Schls., Lakewood, Colo.
Walker, William W., 327 William Ave., Fremont, Nebr.
Wall, G. S., Stout State University, Menomonie, Wis.
Wall, Harry V., 17013 Alwood St., West Covina, Calif.
Wall, Jessie S., Box 194, Univ. of So. Mississippi, Hattiesburg, Miss.
Wallace, Donald G., Col. of Educ., Drake University, Des Moines, Iowa
Wallace, James O., 1001 Howard St., San Antonio, Tex.
Wallace, Marjorie E., Wise State University, Richland, Wis.
Wallace, Morris S., Dept. of Educ., Texas Tech. College, Lubbock, Tex.
Wallace, Richard C., Jr., 793 Mayfield Ave., Stanford, Calif.
Wallen, Norman E., San Francisco State Col., San Francisco, Calif.
Waller, Virginia P., Vance Co. Schls., Henderson, N.C.
Wallin, William H., 1765 Santa Anita, Las Vegas, Nev.

Walsh, John E., Educ. & Training Grp., Oak & Pawnee Sts., Scranton, Pa.
Walter, Raymond L., Box 265, Millbrook, Ala.
Walter, Robert B., 434 N. DelMar Ave., San Gabriel, Calif.
Walthew, John K., 4 Larkspur Lane, Trenton, N.J.
Walz, Garry R., 1718 Arbordale, Ann Arbor, Mich.
Wampler, W. Norman, Superintendent of Schools, Bellflower, Calif.
Wantling, Mrs. Dale, 3261 Edgewood, Granite City, Ill.
Wantoch, Mrs. Ardell H., McNeal Hall, University of Minnesota, St. Paul, Minn.
Ward, Byron J., 155 Park Way, Camillus, N.Y.
Ward, Douglas S., 1044 Warrington Rd., Deerfield, Ill.
Ward, Ted, Michigan State University, East Lansing, Mich.
Ward, Virgil S., Sch. of Educ., University of Virginia, Charlottesville, Va.
Wardeberg, Helen L., Cornell University, Ithaca, New York
Warren, Alex M., R. D. #4, Comfort Road, Ithaca, N.Y.
Warren, John H., 1000 Clove Rd., Staten Island, New York, N.Y.
Warren, Mary Lou, 1334 Division St., Port Huron, Mich.
Warren, Robert A., 1057 S. 9th St., East, Salt Lake City, Utah
Warshavsky, Mrs. Belle, 35 Cooper Dr., Great Neck, N.Y.
Warshavsky, Bernard, 910 West End Ave., New York, N.Y.
Wartenberg, Herbert, Temple Univ., Philadelphia, Pa.
Warwick, Raymond, Box 73, Delmont, N.J.
Warwick, Ronald P., 2222 Scottwood-Apt. 1, Toledo, Ohio
Wasem, G. Leighton, 50 Wedgewood Terr., Springfield, Ill.
Washington, Walter, Alcorn A & M Col., Larmon, Miss.
Wasserman, Mrs. Lillian, 1684 Meadow Lane, East Meadow, N.Y.
Wasson, Margaret, 3705 University Blvd., Dallas, Tex.
Waterman, David C., Indiana State University, Terre Haute, Ind.
Waterman, Floyd T., Univ. of Nebr. at Omaha, Omaha, Nebr.
Waters, E. Worthington, Morgan State College, Baltimore, Md.
Waters, Mrs. Emma B., 228 E. Valley Ave., Holly Springs, Miss.
Watkins, Ralph K., 702 Ingleside Dr., Columbia, Mo.
Watkins, Ray H., Dallas Baptist College, Dallas, Tex.
Watkins, Thomas W., Supt., Wissahickon Sch. Dist., Ambler, Pa.
Watkins, W. O., Eastern New Mexico University, Portales, N.Mex.
Watkins, Yancey Lee, Univ. of Georgia, Athens, Ga.
Watson, Carlos M., Indiana State College, Terre Haute, Ind.
Watson, D. Gene, 5835 Kimbark Ave., Chicago, Ill.
Watson, David R., Highland Park, Ill.
Watson, John E., N. Z. Council for Educ. Res., Wellington, New Zealand
Watson, Norman E., Orange Coast College, Costa Mesa, Calif.
Watson, Paul E., Univ. of Pittsburgh, Pittsburgh, Pa.
Watson, William Crawford, 29 Woodstock Rd., Mt. Waverly, Victoria, Australia
Watt, Ralph W., 1206 Parker Ave., Hyattsville, Md.
Wattenberg, William W., 20220 Murray Hill, Detroit, Mich.
Watters, Velma V., 1365 Mozley Pl., S.W., Atlanta, Ga.
Watts, Mrs. Helen S., University of Dubuque, Dubuque, Iowa
Wawrzyniak, Alex S., 2329 Desmond Dr., Decatur, Ga.
Waxwood, Howard B., Jr., Witherspoon School, Princeton, N.J.
Way, Gail W., 1232 Henderson St., Chicago, Ill.
Wayson, William W., 832 Westmoreland Ave., Syracuse, N.Y.
Weakley, Mrs. Mary L., 1426 Center St., Geneva, Ill.
Weaver, Gladys C., 4708 Tecumseh St., College Park, Md.
Webb, Anne K., 1402 W. Main St., Shelbyville, Ky.
Webb, Clark D., Brigham Young Univ., Austin, Tex.
Webb, E. Sue, 216 West 5th St., Shawano, Wis.
Webb, Holmes, Dept. of Educ., Texas Tech. College, Lubbock, Tex.
Webber, Warren L., Music Dept., Cedarville College, Cedarville, Ohio
Weber, Clarence A., N. Eagleville Rd., Storrs, Conn.
Weber, Martha Gesling, Bowling Green State University, Bowling Green, Ohio
Weber, Wilford A., Syracuse University, Syracuse, N.Y.
Weber, William C., Signal Hill Schl. Dist. # 181, E. St. Louis, Ill.

Weddington, Rachel T., Queens College, 65-30 Kissena Blvd., Flushing, N.Y.
Weeks, Shirley, University of Hawaii, Honolulu, Hawaii
Weele, Jan C. Ter, Hanover Supv. Union # 22, Hanover, N.H.
*Wees, W. R., Ont. Inst. for Studies in Educ., Toronto, Ont., Can.
Weesner, Gary L., 619 Hendricks Court, Marion, Ind.
Wegrzyn, Helen A., 5240 W. Newport Ave., Chicago, Ill.
Wehner, Freda, Wisconsin State College, Oshkosh, Wis.
Wehrer, Charles S., Jc. Box 253, Webster City, Iowa
Weicker, Jack E., South Side High School, Ft. Wayne, Ind.
Weigert, Barbara, Mercyhurst College, Erie, Pa.
Weigler, Diane L., 5733 S.W. Orchid Ct., Portland, Oreg.
Weiland, Mrs. Harry, 67-14 168th St., Flushing, N.Y.
Weilbaker, Charles R., Tchrs. Col., University of Cincinnati, Cincinnati, Ohio
Weiner, Robert I., 1208 Westshore Dr., Ashtabula, Ohio
Weinhold, John D., 1637 Meadow Lane, Seward, Nebr.
Weintraub, Samuel, Indiana University, Bloomington, Ind.
Weis, Harold P., 437—23rd Ave., Moline, Ill.
Weisbender, Leo F., 12792 Topaz St., Garden Grove, Calif.
Weisberg, Patricia H., 9411 S. Pleasant Ave., Chicago, Ill.
Weisiger, Louise P., 2722 Hillcrest Rd., Richmond, Va.
Weiss, Joel, 20 Bernard Ave., Apt. 4, Toronto, Ont., Canada
Weiss, M. Jerry, Jersey City State College, Jersey City, N.J.
Weissleder, Claudette P., 135 Belmont Ave., Jersey City, N.J.
Welcenbach, Frank J., Trombly School, Grosse Pointe, Mich.
Welch, Cornelius A., St. Bonaventure Univ., St. Bonaventure, N.Y.
Welch, Ronald C., Sch. of Educ., Indiana University, Bloomington, Ind.
Welker, Latney C., Jr., Univ. of So. Mississippi, Hattiesburg, Miss.
Welliver, Paul W., 229 S. Patterson St., State College, Pa.
Wells, Carl S., Box 485, Col. Sta., Hammond, La.
Wells, Robert S., Superintendent of Schools, Reading, Mass.
Weltner, William H., Colo. State Coll., McKee Hall #35, Greeley, Colo.
Welton, William B., Prospect Public Schools, Prospect, Conn.
Wendt, Paul R., Southern Illinois University, Carbondale, Ill.
Wenger, Roy E., Kent State University, Kent, Ohio
Wenner, Harry W., 40 Mills St., Morristown, N.J.
Wenrich, Ralph C., Sch. of Educ., University of Michigan, Ann Arbor, Mich.
Wentz, Robert E., 15426 Old Bedford Trail, Mishawaka, Ind.
Werley, Harriet, H., 1447 Hollywood, Grosse Pointe Woods, Mich.
Werstler, Richard E., Adrian College, Adrian, Mich.
Werth, Trostel G., 18549 S.E. Tibbetts Ct., Gresham, Oreg.
Wertheim, Edward G., 512 W. 122nd St., New York, N.Y.
Wesley, Emory J., Henderson State Tchrs. Col., Arkadelphia, Ark.
Wesselman, Roy L., MSU-Macomb Teacher Educ. Ctr., Warren, Mich.
Wessler, Martin, F., 3558 S. Jefferson Ave., St. Louis, Mo.
West, Carole T., N.C. Central Univ., Durham, N.C.
West, Charles K., 501 S. Westlawn, Champaign, Ill.
West, Edna, 648 Sunset Blvd., Baton Rouge, La.
West, Helene, Beverly Hills H.S., 310 S. Altmont Dr., Los Angeles, Calif.
West, Lorraine W., Fresno State College, Fresno, Calif.
West, William H., Supt., County Union Schls., Elizabeth, N.J.
Westbrooks, Sadye Wylena, 1433 Sharon St., N.W., Atlanta, Ga.
Westby-Gibson, Dorothy, San Francisco State College, San Francisco, Calif.
Westover, Frederick L., University of Alabama, University, Ala.
Wetmore, Joseph N., Dept. of Educ., Ohio Wesleyan Univ., Delaware, Ohio
Wetzel, Rev. Chester M., 55 Elizabeth St., Hartford, Conn.
Wewer, William P., 1461 Wedgewood Dr., Anaheim, Calif.
Weyer, F. E., Dept. of Educ., Campbell College, Buies Creek, N.C.
Whalen, Thomas J., 232 Pearl St., Stoughton, Mass.
Whaley, Charles, Kentucky Educ. Assn., 101 W. Walnut St., Louisville, Ky.
Whang, H. Henry, 2620 West Prospect, Milwaukee, Wis.
Wharton, William P., Allegheny College, Meadville, Pa.

Wheat, Leonard B., Southern Illinois University, Edwardsville, Ill.
Wheelock, Warren H., Reading Clinic, Univ. of Missouri, Kansas City, Mo.
Whelan, Gerald J., Pedro de Valdivia, 1423, Santiago, Chile
Whelan, William J., Wells High Schl., Des Plaines, Ill.
Whetton, Annette, 1810 N. Mitchell St., Phoenix, Ariz.
Whetton, Mrs. Betty B., 1810 N. Mitchell St., Phoenix, Ariz.
Whilt, Selma E., Spring Valley, N.Y.
Whitaker, Prevo L., Indiana University, Bloomington, Ind.
White, Andrew W., Col. of Santa Fe, Cerrillos Rd., Santa Fe, N.Mex.
White, George L., Harcourt, Brace & World, Inc., New York, N.Y.
White, Geraldine, 875 Donner Way, Salt Lake City, Utah
White, Jack, Rt. 5, Parker Pl., Franklin, Tenn.
White, John C., Edison School, Mesa, Ariz.
White, Kenneth E., Dept. of Educ., Hamline Univ., St. Paul, Minn.
White, Mary Lou, 15 Park St., Orono, Me.
White, Verna, California Test Bureau, Los Angeles, Calif.
Whited, Frances M., 29 South Ave., Brockport, N.Y.
Whiteford, Emma B., 740 River Dr., St. Paul, Minn.
Whitehead, Willis A., 23351 Chagrin Blvd., Beachwood, Ohio
Whiteside, William R., R.R. 5, Pleasant Hill Rd., Carbondale, Ill.
Whitman, Harold L., Auburn Univ., Auburn, Ala.
Whitmer, Dana P., Superintendent of Schools, Pontiac, Mich.
Whitmore, Keith E., 396 Oakridge Drive, Rochester, N.Y.
Whitt, Robert L., Drake Univ., Des Moines, Iowa
Whittier, C. Taylor, APA Bldg., 1200—17th St., N.W., Washington, D.C.
Wicklund, Lee A., Idaho State Univ., Pocatello, Idaho
Wiebe, Elias H., Pacific College, Fresno, Calif.
Wiebe, Joel A., 315 S. Wilson Ave., Hillsboro, Kans.
* Wieden, Clifford O., 181 Main St., Presque Isle, Maine
Wiggin, Gladys A., Col. of Educ., Univ. of Maryland, College Park, Md.
Wiggin, Richard G., 4151 North 25th St., Arlington, Va.
Wiggins, Thomas W., 1206 Oklahoma, Norman, Okla.
Wilber, Lora Ann, Stony Brook, L.I., N.Y.
Wilburn, D. Banks, Glenville State College, Glenville, W.Va.
Wildebush, Sarah W., 3927 Meridian Ave., Miami, Fla.
Wile, Marcia, 4341 Baintree, University Hghts., Ohio
Wilkerson, Doxey A., 34 Dock Rd., South Norwalk, Conn.
Wilkinson, Harold A., 7744 Sta. ACC, Abilene, Tex.
Willard, Robert L., Utica College, Utica, N.Y.
Willey, Laurence V., Jr., 3001 Veazey Terrace, N.W., Washington, D.C.
Williams, Alfred H., 9712 Nova St., Pico Rivera, Calif.
Williams, Arloff L., 316½ W. Koenig St., Grand Island, Nebr.
Williams, Arthur E., Dillard Comprehensive High School, Fort Lauderdale, Fla.
Williams, Mrs. B. E., Spelman College, Atlanta, Ga.
Williams, Buford W., Southwest Texas State College, San Marcos, Tex.
Williams, Byron B., University of Rochester, Rochester, N.Y.
Williams, Catharine M., Ohio State University, Columbus, Ohio
Williams, Charles C., North Texas State College, Denton, Tex.
Williams, Chester Spring, Indiana State University, Terre Haute, Ind.
Williams, Clarence M., Col. of Educ., Univ. of Rochester, Rochester, N.Y.
Williams, Donald F., Crozer Theological Seminary, Chester, Pa.
*Williams, Fannie C., 3108 Tours St., New Orleans, La.
Williams, Fountie N., 505 Pennsylvania Ave., Clarksburg, W.Va.
Williams, Frances I., Lab. Sch., Indiana State Univ., Terre Haute, Ind.
Williams, Gloria M., Univ. of Minnesota, St. Paul, Minn.
Williams, Harold A., Flat Top, W.Va.
Williams, Herman, 40 Elmwood St., Tiffin, Ohio
Williams, Howard Y., Jr., 3464 Siems Ct., St. Paul, Minn.
Williams, Mrs. Lois, 200 North 18th St., Montebello, Calif.
Williams, Malcolm, Sch. of Educ., Tennessee A. & I. University, Nashville, Tenn.
Williams, Myrtle M., 4631 Annette St., New Orleans, La.

Williams, Nat, Superintendent of Schools, Lubbock, Tex.
Williams, Paul E., Danbury State College, Danbury, Conn.
Williams, Richard H., 380 Moseley Rd., Hillsborough, Calif.
Williams, Robert Alan, San Jose State Col., San Jose, Calif.
Williams, Major Thomas, Maxwell Air Force Base, Ala.
Williams, W. Morris, USAID, Philippines, APO 96528, San Francisco, Calif.
Williams, Wilbur A., Eastern Michigan University, Ypsilanti, Mich.
Williams, William K., 2342 S. Glen Ave., Decatur, Ill.
Williamson, Jane, Pacific Lutheran University, Tacoma, Wash.
Willis, Henry H., Box 2719 S.S. USM, Hattiesburg, Miss.
Wills, Benjamin G., 1145 Stenway Ave., Campbell, Calif.
Willsey, Alan D., SUNY College, Courtland, N.Y.
Wilson, Alan S., Hillyer Col., University of Hartford, Hartford, Conn.
Wilson, Alan T., Faircrest Sch., St. Francis, Wis.
Wilson, David A., 9125 Gross Pt. Rd., Skokie, Ill.
Wilson, David H., Seneca St., Interlaken, N.Y.
Wilson, Dustin W., Jr., 945 Forrest St., Dover, Del.
Wilson, Elizabeth, 3148 Que St., N.W., Washington, D.C.
Wilson, Frederick R., 1633 K., Spartan Village, East Lansing, Mich.
Wilson, Harold M., 3006 N. Trinidad St., Arlington, Va.
Wilson, Herbert B., University of Arizona, Tucson, Ariz.
Wilson, James W., 249 Harris Ave., Needham, Mass.
Wilson, Jean Alice, 715 Tidball Ave., Grove City, Pa.
Wilson, John A. R., 2519 Chapala St., Santa Barbara, Calif.
Wilson, John L., 15800 N.W. 42nd Ave., Miami, Fla.
Wilson, Lois, N.Y. State Teachers Assn., Albany, N.Y
Wilson, Merle A., 2800—62nd St., Des Moines, Iowa
Wilson, Richard, 125 E. Prince Rd., Tucson, Ariz.
Wilson, Robert D., Dept. of Eng., Univ. of Calif., Los Angeles, Calif.
Wilson, Roy K., N.E.A., 1201—16th St., N.W., Washington, D.C.
Wilson, Roy R., Jr., 5647 Harper, Chicago, Ill.
Wilson, William J., Jr., 1821 N.W. 27th Terr., Fort Lauderdale, Fla.
Wilson, Yolande M., Sch. of Educ., Univ. of Chicago, Chicago, Ill.
Wilstach, Mrs. Ilah M., 2127 N. Eastern Ave., Los Angeles, Calif.
Wiltse, Earl W., Northern Illinois Univ., DeKalb, Ill.
Winders, Martha E., 3022 Chapel Hill Rd., Durham, N.C.
Windoes, Frederic C., Okemus, Mich.
Windsor, John G., 4354 West 9th Ave., Vancouver, B.C., Canada
Winebrenner, Neil T., 3844 N. Morris Blvd., Shorewood, Wis.
Winfield, Kenneth, East Stroudsburg State Col., Stroudsburg, Pa.
Wing, Richard L., Directorate USDESEA, APO-09164
Wing, Sherman W., Superintendent of Schools, Provo, Utah
Wingerd, Harold H., Superintendent of Schools, West Chester, Pa.
Wingren, Ralf, Unit 2-77220, Vought Aeronautics Div., Dallas, Tex.
Winkley, Carol K., 125 Forsythe Ln., DeKalb, Ill.
Winnen, Josephine, University of Wisconsin, Milwaukee, Wis.
Winsor, George E., Wilmington College, Wilmington, Ohio
Winter, Nathan B., 3206 Sunnyside Drive, Rockford, Ill.
Wise, Harold L., 7 Delisio Lane, Woodstock, N.Y.
Wise, Pauline, 928 Larchmont Crescent, Norfolk, Va.
Wishart, James S., 1638 Ridge Rd., West, Rochester, N.Y.
Wisniewski, Richard, Ctr. for Urban Educ., 105 Madison Ave., New York, N.Y.
Wisniewski, Virginia, 4623 Ostrom, Lakewood, Calif.
Witchel, Barbara M., 27 Myrtledale Rd., Scarsdale, N.Y.
Witherspoon, W. H., P.O. Box 527, Rockhill, S.C.
Witt, Carl P., 22900 Blythe St., Canoga Park, Calif.
Witt, Marquis G., 4106 Barrett Dr., Newburgh, N.Y.
Witt, Paul W. F., Michigan State Univ., East Lansing, Mich.
Witte, Cyril M., R. 2, Box 264, Mt. Airy, Md.
Witten, Charles H., University of South Carolina, Columbia, S.C.
Witter, Sanford C., 1900 W. County Rd., St. Paul, Minn.

Wittick, Mildred Letton, 300 Pompton Rd., Wayne, N.J.
Wittmer, Arthur E., 315 Park Ave. S., Rm. 1920, New York, N.Y.
Witty, Paul A., 5555 N. Sheridan Rd., Chicago, Ill.
Wixon, John L., 29080 Oxford Ave., The Knolls, Richmond, Calif.
Wochner, Raymond E., Arizona State University, Tempe, Ariz.
Woditsch, June, 6801 Maplewood, Sylvania, Ohio
Woerdehoff, Frank J., Dept. of Educ., Purdue University, Lafayette, Ind.
Woestehoff, Orville W., Oak Park Elementary Schls., Oak Park, Ill.
Wohlers, A. E., Ohio State University, Columbus, Ohio
Wolbrecht, Walter F., 316 Parkwood, Kirkwood, Mo.
Wold, Stanley G., 1924 Orchard Pl., Fort Collins, Colo.
Wolf, Dan B., Indiana Univ., Indianapolis, Ind.
Wolf, Helen S., 2035 Heather Terrace, Northfield, Ill.
Wolf, Ray O., Portland State College, Portland, Oreg.
Wolf, Vivian C., 8802-9th Ave., S.W., Seattle, Wash.
Wolf, William C., Jr., University of Massachusetts, Amherst, Mass.
Wolfe, Deborah P., Queens College, Flushing, N.Y.
Wolfe, Josephine B., Beaver Hill Apts., Jenkintown, Pa.
Wolfendon, Mrs. R., 25 S. Hazelton, B.C., Canada
Wolfson, Bernice J., 2121 E. Capitol Dr., #410, Milwaukee, Wis.
Wolinsky, Gloria F., 69-52 Groton St., Forest Hills, N.Y.
Womack, James, Board of Coop. Educ'l Serv., Huntington, N.Y.
Wong, William T. S., 1640 Paula Dr., Honolulu, Hawaii
Wood, Dan, Center for Urban Educ., 33 W. 42nd St., New York, N.Y.
Wood, Donald I., Dept. of Educ., Rice University, Houston, Tex.
Wood, Joseph E., 18 Duryea Rd., Upper Montclair, N.J.
Wood, Marion C., Hanson RFD, 725 Crescent St., East Bridgewater, Mass.
Wood, Nolan E., Jr., Texas Christian Univ., Ft. Worth, Tex.
Wood, Rebecca H., P.O. Box 3346, Pensacola, Fla.
Wood, Roi S., Superintendent of Schools, Joplin, Mo.
Wood, W. Clement, Fort Hays Kansas State College, Hays, Kans.
Woodard, Prince B., St. Coun. of Higher Educ., Richmond, Va.
Woodburn, A. C., Alamogordo Public Schools, Alamogordo, N.Mex.
Woodburn, John H., Charles E. Woodward H.S., Rockville, Md.
Woodbury, Tom, Livonia Pub. Schools, Livonia, Mich.
Woodin, Ralph J., Ohio St. Univ., Columbus, Ohio
Woods, Joanne, Univ. of Southern Calif., Los Angeles, Calif.
Woods, Robert K., Div. of Elem. Jr. H.S. Educ., Platteville, Wis.
Woodson, C. C., 435 S. Liberty St., Spartanburg, S.C.
Woodworth, Denny, Col. of Educ., Drake University, Des Moines, Iowa
Woodworth, William O., 999 Kedzie Ave., Flossmoor, Ill.
Woolley, Joan, 4615 Via Corona, Torrance, Calif.
Woolson, Edith L., Box 203, Imperial, Calif.
Wootton, John W., 459 Lyons Rd., Liberty Corner, N.J.
Worden, Allen J., Wise State University, Oshkosh, Wis.
Workman, Stanley, 149-07 Sanford Ave., Flushing, N.Y.
Wozencraft, Marian, Eastern Ill. Univ., Charleston, Ill.
Wray, Mabel Elizabeth, 224 Mower St., Worcester, Mass.
Wrenn, Michael P., 6642 Bosworth, Chicago, Ill.
Wright, Adele J., 275 Glencoe St., Denver, Colo.
Wright, Floyd K., 1432 Price Dr., Cape Girardeau, Mo.
Wright, John R., San Jose State College, San Jose, Calif.
Wright, Samuel Lee, 8919—91st Pl., Lanham, Md.
Wright, William H., Jr., 13542 E. Starbuck St., Whittier, Calif.
Wright, William J., 5835 Kimbark Ave., Chicago, Ill.
Wrightstone, J. Wayne, 21 Hickory Rd., Summit, N.J.
Wronski, Stanley P., Col. of Educ., Michigan State Univ., East Lansing, Mich.
Wu, Julia Tu, Hunter Col., New York, N.Y.
Wuolle, Mrs. Ethel, P.O. Box 173, Pine City, Minn.
Wyckoff, D. Campbell, Princeton Theological Seminary, Princeton, N.J.
Wyeth, E. R., 18111 Nordhoff St., Northridge, Calif.
Wyllie, Eugene D., Sch. of Bus., Indiana University, Bloomington, Ind.
Wynn, Willa T., 1122 N. St. Clair St., Pittsburgh, Pa.

Yamamoto, Kaoru, Col. of Educ., Penn. State Univ., University Park, Pa.
Yanis, Martin, 101 S. Second St., Harrisburg, Pa.
Yates, J. W., 223 Wham, Southern Illinois University, Carbondale, Ill.
Yauch, Wilbur A., Northern Illinois University, DeKalb, Ill.
Yeager, John L., LRDC, 160 No. Craig St., Pittsburgh, Pa.
Yee, Albert H., Univ. of Wisconsin, Madison, Wis.
Yelvington, James A., 11809 Goshen Ave. #10, Los Angeles, Calif.
Ylinen, Gerald A., Gustavus Adolphus College, St. Peter, Minn.
Ylisto, Ingrid P., Eastern Michigan University, Ypsilanti, Mich.
Yochim, Louise Dunn, 9545 Drake, Evanston, Ill.
Yockey, Gay J., Box 46, Benton Ridge, Ohio
York, William, Bowling Green University, Bowling Green, Ohio
Young, Carol A., Doane College, Crete, Nebr.
Young, Charles R., 999 Green Bay Road, Glencoe, Ill.
Young, Harold L., Central Missouri State College, Warrensburg, Mo.
Young, J. E. M., Macdonald College Post Office, Quebec, Canada
Young, Jean A., Sonoma State College, Rohnert Park, Calif.
Young, John A., 35 Vincent Rd., Dedham, Mass.
Young, Michael A., 812 W. Wooster St., Bowling Green, Ohio
Young, Paul A., Judson College, Elgin, Ill.
Young, Robert W., 68 E. Main St., Mendham, N.J.
* Young, William E., State Education Department, Albany, N.Y.
Young, W. H., 1150 N. Belsay Rd., Flint, Mich.
Young, William Howard, 1460 Tampa Ave., Dayton, Ohio
Youngblood, Chester E., 1323 Meadow Lane, Weatherford, Okla.
Younie, William J., Tchrs. Col., Columbia University, New York, N.Y.
Yuhas, Theodore Frank, Educ. Dept., Ball State University, Muncie, Ind.
Yunghans, Ernest E., Wartburg College, Waverly, Iowa

Zackmeier, William, Box 710, Diamond Springs, Calif.
Zahn, D. Willard, 7118 McCallum St., Philadelphia, Pa.
Zahorsky, Mrs. Metta, San Francisco State College, San Francisco, Calif.
Zak, Eugene, 7205 Beresford Ave., Parma, Ohio
Zakrzewski, Aurelia R., 2362 Golfview Dr., Troy, Mich.
Zambito, Stephen Charles, Eastern Michigan University, Ypsilanti, Mich.
Zambor, Ronald J., 75 Manalapan Rd., Spotswood, N.J.
Zari, Rosalie V., 1218 - 17th Ave., San Francisco, Calif.
Zavarella, Victor, 388 W. Maple, Canton, Ill.
Zbornik, Joseph J., 3219 Clarence Ave., Berwyn, Ill.
Zdanowicz, Paul J., 7077 Fox Hill Dr., Solon, Ohio
Zebrowski, Kenneth M., Tuslog. Det. 30, Box 404, APO, New York, N.Y.
Zeldin, David, Oriel Cottage, St. Mary's Rd., Mortimer, Berkshire, England
Zeller, William D., Dept. of Educ., Illinois State Univ., Normal, Ill.
Zelmer, A. C. Lynn, 3604—26th Ave., Calgary, Alba., Canada
Zelnick, Joseph, 386 Livingston Ave., New Brunswick, N.J.
Zepper, John T., Educ. Bldg., University of New Mexico, Albuquerque, N.Mex.
Ziebold, Edna B., 6401 Linda Vista Rd., San Diego, Calif.
Ziegler, Lorene E., Eastern Ill. Univ., Charleston, Ill.
Zieman, Orlyn A., Appleton Public Schools, Appleton, Wis.
Ziemba, Walter J., St. Mary's College, Orchard Lake, Mich.
Zierman, Raymond T., 606 Virginia St., Joliet, Ill.
Zim, Herbert Spencer, Box 34, Vacation Village, Fla.
Zimmerman, Gary E., Guilford Col., Greensboro, N.C.
Zimmerman, Herbert M., Roosevelt High School, Chicago, Ill.
Zimmerman, William G., Jr., 26 Winthrop Rd., Hingham, Mass.
Zimnoch, Frances J., Meadowbrook Elem. Schl., East Meadow, L.I., N.Y.
Zintz, Miles V., 3028 Marble Ave., N.E. Albuquerque, N.Mex.
Ziobrowski, Stasia M., Sch. of Educ., New York Univ., New York, N.Y.
Zipper, Joseph H., 1569 West 41st St., Erie, Pa.
Zunigha, Bennie Jean, Box 354, Ft. Wingate, N.Mex.
Zu Wallack, Raymond, Bridgewater State Col., Bridgewater, Mass.
Zweig, Richard L., 20800 Beach Blvd., Huntington Beach, Calif.

INFORMATION CONCERNING THE NATIONAL SOCIETY FOR THE STUDY OF EDUCATION

1. PURPOSE. The purpose of the National Society is to promote the investigation and discussion of educational questions. To this end it holds an annual meeting and publishes a series of yearbooks.

2. ELIGIBILITY TO MEMBERSHIP. Any person who is interested in receiving its publications may become a member by sending to the Secretary-Treasurer information concerning name, title, and address, and a check for $8.00 (see Item 5), except that graduate students, on the recommendation of a faculty member, may become members by paying $6.00 for the first year of their membership. Dues for all subsequent years are the same as for other members (see Item 4).

Membership is not transferable; it is limited to individuals, and may not be held by libraries, schools, or other institutions, either directly or indirectly.

3. PERIOD OF MEMBERSHIP. Applicants for membership may not date their entrance back of the current calendar year, and all memberships terminate automatically on December 31, unless the dues for the ensuing year are paid as indicated in Item 6.

4. DUTIES AND PRIVILEGES OF MEMBERS. Members pay dues of $7.00 annually, receive a cloth-bound copy of each publication, are entitled to vote, to participate in discussion, and (under certain conditions) to hold office. The names of members are printed in the yearbooks.

Persons who are sixty years of age or above may become life members on payment of fee based on average life-expectancy of their age group. For information, apply to Secretary-Treasurer.

5. ENTRANCE FEE. New members are required the first year to pay, in addition to the dues, an entrance fee of one dollar.

6. PAYMENT OF DUES. Statements of dues are rendered in October for the following calendar year. Any member so notified whose dues remain unpaid on January 1, thereby loses his membership and can be reinstated only by paying a reinstatement fee of fifty cents.

School warrants and vouchers from institutions must be accompanied by definite information concerning the name and address of the person for whom membership fee is being paid. Statements of dues are rendered on our own form only. The Secretary's office cannot undertake to fill out special invoice forms of any sort or to affix notary's affidavit to statements or receipts.

Cancelled checks serve as receipts. Members desiring an additional receipt must enclose a stamped and addressed envelope therefor.

7. DISTRIBUTION OF YEARBOOKS TO MEMBERS. The yearbooks, ready prior to each February meeting, will be mailed from the office of the distributor, only to members whose dues for that year have been paid. Members who desire yearbooks prior to the current year must purchase them directly from the distributor (see Item 8).

8. COMMERCIAL SALES. The distribution of all yearbooks prior to the current year, and also of those of the current year not regularly mailed to members in exchange for their dues, is in the hands of the distributor, not of the Secretary. For such commercial sales, communicate directly with the University of Chicago Press, Chicago, Illinois 60637, which will gladly send a price list covering all the publications of this Society. This list is also printed in the yearbook.

9. YEARBOOKS. The yearbooks are issued about one month before the February meeting. They comprise from 600 to 800 pages annually. Unusual effort has been made to make them, on the one hand, of immediate practical value, and, on the other hand, representative of sound scholarship and scientific investigation.

10. MEETINGS. The annual meeting, at which the yearbooks are discussed, is held in February at the same time and place as the meeting of the American Association of School Administrators. Members will be notified of other meetings.

Applications for membership will be handled promptly at any time on receipt of name and address, together with check for $8.00 (or $7.50 for reinstatement). Applications entitle the new members to the yearbook slated for discussion during the calendar year the application is made.

5835 Kimbark Ave.   HERMAN G. RICHEY, *Secretary-Treasurer*
Chicago, Illinois 60637

PUBLICATIONS OF THE NATIONAL SOCIETY FOR THE STUDY OF EDUCATION

POSTPAID PRICE

Distributed by
THE UNIVERSITY OF CHICAGO PRESS, CHICAGO, ILLINOIS 60637
1969